Longman
PREPARATION COURSE
FOR THE TOEFL® TEST

The Paper Test

Deborah Phillips

Longman

**Longman Preparation Course for the TOEFL Test:
The Paper Test**

Pearson Education, 10 Bank Street, White Plains, NY 10606

Acquisitions editor: Virginia L. Blanford
Development editor: Angela Castro
Vice president, director of design and production: Rhea Banker
Executive managing editor: Linda Moser
Production editor: Michael Mone
Production coordinator: Melissa Leyva
Director of manufacturing: Patrice Fraccio
Senior manufacturing buyer: Nancy Flaggman
Cover design: Ann France
CD-ROM project manager: Evelyn Fella
CD-ROM development editor: Lisa Hutchins
Text design adaptation: Page Designs International, Inc.
Text composition: Page Designs International, Inc.

Library of Congress Cataloging-in-Publication Data

Phillips, Deborah, 1952–
    Longman preparation course for the TOEFL test: the paper-based test / Deborah Phillips.
      p. cm.
    ISBN 0-13-140883-6 (SB w/answer key) — ISBN 0-13-140886-0 (SB w/o answer key)
    1. Test of English as a Foreign Language—Study guides. 2. English language—Textbooks
for foreign speakers. 3. English language—Examinations—Study guides. I. Title: Preparation
course for the TOEFL test. II. Title.

PE1128.P4618 2003
428'.0076—dc21

2003047439

LONGMAN ON THE **WEB**

Longman.com offers online resources for teachers
and students. Access our Companion Websites, our
online catalog, and our local offices around the world.

Visit us at **longman.com**.

Printed in the United States of America
13 14–V013–13 12 11

CONTENTS

SECTION THREE: READING COMPREHENSION

SECTION FOUR: Test of Written English (TWE)

INTRODUCTION

ABOUT THIS COURSE

PURPOSE OF THE COURSE

This course is intended to prepare students for the paper version of the TOEFL® (Test of English as a Foreign Language) test. It is based on the most up-to-date information available on the format and content of the paper TOEFL test.

Longman Preparation Course for the TOEFL Test: The Paper Test can be used in a variety of ways, depending on the needs of the reader:

1. It can be used as the primary classroom text in a course emphasizing TOEFL test preparation.
2. It can be used as a supplementary text in a more general ESL course.
3. Along with its companion recording program, it can be used as a tool for individualized study by students preparing for the TOEFL test outside of the ESL classroom.

WHAT IS IN THE BOOK

The book contains a variety of materials that together provide a comprehensive TOEFL preparation program:

- **Diagnostic Pre-Tests** for each section of the test measure students' level of performance and allow students to determine specific areas of weakness.
- **Language Skills** for each section of the test, including the Test of Written English (TWE), provide students with a thorough understanding of the language skills that are regularly tested on the TOEFL test.
- **Test-Taking Strategies** for each section of the test provide students with clearly defined steps to maximize their performance on the test.
- **Exercises** provide practice of one or more skills in a non-TOEFL format.
- **TOEFL Exercises** provide practice of one or more skills in a TOEFL format.
- **TOEFL Review Exercises** provide practice of all of the skills taught up to that point in a TOEFL format.
- **TOEFL Post-Tests** for each section of the test measure the progress that students have made after working through the skills and strategies in the text.
- **Five Complete Tests** allow students to simulate the experience of taking actual TOEFL tests with all of the sections together in one complete test.
- **Scoring Information** allows students to determine their approximate TOEFL scores on the Pre-Tests, Post-Tests, and Complete Tests.
- **Diagnostic Charts** allow students to monitor their progress in specific language skills on the Pre-Tests, Post-Tests, and Complete Tests, so they can easily determine which skills have been mastered and which skills require further study.
- **Progress Charts** allow students to monitor their score improvement from the Pre-Tests to the Post-Tests and Complete Tests.

- **Recording Scripts** allow the students to see the text of all the listening exercises and tests included on the audio cassettes/CDs.
- **Answer Sheets** allow students to practice using appropriate test forms.

Some of the material in this book has been adapted or reprinted from previously published books, including the *Longman Preparation Course for the TOEFL® Test: Volume A* and *Volume B.* Readers familiar with those books will notice that this book includes a much-expanded section on the Test of Written English, longer reading passages to reflect the new length of the actual TOEFL reading passages, expanded Diagnostic Charts which now allow students to track their progress in the Pre-Tests, Post-Tests, and Complete Tests, and the complete recording script for the recording program. All material has also been updated to reflect the most recent information about the TOEFL Test.

WHAT IS ON THE CD-ROM

Longman Student CD-ROM for the TOEFL Test: The Paper Test with over 1,250 questions in the format of the paper TOEFL test and 200 additional writing practice questions, includes a variety of materials that contribute to an effective preparation program for the paper version of the TOEFL test:

- A **Tutorial** provides an overview of the features of the CD-ROM.
- **Skills Practice** for each of the sections on the paper version of the TOEFL test, including the Test of Written English (TWE), provide students with the opportunity to review and master each of the language skills on the test.
- **Test Sections** for each section of the paper version of the TOEFL test allow students to take authentic test sections and to measure their progress. Writing tests can be printed for feedback and review.
- **Answers** and **Explanations** for all practice and test items allow students to understand their errors and learn from their mistakes.
- **Skill Reports** relate the test items on the CD-ROM to the language skills presented in the book.
- **Scoring and Record-Keeping** enable students to record and print out charts that monitor their progress on all practice and test items.

The following chart describes the contents of the Student CD-ROM:

	SKILLS PRACTICE		SECTION TESTS	
LISTENING COMPREHENSION	**Short Dialogues**		**Listening Comprehension Tests**	
	Skills 1–3	10 questions	*Test 1*	50 questions
	Skills 4–6	10 questions	*Test 2*	50 questions
	Skills 7–10	10 questions	*Test 3*	50 questions
	Skills 11–13	10 questions		
	Skills 14–15	10 questions		
	Skills 16–17	10 questions		
	Conversations			
	Conversation 1	4 questions		
	Conversation 2	4 questions		
	Conversation 3	4 questions		
	Talks Practice			
	Talk 1	4 questions		
	Talk 2	4 questions		
	Talk 3	4 questions		
STRUCTURE AND WRITTEN EXPRESSION	**Structure Practice**		**Structure and Written Expression Tests**	
	Skills 1–5	20 questions	*Test 1*	40 questions
	Skills 6–8	20 questions	*Test 2*	40 questions
	Skills 9–12	20 questions	*Test 3*	40 questions
	Skills 13–14	20 questions	*Test 4*	40 questions
	Skills 15–19	20 questions	*Test 5*	40 questions
	Written Expression Practice		*Test 6*	40 questions
			Test 7	40 questions
	Skills 20–23	20 questions	*Test 8*	40 questions
	Skills 24–26	20 questions	*Test 9*	40 questions
	Skills 27–29	20 questions	*Test 10*	40 questions
	Skills 30–32	20 questions		
	Skills 33–36	20 questions		
	Skills 37–38	20 questions		
	Skills 39–42	20 questions		
	Skills 43–45	20 questions		
	Skills 46–48	20 questions		
	Skills 49–51	20 questions		
	Skills 52–55	20 questions		
	Skills 56–57	20 questions		
	Skills 58–60	20 questions		

	SKILLS PRACTICE	SECTION TESTS
READING COMPREHENSION	**Questions about the Ideas of the Passage** *Skills 1–2* 5 questions *Skills 1–2* 4 questions *Skills 1–2* 6 questions	**Reading Comprehension Tests** *Test 1* 50 questions *Test 2* 50 questions *Test 3* 50 questions
	Directly Answered Questions *Skills 3–5* 8 questions *Skills 3–5* 9 questions *Skills 1–5* 9 questions	
	Indirectly Answered Questions *Skills 6–7* 5 questions *Skills 6–7* 5 questions *Skills 1–7* 9 questions	
	Vocabulary Questions *Skills 8–11* 10 questions *Skills 8–11* 10 questions *Skills 1–11* 12 questions	
	Overall Review Questions *Skills 12–13* 7 questions *Skills 12–13* 8 questions *Skills 1–13* 12 questions	
TEST OF WRITTEN ENGLISH (TWE)	**Before and While Writing** *Skills 1–6* 25 questions *Skills 1–6* 25 questions *Skills 1–6* 25 questions **After Writing** *Skill 7 (A–C)* 20 questions *Skill 8A* 20 questions *Skill 8B* 20 questions *Skill 8C* 20 questions *Skill 8D* 20 questions *Skill 8E* 20 questions *Skill 8F* 20 questions	**TWE Tests** *Test 1* 1 question *Test 2* 1 question *Test 3* 1 question *Test 4* 1 question *Test 5* 1 question *Test 6* 1 question *Test 7* 1 question *Test 8* 1 question *Test 9* 1 question *Test 10* 1 question

This CD-ROM has been developed specifically to provide practice opportunities for the TOEFL paper test. To the extent possible, all question formats simulate those on the actual TOEFL paper test and the Test of Written English.

WHAT IS ON THE AUDIO RECORDINGS

The recording program that can be purchased to accompany this book includes all the recorded material from the Listening Comprehension section and the Complete Tests. This program is available on either audio CDs or audiocassettes.

OTHER AVAILABLE MATERIALS

Longman publishes a full suite of materials for TOEFL preparation, for both the paper and the computer-based tests, and for both intermediate and advanced students. Preparation materials are available for both course-based instruction and self-study. Please consult Longman's website—www.longman.com—for a complete list of these products.

ABOUT THE PAPER VERSION OF THE TOEFL TEST

OVERVIEW OF THE TEST

The TOEFL test is a test to measure the English proficiency of nonnative speakers of English. It is required primarily by English-language colleges and universities. Additionally, institutions such as government agencies, businesses, or scholarship programs may require this test. The TOEFL test currently exists in paper and computer formats. (The purpose of this book is to prepare students for the *paper* version of the TOEFL test. There are other Longman products to prepare students for the *computer* version of the TOEFL test.)

DESCRIPTION OF THE TEST

The paper version of the TOEFL test currently has the following sections:

- **Listening Comprehension:** To demonstrate their ability to understand spoken English, examinees must listen to various types of passages on a recording and respond to multiple choice questions about the passages.
- **Structure and Written Expression:** To demonstrate their ability to recognize grammatically correct English, examinees must either choose the correct way to complete sentences or find errors in sentences.
- **Reading Comprehension:** To demonstrate their ability to understand written English, examinees must answer multiple choice questions about the ideas and the meanings of words in reading passages.

- **Test of Written English (TWE):** To demonstrate their ability to produce correct, organized, and meaningful English, examinees must write an essay on a given topic in thirty minutes. The TWE is not given with every administration of the paper TOEFL test and its score is not included in the overall TOEFL score. It is possible for you to determine whether or not the TWE will be given at a particular administration of the TOEFL test when you register for the test.

The probable format of a paper TOEFL test is outlined below. (It should be noted that on certain unannounced occasions a longer version of the paper TOEFL test is given.)

	TOEFL	TIME
Listening Comprehension	50 multiple choice questions	35 minutes
Structure and Written Expression	40 multiple choice questions	25 minutes
Reading Comprehension	50 multiple choice questions	55 minutes
Test of Written English (TWE)	I essay question	30 minutes

REGISTRATION FOR THE TEST

It is important to understand the following information about registration for the TOEFL test:

- The first step in the registration process is to obtain a copy of the *TOEFL Information Bulletin*. This bulletin can be obtained by ordering it or downloading it from the TOEFL website at www.toefl.org, by calling 1-609-771-7100, or by mailing a request to this address.

>   TOEFL Services
>   Educational Testing Service
>   P.O. Box 6151
>   Princeton, NJ 08541-6151 USA

- From the bulletin, it is possible to determine when and where the paper version of the TOEFL test is being given.
- It is important to pay attention to registration deadlines. Registration deadlines are listed in the *TOEFL Information Bulletin*; they are generally four weeks before test dates for test centers in the United States and Canada, and six weeks before test dates for test centers overseas. The registration deadlines listed in the TOEFL Information Bulletin are dates by which registration requests must be received by ETS; they are not dates by which registration requests must be mailed.
- Procedures for completing the registration form and submitting it are listed in the *TOEFL Information Bulletin*. These procedures must be followed exactly. Contact information for submitting registration forms from different parts of the world is listed in the *TOEFL Information Bulletin*.

- It may be possible to take the test on a standby basis. Check the TOEFL website at www.toefl.org for information on the availability of standby testing.

HOW THE TEST IS SCORED

Students should keep the following information in mind about the scoring of the paper TOEFL test:

- The paper version of the TOEFL test is scored on a scale of 217 to 677 points.
- There is no passing score on the TOEFL test, but various institutions and organizations have their own TOEFL requirements. It is important for students to find out from each institution or organization what TOEFL score is required by that institution or organization.
- After students take the Pre-Tests, Post-Tests, and Complete Tests in this book, it is possible for them to calculate estimated TOEFL scores. A description of how to estimate scores on the tests in this book has been provided at the back of the book on pages 549–550.
- The Test of Written English (TWE) may or may not be given at a particular administration of the TOEFL test. If the TWE is given, it is scored on a scale of 1 to 6, and this score is not included in the overall TOEFL score.
- The dates when scores will be mailed out are listed in the *TOEFL Information Bulletin*. Scores are generally mailed out approximately five weeks after the test date for test centers in the United States and Canada, and approximately six weeks after the test date for overseas test centers.

TO THE STUDENT

HOW TO PREPARE FOR THE PAPER VERSION OF THE TOEFL TEST

The paper version of the TOEFL test is a standardized test of English. To do well on this test, you should therefore work in these areas to improve your score:

- You must work to improve your knowledge of the English *language skills* that are covered on the paper version of the TOEFL test.
- You must understand the *test-taking strategies* that are appropriate for the paper version of the TOEFL test.
- You must take *practice tests* with a focus on applying your knowledge of the appropriate language skills and test-taking strategies.

   This book can familiarize you with the English language skills and test-taking strategies necessary for the paper version of the TOEFL test, and it can also provide you with a considerable amount of test practice. Additional practice of the English language skills, test-taking strategies, and tests for the paper version of the TOEFL test are found on the CD-ROM.

HOW TO USE THIS BOOK

This book provides a variety of materials to help you prepare for the paper version of the TOEFL test. Following these steps can help you to get the most out of this book:

- Take the Diagnostic Pre-Test at the beginning of each section. When you take the Pre-Test, try to reproduce the conditions and time pressure of a real TOEFL test.
  - (A) Take each section of the test without interruption.
  - (B) Work on only one section at a time.
  - (C) Use the answer sheets from the back of the book.
  - (D) Use a pencil to completely fill in the answer oval.
  - (E) Erase any changes that you make carefully. If answers are not completely erased on the actual TOEFL sheet, they will be marked wrong.
  - (F) Time yourself for each test section. You need to experience the time pressure that exists on the actual TOEFL test.
  - (G) Play the listening recording one time only during the test. (You may play it more times when you are reviewing the test.)
  - (H) Mark only your answer sheet. You cannot write in a TOEFL test booklet.

- After you complete the Pre-Test, you should score it, diagnose your answers, and record your results.
  - (A) Determine your TOEFL score using the Scoring Information on pages 549–550.
  - (B) Complete the appropriate part of the Diagnostic Charts on pages 551–558 to determine which language skills you have already mastered and which need further study.
  - (C) Record your results on the Progress Chart on page 559.

- Work through the presentations and exercises for each section, paying particular attention to the skills that caused you problems in the Pre-Test. Each time that you complete a TOEFL-format exercise, try to simulate the conditions and time pressure of a real TOEFL test.
  - (A) For listening questions, play the recording one time only. Do not stop the recording between questions.
  - (B) For structure questions, allow yourself one minute for two questions. (For example, you should take five minutes for an exercise with ten questions.)
  - (C) For reading comprehension questions, allow yourself one minute for one question. (For example, if a reading passage has ten questions, you should allow yourself ten minutes to read the passage and answer the ten questions.)
- When further practice on a specific point is included in an Appendix, a note in the text directs you to this practice. Complete the Appendix exercises on a specific point when the text directs you to those exercises and it is an area that you need to improve.
- When you have completed all the skills exercises for a section, take the Post-Test for that section. Follow the directions above to reproduce the conditions and time pressure of a real TOEFL test. After you complete the Post-Test, follow the directions above to score it, diagnose your answers, and record your results.
- As you work through the course material, periodically schedule Complete Tests. There are five Complete Tests in the book. As you take each of the Complete Tests, follow the directions above

to reproduce the conditions and time pressure of a real TOEFL test. After you finish each Complete Test follow the directions above to score it, diagnose your answers, and record your results.

HOW TO USE THE CD-ROM

The CD-ROM provides additional practice of the language skills and paper version tests to supplement the language skills and tests in the book. The material on the CD-ROM is completely different from the material in the book in order to provide the maximum amount of practice. Following these steps can help you to get the most out of the CD-ROM.

Skills Practice
• After you have completed language skills in the book, you should complete the related skills practice exercises on the CD-ROM.

	AFTER THIS IN THE BOOK:	COMPLETE THIS ON THE CD-ROM:
Listening Comprehension	Short Dialogues: Skills 1–3	Short Dialogues: Skills 1–3
	Short Dialogues: Skills 4–6	Short Dialogues: Skills 4–6
	Short Dialogues: Skills 7–10	Short Dialogues: Skills 7–10
	Short Dialogues: Skills 11–13	Short Dialogues: Skills 11–13
	Short Dialogues: Skills 14–15	Short Dialogues: Skills 14–15
	Short Dialogues: Skills 16–17	Short Dialogues: Skills 16–17
	Conversations: Skills 18–22	Conversations: Conversation 1
		Conversations: Conversation 2
		Conversations: Conversation 3
	Talks: Skills 23–27	Talks: Talk 1
		Talks: Talk 2
		Talks: Talk 3
Structure and Written Expression	Structure: Skills 1–5	Structure: Skills 1–5
	Structure: Skills 6–8	Structure: Skills 6–8
	Structure: Skills 9–12	Structure: Skills 9–12
	Structure: Skills 13–14	Structure: Skills 13–14
	Structure: Skills 15–19	Structure: Skills 15–19
	Written Expression: Skills 20–23	Written Expression: Skills 20–23
	Written Expression: Skills 24–26	Written Expression: Skills 24–26
	Written Expression: Skills 27–29	Written Expression: Skills 27–29
	Written Expression: Skills 30–32	Written Expression: Skills 30–32
	Written Expression: Skills 33–36	Written Expression: Skills 33–36
	Written Expression: Skills 37–38	Written Expression: Skills 37–38

	AFTER THIS IN THE BOOK:	COMPLETE THIS ON THE CD-ROM:
Structure and Written Expression (continued)	*Written Expression: Skills 39–42* *Written Expression: Skills 43–45* *Written Expression: Skills 46–48* *Written Expression: Skills 49–51* *Written Expression: Skills 52–55* *Written Expression: Skills 56–57* *Written Expression: Skills 58–60*	*Written Expression: Skills 39–42* *Written Expression: Skills 43–45* *Written Expression: Skills 46–48* *Written Expression: Skills 49–51* *Written Expression: Skills 52–55* *Written Expression: Skills 56–57* *Written Expression: Skills 58–60*
Reading Comprehension	*Reading Comprehension: Skills 1–2* *Reading Comprehension: Skills 3–5* *Reading Comprehension: Skills 6–7* *Reading Comprehension: Skills 8–11* *Reading Comprehension: Skills 12–13*	*Reading Comprehension: Skills 1–2* *Reading Comprehension: Skills 3–5* *Reading Comprehension: Skills 6–7* *Reading Comprehension: Skills 8–11* *Reading Comprehension: Skills 12–13*
Test of Written English (TWE)	*TWE: Skills 1–6* *TWE: Skill 7* *TWE: Skill 8A* *TWE: Skill 8B* *TWE: Skill 8C* *TWE: Skill 8D* *TWE: Skill 8E* *TWE: Skill 8F*	*TWE: Passage 1 (Skills 1–6)* *TWE: Passage 2 (Skills 1–6)* *TWE: Passage 3 (Skills 1–6)* *TWE: Skill 7* *TWE: Skill 8A* *TWE: Skill 8B* *TWE: Skill 8C* *TWE: Skill 8D* *TWE: Skill 8E* *TWE: Skill 8F*

- Work slowly and carefully though the skills practice exercises. The skills practice exercises are not timed but instead are designed to be done in a methodical and thoughtful way.
  (A) Answer a question on the CD-ROM using the skills and strategies that you have learned in the book.
  (B) Use the *Check Answer* button to determine whether the answer to that question is correct or incorrect.
  (C) If your answer is incorrect, reconsider the question and choose a different answer.
  (D) Use the *Check Answer* button to check your new response. (In the Listening Comprehension section, you may listen to a passage again by using the *Listen* button.)
  (E) When you are satisfied that you have figured out as much as you can on your own, use the *Explain Answer* button to see an explanation. (In the Listening Comprehension section, you may see the recording script as you listen to a passage again by using the *View Script* button.)
  (F) Then, move on to the next question and repeat this process.

- As you work your way through the skills practice exercises, monitor your progress on the charts included in the program.
    - (A) The *Score Reports* include a list of each of the exercises that you have completed and how well you have done on each of the exercises. (If you do an exercise more than once, the results of each attempt will be listed.)
    - (B) The *Skill Reports* include a list of each of the language skills in the book, how many questions with each language skill that you have answered, and what percentage of the questions you have answered correctly. In this way, you can see clearly which language skills you have mastered and which language skills require further study.

Section Tests

- Use the section tests on the CD-ROM periodically throughout the course to determine how well you have learned to apply the language skills and test-taking strategies presented in the course. The CD-ROM includes 3 Listening Comprehension section tests, 10 Structure and Written Expression section tests, 3 Reading Comprehension section tests, and 10 Test of Written English (TWE) section tests.
- Take the tests in a manner that is as close as possible to the actual testing environment. Choose a time when you can work on a section without interruption.
- Work straight through each timed test section. The *Check Answer, Explain Answer,* and *Listen* buttons are only available in the Skills Practice activities. The test section is designed to be as close as possible to an actual test.
- After you complete a test section, follow the directions to go to the *Score Report* for the test that you just completed. A TOEFL equivalent score is given in the upper right corner of the *Score Report* for the test that you just completed.
- In the *Score Report,* see which questions you answered correctly and incorrectly and see which language skills were tested in each question. Print this score report if you would like to keep your *Score Reports* together in a notebook.
- In the *Score Report* for the test that you just completed, review each question by double-clicking on a particular question. When you double-click on a question in the *Score Report,* you can see the question, the answer that you chose, the correct answer, and the *Explain Answer* button. You may click on the *Explain Answer* button to see an explanation.
- Return to the *Score Report* for a particular test whenever you would like by entering through the *Scores* button on the Main Menu. You do not need to review a test section immediately but may instead wait to review the test section.

TO THE TEACHER

HOW TO GET THE MOST OUT OF THE EXERCISES

The exercises are a vital part of the TOEFL preparation process presented in this book. Maximum benefit can be obtained from the exercises if the students are properly prepared for the exercises and if the exercises are carefully reviewed after completion.

- Be sure that the students have a clear idea of the appropriate skills and strategies involved in each exercise. Before beginning each exercise, review the skills and strategies that are used in that exercise. Then, when you review the exercises, reinforce the skills and strategies that can be used to determine the correct answers.
- As you review the exercises, be sure to discuss each answer, the incorrect answers as well as the correct answers. Discuss how students can determine that each correct answer is correct and each incorrect answer is incorrect.
- Two different methods are possible to review the listening exercises. One good way to review these exercises is to play back the recording, stopping after each question to discuss the skills and strategies involved in determining which answer is correct and those that are incorrect. Another method is to have the students refer to the recording script at the back of the book to discuss each question.
- The structure exercises in the correct/incorrect format present a challenge for the teacher. In exercises in which the students are asked to indicate which sentences are correct and which are incorrect, it is extremely helpful for the students to correct the incorrect sentences. An indication of the type of error and/or one possible correction for each incorrect sentence is included in the answer key. It should be noted, however, that many of the incorrect sentences can be corrected in several ways. The role of the teacher is to assist the students in finding the various ways that the sentences can be corrected.
- The exercises are designed to be completed in class rather than assigned as homework. The exercises are short and take very little time to complete, particularly since it is important to keep students under time pressure while they are working on the exercises. Considerably more time should be spent in reviewing the exercises than in actually doing them.

HOW TO GET THE MOST OUT OF THE TESTS

There are three different types of tests in this book: Pre-Tests, Post-Tests, and Complete Tests. When the tests are given, it is important that the test conditions be as similar to actual TOEFL test conditions as possible; each section of the test should be given without interruption and under the time pressure of the actual test. Review of the tests should emphasize the function served by each of these different types of tests:

- While reviewing the Pre-Tests, you should encourage students to determine the areas where they require further practice.
- While reviewing the Post-Tests, you should emphasize the language skills and strategies involved in determining the correct answer to each question.

- While reviewing the Complete Tests, you should emphasize overall strategies for the Complete Tests and review the variety of individual language skills and strategies taught throughout the course.

HOW TO GET THE MOST OUT OF THE CD-ROM

The CD-ROM is designed to supplement the practice that is contained in the book and to provide an alternate modality for preparation for the paper version of the TOEFL test. It has a number of features that make it easy to incorporate the CD-ROM into a preparation program for the paper version of the TOEFL test. Here are some ideas to consider as you decide how to incorporate the CD-ROM into your course.

- The CD-ROM is closely coordinated with the book and is intended to provide further practice for the skills and strategies that are presented in the book. This means that the overall organization of the CD-ROM parallels the organization of the book, but the exercise material and test items on the CD-ROM are different from those found in the book. It can thus be quite effective to teach and practice the language skills and strategies in the book and then use the CD-ROM for further practice and assignments.
- The CD-ROM can be used in a computer lab during class time (if you are lucky enough to have access to a computer lab during class time), but it does not need to be used in this way. It can also be quite effective to use the book during class time and to make assignments from the CD-ROM for the students to complete outside of class, either in the school computer lab or on their personal computers. Either method works quite well.
- The CD-ROM contains both a Skills Practice section and a Test section with completely different questions in each of these sections. In the Skills Practice section, the students can practice and assess their mastery of specific skills. In the Test section, the students can see how well they are able to apply their knowledge of the language skills and test-taking strategies to realistic test sections.
- The CD-ROM scores the Skills Practice exercises and the Test sections in different ways. The Skills Practice exercises are given a score that shows the percentage correct. The Test sections are given TOEFL equivalent scores.
- The CD-ROM contains printable Skill Report and Score Report forms so that you can easily and efficiently keep track of your students' progress. You may want to ask your students to print their Score Reports after they complete each exercise and compile the Score Reports in a notebook; you can then ask the students to turn in their notebooks periodically so that you can easily check that the assignments have been completed and monitor the progress that the students are making.
- The CD-ROM allows you to work with the Test of Written English (TWE) tests in a number of ways. In the Test section of the CD-ROM, the TWE task is to write an essay in thirty minutes. The essays can be printed when they are written so that they can be reviewed and analyzed. The essays are also automatically saved and can be accessed through the Scores Menu. It is also possible for the students to copy their essays into a word processing program so that they can make changes, corrections, and improvements to their essays.

SECTION ONE

LISTENING COMPREHENSION

1 □ 1 □ 1 □ 1 □ 1 □ 1 □ 1 □ 1 □ 1

DIAGNOSTIC PRE-TEST

SECTION 1
LISTENING COMPREHENSION
Time—approximately 35 minutes
(including the reading of the directions for each part)

In this section of the test, you will have an opportunity to demonstrate your ability to understand conversations and talks in English. There are three parts to this section, with special directions for each part. Answer all the questions on the basis of what is **stated** or **implied** by the speakers you hear. Do **not** take notes or write in your test book at any time. Do **not** turn the pages until you are told to do so.

Part A

Directions: In Part A you will hear short conversations between two people. After each conversation, you will hear a question about the conversation. The conversations and questions will not be repeated. After you hear a question, read the four possible answers in your test book and choose the best answer. Then, on your answer sheet, find the number of the question and fill in the space that corresponds to the letter of the answer you have chosen.

Listen to an example.

Sample Answer

On the recording, you will hear:

   (man)   *That exam was just awful.*
   (woman)   *Oh, it could have been worse.*
   (narrator) *What does the woman mean?*

In your test book, you will read:
   (A) The exam was really awful.
   (B) It was the worst exam she had ever seen.
   (C) It couldn't have been more difficult.
   (D) It wasn't that hard.

You learn from the conversation that the man thought the exam was very difficult and that the woman disagreed with the man. The best answer to the question, "What does the woman mean?" is (D), "It wasn't that hard." Therefore, the correct choice is (D).

Wait

1. (A) The coffee is much better this morning.
   (B) He's feeling bitter this morning.
   (C) The coffee isn't very good.
   (D) He cannot taste the butter.

2. (A) The two classes meet in an hour and a half.
   (B) The class meets three hours per week.
   (C) Each half of the class is an hour long.
   (D) Two times a week the class meets for an hour.

3. (A) A few minutes ago, the flight departed.
   (B) The fight will start in a while.
   (C) They are frightened about the departure.
   (D) The plane is going to take off soon.

4. (A) He hasn't yet begun his project.
   (B) He's supposed to do his science project next week.
   (C) He needs to start working on changing the due date.
   (D) He's been working steadily on his science project.

5. (A) At the post office.
   (B) In a florist shop.
   (C) In a restaurant.
   (D) In a hospital delivery room.

6. (A) The professor drowned the cells in a lab.
   (B) The topic was presented in a boring way.
   (C) The professor divided the lecture into parts.
   (D) The biologist tried to sell the results of the experiment.

7. (A) She needs to get a driver's license.
   (B) It is impossible to cash a check without two pieces of identification.
   (C) The man should check to see if he needs credit.
   (D) A credit card can be used to get a driver's license.

8. (A) Housing within his budget is hard to locate.
   (B) It's hard to find his house in New York.
   (C) He can't afford to move his house to New York.
   (D) Housing in New York is unavailable.

9. (A) The boss was working on the reports.
   (B) He would have to finish the reports before the end of next month.
   (C) He was directed to stay late and finish some work.
   (D) He could finish the reports at home.

10. (A) The boisterous students made the teacher mad.
    (B) The teacher angered the students with the exam results.
    (C) The students were angry that the teacher was around.
    (D) The angered students complained to the teacher.

11. (A) The prices are reasonable.
    (B) The store is too far out of town.
    (C) He would like the woman to repeat what she said.
    (D) He agrees with the woman.

12. (A) It has rarely rained this much.
    (B) It hardly rained this year.
    (C) It is barely raining this year.
    (D) It seldom rains so little.

13. (A) He needs to do a better job writing questions.
    (B) His writing must certainly be improved.
    (C) Without the questions, he cannot write the answers.
    (D) He needs to understand the written questions better.

GO ON TO THE NEXT PAGE →

14. (A) The agent was standing in line with his passport.
   (B) The line to get new passports is very long.
   (C) The woman must wait her turn to get her passport checked.
   (D) He can check her passport instead of the agent.

15. (A) He couldn't finish closing the library book.
   (B) He hadn't finished the library assignment, but he was close.
   (C) He was working on the assignment when the library closed.
   (D) His homework was incomplete because the library wasn't open.

16. (A) He wishes the hard work had had a better result.
   (B) He thinks the lawyer hardly prepared.
   (C) He wishes the lawyer had prepared.
   (D) He thinks the lawyer worked for free.

17. (A) The history class begins next week.
   (B) He thinks the papers should be turned in next week.
   (C) He has already done the paper for next week.
   (D) The papers are not due next week.

18. (A) He's not really happy.
   (B) The contractor's work was satisfactory.
   (C) He would rather work with the contractor himself.
   (D) He was already contacted about the work.

19. (A) The man should try another type of paper.
   (B) The man should locate a typist tomorrow morning.
   (C) The man should make a tape in the morning.
   (D) The man should complete the paper without help.

20. (A) She'd like some pie.
   (B) It's easy to buy it.
   (C) The task the man's working on isn't difficult.
   (D) It's easier to prepare pie than do what the man is doing.

21. (A) He reported that the time for the budget meeting had been set.
   (B) He is always late in submitting his accounting figures.
   (C) He never manages to budget his time well.
   (D) He is never too late in turning in his reports.

22. (A) The repairs would require an extension.
   (B) The car is going to need a lot of repairs.
   (C) Buying a new car would be quite expensive.
   (D) The mechanic extended the repair warranty.

23. (A) Betty wrote the letter as directed.
   (B) The directions were given to Betty in a letter.
   (C) Betty will follow the instructions later.
   (D) Betty worked exactly as instructed.

24. (A) Walter's had a lack of success with his business.
   (B) Walter's failed in business.
   (C) Walter's new company is doing rather well.
   (D) Walter hoped to succeed in business.

25. (A) He should put the organ in the closet.
   (B) The closet has already been organized.
   (C) He needs to rearrange the closet.
   (D) He wishes the closet were closer.

26. (A) She didn't do the work.
   (B) She gave the assignment her best effort.
   (C) She finished the assignment even though it was difficult.
   (D) She gave the man a signal.

GO ON TO THE NEXT PAGE →

27. (A) She said some terrible things.
    (B) She didn't say anything nice.
    (C) She didn't have any nice things.
    (D) She said really wonderful things.

28. (A) New employees are rarely initiated into the company.
    (B) New workers don't generally undertake actions on their own.
    (C) New employees are initially rated.
    (D) It's rare for employees to make new suggestions.

29. (A) The woman is more than a week late.
    (B) The children would have wrecked the house later.
    (C) The woman was so late that she was a wreck.
    (D) He's glad that she was not any later.

30. (A) He had not gone to the store.
    (B) He was still at the market.
    (C) He was going to take care of the shopping.
    (D) He always went to the market.

GO ON TO THE NEXT PAGE

Part B

Directions: In this part of the test, you will hear longer conversations. After each conversation, you will hear several questions. The conversations and questions will not be repeated.

After you hear a question, read the four possible answers in your test book and choose the best answer. Then, on your answer sheet, find the number of the question and fill in the space that corresponds to the letter of the answer you have chosen.

Remember, you are not allowed to take notes or write in your test book.

31. (A) She's a senior.
    (B) She's a junior.
    (C) She's a transfer student.
    (D) She's a graduate student.

32. (A) How to transfer to a junior college.
    (B) How to find his way around campus.
    (C) The course requirements for a literature major.
    (D) Who won the campus election.

33. (A) Three.
    (B) Five.
    (C) Eight.
    (D) Ten.

34. (A) American literature.
    (B) World literature.
    (C) Literary analysis.
    (D) Surveying.

35. (A) In a book.
    (B) From a television program.
    (C) During a trip that she took.
    (D) From a lecture.

36. (A) To communicate with other dolphins.
    (B) To recognize objects in the water.
    (C) To learn human language.
    (D) To express fear.

37. (A) Five.
    (B) Fifteen.
    (C) Fifty.
    (D) Five hundred.

38. (A) It is limited.
    (B) It is greater than human intelligence.
    (C) It is less than previously thought.
    (D) We are beginning to learn how much they have.

GO ON TO THE NEXT PAGE

Part C

Directions: In this part of the test, you will hear several talks. After each talk, you will hear some questions. The talks and questions will not be repeated.

After you hear a question, you will read the four possible answers in your test book and choose the best answer. Then, on your answer sheet, find the number of the question and fill in the space that corresponds to the letter of the answer you have chosen.

Here is an example.

On the recording, you will hear:

(narrator)   *Listen to an instructor talk to his class about painting.*

(man)   *Artist Grant Wood was a guiding force in the school of painting known as American regionalist, a style reflecting the distinctive characteristics of art from rural areas of the United States. Wood began drawing animals on the family farm at the age of three, and when he was thirty-eight one of his paintings received a remarkable amount of public notice and acclaim. This painting, called "American Gothic," is a starkly simple depiction of a serious couple staring directly out at the viewer.*

Now listen to a sample question.

Sample Answer

(narrator)   *What style of painting is known as American regionalist?*

In your test book, you will read: (A) Art from America's inner cities.
(B) Art from the central region of the U.S.
(C) Art from various urban areas in the U.S.
(D) Art from rural sections of America.

The best answer to the question, "What style of painting is known as American regionalist?" is (D), "Art from rural sections of America." Therefore, the correct choice is (D).

Now listen to another sample question.

Sample Answer

(narrator)   *What is the name of Wood's most successful painting?*

Ⓐ Ⓑ ● Ⓓ

In your test book, you will read: (A) "American Regionalist."
(B) "The Family Farm in Iowa."
(C) "American Gothic."
(D) "A Serious Couple."

The best answer to the question, "What is the name of Wood's most successful painting?" is (C), "American Gothic." Therefore, the correct choice is (C).

Remember, you are **not** allowed to take notes or write in your test book.

39. (A) To protect its members.
    (B) To save the natural environment.
    (C) To honor the memory of John Muir.
    (D) To improve San Francisco's natural beauty.

40. (A) For less than a year.
    (B) Only for a decade.
    (C) For more than a century.
    (D) For at least two centuries.

41. (A) San Francisco.
    (B) All fifty states.
    (C) The Sierra Nevadas.
    (D) The eastern U.S.

42. (A) All over the world.
    (B) In the entire United States.
    (C) Only in California.
    (D) Only in the Sierra Nevadas.

43. (A) Students signing up for athletic teams.
    (B) Students going on a tour of a university campus.
    (C) Students playing various sports.
    (D) Students attending a university dedication ceremony.

44. (A) Membership on an athletic team.
    (B) Enrollment in an exercise class.
    (C) A valid student identification card.
    (D) Permission from a faculty member.

45. (A) To the tennis courts.
    (B) To the arena.
    (C) To the gymnasium.
    (D) To the Athletic Department office.

46. (A) Go to the Art Center.
    (B) Sign up for sports classes.
    (C) Visit the exercise room.
    (D) Watch a football game.

47. (A) Science.
    (B) Art.
    (C) Literature.
    (D) Music.

48. (A) They are completely different.
    (B) They are somewhat similar but have an essential difference.
    (C) They are exactly the same in all respects.
    (D) They are unrelated.

49. (A) Objective.
    (B) Idealistic.
    (C) Philosophical.
    (D) Environmental.

50. (A) Heredity.
    (B) Environment.
    (C) Idealism.
    (D) Natural laws.

This is the end of the Listening Comprehension Pre-Test.

Turn off the recording.

When you finish the test, you may do the following:

- Turn to the **Diagnostic Chart** on pages 551–552, and circle the numbers of the questions that you missed.
- Turn to **Scoring Information** on pages 549–550, and determine your TOEFL score.
- Turn to the **Progress Chart** on page 559, and add your score to the chart.

LISTENING COMPREHENSION

The first section of the TOEFL test is the Listening Comprehension section. This section consists of fifty questions (some tests may be longer). You will listen to recorded materials and respond to questions about the material. You must listen carefully, because you will hear the recording program one time only, and the material on the recording is not written in your test book.

There are three parts in the Listening Comprehension section of the TOEFL test:

1. **Part A** consists of thirty short conversations, each followed by a question. You must choose the best answer to each question from the four choices in your test book.
2. **Part B** consists of two long conversations, each followed by a number of questions. You must choose the best answer to each question from the four choices in your test book.
3. **Part C** consists of three talks, each followed by a number of questions. You must choose the best answer to each question from the four choices in your test book.

GENERAL STRATEGIES

1. **Be familiar with the directions.** The directions on every TOEFL test are the same, so it is not necessary to listen carefully to them each time. You should be completely familiar with the directions before the day of the test.

2. **Listen carefully to the conversations and talks.** You should concentrate fully on what the speakers are saying in the recording program, because you will hear it one time only.

3. **Know where the easier and more difficult questions are generally found.** Within each part of the Listening Comprehension section, the questions generally progress from easy to difficult.

4. **Never leave any answers blank on your answer sheet.** Even if you are unsure of the correct response, you should answer each question. There is no penalty for guessing.

5. **Use any remaining time to look ahead at the answers to the questions that follow.** When you finish with one question, you may have time to look ahead at the answers to the next question.

THE LISTENING PART A QUESTIONS

For each of the thirty questions in Part A of the Listening Comprehension section of the TOEFL test, you will hear a short conversation between two speakers followed by a question. After you listen to the conversation and question, you must choose the best answer to the question from your test book.

Example

On the recording, you hear:

       (man)   *I've always wanted to visit Hawaii with you.*
   (woman)   *Why not next month?*
(narrator)   *What does the woman mean?*

In your test book, you read:

   (A)   Next month isn't a good time for the trip.
   (B)   She doesn't want to go to Hawaii.
   (C)   She suggests taking the trip next month.
   (D)   She's curious about why he doesn't want to go.

Answer (C) is the best answer to the question. *Why not next month?* is a suggestion that they take the trip next month.

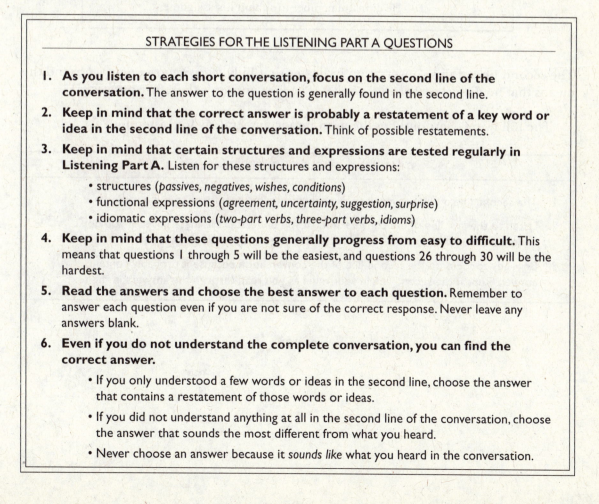

STRATEGIES FOR THE LISTENING PART A QUESTIONS

1. **As you listen to each short conversation, focus on the second line of the conversation.** The answer to the question is generally found in the second line.

2. **Keep in mind that the correct answer is probably a restatement of a key word or idea in the second line of the conversation.** Think of possible restatements.

3. **Keep in mind that certain structures and expressions are tested regularly in Listening Part A.** Listen for these structures and expressions:
   - structures (*passives, negatives, wishes, conditions*)
   - functional expressions (*agreement, uncertainty, suggestion, surprise*)
   - idiomatic expressions (*two-part verbs, three-part verbs, idioms*)

4. **Keep in mind that these questions generally progress from easy to difficult.** This means that questions 1 through 5 will be the easiest, and questions 26 through 30 will be the hardest.

5. **Read the answers and choose the best answer to each question.** Remember to answer each question even if you are not sure of the correct response. Never leave any answers blank.

6. **Even if you do not understand the complete conversation, you can find the correct answer.**
   - If you only understood a few words or ideas in the second line, choose the answer that contains a restatement of those words or ideas.
   - If you did not understand anything at all in the second line of the conversation, choose the answer that sounds the most different from what you heard.
   - Never choose an answer because it *sounds like* what you heard in the conversation.

The following skills will help you to implement these strategies in the Listening Part A section of the TOEFL test.

STRATEGIES

SKILL 1: FOCUS ON THE SECOND LINE

In Listening Part A you will hear a short conversation involving two people; this conversation is followed by a question. It is important to understand that the answer to this type of question is most often (but not always!) found in the second line of the conversation.

Example

On the recording, you hear:

    (man)   *Billy really made a big mistake this time.*
    (woman)   *Yes, he forgot to turn in his research paper.*
    (narrator)   *What does the woman say about Billy?*

In your test book, you read:

    (A) It was the first time he made a mistake.
    (B) He forgot to write his paper.
    (C) He turned in the paper in the wrong place.
    (D) He didn't remember to submit his assignment.

The second line of this conversation indicates that Billy *forgot to turn in his paper,* and this means that he *did not remember to submit it.* The best answer is therefore answer (D).

The following chart outlines the most important strategy for Listening Part A:

STRATEGY #1: FOCUS ON THE SECOND LINE

1. The second line of the conversation probably contains the answer to the question.

2. Listen to the first line of the conversation. If you understand it, that's good. If you don't understand it, don't worry because it probably does not contain the answer.

3. Be ready to focus on the second line of the conversation because it probably contains the answer. Repeat the second line in your mind as you read through the answers in the text.

EXERCISE 1: In this exercise, you should focus on the second line of the conversation, read the question, and then choose the best answer to that question. Remember that you can probably answer the question easily with only the second line.

1.   (man)   *Can you tell me if today's matinee is a comedy, romance, or western?*
     (woman)   *I have no idea.*
     (narrator) *What does the woman mean?*

   (A) She has strong ideas about movies.
   (B) She prefers comedies over westerns and romances.
   (C) She doesn't like today's matinee.
   (D) She does not know.

2.   (woman)   *Was anyone at home at Barb's house when you went there to deliver the package?*
     (man)   *I rang the bell, but no one answered.*
     (narrator) *What does the man imply?*

   (A) Barb answered the bell.
   (B) The house was probably empty.
   (C) The bell wasn't in the house.
   (D) The house doesn't have a bell.

3.   (woman)   *You just got back from the interview for the internship. How do you think it went?*
     (man)   *I think it's highly unlikely that I got the job.*
     (narrator) *What does the man suggest?*

   (A) It's unlikely that he'll go to the interview.
   (B) He thinks he'll be recommended for a high-level job.
   (C) The interview was apparently quite unsuccessful.
   (D) He had an excellent interview.

TOEFL EXERCISE 1: In this exercise, listen carefully to the short conversation and question in the recording program, and then choose the best answer to the question. You should focus carefully on the second line.

NOW BEGIN THE RECORDING PROGRAM AT TOEFL EXERCISE 1.

1.   (A) He is leaving now.
     (B) He has to go out of his way.
     (C) He will not be leaving soon.
     (D) He will do it his own way.

2.   (A) He locked the door.
     (B) He tried unsuccessfully to get into the house.
     (C) He was able to open the door.
     (D) He left the house without locking the door.

3.   (A) She doesn't like to listen to turkeys.
     (B) She thinks the dinner sounds special.
     (C) She especially likes the roast turkey.
     (D) She'd prefer a different dinner.

4.   (A) He'll be busy with her homework tonight.
     (B) He can't help her tonight.
     (C) He's sorry he can't ever help her.
     (D) He'll help her with her physics.

5.   (A) Her eyes hurt.
     (B) She thought the lecture was great.
     (C) The class was boring.
     (D) She didn't want to watch Professor Martin.

6.   (A) Not all the bills have been paid.
     (B) They don't have enough credit to pay the bills.
     (C) What she said on the phone was not credible.
     (D) He used a credit card to pay some of the bills.

7.   (A) She'll call back quickly.
     (B) She'll definitely be back by 4:00.
     (C) She'll give it back by 4:00.
     (D) She'll try to return fast.

8.   (A) She hasn't seen Tim.
     (B) Tim was there only for a moment.
     (C) Tim was around a short time ago.
     (D) Tim will return in a minute.

9. (A) She doesn't like the place he chose.
    (B) She doesn't want to get into the car.
    (C) She's glad the spot is reserved.
    (D) They can't park the car there.

10. (A) There's plenty to eat.
    (B) The refrigerator's broken.
    (C) The food isn't in the refrigerator.
    (D) He's not sure if there's enough.

SKILL 2:   CHOOSE ANSWERS WITH SYNONYMS

Often the correct answer in Listening Part A is an answer that contains synonyms (words with similar meanings but different sounds) for key words in the conversation.

Example

On the recording, you hear:

  (woman) *Why is Barbara feeling so happy?*
   (man) *She just started working in a real estate agency.*
  (narrator) *What does the man say about Barbara?*

In your test book, you read:

  (A) She always liked her work in real estate.
  (B) She began a new job.
  (C) She just bought some real estate.
  (D) She bought a real estate agency.

In this conversation, the key word *started* means *began,* and the key word *working* refers to *job.* The best answer to this question is therefore answer (B).

The following chart outlines a very important strategy for Listening Part A:

STRATEGY #2: CHOOSE ANSWERS WITH SYNONYMS
1. As you listen to the second line of the conversation, focus on key words in that line.
2. If you see any synonyms for key words in a particular answer, then you have probably found the correct answer.

EXERCISE 2: In this exercise, underline key words in the second line of each short conversation. Then underline synonyms for these key words in the answers, and choose the best answer to each question. Remember that the best answer is probably the answer that contains synonyms for the key words in the second line of the conversation.

1. (woman) *Did you see the manager about the job in the bookstore?*
   (man) *Yes, and I also had to fill out an application.*
  (narrator) *What does the man mean?*

(A) He got a job as bookstore manager.
(B) The bookstore was not accepting applications.
(C) He saw a book about how to apply for jobs.
(D) It was necessary to complete a form.

2. (man)   *We're planning to leave for the*   (A) If they could leave at noon.
             trip at about 2:00.

2.	(man)	*We're planning to leave for the trip at about 2:00.*	(A)	If they could leave at noon.
	(woman)	*Couldn't we leave before noon?*	(B)	If it is possible to go by 12:00.
	(narrator)	*What does the woman ask?*	(C)	Why they can't leave at noon.
			(D)	If they could leave the room.

3.	(man)	*Was the concert well received?*	(A)	The performance went on for a long time.
	(woman)	*The audience applauded for a long time after the performance.*	(B)	There was applause throughout the performance.
	(narrator)	*What does the woman say about the concert?*	(C)	The people clapped on and on after the concert.
			(D)	The audience waited for a long time for the concert to begin.

TOEFL EXERCISE 2: In this exercise, listen carefully to the short conversation and question in the recording program, and then choose the best answer to the question. You should look for synonyms for key words in the second line.

    NOW BEGIN THE RECORDING PROGRAM AT TOEFL EXERCISE 2.

1. (A) The final exam was harder than the others.
    (B) There were two exams rather than one.
    (C) He thought the exam would be easier.
    (D) The exam was not very difficult.

2. (A) He's not feeling very well.
    (B) He's rather sick of working.
    (C) He's feeling better today than yesterday.
    (D) He'd really rather not answer the question.

3. (A) The company was founded about a year ago.
    (B) It was just established that he could go into business.
    (C) The family is well established.
    (D) The business only lasted a year.

4. (A) He did not look at the right schedule.
    (B) The plane landed in the right place.
    (C) The plane arrived on time.
    (D) He had to wait for the plane to land.

5. (A) She'd rather go running.
    (B) She doesn't want to go into the pool.
    (C) She'll change clothes quickly and go swimming.
    (D) She needs a sweatsuit to go running.

6. (A) The firefighters saved the homes for last.
    (B) A firefighter saved the hillside last night.
    (C) The homes on the hillside were burned.
    (D) The houses weren't destroyed.

7. (A) There's enough soup.
    (B) The spices are adequate.
    (C) She thinks the soup's too salty.
    (D) The man should add more salt and pepper.

8. (A) He was lucky to receive a grant for his studies.
    (B) He used his fortune to pay his fees.
    (C) He is a scholar at a college with low fees.
    (D) He paid to get a scholarship.

9. (A) It profited from previous mistakes.
    (B) It earned a lot of money.
    (C) This was the last year that it would make a profit.
    (D) It was not so successful.

10. (A) Chuck's bank account has too much money in it.
    (B) He thinks Chuck has the wrong kind of bank account.
    (C) He thinks that Chuck is on his way home from the bank.
    (D) There isn't enough money in Chuck's account.

SKILL 3: AVOID SIMILAR SOUNDS

Often the incorrect answers in Listening Part A are answers that contain words with *similar* sounds but very different meanings from what you hear in the recording program. You should definitely avoid these answers.

Example

On the recording, you hear:

(man)	*Why couldn't Mark come with us?*
(woman)	*He was searching for a new apartment.*
(narrator)	*What does the woman say about Mark?*

In your test book, you read:

(A) He was in the department office.
(B) He was looking for a place to live.
(C) He was working on his research project.
(D) He had an appointment at church.

The key words in the second line of the conversation are *searching* and *apartment*. In answers (C) and (D) the words *research* and *church* sound like *search*, so these answers are incorrect. In answers (A) and (D), the words *department* and *appointment* sound like *apartment*, so these answers are incorrect. The best answer is therefore answer (B).

The following chart outlines a very important strategy for Listening Part A:

STRATEGY #3: AVOID SIMILAR SOUNDS
1. Identify key words in the second line of the conversation.
2. Identify words in the answers that contain similar sounds, and do not choose these answers.

NOTE: In Appendix A there are drills to practice distinguishing similar sounds. You may want to complete these practice drills before trying the following exercises.

EXERCISE 3: In this exercise, underline key words in the second line of each short conversation. Then underline words with sounds similar to these key words in the answers, and choose the best answer to each question. Remember that the best answer is probably the answer that does not contain words with sounds that are similar to the sounds of the key words in the second line of the conversation.

1. (woman) *I heard that Sally just moved into a new, big house near the beach.*
   (man) *But Sally doesn't have a cent!*
   (narrator) *What does the man mean?*

   (A) Sally has no sense of responsibility.
   (B) Sally sent her friend to the house.
   (C) Sally has no money.
   (D) Sally is on the set with her.

2. (woman)   *Did they get the new car they*
                wanted?
    (man)   *No, they lacked the money.*
    (narrator) *What does the man mean?*

    (A) They locked the map in a car.
    (B) They looked many times in the car.
    (C) It cost a lot of money when the car
        leaked oil.
    (D) They didn't have enough money to
        buy another car.

3. (man)   *Have you finished packing yet?*
    (woman)   *You should call the porter to get*
                the suitcases.
    (narrator) *What does the woman mean?*

    (A) It's important to pack the suitcases.
    (B) They need help carrying their bags.
    (C) The man should pack his suit in
        case he needs it.
    (D) The suitcases are quite portable.

TOEFL EXERCISE 3: In this exercise, listen carefully to the short conversation and question in the recording program, and then choose the best answer to the question. You should be careful to avoid answers with similar sounds.

NOW BEGIN THE RECORDING PROGRAM AT TOEFL EXERCISE 3.

1. (A) She has to wait for some cash.
    (B) The waiter is bringing a glass of
         water.
    (C) The lawn is too dry.
    (D) She needs to watch out for a crash.

2. (A) The sweater's the wrong size.
    (B) The man's feet aren't sweating.
    (C) The sweater makes the man seem
         fat.
    (D) The sweet girl doesn't feel right.

3. (A) He has been regularly using a
         computer.
    (B) He communicates with a Boston
         company.
    (C) He regularly goes to communities
         around Boston.
    (D) He has been traveling back and
         forth to Boston.

4. (A) He thought the lesson didn't
         matter.
    (B) He couldn't learn the lesson.
    (C) He learned a massive number of
         details.
    (D) He didn't like most of the lesson.

5. (A) Some animals started the first fire.
    (B) Animals are killed by forest fires.
    (C) In the first frost, animals die.
    (D) Frost can kill animals.

6. (A) Twenty pairs of shoes are on sale.
    (B) The shoe salesclerk spent twenty
         dollars on pears.
    (C) The shoes cost twenty dollars.
    (D) The shoes could be repaired for
         twenty dollars.

7. (A) Tom tended to dislike biology lab.
    (B) Attendance wasn't necessary at
         biology lab.
    (C) Tom went to biology lab.
    (D) There was a tendency to require
         biology lab.

8. (A) The meal will be served at noon.
    (B) The males should be driven there
         by noon.
    (C) He's expecting the ice to melt
         before noon.
    (D) The letters ought to be delivered at
         12:00.

9. (A) The weather will probably get
         worse later.
    (B) The newspaper headlines
         described a bad storm.
    (C) There was news about a headstrong
         man.
    (D) He had a new bed.

10. (A) If she could do the grocery shopping.
    (B) If she prefers cooked vegetables or
         salad.
    (C) If she could help prepare the salad.
    (D) If she minds shopping for
         vegetables.

TOEFL EXERCISE (Skills 1–3): In this exercise, listen carefully to the short conversation and question in the recording program, and then choose the best answer to the question.

 NOW BEGIN THE RECORDING PROGRAM AT TOEFL EXERCISE (SKILLS 1–3).

1. (A) He would like some iced coffee.
   (B) He wants to stop drinking coffee.
   (C) A drink seems like a good idea.
   (D) He needs to drink something to stop his coughing.

2. (A) She would prefer a sunny day.
   (B) The park is too crowded.
   (C) She would like a place that is not so loud.
   (D) She cannot walk because she's too old.

3. (A) He should open an account.
   (B) He should take a ride on a ship.
   (C) He should try to keep the cost cheap.
   (D) He should try something monotonous to get to sleep.

4. (A) The department is not changing the requirements.
   (B) He hasn't heard anything about the change.
   (C) The changes are believable.
   (D) What has happened is incredible to him.

5. (A) The wait has taken close to an hour.
   (B) They were stranded in their car.
   (C) Most of the people have been in line for hours.
   (D) They made a line in the sand.

6. (A) The instructor is selecting several passages.
   (B) The conductor is fair to the passengers.
   (C) The stamp collector is conducting his business.
   (D) The riders are paying for the train trip.

7. (A) The managers will take the train to the program.
   (B) A program to develop new managers will commence soon.
   (C) The new management program is very weak.
   (D) The program will be maintained to the letter.

8. (A) The fire started to attack the building.
   (B) The firefighter stared at the attacker.
   (C) The fire probably began at the top of the building.
   (D) The firefighter started to attack the fire.

9. (A) He assured the woman that he knew the truth.
   (B) He is sure that it isn't new.
   (C) He thought that the woman was aware of what happened.
   (D) He soon will know the truth.

10. (A) The art professor is not one of his fans.
    (B) His drawings were amazing.
    (C) The catches that he made were fantastic.
    (D) His sketches showed a fantasy world.

WHO, WHAT, WHERE _____

SKILL 4: DRAW CONCLUSIONS ABOUT *WHO, WHAT, WHERE*

It is common in Listening Part A to ask you to draw some kind of conclusion. In this type of question the answer is not clearly stated; instead you must draw a conclusion based on clues given in the conversation. One kind of conclusion that is common in this part of the test is to ask you to determine *who* the speaker is, based on clues given in the conversation.

Example

On the recording, you hear:

    (woman)   *Can you tell me what assignments I missed when I was absent from your class?*
    (man)   *You missed one homework assignment and a quiz.*
    (narrator)   *Who is the man?*

In your test book, you read:

    (A) A newspaper editor.
    (B) A police officer.
    (C) A teacher.
    (D) A student.

The clues *your class, homework,* and *quiz* in the conversation tell you that the man is probably a teacher. Answer (C) is therefore the correct answer.

    Another type of conclusion that is common in Listening Part A is to determine *what* will probably happen next, based on clues given in the conversation.

Example

On the recording, you hear:

    (woman)   *Are you going to read those books here in the library?*
    (man)   *I think I'd rather check them out now and take them home.*
    (narrator)   *What will the man probably do next?*

In your test book, you read:

    (A) Sit down in the library.
    (B) Look for some more books.
    (C) Return the books to the shelves.
    (D) Go to the circulation desk.

The man says that he would like to *check the books out now.* Since the *circulation desk* is where you go to check books out from a library, the man will probably go to the circulation desk next. The correct answer is therefore answer (D).

A final type of conclusion that is common in Listening Part A is to determine *where* the conversation probably takes place, based on clues given in the conversation.

Example

On the recording, you hear:

> (woman)   *Are you going into the water, or are you just going to lie there on the sand?*
> (man)   *I think I need to put on some suntan lotion.*
> (narrator)   *Where does this conversation probably take place?*

In your test book, you read:

(A) At a beauty salon.
(B) At the beach.
(C) In a sandbox.
(D) At an outdoor restaurant.

The clues *water, sand,* and *suntan lotion* in the conversation tell you that this conversation probably takes place at the *beach*. Answer (B) is therefore the correct answer.

The following chart outlines the key point that you should remember about this type of question:

CONCLUSIONS ABOUT *WHO, WHAT, WHERE*

It is common for you to be asked to draw one of the following conclusions in Listening Part A:

1. *WHO is probably talking?*

2. *WHAT will s/he probably do next?*

3. *WHERE does the conversation probably take place?*

EXERCISE 4: In this exercise, read the short conversation and question, underline the clues that help you answer the question, and then choose the best answer. You will have to draw conclusions about *who, what,* and *where*.

1. (man) *I'd like to deposit this check in my account, please.*
    (woman) *Would you like any cash back?*
    (narrator) *Who is the woman?*

   (A) A store clerk.
   (B) A bank teller.
   (C) An accountant.
   (D) A waitress.

2. (woman) *Have you deposited your paycheck yet?*
    (man) *No, but that's next on my list of errands.*
    (narrator) *What will the man probably do next?*

   (A) Earn his paycheck.
   (B) Write a check for a deposit on an apartment.
   (C) Go to a bank.
   (D) Make a list of errands to run.

3.   (man)   *Did you get the bread, eggs,*   (A)   In a restaurant.
               and milk?   (B)   At a bakery.
      (woman) *Now we need to stand in line at*   (C)   On a farm.
               the checkout counter.   (D)   In a market.
      (narrator) *Where does this conversation*
                 probably take place?

TOEFL EXERCISE 4: In this exercise, listen carefully to the short conversation and question in the recording program and then choose the best answer to the question. You will have to draw conclusions about *who, what,* and *where.*

NOW BEGIN THE RECORDING PROGRAM AT TOEFL EXERCISE 4.

1.   (A)   In a photography studio.   6.   (A)   On a playground.
      (B)   In a biology laboratory.   (B)   In a parking lot.
      (C)   In an office.   (C)   At a zoo.
      (D)   In the library.   (D)   In a photo studio.

2.   (A)   He's a pilot.   7.   (A)   Respond to the mail.
      (B)   He's a flight attendant.   (B)   Put the letters in a file.
      (C)   He's a member of the grounds   (C)   It depends on where the file is.
            crew.   (D)   File the answers she received to the
      (D)   He works clearing land.   letters.

3.   (A)   Wash the dishes immediately.   8.   (A)   In an airplane.
      (B)   Use as many dishes as possible.   (B)   In a police car.
      (C)   Wash the dishes for as long as   (C)   In a theater.
            possible.   (D)   At a fireworks exhibit.
      (D)   Wait until later to clean up.
                                                  9.   (A)   Take care of Bob.
4.   (A)   In a bank.   (B)   Invite Bob to dinner.
      (B)   In a restaurant.   (C)   Let Bob know that they accept his
      (C)   At a service station.   invitation.
      (D)   In a beauty salon.   (D)   Respond to the woman's question.

5.   (A)   A salesclerk in a shoe store.   10.   (A)   A pharmacist.
      (B)   A shoe repairperson.   (B)   A dentist.
      (C)   A party caterer.   (C)   A teacher.
      (D)   A salesclerk in a fixtures   (D)   A business manager.
            department.

Skill 5: LISTEN FOR *WHO* AND *WHAT* IN PASSIVES

It is sometimes difficult to understand *who* or *what* is doing the action in a passive sentence. This problem is often tested in Listening Part A.

Example

On the recording, you hear:

    (man)   *Did Sally go to the bank this morning?*
    (woman)   *Yes, she did. She got a new checking account.*
    (narrator)   *What does the woman imply?*

In your test book, you read:

    (A)   Sally wrote several checks.
    (B)   Sally wanted to check up on the bank.
    (C)   A new checking account was opened.
    (D)   Sally checked on the balance in her account.

In this conversation, the woman uses an active statement that means that *Sally opened a checking account*. The correct answer uses the passive structure that *a checking account was opened* to express the same idea. Therefore, the best answer to the question above is answer (C).

You should note the following about passive sentences in Listening Part A:

PASSIVE STATEMENTS
1. If the conversation contains a *passive* statement, the answer to the question is often an *active* statement.
2. If the conversation contains an *active* statement, the answer to the question is often a *passive* statement.
NOTE: Check carefully *who* or *what* is doing the action in these questions.

EXERCISE 5: In this exercise each of the correct answers is either a passive restatement of an active sentence or an active restatement of a passive sentence. Read the short conversation and underline the key active or passive statement. Then read the question and choose the best answer to the question. Be careful about *who* and *what* with these passives.

1.   (woman) *Alice needs to pay her tuition today.*
        (man) *But her tuition has already been paid.*
    (narrator) *What does the man imply?*

    (A) Alice's education has paid off.
    (B) Alice's tuition needs to be paid.
    (C) Alice has already paid her fees.
    (D) Alice has already received the money.

2.   (man) *Have you been taking good care of the lawn?*

  (woman) *I watered it only this morning.*

  (narrator) *What does the woman mean?*

(A) She drank some water on the lawn this morning.

(B) She waited for him on the lawn this morning.

(C) The lawn has already been watered today.

(D) She wanted a new lawn this morning.

3.   (man) *Did you hear the news about the child who was lost in the park?*

  (woman) *Yes, and I heard that she was just found!*

  (narrator) *What does the woman mean?*

(A) Someone located the girl.

(B) She heard about the new park from the child.

(C) The child found her lost pet.

(D) The child was the last one in the park.

TOEFL EXERCISE 5: In this exercise, listen carefully to the short conversation and question in the recording program, and then choose the best answer to the question. You should be particularly careful of passives.

NOW BEGIN THE RECORDING PROGRAM AT TOEFL EXERCISE 5.

1. (A) If the restaurant is on the corner.
(B) If the man would like to go to the restaurant.
(C) If the vegetables are fresh.
(D) If vegetarian food can be obtained.

2. (A) He admitted that he wanted to go to law school in the fall.
(B) The law school accepted him as a student.
(C) The law professor admitted that he would be a student in the fall semester.
(D) He would be admitted to law school after the fall semester.

3. (A) Mark's plants were cared for in his absence.
(B) Mark's plan was to be out of town.
(C) Mark was careful about his plans for the out-of-town trip.
(D) She was careful while Mark was gone.

4. (A) The lights in the trees were destroyed in the storm.
(B) The storm damaged the trees.
(C) The falling trees destroyed a store.
(D) In the light the destruction of the storm could be seen.

5. (A) She was broke from skiing.
(B) She went skiing in spite of her accident.
(C) Her leg was hurt on a skiing trip.
(D) Her skis were broken in the mountains.

6. (A) The road the horses took was long and hard.
(B) It was hard to find the hidden houses.
(C) The riders worked the horses too much.
(D) It was hard for people to ride the horses for long.

7. (A) He didn't want the coffee that the woman ordered.
(B) He wasn't sure if the woman wanted coffee.
(C) He assumed the woman had ordered coffee.
(D) He was unaware that coffee had already been ordered.

8. (A) The car was in the left parking lot at the airport.
(B) The friends parked their car at the airport.
(C) The airport couldn't hold a lot of cars.
(D) There were a lot of cars to the left of the parking lot.

9. (A) The students pointed at Mac.
    (B) Mac was present when the other students made the appointment.
    (C) The class representative suggested Mac to the other students.
    (D) Mac was chosen by his classmates to represent them.

10. (A) After the earthquake, the insurance company came out to inspect the damage.
    (B) The insurance company insisted that the building be repaired to meet earthquake safety standards.
    (C) The inhabitants paid their premiums after the earthquake.
    (D) The insurance company paid for the earthquake damage.

SKILL 6: LISTEN FOR *WHO* AND *WHAT* WITH MULTIPLE NOUNS

When there is more than one noun in a sentence in Listening Part A, it is common for the answers to confuse which noun does what.

Example

On the recording, you hear:

  (man)   *Do you know who is in the band now?*
  (woman)   *I heard that Mara replaced Robert in the band.*
  (narrator) *What does the woman say about the band?*

In your test book, you read:

  (A) Robert became a new member of the band.
  (B) Robert took Mara's place in the band.
  (C) Mara didn't have a place in the band.
  (D) Mara took Robert's place in the band.

In the woman's response to the man's question, she talks about two people *(Mara and Robert),* and these two people are confused in the answers. Because *Mara replaced Robert,* this means that Mara is in the band and Robert is not. The best answer is therefore answer (D).

The following chart outlines the key point that you should remember about questions with multiple nouns:

WHO AND *WHAT* WITH MULTIPLE NOUNS
When there are multiple nouns in a sentence, it is common for the answers to confuse which noun does what.

EXERCISE 6: In this exercise, underline the confusing nouns in each short conversation. Then read the question and choose the best answer to that question. Remember to think very carefully about who is doing what.

1.   (man)   *Why is Bill not at work this week?*
     (woman)   *His doctor made him take a week off.*
     (narrator)   *What does the woman mean?*

     (A) The doctor decided to take some time off from work.
     (B) The doctor told Bill he wasn't too weak to work.
     (C) Bill was mad when the doctor took some time off.
     (D) Bill took a vacation on his doctor's orders.

2.   (man)   *Why is Paul going back home this summer?*
     (woman)   *He's returning to Vermont for his sister's wedding.*
     (narrator)   *What does the woman mean?*

     (A) Paul is getting married this summer.
     (B) Paul's sister is returning from Vermont to get married.
     (C) Paul will be there when his sister gets married this summer.
     (D) Paul's sister is coming to his wedding in Vermont.

3.   (man)   *Did you hear that John's uncle died?*
     (woman)   *Yes, and John was named beneficiary in his uncle's will.*
     (narrator)   *What does the woman mean?*

     (A) John received an inheritance when his uncle died.
     (B) It's a benefit that John's name is the same as his uncle's.
     (C) John knows that his uncle will come to the benefit.
     (D) John's uncle gave him a beneficial name.

TOEFL EXERCISE 6: In this exercise, listen carefully to the short conversation and question in the recording program, and then choose the best answer to the question. You should be particularly careful of who is doing what.

   NOW BEGIN THE RECORDING PROGRAM AT TOEFL EXERCISE 6.

1. (A) The passenger waited at the corner.
    (B) The passenger looked for a taxi at the corner.
    (C) The cab driver waited for the passenger.
    (D) The passenger cornered the waiting taxi driver.

2. (A) It was hard for her to hear Jane last night.
    (B) Jane gave a harp recital last night.
    (C) Jane was playing hard while she was hurt.
    (D) She played the harp last night for Jane.

3. (A) The baby sister went to bed quite early.
    (B) The children were forced to go to bed early.
    (C) The baby-sitter made the bed after the children got up.
    (D) The baby-sitter did not stay up late.

4. (A) The man taught his son about football.
    (B) The boy is receiving the ball from his dad.
    (C) The ball is being tossed into the air by the boy.
    (D) The man is playing with the ball in the sun.

5. (A) The students were told to go listen
        to the speaker.
    (B) The professor attended that
        evening's lecture.
    (C) The students were given directions
        to the lecture.
    (D) The professor was directed to the
        lecture hall.

6. (A) The manager went to the supply
        room.
    (B) The clerk set supplies on the floor.
    (C) The clerk went to the supply room
        at the manager's request.
    (D) The clerk backed into the manager
        in the supply room.

7. (A) The librarian was quite reserved
        with the students for two days.
    (B) Within two days the librarian had
        the books for the students.
    (C) The librarian asked the students
        for the books.
    (D) The students put the books on
        hold for two days.

8. (A) The chairman decided that Tony
        would serve on the board for
        another year.
    (B) The chairman elected the board.
    (C) The board decided Tony could be
        chairman after one year.
    (D) Tony became chairman for one
        more year.

9. (A) The judge defended the murderer.
    (B) The judge tried to protect the
        defendant from the murderer.
    (C) The judge said that the defendant
        was a criminal.
    (D) The defense couldn't make a
        judgment about the criminal.

10. (A) The woman should announce the
        names of the committee
        members.
    (B) He is thankful to be appointed to
        the committee.
    (C) He is sure about the time of the
        appointment with the
        committee.
    (D) The woman will serve on the
        committee.

TOEFL EXERCISE (Skills 4–6): In this exercise, listen carefully to the short conversation and question in the recording program, and then choose the best answer to the question.

⌒ NOW BEGIN THE RECORDING PROGRAM AT TOEFL EXERCISE (SKILLS 4–6).

1. (A) In a department store.
    (B) In a stationery store.
    (C) At the post office.
    (D) At the airport.

2. (A) The teacher gave the students a
        hand.
    (B) The term papers were turned in.
    (C) The students got the papers from
        the office.
    (D) The teacher handed the papers to
        the students.

3. (A) The attendant checked the oil in
        Mark's car.
    (B) Mark checked to see if he had
        enough oil in his car.
    (C) Mark checked with the service
        station attendant.
    (D) Mark wrote a check to pay for the
        oil.

4. (A) A delivery man.
    (B) A famous chef.
    (C) A clerk in a fast-food restaurant.
    (D) An airline steward.

5. (A) They need new print for the
        additional copies.
    (B) They can make extra copies if
        necessary.
    (C) Printers are needed for the
        additional copies.
    (D) Additional copies are needed
        immediately.

6. (A) The professor bought two books.
    (B) The students had to purchase two
        books.
    (C) The students sold two books to the
        professor.
    (D) The students were required to read
        two books by the professor.

7. (A) The doctor returned to the office.
   (B) Jim asked the doctor to come to the office.
   (C) The doctor will not return until next week.
   (D) Jim was told to come back.

8. (A) Go to work in the lab.
   (B) Sample the work from the lab.
   (C) Have the samples delivered.
   (D) Send a note to the lab.

9. (A) Mary became the new class president.
   (B) Sue took her place as class president.
   (C) In place of Mary, Sue became senior class president.
   (D) The senior class president replaced Sue and Mary.

10. (A) The panel was analyzed on the television program.
    (B) A committee evaluated recent political events.
    (C) The program featured a psychoanalyst.
    (D) The panel discussed the television program.

TOEFL REVIEW EXERCISE (Skills 1–6): In this exercise, listen carefully to the short conversation and question in the recording program, and then choose the best answer to the question.

NOW BEGIN THE RECORDING PROGRAM AT TOEFL REVIEW EXERCISE (SKILLS 1–6).

1. (A) He seemed to be rather hungry.
   (B) She was quite angry at him.
   (C) He was trying to hang the posters.
   (D) She believes he was mad.

2. (A) The parents are going to stay up late.
   (B) The parents have given Hannah her allowance.
   (C) Lately, the parents have not been so loud.
   (D) Hannah does not have to go to bed early.

3. (A) At a department store.
   (B) At a service station.
   (C) At a collection agency.
   (D) In a delivery room.

4. (A) She just broke some eggs.
   (B) They need to eat fast.
   (C) She is serious about the boat.
   (D) He has a choice to make.

5. (A) It was urgent that Ellen do her best.
   (B) He really urged Ellen to do more.
   (C) He was encouraged by Ellen to try harder.
   (D) Ellen told him that she was trying to do better.

6. (A) The car stalled on the road.
   (B) Someone took the car.
   (C) Rob sold his car.
   (D) Rob heard someone steal his car.

7. (A) Buying the bigger container.
   (B) Putting the milk in the cart.
   (C) Taking a carton that is smaller.
   (D) Getting the milk tomorrow instead.

8. (A) The receptionist welcomed the businesspeople.
   (B) The man created a shipping and receiving business.
   (C) The businesspeople were rather greedy.
   (D) The businesspeople greeted the receptionist.

9. (A) The police officer was stationed near the tourist.
   (B) The tourist was forced to accompany the police officer.
   (C) The tourist became mad at the police station.
   (D) The tourist stated that the police officer never came.

10. (A) He hasn't seen her ideas.
    (B) It was a terrible deal.
    (C) He doesn't like the idea.
    (D) It sounds magnificent to him.

NEGATIVES

SKILL 7:   LISTEN FOR NEGATIVE EXPRESSIONS

Negative expressions are very common in Listening Part A, and the most common kind of correct response to a negative statement is a positive statement containing a word with an opposite meaning.

Example

On the recording, you hear:

      (man)   *How did they get to their grandmother's house in Maine in only five hours?*
    (woman)   *They didn't drive slowly on the trip to Maine.*
    (narrator)   *What does the woman say about the trip?*

In your test book, you read:

    (A) They drove rather quickly.
    (B) They couldn't have driven more slowly.
    (C) They wanted to travel slowly to Maine.
    (D) They didn't drive to Maine.

The correct answer is answer (A). If they *did not* drive *slowly* to Maine, this means that they drove rather *quickly*. Notice that the correct answer uses *quickly*, the opposite of *slowly*. The answers that use *slowly* are not correct.

The following chart outlines the types of negative expressions that you should be careful of:

TYPES OF NEGATIVE EXPRESSIONS		
Expression	Example	Correct Answer
Regular negative: *not* or *n't*	Tom is *not sad* about the results.	*not sad = happy*
Other negatives: *nobody, none, nothing, never*	*Nobody* arrived *on time.* Sal *never works hard.*	*nobody … on time = late* *never works hard = lazy*
Negative prefixes: *un-, in-, dis-*	The patient was *insane.*	*insane = not sane = crazy*

EXERCISE 7: In this exercise, underline the negative in the second line of each short conversation. Then read the question and choose the best answer to that question. Remember that the best answer is one that uses an opposite meaning.

1.   (man) *I can't seem to get the door unlocked.*
    (woman) *That isn't the right key for the door.*
    (narrator) *What does the woman mean?*

    (A) The key in the drawer is on the right.
    (B) The man should write the message on the door.
    (C) The man has the wrong key.
    (D) The right key isn't in the drawer.

2.   (man)   *Were you pleased with last*
                week's convention?
     (woman)   *Nothing went as planned.*
   (narrator)   *What does the woman mean?*

(A)   The convention was disorganized.
(B)   She didn't plan to attend the
      convention.
(C)   She planned the convention last
      week.
(D)   She wasn't pleased with the last
      week of the convention.

3.   (woman)   *Are you planning to go to college*
                next year?
     (man)   *I'm really unsure about the idea.*
   (narrator)   *What does the man mean?*

(A)   He definitely wants to go to
      college.
(B)   He is certain about his plans.
(C)   He's hesitant about attending
      college.
(D)   His idea is to go to college.

TOEFL EXERCISE 7: In this exercise, listen carefully to the short conversation and question in the recording program, and then choose the best answer to the question. You should be particularly careful of negative expressions.

Now begin the recording program at Toefl Exercise 7.

1.   (A)   She is very busy.
     (B)   She has lots of free time.
     (C)   It is not necessary to take out the
           trash.
     (D)   She will do it if she has time.

2.   (A)   The interview is very important.
     (B)   He is worried about the interview.
     (C)   What he's wearing to the interview
           is important.
     (D)   He is not concerned about the
           interview.

3.   (A)   He has almost all the notes.
     (B)   His attendance was perfect.
     (C)   He went to all the lectures but one.
     (D)   He missed more than one
           psychology class.

4.   (A)   They passed the library at
           6:00.
     (B)   The library opens at 6:00 in the
           summer.
     (C)   The library closes at 6:00.
     (D)   You can't check out more than six
           books in the summer.

5.   (A)   Water the plants once a day.
     (B)   Give the plants no more water.
     (C)   Water the plants often while the
           man is gone.
     (D)   Give the plants a limited amount of
           water.

6.   (A)   The service satisfied her.
     (B)   The food was worse than the
           service.
     (C)   She thought the service was bad.
     (D)   Neither the food nor the service
           was satisfying.

7.   (A)   He told his kids to leave.
     (B)   He seriously wanted the woman to
           go.
     (C)   He was joking when he told the
           woman to leave.
     (D)   He left with the woman.

8.   (A)   The project will take all their effort.
     (B)   They have no other work to do.
     (C)   It's impossible to finish.
     (D)   They aren't even close to finishing
           the project.

9.   (A)   She doesn't mind an hour more.
     (B)   She'd rather stay more than an
           hour.
     (C)   It's better to stay than go.
     (D)   She prefers to leave.

10. (A)   The service at the hotel wasn't too
           good.
     (B)   This hotel gave excellent service.
     (C)   The service at the hotel could have
           been improved.
     (D)   This hotel's service was the same as
           the service at other hotels.

SKILL 8:   LISTEN FOR DOUBLE NEGATIVE EXPRESSIONS

It is possible for two negative ideas to appear in one sentence, and the result can be quite confusing.

Example

On the recording, you hear:

        (man)   *I can't believe the news that I heard about the concert.*
    (woman)   *Well, it isn't impossible for the concert to take place.*
   (narrator)   *What does the woman say about the concert?*

In your test book, you read:

    (A)   There's no possibility that the concert will take place.
    (B)   The concert will definitely not take place.
    (C)   The concert might take place.
    (D)   The concert can't take place.

The correct answer to this question is answer (C). If it *isn't impossible* for the concert to take place, then it *is possible,* and the modal *might* indicates possibility.

The following chart outlines the situations where double negatives can occur:

DOUBLE NEGATIVES		
Situation	Example	Meaning
negative word (e.g., *not, no, none*) and a negative prefix (e.g., *in-, un-, dis-*)	He did*n't* like the *un*clean office.	did *not* like *un*clean office = liked clean office
two negative verbs	It *isn't snowing,* so they *aren't going* to the mountains.	implies that they would go if it were snowing
neither or *not … either*	Sue *didn't like* the movie, and *neither did* Mark.	both did not like the movie

EXERCISE 8:   In this exercise, underline the two negatives in the second line of each short conversation. Then read the question and choose the best answer to that question. Remember that two negatives make the sentence positive.

1.   (man)   *Paula, you worked so hard setting up the field trip.*
    (woman)   *I hope no one's unhappy with the arrangements.*
   (narrator)   *What does Paula mean?*

    (A)   She hopes everyone will be pleased.
    (B)   She knows no one is happy with what she has done.
    (C)   She's arranged to take a trip because she's unhappy.
    (D)   Everyone's happy with the condition of the field.

2. (woman)   *How was your history exam?*
    (man)   *I didn't study enough, so I*
              didn't do well.
    (narrator) *What does the man mean?*

   (A) He studied a lot and passed.
   (B) He failed in spite of his effort.
   (C) He got a good grade even though
        he didn't study.
   (D) His grade was poor because of
        inadequate preparation.

3. (man)   *Were your friends able to get*
              tickets for the concert?
    (woman)   *Mark couldn't get tickets for the*
              concert, and neither could Paul.
    (narrator) *What does the woman mean?*

   (A) Although Mark couldn't get both
        tickets, Paul did.
   (B) Both were unable to obtain tickets.
   (C) Neither Mark nor Paul wanted to
        go to the concert.
   (D) Mark tried to get tickets, but Paul
        didn't.

TOEFL EXERCISE 8: In this exercise, listen carefully to the short conversation and question in the recording program, and then choose the best answer to the question. You should be particularly careful of double negatives.

    Now begin the recording program at Toefl Exercise **8.**

1. (A) He'll definitely be elected.
    (B) The election is now complete.
    (C) She has high hopes for his chances.
    (D) It may happen.

2. (A) Both parts of his game were bad.
    (B) He served better than he volleyed.
    (C) Some parts of his game were better
         than others.
    (D) He played rather well.

3. (A) It is a surprise that he was
         prepared.
    (B) He was not ready, as usual.
    (C) He prepared a really big surprise.
    (D) His strong preparation came as no
         surprise.

4. (A) She felt good enough to go out.
    (B) She went out to get some medicine.
    (C) She felt like dancing, so she went
         out with everyone.
    (D) She stayed home because she was
         sick.

5. (A) She has problems that others aren't
         aware of.
    (B) Others aren't aware of her
         problems.
    (C) She knows she's been a problem.
    (D) She doesn't have a care in the
         world.

6. (A) Steve wanted to finish his paper,
         and so did Paul.
    (B) Both Steve's and Paul's papers were
         incomplete.
    (C) Steve and Paul were busy doing
         their term papers.
    (D) When Steve wasn't able to finish his
         paper, Paul couldn't help.

7. (A) It wasn't George's responsibility to
         pay the bill.
    (B) Bill was irresponsible about paying
         George's rent.
    (C) George acted carelessly by not
         taking care of the bill.
    (D) George took responsibility for the
         unpaid bill.

8. (A) It's fortunate that he was accepted.
    (B) It's good that he wasn't admitted.
    (C) Fortunately, the university didn't
         admit him.
    (D) It's too bad he was rejected.

9. (A) The first essay was better than the second.
    (B) The first and second drafts couldn't be better.
    (C) The second draft of the essay was much better than the first.
    (D) Both versions were poorly written.

10. (A) Roger has been bothered.
    (B) Roger wasn't the least bit disturbed.
    (C) The problems have had little effect on Roger.
    (D) Roger hasn't been disturbed.

SKILL 9: LISTEN FOR "ALMOST NEGATIVE" EXPRESSIONS

Certain expressions in English have "almost negative" meanings. These expressions are common on the TOEFL test and need to be reviewed.

Example

On the recording, you hear:

(woman)   *Were you able to pay the electric bill?*
(man)   *I had barely enough money.*
(narrator) *What does the man imply?*

In your test book, you read:

(A) He had plenty of money for the bill.
(B) He did not have enough money for the bill.
(C) He paid the bill but has no money left.
(D) He was unable to pay the bill.

In the man's statement, the word *enough* indicates that there was *enough*, so he did *pay the bill*. However, it was *barely* enough, so he almost did not have enough and certainly *has no money left*. The correct answer is therefore answer (C).

The following chart outlines common "almost negative" expressions:

COMMON "ALMOST NEGATIVE" EXPRESSIONS		
Meaning	Expression	Example
almost none	*hardly, barely, scarcely, only*	There is *hardly* any food in the refrigerator.
almost never	*rarely, seldom*	He *rarely* drives to work.

EXERCISE 9: In this exercise, underline the "almost negative" expression in the second line of each short conversation. Then read the question and choose the best answer. Remember that the best answer is one that means that it *is true* but it is *almost not* true.

1. (man)   *I hear that Mona's been offered the manager's job.*
    (woman) *But she has hardly any work experience!*
    (narrator) *What does the woman say about Mona?*

    (A) Mona hasn't worked hard.
    (B) Mona's experience has been hard.
    (C) Mona's job as manager is hard.
    (D) Mona hasn't worked for very long.

2.   (woman)   *How much time did Sam spend on his paper for economics class?*
        (man)   *Sam has seldom taken so much time on a research paper.*
    (narrator)   *What does the man mean?*

(A) Sam usually spends this much time on his schoolwork.
(B) Sam has rarely worked so hard.
(C) Sam took too much time on this paper.
(D) Sam should've worked harder on this paper.

3.   (woman)   *Does Steve usually park his car there?*
        (man)   *Only once has he parked his car in that lot.*
    (narrator)   *What does the man mean?*

(A) He parks his car there once in a while.
(B) He's parked his car there a lot.
(C) He only leaves his car there for short periods of time.
(D) He left his car there on just one occasion.

TOEFL EXERCISE 9: In this exercise, listen carefully to the short conversation and question in the recording program, and then choose the best answer to the question. You should be particularly careful of "almost negative" expressions.

NOW BEGIN THE RECORDING PROGRAM AT TOEFL EXERCISE 9.

1. (A) There's little rain in July.
    (B) In July it never rains.
    (C) It rains hard in July.
    (D) When it rains in July, it rains hard.

2. (A) The university accepted three students.
    (B) None of the students is going to the university.
    (C) John was not accepted.
    (D) Two were not admitted.

3. (A) Although he did pass, Mark's exam grade wasn't too good.
    (B) Mark failed his history exam.
    (C) The highest grade on the history exam went to Mark.
    (D) Professor Franks didn't pass Mark on the history exam.

4. (A) He often has long waits in Dr. Roberts' office.
    (B) He must wait patiently for Robert.
    (C) Dr. Roberts is generally punctual.
    (D) He doesn't mind waiting for Dr. Roberts.

5. (A) Betty often takes vacations in winter.
    (B) Betty prefers to take vacations in winter.
    (C) Occasionally Betty works one week during vacation.
    (D) A winter vacation is unusual for Betty.

6. (A) He rarely spends time on his courses.
    (B) He's an excellent student.
    (C) He never studies.
    (D) His books are always open.

7. (A) He finished the exam in plenty of time.
    (B) He was scared he wouldn't finish.
    (C) He used every possible minute to finish.
    (D) He was unable to complete the exam.

8. (A) This was a very long staff meeting.
    (B) This was the only staff meeting in a long time.
    (C) The meeting lasted only until one o'clock.
    (D) The one staff meeting should've lasted longer.

9. (A) Meat tastes delicious to him when it's cooked rare.
    (B) He isn't sure if the meal is delicious.
    (C) This meat is the best he's tasted in a long time.
    (D) He'd like to eat some meat from this delicatessen.

10. (A) He broke his arm trying to move it.
    (B) He only hurt the broken arm.
    (C) He only tries to move the broken arm.
    (D) There's no pain if he rests quietly.

SKILL 10:   LISTEN FOR NEGATIVES WITH COMPARATIVES

Negatives can be used with comparatives in Listening Part A of the TOEFL test. A sentence with a negative and a comparative has a superlative, or very strong, meaning.

Example

On the recording, you hear:

(woman)   *What do you think of the new student in math class?*
(man)   *No one is more intelligent than she is.*
(narrator) *What does the man say about the new student?*

In your test book, you read:

(A) She is not very smart.
(B) He is smarter than she is.
(C) Other students are smarter than she is.
(D) She is the smartest student in the class.

The man responds to the woman's question with the negative *no* and the comparative *more intelligent,* and this combination has a superlative meaning. The best answer is therefore answer (D).

The following chart outlines comparisons that you should be careful of when they are used with negatives:

COMPARATIVES WITH NEGATIVES		
Comparative	Example	Meaning
more	*No* one is *more* beautiful than she is.	She is *the most* beautiful.
-er	He *couldn't* be happier.	He is *extremely* happy.

EXERCISE 10: In this exercise, underline the negative and the comparative in the second line of each short conversation. Then read the question and choose the best answer to that question. Remember that the best answer is one that expresses a superlative, or very strong, idea.

1. (woman) *Have you gotten over your cold yet?*
   (man) *I couldn't be feeling any better today.*
   (narrator) *What does the man mean?*

   (A) He's feeling terrific.
   (B) He felt a lot worse today.
   (C) He's not feeling too well today.
   (D) He's a bit better today.

2. (woman) *What did you think of Mike when you first met him?*
   (man) *He couldn't have been more unfriendly.*
   (narrator) *What does the man mean?*

   (A) Mike was extremely friendly when he met him.
   (B) Mike could have met him sooner.
   (C) Mike didn't seem to like him at all.
   (D) When he met Mike, he didn't have a friend.

3. (man) *Did you see Theresa's grade on the math exam? It was unbelievable!*
   (woman) *No one else could have done better.*
   (narrator) *What does the woman mean?*

   (A) Theresa could've gotten a higher grade.
   (B) Anyone could get a good grade.
   (C) Theresa got the highest grade.
   (D) A high grade is impossible for anyone.

TOEFL EXERCISE 10: In this exercise, listen carefully to the short conversation and question in the recording program, and then choose the best answer to the question. You should be particularly careful of comparatives with negatives.

NOW BEGIN THE RECORDING PROGRAM AT TOEFL EXERCISE 10.

1. (A) She's not very happy.
   (B) She didn't do very well on the exam.
   (C) She could be somewhat happier.
   (D) She's delighted with the results.

2. (A) Paula is always lazy.
   (B) Paula didn't work very hard this semester.
   (C) Paula made a strong effort.
   (D) Paula could have worked harder.

3. (A) The prices were great!
   (B) The prices were too high.
   (C) She didn't buy much because of the prices.
   (D) The prices could have been lower.

4. (A) She is not very smart.
   (B) She always tells him everything.
   (C) He doesn't know her very well.
   (D) She's extremely intelligent.

5. (A) The patient absolutely didn't need the surgery.
   (B) The necessity for the surgery was unquestionable.
   (C) The surgeon felt that the operation was necessary.
   (D) It was essential that the surgery be performed immediately.

6. (A) They were not very lucky.
   (B) No one was hurt.
   (C) The accident was unfortunate.
   (D) She wanted to have better luck.

7. (A) Nothing was very difficult.
   (B) The exam wasn't at all easy.
   (C) The exam couldn't have been easier.
   (D) The exam had nothing difficult on it.

8. (A) She wants that job very much.
   (B) No one is going to get the job.
   (C) Everybody else wants that job as much as she does.
   (D) She is not sure about taking the job.

9. (A) She was second in the race.
   (B) She was almost the slowest person in the race.
   (C) She won the race.
   (D) She was not faster than anyone else.

10. (A) This math project was extremely complex.
    (B) This math project was less complicated than the last.
    (C) They seldom complete their math projects.
    (D) Complicated math projects are often assigned.

TOEFL EXERCISE (Skills 7–10): In this exercise, listen carefully to the short conversation and question in the recording program, and then choose the best answer to the question.

NOW BEGIN THE RECORDING PROGRAM AT TOEFL EXERCISE (SKILLS 7–10).

1. (A) She can try a little harder.
   (B) There is a lot more that she can do.
   (C) She's doing the best that she can.
   (D) It is impossible for her to do anything.

2. (A) She's always been late for the bus.
   (B) The bus has always been late.
   (C) The bus only left on time once.
   (D) Only on this trip has the bus been on time.

3. (A) There wasn't enough soup to go around.
   (B) We had so much soup that we couldn't finish it.
   (C) Everyone got one serving of soup, but there wasn't enough for seconds.
   (D) Everyone around the table had a lot of soup.

4. (A) She does want to see the movie.
   (B) It's extremely important to her to go.
   (C) She doesn't want to go there anymore.
   (D) She really couldn't move there.

5. (A) She handed the paper in on time.
   (B) She was able to complete the paper, but she didn't turn it in.
   (C) The paper was a complete mess, so she didn't turn it in.
   (D) The paper was unfinished.

6. (A) Neither Tim nor Sylvia is taking care of Art.
   (B) Sylvia likes modern art even less than Tim does.
   (C) Sylvia doesn't care for anything Tim does.
   (D) Sylvia and Tim agree in their opinion of modern art.

7. (A) They always work hard in the afternoon.
   (B) They don't do much after lunch.
   (C) After noon they never work.
   (D) It's never hard for them to work in the afternoon.

8. (A) It's hard for him to work when it gets warm.
   (B) Whenever it gets warm, he turns on the air conditioner.
   (C) The air conditioner only works when it isn't needed.
   (D) He likes to use the air conditioner when it is warm.

9. (A) He did really poorly.
   (B) He's felt worse before.
   (C) The results could not have been better.
   (D) He's not too unhappy with the results.

10. (A) With so many members present, the committee couldn't reach a decision.
    (B) The committee should've waited until more members were present.
    (C) The issue shouldn't have been decided by all the committed members.
    (D) The issue wasn't decided because so many members were absent.

TOEFL REVIEW EXERCISE (Skills 1–10): In this exercise, listen carefully to the short conversation and question in the recording program, and then choose the best answer to the question.

NOW BEGIN THE RECORDING PROGRAM AT TOEFL REVIEW EXERCISE (SKILLS 1–10).

1. (A) In a doctor's office.
   (B) At a bar.
   (C) In a travel agency.
   (D) In a business office.

2. (A) She bought some sheets.
   (B) She got a new piece of clothing.
   (C) She couldn't find anything because she's too short.
   (D) She was sure to greet her boss.

3. (A) The hotel was all right, except for the poor view.
   (B) The view from the hotel room was spectacular.
   (C) She would have preferred a better hotel.
   (D) Only a few hotels would have been better.

4. (A) Take a nap.
   (B) Try the rest of the work.
   (C) See a doctor.
   (D) Have a bite to eat.

5. (A) She's an exacting person.
   (B) She can't be expected to give you four of them.
   (C) She generally forgives others.
   (D) She isn't exact about what she gives to others.

6. (A) She's unable to take her vacation this year.
   (B) Her vacation next week has been postponed.
   (C) She'll go on vacation next week.
   (D) She'll return from vacation in a week.

7. (A) The waitress was sitting in the back of the restaurant.
   (B) They were waiting for a seat in the restaurant.
   (C) The customers had a table in the back.
   (D) The waitress sat down behind the table.

8. (A) It's hard for the market to sell its fruit.
   (B) All of the fresh fruit at the market is hard.
   (C) She hardly ever goes to the market to buy fresh fruit.
   (D) There was a scarcity of fresh fruit at the market.

9. (A) The man should never be late for school.
   (B) The man can always return to school.
   (C) The man should never go back to school.
   (D) If the man's late to school, he should go through the back door.

10. (A) She can't bear to try.
    (B) She is a daring person.
    (C) She doesn't want the man even to try.
    (D) She is challenging the man to make the effort.

FUNCTIONS

Skill 11: LISTEN FOR EXPRESSIONS OF AGREEMENT

Expressions of agreement are common in Listening Part A, so you should become familiar with them. The following example shows agreement with a *positive* statement.

Example

On the recording, you hear:

(man)	*I think that the hypothesis is indefensible.*
(woman)	*So do I.*
(narrator)	*What does the woman mean?*

In your test book, you read:

(A)   She is unsure about the hypothesis.
(B)   The hippopotamus is behind the fence.
(C)   She thinks that the hypothesis can be defended.
(D)   She agrees with the man.

The expression *so do I* is an expression that shows agreement with a positive statement, so the woman means that she *agrees* with the man. The best answer is therefore answer (D).

Other expressions are used to show agreement with negative statements.

Example

On the recording, you hear:

(woman)	*I don't think that our history teacher is very interesting.*
(man)	*Neither do I.*
(narrator)	*What does the man mean?*

In your test book, you read:

(A)   He disagrees with the woman.
(B)   He thinks the history teacher is interesting.
(C)   He shares the woman's opinion.
(D)   He doesn't think the woman's idea is good.

The expression *neither do I* is an expression that shows agreement with a negative statement, so the man *agrees* with the woman. The best answer is therefore answer (C).

The following chart lists common expressions that show agreement. You should become familiar with these expressions:

EXPRESSIONS OF AGREEMENT	
Agreement with Positive Statements	Agreement with Negative Statements
So do I. *Me, too.* *I'll say!* *Isn't it!* *You can say that again!*	*Neither do I.* *I don't either.*

EXERCISE 11: In this exercise, underline the expression of agreement in each short conversation. Then read the question and choose the best answer to that question. Remember that the best answer is one that shows agreement.

1. (woman)   *These paintings are really fascinating!*
    (man)   *Aren't they!*
    (narrator) *What does the man mean?*

    (A) These paintings aren't very interesting.
    (B) He isn't fascinated by these paintings.
    (C) He isn't sure how he feels.
    (D) He finds these paintings quite interesting.

2. (woman)   *I don't really care for the way the building was renovated.*
    (man)   *I don't either.*
    (narrator) *What does the man mean?*

    (A) He thinks the building was not renovated.
    (B) He has the same opinion of the building as the woman.
    (C) He doesn't care about the renovation of the building.
    (D) He suggests being careful in the renovated building.

3. (man)   *I think that both candidates for county supervisor are unqualified.*
    (woman)   *Me, too.*
    (narrator) *What does the woman mean?*

    (A) She agrees with the man.
    (B) She thinks he should become county supervisor.
    (C) She thinks the candidates are qualified.
    (D) She has no opinion about the candidates for county supervisor.

TOEFL EXERCISE 11: In this exercise, listen carefully to the short conversation and question in the recording program, and then choose the best answer to the question. You should pay attention to expressions of agreement.

🎧 NOW BEGIN THE RECORDING PROGRAM AT TOEFL EXERCISE 11.

1. (A) The trip would cost too much.
    (B) She doesn't think that a trip would be a good idea.
    (C) She would like to take two trips rather than one.
    (D) She would also like to take a trip.

2. (A) He would like to see the elections for town council.
    (B) He agrees that Matt should be elected.
    (C) He thinks the elections should take place next month.
    (D) He disagrees with the woman.

3. (A) She is not sure which course she
         should take.
    (B) She's not sure if she should take a
         trip to France.
    (C) She knows that she is not ready for
         intermediate French.
    (D) She wants to take neither
         beginning nor intermediate
         French.

4. (A) The man should repeat what he
         said.
    (B) The man said something foolish.
    (C) She thinks that the food is the best
         she has ever tasted.
    (D) She agrees that the food is pretty
         bad.

5. (A) This party hasn't been any fun at all.
    (B) He wonders if the woman enjoyed
         herself.
    (C) He wants to know what she said.
    (D) He's enjoyed himself
         tremendously.

6. (A) She condones what happened.
    (B) She does not like what the man said.
    (C) She agrees with the man about
         what happened.
    (D) She says that she did not do it.

7. (A) He thinks the parties aren't loud.
    (B) He says that the neighbors don't
         have many parties.
    (C) He agrees that the upstairs
         neighbors are noisy.
    (D) The loud parties don't bother him.

8. (A) She doesn't like this meal too much.
    (B) This food tastes wonderful to her.
    (C) She's not sure if she likes it.
    (D) She can't stand this meal.

9. (A) She agrees that getting the car was
         not a good idea.
    (B) She imagines that she would like to
         have a similar car.
    (C) She thinks that the man is mistaken
         about the car.
    (D) She thinks the man has no
         imagination.

10. (A) He would like the woman to repeat
         what she said.
    (B) He thinks that one semester is
         enough time for the course.
    (C) He also thinks that the course
         should be extended.
    (D) He would like to take the course
         two semesters from now.

SKILL 12:   LISTEN FOR EXPRESSIONS OF UNCERTAINTY AND SUGGESTION

Expressions of uncertainty and suggestion are common in Listening Part A, so you should become familiar with them. The following example shows an expression of uncertainty.

Example

On the recording, you hear:

(man)   *Do you know anything about the final exam in Physics?*
(woman)   *It's going to be rather difficult, isn't it?*
(narrator) *What does the woman mean?*

In your test book, you read:

(A) The exam is not going to be too difficult.
(B) She's positive that it's going to be hard.
(C) She thinks that it might be hard.
(D) She has no idea about the exam.

The tag question *isn't it* changes a definite statement into a statement that shows uncertainty, so the best answer is one that expresses uncertainty. The best answer to this question is answer (C) because the words *thinks* and *might* express uncertainty.

Other expressions that are common in Listening Part A are expressions of suggestion.

Example

On the recording, you hear:

(man)	*I'll never have time to type my paper tomorrow.*
(woman)	*Why not do it now?*
(narrator)	*What does the woman suggest?*

In your test book, you read:

(A) Finishing the paper today.
(B) Not working on the paper now.
(C) Never typing the paper.
(D) Taking time out from the paper now.

In this example, the expression *why not* is an expression of suggestion, so the woman suggests *doing it now*. In this suggestion, the woman is referring to the paper that the man needs to type, so the best answer is answer (A).

The following chart lists common expressions that show uncertainty and suggestion:

EXPRESSIONS OF UNCERTAINTY AND SUGGESTION	
Uncertainty	Suggestion
. . . *isn't it* (tag)? *As far as I know.* *As far as I can tell.*	*Why not* . . . ? *Let's* . . .

EXERCISE 12: In this exercise, underline the expression of uncertainty or suggestion in each short conversation. Then read the question and choose the best answer to that question. Remember that the best answer is one that shows uncertainty or suggestion.

1.   (man) *Do you know what time they're leaving for the city?*
   (woman) *They have to leave at four o'clock, don't they?*
   (narrator) *What does the woman mean?*

(A) She's not completely sure when they are leaving.
(B) They are returning from the city at about 4:00.
(C) She knows when they are leaving.
(D) She doesn't have any idea when they are leaving.

2.   (woman) *I'm so thirsty from all this walking.*
   (man) *Let's stop and get a drink.*
   (narrator) *What does the man suggest?*

(A) They should stop drinking.
(B) They should go for a walk.
(C) They should walk thirty miles.
(D) They should take a break and have a drink.

3.   (man)   *Is the exam still scheduled for*
                3:00 on Thursday?
    (woman)   *As far as I know.*
    (narrator)   *What does the woman mean?*

(A) The exam is far away.
(B) She knows that the exam schedule
     has been changed.
(C) She is sure that the exam is set for
     Thursday.
(D) She thinks she knows when the
     test is.

TOEFL EXERCISE 12: In this exercise, listen carefully to the short conversation and question in the recording program, and then choose the best answer to the question. You should be particularly careful of expressions of uncertainty and suggestion.

NOW BEGIN THE RECORDING PROGRAM AT TOEFL EXERCISE 12.

1. (A) He's sure about which chapters
         they are to read.
    (B) He thinks he knows what the
         assignment is.
    (C) He has to tell her how far she
         should go.
    (D) The professor told them to read
         the chapters after the exam.

2. (A) The man should take the pie out.
    (B) The man should try something
         else.
    (C) The man shouldn't try cherry pie.
    (D) The man should feel sorry.

3. (A) He knows the movie starts at 8:00.
    (B) He is not quite sure when the
         movie begins.
    (C) He thinks the start of the movie has
         been changed.
    (D) He will start the movie himself at
         8:00.

4. (A) Not doing the dishes now.
    (B) Leaving the house with the dishes.
    (C) Leaving later so that they can do
         the dishes now.
    (D) Washing the dishes before they
         leave.

5. (A) She's told Matt he'll go far.
    (B) Matt has far from enough talent.
    (C) She told Matt to roll farther.
    (D) She believes Matt has the ability for
         the part.

6. (A) They should go to the hospital.
    (B) Mary should visit the man.
    (C) The woman should try not to break
         her leg.
    (D) They should go on a trip with Mary.

7. (A) She knows where the children are.
    (B) The children have finished playing
         ball.
    (C) She's going to the park to find the
         children.
    (D) She believes that the children are
         in the park.

8. (A) The man should try to borrow
         some from a neighbor.
    (B) The man should take a check to
         Tom.
    (C) The man should work on his math
         assignment with Tom.
    (D) The man should check behind the
         door.

9. (A) He thinks the bill is due in the middle of the month.
    (B) The bill is approximately fifteen dollars.
    (C) He knows when they should pay the bill.
    (D) The bill is going to be fifteen days late.

10. (A) They should postpone their decision until morning.
    (B) They should go to sleep in the new house.
    (C) They should not buy such a big house.
    (D) They should decide where to go to sleep.

SKILL 13:   LISTEN FOR EMPHATIC EXPRESSIONS OF SURPRISE

Emphatic expressions of surprise are common in Listening Part A, so you should become familiar with them. When surprise is expressed, it implies that the speaker did not expect something to be true.

Example

On the recording, you hear:

   (woman)   *Did you see Paul driving around in his Mustang?*
   (man)   *Then, he DID get a new car.*
   (narrator)   *What had the man thought?*

In your test book, you read:

   (A) Paul would definitely get a Mustang.
   (B) Paul did not know how to drive.
   (C) Paul did not like Mustangs.
   (D) Paul would not get a new car.

In this conversation the emphatic form *he did get* is used to show the man's surprise that Paul got a new car. It means that the man expected that Paul *would not get* a new car, so the best answer is answer (D).

The following chart outlines various ways to express emphatic surprise:

EXPRESSIONS OF EMPHATIC SURPRISE			
Verb	Emphatic Form	Example	Meaning
be	*be,* with emphasis	Then, he *is* here!	I thought he was not here.
modal	modal, with emphasis	Then, you *can* go!	I thought you could not go.
present tense	*do(es),* with emphasis	Then, you *do* play tennis!	I thought you did not play tennis.
past tense	*did,* with emphasis	Then, she *did* read it.	I thought she had not read it.
perfect tense	*have,* with emphasis	Then, he *has* gone there.	I thought he had not gone there.

EXERCISE 13: In this exercise, underline the expression of emphatic surprise in each short conversation. Then read the question and choose the best answer to that question. Remember that the best answer is one that shows surprise.

1.   (man)   *I just got 600 on the TOEFL test!*
   (woman)   *Then you did pass.*
   (narrator)   *What had the woman assumed?*

   (A) The man had not passed.
   (B) The man would pass easily.
   (C) The man had already passed.
   (D) The man got the score he was expected to get.

2.   (woman)   *Would you like to go skiing this weekend?*
   (man)   *So you can ski!*
   (narrator)   *What had the man assumed?*

   (A) The woman was a good skier.
   (B) The woman was going skiing this weekend.
   (C) The woman did not know how to ski.
   (D) The woman did not intend to go skiing.

3.   (man)   *I just got this letter from my sister.*
   (woman)   *So the mail has come already.*
   (narrator)   *What had the woman assumed?*

   (A) The man's sister never wrote to him.
   (B) The mail had not yet arrived.
   (C) The mail always came early.
   (D) The mail had already arrived.

TOEFL EXERCISE 13: In this exercise, listen carefully to the short conversation and question in the recording program, and then choose the best answer to the question. You should be particularly careful of expressions of emphatic surprise.

NOW BEGIN THE RECORDING PROGRAM AT TOEFL EXERCISE 13.

1. (A) Greg always comes to parties.
   (B) Greg would come to the party later.
   (C) Greg was unable to attend the party.
   (D) Greg would stay at the party for only a moment.

2. (A) The woman always rode her motorcycle to school.
   (B) The woman was not coming to school today.
   (C) The woman was an expert motorcycle rider.
   (D) The woman did not know how to ride a motorcycle.

3. (A) The man was not a very good cook.
   (B) The man never invited friends over for dinner.
   (C) The man would never invite him over for dinner.
   (D) The man was an excellent cook.

4. (A) The woman had run more than three miles.
   (B) The woman always got lots of exercise.
   (C) The woman ran for three hours in the morning.
   (D) The woman had not gotten much exercise.

5. (A) He had been somewhere else.
   (B) He had been in the library.
   (C) He had been working on his research project.
   (D) He would start working on his project in five hours.

6. (A) He had changed apartments.
   (B) He did not like his new apartment.
   (C) He was still in his old apartment.
   (D) He had moved from a house to an apartment.

7. (A) The woman did not like desserts.
    (B) The woman ate sweets regularly.
    (C) The woman would not share her chocolate cake.
    (D) The woman had eaten his piece of cake.

8. (A) The man was going to study hard.
    (B) The man already had a driver's license.
    (C) The man would not take the test.
    (D) The man had already taken the test.

9. (A) She had registered in physics.
    (B) She would go to physics class later.
    (C) She had already taken a physics class.
    (D) She had not enrolled in physics.

10. (A) The pipes were not clear.
    (B) The plumber would be late.
    (C) The plumber had already cleared the pipes.
    (D) The pipes did not need to be cleared.

TOEFL EXERCISE (Skills 11–13): In this exercise, listen carefully to the short conversation and question in the recording program, and then choose the best answer to the question.

NOW BEGIN THE RECORDING PROGRAM AT TOEFL EXERCISE (SKILLS 11–13).

1. (A) She plans to talk a lot this month.
    (B) She has a lot to say about the phone bill.
    (C) The bill is high because she has a lot to say.
    (D) She agrees with the man.

2. (A) Bill had never really been sick.
    (B) Bill was too sick to come to class.
    (C) Bill was sick of calculus class.
    (D) Bill had forgotten about the calculus class that morning.

3. (A) The man should go out tonight.
    (B) The man should stay home and relax.
    (C) The man should work on the paper tonight.
    (D) The man should go out Monday instead.

4. (A) The cafeteria was open in the morning.
    (B) The cafeteria did not serve breakfast.
    (C) The breakfast in the cafeteria was not very tasty.
    (D) The woman never ate breakfast in the cafeteria.

5. (A) He believes that it is acceptable to park there.
    (B) The parking lot is too far from their destination.
    (C) He knows that they won't get a ticket.
    (D) He knows where the parking lot is.

6. (A) He would be glad to say it over again.
    (B) He would like the woman to repeat what she said.
    (C) He says that he would like to take the class again.
    (D) He's happy the class is over, too.

7. (A) He finished all the problems.
    (B) He doesn't believe what the woman said.
    (C) He was able to finish some of the problems.
    (D) Both he and the woman were unsuccessful on the math problems.

8. (A) The man had mailed the package.
    (B) The man had forgotten to go to the post office.
    (C) The man had given the package to the woman to mail.
    (D) The man remembered the package after he went to the post office.

9. (A) They should take both cars.
    (B) The woman should try not to be afraid.
    (C) The woman should buy a bigger car.
    (D) They should go together in his car.

10. (A) He wants to know if the muffins taste good.
    (B) He thinks the muffins were recently prepared.
    (C) The muffins are not really fresh.
    (D) He's sure that the muffins were just made.

TOEFL REVIEW EXERCISE (Skills 1–13): In this exercise, listen carefully to the short conversation and question in the recording program, and then choose the best answer to the question.

 NOW BEGIN THE RECORDING PROGRAM AT TOEFL REVIEW EXERCISE (SKILLS 1–13).

1. (A) Write a message to the man.
    (B) Make some phone calls.
    (C) Respond to the man's questions.
    (D) Get a new phone installed.

2. (A) She's not sure if she's free.
    (B) She's marked it on her calendar.
    (C) She'll write a check for the calendar.
    (D) Her calendar says she has to have a meeting at 3:00.

3. (A) He barely rode the bicycle.
    (B) He didn't have enough money.
    (C) The bicycle didn't need to be paid for.
    (D) He paid for the bicycle.

4. (A) She fixed the television.
    (B) Bob made the television work.
    (C) The woman looked at Bob on television.
    (D) Bob works for the woman.

5. (A) He helped her say what she couldn't say.
    (B) She was unable to say anything about him.
    (C) He hasn't helped her very much.
    (D) What he said was very helpful.

6. (A) The man should spend more time on registration.
    (B) The man should walk more quickly through registration.
    (C) The man should send in his registration materials.
    (D) The man should try to avoid registering next semester.

7. (A) He couldn't find Paula's phone number, so he didn't call her.
    (B) He couldn't give Paula the list over the phone.
    (C) When he went to call Paula, he couldn't find the list.
    (D) He couldn't recollect the number that was on the list.

8. (A) She couldn't take her luggage to the store.
    (B) She stored her luggage at the train station.
    (C) She carried her luggage from the train station to the store.
    (D) There were no lockers for her bags.

9. (A) The woman had taken a different major.
    (B) The woman had chosen psychology as a major.
    (C) The woman was uninformed.
    (D) The woman needed to see a psychiatrist.

10. (A) She would like the man to repeat what he said.
    (B) She thinks the exam could have been a little more difficult.
    (C) She shares the same opinion of the exam as the man.
    (D) She believes that the exam was easy.

CONTRARY MEANINGS

SKILL 14:   LISTEN FOR WISHES

Conversations about wishes can appear in Listening Part A. The important idea to remember about wishes is that a wish implies that *the opposite of the wish is true.*

Skill 15: Listen for Untrue Conditions

Conversations containing conditions can appear in Listening Part A. The important idea to remember about conditions is that a condition implies that the *opposite of the condition is true*.

Example

On the recording, you hear:

     (man)   *Do you think that you'll be able to go to the party?*
    (woman)   *If I had time, I would go.*
    (narrator)   *What does the woman say about the party?*

In your test book, you read:

    (A) Maybe she'll go.
    (B) She has time, so she'll go.
    (C) She is going even if she doesn't have time.
    (D) It's impossible to go.

In this question, the condition *if I had time* implies that the opposite is true: The woman does not have time for the party, so she *cannot go*. Therefore, the best answer to this question is answer (D).

The following box outlines the key points that you should know about untrue conditions:

KEY INFORMATION ABOUT UNTRUE CONDITIONS		
Point	Example	Meaning
• An *affirmative* condition implies a *negative* reality.	If she *were at home,* she could do it.*	= not at home
• A *negative* condition implies an *affirmative* reality.	If she *weren't at home,* she could do it.	= at home
• A *past* tense implies a *present* reality.	If I *had* money, I would buy it.	= do not have money
• A *past perfect* verb implies a *past* reality.	If I *had had* money, I would have bought it.	= did not have money
• *Had* can be used without *if.*	*Had I had* money, I would have bought it.**	= did not have money

*Remember that *were* is used instead of *was* in untrue conditions: "If I *were* there, I would help."
**This has the same meaning as "If I had had money. . . ." Note that the subject and "had" are inverted.

EXERCISE 15: In this exercise, underline the condition in each short conversation. Then, read the question and choose the best answer to that question. Remember that the best answer is one that implies the opposite of what is said.

1.   (man) *Are you going to have something to eat?*
    (woman) *If the food looked fresh, I would eat some.*
    (narrator) *What does the woman mean?*

(A) She is not going to eat.
(B) The food looks fresh.
(C) She doesn't like fresh food.
(D) She already ate something.

2.   (woman) *The flight must have taken longer than usual.*
    (man) *Had the flight left on time, we would not have arrived so late.*
    (narrator) *What does the man say about the flight?*

(A) It arrived early.
(B) It was unusually short.
(C) It left on time.
(D) It departed late.

3.   (man) *Are you sure you want to go out? You do not seem to be feeling very well.*
    (woman) *If there were some aspirin in the medicine cabinet, I would not need to go to the drugstore.*
    (narrator) *What does the woman mean?*

(A) She really is feeling fine.
(B) There is plenty of aspirin in the medicine cabinet.
(C) It is necessary to get some aspirin.
(D) She does not need to go out.

TOEFL EXERCISE 15: In this exercise, listen carefully to the short conversation and question in the recording program, and then choose the best answer to the question. You should be particularly careful of untrue conditions.

NOW BEGIN THE RECORDING PROGRAM AT TOEFL EXERCISE 15.

1. (A) The woman did not need to call him.
(B) The woman called to let him know about the meeting.
(C) He's not glad that the woman called.
(D) He already knew about the meeting when the woman called.

2. (A) The man often drives too quickly.
(B) The police do not stop the man too much.
(C) The man drove rather slowly.
(D) The police should not stop the man so often.

3. (A) She's so happy they don't have to work on Friday.
(B) It would be nice if they could finish their work on Friday.
(C) She wonders if the man would be nice enough to come in to work in her place on Friday.
(D) It's too bad they must work on Friday.

4. (A) She did not put enough postage on the letter.
(B) The letter arrived last week.
(C) The letter did not need more postage.
(D) She did not put any postage on the letter.

5. (A) He has a dog.
(B) He doesn't pay attention to dogs.
(C) He wishes he had a dog.
(D) Dogs do not need much attention.

6. (A) They knew they had to prepare for the exam.
(B) They didn't prepare for the exam.
(C) As soon as they knew about the exam, they began to prepare for it.
(D) They knew that the preparation for the exam would take a lot of time.

7. (A) It costs too much for him to go.
   (B) He agrees to go with them.
   (C) He is unworried about the cost of the restaurant.
   (D) The restaurant is rather inexpensive.

8. (A) When Joe saw the car coming, he tried to get out of the way.
   (B) Joe was able to get out of the way because he saw the car coming.
   (C) Joe jumped out of the way of the oncoming car.
   (D) Because Joe didn't see the car coming, he couldn't get out of the way.

9. (A) The woman didn't come.
   (B) The woman wanted to be there.
   (C) The woman was going to leave immediately.
   (D) The woman was not really there.

10. (A) Kathy didn't work as hard as possible because she didn't know what the reward was.
    (B) Kathy couldn't have put more effort into the project to win the prize.
    (C) Kathy won first prize because of her hard work on the art project.
    (D) Kathy worked so hard that she knew first prize was hers.

TOEFL EXERCISE (Skills 14–15): In this exercise, listen carefully to the short conversation and question in the recording program, and then choose the best answer to the question.

🎧 Now begin the recording program at Toefl Exercise (Skills 14–15).

1. (A) She enjoys violent movies.
   (B) She would have preferred a more violent movie.
   (C) She thinks the film was too violent.
   (D) She enjoyed the movie.

2. (A) He left the windows open.
   (B) The rain did not get in.
   (C) He forgot to close the windows.
   (D) The rain got into the house.

3. (A) Her family is unable to come to graduation.
   (B) It is possible that her family will come.
   (C) Her parents are coming to the ceremonies.
   (D) She is not graduating this year.

4. (A) He is going to miss the conference.
   (B) He will take his vacation next week.
   (C) He will attend the conference.
   (D) He won't miss his vacation.

5. (A) He enjoys chemistry lab.
   (B) He doesn't have chemistry lab this afternoon.
   (C) He isn't taking chemistry class.
   (D) He has to go to the lab.

6. (A) They filled up the gas tank at the last service station.
   (B) Although they filled up the tank, they still ran out of gas.
   (C) Even though they didn't stop at the service station, they didn't run out of gas.
   (D) They ran out of gas because they didn't stop at the gas station.

7. (A) His schedule is not really heavy.
   (B) He needs to add a few more courses.
   (C) He enrolled in more courses than he really wants.
   (D) He will register for a lot of courses next semester.

8. (A) She never took the bus to work.
   (B) She regularly takes the bus.
   (C) She doesn't know how to get to work.
   (D) She gets lost on the bus.

9. (A) She bought some eggs at the store.
    (B) She doesn't have any eggs to lend him.
    (C) He can borrow some eggs.
    (D) She didn't go to the store.

10. (A) Teresa is feeling a lot better.
    (B) The doctor didn't prescribe the medicine.
    (C) Teresa didn't follow the doctor's orders.
    (D) Teresa did exactly what the doctor said.

TOEFL REVIEW EXERCISE (Skills 1–15): In this exercise, listen carefully to the short conversation and question in the recording program, and then choose the best answer to the question.

NOW BEGIN THE RECORDING PROGRAM AT TOEFL REVIEW EXERCISE (SKILLS 1–15).

1. (A) Drinking the hot tea.
    (B) Making more tea in a few minutes.
    (C) Letting the tea cool off a bit.
    (D) Having the tea immediately.

2. (A) In a bus station.
    (B) In a store.
    (C) In a restaurant.
    (D) In a theater.

3. (A) He's unhappy to end the semester.
    (B) He's glad to be finishing school.
    (C) He couldn't be happier to begin the semester.
    (D) The end of the semester is making him feel sad.

4. (A) The storm destroyed the house.
    (B) The house blocked the trees.
    (C) The stormy weather caused the trees to fall.
    (D) During the storm, someone knocked on the door of the house.

5. (A) The team hasn't won often.
    (B) He usually doesn't pay attention to the football team.
    (C) It's out of the ordinary for the team to lose.
    (D) He usually hears about the football games.

6. (A) He went to the office every morning.
    (B) He was not working.
    (C) He had to arrive at work earlier than 8 o'clock.
    (D) He had a job.

7. (A) He did not enjoy his vacation as much as possible.
    (B) He got lost on his vacation.
    (C) The vacation was really enjoyable.
    (D) He did not really lose his passport.

8. (A) It will take eight hours to get to Riverdale on the bus.
    (B) He believes he knows the correct bus.
    (C) He doesn't know where Riverdale is.
    (D) He assures the woman that he knows the way to Riverdale.

9. (A) The laboratory assistant completed one experiment.
    (B) The laboratory assistant couldn't finish one experiment.
    (C) The laboratory assistant didn't want to do more experiments.
    (D) None of the experiments could be completed.

10. (A) She would like the man to repeat what he said.
    (B) The semester is really over!
    (C) The semester will never end.
    (D) She has the same wish as the man.

IDIOMATIC LANGUAGE_____

SKILL 16:   LISTEN FOR TWO- AND THREE-PART VERBS

Two- and three-part verbs appear in some questions in Listening Part A. These verbs are expressions that include a verb and one or more particles (such as *in, on,* or *at*); the particle changes the meaning of the verb. Questions involving two- and three-part verbs can be difficult for students because the addition of the particle changes the meaning of the verb in an idiomatic way.

Example

On the recording, you hear:

　　　　(man)　　*What time does the meeting start?*
　　　(woman)　*Didn't you hear that it was called off by the director?*
　　(narrator)　*What does the woman say about the meeting?*

In your test book, you read:

　　(A)　The director called a meeting.
　　(B)　The director phoned her about the meeting.
　　(C)　The director called the meeting to order.
　　(D)　The director canceled the meeting.

In this question, the two-part verb *called off* has a different meaning than the verb *call,* which means *phone.* The two-part verb *call off* means *cancel,* so the best answer is answer (D).

NOTE:　A list of common two- and three-part verbs and exercises using these verbs appear in Appendix B. You may want to study these two- and three-part verbs before you try the following exercises.

EXERCISE 16: In this exercise, underline the two- or three-part verb in each short conversation. Then read the question and choose the best answer to that question. Remember that the best answer is one that is related to the meaning of the two- or three-part verb and might not seem to be related to the meaning of the verb without the particle.

1.　　(man)　*Did you have your history exam today?*
　　(woman)　*No, the professor put it off for another week.*
　　(narrator)　*What does the woman say about the exam?*

　　(A)　She would like to put it out of her mind.
　　(B)　The professor canceled it.
　　(C)　It was moved to another location.
　　(D)　It was delayed.

2.　　(woman)　*Do we have any more soap?*
　　(man)　*We've run out of it. Someone will have to go to the store.*
　　(narrator)　*What does the man mean?*

　　(A)　He will run to the store.
　　(B)　He needs soap to wash himself after running.
　　(C)　There is no more soap.
　　(D)　They have a store of soap at home.

3.   (man)   *I need to take the written test to renew my driver's license.*

      (woman)   *Then, you'll have to brush up on the laws.*

      (narrator)   *What does the man need to do?*

(A) Reapply for his driver's license.
(B) Sweep around the lawn.
(C) Learn the laws for the first time.
(D) Review the information that will be on the test.

TOEFL EXERCISE 16: In this exercise, listen carefully to the short conversation and question in the recording program, and then choose the best answer to the question. You should be particularly careful of two- and three-part verbs.

NOW BEGIN THE RECORDING PROGRAM AT TOEFL EXERCISE 16.

1. (A) Phone their neighbors.
    (B) Call to their neighbors over the fence.
    (C) Help the neighbors move in.
    (D) Visit their neighbors.

2. (A) The course is becoming more interesting.
    (B) The course used to be more interesting.
    (C) The course is about the same as it was.
    (D) He's not as bored in the class as the woman.

3. (A) Her headache is getting worse.
    (B) She felt better this morning than now.
    (C) She seems to be feeling better now.
    (D) She is just getting another headache now.

4. (A) The man should stop breaking his cigarettes in half.
    (B) The man should decrease the number of cigarettes he smokes.
    (C) The man should cut the ends off his cigarettes.
    (D) The man should stop smoking completely.

5. (A) The client presented his case to the lawyer.
    (B) The client was upset about the lawyer's rejection.
    (C) The client was annoyed because the lawyer returned the suitcase.
    (D) The client made the lawyer unhappy about the case.

6. (A) She gets along with lots of people.
    (B) She gets back at people who cross her.
    (C) She gets rid of people she doesn't want to spend time with.
    (D) She tries to get ahead of everyone else.

7. (A) He must try to find the children.
    (B) It is necessary for him to clean up after the children.
    (C) The children need to be watched.
    (D) He's going to see what the children have done.

8. (A) They are going on strike.
    (B) They are lying down on the job.
    (C) They are being released from their jobs.
    (D) They are relaxing too much at the factory.

9. (A) He is betting that the football team will win.
    (B) He really wants to succeed.
    (C) It is not so difficult to play on the football team.
    (D) He pulled a muscle while playing football.

10. (A) She's unsure why she tolerates the man.
     (B) She doesn't know where she put her keys.
     (C) She is actually the one who put the keys in the car.
     (D) She can't understand why the man did what he did.

Skill 17:   LISTEN FOR IDIOMS

Idioms appear in some questions in Listening Part A. Idioms are special expressions in a language that all speakers of the language know; these special expressions describe one situation in life but are applied to many different areas of life. Idiom questions can be difficult for students because they seem to be describing one situation when they are really describing a different situation.

Example

On the recording, you hear:

> (man)   *Tom is a full-time student and is holding down a full-time job.*
>
> (woman)   *He's really burning the candle at both ends.*
>
> (narrator)   *What does the woman say about Tom?*

In your test book, you read:

(A) He's lighting a candle.
(B) He's holding the candle at the top and the bottom.
(C) He's doing too much.
(D) He's working as a firefighter.

In this question, the idiom *burning the candle at both ends* has nothing to do with candles and nothing to do with burning or fires, so answers (A), (B), and (D) are not correct. Instead, this idiom is an expression that is used in a situation when someone is trying to do more than he or she really can do; after all, a candle usually only burns at one end, so a candle that burns at two ends is *doing more than it can*. Therefore, the best answer to the question above is answer (C).

NOTE: A list of common idioms and exercises using these idioms appear in Appendix C. You may want to study these idioms before you try the following exercises.

EXERCISE 17: In this exercise, underline the idiom in each short conversation. Then read the question and choose the best answer to that question. Remember that the best answer is one that might not seem to be related to the idiom in the second line.

1.   (man) *I have to take Advanced Biology from Professor Stanton next semester.*
    (woman) *Don't worry about it. It's a piece of cake.*
    (narrator) *What does the woman mean?*

(A) The man should try a piece of cake.
(B) The man should worry about the course.
(C) The man shouldn't take part in the course.
(D) The course is easy.

2.   (woman) *Thanks for changing the oil AND putting air in the tires.*
    (man) *It's all in a day's work.*
    (narrator) *What does the man mean?*

(A) It will take him a whole day to do the job.
(B) This is a regular part of his job.
(C) He can do the work at the end of the day.
(D) He's too busy today to do the work.

3.   (man)   *What was it like while the*   (A) The president dropped his pen.
              president was giving his speech?   (B) The audience was very quiet.
      (woman) *You could hear a pin drop.*   (C) The speech contained several puns.
      (narrator) *What does the woman mean?*   (D) The president discussed dropping
                                                           a bomb.

TOEFL EXERCISE 17: In this exercise, listen carefully to the short conversation and question in the recording program, and then choose the best answer to the question. You should be particularly careful of idioms.

Now begin the recording program at Toefl Exercise 17.

1. (A) The man's never late.
    (B) It's good that the man was fifteen
         minutes late.
    (C) It's never good to be late for class.
    (D) It's good that the man went to
         class, on time or not.

2. (A) The woman's work is all in her
         head.
    (B) The woman has to do two
         experiments rather than one.
    (C) It's a good idea to work together.
    (D) The biology experiment concerns
         two-headed animals.

3. (A) She has no time to work now.
    (B) She doesn't want to work on the
         report either.
    (C) It's best to get it over with now.
    (D) There's no time to present the
         report now.

4. (A) She's very lucky to get the last
         book.
    (B) She's sorry she can't get the book
         today.
    (C) She always has good luck with
         books.
    (D) She just wanted to look at the book.

5. (A) The man doesn't like eating in
         restaurants.
    (B) She doesn't really like that
         restaurant.
    (C) Each of them has his own
         restaurant.
    (D) Everyone has different tastes.

6. (A) She'll do it immediately.
    (B) It is not possible to do it.
    (C) The man should have told her
         sooner.
    (D) She would have done it if the man
         had asked.

7. (A) Abbie used a feather in his art
         project.
    (B) He was knocked down.
    (C) He was really surprised.
    (D) Abbie's father knocked on the
         door.

8. (A) They are taking a boat trip
         together.
    (B) The six chapters are all about the
         boat.
    (C) Everyone has to do the same thing.
    (D) The man will read while he's on
         the boat.

9. (A) She is taller than the others.
    (B) She put her science project on top
         of the others.
    (C) She has a really good head on her
         shoulders.
    (D) She's the best of them all.

10. (A) The man needs to improve his
         penmanship.
    (B) The man doesn't really need to
         apply for the scholarship.
    (C) The man needs to fill out the
         application with dots and crosses.
    (D) The man needs to pay attention to
         every detail.

TOEFL EXERCISE (Skills 16–17): In this exercise, listen carefully to the short conversation and question in the recording program, and then choose the best answer to the question.

🎧 NOW BEGIN THE RECORDING PROGRAM AT TOEFL EXERCISE (SKILLS 16–17).

1. (A) She gets lots of take-out dinners.
   (B) She and her roommate alternate cooking responsibilities.
   (C) Her roommate cooks more often than she does.
   (D) Her roommate does the cooking while she does other chores.

2. (A) He resembles his father.
   (B) He has a chipped tooth.
   (C) He lives one block from his father.
   (D) He and his father were playing a game with blocks.

3. (A) She's going somewhere else.
   (B) She does not like football.
   (C) She has a lot of work to do.
   (D) She is getting sick.

4. (A) He put his foot where he should not have.
   (B) He put the food that the teacher gave him into his mouth.
   (C) He said something embarrassing.
   (D) He told the teacher that his foot was hurt.

5. (A) She'd like the man to delay his trip.
   (B) She prefers that the man leave a few minutes earlier than he planned.
   (C) She wants to know if the man will stay in the market for only a few minutes.
   (D) She'd like to talk to the man for a few minutes.

6. (A) The man might start a fire in the park.
   (B) The man parked his car near the fire.
   (C) The man's thinking of doing something dangerous.
   (D) The man's playing a game in the park.

7. (A) The machines do not act very well.
   (B) The machines don't really bother her.
   (C) She would like them to stop the noise.
   (D) She wishes the machines would cut the wood.

8. (A) Fred has a dog that barks a lot.
   (B) Fred has hidden the money in a tree.
   (C) Fred has backed into a tree.
   (D) Fred has made a mistake.

9. (A) She will give him any help he needs.
   (B) He has to give away what he doesn't need.
   (C) He should not give up.
   (D) He should give back what he borrowed.

10. (A) She'd rather go swimming than do the homework.
    (B) The chemistry homework is really difficult.
    (C) She's doing the homework by the swimming pool.
    (D) The stream is drying up.

TOEFL REVIEW EXERCISE (Skills 1–17): In this exercise, listen carefully to the short conversation and question in the recording program, and then choose the best answer to the question.

🎧 NOW BEGIN THE RECORDING PROGRAM AT TOEFL REVIEW EXERCISE (SKILLS 1–17).

1. (A) There's no more wood inside.
   (B) The wood in the fireplace should be put outside.
   (C) There's a fire outside.
   (D) He needs to bring some wood outside.

2. (A) She worked late at a conference.
   (B) Her meeting was canceled.
   (C) She called a conference at work.
   (D) She was late to a conference.

3. (A) In a hospital.
   (B) At a police station.
   (C) At the beach.
   (D) In a locker room.

4. (A) There was too much room on the
       dance floor.
   (B) He enjoyed the room where they
       went dancing.
   (C) The dance floor was too crowded.
   (D) The club needed more rooms for
       dancing.

5. (A) He could not understand the fax
       machine.
   (B) He wrote the letter that was sent.
   (C) The fax machine was easy for him
       to use.
   (D) He was not very good with figures.

6. (A) The woman hit her head on a nail.
   (B) The woman hit his new car.
   (C) The woman was exactly right.
   (D) The woman bought the new car.

7. (A) He would like the woman to help
       him find his paper.
   (B) He wants the woman to put the
       paper away.
   (C) He needs the woman to review the
       paper.
   (D) He would like the woman to write
       the paper for him.

8. (A) Information about the problem is
       unavailable.
   (B) No one has been informed.
   (C) Everybody knows what is going on.
   (D) Nobody is aware that the problem
       is serious.

9. (A) He did not sleep well.
   (B) He never woke up this morning.
   (C) The alarm failed to go off.
   (D) He needed a loud alarm to wake
       up.

10. (A) The pilot made an emergency
        landing.
    (B) The pilot was forced to leave the
        plane in a hurry.
    (C) The pilot fielded questions about
        the forced landing.
    (D) The plane was damaged when it
        landed forcefully.

THE LISTENING PART B QUESTIONS

Part B of the Listening Comprehension section of the TOEFL test consists of two long conversations, each followed by a number of questions. You will hear the conversations and the questions on the recording; they are not written in your test book. You must choose the best answer to each question from the four choices that are written in your test book.

The conversations are often about some aspect of school life (how difficult a class is, how to write a research paper, how to register for a course). The conversations can also be about topics currently in the news in the United States (desalination of the water supply, recycling of used products, damage from a storm or some other type of natural phenomenon).

Example

On the recording, you hear:

(narrator)	***Questions 1 through 4.*** *Listen to a conversation between a professor and a student.*
(man)	*Hello, Professor Denton. Are you free for a moment? Could I have a word with you?*
(woman)	*Come on in, Michael. Of course I have some time. These are my office hours, and this is the right time for you to come and ask questions. Now, how can I help you?*
(man)	*Well, I have a quick question for you about the homework assignment for tomorrow. I thought the assignment was to answer the first three questions at the top of page 67 in the text, but when I looked, there weren't any questions there. I'm confused.*
(woman)	*The assignment was to answer the first three questions at the top of page 76, not 67.*
(man)	*Oh, now I understand. I'm glad I came in to check. Thanks for your help.*
(woman)	*No problem. See you tomorrow.*

Questions:

1. On the recording, you hear:

    (narrator)   *Who is the man?*

  In your test book, you read:

    (A) A professor.
    (B) An office worker.
    (C) Professor Denton's assistant.
    (D) A student.

2. On the recording, you hear:

    (narrator)   *When does the man come to see Professor Denton?*

  In your test book, you read:

    (A) During regular class hours.
    (B) Just before class time.
    (C) As soon as class is finished.
    (D) During office hours.

(continued on next page)

3. On the recording, you hear:

(narrator)   *Why does the man come to see Professor Denton?*

In your test book, you read:
   (A)   To turn in an assignment.
   (B)   To ask a question.
   (C)   To pick up a completed test.
   (D)   To explain why he did not attend class.

4. On the recording, you hear:

(narrator)   *What incorrect information did the man have?*

In your test book, you read:
   (A)   The date the assignment was due.
   (B)   The page number of the assignment.
   (C)   The length of the assignment.
   (D)   The numbers of the assignment questions.

The first question asks you to determine who the man is. Since the man opens the conversation with *Professor Denton* and he asks about the page number of an assignment for tomorrow, he is probably a student. The best answer to this question is therefore answer (D). The second question asks about when the man comes to see the professor. The professor says that *these are my office hours,* so the best answer to this question is answer (D). The third question asks why the man comes to see the professor. Since the man says *I have a quick question for you,* the best answer to this question is answer (B). The last question asks what incorrect information the man had. The man thought that the assignment was on page 67 and not on page 76, so he was mistaken about the *page number* of the assignment. The best answer to this question is answer (B).

STRATEGIES FOR THE LISTENING PART B QUESTIONS

1. **If you have time, preview the answers to the Listening Part B questions.** While you are looking at the answers, you should try to do the following:
   - Anticipate the **topics** of the conversations you will hear.
   - Anticipate the **questions** for each of the groups of answers.

2. **Listen carefully to the first line of the conversation.** The first line of the conversation often contains the main idea, subject, or topic of the conversation, and you will often be asked to answer such questions.

3. **As you listen to the conversation, draw conclusions about the situation of the conversation: who is talking, where the conversation takes place, or when it takes place.** You will often be asked to make such inferences about the conversation.

4. **As you listen to the conversation, follow along with the answers in your test book and try to determine the correct answers.** Detail questions are generally answered in order in the conversation, and the answers often sound the same as what is said in the recording program.

5. **You should guess even if you are not sure.** Never leave any answers blank.

6. **Use any remaining time to look ahead at the answers to the questions that follow.**

The following skills will help you to implement these strategies in Part B of the Listening Comprehension section of the TOEFL test.

BEFORE LISTENING

SKILL 18:   ANTICIPATE THE TOPICS

It is very helpful to your overall comprehension if you know what topics to expect in Listening Part B. You should therefore try to anticipate the topics you will be hearing. For example, are the conversations about some aspect of school life, or some type of social issue, or a trip someone is planning? A helpful strategy is therefore to look briefly at the answers in the test book, before you actually hear the conversations in the recording program, and try to determine the topics of the conversations that you will hear.

EXERCISE 18: Look at the answers to the five questions together, and try to anticipate the topic of the conversation for those five questions. (Of course, you cannot always determine exactly what the topic is, but you often can get a general idea.) Questions 1 through 5 have been answered for you.

1. (A) Find *work on campus*.
   (B)   *Work* in the *employment office*.
   (C) Help *students* find *jobs*.
   (D) Ask the woman questions.

2. (A) In the library.
   (B) In a classroom.
   (C) In a campus office.
   (D) In an apartment.

3. (A) No more than ten.
   (B) At least twenty.
   (C) Not more than twenty.
   (D) Up to ten.

4. (A) Every morning.
   (B) Afternoons and weekends.
   (C) When he's in class.
   (D) Weekdays.

5. (A) Fill out a form.
   (B) Give her some additional
        information.
   (C) Tell her some news.
   (D) Phone her.

What is the topic of the conversation for questions 1 through 5?

looking for a job on campus

You can guess this because of the following clues:

- *work on campus*
- *employment office*
- *students*
- *jobs*

6. (A) Just before a vacation.
    (B) Just after the end of a school
         semester.
    (C) At the end of the summer.
    (D) Just after a break from school.

7. (A) A trip to visit the Eskimos.
    (B) A trip the woman is planning to
         take.
    (C) A trip the man has already taken.
    (D) A camping trip the man and
         woman took.

8. (A) Three hours.
    (B) Three complete days.
    (C) Three classes.
    (D) Three weeks.

9. (A) Sleeping outside on the ground.
    (B) Spending time in a sauna or hot
         tub.
    (C) Relaxing at the lodge.
    (D) Enjoying excellent food.

10. (A) She'd be scared, but she'd like to
         try.
    (B) She can't wait.
    (C) It would be quite exciting for her.
    (D) She'd prefer not to try.

What is the topic of the conversation for questions 6 through 10?

_____

11. (A) All types of pollution.
    (B) How acid rain has harmed the
         earth.
    (C) Pollution from cars and factories.
    (D) The causes and possible effects of
         acid rain.

12. (A) Nuclear power.
    (B) Electricity.
    (C) Burning coal and oil.
    (D) Solar power.

13. (A) From sulfur dioxide and water
         vapor.
    (B) From sulfur dioxide and nitrogen
         oxide.
    (C) From nitric acid and sulfur
         dioxide.
    (D) From water vapor and nitric acid.

14. (A) Only in North America.
    (B) At the North and South Poles.
    (C) In parts of several northern
         continents.
    (D) In equatorial areas.

15. (A) She should protect herself from
         the rain.
    (B) She should clean up the water
         supply.
    (C) She should read a novel.
    (D) She should get more information
         about acid rain.

What is the topic of the conversation for questions 11 through 15?

_____

Skill 19: ANTICIPATE THE QUESTIONS

It is very helpful to your ability to answer individual questions in Listening Part B if you can anticipate what the questions will be and listen specifically for the answers to those questions.

Example

In your test book, you read:

    (A) In the airport.
    (B) In the library.
    (C) In the dormitory.
    (D) In the travel agent's office.

You try to anticipate the question:

Where does the conversation probably take place?

In this example, you can be quite certain that one of the questions will be about where the conversation takes place. Since you are sure that this is one of the questions, you can listen carefully for clues that will give you the answer. This example shows that a helpful strategy is therefore to look briefly at the answers in the test book, before you actually hear the conversations in the recording program, and try to determine the questions that you will be asked to answer.

EXERCISE 19: Study the following answers and try to determine what the questions will be. (You should note that perhaps you will only be able to predict part of a question, rather than the complete question.) If you cannot predict the question in a short period of time, then move on to the next group of answers. Question 1 has been answered for you.

1. Question: ___What does (someone) want to do?___
    (A) Find work on campus.
    (B) Work in the employment office.
    (C) Help students find jobs.
    (D) Ask the woman questions.

2. Question: _____
    (A) In the library.
    (B) In a classroom.
    (C) In a campus office.
    (D) In an apartment.

3. Question: _____
    (A) No more than ten.
    (B) At least twenty.
    (C) Not more than twenty.
    (D) Up to ten.

4. Question: _____
    (A) Every morning.
    (B) Afternoons and weekends.
    (C) When he's in class.
    (D) Weekdays.

5. Question: _____
    (A) Fill out a form.
    (B) Give her some additional information.
    (C) Tell her some news.
    (D) Phone her.

6. Question: _____
    (A) Just before a vacation.
    (B) Just after the end of a school semester.
    (C) At the end of the summer.
    (D) Just after a break from school.

7. Question: _____
    (A) A trip to visit the Eskimos.
    (B) A trip the woman is planning to take.
    (C) A trip the man has already taken.
    (D) A camping trip the man and woman took.

8. Question: _____
    (A) Three hours.
    (B) Three complete days.
    (C) Three classes.
    (D) Three weeks.

9. Question: _____
    (A) Sleeping outside on the ground.
    (B) Spending time in a sauna or hot tub.
    (C) Relaxing at the lodge.
    (D) Enjoying excellent food.

10. Question: _____
    (A) She'd be scared, but she'd like to try.
    (B) She can't wait.
    (C) It would be quite exciting for her.
    (D) She'd prefer not to try.

11. Question: _____
    (A) All kinds of pollution.
    (B) How acid rain has harmed the earth.
    (C) Pollution from cars and factories.
    (D) The causes and possible effects of acid rain.

12. Question: _____
    (A) Nuclear power.
    (B) Electricity.
    (C) Burning coal and oil.
    (D) Solar power.

13. Question: _____
    (A) From sulfur dioxide and water vapor.
    (B) From sulfur dioxide and nitrogen oxide.
    (C) From nitric acid and sulfur dioxide.
    (D) From water vapor and nitric acid.

14. Question: _____
    (A) Only in North America.
    (B) At the North and South Poles.
    (C) In parts of several northern continents.
    (D) In equatorial areas.

15. Question: _____
(A) She should protect herself from the rain.
(B) She should clean up the water supply.
(C) She should read a novel.
(D) She should get more information about acid rain.

WHILE LISTENING

SKILL 20: DETERMINE THE TOPIC

As you listen to each conversation in Listening Part B, you should be thinking about the topic (subject) or main idea for each conversation. Since the first one or two sentences generally give the topic, you should be asking yourself what the topic is while you are listening carefully to the first part of the conversation.

Example

On the recording, you hear:

(man)   *You can't believe what I just got!*
(woman)   *I bet you got that new car you've always wanted.*
(man)   *Now, how in the world did you figure that out?*

You think:

The topic of the conversation is the new car that the man just got.

EXERCISE 20: Listen to the first part of each of the conversations, and decide on the topic of each conversation.

🎧 NOW BEGIN THE RECORDING PROGRAM AT EXERCISE 20.

1. What is the topic of Conversation 1?

_____

2. What is the topic of Conversation 2?

_____

3. What is the topic of Conversation 3?

_____

SKILL 21: DRAW CONCLUSIONS ABOUT *WHO, WHAT, WHEN, WHERE*

As you listen to each conversation in Listening Part B, you should be trying to set the situation in your mind. You should be thinking the following thoughts:

- ***Who*** *is talking?*
- ***When*** *does the conversation probably take place?*
- ***Where*** *does the conversation probably take place?*
- ***What*** *is the source of information for the conversation?*

Example

On the recording, you hear:

(man)	*Why do you have so many books?*
(woman)	*I need them for my paper on George Washington. Do you know how I can check them out?*
(man)	*Yes, you should go downstairs to the circulation desk and fill out a card for each book.*

You think:

Who is probably talking?	(two students)
Where are they?	(in the library)
What course are they discussing?	(American History)

EXERCISE 21: Listen to the first part of each of the conversations and try to imagine the situation. Then answer the questions in the text.

NOW BEGIN THE RECORDING PROGRAM AT EXERCISE 21.

Conversation 1
1.   Who is probably talking?   _____

2.   Where does the conversation take place?   _____

Conversation 2
1.   Who is probably talking?   _____

2.   When does the conversation take place?   _____

3.   What is the source of the man's information? _____

Conversation 3
1.   Who is probably talking?   _____

2.   When does the conversation take place?   _____

3.   What is the source of the information?   _____

SKILL 22: LISTEN FOR ANSWERS IN ORDER

There are two possible methods to use while you listen to a conversation in the Listening Part B of the TOEFL test.

- *You can just listen to the conversation (and ignore the answers).*
- *You can follow along with the answers while you listen.*

Some students prefer to just listen to the conversation while it is being spoken, and if that method works well for you, then that is what you should do. Other students find that they can answer more questions correctly if they read along with the answers while the conversation is being spoken. Because the detail questions are answered in order, it is possible to read along while you listen to the conversation in the recording program.

Example

On the recording, you hear:

(man)	*Can I help you?*
(woman)	*I'm interested in opening an account.*
(man)	*Well, we have several different types of accounts: checking accounts, savings accounts, money market accounts, time deposit accounts.*
(woman)	*It's a checking account that I am interested in.*
(man)	*I can help you with that. First, you have to fill out a form, and then I need to see some identification. That's about all there is to it.*
(woman)	*That sounds easy enough. Thanks for your help.*

In your test book, you read (same time):

1. (A) A checking account.
   (B) A savings account.
   (C) A money market account.
   (D) A time deposit account.

2. (A) A form.
   (B) An account.
   (C) A piece of identification.
   (D) A check.

On the recording, you hear:

(narrator) 1. *What type of account does the woman want?*

2. *What does the man need for her to show him?*

When you read the answers to the first question, you can anticipate that the first question is: *What type of account?* As you listen, you determine that the woman wants *a checking account.* Therefore, you can anticipate that the best answer to the first question is (A).

When you read the answers to the second question, you can anticipate that the second question is going to ask *What thing . . . ?* In the conversation, the man asks her to fill out a *form* and show some *identification,* so as you are listening you can anticipate that the correct answer to the second question is either (A) or (C). When you hear the question, you can determine that the best answer is answer (C).

TOEFL EXERCISE 22: Listen to each complete conversation and answer the questions that follow.

 NOW BEGIN THE RECORDING PROGRAM AT TOEFL EXERCISE 22.

1. (A) Find work on campus.
    (B) Work in the employment office.
    (C) Help students find jobs.
    (D) Ask the woman questions.

2. (A) In the library.
    (B) In a classroom.
    (C) In a campus office.
    (D) In an apartment.

3. (A) No more than ten.
    (B) At least twenty.
    (C) Not more than twenty.
    (D) Up to ten.

4. (A) Every morning.
    (B) Afternoons and weekends.
    (C) When he's in class.
    (D) Weekdays.

5. (A) Fill out a form.
    (B) Give her some additional information.
    (C) Tell her some news.
    (D) Phone her.

6. (A) Just before a vacation.
    (B) Just after the end of a school semester.
    (C) At the end of the summer.
    (D) Just after a break from school.

7. (A) A trip to visit the Eskimos.
    (B) A trip the woman is planning to take.
    (C) A trip the man has already taken.
    (D) A camping trip the man and woman took.

8. (A) Three hours.
    (B) Three complete days.
    (C) Three classes.
    (D) Three weeks.

9. (A) Sleeping outside on the ground.
    (B) Spending time in a hot tub.
    (C) Relaxing at the lodge.
    (D) Enjoying excellent food.

10. (A) She'd be scared, but she'd like to try.
    (B) She can't wait.
    (C) It would be quite exciting for her.
    (D) She'd prefer not to try.

11. (A) All kinds of pollution.
    (B) How acid rain has harmed the earth.
    (C) Pollution from cars and factories.
    (D) The causes and possible effects of acid rain.

12. (A) Nuclear power.
    (B) Electricity.
    (C) Burning coal and oil.
    (D) Solar power.

13. (A) From sulfur dioxide and water vapor.
    (B) From sulfur dioxide and nitrogen oxide.
    (C) From nitric acid and sulfur dioxide.
    (D) From water vapor and nitric acid.

14. (A) Only in North America.
    (B) At the North and South Poles.
    (C) In parts of several northern continents.
    (D) In equatorial areas.

15. (A) She should protect herself from the rain.
    (B) She should clean up the water supply.
    (C) She should read a novel.
    (D) She should get more information about acid rain.

TOEFL REVIEW EXERCISE (Skills 18–22): In this exercise, you will use all of the information that you learned in Skills 18 through 22.

Before the recording program begins, you should read over the answers to questions 1 through 15 and do the following:

- *Anticipate the topics you will hear.*
- *Anticipate the questions.*

While you are listening to the conversations, you should do the following:

- *Listen for the topic in the first lines.*
- *Draw conclusions about the situation (who, what, when, where).*
- *Listen for the answers in order.*

 Now begin the recording program at Toefl Review Exercise Skills (18–22).

1. (A) To a concert.
   (B) To a rehearsal.
   (C) To a lecture.
   (D) To the library.

2. (A) One.
   (B) Two.
   (C) Three.
   (D) Four.

3. (A) The bus does not go directly to the Music Building.
   (B) The bus goes very slowly to the Music Building.
   (C) The bus sometimes does not come.
   (D) The bus will not arrive for a while.

4. (A) Walk.
   (B) Wait for the bus.
   (C) Miss the lecture.
   (D) Think of another plan.

5. (A) Boring.
   (B) Fantastic.
   (C) Lengthy.
   (D) Faithful.

6. (A) By car.
   (B) By plane.
   (C) By train.
   (D) By bicycle.

7. (A) She went directly to Yellowstone.
   (B) She spent a few weeks in Laramie.
   (C) She stopped at the Devil's Tower National Monument.
   (D) She made a few stops before going on to Yellowstone.

8. (A) Laramie.
   (B) Devil's Tower National Monument.
   (C) Old Faithful.
   (D) Wyoming.

9. (A) Hear again about Yellowstone.
   (B) Take a trip to Yellowstone.
   (C) Get a job in a national park.
   (D) Move to Yellowstone.

10. (A) How and when we celebrate Thanksgiving.
    (B) The traditional Thanksgiving dinner.
    (C) When Thanksgiving began.
    (D) Abraham Lincoln.

11. (A) With colonists in Massachusetts.
    (B) Alone and thinking about how Thanksgiving developed.
    (C) With a big Thanksgiving dinner.
    (D) In an untraditional manner.

12. (A) The terrible winter.
    (B) The corn harvest.
    (C) The development of Thanksgiving Day.
    (D) For getting the whole family together.

13. (A) At many different times.
    (B) In July.
    (C) Any time in November.
    (D) On a Thursday in November.

THE LISTENING PART C QUESTIONS

Part C of the Listening Comprehension section of the TOEFL test consists of three talks, each followed by a number of questions. You will hear the talks and the questions on a recording; they are not written in your test book. You must choose the best answer to each question from the four choices that are written in your test book. Like the conversations in Listening Part B, the talks are often about some aspect of school life or topics currently in the news. It is also very common for the talks to be shortened versions of lectures from courses taught in American colleges and universities.

Example

On the recording, you hear:

(narrator)	***Questions 1 through 4.*** *Listen to a talk about the settlement of America.*
(woman)	*The settling of the vast farmlands in central North America was delayed at least partly because of an error by one man. In the early nineteenth century, Lieutenant Zebulon Pike of the U.S. Army was sent out to explore and chart the huge expanses of land in the center of the continent. When he returned from his explorations, he wrote a report in which he erroneously stated that the vast plains in the central part of the continent were desertlike, comparable to the Sahara in Africa. In reality, however, these vast plains contained some of the most fertile farmland in the world. Because of Pike's mistake, the maps of the day depicted the central part of what is today the United States as a vast desert rather than the excellent and available farmland that it was. This mistaken belief about the nature of those lands caused settlers to avoid the central plains for years.*

Questions:

1. On the recording, you hear:

    (narrator)   *What is the topic of this talk?*

    In your test book, you read:

    (A) Zebulon Pike's career.
    (B) A mistake that influenced the
            settlement of America.
    (C) A report for the army.
    (D) The farmlands.

2. On the recording, you hear:

    (narrator)   *How did Pike describe the area that he explored?*

    In your test book, you read:

    (A) As a desert.
    (B) As usable for army purposes.
    (C) As located in the Sahara.
    (D) As available for farmland.

(continued on next page)

3. On the recording, you hear:

    (narrator)   *What was this area really like?*

    In your test book, you read: (A) It was a vast desert.
                                     (B) It was covered with farms.
                                     (C) It was excellent farmland.
                                     (D) It was similar to the Sahara.

4. On the recording, you hear:

    (narrator)   *his talk would probably be given in*
                  hich of the following courses?

    In your test book, you read:) Agricultural Science.
) American History.
                                        Geology of the United States.
                                    (Military Science.

The first question asks about the topic of th alk. The topic of the talk is found in the
first sentence of the talk: *The settling of the vast rmlands in central North America was delayed
at least partly because of an error by one man.* Th efore, the best answer to the question is
(B). The second question is a detail question t t asks how Pike described this area. It is
stated in the talk that Pike *wrote a report in which erroneously stated that the vast plains in the
central part of the continent were desertlike. . . .* The fore, the best answer to this question is
(A). The third question is an additional detail q stion that asks what the area was really
like. Because the talk indicates that *in reality . . . ese vast plains contained some of the most
fertile farmland in the world,* the best answer to thi uestion is (C). The fourth question is
an inference question. It asks in which course th lecture would probably be given. The
word *probably* indicates to you that the question is ot answered directly in the talk. You
must draw a conclusion from the information in th talk to answer this question. Because
this talk refers to *the early nineteenth century* and disc ses the *settling of the vast farmlands in
central North America,* it would probably be given in American History course. The best
answer to this question is (B).

STRATEGIES FOR THE LISTENING PA   C QUESTIONS

1. **If you have time, preview the answers to the Liste ng Part C questions.** While you
    are looking at the answers, you should try to do the follo ng:

    •Anticipate the **topics** of the talks you will hear.
    •Anticipate the **questions** for each of the groups of swers.

2. **Listen carefully to the first line of the talk.** The first l e of the talk often contains the
    main idea, subject, or topic of the talk, and you will often be ked this type of question.

3. **As you listen to the talk, draw conclusions about the situation of the talk: who is
    talking, where or when the talk takes place, which course this lecture might be
    given in.** You will often be asked to make such inferences about the talk.

4. **As you listen to the talk, follow along with the answers in your test book and try
    to determine the correct answers.** Detail questions are generally answered in order in
    the talk, and the answers often sound the same as what is said on the recording.

5. **You should guess even if you are not sure.** Never leave any answers blank.

6. **Use any remaining time to look ahead at the answers to the questions that follow.**

The following skills will help you to implement these strategies in Part C of the Listening Comprehension section of the TOEFL test.

BEFORE LISTENING_____

SKILL 23:   ANTICIPATE THE TOPICS

It is very helpful to your overall comprehension if you know what topics to expect in Listening Part C. You should therefore try to anticipate the topics that you will be hearing (as you did in Listening Part B). For example, are the talks about American history, or literature, or some aspect of school life? A helpful strategy is therefore to look briefly at the answers in the test book, before you actually hear the talks on the recording, and try to determine the topics of the talks that you will hear.

EXERCISE 23:   Look at the answers to the five questions together, and try to anticipate the topic of the talk for those five questions. (Of course, you cannot always determine exactly what the topic is, but you often can get a general idea.) Questions 1 through 5 have been answered for you.

1. (A) During a *biology* laboratory session.
    (B) In a biology study group.
    (C) On the *first day of class.*
    (D) Just before the final exam.

2. (A) Once a week.
    (B) Two times a week.
    (C) Three times a week.
    (D) For fifteen hours.

3. (A) To do the first laboratory assignment.
    (B) To take the first *exam.*
    (C) To study the laboratory manual.
    (D) To read one chapter of the text.

4. (A) Room assignments.
    (B) Exam topics.
    (C) *Reading assignments.*
    (D) The first lecture.

5. (A) *Exams and lab work.*
    (B) Reading and writing assignments.
    (C) Class participation and grades on examinations.
    (D) Lecture and laboratory attendance.

What is the topic of the talk for questions 1 through 5?

the requirements of a biology class

You can guess this because of the following clues:

- *biology*
- *first day of class*
- *reading assignments*
- *exams*
- *lab work*

6. (A) What caused the Ring of Fire.
    (B) The volcanoes of the Ring of Fire.
    (C) Hawaiian volcanoes.
    (D) Different types of volcanoes.

7. (A) The Ring of Fire.
    (B) The characteristics of volcanoes in
         the Ring of Fire.
    (C) The volcanoes of Hawaii.
    (D) Mauna Loa.

8. (A) In Hawaii.
    (B) In the United States.
    (C) Along the Ring of Fire.
    (D) Within the Ring of Fire.

9. (A) They are not so violent.
    (B) They are located along the Ring of
         Fire.
    (C) They contain a lot of gas.
    (D) They contain thick lava.

10. (A) A volcano on the Ring of Fire.
    (B) An island in Hawaii.
    (C) A long, low volcanic mountain.
    (D) An explosive volcano.

What is the topic of the talk for questions 6 through 10?

_____

11. (A) An artist.
    (B) A tour guide.
    (C) An Indian.
    (D) Orville Wright.

12. (A) Several.
    (B) Sixty thousand.
    (C) Sixteen million.
    (D) Millions and millions.

13. (A) The National Air and Space
         Museum.
    (B) The Museum of Natural History.
    (C) The American History Museum.
    (D) The Smithsonian Arts and
         Industries Building.

14. (A) The American History Museum.
    (B) The Smithsonian Arts and
         Industries Building.
    (C) The Washington Museum.
    (D) The National Air and Space
         Museum.

15. (A) To the White House.
    (B) To the Smithsonian.
    (C) To the mall.
    (D) To various other museums.

What is the topic of the talk for questions 11 through 15?

_____

SKILL 24:   ANTICIPATE THE QUESTIONS

It is very helpful to your ability to answer individual questions in Listening Part C if you can anticipate what the questions will be and listen specifically for the answers to those questions (as you did in Listening Part B).

Example

In your test book, you read:

(A)   For three weeks.
(B)   For three days.
(C)   For three months.
(D)   For three hours.

You try to anticipate the question:

How long does (something) ¹

In this example, you can be quite ce.... ...at one of the questions will be about how long something lasts. Since you are su.... ...at this is one of the questions, you can listen carefully for clues that will gi.... ...answer. This example shows that a helpful strategy is therefore to look b.... .....swers in the test book, before you actually hear the talks on the ....y to determine the questions that you will be asked to answer.

E. RCISE 24: Study the following answers and try to determine what the questions will (You should note that perhaps you will only be able to predict part of a question, rather ....an the complete question.) If you cannot predict the question in a short period of time, then move on to the next group of answers. Question 1 has been answered for you.

1. Question: __When does the talk probably take place?__
    (A)   During a biology laboratory session.
    (B)   In a biology study group.
    (C)   On the first day of class.
    (D)   Just before the final exam.

2. Question: _____
    (A)   Once a week.
    (B)   Two times a week.
    (C)   Three times a week.
    (D)   For fifteen hours.

3. Question: _____
    (A)   To do the first laboratory assignment.
    (B)   To take the first exam.
    (C)   To study the laboratory manual.
    (D)   To read one chapter of the text.

4. Question: _____
    (A)   Room assignments.
    (B)   Exam topics.
    (C)   Reading assignments.
    (D)   The first lecture.

5. Question: _____
    (A) Exams and lab work.
    (B) Reading and writing assignments.
    (C) Class participation and grades on examinations.
    (D) Lecture and laboratory attendance.

6. Question: _____
    (A) What caused the Ring of Fire.
    (B) The volcanoes of the Ring of Fire.
    (C) Hawaiian volcanoes.
    (D) Different types of volcanoes.

7. Question: _____
    (A) The Ring of Fire.
    (B) The characteristics of volcanoes in the Ring of Fire.
    (C) The volcanoes of Hawaii.
    (D) Mauna Loa.

8. Question: _____
    (A) In Hawaii.
    (B) In the United States.
    (C) Along the Ring of Fire.
    (D) Within the Ring of Fire.

9. Question: _____
    (A) They are not so violent.
    (B) They are located along the Ring of Fire.
    (C) They contain a lot of gas.
    (D) They contain thick lava.

10. Question: _____
    (A) A volcano on the Ring of Fire.
    (B) An island in Hawaii.
    (C) A long, low volcanic mountain.
    (D) An explosive volcano.

11. Question: _____
    (A) An artist.
    (B) A tour guide.
    (C) An Indian.
    (D) Orville Wright.

12. Question: _____
    (A) Several.
    (B) Sixty thousand.
    (C) Sixteen million.
    (D) Millions and millions.

13. Question: _____
    (A) The National Air and Space Museum.
    (B) The Museum of Natural History.
    (C) The American History Museum.
    (D) The Smithsonian Arts and Industries Building.

14. Question: _____
    (A) The American History Museum.
    (B) The Smithsonian Arts and Industries Building.
    (C) The Washington Museum.
    (D) The National Air and Space Museum.

15. Question: _____
    (A) To the White House.
    (B) To the Smithsonian.
    (C) To the mall.
    (D) To various other museums.

WHILE LISTENING

SKILL 25:   DETERMINE THE TOPIC

As you listen to each talk in Listening Part C, you should be thinking about the topic (subject) or main idea for the talk (as you did in Listening Part B). Since the first sentence is generally a topic sentence, you should be asking yourself what the topic is while you are listening carefully to the first part of the talk.

Example

On the recording, you hear:

    (man)   *The major earthquake that occurred east of Los Angeles in*
                  1971 is still affecting the economy of the area today.

You think:

    The topic of the talk is the effect of the 1971 earthquake on
    Los Angeles today.

EXERCISE 25: Listen to the first part of each of the talks, and decide on the topic of each talk.

🎧 Now begin the recording program at Exercise 25.

1. What is the topic of Talk 1?

_____

2. What is the topic of Talk 2?

_____

3. What is the topic of Talk 3?

_____

SKILL 26:   DRAW CONCLUSIONS ABOUT *WHO, WHAT, WHEN, WHERE*

As you listen to each talk in Listening Part C, you should be trying to set the situation in your mind (as you did in Listening Part B). You should be thinking the following thoughts:

- *Who* is talking?
- *When* does the talk probably take place?
- *Where* does the talk probably take place?
- *What* course is the talk concerned with?
- *What* is the source of information for the talk?

Example

On the recording, you hear:

> (woman)   *The next stop on our tour of Atlanta will be the original home of Coca-Cola, at 107 Marietta Street. Coca-Cola was manufactured at this location until early in September of 1888.*

You think:

Who is probably talking?	(a tour guide)
Where are they?	(in Atlanta)
When does the talk take place?	(in the middle of a tour)

EXERCISE 26: Listen to the first part of each of the talks and try to imagine the situation. Then answer the questions in the text.

NOW BEGIN THE RECORDING PROGRAM AT EXERCISE 26.

Talk 1
1.   Who is probably talking?   _____

2.   Where does the talk probably take place?   _____

3.   When does the talk probably take place?   _____

4.   What course is being discussed?   _____

Talk 2
1.   Who is probably talking?   _____

2.   Where does the talk probably take place?   _____

3.   When does the talk probably take place?   _____

4.   What course is being discussed?   _____

Talk 3
1.   Who is probably talking?   _____

2.   Where does the talk take place?   _____

3.   When does the talk take place?   _____

SKILL 27:   LISTEN FOR ANSWERS IN ORDER

There are two possible methods to use while you listen to the talks in Listening Part C.

- *You can just listen to the talk (and ignore the answers).*
- *You can follow along with the answers while you listen.*

Some students prefer to just listen to the talk while it is being spoken, and if that method works well for you, then that is what you should do. Other students find that they can answer more questions correctly if they read along with the answers while the talk is being given. Because the detail questions are answered in order, it is possible to read along while you listen to the talk in the recording program.

Example

On the recording, you hear:

(woman)   *The Great Chicago Fire began on
          October 8, 1871, and, according to
          legend, began when a cow knocked
          over a lantern in Mrs. O'Leary's
          barn. No matter how it began, it
          was a disastrous fire. The preceding
          summer had been exceedingly dry
          in the Chicago area, and the extreme
          dryness accompanied by Chicago's
          infamous winds created an inferno
          that destroyed 18,000 buildings and
          killed more than 300 people before
          it was extinguished the following day.*

In your test book, you read (same time):

1.   (A)   In a barn.
     (B)   In Mrs. O'Leary's home.
     (C)   In a cow pasture.
     (D)   In a lantern factory.

2.   (A)   The dry weather prior to the fire
             made it worse.
     (B)   It happened during the summer.
     (C)   Chicago's winds made it worse.
     (D)   It killed many people.

On the recording, you hear:

(narrator)   1.   *According to legend, where did
                  the Great Chicago Fire begin?*

             2.   *Which of the following is **not**
                  true about the Great Chicago Fire?*

When you read the answers to the first question, you can anticipate that the first question is: *Where did something happen?* As you listen, you determine that the fire began *in Mrs. O'Leary's barn.* Therefore, you can anticipate that the best answer to the first question is (A).

   If you read the answers to the second question while you listen to the talk, you can determine that answers (A), (C), and (D) are true. Answer (B) is not true: the fire did not begin in the summer, it began in *October,* which is in the autumn. Therefore, answer (B) is the best answer to the question *Which of the following is **not** true about the Great Chicago Fire?*

TOEFL EXERCISE 27: Listen to each complete talk and answer the questions that follow.

NOW BEGIN THE RECORDING PROGRAM AT TOEFL EXERCISE 27.

1. (A) During a biology laboratory session.
    (B) In a biology study group.
    (C) On the first day of class.
    (D) Just before the final exam.

2. (A) Once a week.
    (B) Two times a week.
    (C) Three times a week.
    (D) For fifteen hours.

3. (A) To do the first laboratory assignment.
    (B) To take the first exam.
    (C) To study the laboratory manual.
    (D) To read one chapter of the text.

4. (A) Room assignments.
    (B) Exam topics.
    (C) Reading assignments.
    (D) The first lecture.

5. (A) Exams and lab work.
    (B) Reading and writing assignments.
    (C) Class participation and grades on examinations.
    (D) Lecture and laboratory attendance.

6. (A) What caused the Ring of Fire.
    (B) The volcanoes of the Ring of Fire.
    (C) Hawaiian volcanoes.
    (D) Different types of volcanoes.

7. (A) The Ring of Fire.
    (B) The characteristics of volcanoes in the Ring of Fire.
    (C) The volcanoes of Hawaii.
    (D) Mauna Loa.

8. (A) In Hawaii.
    (B) In the United States.
    (C) Along the Ring of Fire.
    (D) Within the Ring of Fire.

9. (A) They are not so violent.
    (B) They are located along the Ring of Fire.
    (C) They contain a lot of gas.
    (D) They contain thick lava.

10. (A) A volcano on the Ring of Fire.
    (B) An island in Hawaii.
    (C) A long, low volcanic mountain.
    (D) An explosive volcano.

11. (A) An artist.
    (B) A tour guide.
    (C) An Indian.
    (D) Orville Wright.

12. (A) Several.
    (B) Sixty thousand.
    (C) Sixteen million.
    (D) Millions and millions.

13. (A) The National Air and Space Museum.
    (B) The Museum of Natural History.
    (C) The American History Museum.
    (D) The Smithsonian Arts and Industries Building.

14. (A) The American History Museum.
    (B) The Smithsonian Arts and Industries Building.
    (C) The Washington Museum.
    (D) The National Air and Space Museum.

15. (A) To the White House.
    (B) To the Smithsonian.
    (C) To the mall.
    (D) To various other museums.

TOEFL REVIEW EXERCISE (Skills 23–27): In this exercise, you will use all of the information that you learned in Skills 23 through 27.

Before the recording program begins, you should read over the answers to questions 1 through 12 and do the following:

- *Anticipate the topics you will hear.*
- *Anticipate the questions.*

While you are listening to the talks, you should do the following:

- *Listen for the topic in the first sentence.*
- *Draw conclusions about the situation (who, what, when, where).*
- *Listen for the answers in order.*

NOW BEGIN THE RECORDING PROGRAM AT TOEFL REVIEW EXERCISE (SKILLS 23–27).

1. (A) Other librarians.
   (B) Undergraduate students.
   (C) Students who are not in the business department.
   (D) Graduate business students.

2. (A) It opens at 7:00 A.M.
   (B) It closes at 7:00 P.M.
   (C) It closes at midnight.
   (D) It is always open.

3. (A) Computer area and business materials.
   (B) Magazines and newspapers.
   (C) Business department and library staff offices.
   (D) First and second floors of the library.

4. (A) Go home.
   (B) Return to class.
   (C) Work on the computers.
   (D) Tour the library.

5. (A) A student in health services.
   (B) A drug abuse lecturer.
   (C) A dermatologist.
   (D) A representative of the tobacco industry.

6. (A) How to reduce nicotine and other addictions.
   (B) How stress affects the skin.
   (C) The effects of alcohol on health.
   (D) How to achieve optimal health.

7. (A) Alcohol.
   (B) Nicotine.
   (C) Caffeine.
   (D) A reduced supply of blood.

8. (A) It increases the flow of blood to the skin.
   (B) It causes increased consumption of alcohol.
   (C) It prevents the skin from receiving enough nourishment.
   (D) It causes stress.

9. (A) Before the Civil War.
   (B) At the end of the Civil War.
   (C) At the beginning of the twentieth century.
   (D) Within the last decade.

10. (A) The Civil War ended.
    (B) The U.S. government issued a large amount of paper currency.
    (C) The price of gold plummeted.
    (D) The value of gold became inflated.

11. (A) The president.
    (B) The president's brother.
    (C) The president's brother-in-law.
    (D) The president's wife.

12. (A) Issue greenbacks.
    (B) Sell gold.
    (C) Corner the gold market.
    (D) Hold its gold reserves.

1 □ 1 □ 1 □ 1 □ 1 □ 1 □ 1 □ 1

TOEFL POST-TEST

SECTION 1
LISTENING COMPREHENSION
Time—approximately 35 minutes
(including the reading of the directions for each part)

In this section of the test, you will have an opportunity to demonstrate your ability to understand conversations and talks in English. There are three parts to this section, with special directions for each part. Answer all the questions on the basis of what is **stated** or **implied** by the speakers you hear. Do **not** take notes or write in your test book at any time. Do **not** turn the pages until you are told to do so.

Part A

Directions: In Part A you will hear short conversations between two people. After each conversation, you will hear a question about the conversation. The conversations and questions will not be repeated. After you hear a question, read the four possible answers in your test book and choose the best answer. Then, on your answer sheet, find the number of the question and fill in the space that corresponds to the letter of the answer you have chosen.

Listen to an example.   **Sample Answer**

                                                                             Ⓐ

On the recording, you will hear: Ⓑ
                                                                    Ⓒ

    (man)   *That exam was just awful.*   ●
  (woman) *Oh, it could have been worse.*
(narrator) *What does the woman mean?*

In your test book, you will read: (A) The exam was really awful.
                                        (B) It was the worst exam she had ever seen.
                                        (C) It couldn't have been more difficult.
                                        (D) It wasn't that hard.

You learn from the conversation that the man thought the exam was very difficult and that the woman disagreed with the man. The best answer to the question, "What does the woman mean?" is (D), "It wasn't that hard." Therefore, the correct choice is (D).

Ⓦⓐⓘⓣ **Wait**

1. (A) He'll correct the exams this afternoon.
   (B) The exam will be at noon.
   (C) He will collect the exams at 12:00.
   (D) The tests have not yet been graded.

2. (A) Martha applied for a visa last month.
   (B) Martha's visa will last for only a month.
   (C) Martha arrived last month without her visa.
   (D) Martha's visa was already delivered.

3. (A) The professor described what the students should do.
   (B) There was a long line to register for the required class.
   (C) The professor required an outline.
   (D) The professor lined up for retirement.

4. (A) Chuck had improved.
   (B) This visit was better than the last.
   (C) Chuck looked at him in the hospital.
   (D) Chuck didn't seem to be doing very well.

5. (A) She thinks the tuition should be increased.
   (B) The semester's tuition is quite affordable.
   (C) It costs too much.
   (D) She has more than enough for tuition.

6. (A) He thinks he got a good grade.
   (B) The history grades were all C or above.
   (C) No one got history grades.
   (D) All the grades were C or lower.

7. (A) The parking lots were full before 10:00.
   (B) It was impossible to start class by 10:00.
   (C) He parked the car before class at 10:00.
   (D) The possibility of finding a place to park increased.

8. (A) She's found a new ring.
   (B) She would like a hug.
   (C) She's shopping for a carpet.
   (D) She's thankful she has a rag.

9. (A) In a department store.
   (B) In a bank.
   (C) In an accounting firm.
   (D) In a checkout line.

10. (A) Jane usually visits San Francisco for her vacations.
    (B) Jane's cousin often visits San Francisco.
    (C) Whenever there's a holiday, Jane's cousin goes to San Francisco.
    (D) Whenever there's a holiday, Jane leaves San Francisco.

11. (A) He wishes he had something to eat.
    (B) He hopes he won't eat for weeks.
    (C) He wishes he hadn't eaten so much.
    (D) He wishes he weren't eating.

12. (A) Traffic should not be allowed.
    (B) She thinks that the traffic should stay outside.
    (C) She agrees that the traffic is noisy.
    (D) She'll stay outside with the man.

13. (A) The headings for today's reading assignment.
    (B) The chance to make the headlines.
    (C) Her reading ability.
    (D) The daily newspaper.

14. (A) The bus trip is only five minutes long.
    (B) The man missed the bus by five minutes.
    (C) The man doesn't have time to waste.
    (D) The bus was five minutes late.

15. (A) It's not possible to pass the class.
    (B) She'll definitely fail.
    (C) It's always possible.
    (D) She shouldn't say anything about the class.

GO ON TO THE NEXT PAGE →

16. (A) She gave Tom money to pay the rent.
    (B) She was given money for the rent.
    (C) Tom borrowed money for the rent.
    (D) She had some money to lend.

17. (A) The cake is extremely good.
    (B) He never tasted the cake.
    (C) He wished he hadn't tasted the cake.
    (D) The cake has never been very good.

18. (A) At the corner she ran into another car.
    (B) She ran to Carl because she cared.
    (C) She unexpectedly met one of her relatives.
    (D) Carl was running from place to place.

19. (A) She shouldn't leave her purse here.
    (B) She's probably in the apartment.
    (C) Her purse must not be in the apartment.
    (D) She left without taking her purse.

20. (A) The landlord failed to collect rent on the first of last month.
    (B) The tenants absolutely must pay rent by the first of the month.
    (C) The landlord will not fail to collect your rent on the first of next month.
    (D) It is important to call the landlord about rent on the first of the month.

21. (A) Taking the car out for a test drive.
    (B) Listening to the noises.
    (C) Fixing the car herself.
    (D) Getting the car repaired.

22. (A) Martha's jobs are easy.
    (B) It's easy to hold two jobs.
    (C) It's better for Martha to have two jobs.
    (D) Martha should slow down.

23. (A) The plane took off just after he arrived.
    (B) He arrived just after the plane took off.
    (C) He wasn't in time to catch the plane.
    (D) He arrived too late to catch the plane.

24. (A) He agrees with the woman's suggestion.
    (B) Parking is not free on the weekend.
    (C) It is not necessary for them to park.
    (D) He thinks they don't have to pay.

25. (A) He is eager to leave his job.
    (B) He is unhappy at the thought of retiring.
    (C) He couldn't be unhappier about retiring.
    (D) He is retiring too soon.

26. (A) He got the car he really wanted.
    (B) He didn't get a new car.
    (C) The car that he got was not his first choice.
    (D) He didn't really want a new car.

27. (A) Mr. Drew pointedly asked the president about the committee.
    (B) The president pointed to Mr. Drew's head.
    (C) Mr. Drew became head of the new commission.
    (D) Mr. Drew was committed to the president's appointments.

28. (A) She felt inferior.
    (B) She wasn't furious.
    (C) She felt there should have been more fairness.
    (D) She was extremely angry.

29. (A) The man would do the dishes.
    (B) The plates did not need to be washed.
    (C) The man would not be ready to go.
    (D) The dishes would not be done.

30. (A) He knew that grapes were cheaper than cherries.
    (B) He didn't know that grapes were cheaper than cherries.
    (C) He bought grapes because they were cheaper than cherries.
    (D) He didn't buy either grapes or cherries because of the price.

GO ON TO THE NEXT PAGE

1 □ 1 □ 1 □ 1 □ 1 □ 1 □ 1 □ 1

Part B

Directions: In this part of the test, you will hear longer conversations. After each conversation, you will hear several questions. The conversations and questions will not be repeated.

After you hear a question, read the four possible answers in your test book and choose the best answer. Then, on your answer sheet, find the number of the question and fill in the space that corresponds to the letter of the answer you have chosen.

Remember, you are not allowed to take notes or write in your test book.

31. (A) Attend a football game alone.
    (B) Go to a sporting event.
    (C) Eat in the cafeteria and study.
    (D) See a play.

32. (A) It's the final game of the season.
    (B) It's better than the drama department's play.
    (C) It's a very important game.
    (D) It's close to the cafeteria.

33. (A) A play.
    (B) A game.
    (C) A study group meeting.
    (D) Dinner in the cafeteria.

34. (A) Saturday night.
    (B) After dinner in the cafeteria.
    (C) Sunday afternoon.
    (D) Maybe next weekend.

35. (A) Trash orbiting Earth.
    (B) A trip by an astronaut to the Moon.
    (C) The overabundance of garbage on Earth.
    (D) Becoming space scientists.

36. (A) From a lecture.
    (B) In a magazine article.
    (C) In a book.
    (D) On a television program.

37. (A) 17,000 pounds.
    (B) 3,000 tons.
    (C) 3,000 pounds.
    (D) 300 tons.

38. (A) She will be able to travel in space.
    (B) The problem will take care of itself.
    (C) Scientists will find solutions to the problem.
    (D) The junk will fall to Earth.

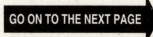

GO ON TO THE NEXT PAGE

1 □ 1 □ 1 □ 1 □ 1 □ 1 □ 1 □ 1

Part C

Directions: In this part of the test, you will hear several talks. After each talk, you will hear some questions. The talks and questions will not be repeated.

After you hear a question, you will read the four possible answers in your test book and choose the best answer. Then, on your answer sheet, find the number of the question and fill in the space that corresponds to the letter of the answer you have chosen.

Here is an example.

On the recording, you will hear:

(narrator) *Listen to an instructor talk to his class about painting.*

(man) *Artist Grant Wood was a guiding force in the school of painting known as American regionalist, a style reflecting the distinctive characteristics of art from rural areas of the United States. Wood began drawing animals on the family farm at the age of three, and when he was thirty-eight one of his paintings received a remarkable amount of public notice and acclaim. This painting, called "American Gothic," is a starkly simple depiction of a serious couple staring directly out at the viewer.*

Now listen to a sample question.   **Sample Answer**

(narrator) *What style of painting is known as American regionalist?*

In your test book, you will read: (A) Art from America's inner cities.
                                        (B) Art from the central region of the U.S.
                                        (C) Art from various urban areas in the U.S.
                                        (D) Art from rural sections of America.

The best answer to the question, "What style of painting is known as American regionalist?" is (D), "Art from rural sections of America." Therefore, the correct choice is (D).

Now listen to another sample question.   **Sample Answer**

(narrator) *What is the name of Wood's most successful painting?*

In your test book, you will read: (A) "American Regionalist."
                                        (B) "The Family Farm in Iowa."
                                        (C) "American Gothic."
                                        (D) "A Serious Couple."

The best answer to the question, "What is the name of Wood's most successful painting?" is (C), "American Gothic." Therefore, the correct choice is (C).

Remember, you are **not** allowed to take notes or write in your test book.

39. (A) On the first day of class.
    (B) In the middle of the semester.
    (C) At the end of
    (D) In the final of the semester.

40. (A) Later
    (B) By F this week.
    (C) In eks.
    (D) I weeks.

41. (A) nal and magazine articles.
    (B) oks from outside the library.
    (C) ooks listed in student journals.
    (Both books and journals.

42. Two.
) Three.
    C) Five.
    (D) Seven.

    (A) In winter.
    (B) In spring.
    (C) In summer.
    (D) In fall.

44. (A) Seasonable, with warm summers and cold winters.
    (B) Fairly constant and moderate.
    (C) Very humid.
    (D) Extremely hot year-round.

45. (A) They come from the southwest.
    (B) They come most days of the year.
    (C) They are the hardest during the night.
    (D) They increase the humidity.

46. (A) Preparing for a trip.
    (B) Writing a report about the weather.
    (C) Beginning a study of the weather.
    (D) Buying warm clothes for a trip.

47. (A) Modern American Authors.
    (B) United States History.
    (C) American Democracy.
    (D) Nineteenth-Century American Literature.

48. (A) The death of Abraham Lincoln.
    (B) The beauty of American democracy.
    (C) The raising of plants.
    (D) The maturity of poetry.

49. (A) It's a poem about the author.
    (B) It's a poem about Abraham Lincoln.
    (C) It's a collection of twelve poems that remained unchanged.
    (D) It's a volume of poetry that grew with its author.

50. (A) "Leaves of Grass."
    (B) "Song of Myself."
    (C) "When Lilacs Last in the Dooryard Bloomed."
    (D) "American Democracy."

This is the end of Section 1. Stop work on Section 1.

Turn off the recording.

When you finish the test, you may do the following:

• Turn to the **Diagnostic Chart** on pages 551–552, and circle the numbers of the questions that you missed.

• Turn to **Scoring Information** on pages 549–550, and determine your TOEFL score.

• Turn to the **Progress Chart** on page 559, and add your score to the chart.

SECTION TWO

STRUCTURE AND WRITTEN EXPRESSION

DIAGNOSTIC PRE-TEST

SECTION 2
STRUCTURE AND WRITTEN EXPRESSION
Time—25 minutes
(including the reading of the directions)
Now set your clock for 25 minutes.

This section is designed to measure your ability to recognize language that is appropriate for standard written English. There are two types of questions in this section, with special directions for each type.

Structure

Directions: These questions are incomplete sentences. Beneath each sentence you will see four words or phrases, marked (A), (B), (C), and (D). Choose the **one** word or phrase that best completes the sentence. Then, on your answer sheet, find the number of the question and fill in the space that corresponds to the letter of the answer you have chosen.

Look at the following examples.

Example I

The president _____ the election by a landslide.

Sample Answer

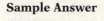

(A) won
(B) he won
(C) yesterday
(D) fortunately

The sentence should read, "The president won the election by a landslide." Therefore, you should choose answer (A).

Example II

When _____ the conference?

Sample Answer

(A) the doctor attended
(B) did the doctor attend
(C) the doctor will attend
(D) the doctor's attendance

The sentence should read, "When did the doctor attend the conference?" Therefore, you should choose answer (B).

1. The North Pole _____ a latitude of 90 degrees north.

    (A) has
    (B) is having
    (C) which is having
    (D) it has

2. _____ greyhound, can achieve speeds up to thirty-six miles per hour.

    (A) The
    (B) The fastest
    (C) The fastest dog
    (D) The fastest dog, the

3. The *Mayflower* was bo___ d for Virginia, but a hurricane _____ off ___ urse.

    (A) blew it
    (B) to blow it
    (C) it blew
    (D) blowin___

4. The gr___ use effect occurs _____ heat radia___ rom the Sun.

    (A) ___ hen does the Earth's atmosphere trap
    ___ does the Earth's atmosphere trap
    ___) when the Earth's atmosphere traps
    (D) the Earth's atmosphere traps

___. The Rose Bowl, _____ place on New Year's Day, is the oldest postseason collegiate football game in the United States.

    (A) takes
    (B) which takes
    (C) it takes
    (D) took

6. Experiments _____ represent a giant step into the medicine of the future.

    (A) using gene therapy
    (B) use gene therapy
    (C) they use
    (D) gene therapy uses

7. _____ off the Hawaiian coastline are living, others are dead.

    (A) Coral reefs
    (B) Some types of coral reefs
    (C) There are many types of coral reefs
    (D) While some types of coral reefs

8. People who reverse the letters of words _____ to read suffer from dyslexia.

    (A) if they tried
    (B) when trying
    (C) when tried
    (D) if he tries

9. Featured at the Henry Ford Museum _____ of antique cars dating from 1865.

    (A) an exhibit is
    (B) an exhibit
    (C) is an exhibit
    (D) which is an exhibit

10. Rubber _____ from vulcanized silicones with a high molecular weight is difficult to distinguish from natural rubber.

    (A) is produced
    (B) producing
    (C) that produces
    (D) produced

11. _____ in scope, romanticism was a reaction against neoclassical principles.

    (A) Mainly literary
    (B) It was mainly literary
    (C) The main literature was
    (D) The literature was mainly

12. The Central Intelligence Agency (CIA) _____ came about as a result of the National Security Act of 1947.

    (A) what
    (B) it was
    (C) was what
    (D) it was what

GO ON TO THE NEXT PAGE

13. Oil shale is a soft, fine-grained sedimentary rock _____ oil and natural gas are obtained.

   (A) from
   (B) is from
   (C) is which
   (D) from which

14. _____ appears considerably larger at the horizon than it does overhead is merely an optical illusion.

   (A) The Moon
   (B) That the Moon
   (C) When the Moon
   (D) The Moon which

15. According to the World Health Organization, _____ there to be an outbreak of any of the six most dangerous diseases, this could be cause for quarantine.

   (A) were
   (B) they were
   (C) there were
   (D) were they

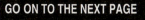

GO ON TO THE NEXT PAGE

Written Expression

Directions: In these questions, each sentence has four underlined words or phrases. The four underlined parts of the sentence are marked (A), (B), (C), and (D). Identify the **one** underlined word or phrase that must be changed in order for the sentence to be correct. Then, on your answer sheet, find the number of the question and fill in the space that corresponds to the letter of the answer you have chosen.

Look at the following examples.

Example I   **Sample Answer**

The four string on a violin are tuned
 A   B   C   D
in fifths.

The sentence should read, "The four strings on a violin are tuned in fifths." Therefore, you should choose answer (B).

Example II   **Sample Answer**

The research for the book *Roots* taking   Ⓐ Ⓑ ● Ⓓ
    A   B   C
Alex Haley twelve years.
          D

The sentence should read, "The research for the book *Roots* took Alex Haley twelve years." Therefore, you should choose answer (C).

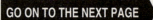
GO ON TO THE NEXT PAGE

16. Segregation in public schools was declare unconstitutional by the Supreme Court in
             A   B   C   D

    1954.

17. Sirius, the Dog Star, is the most brightest star in the sky with an absolute magnitude
                            A   B

    about twenty-three times that of the Sun.
                      C   D

18. Killer whales tend to wander in family clusters that hunt, play, and resting together.
                A   B   C   D

19. Some of the most useful resistor material are carbon, metals, and metallic alloys.
                 A   B   C   D

20. The community of Bethesda, Maryland, was previous known as Darcy's Store.
         A   B   C D

21. J. H. Pratt used group therapy early in the past century when he brought
                    A   B   C

    tuberculosis patients together to discuss its disease.
                                       D

22. Alloys of gold and copper have been widely using in various types of coins.
                             A   B   C   D

23. The United States has import all carpet wools in recent years because domestic
                   A   B   C

    wools are too fine and soft for carpets.
              D

24. Banks are rushing to merge because consolidations enable them to slash theirs costs
                                          A   B   C

    and expand.
       D

25. That water has a very high specific heat means that, without a large temperature
      A   B

    change, water can add or lose a large number of heat.
                    C   D

26. Benny Goodman was equally talented as both a jazz performer as well as a classical
                  A   B   C

    musician.
     D

GO ON TO THE NEXT PAGE →

27. No longer satisfied with the emphasis of the Denishawn School, Martha Graham
        A   B   C

    is moving to the staff of the Eastman School in 1925.
        D

28. Irving Berlin wrote "Oh, How I Hate to Get Up in the Morning" while serving in a
              A   B   C

    U.S. Army during World War I.
             D

29. Shortly before the Allied invasion of Normandy, Ernest Hemingway has gone to
      A   B   C

    London as a war correspondent for *Collier's*.
              D

30. During the 1960s, the Berkeley campus of the University of California came to
                                                  A

    national attention as a result its radical political activity.
               B   C   D

31. Because of the flourish with which John Hancock signed the Declaration of
                      A

    Independence, his name become synonymous with *signature*.
               B   C   D

32. On the floor of the Pacific Ocean is hundreds of flat-topped mountains more than a
          A   B   C   D

    mile beneath sea level.

33. William Hart was an act best known for his roles as western heros in silent films.
                A   B   C   D

34. Prior to an extermination program early in the last century, alive wolves roamed
      A   B   C

    across nearly all of North America.
           D

35. The state seal still used in Massachusetts designed by Paul Revere, who also
                 A   B   C

    designed the first Continental currency.
                        D

36. Artist Gutzon Borglum designed the Mount Rushmore Memorial and worked on
                 A

    project from 1925 until his death in 1941.
      B   C D

GO ON TO THE NEXT PAGE →

37. It is proving less <u>costly</u> and more <u>profitably</u> for drugmakers to <u>market</u> <u>directly to</u>
       A   B   C   D

 patients.

38. Sapphires <u>weighing</u> as much as <u>two pounds</u> have on occasion <u>mined</u>.
      A   B   C   D

39. <u>Like</u> snakes, lizards can be <u>found</u> on all <u>others</u> continents <u>except</u> Antarctica.
  A   B   C   D

40. Banks, savings and loans, and finance companies <u>have recently</u> been <u>doing h</u> e
                    A   B

 equity loans with <u>greater frequency</u> than <u>ever before</u>.
         C   D

This is the end of the Structure and Written Expression Pre-T   **.**

When you finish the test, you may do the followir

- Turn to the **Diagnostic Chart** on pages 553–55   nd circle the numbers of the questions that you m sed.

- Turn to **Scoring Information** on pages 549–5 , and determine your TOEFL score.

- Turn to the **Progress Chart** on page 559, an dd your score to the chart.

STRUCTURE AND WRITTEN EXPRESSION

The second section of the TOEFL test is the Structure and Written Expression section. This section consists of forty questions (some tests may be longer). You have twenty-five minutes to complete the forty questions in this section.

There are two types of questions in the Structure and Written Expression section of the TOEFL test:

1. **Structure** (questions 1–15) consists of fifteen sentences in which part of the sentence has been replaced with a blank. Each sentence is followed by four answer choices. You must choose the answer that completes the sentence in a grammatically correct way.
2. **Written Expression** (questions 16–40) consists of twenty-five sentences in which four words or groups of words have been underlined. You must choose the underlined word or group of words that is *not* correct.

GENERAL STRATEGIES

1. **Be familiar with the directions.** The directions on every TOEFL test are the same, so it is not necessary to spend time reading the directions carefully when you take the test. You should be completely familiar with the directions before the day of the test.

2. **Begin with questions 1 through 15.** Anticipate that questions 1 through 5 will be the easiest. Anticipate that questions 11 through 15 will be the most difficult. Do not spend too much time on questions 11 through 15. There will be easier questions that come later.

3. **Continue with questions 16 through 40.** Anticipate that questions 16 through 20 will be the easiest. Anticipate that questions 36 through 40 will be the most difficult. Do not spend too much time on questions 36 through 40.

4. **If you have time, return to questions 11 through 15.** You should spend extra time on questions 11 through 15 only after you spend all the time that you want on the easier questions.

5. **Never leave any answers blank on your answer sheet.** Even if you are not sure of the correct response, you should answer each question. There is no penalty for guessing.

THE STRUCTURE QUESTIONS

In the TOEFL test, questions 1 through 15 of the Structure and Written Expression section test your knowledge of the correct structure of English sentences. The questions in this section are multiple-choice questions in which you must choose the letter of the answer that best completes the sentence.

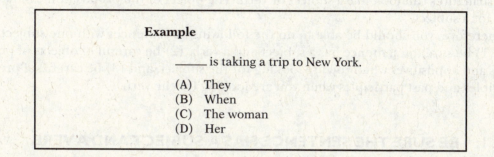

Example

_____ is taking a trip to New York.

(A) They
(B) When
(C) The woman
(D) Her

In this example, you should notice immediately that the sentence has a verb (*is taking*), and that the verb needs a subject. Answers (B) and (D) are incorrect because *when* and *her* are not subjects. In answer (A), *they* is a subject, but *they* is plural and the verb *is taking* is singular. The correct answer is answer (C); *the woman* is a singular subject. You should therefore choose answer (C).

STRATEGIES FOR THE STRUCTURE QUESTIONS

1. **First study the sentence.** Your purpose is to determine what is needed to complete the sentence correctly.

2. **Then study each answer based on how well it completes the sentence.** Eliminate answers that do not complete the sentence correctly.

3. **Do not try to eliminate incorrect answers by looking only at the answers.** The incorrect answers are generally correct by themselves. The incorrect answers are generally incorrect only when used to complete the sentence.

4. **Never leave any answers blank.** Be sure to answer each question even if you are unsure of the correct response.

5. **Do not spend too much time on the Structure questions.** Be sure to leave adequate time for the Written Expression questions.

The following skills will help you to implement these strategies in the Structure section of the TOEFL test.

SENTENCES WITH ONE CLAUSE

Some sentences in English have just one subject and verb, and it is very important for you to find the subject and verb in these sentences. In some sentences it is easy to find the subject and verb. However, certain structures, such as objects of prepositions, appositives, and participles, can cause confusion in locating the subject and verb because each of these structures can look like a subject or verb. The object of the preposition can be mistaken for a subject.

Therefore, you should be able to do the following in sentences with one subject and verb: (1) be sure the sentence has a subject and a verb, (2) be careful of objects of prepositions and appositives when you are looking for the subject, and (3) be careful of present participles and past participles when you are looking for the verb.

SKILL 1: BE SURE THE SENTENCE HAS A SUBJECT AND A VERB

You know that a sentence in English should have a subject and a verb. The most common types of problems that you will encounter in the Structure section of the TOEFL test have to do with subjects and verbs: perhaps the sentence is missing either the subject or the verb or both, or perhaps the sentence has an extra subject or verb.

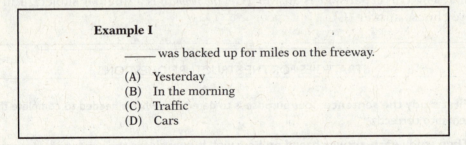

Example I

_____ was backed up for miles on the freeway.

(A) Yesterday
(B) In the morning
(C) Traffic
(D) Cars

In this example you should notice immediately that there is a verb (*was*), but there is no subject. Answer (C) is the best answer because it is a singular subject that agrees with the singular verb *was*. Answer (A), *yesterday,* and answer (B), *in the morning,* are not subjects, so they are not correct. Although answer (D), *cars,* could be a subject, it is not correct because *cars* is plural and it does not agree with the singular verb *was.*

Example II

Engineers _____ for work on the new space program.

(A) necessary
(B) are needed
(C) hopefully
(D) next month

In this example you should notice immediately that the sentence has a subject (*engineers*), and that there is no verb. Because answer (B), *are needed,* is a verb, it is the best answer. Answers (A), (C), and (D) are not verbs, so they are not correct.

_____ 9.   For the fever and headache took two aspirin tablets.

_____10.   The report with complete documentation was delivered at the conference.

SKILL 3:   BE CAREFUL OF APPOSITIVES

Appositives can cause confusion in the Structure section of the TOEFL test because an appositive can be mistaken for the subject of a sentence. An appositive is a noun that comes before or after another noun and has the same meaning.

Sally, the best *student* in the class, got an A on the exam.

In this example *Sally* is the subject of the sentence and *the best student in the class* can easily be recognized as an appositive phrase because of the noun *student* and because of the commas. The sentence says that *Sally* and *the best student in the class* are the same person. Note that if you leave out the appositive phrase, the sentence still makes sense (*Sally got an A on the exam*).

The following example shows how an appositive can be confused with the subject of a sentence in the Structure section of the TOEFL test.

Example I

_____, George, is attending the lecture.

(A)   Right now
(B)   Happily
(C)   Because of the time
(D)   My friend

In this example you should recognize from the commas that *George* is not the subject of the sentence. *George* is an appositive. Because this sentence still needs a subject, the best answer is (D), *my friend*. Answers (A), (B), and (C) are incorrect because they are not subjects.

The next example shows that an appositive does not always come after the subject; an appositive can also come at the beginning of the sentence.

Example II

_____, Sarah rarely misses her basketball shots.

(A)   An excellent basketball player
(B)   An excellent basketball player is
(C)   Sarah is an excellent basketball player
(D)   Her excellent basketball play

In this example you can tell that *Sarah* is the subject and *misses* is the verb because there is no comma separating them. In the space you should put an appositive for Sarah, and Sarah is *an excellent basketball player,* so answer (A) is the best answer. Answers (B) and (C) are not correct because they each contain the verb *is*, and an appositive does not need a verb. Answer (D) contains a noun, *play,* that could possibly be an appositive, but *play* is not the same as *Sarah,* so this answer is not correct.

The following chart outlines the key information that you should remember about appositives:

APPOSITIVES
An *appositive* is a noun that comes before or after another noun and is generally set off from the noun with commas. **If a word is an *appositive*, it is not the *subject*.** The following appositive structures are both possible in English:
S,   APP,   V **Tom, a really good mechanic, is fixing the car.**
APP,   S   V **A really good mechanic, Tom is fixing the car.**

EXERCISE 3: Each of the following sentences contains an appositive. Underline the subjects once and the verbs twice. Circle the appositive phrases. Then, indicate if the sentences are correct (C) or incorrect (I).

___C___ 1. (The son of the previous owner,) the new owner is undertaking some fairly broad changes in management policy.

___I___ 2. Last semester, (a friend,) graduated *cum laude* from the university.

_____ 3. Valentine's Day, February 14, is a special holiday for sweethearts.

_____ 4. At long last, the chief executive officer, has decided to step down.

_____ 5. Tonight's supper, leftovers from last night, did not taste any better tonight than last night.

_____ 6. The only entrance to the closet, the door was kept locked at all times.

_____ 7. In the cold of winter, a wall heating unit, would not turn on.

_____ 8. The new tile pattern, yellow flowers on a white background, really brightens up the room.

_____ 9. The high-powered computer the most powerful machine of its type, was finally readied for use.

_____10. A longtime friend and confident, the psychologist was often invited over for Sunday dinner.

SKILL 4: BE CAREFUL OF PRESENT PARTICIPLES

A present participle is the *-ing* form of the verb (*talking, playing*). In the Structure section of the TOEFL test a present participle can cause confusion because it can be either a part of the verb or an adjective. It is part of the verb when it is preceded by some form of the verb *be*.

The man *is talking* to his friend.
VERB

In this sentence *talking* is part of the verb because it is accompanied by *is*.

A present participle is an adjective when it is not accompanied by some form of the verb *be*.

The man *talking* to his friend has a beard.
                    ADJECTIVE

In this sentence *talking* is an adjective and not part of the verb because it is not accompanied by some form of *be*. The verb in this sentence is *has*.

The following example shows how a present participle can be confused with the verb in the Structure section of the TOEFL test.

Example

The child _____ playing in the yard is my son.

(A) now
(B) is
(C) he
(D) was

In this example, if you look at only the first words of the sentence, it appears that *child* is the subject and *playing* is part of the verb. If you think that *playing* is part of the verb, you might choose answer (B), *is*, or answer (D), *was*, to complete the verb. However, these two answers are incorrect because *playing* is not part of the verb. You should recognize that *playing* is a participial adjective rather than a verb because there is another verb in the sentence (*is*). In this sentence there is a complete subject (*child*) and a complete verb (*is*), so this sentence does not need another subject or verb. The best answer here is (A).

The following chart outlines what you should remember about present participles:

PRESENT PARTICIPLES

A *present participle* is the *-ing* form of the verb. **The *present participle* can be (1) part of the verb or (2) an *adjective*.** It is part of the *verb* when it is accompanied by some form of the verb *be*. It is an *adjective* when it is not accompanied by some form of the verb *be*.

1. *The boy is* **standing** *in the corner.*
2. *The boy* **standing** *in the corner was naughty.*

EXERCISE 4: Each of the following sentences contains one or more present participles. Underline the subjects once and the verbs twice. Circle the present participles and label them as adjectives or verbs. Then indicate if the sentences are correct (C) or incorrect (I).

__C__   1. The companies (offering) the lowest prices will have the most customers.
                                    ADJ.

__I__   2. Those travelers are (completing) their trip on Delta should report to Gate Three.
                                   VERB

_____   3. The artisans were demonstrating various handicrafts at booths throughout the fair.

_____   4. The fraternities are giving the wildest parties attract the most new pledges.

_____   5. The first team winning four games is awarded the championship.

_____ 6.   The speaker was trying to make his point was often interrupted vociferously.

_____ 7.   The fruits were rotting because of the moisture in the crates carrying them to market.

_____ 8.   Any students desiring official transcripts should complete the appropriate form.

_____ 9.   The advertisements were announcing the half-day sale received a lot of attention.

_____ 10. The spices flavoring the meal were quite distinctive.

Skill 5:   BE CAREFUL OF PAST PARTICIPLES

Past participles can cause confusion in the Structure section of the TOEFL test because a past participle can be either an adjective or a part of a verb. The past participle is the form of the verb that appears with *have* or *be*. It often ends in *-ed*, but there are also many irregular past participles in English. (See Appendix F for a list of irregular past participles.)

The family *has purchased* a television.
VERB

The poem *was written* by Paul.
VERB

In the first sentence the past participle *purchased* is part of the verb because it is accompanied by *has*. In the second sentence the past participle *written* is part of the verb because it is accompanied by *was*.

A past participle is an adjective when it is not accompanied by some form of *be* or *have*.

The television *purchased* yesterday was expensive.
ADJECTIVE

The poem *written* by Paul appeared in the magazine.
ADJECTIVE

In the first sentence *purchased* is an adjective rather than a verb because it is not accompanied by a form of *be* or *have* (and there is a verb, *was*, later in the sentence). In the second sentence *written* is an adjective rather than a verb because it is not accompanied by a form of *be* or *have* (and there is a verb, *appeared*, later in the sentence).

The following example shows how a past participle can be confused with the verb in the Structure section of the TOEFL test.

Example

The packages _____ mailed at the post office will arrive Monday.

(A) have
(B) were
(C) them
(D) just

In this example, if you look only at the first few words of the sentence, it appears that *packages* is the subject and *mailed* is either a complete verb or a past participle that needs a helping verb. But if you look further in the sentence, you will see that the verb is *will arrive*. You will then recognize that *mailed* is a participial adjective and is therefore not part of the verb. Answers (A) and (B) are incorrect because *mailed* is an adjective and does not need a helping verb such as *have* or *were*. Answer (C) is incorrect because there is no need for the object *them*. Answer (D) is the best answer to this question.

The following chart outlines what you should remember about past participles:

PAST PARTICIPLES

A *past participle* often ends in *-ed,* but there are also many irregular past participles. For many verbs, including *-ed* verbs, the *simple past* and the *past participle* are the same and can be easily confused. **The *-ed* form of the verb can be (1) the *simple past,* (2) the *past participle* of a verb, or (3) an *adjective.***

1. She **painted** this picture.
2. She has **painted** this picture.
3. The picture **painted** by Karen is now in a museum.

EXERCISE 5: Each of the following sentences contains one or more past participles. Underline the subjects once and the verbs twice. Circle the past participles and label them as adjectives or verbs. Then indicate if the sentences are correct (C) or incorrect (I).

__I__   1.   The money was (offered) by the client was not (accepted.)
                         VERB   VERB

__C__   2.   The car (listed) in the advertisement had already (stalled.)
                         ADJ.   VERB

_____   3.   The chapters were taught by the professor this morning will be on next week's exam.

_____   4.   The loaves of bread were baked in a brick oven at a low temperature for many hours.

_____   5.   The ports were reached by the sailors were under the control of a foreign nation.

_____   6.   Those suspected in the string of robberies were arrested by the police.

_____   7.   The pizza is served in this restaurant is the tastiest in the county.

_____   8.   The courses are listed on the second page of the brochure have several prerequisites.

_____   9.   All the tenants were invited to the Independence Day barbecue at the apartment complex.

_____   10. Any bills paid by the first of the month will be credited to your account by the next day.

EXERCISE (Skills 1–5): Underline the subjects once and the verbs twice in each of the following sentences. Then indicate if the sentences are correct (C) or incorrect (I).

_____   1. For three weeks at the beginning of the semester students with fewer than the maximum number of units can add additional courses.

_____   2. On her lunch hour went to a nearby department store to purchase a wedding gift.

_____   3. The fir trees were grown for the holiday season were harvested in November.

_____   4. In the grove the overripe oranges were falling on the ground.

_____   5. The papers being delivered at 4:00 will contain the announcement of the president's resignation.

_____   6. A specialty shop with various blends from around the world in the shopping mall.

_____   7. The portraits exhibited in the Houston Museum last month are now on display in Dallas.

_____   8. With a sudden jerk of his hand threw the ball across the field to one of the other players.

_____   9. Construction of the housing development it will be underway by the first of the month.

_____   10. Those applicants returning their completed forms at the earliest date have the highest priority.

TOEFL EXERCISE (Skills 1–5): Choose the letter of the word or group of words that best completes the sentence.

1. The North Platte River _____ from Wyoming into Nebraska.

    (A) it flowed
    (B) flows
    (C) flowing
    (D) with flowing water

2. _____ Biloxi received its name from a Sioux word meaning "first people."

    (A) The city of
    (B) Located in
    (C) It is in
    (D) The tour included

3. A pride of lions _____ up to forty lions, including one to three males, several females, and cubs.

    (A) can contain
    (B) it contains
    (C) contain
    (D) containing

4. _____ tea plant are small and white.

    (A) The
    (B) On the
    (C) Having flowers the
    (D) The flowers of the

5. The tetracyclines, _____ antibiotics, are used to treat infections.

    (A) are a family of
    (B) being a family
    (C) a family of
    (D) their family is

6. Any possible academic assistance from taking stimulants _____ marginal at best.

    (A) it is
    (B) there is
    (C) is
    (D) as

7. Henry Adams, born in Boston, _____ famous as a historian and novelist.

   (A) became
   (B) and became
   (C) he was
   (D) and he became

8. The major cause _____ the pull of the Moon on the Earth.

   (A) the ocean tides are
   (B) of ocean tides is
   (C) of the tides in the ocean
   (D) the oceans' tides

9. Still a novelty in the late nineteenth century, _____ limited to the rich.

   (A) was
   (B) was photography
   (C) it was photography
   (D) photography was

10. A computerized map of the freeways using information gathered by sensors embedded in the pavement _____ on a local cable channel during rush hours.

   (A) airs
   (B) airing
   (C) air
   (D) to air

SENTENCES WITH MULTIPLE CLAUSES

Many sentences in English have more than one clause. (A clause is a group of words containing a subject and a verb.) Whenever you find a sentence on the TOEFL test with more than one clause, you need to make sure that every subject has a verb and every verb has a subject. Next you need to check that the various clauses in the sentence are correctly joined. There are various ways to join clauses in English. Certain patterns appear frequently in English and on the TOEFL test. You should be very familiar with these patterns.

SKILL 6:   USE COORDINATE CONNECTORS CORRECTLY

When you have two clauses in an English sentence, you must connect the two clauses correctly. One way to connect two clauses is to use *and, but, or, so,* or *yet* between the clauses.

> Tom is singing, *and* Paul is dancing.
>
> Tom is tall, *but* Paul is short.
>
> Tom must write the letter, *or* Paul will do it.
>
> Tom told a joke, *so* Paul laughed.
>
> Tom is tired, *yet* he is not going to sleep.

In each of these examples, there are two clauses that are correctly joined with a coordinate conjunction *and, but, or, so,* or *yet,* and a comma (,).

The following example shows how this sentence pattern could be tested in the Structure section of the TOEFL test.

Example

A power failure occurred, _____ the lamps went out.

(A) then
(B) so
(C) later
(D) next

In this example you should notice quickly that there are two clauses, *a power failure occurred* and *the lamps went out*. This sentence needs a connector to join the two clauses. *Then, later,* and *next* are not connectors, so answers (A), (C), and (D) are not correct. The best answer is answer (B) because *so* can connect two clauses.

The following chart lists the coordinate connectors and the sentence pattern used with them:

COORDINATE CONNECTORS				
and	*but*	*or*	*so*	*yet*
S V,		(coordinate connector)	S V	
She laughed,		**but**	**she wanted to cry.**	

EXERCISE 6: Each of the following sentences contains more than one clause. Underline the subjects once and the verbs twice. Circle the connectors. Then indicate if the sentences are correct (C) or incorrect (I).

__C__ 1. The software should be used on an IBM computer, (and) this computer is an IBM.

__I__   2. The rain clouds can be seen in the distance, (but) no has fallen.

_____ 3. They are trying to sell their house, it has been on the market for two months.

_____ 4. So the quality of the print was not good, I changed the toner cartridge.

_____ 5. The lifeguard will warn you about the riptides, or she may require you to get out of the water.

_____ 6. You should have finished the work yesterday, yet is not close to being finished today.

_____ 7. The phone rang again and again, so the receptionist was not able to get much work done.

_____ 8. The missing wallet was found, but the cash and credit cards had been removed.

_____ 9. Or you can drive your car for another 2,000 miles, you can get it fixed.

_____ 10. The chemist was awarded the Nobel Prize, he flew to Europe to accept it.

SKILL 7:   USE ADVERB *TIME* AND *CAUSE* CONNECTORS CORRECTLY

Sentences with adverb clauses have two basic patterns in English. Study the clauses and connectors in the following sentences:

<u>I</u> will <u>sign</u> the check *before* <u>you</u> <u>leave</u>.

Before <u>you</u> <u>leave</u>, <u>I</u> will <u>sign</u> the check.

In each of these examples, there are two clauses: *you leave* and *I will sign the check,* and the clause *you leave* is an adverb time clause because it is introduced with the connector *before.* In the first example the connector *before* comes in the middle of the sentence, and no comma (,) is used. In the second example the connector *before* comes at the beginning of the sentence. In this pattern, when the connector comes at the beginning of the sentence, a comma (,) is required in the middle of the sentence.

The following example shows how this sentence pattern could be tested in the Structure section of the TOEFL test.

Example

_____ was late, I missed the appointment.

(A) I
(B) Because
(C) The train
(D) Since he

In this example you should recognize easily that there is a verb, *was,* that needs a subject. There is also another clause, *I missed the appointment.* If you choose answer (A) or answer (C), you will have a subject for the verb *was,* but you will not have a connector to join the two clauses. Because you need a connector to join two clauses, answers (A) and (C) are incorrect. Answer (B) is incorrect because there is no subject for the verb *was.* Answer (D) is the best answer because there is a subject, *he,* for the verb *was,* and there is a connector, *since,* to join the two clauses.

The following chart lists adverb *time* and *cause* connectors and the sentence patterns used with them:

ADVERB *TIME* AND *CAUSE* CONNECTORS						
TIME				CAUSE		
after	*as soon as*	*once*	*when*	*as*		*now that*
as	*before*	*since*	*whenever*	*because*		*since*
as long as	*by the time*	*until*	*while*	*inasmuch as*		
S V			(adverb connector)	S V		
Teresa went inside			***because***	***it was raining.***		
(adverb connector)	S V,		S V			
Because	***it was raining,***		***Teresa went inside.***			

EXERCISE 7: Each of the following sentences contains more than one clause. Underline the subjects once and the verbs twice. Circle the connectors. Then indicate if the sentences are correct (C) or incorrect (I).

__C__ 1. (Since) the bank closes in less than an hour, the deposits need to be tallied immediately.

__I__ 2. Their backgrounds are thoroughly investigated (before) are admitted to the organization.

_____ 3. The citizens are becoming more and more incensed about traffic accidents whenever the accidents occur at that intersection.

_____ 4. The ground had been prepared, the seedlings were carefully planted.

_____ 5. We can start the conference now that all the participants have arrived.

_____ 6. The building quite vulnerable to damage until the storm windows are installed.

_____ 7. Once the address label for the package is typed, can be sent to the mail room.

_____ 8. Because the recent change in work shifts was not posted, several workers missed their shifts.

_____ 9. The mother is going to be quite upset with her son as long he misbehaves so much.

_____ 10. Inasmuch as all the votes have not yet been counted the outcome of the election cannot be announced.

SKILL 8:   USE OTHER ADVERB CONNECTORS CORRECTLY

Adverb clauses can express the ideas of time and cause, as you saw in Skill 7; adverb clauses can also express a number of other ideas, such as contrast, condition, manner, and place. Because these clauses are adverb clauses, they have the same structure as the time and cause clauses in Skill 7. Study the following examples:

> I will leave at 7:00 *if* I am ready.
>
> *Although* I was late, I managed to catch the train.

In each of these examples, there are two clauses that are correctly joined with adverb connectors. In the first sentence the adverb condition connector *if* comes in the middle of the sentence. In the second sentence the adverb contrast connector *although* comes at the beginning of the sentence, and a comma (,) is used in the middle of the sentence.

The following example shows a way that this sentence pattern can be tested in the Structure section of the TOEFL test.

Example

You will get a good grade on the exam provided _____.

(A) studying
(B) study
(C) to study
(D) you study

In this example you should quickly notice the adverb condition connector *provided*. This connector comes in the middle of the sentence; because it is a connector, it must be followed by a subject and a verb. The best answer to this question is answer (D), which contains the subject and verb *you study*.

The following chart lists the adverb contrast, condition, manner, and place connectors and the sentence patterns used with them:

OTHER ADVERB CONNECTORS			
CONDITION	CONTRAST	MANNER	PLACE
if in case provided providing unless whether	although even though though while whereas	as in that	where wherever

S   V   (adverb connector)   S   V

Bob went to school   even though   he felt sick.

(adverb connector)   S   V,   S   V

Even though   Bob felt sick,   he went to school.

NOTE: A comma is often used in the middle of the sentence with a contrast connector.

The Smith family arrived at 2:00, **while** the Jones family arrived an hour later.

EXERCISE 8: Each of the following sentences contains more than one clause. Underline the subjects once and the verbs twice. Circle the connectors. Then indicate if the sentences are correct (C) or incorrect (I).

___C___ 1. It is impossible to enter that program (if) you lack experience as a teacher.

___I___ 2. The commandant left strict orders about the passes, several soldiers left the post anyway.

_____ 3. No one is admitted to the academy unless he or she the education requirements.

_____ 4. While most students turned the assignment in on time, a few asked for an extension.

_____ 5. I will take you wherever need to go to complete the registration procedures.

_____ 6. I will wait here in the airport with you whether the plane leaves on time or not.

_____ 7. Providing the envelope is postmarked by this Friday, your application still acceptable.

_____ 8. As the nurse already explained all visitors must leave the hospital room now.

_____ 9. This exam will be more difficult than usual in that it covers two chapters instead of one.

_____ 10. Though snow had been falling all day long, everyone got to the church on time for the wedding.

EXERCISE (Skills 6–8): Underline the subjects once and the verbs twice in each of the following sentences. Circle the connectors. Then indicate if the sentences are correct (C) or incorrect (I).

_____ 1. Until the registrar makes a decision about your status, you must stay in an unclassified category.

_____ 2. Or the bills can be paid by mail by the first of the month.

_____ 3. The parents left a phone number with the baby-sitter in case a problem with the children.

_____ 4. The furniture will be delivered as soon it is paid for.

_____ 5. Whenever you want to hold the meeting, we will schedule it.

_____ 6. The government was overthrown in a revolution, the king has not returned to his homeland.

_____ 7. Whereas most of the documents are complete, this form still needs to be notarized.

_____ 8. Trash will be collected in the morning, so you should put the trash cans out tonight.

_____ 9. It is impossible for the airplane to take off while is snowing so hard.

_____ 10. We did not go out to dinner tonight eventhough I would have preferred not to cook.

TOEFL EXERCISE (Skills 6–8): Choose the letter of the word or group of words that best completes the sentence.

1. The president of the U. S. appoints the cabinet members, _____ appointments are subject to Senate approval.

   (A) their
   (B) with their
   (C) because their
   (D) but their

2. The prisoners were prevented from speaking to reporters because _____

   (A) not wanting the story in the papers.
   (B) the story in the papers the superintendent did not want
   (C) the public to hear the story
   (D) the superintendent did not want the story in the papers

3. Like Thomas Berger's fictional character _Little Big Man,_ Lauderdale managed to find himself where _____ of important events took place.

   (A) it was an extraordinary number
   (B) there was an extraordinary number
   (C) an extraordinary number
   (D) an extraordinary number existed

4. _____ sucked groundwater from below, some parts of the city have begun to sink as much as ten inches annually.

   (A) Pumps have
   (B) As pumps have
   (C) So pumps have
   (D) With pumps

5. Case studies are the target of much skepticism in the scientific community, _____ used extensively by numerous researchers.

   (A) they are
   (B) are
   (C) yet they
   (D) yet they are

6. According to the hypothesis in the study, the monarchs pick up the magnetic field of the _____ migrate by following magnetic fields.

   (A) target monarchs
   (B) target since monarchs
   (C) target since monarchs are
   (D) target

7. _____ show the relations among neurons, they do not preclude the possibility that other aspects are important.

(A) Neural theories
(B) A neural theory
(C) Although neural theories
(D) However neural theories

8. _____ or refinanced, the lender will generally require setting up an escrow account to ensure the payment of property taxes and homeowner's insurance.

(A) A home is
(B) A home is bought
(C) When a home
(D) When a home is bought

9. If ultraviolet radiation enters the Earth's atmosphere, _____ generally blocked by the ozone concentrated in the atmosphere.

(A) it
(B) it is
(C) so it is
(D) then it

10. Among human chromosomes, the Y chromosome is unusual _____ most of the chromosome does not participate in meiotic recombination.

(A) in
(B) so
(C) and
(D) in that

TOEFL REVIEW EXERCISE (Skills 1–8): Choose the letter of the word or group of words that best completes the sentence.

1. The three basic chords in _____ the tonic, the dominant, and the subdominant.

(A) functional harmony
(B) functional harmony is
(C) functional harmony are
(D) functional harmony they are

2. _____ Hale Telescope, at the Palomar Observatory in southern California, scientists can photograph objects several billion light years away.

(A) The
(B) With the
(C) They use the
(D) It is the

3. Without the proper card installed inside the computer, _____ impossible to run a graphical program.

(A) is definitely
(B) because of
(C) it is
(D) is

4. The charter for the Louisiana lottery was coming up for renewal, _____ spared no expense in the fight to win renewal.

(A) the lottery committee
(B) so the lottery committee and
(C) so the lottery committee
(D) the lottery committee made

5. While in reality Alpha Centauri is a triple star, _____ to the naked eye to be a single star.

(A) it appears
(B) but it appears
(C) appears
(D) despite it

6. The Sun's gravity severely distorted the path of the comet _____ entered its wildly erratic orbit around Jupiter.

(A) it
(B) when
(C) after the comet came into it
(D) once the comet

7. Each object _____ Jupiter's magnetic field is deluged with electrical charges.

(A) enters
(B) it enters
(C) entering
(D) enter

8. As its name suggests, the Prairie Wetlands Resource Center _____ the protection of wetlands on the prairies of the Dakotas, Montana, Minnesota, and Nebraska.

(A) it focuses
(B) focuses on
(C) focusing
(D) to focus on

9. One of the largest and most powerful birds of prey in the world, _____ a six-foot wingspan and legs and talons roughly the size of a man's arms and legs.

(A) so the harpy has
(B) the harpy having
(C) with the harpy having
(D) the harpy has

10. _____ creation of such a community was a desirable step, the requisite political upheaval had to be accepted.

(A) Since the
(B) The
(C) Later, the
(D) It was the

MORE SENTENCES WITH MULTIPLE CLAUSES_____

As we saw in Skills 6 through 8, many sentences in English have more than one clause. In Skills 9 through 12, we will see more patterns for connecting the clauses in sentences with multiple clauses. Because these patterns appear frequently in English and on the TOEFL test, you should be very familiar with them.

SKILL 9:   USE NOUN CLAUSE CONNECTORS CORRECTLY

A noun clause is a clause that functions as a noun; because the noun clause is a noun, it is used in a sentence as either an object of a verb, an object of a preposition, or the subject of the sentence.

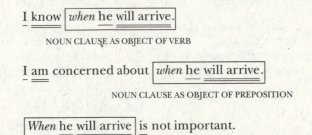

I know | *when* he will arrive. |
NOUN CLAUSE AS OBJECT OF VERB

I am concerned about | *when* he will arrive. |
NOUN CLAUSE AS OBJECT OF PREPOSITION

| *When* he will arrive | is not important.
NOUN CLAUSE AS SUBJECT

In the first example there are two clauses, *I know* and *he will arrive*. These two clauses are joined with the connector *when*. *When* changes the clause *he will arrive* into a noun clause that functions as the object of the verb *know*.

In the second example the two clauses *I am concerned* and *he will arrive* are also joined by the connector *when*. *When* changes the clause *he will arrive* into a noun clause that functions as the object of the preposition *about*.

The third example is more difficult. In this example there are two clauses, but they are a little harder to recognize. *He will arrive* is one of the clauses, and the connector *when* changes it into a noun clause that functions as the subject of the sentence. The other clause has the noun clause *when he will arrive* as its subject and *is* as its verb.

The following example shows how these sentence patterns could be tested in the Structure section of the TOEFL test.

> **Example**
>
> _____ was late caused many problems.
>
> (A) That he
> (B) The driver
> (C) There
> (D) Because

In this example there are two verbs (_was_ and _caused_), and each of these verbs needs a subject. Answer (B) is wrong because _the driver_ is one subject, and two subjects are needed. Answers (C) and (D) are incorrect because _there_ and _because_ are not subjects. The best answer is answer (A). If you choose answer (A), the completed sentence would be: _That he was late caused many problems._ In this sentence _he_ is the subject of the verb _was_, and the noun clause _that he was late_ is the subject of the verb _caused_.

The following chart lists the noun clause connectors and the sentence patterns used with them:

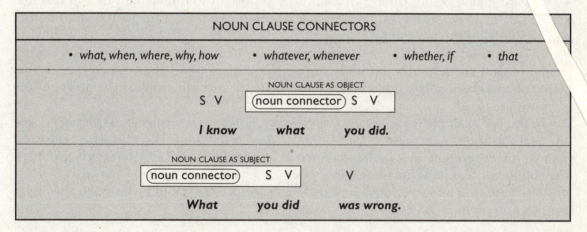

NOUN CLAUSE CONNECTORS
• _what, when, where, why, how_   • _whatever, whenever_   • _whether, if_   • _that_

NOUN CLAUSE AS OBJECT

S V   (noun connector) S V

I know   what   you did.

NOUN CLAUSE AS SUBJECT

(noun connector)   S V   V

What   you did   was wrong.

EXERCISE 9: Each of the following sentences contains more than one clause. Underline the subjects once and the verbs twice. Circle the connectors. Put boxes around the noun clauses. Then indicate if the sentences are correct (C) or incorrect (I).

__C__   1.   (When) the season starts is determined by the weather.

__I__   2.   The manual (how) the device should be built.

_____   3.   The schedule indicated if the teams would be playing in the final game.

_____   4.   He refused to enter a plea could not be determined by the lawyer.

_____   5.   Talked about where we should go for lunch.

_____   6.   Why the condition of the patient deteriorated so rapidly it was not explained.

_____   7.   Whether or not the new office would be built was to be determined at the meeting.

_____   8.   That the professor has not yet decided when the paper is due.

_____   9.   The contract will be awarded is the question to be answered at the meeting.

_____   10.   He always talked with whomever he pleased and did whatever he wanted.

SKILL 10:   USE NOUN CLAUSE CONNECTOR/SUBJECTS CORRECTLY

In Skill 9 we saw that noun clause connectors were used to introduce noun subject clauses or noun object clauses. In Skill 10 we will see that in some cases a noun clause connector is not just a connector; a noun clause connector can also be the subject of the clause at the same time.

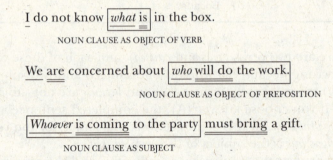

I do not know | *what* is | in the box.

NOUN CLAUSE AS OBJECT OF VERB

We are concerned about | *who* will do the work.|

NOUN CLAUSE AS OBJECT OF PREPOSITION

|*Whoever* is coming to the party| must bring a gift.

NOUN CLAUSE AS SUBJECT

In the first example there are two clauses: *I do not know* and *what is in the box.* These two clauses are joined by the connector *what.* It is important to understand that in this sentence the word *what* serves two functions. It is both the subject of the verb *is* and the connector that joins the two clauses.

In the second example there are two clauses. In the first clause *we* is the subject of *are.* In the second clause *who* is the subject of *will do. Who* also serves as the connector that joins the two clauses. The noun clause *who will do the work* functions as the object of the preposition *about.*

In the last example there are also two clauses: *whoever* is the subject of the verb *is coming,* and the noun clause *whoever is coming to the party* is the subject of *must bring.* The word *whoever* serves two functions in the sentence: It is the subject of the verb *is coming,* and it is the connector that joins the two clauses.

The following example shows how this sentence pattern could be tested in the Structure section of the TOEFL test.

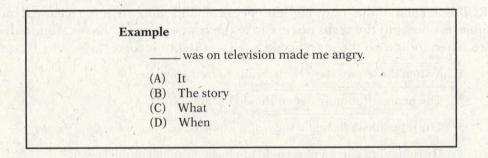

Example

_____ was on television made me angry.

(A) It
(B) The story
(C) What
(D) When

In this example you should notice immediately that there are two verbs, *was* and *made,* and each of those verbs needs a subject. Answers (A) and (B) are incorrect because *it* and *the story* cannot be the subject for both *was* and *made* at the same time. Answer (D) is incorrect because *when* is not a subject. In answer (C) *what* serves as both the subject of the verb *was* and the connector that joins the two clauses together; the noun clause *what was on television* is the subject of the verb *made.* Answer (C) is therefore the best answer.

The following chart lists the noun clause connector/subjects and the sentence patterns used with them:

NOUN CLAUSE CONNECTOR/SUBJECTS		
who	*what*	*which*
whoever	*whatever*	*whichever*

	NOUN CLAUSE AS OBJECT	
S V	(noun connector/subject)	V
I know	*what*	*happened.*

NOUN CLAUSE AS SUBJECT		
(noun connector/subject)	V	V
What	*happened*	*was great.*

EXERCISE 10: Each of the following sentences contains more than one clause. Underline the subjects once and the verbs twice. Circle the connectors. Put boxes around the noun clauses. Then indicate if the sentences are correct (C) or incorrect (I).

__C__ 1. The game show contestant was able to respond to [(whatever) was asked.]

__I__ 2. You should find out [(which) the best physics department.]

_____ 3. The employee was unhappy about what was added to his job description.

_____ 4. Whoever wants to take the desert tour during spring break signing up at the office.

_____ 5. The motorist was unable to discover who he had struck his car.

_____ 6. The voters should elect whichever of the candidates seems best to them.

_____ 7. It was difficult to distinguish what was on sale and what was merely on display.

_____ 8. You should buy whatever the cheapest and most durable.

_____ 9. What was written in the letter angered him beyond belief.

_____ 10. You can spend your time with whoever important to you.

SKILL 11: USE ADJECTIVE CLAUSE CONNECTORS CORRECTLY

An adjective clause is a clause that describes a noun. Because the clause is an adjective, it is positioned directly after the noun that it describes.

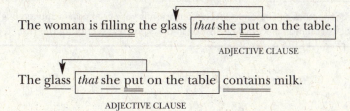

The woman is filling the glass *that* she put on the table.
ADJECTIVE CLAUSE

The glass *that* she put on the table contains milk.
ADJECTIVE CLAUSE

In the first example there are two clauses: *woman* is the subject of the verb *is filling*, and *she* is the subject of the verb *put*. *That* is the adjective clause connector that joins these two clauses, and the adjective clause *that she put on the table* describes the noun *glass*.

In the second example there are also two clauses: *glass* is the subject of the verb *contains*, and *she* is the subject of the verb *put*. In this sentence also, *that* is the adjective clause connector that joins these two clauses, and the adjective clause *that she put on the table* describes the noun *glass*.

The following example shows how these sentence patterns could be tested in the Structure section of the TOEFL test.

Example

The gift _____ selected for the bride was rather expensive.

(A) because
(B) was
(C) since
(D) which we

In this example you should notice quickly that there are two clauses: *gift* is the subject of the verb *was,* and the verb *selected* needs a subject. Because there are two clauses, a connector is also needed. Answers (A) and (C) have connectors, but there are no subjects, so these answers are not correct. Answer (B) changes *selected* into a passive verb; in this case the sentence would have one subject and two verbs, so answer (B) is not correct. The best answer to this question is answer (D). The correct sentence should say: *The gift which we selected for the bride was rather expensive.* In this sentence *gift is* the subject of the verb *was, we* is the subject of the verb *selected,* and the connector *which* joins these two clauses.

The following chart lists the adjective clause connectors and the sentence patterns used with them:

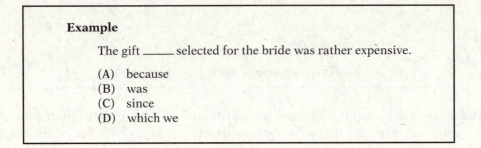

ADJECTIVE CLAUSE CONNECTORS		
whom (for people)	*which* (for things)	*that* (for people or things)
S V	(adjective connector) S V	
I liked the book	*which* *you recommended.*	
S	(adjective connector) S V	V
The book	*which* *you recommended*	*was interesting.*
NOTE: The adjective connectors can be omitted. This omission is very common in spoken English or in casual written English. It is not as common in formal English or in the Structure section of the TOEFL test.		

EXERCISE 11: Each of the following sentences contains more than one clause. Underline the subjects once and the verbs twice. Circle the connectors. Put boxes around the adjective clauses. Then indicate if the sentences are correct (C) or incorrect (I).

__C__   1.   It is important to fill out the form in the way (that) you have been instructed.

__I__   2.   The car (which) I having been driving for five years for sale at a really good price.

_____   3.   I just finished reading the novel whom the professor suggested for my book report.

_____   4.   The plane that he was scheduled to take to Hawaii was delayed.

_____   5.   The movie which we watched on cable last night it was really frightening.

_____   6.   I made an appointment with the doctor whom you recommended.

_____   7.   The enthusiasm with which he greeted me made me feel welcome.

_____   8.   The story that you told me about Bob.

_____   9.   The men with whom were having the discussion did not seem very friendly.

_____   10.   I'm not really sure about taking part in the plans that we made last night.

Skill 12:   USE ADJECTIVE CLAUSE CONNECTOR/SUBJECTS CORRECTLY

In Skill 11 we saw that adjective clause connectors were used to introduce clauses that describe nouns. In Skill 12 we will see that in some cases an adjective clause connector is not just a connector; an adjective clause connector can also be the subject of the clause at the same time.

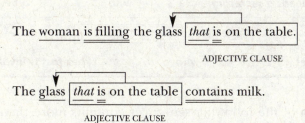

In the first example there are two clauses: *woman* is the subject of the verb *is filling,* and *that* is the subject of the verb *is.* These two clauses are joined with the connector *that.* Notice that in this example the word *that* serves two functions at the same time: it is the subject of the verb *is,* and it is the connector that joins the two clauses. The adjective clause *that is on the table* describes the noun *glass.*

In the second example, there are also two clauses: *glass* is the subject of the verb *contains,* and *that* is the subject of the verb *is.* In this example *that* also serves two functions: it is the subject of the verb *is,* and it is the connector that joins the two clauses. Because *that is on the table* is an adjective clause describing the noun *glass,* it directly follows *glass.*

The following example shows how these sentence patterns could be tested in the Structure section of the TOEFL test.

Example

_____ is on the table has four sections.

(A)   The notebook
(B)   The notebook which
(C)   Because the notebook
(D)   In the notebook

In this example you should notice immediately that the sentence has two verbs, *is* and *has*, and each of them needs a subject. (You know that *table* is not a subject because it follows the preposition *on; table* is the object of the preposition.) The only answer that has two subjects is answer (B), so answer (B) is the correct answer. The correct sentence should say: *The notebook which is on the table has four sections.* In this sentence *notebook* is the subject of the verb *has,* and *which* is the subject of the verb *is. Which* is also the connector that joins the two clauses.

The following chart lists the adjective clause connector/subjects and the sentence patterns used with them:

ADJECTIVE CLAUSE CONNECTOR/SUBJECTS		
who (for people)	*which* (for things)	*that* (for people or things)
S V	adjective connector/subject V	
She needs a secretary	*who*	*types fast.*
S	adjective connector/subject V	V
A secretary	*who*	*types fast is invaluable.*

EXERCISE 12: Each of the following sentences contains more than one clause. Underline the subjects once and the verbs twice. Circle the connectors. Put boxes around the adjective clauses. Then indicate if the sentences are correct (C) or incorrect (I).

__C__   1.   The ice cream (that) is served in the restaurant has a smooth, creamy texture.

__I__   2.   The cars are trying to enter the freeway system are lined up for blocks.

_____   3.   I have great respect for everyone who on the Dean's List.

_____   4.   It is going to be very difficult to work with the man which just began working here.

_____   5.   The door that leads to the vault it was tightly locked.

_____   6.   The neighbors reported the man who was trying to break into the car to the police.

_____ 7. These plants can only survive in an environment is extremely humid.

_____ 8. The boss meets with any production workers who they have surpassed their quotas.

_____ 9. The salesclerk ran after the woman who had left her credit card in the store.

_____ 10. The shoes which matched the dress that was on sale.

EXERCISE (Skills 9–12): Each of the following sentences contains more than one clause. Underline the subjects once and the verbs twice. Circle the connectors. Put boxes around the clauses. Then indicate if the sentences are correct (C) or incorrect (I).

_____ 1. No one explained to me whether was coming or not.

_____ 2. The part of the structure that has already been built needs to be torn down.

_____ 3. The girl who she just joined the softball team is a great shortstop.

_____ 4. I have no idea about when the meeting is supposed to start.

_____ 5. We have been told that we can leave whenever want.

_____ 6. The racquet with whom I was playing was too big and too heavy for me.

_____ 7. I will never understand that he did.

_____ 8. He was still sick was obvious to the entire medical staff.

_____ 9. What is most important in this situation it is to finish on time.

_____ 10. The newspapers that were piled up on the front porch were an indication that the residents had not been home in some time.

TOEFL EXERCISE (Skills 9–12): Choose the letter of the word or group of words that best completes the sentence.

1. Dolphins form extremely complicated allegiances and _____ continually change.

   (A) enmities that
   (B) that are enmities
   (C) enmities that are
   (D) that enmities

2. Scientists are now beginning to conduct experiments on _____ trigger different sorts of health risks.

   (A) noise pollution can
   (B) that noise pollution
   (C) how noise pollution
   (D) how noise pollution can

3. The *Apollo 11* astronauts _____ of the Earth's inhabitants witnessed on the famous first moonwalk on July 20, 1969, were Neil Armstrong and Buzz Aldrin.

   (A) whom
   (B) whom millions
   (C) were some
   (D) whom some were

4. At the end of the nineteenth century, Alfred Binet developed a test for measuring intelligence _____ served as the basis of modern IQ tests.

   (A) has
   (B) it has
   (C) and
   (D) which has

5. _____ have at least four hours of hazardous materials response training is mandated by federal law.

(A) All police officers
(B) All police officers must
(C) That all police officers
(D) For all police officers

6. A cloud's reservoir of negative charge extends upward from the altitude at _____ the freezing point.

(A) temperatures hit
(B) hit temperatures
(C) which temperatures hit
(D) which hit temperatures

7. In a 1988 advanced officers' training program, Sampson developed a plan to incorporate police in enforcing environmental protection laws whenever _____ feasible.

(A) it is
(B) is
(C) has
(D) it has

8. _____ will be carried in the next space shuttle payload has not yet been announced to the public.

(A) It
(B) What
(C) When
(D) That

9. During free fall, _____ up to a full minute, a skydiver will fall at a constant speed of 120 m.p.h.

(A) it is
(B) which is
(C) being
(D) is

10. The fact _____ the most important ratings period is about to begin has caused all three networks to shore up their schedules.

(A) is that
(B) of
(C) that
(D) what

TOEFL REVIEW EXERCISE (Skills 1–12): Choose the letter of the word or group of words that best completes the sentence.

1. _____ loom high above the north and northeastern boundaries of the expanding city of Tucson.

(A) The Santa Catalina mountains
(B) Because the Santa Catalina mountains
(C) The Santa Catalina mountains are
(D) That the Santa Catalina mountains

2. Radioactive _____ provides a powerful way to measure geologic time.

(A) it
(B) dates
(C) dating
(D) can

3. _____ contained in the chromosomes, and they are thought of as the units of heredity.

(A) Genes which are
(B) Genes are
(C) When genes
(D) Because of genes

4. The benefit _____ the study is that it provides necessary information to anyone who needs it.

(A) of
(B) which
(C) that
(D) because

5. The same symptoms that occur _____ occur with cocaine.

(A) amphetamines can
(B) with amphetamines can
(C) so amphetamines
(D) with amphetamines they

6. Many companies across the country have molded the concepts _____ describes into an integrated strategy for preventing stress.

(A) and Wolf
(B) that Wolf
(C) what Wolf
(D) so Wolf

7. _____ in the first draft of the budget will not necessarily be in the final draft.

    (A) Although it appears
    (B) It appears
    (C) What appears
    (D) Despite its appearance

8. If a food label indicates that a food is mostly carbohydrate, it does not mean _____ is a good food to eat.

    (A) and it
    (B) and
    (C) that it
    (D) when

9. A need for space law to include commercial concerns has been recognized inasmuch _____ been expanding drastically in recent years.

    (A) the commercial launch industry
    (B) the commercial launch industry has
    (C) as has the commercial launch industry
    (D) as the commercial launch industry has

10. The report on the nuclear power plant indicated that when the plant had gone on line _____ unsafe.

    (A) and it had been
    (B) it had been
    (C) had been
    (D) that it had been

SENTENCES WITH REDUCED CLAUSES_____

It is possible in English for a clause to appear in a complete form or in a reduced form.

> My friend should be on the train *which is arriving at the station now.*

> *Although it was not really difficult,* the exam took a lot of time.

The first sentence shows an adjective clause in its complete form, *which is arriving at the station now,* and in its reduced form, *arriving at the station now.* The second sentence shows an adverb clause in its complete form, *although it was not really difficult,* and its reduced form, *although not really difficult.*

The two types of clauses that can reduce in English are: (1) adjective clauses and (2) adverb clauses. It is important to become familiar with these reduced clauses because they appear frequently on the TOEFL test.

SKILL 13:   USE REDUCED ADJECTIVE CLAUSES CORRECTLY

Adjective clauses can appear in a reduced form. In the reduced form, the adjective clause connector and the *be*-verb that directly follow it are omitted.

> The woman *who is waving to us* is the tour guide.

> The letter *which was written last week* arrived today.

> The pitcher *that is on the table* is full of iced tea.

Each of these sentences may be used in the complete form or in the reduced form. In the reduced form the connector *who, which,* or *that* is omitted along with the *be*-verb *is* or *was.*

If there is no *be*-verb in the adjective clause, it is still possible to have a reduced form. When there is no *be*-verb in the adjective clause, the connector is omitted and the verb is changed into the *-ing* form.

appearing
I don't understand the article *which appears in today's paper.*

In this example there is no *be*-verb in the adjective clause *which appears in today's paper,* so the connector *which* is omitted and the main verb *appears* is changed to the *-ing* form *appearing.*

It should be noted that not all adjective clauses can appear in a reduced form. An adjective clause can appear in a reduced form only if the adjective clause connector is followed directly by a verb. In other words, an adjective clause can only be reduced if the connector is also a subject.

The woman *that I just met* is the tour guide.   (*does not reduce*)
The letter *which you sent me* arrived yesterday.   (*does not reduce*)

In these two examples the adjective clauses cannot be reduced because the adjective clause connectors *that* and *which* are not directly followed by verbs; *that* is directly followed by the subject *I,* and *which* is directly followed by the subject *you.*

A final point to note is that some adjective clauses are set off from the rest of the sentence with commas, and these adjective clauses can also be reduced. In addition, when an adjective clause is set off with commas, the reduced adjective clause can appear at the front of the sentence.

The White House, *which is located in Washington,* is the home of the president.
The White House, *located in Washington,* is the home of the president.
Located in Washington, the White House is the home of the president.

The president, *who is now preparing to give a speech,* is meeting with his advisors.
The president, *now preparing to give a speech,* is meeting with his advisors.
Now preparing to give a speech, the president is meeting with his advisors.

In these two examples, the adjective clauses are set off from the rest of the sentence with commas, so each sentence can be structured in three different ways: (1) with the complete clause, (2) with the reduced clause following the noun that it describes, and (3) with the reduced clause at the beginning of the sentence.

The following example shows how reduced adjective clauses could be tested in the Structure section of the TOEFL test.

Example

_____ on several different television programs, the witness gave conflicting accounts of what had happened.

(A)   He appeared
(B)   Who appeared
(C)   Appearing
(D)   Appears

In this example, answer (A) is incorrect because there are two clauses, *He appeared . . .* and *the witness gave . . . ,* and there is no connector to join them. Answer (B) is incorrect because an adjective clause such as *who appeared* . . . cannot appear at the beginning of a sentence (unless it is in a reduced form). Answer (C) is the correct answer because it is the reduced form of the clause *who appeared,* and this reduced form can appear at the front of the sentence. Answer (D) is not the reduced form of a verb; it is merely a verb in the present tense; a verb such as *appears* needs a subject and a connector to be correct.

The following chart lists the structure for reduced adjective clauses and rules for how and when reduced forms can be used:

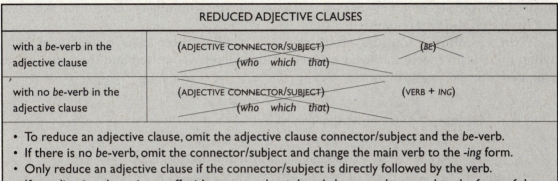

REDUCED ADJECTIVE CLAUSES		
with a *be*-verb in the adjective clause	~~(ADJECTIVE CONNECTOR/SUBJECT)~~ ~~(who which that)~~	~~(BE)~~
with no *be*-verb in the adjective clause	~~(ADJECTIVE CONNECTOR/SUBJECT)~~ ~~(who which that)~~	(VERB + *ING*)

- To reduce an adjective clause, omit the adjective clause connector/subject and the *be*-verb.
- If there is no *be*-verb, omit the connector/subject and change the main verb to the *-ing* form.
- Only reduce an adjective clause if the connector/subject is directly followed by the verb.
- If an adjective clause is set off with commas, the reduced clause can be moved to the front of the sentence.

EXERCISE 13: Each of the following sentences contains an adjective clause, in a complete or reduced form. Underline the adjective clauses. Then indicate if the sentences are correct (C) or incorrect (I).

___C___ 1. We will have to return the merchandise <u>purchased yesterday</u> at the Broadway.

___I___ 2. The children <u>sat in the fancy restaurant</u> found it difficult to behave.

_____ 3. Serving a term of four years, the mayor of the town will face reelection next year.

_____ 4. The brand new Cadillac, purchasing less than two weeks ago, was destroyed in the accident.

_____ 5. The fans who supporting their team always come out to the games in large numbers.

_____ 6. The suspect can be seen in the photographs were just released by the police.

_____ 7. The food placing on the picnic table attracted a large number of flies.

_____ 8. Impressed with everything she had heard about the course, Marie signed her children up for it.

_____ 9. The passengers in the airport waiting room, heard the announcement of the canceled flight, groaned audibly.

_____ 10. Dissatisfied with the service at the restaurant, the meal really was not enjoyable.

SKILL 14:   USE REDUCED ADVERB CLAUSES CORRECTLY

Adverb clauses can also appear in a reduced form. In the reduced form, the adverb connector remains, but the subject and *be*-verb are omitted.

> *Although ~~he is~~ rather unwell,* the speaker will take part in the seminar.

> *When ~~you are~~ ready,* you can begin your speech.

These two examples may be used in either the complete or reduced form. In the reduced form, the adverb connectors *although* and *when* remain; the subjects *he* and *you* as well as the *be*-verbs *is* and *are* are omitted.

If there is no *be*-verb in the adverb clause, it is still possible to have a reduced form. When there is no *be*-verb in the adverb clause, the subject is omitted and the main verb is changed into the *-ing* form.

> *feeling*
> *Although ~~he feels~~ rather sick,* the speaker will take part in the seminar.

> *giving*
> *When ~~you give~~ your speech,* you should speak loudly and distinctly.

In the first example the adverb clause *although he feels rather sick* does not include a *be*-verb; to reduce this clause, the subject *he* is omitted and the main verb *feels* is changed to *feeling*. In the second example the adverb clause *when you give your speech* also does not include a *be*-verb; to reduce this clause, the subject *you* is omitted and the main verb *give* is changed to *giving*.

The following example shows how this sentence pattern could be tested in the Structure section of the TOEFL test.

Example

When _____ , you are free to leave.

(A)   the finished report
(B)   finished with the report
(C)   the report
(D)   is the report finished

In this example you should notice the adverb connector *when,* and you should know that this time word could be followed by either a complete clause or a reduced clause. Answers (A) and (C) contain the subjects *the finished report* and *the report* and no verb, so these answers are incorrect. In answer (D) the subject and verb are inverted, and this is not a question, so answer (D) is incorrect. The correct answer is answer (B); this answer is the reduced form of the clause *when you are finished with the report.*

It should be noted that not all adverb clauses can appear in a reduced form, and a number of adverb clauses can only be reduced if the verb is in the passive form.

Once you submit your thesis, you will graduate.   *Once ~~it is~~ submitted,* your thesis will be reviewed.
(active — does not reduce)   (passive — does reduce)

In the first example, the adverb clause *once you submit your thesis* does not reduce because clauses introduced by *once* only reduce if the verb is passive, and the verb *submit* is active. In the second example, the adverb clause *once it is submitted* does reduce to *once submitted* because the clause is introduced by *once* and the verb *is submitted* is passive.

The following chart lists the structures for reduced adverb clauses and which adverb clause connectors can be used in a reduced form:

REDUCED ADVERB CLAUSES					
with a *be*-verb in the adverb clause	(ADVERB CONNECTOR)		~~(SUBJECT)~~		~~(BE)~~
with no *be*-verb in the adverb clause	(ADVERB CONNECTOR)		~~(SUBJECT)~~	(VERB + *ING*)	
	Time	Condition	Contrast	Place	Manner
reduces in ACTIVE	*after* *before* *since* *while* *when*	*if* *unless* *whether*	*although* *though*		
reduces in PASSIVE	*once* *until* *when* *whenever*	*if* *unless* *whether*	*although* *though*	*where* *wherever*	*as*

- To reduce an adverb clause, omit the subject and the *be*-verb from the adverb clause.
- If there is no *be*-verb, then omit the subject and change the verb to the *-ing* form.

EXERCISE 14: Each of the following sentences contains a reduced adverb clause. Circle the adverb connectors. Underline the reduced clauses. Then indicate if the sentences are correct (C) or incorrect (I).

__C__ 1. (If) not completely satisfied, you can return the product to the manufacturer.

__I__ 2. Steve has had to learn how to cook and clean (since) left home.

_____ 3. The ointment can be applied where needed.

_____ 4. Tom began to look for a job after completing his master's degree in engineering.

_____ 5. Although not selecting for the team, he attends all of the games as a fan.

_____ 6. When purchased at this store, the buyer gets a guarantee on all items.

_____ 7. The medicine is not effective unless taken as directed.

_____ 8. You should negotiate a lot before buy a new car.

_____ 9. Once purchased, the swimsuits cannot be returned.

_____ 10. Though located near the coast, the town does not get much of an ocean breeze.

EXERCISE (Skills 13–14): Each of the following sentences contains a reduced clause. Underline the reduced clauses. Then indicate if the sentences are correct (C) or incorrect (I).

_____   1.   Though was surprised at the results, she was pleased with what she had done.

_____   2.   Wearing only a light sweater, she stepped out into the pouring rain.

_____   3.   The family stopped to visit many relatives while driving across the country.

_____   4.   The company president, needed a vacation, boarded a plane for the Bahamas.

_____   5.   When applying for the job, you should bring your letters of reference.

_____   6.   She looked up into the dreary sky was filled with dark thunderclouds.

_____   7.   Feeling weak after a long illness, Sally wanted to try to get back to work.

_____   8.   Before decided to have surgery, you should get a second opinion.

_____   9.   The construction material, a rather grainy type of wood, gave the room a rustic feeling.

_____   10. The application will at least be reviewed if submitted by the fifteenth of the month.

TOEFL EXERCISE (Skills 13–14): Choose the letter of the word or group of words that best completes the sentence.

1.   When _____ nests during spring nesting season, Canadian geese are fiercely territorial.

(A) building
(B) are building
(C) built
(D) are built

2.   In 1870, Calvin, along with Adirondack hunter Alvah Dunning, made the first known ascent of Seward Mountain, _____ far from roads or trails.

(A) a remote peak
(B) it is a remote peak
(C) a remote peak is
(D) which a remote peak

3.   Kokanee salmon begin to deteriorate and die soon _____ at the age of four.

(A) they spawn
(B) after spawning
(C) spawn
(D) spawned the salmon

4.   _____ behind government secrecy for nearly half a century, the Hanford plant in central Washington produced plutonium for the nuclear weapons of the Cold War.

(A) It is hidden
(B) Hidden
(C) Which is hidden
(D) The plant is hiding

5.   Until _____ incorrect, astronomers had assumed that the insides of white dwarfs were uniform.

(A) they
(B) their proof
(C) the astronomers recently proven
(D) recently proven

6.   _____ artifacts from the early Chinese dynasties, numerous archeologists have explored the southern Silk Road.

(A) They were searching for
(B) It was a search for
(C) Searched for
(D) Searching for

7. In Hailey, the best-known lecturer was women's rights activist Abigail Scott Duniway of Portland, Oregon, who could usually be persuaded to speak _____ town visiting her son.

   (A) she was in
   (B) while in
   (C) while she was
   (D) was in

8. The National Restaurant _____ Washington, says that federal efforts to regulate workplace smoking would limit restaurants' ability to respond to the desires of their patrons.

   (A) Association in
   (B) Association is in
   (C) Association which is in
   (D) Association, based in

9. _____ in North American waterways less than a decade ago, zebra mussels have already earned a nasty reputation for their expensive habit of clogging water pipes in the Great Lakes area.

   (A) The first sighting
   (B) Although first sighted
   (C) Zebra mussels were first sighted
   (D) First sighting

10. Small companies may take their goods abroad for trade shows without paying foreign value-added taxes by acquiring _____ an ATA carnet.

   (A) a document calls
   (B) a document called
   (C) calls a document
   (D) called a document

TOEFL REVIEW EXERCISE (Skills 1–14): Choose the letter of the word or group of words that best completes the sentence.

1. In the United States _____ approximately four million miles of roads, streets, and highways.

   (A) there
   (B) is
   (C) they
   (D) there are

2. _____ twelve million immigrants entered the United States via Ellis Island.

   (A) More than
   (B) There were more than
   (C) Of more than
   (D) The report of

3. The television, _____ so long been a part of our culture, has an enormous influence.

   (A) has
   (B) it has
   (C) which
   (D) which has

4. Psychologists have traditionally maintained that infants cannot formulate long-term memories until _____ the age of eight or nine months.

   (A) they
   (B) they reach
   (C) to reach
   (D) reach

5. _____ a cheese shop has since grown into a small conglomerate consisting of a catering business and two retail stores.

   (A) In the beginning of
   (B) It began as
   (C) Its beginning which was
   (D) What began as

6. Primarily a government contractor, _____ preferential treatment from government agencies as both a minority-group member and a woman.

   (A) receives Weber
   (B) Weber receives
   (C) the reception of Weber
   (D) according to Weber's reception

7. Because the project depends on _____ at the federal level, the city and county may have to wait until the budget cutting ends.

   (A) it happens
   (B) which happening
   (C) what happens
   (D) that it happens

8. _____ definitive study of a western hard-rock mining community cemetery appears to have been done is in Silver City, Nevada.

    (A) Most
    (B) The most
    (C) Where most
    (D) Where the most

9. One of the areas of multimedia that is growing quickly _____ is sound.

    (A) yet is easily overlooked
    (B) is easily overlooked
    (C) it is easily overlooked
    (D) that is easily overlooked

10. _____, early approaches for coping with workplace stress dealt with the problem only after its symptoms had appeared.

    (A) Although well intending
    (B) Although it is a good intention
    (C) Although a good intention
    (D) Although well intended

SENTENCES WITH INVERTED SUBJECTS AND VERBS _____

Subjects and verbs are inverted in a variety of situations in English. Inverted subjects and verbs occur most often in the formation of a question. To form a question with a helping verb (*be, have, can, could, will, would,* etc.), the subject and helping verb are inverted.

He can go to the movies.
Can he go to the movies?

You would tell me the truth.
Would you tell me the truth?

She was sick yesterday.
Was she sick yesterday?

To form a question when there is no helping verb in the sentence, the helping verb *do* is used.

He goes to the movies.
Does he go to the movies?

You told me the truth.
Did you tell me the truth?

There are many other situations in English when subjects and verbs are inverted, but if you just remember this method of inverting subjects and verbs, you will be able to handle the other situations. The most common problems with inverted subjects and verbs on the TOEFL test occur in the following situations: (1) with question words such as *what, when, where, why,* and *how;* (2) after some place expressions; (3) after negative expressions; (4) in some conditionals; and (5) after some comparisons.

SKILL 15: INVERT THE SUBJECT AND VERB WITH QUESTION WORDS

There is some confusion about when to invert the subject and verb after question words such as *what, when, where, why,* and *how.* These words can have two very different functions in a sentence. First, they can introduce a question, and in this case the subject and verb that follow are inverted.

> *What* is the homework?
> *When* can I leave?
> *Where* are you going?

Also, these words can join together two clauses, and in this case the subject and verb that follow are not inverted.

> I do not know *what* the homework is.
> *When* I can leave, I will take the first train.
> Do you know *where* you are going?

In each of these examples there are two clauses joined by a question word. Notice that the subjects and verbs that follow the question words *what, when,* and *where* are not inverted in this case.

The following example shows how this sentence pattern could be tested in the Structure section of the TOEFL test.

Example

The lawyer asked the client why _____ it.

(A) did he do
(B) did he
(C) he did
(D) did

In this example the question word *why* is used to connect the two clauses, so a subject and verb are needed after this connector; this is not a question, so the subject and verb should not be inverted. The best answer is therefore answer (C).

The following chart lists the question words and their sentence patterns:

INVERTED SUBJECTS AND VERBS WITH QUESTION WORDS					
who	*what*	*when*	*where*	*why*	*how*
When the question word introduces a question, the subject and verb *are* inverted.					
(question word) V S ?					
What are they?					
When the question word connects two clauses, the subject and verb that follow *are not* inverted.					
S V (question word) S V.					
I know what they are.					

EXERCISE 15: Each of the following sentences contains a question word. Circle the question words. Underline the subjects once and the verbs twice. Then indicate if the sentences are correct (C) or incorrect (I).

__I__   1. The phone company is not certain (when) will the new directories be ready.

__C__   2. The professor does not understand (why) so many students did poorly on the exam.

_____   3. How new students can get information about parking?

_____   4. Where is it cheapest to get typeset copies printed?

_____   5. Only the pilot can tell you how far can the plane go on one tank of fuel.

_____   6. What type of security does he prefer for his investments?

_____   7. Not even the bank president knows when the vault will be opened.

_____   8. How long it has been since you arrived in the United States?

_____   9. The jury doubts what the witness said under cross-examination.

_____   10. Do you know why he wants to take an extended leave of absence?

SKILL 16:   INVERT THE SUBJECT AND VERB WITH PLACE EXPRESSIONS

After ideas expressing place, the subject and the verb sometimes invert in English. This can happen with single words expressing place, such as *here, there,* or *nowhere.*

> *Here* is the book that you lent me.
> *There* are the keys that I thought I lost.
> *Nowhere* have I seen such beautiful weather.

In the first example the place word *here* causes the subject *book* to come after the verb *is.* In the second example the place word *there* causes the subject *keys* to come after the verb *are.* In the last example the place word *nowhere* causes the subject *I* to come after the verb *have.*

The subject and verb can also be inverted after prepositional phrases expressing place.

> *In the closet* are the clothes that you want.
> *Around the corner* is Sam's house.
> *Beyond the mountains* lies the town where you will live.

In the first example the prepositional phrase of place *in the closet* causes the subject *clothes* to come after the verb *are.* In the second example the prepositional phrase of place *around the corner* causes the subject *house* to come after the verb *is.* In the last example the prepositional phrase of place *beyond the mountains* causes the subject *town* to come after the verb *lies.*

It is important (and a bit difficult) to understand that the subject and verb will invert after place expressions at the beginning of a sentence only when the place expression is *necessary* to complete the sentence. Study the following examples:

> *In the forest* are many exotic birds.
> *In the forest* I walked for many hours.

In the first example the subject *birds* and verb *are* are inverted because the place expression *in the forest* is needed to complete the idea *many exotic birds are.* . . . In the second example the subject *I* and the verb *walked* are not inverted because the idea *I walked for many hours* is complete without the place expression *in the forest;* the place expression is therefore not needed to complete the sentence.

The following example shows how this sentence pattern could be tested in the Structure section of the TOEFL test.

Example

On the second level of the parking lot _____.

(A) is empty
(B) are empty
(C) some empty stalls are
(D) are some empty stalls

This example begins with the place expression *on the second level of the parking lot,* which consists of two prepositional phrases, *on the second level* and *of the parking lot.* This sentence needs a subject and a verb to be complete, and the two answers that contain both a subject, *stalls,* and verb, *are,* are answers (C) and (D). The subject and verb should be inverted because the place expression is necessary to complete the idea *some empty stalls are.* . . . The best answer is therefore answer (D).

The following chart lists the sentence patterns used with place expressions:

INVERTED SUBJECTS AND VERBS WITH PLACE EXPRESSIONS
When a place expression at the front of the sentence is *necessary* to complete the sentence, the subject and verb that follow *are* inverted.
PLACE (necessary)   V   S
In the classroom   were some old desks.
When a place expression at the front of the sentence contains *extra* information that is *not* needed to complete the sentence, the subject and verb that follow *are not* inverted.
PLACE (extra)   S   V
In the classroom,   I studied very hard.

EXERCISE 16: Each of the following sentences contains an expression of place at the beginning of the sentence. Circle the expressions of place. Look at the clauses that immediately follow the place expressions and underline the subjects once and the verbs twice. Then indicate if the sentences are correct (C) or incorrect (I).

___C___   1. (In front of the house) were some giant trees.

___I___   2. (There) a big house is on the corner.

_____   3. In the cave was a vast treasure of gems and jewels.

_____   4. To the north the stream is that the settlers will have to cross.

_____   5. Around the corner are the offices that you are trying to find.

_____   6. At the Italian restaurant was the food too spicy for my taste.

_____   7. Nowhere in the world farmers can grow such delicious food.

_____   8. In the backyard the two trees are that need to be pruned.

_____   9. Around the recreation hall and down the path are the tents where we will be staying this week.

_____   10. In the apartment next to mine, a family was that had a lot of pets.

SKILL 17: INVERT THE SUBJECT AND VERB WITH NEGATIVES

The subject and verb can also be inverted after certain negatives and related expressions. When negative expressions, such as *no*, *not*, or *never*, come at the beginning of a sentence, the subject and verb are inverted.

> *Not once* did I miss a question.
> *Never* has Mr. Jones taken a vacation.
> *At no time* can the woman talk on the telephone.

In the first example the negative expression *not once* causes the subject *I* to come after the helping verb *did*. In the second example the negative word *never* causes the subject *Mr. Jones* to come after the helping verb *has*. In the last example the negative expression *at no time* causes the subject *woman* to come after the helping verb *can*.

Certain words in English, such as *hardly*, *barely*, *scarcely*, and *only*, act like negatives. If one of these words comes at the beginning of a sentence, the subject and verb are also inverted.

> *Hardly ever* does he take time off.
> (This means that he *almost never* takes time off.)

> *Only once* did the manager issue overtime paychecks.
> (This means that the manager *almost never* issued overtime paychecks.)

In the first example the "almost negative" expression *hardly ever* causes the subject *he* to come after the helping verb *does*. In the second example the "almost negative" expression *only once* causes the subject *manager* to come after the helping verb *did*.

When a negative expression appears in front of a subject and verb in the middle of a sentence, the subject and verb are also inverted. This happens often with the negative words *neither* and *nor*.

> I do not want to go, and *neither* does Tom.
> The secretary is not attending the meeting, *nor* is her boss.

In the first example the negative *neither* causes the subject *Tom* to come after the helping verb *does*. In the second example the negative *nor* causes the subject *boss* to come after the verb *is*.

The following example shows how this sentence pattern could be tested in the Structure section of the TOEFL test.

Example

Only in extremely dangerous situations _____ stopped.

(A) will be the printing presses
(B) the printing presses will be
(C) that the printing presses will be
(D) will the printing presses be

In this example you should notice that the sentence begins with the negative *only*, so an inverted subject and verb are needed. Answer (D) contains a correctly inverted subject and verb, with the helping verb *will*, the subject *printing presses*, and the main verb *be*, so answer (D) is the best answer.

The following chart lists the negative expressions and the sentence pattern used with them:

INVERTED SUBJECTS AND VERBS WITH NEGATIVES					
no	*not*	*never*	*neither*	*nor*	
barely	*hardly*	*only*	*rarely*	*scarcely*	*seldom*

When a negative expression appears *in front of* a subject and verb (at the beginning of a sentence or in the middle of a sentence), the subject and verb *are* inverted.

(negative expression)   V   S

Rarely   **were they so happy.**

EXERCISE 17: Each of the following sentences contains a negative or "almost negative" expression. Circle the negative expressions. Look at the clauses that follow and underline the subjects once and the verbs twice. Then indicate if the sentences are correct (C) or incorrect (I).

___I___   1. (Never) the boy wrote to his sisters.

___C___   2. (On no occasion) did they say that to me.

_____   3. Steve did not win the prize, nor did he expect to do so.

_____   4. Only once in my life gone I have to New York City.

_____   5. Did he go out of the house at no time.

_____   6. Seldom their secretary has made such mistakes.

_____   7. No sooner had she hung up the phone than it rang again.

_____   8. Sheila did not arrive late for work, nor she left early.

_____   9. Barely had he finished the exam when the graduate assistant collected the papers.

_____ 10. The police did not arrive in time to save the girl, and neither did the paramedics.

SKILL 18:   INVERT THE SUBJECT AND VERB WITH CONDITIONALS

In certain conditional structures, the subject and verb may also be inverted. This can occur when the helping verb in the conditional clause is *had, should,* or *were,* and the conditional connector *if* is omitted.

> *If* he had taken more time, the results would have been better.
> Had he taken more time, the results would have been better.

> I would help you *if* I were in a position to help.
> I would help you were I in a position to help.

> *If* you should arrive before 6:00, just give me a call.
> Should you arrive before 6:00, just give me a call.

In each of these examples you can see that when *if* is included, the subject and verb are in the regular order (*if he had taken, if I were, if you should arrive*). It is also possible to omit *if*; in this case, the subject and verb are inverted (*had he taken, were I, should you arrive*).

The following example shows how this sentence pattern could be tested in the Structure section of the TOEFL test.

Example

The report would have been accepted _____ in checking its accuracy.

(A) if more care
(B) more care had been taken
(C) had taken more care
(D) had more care been taken

In this example a connector (*if*) and a subject and verb are needed, but *if* could be omitted and the subject and verb inverted. Answer (A) is incorrect because it contains the connector *if* and the subject *care* but no verb. Answer (B) is incorrect because it contains the subject *care* and the verb *had been taken* but does not have a connector. In answers (C) and (D), *if* has been omitted. Because it is correct to invert the subject *more care* and the helping verb *had,* answer (D) is correct.

The following chart lists the conditional verbs that may invert and the sentence patterns used with them:

INVERTED SUBJECTS AND VERBS WITH CONDITIONALS
had   *should*   *were*
When the verb in the conditional clause is *had, should,* or *were,* it is possible to omit *if* and invert the subject and verb. (omitted *if*)   V   S   **Were he   here, he would help.**
It is also possible to keep *if.* Then the subject and verb *are not* inverted. *if*   S   V **If   he were   here, he would help.**

EXERCISE 18: Each of the following sentences contains a conditional (with a stated or implied *if*). Circle the conditionals, or put an asterisk (*) where *if* has been omitted. Look at the clauses that follow and underline the subjects once and the verbs twice. Then indicate if the sentences are correct (C) or incorrect (I).

____C____ 1. *Were our neighbors a bit more friendly, it would be somewhat easier to get to know them.

____I____ 2. There are plenty of blankets in the closet if should you get cold during the night.

_____ 3. Has he enough vacation days left this year, he will take two full weeks off in December.

_____ 4. Had we been informed of the decision, we might have had something to say about it.

_____   5.   I would like to know could you help me pack these boxes.

_____   6.   He would have been in big trouble had not he remembered the assignment at the last minute.

_____   7.   If your friends come to visit, will they stay in a hotel or at your house?

_____   8.   He might be a little more successful today was he a little more willing to do some hard work.

_____   9.   Should you ever visit this town again, I would be delighted to show you around.

_____   10.   Do you think that she would give the speech were she asked to do so?

SKILL 19: INVERT THE SUBJECT AND VERB WITH COMPARISONS

An inverted subject and verb may occur also after a comparison. The inversion of a subject and verb after a comparison is optional, rather than required, and it is a rather formal structure. There have been a number of inverted comparisons on recent TOEFL tests, so you should be familiar with this structure.

> My sister spends *more* hours in the office *than* John.
> My sister spends *more* hours in the office *than* John does.
> My sister spends *more* hours in the office *than* does John.

All three of these examples contain the comparison *more . . . than,* and all three are correct in English. It is possible to have the noun *John* alone, as in the first example; it is possible that the comparison is followed by the subject and verb *John does,* as in the second example; it is also possible that the comparison is followed by the inverted subject and verb *does John,* as in the third example.

   The following example shows how this sentence pattern could be tested in the Structure section of the TOEFL test.

Example

The results of the current experiment appear to be more consistent than _____ the results of any previous tests.

(A) them
(B) were
(C) they were
(D) were they

In this example you should notice the comparison *more consistent than,* and you should also understand that *the results of the current experiment* is being compared with *the results of any previous tests.* Because *the results of any previous tests* is the subject, only a verb is needed; the best answer to this question is therefore answer (B). We know that it is possible for a subject and a verb to be inverted after a comparison, and in this case the subject *the results of any previous tests* comes after the verb *were.*

The following chart lists the sentence patterns used with comparisons:

INVERTED SUBJECTS AND VERBS WITH COMPARISONS				
The subject and verb *may* invert after a comparison. The following structures are both possible.				
S	V	(comparison)	S	V
We	were	*more prepared than*	*the other performers*	*were.*
S	V	(comparison)	V	S
We	were	*more prepared than*	*were*	*the other performers.*

NOTE: A subject–verb inversion after a comparison sounds rather formal.

EXERCISE 19: Each of the following sentences contains a comparison. Circle the comparisons. Look at the clauses that follow and underline the subjects once and the verbs twice. Then indicate if the sentences are correct (C) or incorrect (I).

__C__   1. This candidate has received (more votes than) has any other candidate in previous years.

__I__   2. Obviously we were much (more impressed with the performance than) did the other members of the audience.

_____   3. The film that we saw last night at the festival was far better than any of the other films.

_____   4. The vegetables at the market this morning were far fresher than were those at the market yesterday.

_____   5. I am afraid that is the condition of these tires as bad as the condition of the others.

_____   6. We firmly believed that our team could achieve a much faster time than any of the others.

_____   7. This apple pie is not as good as the last one that you made.

_____   8. On the fishing trip, Bobby caught twice as many fish as anyone else did.

_____   9. The final speaker gave us more details than had any of the previous speakers.

_____ 10. Do you know why does he need to sleep so many more hours than do the others?

EXERCISE (Skills 15–19): Each of these sentences contains a structure that could require an inverted subject and verb. Circle the structures that may require inverted subjects and verbs. Underline the subjects once and the verbs twice. Then indicate if the sentences are correct (C) or incorrect (I).

_____ 1. The town council is not sure why have the land developers changed their plans.

_____ 2. Never in the world I believed that this would happen.

_____ 3. The day might have been a little more enjoyable had the sun been out a little more.

_____ 4. Only once did the judge take the defense lawyer's suggestion.

_____ 5. Down the hall to the left the offices are that need to be painted.

_____ 6. Did the scientist explain what he put in the beaker?

_____ 7. Hardly ever it snows in this section of the country.

_____ 8. Elijah scored more points in yesterday's basketball final than had any other player in history.

_____ 9. In the state of California, earthquakes occur regularly.

_____ 10. He should ever call again, please tell him that I am not at home.

TOEFL EXERCISE (Skills 15–19): Choose the letter of the word or group of words that best completes the sentence.

1. Rarely _____ located near city lights or at lower elevations.

   (A) observatories are
   (B) are
   (C) in the observatories
   (D) are observatories

2. There are geographic, economic, and cultural reasons why _____ around the world.

   (A) diets differ
   (B) do diets differ
   (C) are diets different
   (D) to differ a diet

3. Were _____ millions of dollars each year replenishing eroding beaches, the coastline would be changing even more rapidly.

   (A) the U.S. Army Corps of Engineers not spending
   (B) the U.S. Army Corps of Engineers not spend
   (C) the U.S. Army Corps of Engineers does not spend
   (D) not spending the U.S. Army Corps of Engineers

4. Nowhere _____ more skewed than in the auto industry.

   (A) that retail trade figures
   (B) retail trade figures
   (C) are retail trade figures
   (D) retail trade figures

5. New York City's Central Park is nearly twice as large _____ second smallest country, Monaco.

    (A) as
    (B) is the
    (C) as is
    (D) as is the

6. Potassium has a valence of positive one because it usually loses one electron when _____ with other elements.

    (A) does it combine
    (B) it combines
    (C) in combining
    (D) combination

7. The economic background of labor legislation will not be mentioned in this course, _____ be treated.

    (A) trade unionism will not
    (B) nor trade unionism will
    (C) nor will trade unionism
    (D) neither trade unionism will

8. _____ test positive for antibiotics when tanker trucks arrive at a milk processing plant, according to federal law, the entire truckload must be discarded.

    (A) Should milk
    (B) If milk
    (C) If milk is
    (D) Milk should

9. Located behind _____ the two lacrimal glands.

    (A) each eyelid
    (B) is each eyelid
    (C) each eyelid are
    (D) each eyelid which is

10. Only for a short period of time _____ run at top speed.

    (A) cheetahs
    (B) do cheetahs
    (C) that a cheetah can
    (D) can

TOEFL REVIEW EXERCISE (Skills 1–19): Choose the letter of the word or group of words that best completes the sentence.

1. _____ variety of flowers in the show, from simple carnations to the most exquisite roses.

    (A) A wide
    (B) There was a wide
    (C) Was there
    (D) Many

2. The wedges _____ dartboard are worth from one to twenty points each.

    (A) they are on a
    (B) are on a
    (C) are they on a
    (D) on a

3. _____ producing many new movies for release after the new season begins.

    (A) His company is
    (B) His companies
    (C) The company
    (D) Why the company is

4. _____ that Emily Dickinson wrote, 24 were given titles and 7 were published during her lifetime.

    (A) Of the 1,800 poems
    (B) There were 1,800 poems
    (C) Because the 1,800 poems
    (D) The 1,800 poems

5. Since an immediate change was needed on an emergency basis, _____ by the governor to curtail railway expenditure.

    (A) so it was proposed
    (B) was proposed
    (C) because of the proposal
    (D) it was proposed

6. In the Morgan Library in New York City _____ of medieval and renaissance manuscripts.

    (A) a collection is
    (B) in a collection
    (C) is a collection
    (D) which is a collection

7. Some fishing fleets might not have been so inefficient in limiting their catch to target species _____ more strict in enforcing penalties.

    (A) the government had been
    (B) if the government had
    (C) had the government been
    (D) if the government

8. The Dewey decimal system, currently used in libraries throughout the world, _____ all written works into ten classes according to subject.

    (A) dividing
    (B) divides
    (C) it would divide
    (D) was divided

9. Individual differences in brain-wave activity may shed light on why some people are more prone to emotional stress disorders _____.

    (A) that others are
    (B) and others are
    (C) others are
    (D) than are others

10. _____ squeezed, the orange juice in a one-cup serving provides twice the minimum daily requirement for vitamin C.

    (A) It is freshly
    (B) If freshly
    (C) You freshly
    (D) If it freshly

THE WRITTEN EXPRESSION QUESTIONS

Questions 16 through 40 in the Structure and Written Expression section of the TOEFL test examine your knowledge of the correct way to express yourself in English writing. Each question in this section consists of one sentence in which four words or groups of words have been underlined. You must choose the letter of the word or group of words that is *not* correct.

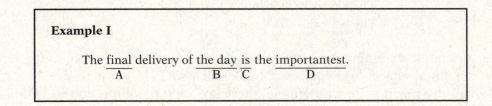

Example I

The final delivery of the day is the importantest.
    A   B C   D

If you look at the underlined words in this example, you should notice immediately that *importantest* is not correct. The correct superlative form of *important* is *the most important*. Therefore, you should choose answer (D) because (D) is not correct.

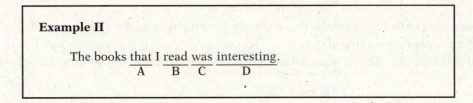

Example II

The books that I read was interesting.
    A B C   D

If you look at the underlined words in this example, each word by itself appears to be correct. However, the singular verb *was* is incorrect because it does not agree with the plural subject *books*; the verb should be *were* instead. Therefore, you should choose answer (C) because (C) is not correct.

STRATEGIES FOR THE WRITTEN EXPRESSION QUESTIONS

1. **First look at the underlined word or groups of words.** You want to see if you can spot which of the four answer choices is *not* correct.

2. **If you have been unable to find the error by looking only at the four underlined expressions, then read the complete sentence.** Often an underlined expression is incorrect because of something in another part of the sentence.

3. **Never leave any answers blank.** Be sure to answer each question even if you are unsure of the correct response.

The following skills will help you to implement these strategies in the Written Expression questions.

PROBLEMS WITH SUBJECT/VERB AGREEMENT_____

Subject/verb agreement is simple: if the subject of a sentence is singular, then the verb must be singular; if the subject of the sentence is plural, then the verb must be plural. An *s* on a verb usually indicates that a verb is singular, while an *s* on a noun usually indicates that the noun is plural. (Do not forget irregular plurals of nouns, such as *women*, *children*, and *people*.)

> The boy walks to school.
> The boys walk to school.

In the first example the singular subject *boy* requires a singular verb, *walks*. In the second example the plural subject *boys* requires a plural verb, *walk*.

Although this might seem quite simple, there are a few situations on the TOEFL test when subject/verb agreement can be a little tricky. You should be careful of subject/verb agreement in the following situations: (1) after prepositional phrases, (2) after expressions of quantity, (3) after inverted verbs, and (4) after certain words, such as *anybody*, *everything*, *no one*, *something*, *each*, and *every*.

Skill 20:   MAKE VERBS AGREE AFTER PREPOSITIONAL PHRASES

Sometimes prepositional phrases can come between the subject and the verb. If the object of the preposition is singular and the subject is plural, or if the object of the preposition is plural and the subject is singular, there can be confusion in making the subject and verb agree.

> The key (to the doors) are* in the drawer.
> SINGULAR   PLURAL
>
> The keys (to the door) is* in the drawer.
> PLURAL   SINGULAR
>
> (* indicates an error)

In the first example you might think that *doors* is the subject because it comes directly in front of the verb *are*. However, *doors* is not the subject because it is the object of the preposition *to*. The subject of the sentence is *key*, so the verb should be *is*. In the second example you might think that *door* is the subject because it comes directly in front of the verb *is*. You should recognize in this example that *door* is not the subject because it is the object of the preposition *to*. Because the subject of the sentence is *keys*, the verb should be *are*.

The following chart outlines the key information that you should understand about subject/verb agreement with prepositional phrases:

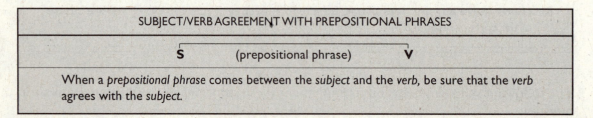

SUBJECT/VERB AGREEMENT WITH PREPOSITIONAL PHRASES		
S	(prepositional phrase)	V
When a *prepositional phrase* comes between the *subject* and the *verb*, be sure that the *verb* agrees with the *subject*.		

EXERCISE 20: Each of the following sentences has one or more prepositional phrases between the subject and verb. Circle the prepositional phrases. Underline the subjects once and the verbs twice. Then indicate if the sentences are correct (C) or incorrect (I).

__C__ 1. The climbers (on the sheer face) (of the mountain) need to be rescued.

__I__ 2. The interrogation, conducted (by three police officers,) have lasted for several hours.

_____ 3. The tenants in the apartment next to mine is giving a party this evening.

_____ 4. The president, surrounded by Secret Service agents, is trying to make his way to the podium.

_____ 5. The buildings destroyed during the fire are being rebuilt at the taxpayers' expense.

_____ 6. Because of the seriousness of the company's financial problems, the board of directors have called an emergency meeting.

_____ 7. Manufacture of the items that you requested have been discontinued because of lack of profit on those items.

_____ 8. Further development of any new ideas for future products has to be approved in advance.

_____ 9. The scheduled departure time of the trams, posted on panels throughout the terminal buildings, are going to be updated.

_____ 10. Any houses built in that development before 1970 have to be upgraded to meet current standards.

SKILL 21:   MAKE VERBS AGREE AFTER EXPRESSIONS OF QUANTITY

A particular agreement problem occurs when the subject is an expression of quantity, such as *all, most,* or *some,* followed by the preposition *of.* In this situation, the subject (*all, most,* or *some*) can be singular or plural, depending on what follows the preposition *of.*

All (of the *book*) was interesting.
SINGULAR

All (of the *books*) were interesting.
PLURAL

All (of the *information*) was interesting.
UNCOUNTABLE

In the first example the subject *all* refers to the singular noun *book,* so the correct verb is therefore the singular verb *was.* In the second example the subject *all* refers to the plural noun *books,* so the correct verb is the plural verb *were.* In the third example the subject *all* refers to the uncountable noun *information,* so the correct verb is therefore the singular verb *was.*

The following chart outlines the key information that you should understand about subject/verb agreement after expressions of quantity:

SUBJECT/VERB AGREEMENT AFTER EXPRESSIONS OF QUANTITY
all *most* *some* *half*   OF THE (OBJECT)   **V**
When an expression of quantity is the subject, the verb agrees with the object.

EXERCISE 21: Each of the following sentences has a quantity expression as the subject. Underline the subjects once and the verbs twice. Circle the objects that the verbs agree with. Then indicate if the sentences are correct (C) or incorrect (I).

_C_   1. The witnesses saw that most of the (fire) in the hills was extinguished.

_I_   2. Some of the (animals) from the zoo was released into the animal preserve.

_____   3. All of the students in the class taught by Professor Roberts is required to turn in their term papers next Monday.

_____   4. Half of the food that we are serving to the guests are still in the refrigerator.

_____   5. We believe that some of the time of the employees is going to be devoted to quality control.

_____   6. All of the witnesses in the jury trial, which lasted more than two weeks, have indicated that they believed that the defendant was guilty.

_____   7. She did not know where most of the people in the room was from.

_____   8. In spite of what was decided at the meeting, half of the procedures was not changed.

_____   9. I was sure that all of the questions on the test were correct.

_____ 10. Most of the trouble that the employees discussed at the series of meetings was resolved within a few weeks.

SKILL 22: MAKE INVERTED VERBS AGREE

We have seen that sometimes in English the subject comes after the verb. This can occur after question words (Skill 15), after place expressions (Skill 16), after negative expressions (Skill 17), after omitted conditionals (Skill 18), and after some comparisons (Skill 19). When the subject and verb are inverted, it can be difficult to locate them, and it can therefore be a problem to make them agree.

(Behind the house) was* the bicycles I wanted.
(Behind the houses) were* the bicycle I wanted.

In the first example it is easy to think that *house* is the subject, because it comes directly in front of the verb *was*. *House* is not the subject, however, because it is the object of the preposition *behind*. The subject of the sentence is *bicycles*, and the subject *bicycles* comes after the verb because of the place expression *behind the house*. Because the subject *bicycles* is plural, the verb should be changed to the plural *were*. In the second example the subject *bicycle* comes after the verb *were* because of the place expression *behind the houses*. Because the subject *bicycle* is singular, the verb should be changed to the singular *was*.

The following chart outlines the key information that you should understand about subject/verb agreement after inverted verbs:

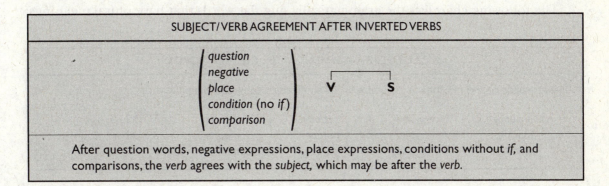

SUBJECT/VERB AGREEMENT AFTER INVERTED VERBS

question
negative
place
condition (no *if*)
comparison

V   S

After question words, negative expressions, place expressions, conditions without *if*, and comparisons, the *verb* agrees with the *subject*, which may be after the *verb*.

EXERCISE 22: Each of the following sentences contains an inverted subject and verb. Circle the word or group of words that causes the subject and verb to invert. Find the subject and verb that follow these words. Underline the subject once and the verb twice. Then indicate if the sentences are correct (C) or incorrect (I).

___C___ 1. (Only once) this morning <u>were</u> the <u>letters</u> <u>delivered</u> by the campus mail service.

___I___ 2. (Around the corner and to the right) <u>is</u> the <u>rooms</u> that have been assigned to that program.

_____ 3. What in the world is the children trying to do?

_____ 4. John would be studying the chapters were he able to get hold of the book.

_____ 5. This chapter has many more exercises than do the next one.

_____ 6. The computer programmer was unaware that there was so many mistakes in the program he had written.

_____ 7. Seldom in the history of television has two new comedies been so successful in one season.

_____ 8. How many huge mistakes have the teacher actually found in the research paper?

_____ 9. The new phone system is able to hold far more messages than was the phone system that had previously been used.

_____ 10. In the parking lot south of the stadium was the cars that were about to be towed.

Skill 23:   MAKE VERBS AGREE AFTER CERTAIN WORDS

Certain words in English are always grammatically singular, even though they might have plural meanings.

Everybody are going* to the theater.

Even though we understand from this example that a lot of people are going to the theater, *everybody* is singular and requires a singular verb. The plural verb *are going* should be changed to the singular verb *is going*.

The following chart lists the grammatically singular words that have plural meanings:

SUBJECT/VERB AGREEMENT AFTER CERTAIN WORDS
These words or expressions are grammatically singular, so they take singular verbs:

anybody	everybody	nobody	somebody	each (+ noun)
anyone	everyone	no one	someone	every (+ noun)
anything	everything	nothing	something	

EXERCISE 23: Each of the following sentences contains one of the words that are grammatically singular but have plural meanings. Underline these words once and underline the verbs twice. Then indicate if the sentences are correct (C) or incorrect (I).

___I___   1.   It is impossible to believe that somebody actually admire that man.

___C___   2.   Each of the doctors in the building needs to have a separate reception area.

_____   3.   The president felt that no one were better suited for the position of chief staff advisor.

_____   4.   Everybody participating in the fund-raiser are to turn in the tickets by 8:00.

_____   5.   Because of the low number of orders, nothing has to be done now.

_____   6.   Every time someone take unnecessary breaks, precious moments of production time are lost.

_____   7.   Anybody who goes to the top of the Empire State Building is impressed with the view.

_____   8.   Every man, woman, and child in this line are required to sign the forms in order to complete the registration process.

_____   9.   It is nice to believe that anything is possible if a person tries hard enough.

_____   10.   The company reiterated to reporters that nobody have been dismissed because of the incident.

EXERCISE (Skills 20–23): Underline the subjects once and the verbs twice in each of the following sentences. Then indicate if the sentences are correct (C) or incorrect (I).

_____   1. The contracts signed by the company has been voided because some stipulations were not met.

_____   2. Ten miles beyond the river was the farmlands that they had purchased with their life savings.

_____   3. Each package that is not properly wrapped have to be returned to the sender.

_____   4. She would not have to enter the house through the bedroom window were the keys where they were supposed to be.

_____   5. The proposal brought so much new work to the partnership that there was not enough hours to complete all of it.

_____   6. The box of cartridges for the printer have been misplaced.

_____   7. It is disconcerting to believe that every possible candidate has been rejected for one reason or another.

_____   8. Only once have there been more excitement in this city about a sporting event.

_____   9. Bobby has a bigger bicycle than does the other children in the neighborhood.

_____ 10. If nobody have bought that car from the dealer, then you should return and make another offer.

TOEFL EXERCISE (Skills 20–23): Choose the letter of the word or group of words that best completes the sentence.

1. Among bees _____ a highly elaborate form of communication.

    (A) occur
    (B) occurs
    (C) it occurs
    (D) they occur

2. _____ heated by solar energy have special collectors on the roofs to trap sunlight.

    (A) A home is
    (B) Homes are
    (C) A home
    (D) Homes

Choose the letter of the underlined word or group of words that is not correct.

_____ 3. Each number in a <u>binary</u> system <u>are</u> <u>formed</u> from <u>only two</u> symbols.
                                     A   B   C   D

_____ 4. Scientists at the medical center <u>is trying</u> <u>to determine</u> if there <u>is</u> a relationship
                                                  A   B   C
            between <u>saccharine and cancer.</u>
                         D

_____ 5. On <u>the rim</u> of the Kilauea volcano in the <u>Hawaiian Islands</u> <u>are</u> a hotel <u>called</u> the
                   A   B   C   D
            Volcano Hotel.

_____ 6. The great <u>digital</u> advances of the electronic age, such as integrated <u>circuitry</u> and a
                    A   B

microcomputer, <u>has</u> been <u>planted</u> in tiny chips.
                 C   D

_____ 7. There are many <u>frequently</u> <u>mentioned</u> reasons why one out of <u>four arrests</u> <u>involve</u> a
                          A   B   C   D

juvenile.

_____ 8. Kepler's Laws, principles outlining planetary movement, <u>was</u> <u>formulated</u> <u>based on</u>
                                                                  A   B   C

observations <u>made</u> without a telescope.
              D

_____ 9. Only with a <u>two-thirds vote</u> by both houses are the U.S. Congress <u>able</u> to override a
                      A   B   C

presidential <u>veto</u>.
              D

_____10. Of all the evidence that <u>has piled</u> up since Webster's paper was published, there is <u>no</u>
                                   A   B

<u>new ideas</u> to <u>contradict</u> his original theory.
 C   D

TOEFL REVIEW EXERCISE (Skills 1–23): Choose the letter of the word or group of words that best completes the sentence.

1. _____ several unsuccessful attempts, Robert Peary reached the North Pole on April 6, 1909.

   (A) After
   (B) He made
   (C) When
   (D) His

2. The musical instrument _____ is six feet long.

   (A) is called the bass
   (B) it is called the bass
   (C) called the bass
   (D) calls the bass

3. One problem with all languages _____ they are full of irregularities.

   (A) when
   (B) so
   (C) is that
   (D) in case

4. _____ of economic cycles been helpful in predicting turning points in cycles, they would have been used more consistently.

   (A) Psychological theories
   (B) Psychological theories have
   (C) Had psychological theories
   (D) Psychologists have theories

5. Hospital committees _____ spent weeks agonizing over which artificial kidney candidate would receive the treatments now find that the decision is out of their hands.

   (A) once
   (B) that once
   (C) have
   (D) once had

Choose the letter of the underlined word or group of words that is not correct.

_____ 6.   More than half of the children in the 1,356-member district qualifies for
           A   B   C

reduced-price or free lunches.
      D

_____ 7.   Five miles beyond the hills were a fire with its flames reaching up to the sky.
                        A   B   C   D

_____ 8.   Kettledrums, what were first played on horseback, were incorporated into the
               A   B   C   D

orchestra in the eighteenth century.

_____ 9.   When is a flag hung upside down, it is an internationally recognized symbol of distress.
             A   B   C   D

_____10.   The Museum of the Confederation in Richmond hosts an exhibition which
                                               A

documenting the origins and history of the banner that most Americans think of as
     B   C   D

the Confederate flag.

PROBLEMS WITH PARALLEL STRUCTURE

In good English an attempt should be made to make the language as even and balanced as possible. This balance is called "parallel structure." You can achieve parallel structure by making the forms of words as similar as possible. The following is an example of a sentence that is not parallel:

I like to sing and dancing.*

The problem in this sentence is not the expression *to sing*, and the problem is not the word *dancing*. The expression *to sing* is correct by itself, and the word *dancing* is correct by itself. Both of the following sentences are correct:

I like to sing.
I like dancing.

The problem in the incorrect example is that *to sing* and *dancing* are joined together in one sentence with *and*. They are different forms where it is possible to have similar forms; therefore the example is not parallel. It can be corrected in two different ways: we can make the first expression like the second, or we can make the second expression like the first.

I like to sing and to dance.
I like singing and dancing.

There are several situations in which you should be particularly careful of parallel structure. Parallel structures are required in the following situations: (1) with coordinate conjunctions, such as *and, but, or;* (2) with paired conjunctions, such as *both . . . and, either . . . or, neither . . . nor, not only . . . but also;* and (3) with comparisons.

Skill 24:   USE PARALLEL STRUCTURE WITH COORDINATE CONJUNCTIONS

The job of the coordinate conjunctions (*and, but, or*) is to join together equal expressions. In other words, what is on one side of these words must be parallel to what is on the other side. These conjunctions can join nouns, or verbs, or adjectives, or phrases, or subordinate clauses, or main clauses; they just must join together two of the same thing. Here are examples of two nouns joined by a coordinate conjunction:

> I need to talk to the manager *or* the assistant manager.
> She is not a teacher *but* a lawyer.
> You can choose from activities such as hiking *and* kayaking.

Here are examples of two verbs joined by a coordinate conjunction:

> He eats *and* sleeps only when he takes a vacation.
> She invites us to her home *but* never talks with us.
> You can stay home *or* go to the movies with us.

Here are examples of two adjectives joined by a coordinate conjunction:

> My boss is sincere *and* nice.
> The exam that he gave was short *but* difficult.
> Class can be interesting *or* boring.

Here are examples of two phrases joined by a coordinate conjunction:

> There are students in the classroom *and* in front of the building.
> The papers are on my desk *or* in the drawer.
> The checks will be ready not at noon *but* at 1:00.

Here are examples of two clauses joined by a coordinate conjunction:

> They are not interested in what you say *or* what you do.
> I am here because I have to be *and* because I want to be.
> Mr. Brown likes to go home early, *but* his wife prefers to stay late.

The following chart outlines the use of parallel structures with coordinate conjunctions:

PARALLEL STRUCTURE WITH COORDINATE CONJUNCTIONS		
(same structure)	*and* *but* *or*	(same structure)
(same structure), (same structure),	*and* *but* *or*	(same structure)

EXERCISE 24: Each of the following sentences contains words or groups of words that should be parallel. Circle the word that indicates that the sentence should have parallel parts. Underline the parts that should be parallel. Then indicate if the sentences are correct (C) or incorrect (I).

__I__	1.	She held jobs as <u>a typist</u>, <u>a housekeeper</u>, (and) <u>in a restaurant</u>.
__C__	2.	The report you are looking for could be <u>in the file</u> (or) <u>on the desk</u>.
_____	3.	She works very hard but usually gets below-average grades.
_____	4.	The speaker introduced himself, told several interesting anecdotes, and finishing with an emotional plea.
_____	5.	You should know when the program starts and how many units you must complete.
_____	6.	The term paper he wrote was rather short but very impressive.
_____	7.	She suggested taking the plane this evening or that we go by train tomorrow.
_____	8.	The dean or the assistant dean will inform you of when and where you should apply for your diploma.
_____	9.	There are papers to file, reports to type, and those letters should be answered.
_____	10.	The manager needed a quick but thorough response.

SKILL 25:   USE PARALLEL STRUCTURE WITH PAIRED CONJUNCTIONS

The paired conjunctions *both . . . and, either . . . or, neither . . . nor,* and *not only . . . but also* require parallel structures.

> I know *both* <u>where you went</u> *and* <u>what you did</u>.
> *Either* <u>Mark</u> *or* <u>Sue</u> has the book.
> The tickets are *neither* <u>in my pocket</u> *nor* <u>in my purse</u>.
> He is *not only* <u>an excellent student</u> *but also* <u>an outstanding athlete</u>.

The following is not parallel and must be corrected:

> He wants *either* <u>to go by train</u> *or* <u>by plane</u>*.

It is not correct because *to go by train* is not parallel to *by plane*. It can be corrected in several ways.

> He wants *either* <u>to go by train</u> *or* <u>to go by plane</u>.
> He wants to go *either* <u>by train</u> *or* <u>by plane</u>.
> He wants to go by *either* <u>train</u> *or* <u>plane</u>.

When you are using these paired conjunctions, be sure that the correct parts are used together. The following are incorrect:

> I want *both* <u>this book</u> *or** <u>that one</u>.
> *Either* <u>Sam</u> *nor** <u>Sue</u> is taking the course.

These sentences are incorrect because the wrong parts of the paired conjunctions are used together. In the first example, *and* should be used with *both*. In the second example, *or* should be used with *either*.

The following chart outlines the use of parallel structure with paired conjunctions:

PARALLEL STRUCTURE WITH PAIRED CONJUNCTIONS			
both either neither not only	(same structure)	and or nor but also	(same structure)

EXERCISE 25: Each of the following sentences contains words or groups of words that should be parallel. Circle the word or words that indicate that the sentence should have parallel parts. Underline the parts that should be parallel. Then indicate if the sentences are correct (C) or incorrect (I).

_I_ 1. According to the syllabus, you can (either) write a paper (or) you can take an exam.

_C_ 2. It would be (both) noticed (and) appreciated if you could finish the work before you leave.

_____ 3. She would like neither to see a movie or to go bowling.

_____ 4. Either the manager or her assistant can help you with your refund.

_____ 5. She wants not only to take a trip to Europe but she also would like to travel to Asia.

_____ 6. He could correct neither what you said nor you wrote.

_____ 7. Both the tailor or the laundress could fix the damage to the dress.

_____ 8. He not only called the police department but also called the fire department.

_____ 9. You can graduate either at the end of the fall semester or you can graduate at the end of the spring semester.

_____ 10. The movie was neither amusing nor was it interesting.

SKILL 26:   USE PARALLEL STRUCTURE WITH COMPARISONS

When you make a comparison, you point out the similarities or differences between two things, and those similarities or differences must be in parallel form. You can recognize a comparison showing how two things are different from the *-er . . . than* or the *more . . . than*.

My school is farth*er than* your school.
To be rich is bett*er than* to be poor.
What is written is *more* easily understood *than* what is spoken.

A comparison showing how two things are the same might contain *as . . . as* or expressions such as *the same as* or *similar to*.

> Their car is *as* big *as* a small house.
> Renting those apartments costs about *the same as* leasing them.
> The work that I did is *similar to* the work that you did.

The following chart outlines the use of parallel structures with comparisons:

PARALLEL STRUCTURE WITH COMPARISONS		
(same structure)	more ... than -er ... than less ... than as ... as the same ... as similar ... to	(same structure)

EXERCISE 26: Each of the following sentences contains words or groups of words that should be parallel. Circle the word or words that indicate that the sentence should have parallel parts. Underline the parts that should be parallel. Then indicate if each sentence is correct (C) or incorrect (I).

___C___ 1. His <u>research</u> for the thesis was (more useful than) <u>hers</u>.

___I___ 2. <u>Dining</u> in a restaurant is (more fun than) <u>to eat</u> at home.

_____ 3. I want a new secretary who is as efficient as the previous one.

_____ 4. What you do today should be the same as did yesterday.

_____ 5. This lesson is more difficult than we had before.

_____ 6. You have less homework than they do.

_____ 7. What you do has more effect than what you say.

_____ 8. Music in your country is quite similar to my country.

_____ 9. The collection of foreign journals in the university library is more extensive than the high school library.

_____ 10. How to buy a used car can be as difficult as buying a new car.

EXERCISE (Skills 24–26): Circle the word or words that indicate that the sentence should have parallel parts. Underline the parts that should be parallel. Then indicate if the sentences are correct (C) or incorrect (I).

_____   1. After retirement he plans on traveling to exotic locations, dine in the finest restaurants, and playing a lot of golf.

_____   2. She was both surprised by and pleased with the seminar.

_____   3. What came after the break was even more boring than had come before.

_____   4. He would find the missing keys neither under the bed or behind the sofa.

_____   5. Depending on the perspective of the viewer, the film was considered laudable, mediocrity, or horrendous.

_____   6. He exercised not only in the morning, but he also exercised every afternoon.

_____   7. Working four days per week is much more relaxing than working five days per week.

_____   8. Sam is always good-natured, generous, and helps you.

_____   9. Either you have to finish the project, or the contract will be canceled.

_____   10. The courses that you are required to take are more important than the courses that you choose.

TOEFL EXERCISE (Skills 24–26): Choose the letter of the word or group of words that best completes the sentence.

1. Truman Capote's _In Cold Blood_ is neither journalistically accurate _____.

    (A) a piece of fiction
    (B) nor a fictitious work
    (C) or written in a fictitious way
    (D) nor completely fictitious

2. Vitamin C is necessary for the prevention and _____ of scurvy.

    (A) it cures
    (B) cures
    (C) cure
    (D) for curing

3. A baby's development is influenced by both heredity and _____.

    (A) by environmental factors
    (B) environmentally
    (C) the influence of the environment
    (D) environment

4. Because bone loss occurs earlier in women than _____, the effects of osteoporosis are more apparent in women.

    (A) men do
    (B) in men
    (C) as men
    (D) similar to men

Choose the letter of the underlined word or group of words that is not correct.

_____ 5. Fire <u>extinguishers</u> <u>can contain</u> liquefied gas, dry chemicals, <u>or</u> <u>watery</u>.
              A   B   C D

_____ 6. The U.S. Congress <u>consists</u> <u>of</u> both the Senate <u>as well as</u> the House of Representatives.
                             A B   C   D

_____ 7. The prison <u>population</u> in this state, <u>now at an all time high</u>, is <u>higher</u> than <u>any state</u>.
                       A   B   C   D

_____ 8. A <u>well-composed</u> baroque opera <u>achieves</u> a delicate balance by <u>focusing</u> alternately
               A   B   C

on the aural, visual, emotional, and <u>philosophy</u> elements.
                                     D

_____ 9. Manufacturers <u>may use</u> food additives for <u>preserving</u>, to color, to flavor, or <u>to fortify</u>
                       A   B   C

<u>foods</u>.
 D

_____10. A <u>bankruptcy</u> <u>may be</u> either <u>voluntary</u> <u>nor</u> involuntary.
         A   B   C   D

TOEFL REVIEW EXERCISE (Skills 1–26): Choose the letter of the word or group of words that best completes the sentence.

1. The growth of hair _____ cyclical process, with phases of activity and inactivity.

   (A) it is
   (B) is a
   (C) which is
   (D) a regular

2. The fire _____ to have started in the furnace under the house.

   (A) is believed
   (B) that is believed
   (C) they believe
   (D) that they believe

3. In Roman numerals, _____ symbols for numeric values.

   (A) are letters of the alphabet
   (B) letters of the alphabet are
   (C) which uses letters of the alphabet
   (D) in which letters of the alphabet are

4. The legal systems of most countries can be classified _____ common law or civil law.

   (A) as either
   (B) either as
   (C) either to
   (D) to either

5. One difference between mathematics and language is that mathematics is precise _____.

   (A) language is not
   (B) while language is not
   (C) but language not
   (D) while is language

6. Your criticism of the three short stories should not be less than 2,000 words, nor _____ more than 3,000.

   (A) should it be
   (B) it should be
   (C) it is
   (D) should be it

Choose the letter of the underlined word or group of words that is not correct.

_____ 7. In 1870, the attorney general <u>was made</u> head of the Department of Justice, given an
                                         A

enlarged staff, and <u>endow</u> with <u>clear-cut</u> law-enforcement <u>functions</u>.
        B   C   D

_____ 8. The General Sherman Tree, <u>the largest</u> of all the giant sequoias, <u>are</u> <u>reputed</u> to be the
                                     A   B   C

world's largest <u>living</u> thing.
                 D

_____ 9. The skeleton of a shark <u>is made</u> of <u>cartilage</u> rather than <u>having</u> bone.
                                   A   B   C   D

_____10. At least one sample <u>of each of</u> the brands <u>contains</u> measurable amounts of aflatoxin,
                               A   B

and <u>there is</u> three <u>which exceed</u> the maximum.
     C   D

PROBLEMS WITH COMPARATIVES AND SUPERLATIVES _____

Sentences with incorrect comparatives and superlatives can appear on the TOEFL test. It is therefore important for you to know how to do the following: (1) form the comparative and superlative correctly; (2) use the comparative and superlative correctly; and (3) use the irregular *-er, -er* structure that has been appearing frequently on the TOEFL test.

SKILL 27:   FORM COMPARATIVES AND SUPERLATIVES CORRECTLY

The problem with some of the comparative and superlative sentences on the TOEFL test is that the comparative or superlative is formed incorrectly. You should therefore understand how to form the comparative and superlative to answer such questions correctly.

The comparative is formed with either *-er* or *more* and *than*. In the comparative, *-er* is used with short adjectives such as *tall*, and *more* is used with longer adjectives such as *beautiful*.

> Bob is tall*er than* Ron.
> Sally is *more* beautiful *than* Sharon.

The superlative is formed with *the*, either *-est* or *most*, and sometimes *in, of*, or a *that*-clause. In the superlative, *-est* is used with short adjectives such as *tall*, and *most* is used with longer adjectives such as *beautiful*.

> Bob is *the* tall*est* man *in* the room.
> Sally is *the most* beautiful *of* all the women at the party.
> The spider over there is *the* larg*est* one *that* I have ever seen.
> *The* fast*est* runner wins the race.   (no *in, of*, or *that*)

The following chart outlines the possible forms of comparatives and superlatives:

THE FORM OF COMPARATIVES AND SUPERLATIVES		
COMPARATIVE	*more* (long adjective) (short adjective) + *er*	*than*
SUPERLATIVE	*the* *most* (long adjective) (short adjective) + *est*	maybe *in, of, that*

EXERCISE 27: Each of the following sentences contains a comparative or superlative. Circle the comparative or superlative. Then indicate if the sentences are correct (C) or incorrect (I).

__I__   1. Oxygen is (abundanter than) nitrogen.

__C__   2. The directions to the exercise say to choose (the most appropriate) response.

_____   3. The lesson you are studying now is the most importantest lesson that you will have.

_____   4. Fashions this year are shorter and more colorful than they were last year.

_____   5. The professor indicated that Anthony's research paper was more long than the other students' papers.

_____   6. Alaska is the coldest than all the states in the United States.

_____   7. The workers on the day shift are more rested than the workers on the night shift.

_____   8. She was more happier this morning than she had been yesterday.

_____   9. The quarterback on this year's football team is more versatile than the quarterback on last year's team.

_____   10. She always tries to do the best and most efficient job that she can do.

Skill 28: USE COMPARATIVES AND SUPERLATIVES CORRECTLY

Another problem with the comparative and superlative on the TOEFL test is that they can be used incorrectly. The comparative and superlative have different uses, and you should understand these different uses to answer such questions correctly. The comparative is used to compare two equal things.

> The history class is *larger than* the math class.
> Mary is *more intelligent than* Sue.

In the first example *the history class* is being compared with *the math class*. In the second example *Mary* is being compared with *Sue*.

The superlative is used when there are more than two items to compare and you want to show the one that is the best, the biggest, or in some way the most outstanding.

> The history class is *the largest* in the school.
> Mary is *the most intelligent* of all the students in the class.

In the first example *the history class* is compared with all the other classes in the school, and the history class is larger than each of the other classes. In the second example, *Mary* is compared with all the other students in the class, and Mary is more intelligent than each of the other students.

The following chart outlines the uses of comparatives and superlatives:

THE USES OF COMPARATIVES AND SUPERLATIVES
The COMPARATIVE is used to compare *two equal things*.
The SUPERLATIVE is used to show which *one of many* is in some way the most outstanding.

EXERCISE 28: Each of the following sentences contains a comparative or superlative. Circle the comparative or superlative. Then indicate if the sentences are correct (C) or incorrect (I).

___C___ 1. Harvard is probably (the most prestigious) university in the United States.

___I___ 2. Rhonda is (more hard working) of the class.

_____ 3. The engineers hired this year have more experience than those hired last year.

_____ 4. The graduate assistant informed us that the first exam is the most difficult of the two.

_____ 5. He bought the more powerful stereo speakers that he could find.

_____ 6. The afternoon seminar was much more interesting than the morning lecture.

_____ 7. The food in this restaurant is the best of the restaurant we visited last week.

_____ 8. The plants that have been sitting in the sunny window are far healthier than the other plants.

_____ 9. The photocopies are the darkest that they have ever been.

_____ 10. The first journal article is the longest of the second article.

SKILL 29:   USE THE IRREGULAR *-ER, -ER* STRUCTURE CORRECTLY

An irregular comparative structure that has been appearing frequently on the TOEFL test consists of two parallel comparatives introduced by *the*.

> *The harder* he tried, *the further* he fell behind.
> *The older* the children are, *the more* their parents expect from them.

The first example contains the two parallel comparatives *the harder* and *the further*. The second example contains the two parallel comparatives *the older* and *the more*.

In this type of sentence, *the* and the comparison can be followed by a number of different structures.

> *The more* children you have, *the bigger* the house you need.
> *The harder* you work, *the more* you accomplish.
> *The greater* the experience, *the higher* the salary.

In the first example, *the more* is followed by the noun *children* and the subject and verb *you have*, while *the bigger* is followed by the noun *the house* and the subject and verb *you need*. In the second example, *the harder* is followed by the subject and verb *you work*, while *the more* is followed by the subject and verb *you accomplish*. In the third example, *the greater* is followed only by the noun *the experience*, while *the higher* is followed only by the noun *the salary*. You should note that this last example does not even contain a verb, yet it is a correct structure in English.

The following chart outlines this irregular *-er, -er* structure:

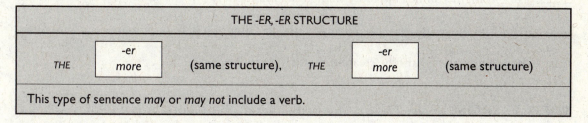

THE *-ER, -ER* STRUCTURE					
THE	-er / more	(same structure),	THE	-er / more	(same structure)
This type of sentence *may* or *may not* include a verb.					

EXERCISE 29: Each of the following sentences contains the irregular *-er, -er* structure. Circle the two comparisons with *the*. Underline the parts that should be parallel. Then indicate if the sentences are correct (C) or incorrect (I).

___I___ 1. (The hotter) the food is, (harder) it is to eat.

___C___ 2. (The warmer) the weather, (the greater) the attendance at the outdoor concert.

_____ 3. The more you say, the worst the situation will be.

_____ 4. The more time they have to play, the happier the children are.

_____ 5. The thicker the walls, the noise that comes through is less.

_____ 6. If you run faster, the more quickly you'll arrive.

_____ 7. The more you use the phone, the higher the bill will be.

_____ 8. The harder you serve, the easier it is to win the point.

_____ 9. The earliest you send in your tax forms, the sooner you will receive your refund.

_____ 10. The more people there are at the party, you'll have a good time.

EXERCISE (Skills 27–29): Circle the comparatives and superlatives in the following sentences. Then indicate if the sentences are correct (C) or incorrect (I).

_____   1. The coffee is more stronger today than it was yesterday.

_____   2. The tree that was struck by lightning had been the tallest of the two trees we had in the yard.

_____   3. He will buy the most fuel-efficient car that he can afford.

_____   4. The closest it gets to summer, the longer the days are.

_____   5. The business department is bigger of the departments in the university.

_____   6. I really do not want to live in the Southeast because it is one of the most hot areas in the United States.

_____   7. It is preferable to use the most efficient and most effective method that you can.

_____   8. Tonight's dinner was more filling than last night's.

_____   9. The sooner the exam is scheduled, the less time you have to prepare.

_____   10. The house is now the cleanest that it has ever been.

TOEFL EXERCISE (Skills 27–29): Choose the letter of the word or group of words that best completes the sentence.

1. The speed of light is _____ the speed of sound.

   (A) faster
   (B) much faster than
   (C) the fastest
   (D) as fast

2. The use of detail is _____ method of developing a controlling idea, and almost all students employ this method.

   (A) more common
   (B) common
   (C) most common
   (D) the most common

3. _____ in Stevenson's landscapes, the more vitality and character the paintings seem to possess.

   (A) The brushwork is loose
   (B) The looser brushwork
   (C) The loose brushwork is
   (D) The looser the brushwork is

Choose the letter of the underlined word or group of words that is not correct.

_____ 4. Certain types of snakes <u>have been known</u> to survive <u>fasts</u> more <u>as</u> a year long.
                          A   B   C   D

_____ 5. The grizzly bear, <u>which can</u> grow up to eight feet tall, <u>has been</u> called <u>a</u> <u>more</u>
                          A   B   C   D

dangerous animal of North America.

——— 6. Climate, soil type, and availability of water are the most critical factors than
                                      A   B   C

selecting the best type of grass for a lawn.
               D

——— 7. Peter Abelard, a logician and theologian, was the controversialest teacher of his age.
                              A   B   C   D

——— 8. Protein molecules are the most complex than the molecules of carbohydrates.
                            A   B   C   D

——— 9. The leek, a member of the lily family, has a mildest taste than the onion.
                  A   B   C   D

———10. The widely used natural fiber of all is cotton.
              A   B   C   D

TOEFL REVIEW EXERCISE (Skills 1–29): Choose the letter of the word or group of words that best completes the sentence.

1. ——, a liberal arts college specifically for deaf people, is located in Washington, D.C.

    (A) Gallaudet College
    (B) Gallaudet College is
    (C) About Gallaudet College
    (D) Because of Gallaudet College

2. —— varieties of dogs at the show, including spaniels, poodles, and collies.

    (A) The several
    (B) Those
    (C) Several
    (D) There were several

3. While the discovery that many migratory songbirds can thrive in deforested wintering spots ——, the fact remains that these birds are dying at unusual rates.

    (A) it is heartening
    (B) hearten
    (C) heartening
    (D) is heartening

Choose the letter of the underlined word or group of words that is not correct.

——— 4. The coyote is somewhat smaller in size that a timber wolf.
                            A   B   C D

——— 5. The weather reports all showed that there were a tremendous storm front moving in.
                        A   B   C   D

——— 6. Seldom cactus plants are found outside of North America.
                  A   B   C   D

——— 7. In a basketball game a player what is fouled receives one or two free throws.
                                      A   B   C   D

——— 8. Until recently, California was largest producer of oranges in the United States.
              A   B   C   D

_____ 9.   An understanding of <u>engineering theories</u> and problems <u>are</u> impossible until basic
                             A   B

arithmetic <u>is</u> fully <u>mastered</u>.
           C   D

_____ 10.   The earliest <u>the</u> CVS (chorionic villus sampling) <u>procedure</u> in the pregnancy, the
             A B   C

greater the <u>risk to</u> the baby.
            D

PROBLEMS WITH THE FORM OF THE VERB_____

It is common in the Written Expression part of the TOEFL test for the verbs to be formed incorrectly. Therefore, you should check the form of the verb carefully. You should be familiar with the following verb forms: the base form, the present tense, the present participle, and the past participle. The following are examples of each of these verb forms as they are used in this text:

BASE FORM	PRESENT	PRESENT PARTICIPLE	PAST	PAST PARTICIPLE
walk	walk(s)	walking	walked	walked
hear	hear(s)	hearing	heard	heard
cook	cook(s)	cooking	cooked	cooked
sing	sing(s)	singing	sang	sung
come	come(s)	coming	came	come
begin	begin(s)	beginning	began	begun

You should be particularly aware of the following three problematic situations with verbs because they are the most common and the easiest to correct: (1) check what comes after *have;* (2) check what comes after *be;* and (3) check what comes after *will, would,* and other modals.

> NOTE: A more complete list of verb forms and an exercise to practice their use are included at the back of the text in Appendix F. You may want to complete this exercise before you continue with skills 30 through 32.

SKILL 30:   AFTER *HAVE*, USE THE PAST PARTICIPLE

Whenever you see the verb *have* in any of its forms (*have, has, having, had*), be sure that the verb that follows it is in the past participle form.

They *had walk** to school.	(should be *had walked*)
We *have see** the show.	(should be *have seen*)
He *has took** the test.	(should be *has taken*)
*Having ate**, he went to school.	(should be *Having eaten*)
She *should have did** the work.	(should be *should have done*)

In addition, you should be sure that if you have a subject and a past participle, you also have the verb *have*. This problem is particularly common with those verbs (such as *sing*, *sang*, *sung*) that change from present to past to past participle by changing only the vowel.

My friend *sung** in the choir.   (should be *sang* or *has sung*)
He *become** angry at his friend.   (should be *became* or *has become*)
The boat *sunk** in the ocean.   (should be *sank* or *has sunk*)

The following chart outlines the use of verb forms after *have*:

VERB FORMS AFTER *HAVE*
HAVE   +   past participle

EXERCISE 30: Each of the following sentences contains a verb in the past or a past participle. Underline the verbs or past participles twice. Then indicate if the sentences are correct (C) or incorrect (I).

___I___ 1. The young girl <u>drunk</u> a glass of milk.

___C___ 2. Before she <u>left</u>, she <u>had asked</u> her mother for permission.

_____ 3. Having finished the term paper, he began studying for the exam.

_____ 4. The secretary has broke her typewriter.

_____ 5. The installer should have completes the task more quickly.

_____ 6. He has often become angry during meetings.

_____ 7. She has rarely rode her horse in the park.

_____ 8. Having saw the film, he was quite disappointed.

_____ 9. Tom has thought about taking that job.

_____ 10. You might have respond more effectively.

SKILL 31:   AFTER *BE*, USE THE PRESENT PARTICIPLE OR THE PAST PARTICIPLE

The verb *be* in any of its forms (*am, is, are, was, were, be, been, being*) can be followed by another verb. This verb should be in the present participle or the past participle form.

We *are do** our homework.   (should be *are doing*)
The homework *was do** early.   (should be *was done*)
Tom *is take** the book.   (should be *is taking*)
The book *was take** by Tom.   (should be *was taken*)

The following chart outlines the use of verb forms after *be*:

VERB FORMS AFTER *BE*
BE   +   (1) present participle (2) past particple

EXERCISE 31: Each of the following sentences contains a verb formed with *be*. Underline the verbs twice. Then indicate if the sentences are correct (C) or incorrect (I).

__I__   1.   At 12:00 Sam <u>is eat</u> his lunch.

__C__   2.   We <u>are meeting</u> them later today.

_____   3.   The message was took by the receptionist.

_____   4.   Being heard was extremely important to him.

_____   5.   The Smiths are build their house on some property that they own in the desert.

_____   6.   It had been noticed that some staff members were late.

_____   7.   The report should have been submit by noon.

_____   8.   Are the two companies merge into one?

_____   9.   He could be taking four courses this semester.

_____ 10.   The score information has been duplicates on the back-up disk.

SKILL 32:   AFTER *WILL, WOULD,* OR OTHER MODALS, USE THE BASE FORM OF THE VERB

Whenever you see a modal, such as *will, would, shall, should, can, could, may, might,* or *must,* you should be sure that the verb that follows it is in its base form.

The boat *will leaving** at 3:00.	(should be *will leave*)
The doctor *may arrives** soon.	(should be *may arrive*)
The students *must taken** the exam.	(should be *must take*)

The following chart outlines the use of verb forms after modals:

VERBS FORMS AFTER MODALS		
MODAL	+	main form of the verb

EXERCISE 32: Each of the following sentences contains a verb formed with a modal. Underline the verbs twice. Then indicate if the sentences are correct (C) or incorrect (I).

__C__   1.   The salesclerk <u>might lower</u> the price.

__I__   2.   The television movie <u>will finishes</u> in a few minutes.

_____   3.   Should everyone arrive by 8:00?

_____   4.   The method for organizing files can be improved.

_____   5. The machine may clicks off if it is overused.

_____   6. Every morning the plants must be watered.

_____   7. The houses with ocean views could sell for considerably more.

_____   8. Would anyone liked to see that movie?

_____   9. I do not know when it will depart.

_____   10. She will work on the project only if she can has a full-time secretary.

EXERCISE (Skills 30–32): Underline the verbs twice in the following sentences. Then indicate if the sentences are correct (C) or incorrect (I).

_____   1. I have gave you all the money that I have.

_____   2. The articles were put in the newspaper before he was able to stop production.

_____   3. All the tickets for the concert might already be sold.

_____   4. He was so thirsty that he drunk several large glasses of water.

_____   5. The deposit will has to be paid before the apartment can be rented.

_____   6. He objects to being held without bail.

_____   7. Having completed the first chapter of the manuscript, she decided to take a break.

_____   8. If Steve had really wanted to pass his exam, he would has studied much more.

_____   9. He thought that he should have be invited to attend the conference.

_____   10. Before the speaker finished, many guests had rose from their seats and started for the door.

TOEFL EXERCISE (Skills 30–32): Choose the letter of the underlined word or group of words that is not correct.

_____   1. *Alice in Wonderland,* first published in 1865, has since being translated into thirty
                              A   B   C   D

          languages.

_____   2. The Peace Corps was establish on March 1, 1961, by then President John F. Kennedy.
                A   B   C   D

_____   3. The advisor told himself, while listening to the speech, that a dozen other reporters
                      A   B

          would has already asked that question.
             C   D

_____ 4. At the start of the American Revolution, lanterns were hung in the Old North Church
           A   B   C

as a signal that the British were came.
                                   D

_____ 5. Before he died, Linus Pauling had wins two Nobel Prizes: the 1954 Nobel Prize
                                     A   B   C

in Chemistry and the 1962 Nobel Peace Prize.
   D

_____ 6. On the huge Ferris wheel constructed for a world exhibition in Chicago in 1893,
              A   B

each of the thirty-six cabs could held sixty people.
     C   D

_____ 7. To overcome rejection of a skin graft, a system for matching donor and recipient
              A   B   C

tissues has be developed.
          D

_____ 8. Nails are commonly make of steel but also can contain substances such as aluminum
              A   B   C   D

or brass.

_____ 9. A patient suffering from amnesia may had partial or total loss of memory.
                   A   B   C   D

_____10. The idea of using pure nicotine to help smokers stop was first tries in the mid-1980s
                         A   B   C   D

with the nicotine-laced chewing gum Nicotette.

TOEFL REVIEW EXERCISE (Skills 1–32): Choose the letter of the word or group of words that best completes the sentence.

1. _____ separates Manhattan's Upper East Side from the Upper West Side.

   (A) Central Park
   (B) Where Central Park
   (C) Where is Central Park
   (D) Central Park which

2. Bioluminescent animals _____ the water or on land.

   (A) live
   (B) are living either
   (C) they are found in
   (D) can be found in

3. The purpose of a labor union is to improve the working conditions, _____, and pay of its members.

   (A) jobs are secure
   (B) to be secure
   (C) job security
   (D) the job's security

4. When _____ on July 4, 1789, the federal tariff, intended by the Founding Fathers to be the government's primary source of revenue, was remarkably evenhanded.

   (A) was first enacted
   (B) first enacted
   (C) was enacted first
   (D) it first

5. _____ inclined to push for such a reduction, it would probably not be successful.

   (A) The Office of Management
   (B) The Office of Management was
   (C) In the Office of Management
   (D) Were the Office of Management

Choose the letter of the underlined word or group of words that is not correct.

_____ 6.   Helium has the most low boiling point of all substances.
                      A   B   C   D

_____ 7.   There is twenty-six bones in the human foot, fourteen of them in the toes.
                   A   B   C   D

_____ 8.   Extension of the countdown hold to fourteen hours was order to give crews
                                              A   B

more time to repair wiring and clear away equipment.
         C   D

_____ 9.   The study demonstrates that neither experience or awareness will improve chances
                          A   B   C   D

of success.

_____ 10.   Some of the eye movements used in reading is actually unnecessary.
                                              A   B   C   D

PROBLEMS WITH THE USE OF THE VERB_____

Many different problems in using the correct verb tense are possible in English. However, four specific problems occur frequently on the TOEFL test, so you need to pay careful attention to these four: (1) knowing when to use the past with the present, (2) using *had* and *have* correctly, (3) using the correct tense with time expressions, and (4) using the correct tense with *will* and *would*.

SKILL 33:   KNOW WHEN TO USE THE PAST WITH THE PRESENT

One verb tense problem that is common both in student writing and on the TOEFL test is the switch from the past tense to the present tense for no particular reason. Often when a sentence has both a past tense and a present tense, the sentence is incorrect.

> He *took* the money when he *wants** it.

This sentence says that *he took the money* (in the past) *when he wants it* (in the present). This meaning does not make any sense; it is impossible to do something in the past as a result of something you want in the present. This sentence can be corrected in several ways, depending on the desired meaning.

> He *took* the money when he *wanted* it.
> He *takes* the money when he *wants* it.

The first example means that *he took the money* (in the past) *when he wanted it* (in the past). This meaning is logical, and the sentence is correct. The second example means that *he takes the money* (habitually) *when he wants it* (habitually). This meaning is also logical, and the second example is also correct.

It is necessary to point out, however, that it is possible for a logical sentence in English to have both the past and the present tense.

I know that he *took* the money yesterday.

The meaning of this sentence is logical: *I know* (right now, in the present) that *he took the money* (yesterday, in the past). You can see from this example that it is possible for an English sentence to have both the past and the present tense. The error you need to avoid is the switch from the past to the present for no particular reason. Therefore, when you see a sentence on the TOEFL test with both the past and the present tense, you must check the meaning of the sentence carefully to see if it is logical in English.

The following chart outlines the use of the past tense with the present tense in English:

USING THE PAST WITH THE PRESENT
1. If you see a sentence with one verb in the *past* and one verb in the *present,* the sentence is probably incorrect.
2. However, it is possible for a correct sentence to have both *past* and *present* together.
3. If you see the *past* and *present* together, you must *check the meaning* to determine whether or not the sentence is correct.

EXERCISE 33: Each of the following sentences has at least one verb in the past and one verb in the present. Underline the verbs twice and decide if the meanings are logical. Then indicate if the sentences are correct (C) or incorrect (I).

_ I _   1. I tell him the truth when he asked me the question.

_ C _   2. I understand that you were angry.

_____   3. When he was a child, he always goes to the circus.

_____   4. Last semester he reads seven books and wrote five papers.

_____   5. Steve wakes up early every morning because he went to work early.

_____   6. Mark studied at the American University when he is in Washington, D.C.

_____   7. He is telling the teacher why he did not have time to finish his homework.

_____   8. He put some money in his account when he goes to the bank.

_____   9. Tom keeps studying hard because he intended to go to dental school.

_____   10. She is where she is today because she worked hard when she was a student.

SKILL 34:   USE *HAVE* AND *HAD* CORRECTLY

Two tenses that are often confused are the present perfect (*have* + past participle) and the past perfect (*had* + past participle). These two tenses have completely different uses, and you should understand how to differentiate them.

The present perfect (*have* + past participle) refers to the period of time *from the past until the present.*

> Sue *has lived* in Los Angeles for ten years.

This sentence means that Sue has lived in Los Angeles for the ten years up to now. According to this sentence, Sue is still living in Los Angeles.

Because the present perfect refers to a period of time from the past until the present, it is not correct in a sentence that indicates past only.

> *At the start of the nineteenth century,* Thomas Jefferson *has become** president of the United States. Every time Jim *worked* on his car, he *has improved** it.

In the first example, the phrase *at the start of the nineteenth century* indicates that the action of the verb was in the past only, but the verb indicates the period of time from the past until the present. Since this is not logical, the sentence is not correct. The verb in the first example should be *became.* The second example indicates that Jim *worked* on his car in the past, but he improved it in the period from the past until the present. This idea also is not logical. The verb in the second example should be the simple past *improved.*

The past perfect (*had* + past participle) refers to a period of time *that started in the past and ended in the past, before something else happened in the past.*

> Sue *had lived* in Los Angeles for ten years when she *moved* to San Diego.

This sentence means that Sue lived in Los Angeles for ten years in the past before she moved to San Diego in the past. She no longer lives in Los Angeles.

Because the past perfect begins in the past and ends in the past, it is generally not correct in the same sentence with the present tense.

> Tom *had finished* the exam when the teacher *collects** the papers.

This sentence indicates that *Tom finished the exam* (in the past) and that action ended *when the teacher collects the papers* (in the present). This is not logical, so the sentence is not correct. Tom finished the exam (in the past), and the action of finishing the exam ended when the teacher collected the papers. Therefore, the second verb in this example should be in the past tense, *collected.*

The following chart outlines the uses of the present perfect and the past perfect:

USING (*HAVE* + PAST PARTICIPLE) AND (*HAD* + PAST PARTICIPLE)			
TENSE	FORM	MEANING	USE
present perfect	*have* + past participle	past up to now	not with a past tense**
past perfect	*had* + past participle	before past up to past	not with a present tense
**Except when the time expression *since* is part of the sentence (see Skill 35).			

EXERCISE 34: Each of the following sentences contains *had* or *have*. Underline the verbs twice and decide if the meanings are logical. Then indicate if the sentences are correct (C) or incorrect (I).

   _C_   1.   I have always liked the designs that are on the cover.

   _I_   2.   Because her proposal had been rejected, she is depressed.

   ___   3.   The students have registered for classes before the semester started.

   ___   4.   When she had purchased the car, she contacted the insurance agent.

   ___   5.   He said that he had finished the typing when you finish the reports.

   ___   6.   She has enjoyed herself every time that she has gone to the zoo.

   ___   7.   He drove to the post office after he had finished preparing the package.

   ___   8.   After the votes were counted, it had been determined that Steve was the winner.

   ___   9.   Last night all the waiters and waitresses have worked overtime.

   ___ 10.   He had fastened his seat belt before the airplane took off.

Skill 35:   USE THE CORRECT TENSE WITH TIME EXPRESSIONS

Often in sentences in the Written Expression section of the TOEFL test there is a time expression that clearly indicates what verb tense is needed in the sentence.

> We moved to New York *in 1970*.
> We had left there *by 1980*.
> We have lived in San Francisco *since 1982*.

In the first example, the time expression *in 1970* indicates that the verb should be in the simple past (*moved*). In the second example, the time expression *by 1980* indicates that the verb should be in the past perfect (*had left*). In the third example, the time expression *since* 1982 indicates that the verb should be in the present perfect (*have lived*).

Some additional time expressions that clearly indicate the correct tense are *ago*, *last*, and *lately*.

> She got a job *two years ago*.
> She started working *last week*.
> She has worked very hard *lately*.

In the first example, the time expression *two years ago* indicates that the verb should be in the simple past (*got*). In the second example, the time expression *last week* indicates that the verb should be in the simple past (*started*). In the third example, the time expression *lately* indicates that the verb should be in the present perfect (*has worked*).

The following chart lists time expressions that indicate the correct verb tense:

USING CORRECT TENSES WITH TIME EXPRESSIONS		
PAST PERFECT	SIMPLE PAST	PRESENT PERFECT
by (1920)	(two years) ago last (year) in (1920)	since (1920) lately

EXERCISE 35: Each of the following sentences contains a time expression. Circle the time expressions and underline the verbs twice. Then indicate if the sentences are correct (C) or incorrect (I).

__C__   1.   The phone <u>rang</u> incessantly (last night.)

__I__   2.   They <u>have finished</u> contacting everyone (by 4:00 yesterday.)

_____   3.   The Pilgrims have arrived in the New World in 1612.

_____   4.   Since the new law was passed, it has been difficult to estimate taxes.

_____   5.   The cashier put the money into the account two hours ago.

_____   6.   All the votes have been counted last week.

_____   7.   The students are writing many compositions lately.

_____   8.   The Senate votes on the law to ban cigarette smoking in public in 1990.

_____   9.   By the time the main course was served, all the guests had arrived and been seated.

_____   10.   I had not done much more work since I talked to you on Wednesday.

SKILL 36:   USE THE CORRECT TENSE WITH *WILL* AND *WOULD*

Certain combinations of verbs are very common in English. One is the combination of the simple present and *will*.

> I *know* that they *will arrive* soon.
> It *is* certain that he *will graduate.*

Another combination that is quite common is the combination of the simple past and *would*.

> I *knew* that he *would arrive.*
> It *was* certain that he *would graduate.*

It is important to stress that in the combination discussed here, the present should be used with *will* and the past should be used with *would*; they generally should not be mixed.

The common errors that must generally be avoided are the combination of the past with *will* and the combination of the present with *would*.

> I *know* that he *would** arrive soon.
> It *was* certain that he *will** graduate.

In the first example, the present, *know*, is illogical with *would*. It can be corrected in two different ways.

> I *knew* that he *would arrive* soon.
> I *know* that he *will arrive* soon.

In the second example, the past, *was*, is illogical with *will*. It can also be corrected in two different ways.

> It *was* certain that he *would graduate*.
> It *is* certain that he *will graduate*.

The following chart outlines the use of tenses with *will* and *would*:

USING CORRECT TENSES WITH *WILL* AND *WOULD*		
VERB	MEANING	USE
will	after the present	do not use with past
would	after the past	do not use with present
NOTE: There is a different modal *would* that is used to make polite requests. This type of *would* is often used with the present tense.		
I **would** like to know if you **have** a pencil that I could borrow.		

EXERCISE 36: Each of the following sentences contains *will* or *would*. Underline the verbs twice and decide if the meanings are logical. Then indicate if the sentences are correct (C) or incorrect (I).

__I__   1. He <u>knew</u> that he <u>will</u> be able to pass the exam.

__C__   2. I <u>think</u> that I <u>will</u> leave tomorrow.

_____   3. Paula did not say when she will finish the project.

_____   4. Jake doubts that he would have time to finish the project.

_____   5. I know that I will go if I can afford it.

_____   6. The police officer indicated that he would write a ticket if he has the time.

_____   7. Students will often study in the library before they go to classes or before they go home.

_____   8. He told me that he thought he will get the job in spite of his lack of education.

_____   9. The executive vice president emphasizes at the conferences that the board would not change its position.

_____   10. Students will register for classes according to who has the highest number of units.

EXERCISE (Skills 33–36): Underline the verbs twice in each of the following sentences. Then indicate if the sentences are correct (C) or incorrect (I).

_____   1. When he receives the money from the insurance company two days ago, he had already rebuilt the house.

_____   2. The position on the city council will be filled next week when the electorate votes.

_____   3. The dentist fills the cavities every time the X-rays show that it was necessary.

_____   4. When the bell rang, the students have left the class.

_____   5. The space shuttle would be launched next month if the weather is good.

_____   6. The special delivery package has arrived by noon yesterday.

_____   7. It is probable that the students who were tested yesterday were quite successful.

_____   8. After forty-five students had signed up for the class, the class was closed.

_____   9. The parking at the arena was inadequate for the tremendous number of drivers who will want to park there.

_____   10. They have not returned to Rhode Island since they left in 1970.

TOEFL EXERCISE (Skills 33–36): Choose the letter of the underlined word or group of words that is not correct.

_____ 1. In several of his paintings, Edward Hicks depicted the Quaker farm in Pennsylvania
                    A

   where he spends his youth.
     B   C   D

_____ 2. Florida has become the twenty-seventh state in the United States on March 3, 1845.
                 A   B   C   D

_____ 3. After last week's meeting, the advertising department quickly realized that the
                A   B

   product will need a new slogan.
         C   D

_____ 4. John F. Kennedy's grandfather, John F. Fitzgerald, serves two terms as the mayor of
                    A   B   C

   Boston in the beginning of the twentieth century.
         D

_____ 5. Fort Ticonderoga, a strategically important fortification during the Revolution, had
                                                        A

   since been reconstructed and turned into a museum.
     B   C   D

_____ 6. In making their calculations, Institute researchers assume that the least costly form
             A   B

   of energy would be used.
         C   D

_____ 7. A twenty-one-year-old man became the second casualty yesterday when he loses
                                            A   B   C

control of his truck.
   D

_____ 8. Most people had written with quill pens until pens with metal points become popular
                              A   B   C   D

in the middle of the nineteenth century.

_____ 9. In a determined drive to pare its debt, Time Warner is launching a stock offering
                     A   B   C

plan that would potentially raise $2.8 billion.
                  D

_____10. The formula used in the study calls for either peroxide or metaldehyde, but
                              A   B   C

metaldehyde was not always available.
                     D

TOEFL REVIEW EXERCISE (Skills 1–36): Choose the letter of the word or group of
words that best completes the sentence.

1. _____ in the United States declined from
   twenty million in 1910 to nine million in
   the 1970s.

   (A) For a number of horses
   (B) The number of horses
   (C) When the number of horses
   (D) That the number of horses

2. Because of his reservations about the
   issue, _____ refused to vote for it.

   (A) who
   (B) and
   (C) which the senator
   (D) the senator

3. Bats avoid running into objects by _____
   high-frequency sounds and listening for
   echoes.

   (A) the emission
   (B) emitted
   (C) emitting
   (D) they emit

4. It has been estimated that if we intend to
   stay above the starvation level, _____ the
   food supply.

   (A) so we will have to double
   (B) and it must double
   (C) which it must be doubled
   (D) we must double

Choose the letter of the underlined word or group of words that is not correct.

_____ 5. To determine an object's force, the mass and speed of the object must be measure.
                     A   B   C   D

_____ 6. The most common time for tornados to occur are in the afternoon or evening on a
                     A   B   C

hot, humid spring day.
         D

_____ 7. Automakers Nissan and Ford and several aerospace research facilities in Great
                                                            A

Britain are working lately to apply active noise cancellation to entire cars and planes.
            B   C   D

_____ 8. When a <u>country in</u> an early stage of development, <u>investments</u> in <u>fixed</u> capital
                            A   B   C

       <u>are vital</u>.
         D

_____ 9. John Chapman became <u>famous</u> in American folklore as "Johnny Appleseed" after he
                                 A

       <u>plants</u> apple trees <u>throughout</u> the northeastern <u>part</u> of the United States.
        B   C   D

_____ 10. <u>Inasmuch</u> he kept <u>mostly</u> <u>to himself</u>, the author of *The Treasure of the Sierra Madre*
         A   B   C

       <u>was known</u> as "the mysterious B. Treuen."
         D

PROBLEMS WITH PASSIVE VERBS

Sentences in which the error is an incorrect passive are common in the Written Expression section of the TOEFL test. You therefore need to be able to recognize the correct form of the passive and to be able to determine when a passive verb rather than an active verb is needed in a sentence.

The difference between an active and a passive verb is that the subject in an active sentence *does* the action of the verb, and the subject in a passive sentence *receives* the action of the verb. To convert a sentence from active to passive, two changes must be made. (1) The subject of the active sentence becomes the object of the passive sentence, while the object of the active sentence becomes the subject of the passive sentence. (2) The verb in the passive sentence is formed by putting the helping verb *be* in the same form as the verb in the active sentence and then adding the past participle of this verb.

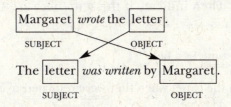

The first example is an active sentence. To convert this active sentence to a passive sentence, you must first make the subject of the active sentence, *Margaret,* the object of the passive sentence with *by.* The object of the active sentence, *letter,* becomes the subject of the passive sentence. Next, the passive verb can be formed. Because *wrote* is in the past tense in the active sentence, the past tense of *be (was)* is used in the passive sentence. Then the verb *wrote* in the active sentence is changed to the past participle *written* in the passive sentence.

It should be noted that in a passive sentence, *by + object* does not need to be included to have a complete sentence. The following are both examples of correct sentences.

> The letter was written yesterday *by Margaret.*
> The letter was written yesterday.

Notice that these passive sentences are correct if *by Margaret* is included (as in the first example) or if *by Margaret* is omitted (as in the second example).

> NOTE: Exercises to practice active and passive forms can be found in Appendix G at the back of the text. You may want to complete these exercises before you begin Skill 37.

SKILL 37:   USE THE CORRECT FORM OF THE PASSIVE

One way that the passive can be tested on the TOEFL test is simply with an incorrect form of the passive. The following are examples of passive errors that might appear on the TOEFL test:

> The portrait *was painting** by a famous artist.
> The project *will finished** by Tim.

In the first example, the passive is formed incorrectly because the past participle *painted* should be used rather than the present participle *painting*. In the second example, the verb *be* has not been included, and some form of *be* is necessary for a passive verb. The verb in the second sentence should be *will be finished*.

The following chart outlines the way to form the passive correctly:

THE FORM OF THE PASSIVE
BE   +   past participle (BY + object)

EXERCISE 37: Each of the following sentences has a passive meaning. Underline twice the verbs that should be passive. Then indicate if the sentences are correct (C) or incorrect (I).

__I__   1.   The boy had never be stung by a bee.

__C__   2.   The suits were hung in the closet when they were returned from the cleaners.

_____   3.   Money is lending by the credit union to those who want to buy homes.

_____   4.   The record had been chose by dancers near the jukebox.

_____   5.   The topic for your research paper should have been approved by your advisor.

_____   6.   That song has been playing over and over again by Steve.

_____   7.   Their utility bills have been increased again and again.

_____   8.   The patients who are too sick to sit up are being assisted by the orderlies.

_____   9.   The offices were thoroughly clean last evening by the night crew.

_____   10. The car that was struck in the intersection yesterday is being repaired today.

SKILL 38:   RECOGNIZE ACTIVE AND PASSIVE MEANINGS

When there is no object (with or without *by*) after a verb, you must look at the meaning of the sentence to determine if the verb should be active or passive. Sentences with an incorrect passive verb and no *by + object* to tell you that the verb should be passive are the most difficult passive errors to recognize on the TOEFL test. Study the examples:

> We mailed *the package* at the post office.
> The letter was mailed *by us* today before noon.
> The letter was mailed today before noon.
> The letter mailed* today before noon.

The first three examples above are correct. The first example has the active verb *mailed* used with the object *package*; the second example has the passive verb *was mailed* used with *by us*; the third sentence has the passive verb *was mailed* used without an object.

The fourth example is the type of passive error that appears most often on the TOEFL test. This type of sentence has the following characteristics: (1) an incorrect passive verb that looks like a correct active verb, and (2) no *by + object* to tell you that a passive is needed. To correct the fourth example, the active verb needs to be changed to the passive *was mailed*.

To determine that such a sentence is incorrect, you must study the meaning of the subject and the verb. You must ask yourself if the subject *does* the action of the verb (so an active verb is needed) or if the subject *receives* the action of the verb (so a passive verb is needed). In the incorrect example, you should study the meaning of the subject and verb, *the letter mailed*. You should ask yourself if *a letter mails itself* (the letter *does* the action) or if someone *mails a letter* (the letter *receives* the action of being mailed). Since a letter does not mail itself, the passive is required in this sentence.

The following chart outlines the difference in meaning between active and passive verbs:

ACTIVE AND PASSIVE MEANINGS	
ACTIVE	The subject *does* the action of the verb.
PASSIVE	The subject *receives* the action of the verb.

EXERCISE 38: Each of the following sentences contains at least one active verb; however, some of the verbs should be passive. Underline the verbs twice. Then indicate if the sentences are correct (C) or incorrect (I).

___I___ 1. The car parked in a no-parking zone.

___C___ 2. The physics exam began just a few minutes ago.

_____ 3. Everything to organize the picnic has already done.

_____ 4. The police investigated him because of his unusual actions.

_____ 5. The package containing the necessary samples has just sent.

_____ 6. The vacation to Europe will plan carefully before the scheduled departure date.

_____ 7. The coffee turned bitter when it left on the stove for so long.

_____ 8. The soccer game won in the closing minutes.

_____ 9. The clothes made to rival the latest fashions of the season.

_____ 10. When the roads are icy, the buses do not drive.

EXERCISE (Skills 37–38): Underline the verbs twice in the following sentences. Then indicate if the sentences are correct (C) or incorrect (I).

_____ 1. After the old radiator had be replaced, the travelers continued their cross-country trip.

_____ 2. During the lightning storm, he struck in the head by a falling tree.

_____ 3. While I am on vacation, the pets should be feeds every morning and evening.

_____ 4. A book being written now by a team of writers will be published in the fall.

_____ 5. I found out that the real estate agent had already been leased the condominium.

_____ 6. The house that Mrs. Martin has always wanted to buy has just placed on the market.

_____ 7. The foundation should have been finishing by the construction workers before they left the construction site.

_____ 8. We must leave that money in the checking account because the bills pay on the first of the month.

_____ 9. The horses can't be taken out now because they have been rode for the past few hours.

_____ 10. It is being announced by a presidential aide that a lawyer from Virginia has been named attorney general.

TOEFL EXERCISE (Skills 37–38): Choose the letter of the word or group of words that best completes the sentence.

1. _____ discussed by the board of directors when it was proposed again by the supervisors.

    (A) The problem had already
    (B) The problem is already
    (C) The problem had already been
    (D) The problem has already

2. Much of the carnage of elephants, giraffes, and big cats _____ uncaring hunters.

    (A) must commit by
    (B) must be committed
    (C) must have committed
    (D) must have been committed by

3. The X-ray treatments _____ up to the time that he was dismissed from the hospital.

    (A) gave daily
    (B) were given daily
    (C) basically have given
    (D) daily had been given

Choose the letter of the underlined word or group of words that is not correct.

_____ 4. Particular <u>issues</u> that <u>concern</u> teenagers <u>were</u> <u>covering</u> in the half-hour program.
                    A   B   C   D

_____ 5. Electrical <u>impulses</u> <u>may</u> <u>also</u> <u>picked</u> up <u>by</u> the optic nerve.
                      A   B   C   D

_____ 6. Workers <u>training</u> for a specific job <u>have</u> a strong possibility of <u>being</u> <u>replace</u> by a
                       A   B   C   D

        machine.

_____ 7. On June 30, 1992, international timekeepers in Paris <u>were added</u> an extra <u>second</u> to
        A   B   C

        the day.
        D

_____ 8. The report <u>could not be</u> <u>turned in</u> on time because all the <u>needed</u> work <u>lost</u>.
                     A   B   C   D

_____ 9. In English these questions <u>have be</u> <u>formed</u> by <u>changing</u> the word order of a
                                     A   B   C

        statement, whereas in some languages the word order <u>remains</u> the same.
                                                                              D

_____10. He was <u>not able</u> to <u>define</u> the process <u>by which</u> the body <u>had protected</u> by the
             A   B   C   D

        immunologic system.

TOEFL REVIEW EXERCISE (Skills 1–38): Choose the letter of the word or group of words that best completes the sentence.

1. _____ Big Dipper, a seven-star constellation in the shape of a cup, is part of Ursa Major.

   (A) The
   (B) It is the
   (C) With the
   (D) That the

2. The Military Academy at West Point _____ on the west bank of the Hudson River, north of New York City.

   (A) located
   (B) is located
   (C) which is located
   (D) whose location is

3. _____ impressive chapter in the book was the chapter on Stuart's scientific theories.

   (A) It was the most
   (B) The most
   (C) Most
   (D) Most of the

Choose the letter of the underlined word or group of words that is not correct.

_____ 4. The first fish have appeared on the earth approximately 500 million years ago.
                    A   B   C   D

_____ 5. Only rarely sound waves are of a single frequency encountered in practice.
                    A   B   C   D

_____ 6. Cameos can be carved not only from onyx and sardonyx or from agate.
                    A   B   C   D

_____ 7. Although most of the wild horses in the western range have already been rounded
                         A   B

          up, the most remote the area, the greater the possibility that wild horses can still be
                  C   D

          found.

_____ 8. During this period, $206 was spend annually on food by families in the lower third
                                    A   B   C   D

          income bracket.

_____ 9. The dangers of noise are, unfortunately, not as clear-cut than are those from
                                A   B   C

          most other health hazards.
              D

_____10. In a recent survey of Americans, more than 75 percent expressed the view that the
                    A   B

          government it should take a more active role in health care.
                        C   D

PROBLEMS WITH NOUNS _____

The same types of problems with nouns appear often in the Written Expression section of the TOEFL test. You should be familiar with these problems so that you will recognize them easily. You should be able to do the following: (1) use the correct singular or plural noun, (2) distinguish countable and uncountable nouns, (3) recognize irregular singular and plural nouns, and (4) distinguish the person from the thing.

SKILL 39:   USE THE CORRECT SINGULAR OR PLURAL NOUN

A problem that is common in the Written Expression section of the TOEFL test is a singular noun used where a plural noun is needed, or a plural noun used where a singular noun is needed.

> On the table there were many *dish**.
> The lab assistant finished every *tests**.

In the first example, *many* indicates that the plural *dishes* is needed. In the second example, *every* indicates that the singular *test* is needed.

In the Written Expression section of the TOEFL test, you should watch very carefully for key words, such as *each, every, a, one,* and *single,* that indicate that a noun should be singular. You should also watch carefully for such key words as *many, several, both, various,* and *two* (or any other number except *one*) that indicate that a noun should be plural.

The following chart lists the key words that indicate to you whether a noun should be singular or plural:

KEY WORDS FOR SINGULAR AND PLURAL NOUNS					
For Singular Nouns	*each*	*every*	*single*	*one*	*a*
For Plural Nouns	*both*	*two*	*many*	*several*	*various*

EXERCISE 39: Each of the following sentences contains at least one key word to tell you if a noun should be singular or plural. Circle the key words. Draw arrows to the nouns they describe. Then indicate if the sentences are correct (C) or incorrect (I).

__I__   1. The automotive shop stocked (many) part for the (various) types of Hondas.

__C__   2. (Every) receipt must be removed from the cashier's drawer and tallied.

_____   3. The salesclerk demonstrated various additional way that the machine could be used.

_____   4. The woman found it difficult to believe that both of the piece of jewelry had disappeared.

_____   5. The unhappy man became more and more discouraged with each passing days.

_____   6. An extended cruise would be a nice way to spend a vacation one days.

_____   7. The manager was surprised that not a single worker was available on Tuesday.

_____   8. The housekeeper cleaned the room and took two of the occupant's dress to the laundry.

_____   9. When the first bill was defeated, the Senate immediately began work on a different bills.

_____   10. There were several boxes in the cupboard, and each box contained a dozen glasses.

SKILL 40: DISTINGUISH COUNTABLE AND UNCOUNTABLE NOUNS

In English nouns are classified as countable or uncountable. For certain questions on the TOEFL test, it is necessary to distinguish countable and uncountable nouns in order to use the correct modifiers with them.

As the name implies, countable nouns are nouns that can be counted. Countable nouns can come in quantities of one, or two, or a hundred, etc. The noun *book* is countable because you can have one book or several books.

Uncountable nouns, on the other hand, are nouns that cannot be counted because they come in some indeterminate quantity or mass. A noun such as *milk* or *happiness* cannot be counted; you cannot have one milk or two milks, and you cannot find one happiness or two happinesses. Uncountable nouns are often liquid items, such as *water, oil*, or *shampoo*. Uncountable nouns can also refer to abstract ideas, such as *security, friendship,* or *hope.*

It is important for you to recognize the difference between countable and uncountable nouns when you come across such key words as *much* and *many*.

> He has seen *much** foreign *films.*
> He didn't have *many* fun* at the movies.

In the first example, *much* is incorrect because *films* is countable. This sentence should say *many foreign films.* In the second example, *many* is incorrect because *fun* is uncountable. This sentence should say *much fun.*

The following chart lists the key words that indicate to you whether a noun should be countable or uncountable:

KEY WORDS FOR COUNTABLE AND UNCOUNTABLE NOUNS				
For Countable Nouns	*many*	*number*	*few*	*fewer*
For Uncountable Nouns	*much*	*amount*	*little*	*less*

EXERCISE 40: Each of the following sentences contains at least one key word to tell you if a noun should be countable or uncountable. Circle the key words. Draw arrows to the nouns they describe. Then indicate if the sentences are correct (C) or incorrect (I).

__C__   1.   He received (little) notice that the bill would have to be paid in full.

__I__   2.   The police had (few) opportunities to catch the thief who had committed a large (amount) of crimes.

_____   3.   You will have fewer problems with your income taxes if you get professional help.

_____   4.   After the strike, the company dismissed many employees.

_____   5.   Because the bottom corner of the pocket was torn, much coins fell out.

_____   6.   Since he bought the new adapter, he has had less trouble with the machine.

_____   7.   There are much new items to purchase before leaving, and there is such a short amount of time.

_____   8. The less time you take on the assignment, the less pages you will complete.

_____   9. A few soldiers who had been in heavy combat were brought back for a little rest.

_____ 10. It is better to go shopping in the late evening because there are less people in the market, and you can accomplish a number of tasks in a short period of time.

SKILL 41:   RECOGNIZE IRREGULAR PLURALS OF NOUNS

Many nouns in English have irregular plurals, and these irregular forms can cause confusion in the Written Expression section of the TOEFL test. The irregular forms that are the most problematic are plural forms that do not end in *s*.

Different *criteria* was* used to evaluate the performers.

In this example the plural noun *criteria* looks singular because it does not end in *s*; you might incorrectly assume that it is singular because there is no final *s*. However, *criteria* is a plural noun, so the singular verb *was used* is incorrect. The verb should be the plural form *were used*.

The following chart lists the irregular plurals that you should become familiar with:

IRREGULAR PLURALS			
Vowel change	*man / men* *woman / women*	*foot / feet* *tooth / teeth*	*goose / geese* *mouse / mice*
Add -*EN*	*child / children*	*ox / oxen*	
Same as singular	*deer / deer* *fish / fish*	*salmon / salmon* *sheep / sheep*	*trout / trout*
-*IS* ⟶ -*ES*	*analysis / analyses* *axis / axes* *crisis / crises*	*diagnosis / diagnoses* *hypothesis / hypotheses* *parenthesis / parentheses*	*synthesis / syntheses* *thesis / theses*
Ends in -*A*	*bacterium / bacteria* *curriculum / curricula*	*datum / data* *phenomenon / phenomena*	*criterion / criteria*
-*US* ⟶ -*I*	*alumnus / alumni* *bacillus / bacilli* *cactus / cacti*	*fungus / fungi* *nucleus / nuclei* *radius / radii*	*stimulus / stimuli* *syllabus / syllabi*

NOTE: Additional exercises to practice these irregular plurals of nouns appear in Appendix H at the back of the text. You may want to complete these exercises before you begin Exercise 41.

EXERCISE 41: Each of the following sentences contains at least one noun with an irregular plural. Circle the nouns with irregular plurals. Then indicate if the sentences are correct (C) or incorrect (I).

_I_   1.   (Parentheses) is needed around that expression.

_C_   2.   He wants to go on a fishing trip this weekend because he has heard that the (fish) are running.

_____   3.   The syllabi for the courses is included in the packet of materials.

_____   4.   The diagnosis that he heard today were not very positive.

_____   5.   The crisis is not going to be resolved until some of the pressure is relieved.

_____   6.   All of the alumni are attending the reception at the president's house.

_____   7.   A flock of geese were seen heading south for the winter.

_____   8.   The teeth in the back of his mouth needs to be capped.

_____   9.   The fungi has spread throughout the garden.

_____   10.   The sheepdog is chasing after the sheep which are heading over the hill.

SKILL 42:   DISTINGUISH THE PERSON FROM THE THING

Nouns in English can refer to persons or things. Sometimes in the Written Expression section of the TOEFL test the person is used in place of the thing, or the thing is used in place of the person.

> Ralph Nader is an *authorization** in the field of consumer affairs.
> There are many job opportunities in *accountant**.

In the first example, *authorization* is incorrect because *authorization* is a thing and Ralph Nader is a person. The person *authority* should be used in this sentence. In the second example, *accountant* is incorrect because *accountant* is a person and the field in which an accountant works is *accounting*. The thing *accounting* should be used in this sentence.

The following chart outlines what you should remember about the person or thing:

PERSON OR THING
1.   It is common to confuse a person with a thing in the Written Expression section of the TOEFL test.
2.   This type of question generally appears near the end of the Written Expression section.

EXERCISE 42: Some of the following sentences contain incorrectly used *persons* or *things*. Circle the incorrectly used words. Then indicate if the sentences are correct (C) or incorrect (I).

__I__   1.   In the evening he relaxes in front of the fire and writes long (poets.)

__C__   2.   Service in the restaurant was slow because one cook had called in sick.

_____   3.   The sculpture worked from sunrise until sunset on his new project.

_____   4.   She has received several awards for her research in engineer.

_____   5.   The economist's radical views were printed in a column in the Sunday newspaper.

_____   6.   You must have remarkable looks to work as a model for *Vogue*.

_____   7.   He had several critics to offer about the new play.

_____   8.   The gardener worked feverishly after the frost to save as many plants as possible.

_____   9.   The company hired a statistic to prepare marketing studies for the new product.

_____   10.   The famous acting has appeared in more than fifty Broadway plays.

EXERCISE (Skills 39–42): Study the nouns in the following sentences. Then indicate if the sentences are correct (C) or incorrect (I).

_____   1.   The professor does not give many exam in chemistry class, but the ones she gives are difficult.

_____   2.   His thesis includes an analyses of the hypotheses.

_____   3.   It was his dream to be a musical in the New York Philharmonic.

_____   4.   For the reception, the caterers prepared a large amount of food to serve a large number of people.

_____   5.   Many job opportunities exist in the field of nurse if you will accept a low-paying position.

_____   6.   For each business trip you make, you can choose from many different airlines.

_____   7.   The stimulus for his career change is his acknowledgment that he is in a dead-end job.

_____   8.   She wants to undergo a series of treatments, but she thinks it costs a little too much money.

_____   9.   The television producer that was shown last night on the CBS network from 9:00 to 11:00 was one of the best shows of the season.

_____   10.   Various sight-seeing excursion were available from the tourist agency.

TOEFL EXERCISE (Skills 39–42): Choose the letter of the underlined word or group of words that is not correct.

_____ 1.   As a compilation of useful details, a weekly magazine commends itself in several
                                   A   B   C

respect.
D

_____ 2.   Through aquaculture, or fish farming, more than 500 million tons of fish
                                                        A   B

are produced each years.
        C   D

_____ 3.   The legal system has much safeguards to protect the right of a defendant to an
                                         A   B   C

impartial jury.
D

_____ 4.   The mystery bookstore was largely a phenomena of the last decade.
                                              A   B   C   D

_____ 5.   The _Song of Hiawatha_, by Longfellow, tells the story of the Indian heroism who
                                                           A   B   C

married Minehaha.
D

_____ 6.   Uranus is the seventh planets from the Sun.
                      A   B   C   D

_____ 7.   The sycamore has broad leaves with a large amount of pointed teeth.
                                        A   B   C   D

_____ 8.   The first of two such investigation requires the students to read continuously over a
                                          A   B

period of four hours.
        C   D

_____ 9.   A quantitative analysis, using both the computer and quantitative techniques,
                                            A   B

are used to optimize financial decisions.
        C   D

_____ 10. To enter the FBI National Academy, an application must be between the ages of
                      A   B   C   D

twenty-three and thirty-four.

TOEFL REVIEW EXERCISE (Skills 1–42): Choose the letter of the word or group of words that best completes the sentence.

1. Presidential ____ held every four years on the first Tuesday after the first Monday in November.

    (A) electing
    (B) elections are
    (C) is elected
    (D) elected and

2. Studies of carcinogenesis in animals can provide data on ____ in human susceptibility.

    (A) differences are
    (B) that differences are
    (C) differences have
    (D) differences

3. Those who favor the new law say that the present law does not set spending limits on lobbyists' gifts to politicians, nor ____ statewide funds.

    (A) it limits
    (B) limits it
    (C) does it limit
    (D) does it

4. The population of the earth is increasing at a tremendous rate and ____ out of control.

    (A) they have become
    (B) are soon going to be
    (C) soon will be
    (D) why it will be

5. Starting in 1811, traders and manufacturers were more easily able to send goods upriver in ____ provided the necessary power to counteract the flow of the waters.

    (A) steamboats
    (B) which
    (C) that
    (D) that steamboats

Choose the letter of the underlined word or group of words that is not correct.

____ 6. Temperature <u>indicates</u> on a <u>bimetallic</u> thermometer by the <u>amount</u> <u>that</u> the
                        A   B   C   D

   bimetallic strip bends.

____ 7. <u>Many</u> of the food <u>consumed</u> by penguins <u>consists</u> of fish <u>obtained from</u> the ocean.
            A   B   C   D

____ 8. Before the newspaper became <u>widespread</u>, a town <u>crier</u> <u>has</u> walked throughout a
                                          A   B   C

   village or town <u>singing out</u> the news.
                        D

____ 9. All of NASA's <u>manned</u> spacecraft <u>project</u> are <u>headquartered</u> at the Lyndon B.
            A   B   C   D

   Johnson Space Center in Houston.

____10. Fungi <u>cause</u> more <u>serious</u> plant <u>diseased</u> than <u>do</u> other parasites.
                  A   B   C   D

PROBLEMS WITH PRONOUNS _____

Pronouns are words, such as *he, she,* or *it,* that take the place of nouns. When you see a pronoun in the Written Expression section of the TOEFL test, you need to check that it serves the correct function in the sentence (as a subject or object, for example) and that it agrees with the noun it is replacing. The following pronoun problems are the most common on the TOEFL test: (1) distinguishing subject and object pronouns, (2) distinguishing possessive pronouns and possessive adjectives, and (3) checking pronoun reference for agreement.

SKILL 43:   DISTINGUISH SUBJECT AND OBJECT PRONOUNS

Subject and object pronouns can be confused on the TOEFL test, so you should be able to recognize these two types of pronouns:

SUBJECT	OBJECT
I	me
you	you
he	him
she	her
it	it
we	us
they	them

A subject pronoun is used as the subject of a verb. An object pronoun can be used as the object of a verb or the object of a preposition. Compare the following two sentences.

Sally gave *the book* to *John.*

She gave *it* to *him.*

In the second sentence the subject pronoun *she* is replacing the noun *Sally.* The object of the verb *it* is replacing the noun *book,* and the object of the preposition *him* is replacing the noun *John.*

The following are examples of the types of subject or object pronoun errors that you might see on the TOEFL test.

*Him** and the girl are going shopping.
The gift was intended for you and *I*.*

In the first example, the object pronoun *him* is incorrect because this pronoun serves as the subject of the sentence. The object pronoun *him* should be changed to the subject pronoun *he.* It can be difficult to recognize that *him* is the subject because the verb *are* has a double subject, *him* and *girl.* In the second example, the subject pronoun *I* is incorrect because this pronoun serves as the object of the preposition *for.* The subject pronoun *I* should be changed to the object pronoun *me.* It can be difficult to recognize that *I* is the object of the preposition *for* because the preposition *for* has two objects: the correct object *you* and the incorrect object *I.*

EXERCISE 43: Each of the following sentences contains at least one subject or object pronoun. Circle the pronouns. Then indicate if the sentences are correct (C) or incorrect (I).

_C_   1. The worst problem with (it) is that (he) cannot afford (it.)

_I_   2. (They) saw Steve and (I) at the movies last night after class.

_____   3. Perhaps you would like to go to the seminar with they and their friends.

_____   4. The mother took her son to the doctor's office because he was feeling sick.

_____   5. I did not know that you and her were working together on the project.

_____   6. She did not buy the sweater because it had a small hole in it.

_____   7. The man leading the seminar gave me all the information I needed to make a decision.

_____   8. The cards connecting the computer to its printer need to be replaced before them wear down.

_____   9. He is going to the party with you and me if you do not mind.

_____   10. You and her ought to return the books to the library because they are already overdue.

Skill 44:   DISTINGUISH POSSESSIVE ADJECTIVES AND PRONOUNS

Possessive adjectives and pronouns both show who or what "owns" a noun. However, possessive adjectives and possessive pronouns do not have the same function, and these two kinds of possessives can be confused on the TOEFL test. A possessive adjective describes a noun: it must be accompanied by a noun. A possessive pronoun takes the place of a noun: it cannot be accompanied by a noun.

They lent me *their* book.
ADJECTIVE

They lent me *theirs*.
PRONOUN

Notice that in the first example the possessive adjective *their* is accompanied by the noun *book*. In the second example the possessive pronoun *theirs* is not accompanied by a noun.

These examples show the types of errors that are possible with possessive adjectives and possessive pronouns on the TOEFL test.

Each morning they read *theirs** newspapers.
Could you give me *your**?

In the first example, the possessive pronoun *theirs* is incorrect because it is accompanied by the noun *newspapers,* and a possessive pronoun cannot be accompanied by a noun. The possessive adjective *their* is needed in the first example. In the second example, the possessive adjective *your* is incorrect because it is not accompanied by a noun, and a possessive adjective must be accompanied by a noun. The possessive pronoun *yours* is needed in the second example.

The following chart outlines the possessives and their uses:

POSSESSIVE ADJECTIVES	POSSESSIVE PRONOUNS
my	*mine*
your	*yours*
his	*his*
her	*hers*
its	—
our	*ours*
their	*theirs*
must be accompanied by a noun	*cannot* be accompanied by a noun

EXERCISE 44: Each of the following sentences contains at least one possessive pronoun or adjective. Circle the possessives in these sentences. Then indicate if the sentences are correct (C) or incorrect (I).

_I_   1. If she borrows (your) coat, then you should be able to borrow (her.)

_C_   2. Each pot and pan in (her) kitchen has (its) own place on the shelf.

_____   3. Mary and Mark invited theirs parents to see their new apartment.

_____   4. When my roommate paid her half of the rent, I paid mine.

_____   5. All students need to bring theirs own pencils and answer sheets to the exam.

_____   6. All her secretaries are working late tonight to finish her report.

_____   7. The horse trotting around the track won its race a few minutes ago.

_____   8. Before the report is finalized, the information in their notes and our must be proofed.

_____   9. She worked all day cooking food and making decorations for her son's birthday party.

_____   10. The weather in the mountains this weekend will be extremely cold, so please take yours heavy jackets.

Skill 45: CHECK PRONOUN REFERENCE FOR AGREEMENT

After you have checked that the subject and object pronouns and the possessives are used correctly, you should also check each of these pronouns and possessives for agreement. The following are examples of errors of this type that you might find on the TOEFL test:

> The boys will cause trouble if you let *him**.
> Everyone must give *their** name.

In the first example, the singular pronoun *him* is incorrect because it refers to the plural noun *boys*. This pronoun should be replaced with the plural noun *them*. In the second example, the plural possessive adjective *their* is incorrect because it refers to the singular *everyone*. This adjective should be replaced with the singular *his* or *his or her.*

The following chart outlines what you should remember about checking pronoun reference:

PRONOUN AGREEMENT
1. Be sure that every pronoun and possessive agrees with the noun it refers to.
2. You generally check *back* in the sentence for agreement.

EXERCISE 45: Each of the following sentences contains at least one pronoun or possessive. Circle the pronouns and possessives. Draw arrows to the nouns they refer to. Then indicate if the sentences are correct (C) or incorrect (I).

___I___   1.   If a person really wants to succeed, (they) must always work hard.

___C___   2.   If you see the students from the math class, could you return (their) exam papers to (them?)

_____   3.   Some friends and I went to see a movie, and afterwards we wrote a critique about them.

_____   4.   If you have a problem, you are welcome to discuss it with me before you try to resolve them.

_____   5.   I know you had a terrible time last week, but you must try to forget about it.

_____   6.   At the start of the program, each student needs to see his advisor about his schedule.

_____   7.   In spite of its small size, these video recorders produce excellent tapes.

_____   8.   Whatever the situation, you should reflect profoundly about them before coming to a decision.

_____   9.   The people I admire most are those who manage to solve their own problems.

_____   10.   If anyone stops by while I am at the meeting, please take a message from them.

EXERCISE (Skills 43–45): Circle the pronouns and possessives in the following sentences. Then indicate if the sentences are correct (C) or incorrect (I).

_____ 1. Helicopters are being used more and more in emergency situations because of its ability to reach out-of-the-way places.

_____ 2. The worker was fired by the chemical company because his refused to work with certain dangerous chemicals.

_____ 3. If you have car trouble while driving on the freeway, you should pull your car over to the side of the freeway and wait for help.

_____ 4. The administration will not install the new security system because they cost so much.

_____ 5. Some parents prefer to send their children to private schools because they believe the children will be better educated.

_____ 6. The air traffic controller was not blamed for the accident because he had strictly followed the correct procedures.

_____ 7. The new student has been assigned to work on the project with you and I.

_____ 8. Many different kinds of aspirin are on the market, but theirs effectiveness seems to be equal.

_____ 9. You must bring a tent and a sleeping bag for your trip to the Sierras.

_____ 10. Each of the team members had their new uniform.

TOEFL EXERCISE (Skills 43–45): Choose the letter of the underlined word or group of words that is not correct.

_____ 1. Superman made their comic debut in 1938 in *Action Comics*.
              A   B   C   D

_____ 2. Commercial letters of credit are often used to finance export trade, but them can
                         A   B   C

     have other uses.
            D

_____ 3. When children experience too much frustration, its behavior ceases to be integrated.
                    A   B   C   D

_____ 4. On March 30, 1981, President Reagan was shot as his was leaving a Washington hotel.
                             A B C   D

_____ 5. Although the destruction that it causes is often terrible, cyclones benefit a
                         A   B

     much wider belt than they devastate.
            C   D

_____ 6. President Andrew Jackson had <u>an official</u> cabinet, but <u>him</u> <u>preferred</u> the advice of
                                            A   B   C

his informal advisors, the Kitchen Cabinet.
<u>   </u>
D

_____ 7. After <u>Clarence Day's book</u> *Life with Father* was <u>rewritten</u> as a play, <u>they</u> ran for
                        A   B   C

<u>six years</u> on Broadway.
      D

_____ 8. <u>Almost</u> <u>half of the</u> Pilgrims did not survive <u>theirs</u> <u>first</u> winter in the New World.
              A   B   C   D

_____ 9. There was <u>no indication</u> from the Senate that <u>he</u> would agree with the decision <u>made</u>
              A   B   C   D

in the House.

_____ 10. A baby learns the meanings of words as <u>they</u> are spoken by <u>others</u> and <u>later</u> uses <u>him</u>
                                                      A   B   C   D

in sentences.

TOEFL REVIEW EXERCISE (Skills 1–45): Choose the letter of the word or group of words that best completes the sentence.

1. _____ worst phase of the Depression, more than thirteen million Americans had no jobs.

   (A) It was in the
   (B) During the
   (C) While the
   (D) The

2. When reading a book, you must keep your point of view separate from the point of view in _____ you are studying.

   (A) that
   (B) the material and
   (C) the materials that
   (D) the materials that are

3. Speech consists not merely of sounds but _____ that follow various structural patterns.

   (A) of organized sound patterns
   (B) organized sound patterns
   (C) that sound patterns are organized
   (D) in organizing sound patterns

Choose the letter of the underlined word or group of words that is not correct.

_____ 4. <u>The latest</u> medical report indicated that the patient's temperature was <u>near normal</u>
              A   B

and <u>their</u> lungs <u>were</u> partially cleared.
        C   D

_____ 5. <u>Most</u> oxygen atoms have <u>eight</u> neutrons, but a small <u>amount</u> have <u>nine or ten</u>.
              A   B   C   D

_____ 6. When Paine expressed <u>his</u> <u>belief</u> in independence, he <u>praised</u> by <u>the public</u>.
                                    A   B   C   D

_____ 7. A vast quantity of radioactive material is made when does a hydrogen bomb explode .
          ‾‾‾‾‾‾‾‾‾‾‾‾‾‾‾‾   ‾‾‾‾‾‾‾‾‾‾‾‾   ‾‾‾‾‾‾   ‾‾‾‾‾‾‾‾‾‾‾‾‾‾‾‾‾‾‾‾‾‾‾‾‾‾‾
                A   B   C   D

_____ 8. Genes have several alternative form, or alleles, which are produced by mutations.
                  ‾‾‾‾‾‾‾‾‾‾‾‾‾‾‾‾‾‾‾‾   ‾‾‾‾‾‾‾‾   ‾‾‾‾‾‾‾‾‾‾‾‾   ‾‾‾‾‾‾‾‾‾
                          A   B   C   D

_____ 9. A star that has used up its energy and has lost its heat became a black dwarf.
               ‾‾‾‾   ‾‾‾‾‾‾‾‾‾‾‾‾‾‾   ‾‾‾‾   ‾‾‾‾‾‾‾
               A   B   C   D

_____ 10. Each lines of poetry written in blank verse has ten syllables, which are alternately
          ‾‾‾‾‾‾‾‾‾   ‾‾‾‾‾‾‾‾   ‾‾‾‾   ‾‾‾‾‾‾‾‾‾‾‾
              A   B   C   D

          stressed and unstressed.

PROBLEMS WITH ADJECTIVES AND ADVERBS _____

Many different problems with adjectives and adverbs are possible in the Written Expression section of the TOEFL test. To identify these problems, you must first be able to recognize adjectives and adverbs.

Often adverbs are formed by adding *-ly* to adjectives, and these *-ly* adverbs are very easy to recognize. The following examples show adverbs that are formed by adding *-ly* to adjectives:

ADJECTIVE	ADVERB
recent	*recently*
public	*publicly*
evident	*evidently*

However, there are many adverbs in English that do not end in *-ly*. These adverbs can be recognized from their meanings. They can describe *when* something happens (*often, soon, later*), *how* something happens (*fast, hard, well*), or *where* something happens (*here, there, nowhere*).

There are three skills involving adjectives and adverbs that will help you on the Written Expression section of the TOEFL test: (1) knowing when to use adjectives and adverbs, (2) using adjectives rather than adverbs after linking verbs, and (3) positioning adjectives and adverbs correctly.

SKILL 46:   USE BASIC ADJECTIVES AND ADVERBS CORRECTLY

Sometimes in the Written Expression section of the TOEFL test, adjectives are used in place of adverbs, or adverbs are used in place of adjectives. Adjectives and adverbs have very different uses. Adjectives have only one job: they describe nouns or pronouns.

She is a *beautiful* woman.
       ADJ.   NOUN

She is *beautiful*.
PRO.   ADJ.

In the first example, the adjective *beautiful* describes the noun *woman*. In the second example, the adjective *beautiful* describes the pronoun *she*.

Adverbs do three different things. They describe verbs, adjectives, or other adverbs.

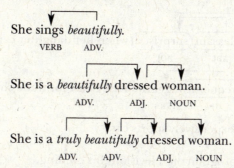

In the first example, the adverb *beautifully* describes the verb *sings*. In the second example, the adverb *beautifully* describes the adjective *dressed* (which describes the noun *woman*). In the third example, the adverb *truly* describes the adverb *beautifully*, which describes the adjective *dressed* (which describes the noun *woman*).

The following are examples of incorrect sentences as they might appear on the TOEFL test.

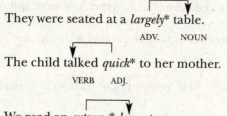

In the first example, the adverb *largely* is incorrect because the adjective *large* is needed to describe the noun *table*. In the second example, the adjective *quick* is incorrect because the adverb *quickly* is needed to describe the verb *talked*. In the last example, the adjective *extreme* is incorrect because the adverb *extremely* is needed to describe the adjective *long*.

The following chart outlines the important information that you should remember about the basic use of adjectives and adverbs:

BASIC USE OF ADJECTIVES AND ADVERBS	
ADJECTIVES	Adjectives describe *nouns* or *pronouns*.
ADVERBS	Adverbs describe *verbs*, *adjectives*, or other *adverbs*.

EXERCISE 46: Each of the following sentences has at least one adjective or adverb. Circle the adjectives and adverbs, and label them. Draw arrows to the words they describe. Then indicate if the sentences are correct (C) or incorrect (I).

__I__   1.   The mother was (pleasant)(surprised) when her daughter came to visit.
              ADJ.   ADJ.

__C__   2.   The salespeople (frequently) visit the East Coast for trade shows.
              ADV.   VERB

_____   3.   He was driving an expensively sports car.

_____   4.   There is a special program on television this evening.

_____   5.   She was chosen for the leading part because she sings so well.

_____   6.   The car was not complete ready at 3:00.

_____   7.   It was difficult to believe that what we read in the newspaper was a truly story.

_____   8.   Points will be subtracted for each incorrect answered question.

_____   9.   The production manager quietly requested a completely report of the terribly incident.

_____   10.   The children finished their homework quickly so they could watch television.

SKILL 47:   USE ADJECTIVES AFTER LINKING VERBS

Generally an adverb rather than an adjective will come directly after a verb because the adverb is describing the verb.

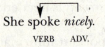

She spoke *nicely.*
VERB   ADV.

In this example, the verb *spoke* is followed by the adverb *nicely.* This adverb describes the verb *spoke.*

However, you must be very careful if the verb is a *linking* verb. A *linking* verb is followed by an adjective rather than an adverb.

She looks *nice.*
SUB.   ADJ.

In this example, the linking verb *looks* is followed by the adjective *nice.* This adjective describes the subject *she.*

You should be sure to use an adjective rather than an adverb after a linking verb. Be careful, however, because the adjective that goes with the linking verb does not always directly follow the linking verb.

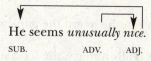

He seems *unusually nice*.
SUB.   ADV.   ADJ.

In this example, the adjective *nice,* which describes the subject *he,* is itself described by the adverb *unusually.* From this example, you should notice that it is possible to have an adverb directly after a linking verb, but only if the adverb describes an adjective that follows.

The following chart lists commonly used linking verbs and outlines the different uses of adjectives and adverbs after regular verbs and linking verbs:

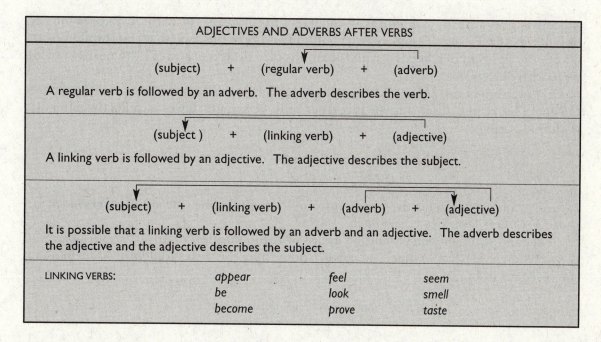

ADJECTIVES AND ADVERBS AFTER VERBS

(subject)   +   (regular verb)   +   (adverb)

A regular verb is followed by an adverb. The adverb describes the verb.

(subject)   +   (linking verb)   +   (adjective)

A linking verb is followed by an adjective. The adjective describes the subject.

(subject)   +   (linking verb)   +   (adverb)   +   (adjective)

It is possible that a linking verb is followed by an adverb and an adjective. The adverb describes the adjective and the adjective describes the subject.

LINKING VERBS:

appear	*feel*	*seem*
be	*look*	*smell*
become	*prove*	*taste*

EXERCISE 47: Each of the following sentences contains at least one adjective or adverb. Circle the adjectives and adverbs, and label them. Draw arrows to the words they describe. Then indicate if the sentences are correct (C) or incorrect (I).

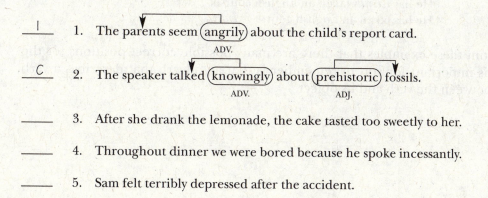

___I___ 1. The parents seem (angrily) about the child's report card.
                        ADV.

___C___ 2. The speaker talked (knowingly) about (prehistoric) fossils.
                        ADV.   ADJ.

_____ 3. After she drank the lemonade, the cake tasted too sweetly to her.

_____ 4. Throughout dinner we were bored because he spoke incessantly.

_____ 5. Sam felt terribly depressed after the accident.

_____ 6. The neighbor appeared calm in spite of the fact that his house was on fire.

_____ 7. He looked quite unhappily at the thought of leaving his job.

_____ 8. Marla jumped up quick when she heard the gunshot.

_____ 9. Even though we were not really hungry, the food smelled delicious.

_____ 10. The history course that I took last semester proved more difficultly than I had expected.

SKILL 48:   POSITION ADJECTIVES AND ADVERBS CORRECTLY

Adjectives and adverbs can appear in incorrect positions in the Written Expression section of the TOEFL test. There are two common errors of this type that you should beware of: (1) the position of adjectives with the nouns they describe, and (2) the position of adverbs with objects.

In English it is correct to place a one-word adjective in front of the noun it describes. On the TOEFL test, however, an incorrect sentence might have an adjective after the noun it describes.

The information *important** is on the first page.
NOUN   ADJ.

In this example, the adjective *important* should come before the noun *information,* because *important* describes *information.*

A second problem you should be aware of is the position of adverbs with objects of verbs. When a verb has an object, an adverb describing the verb should not come between the verb and its object.

He has taken *recently** an English course.
ADV.   OBJECT

This example is incorrect because the adverb *recently* comes between the verb *has taken* and its object *an English course.* There are many possible corrections for this sentence.

Recently he has taken an English course.
He has *recently* taken an English course.
He has taken an English course *recently.*

You can see from these examples that there are many possible correct positions for the adverb. What is important for you to remember is that an adverb that describes a verb cannot come between the verb and its object.

The following chart outlines the key points that you should remember about the position of adjectives and adverbs:

THE POSITION OF ADJECTIVES AND ADVERBS	
ADJECTIVES	A one-word *adjective* comes before the noun it describes. It does not come directly after.
ADVERBS	An *adverb* can appear in many positions. It cannot be used between a verb and its object.

EXERCISE 48: Each of the following sentences contains at least one adjective or adverb. Circle the adjectives and adverbs, and label them. Draw arrows to the words they describe. Then indicate if the sentences are correct (C) or incorrect (I).

___I___   1. The store opened with a sale (fantastic.)
                                          ADJ.

___C___   2. The pharmacist has (always) filled our order (quickly.)
                                 ADV.   ADV.

_____   3. The political candidates expressed their opposing views.

_____   4. The lawyer has selected carefully a new case.

_____   5. Frequently the coffee has tasted bitter.

_____   6. The wedding reception was held at a restaurant expensive.

_____   7. The salesclerk has often traveled to New York.

_____   8. Following the failure of the first set of plans, the manager has altered subsequently them.

_____   9. The students had to study many hours daily during the program intensive.

_____ 10. The naval officer was asked to transfer to a foreign country.

EXERCISE (Skills 46–48): Circle the adjectives and adverbs in the following sentences. Draw arrows to the words they describe. Then indicate if the sentences are correct (C) or incorrect (I).

_____   1. They were unable to see where their friends were sitting in the theater because of the lights dim.

_____   2. After the comprehensive exam, she looked exhaustedly by the experience.

_____   3. The project was remarkable close to being finished.

_____   4. Mark always does his homework careful.

_____   5. The program proved far more interesting than I had imagined it would be.

_____   6. The student had attended regularly all the lectures in the series.

_____   7. The patient became healthy after the operation.

_____   8. The grandparents speak proudly about all their offspring.

_____   9. The manager seemed certainly that the project would be finished under budget.

_____   10. The firefighters worked feverishly, and they put out immediately the fire.

TOEFL EXERCISE (Skills 46–48): Choose the letter of the underlined word or group of words that is not correct.

_____   1. Modern art is on display at the Guggenhein Museum, a building with an unusually
                   A   B   C   D

             design.

_____   2. By the beginning of the 1980s fifteen states had adopted already no-fault insurance
                            A   B   C   D

             laws.

_____   3. Heart attacks are fatally in 75 percent of occurrences.
                   A   B   C   D

_____   4. In spite of a tremendous amount of electronic gadgetry, air traffic control still
                           A   B   C

             depends heavy on people.
                      D

_____   5. Only recently have Gooden's industrially designers and engineers been able to
                   A   B

             optimize Watertred's unusual tread patterns for mass production.
                        C   D

_____   6. A baboon's arms appear as lengthily as its legs.
                   A   B   C   D

_____   7. A serious problem is how to communicate reliable with a submerged submarine.
                   A   B   C   D

_____   8. Americans are destroying rapidly wetlands, faster than an acre every two minutes.
                   A   B   C   D

_____   9. The central banking system of the United States consists of twelve banks district.
                   A   B   C   D

_____   10. Telegraph service across the Atlantic was successful established in 1866.
                     A   B   C   D

TOEFL REVIEW EXERCISE (Skills 1–48): Choose the letter of the word or group of words that best completes the sentence.

1. Patty Berg, the top tournament winner in women's golf, _____ eighty-three golf tournaments from 1935 through 1964.

    (A) she won
    (B) winning
    (C) won
    (D) who won

2. _____ with about fifteen times its weight in air does gasoline allow the carburetor to run smoothly.

    (A) It is mixed
    (B) To mix it
    (C) When mixed
    (D) Only when mixed

Choose the letter of the underlined word or group of words that is not correct.

_____ 3. The Colorado River reaches their maximum height during April and May.
                              A   B   C   D

_____ 4. Plant proteins tend to have few amino acids than proteins from animal sources.
                A   B   C   D

_____ 5. The Viking spacecraft has landed on Mars in July of 1976.
                A   B   C   D

_____ 6. Admiral Byrd commanded airplane expeditions over both the Arctic or the
                              A   B   C   D

Antarctic.

_____ 7. The advertising campaign will be based on the recent completed study.
                    A   B   C   D

_____ 8. Coronary occlusion results from a disease in which fatty substances with a large
                                A   B

amount of cholesterol is deposited in the arteries.
    C   D

_____ 9. Her money gave back as soon as she threatened to take the matter to court.
                        A   B   C   D

_____ 10. Other sites of fossil discoveries throughout Wyoming, ranging from the fiery
                A   B

Tyrannosaurus rex to the milder *Triceratops,* have proven equally excite.
                            C   D

MORE PROBLEMS WITH ADJECTIVES_____

The previous section dealt with various problems related to both adjectives and adverbs. This section deals with a few problems that are related only to adjectives: (1) -*ly* adjectives, (2) predicate adjectives, and (3) -*ed* and -*ing* adjectives.

SKILL 49:   RECOGNIZE -*LY* ADJECTIVES

Generally when a word ends in -*ly* in English, it is an adverb. However, there are a few words ending in -*ly* that are adjectives, and these -*ly* adjectives can cause confusion in the Written Expression section of the TOEFL test.

The manager turned in his *weekly* report.

ADJ.   NOUN

This example is correct, but it appears to be incorrect; it appears that there is an -*ly* adverb in front of the noun *report*. However, *weekly* is an adjective that describes the noun *report*.

The following chart lists common -*ly* adjectives that can appear in English:

-LY ADJECTIVES				
costly	likely	daily	quarterly	northerly
early	lively	hourly	weekly	easterly
friendly	lonely	monthly	yearly	southerly
kindly	manly	nightly	lovely	westerly

EXERCISE 49: Each of the following sentences contains at least one adjective or adverb ending in -*ly*. Circle the -*ly* words, and label them as either adjectives or adverbs. Draw arrows to the words they describe. Then indicate if the sentences are correct (C) or incorrect (I).

___C___   1. Federal taxes are (yearly) taxes which must be paid every April.
                   ADJ.

___I___   2. At the fashion show, the new (seasonally) fashions will be shown.
                   ADV.

_____   3. Do you want to go to the early movie or the lately movie?

_____   4. She offered me some friendly advice about how to deal with the terribly problem.

_____   5. The quarterly reports need to be turned in at the next weekly meeting.

_____   6. He did not have a manly reaction to the negatively comments.

_____   7. The likely outcome of the purchase of the costly car is that he will not be able to pay his monthly bills.

_____ 8. The days she spent at the beach house were lonely and solitarily.

_____ 9. She takes her daily medication on a regularly schedule.

_____ 10. The kindly neighbor paid hourly visits to her unhealthily friend.

SKILL 50:   USE PREDICATE ADJECTIVES CORRECTLY

Certain adjectives appear only in the predicate of the sentence; that is, they appear after a linking verb such as *be,* and they cannot appear directly in front of the nouns that they describe.

> The snake on the rock was *alive.*
> The *alive** snake was lying on the rock.

In the first example, the predicate adjective *alive* is used correctly after the linking verb *was* to describe the subject *snake.* In the second example, the predicate adjective *alive* is used incorrectly in front of the noun *snake.* In this position, the adjective *live* should be used.

The following chart lists some common predicate adjectives and the corresponding forms that can be used in front of the noun:

PREDICATE ADJECTIVES	
PREDICATE ADJECTIVES	FORMS USED IN FRONT OF NOUN
alike	*like, similar*
alive	*live, living*
alone	*lone*
afraid	*frightened*
asleep	*sleeping*
A predicate adjective appears after a linking verb such as *be.* It cannot appear directly in front of the noun that it describes.	

EXERCISE 50: Each of the following sentences contains a predicate adjective or its related form. Circle the predicate adjectives or related forms. Then indicate if the sentences are correct (C) or incorrect (I).

__C__ 1. The two brothers do not look at all (alike.)

__I__ 2. My friend brought the (alive) lobster to my house and expected me to cook it.

_____ 3. Are you going to be lone in the house tonight?

_____ 4. The afraid child cried for his mother.

_____ 5. Everyone else was asleep by the time I arrived home.

_____ 6. We completed our two projects in a like manner.

_____ 7. All of the crash victims were alive when they were found.

_____ 8. She tried to walk quietly by the asleep dogs without waking them.

_____ 9. Were you feeling afraid when you heard the noise?

_____ 10. According to the report, the president was shot by an alone gunman.

SKILL 51: USE -*ED* AND -*ING* ADJECTIVES CORRECTLY

Verb forms ending in -*ed* and -*ing* can be used as adjectives. For example, the verbal adjectives *cleaned* and *cleaning* come from the verb *to clean*.

The woman *cleans* the car.
VERB

The *cleaning* woman worked on the car.
ADJECTIVE

The woman put the *cleaned* car back in the garage.
ADJECTIVE

In the first example, *cleans* is the verb of the sentence. In the second example, *cleaning* is a verbal adjective describing *woman*. In the third example, *cleaned* is a verbal adjective describing *car*.

Verbal adjectives ending in -*ed* and -*ing* can be confused in the Written Expression section of the TOEFL test.

The *cleaning** car . . .
The *cleaned** woman . . .

The difference between an -*ed* and an -*ing* adjective is similar to the difference between the active and the passive (see Skills 37 and 38). An -*ing* adjective (like the active) means that the noun it describes is *doing* the action. The above example about the *cleaning* car is not correct because a car cannot do the action of cleaning: you cannot say that *a car cleans itself*. An -*ed* adjective (like the passive) means that the noun it describes is *receiving* the action from the verb. The above example about *the cleaned woman* is not correct because in this example a woman cannot receive the action of the verb *clean*: this sentence does not mean that *someone cleaned the woman*.

The following chart outlines the key information that you should remember about *-ed* and *-ing* adjectives:

-ED AND -ING ADJECTIVES			
TYPE	MEANING	USE	EXAMPLE
-ING	active	It *does* the action of the verb.	. . . the happily *playing* children . . . (The children *play*.)
-ED	passive	It *receives* the action of the verb.	. . . the frequently *played* record . . . (Someone *plays* the record.)

EXERCISE 51: Each of the following sentences contains either an *-ed* or an *-ing* verbal adjective. Circle the verbal adjectives. Draw arrows to the words they describe. Then indicate if the sentences are correct (C) or incorrect (I).

_ I _   1. The teacher gave a quiz on the just (completing) lesson.

_ C _   2. There is a (fascinating) movie at the theater tonight.

_____   3. They thought that it had been a very satisfied dinner.

_____   4. The empty bottles are to the left, and the filling bottles are to the right.

_____   5. For lunch at the restaurant she ordered a mixed salad.

_____   6. The students thought that it was an interesting assignment.

_____   7. The shoppers were impressed by the reducing prices.

_____   8. He can't afford to take long vacations to exotic places because he is a worked man.

_____   9. I recently received several annoying phone calls from the insurance agent.

_____ 10. Today the bookkeeper is working on the unpaying bills.

EXERCISE (Skills 49–51): Circle the adjectives in each of the following sentences. Draw arrows to the nouns or pronouns they describe. Then indicate if the sentences are correct (C) or incorrect (I).

_____   1. Her kindly words of thanks made me feel appreciating.

_____   2. After the earthquake, assistance was sent to the damaging areas.

_____   3. Your view has some validity; however, we do not have alike opinions on the matter.

_____   4. It is likely that the early seminar will not be the most interested.

_____   5. I prefer a live theater show to a movie.

_____ 6. The thesis of your essay was not very well developed.

_____ 7. The asleep children were wakened by the loud sound of the crashing thunder.

_____ 8. During the nightly news show there was a lively and fascinating debate.

_____ 9. His car was struck by an uninsured motorist.

_____ 10. The girl was all alone and feeling lonely in the darkened, frightened house.

TOEFL EXERCISE (Skills 49–51): Choose the letter of the underlined word or group of words that is not correct.

_____ 1. As the only major American river that flowed in a west direction, the Ohio was the
             A   B   C

preferred route for settlers.
   D

_____ 2. During the annually salmon migration from the sea to fresh water, Alaska's McNeil
                    A   B

River becomes a gathering place for brown bears waiting eagerly to catch their fill.
                    C   D

_____ 3. Edelman stresses the mounting evidence showing that greatly variation on a
                            A   B   C

microscopic scale is likely.
                      D

_____ 4. Perhaps the most welcoming and friendly of the park's wild places is the live oak
                          A   B   C

forest that surrounds the district's alone visitors' center in Gulf Breeze.
                                     D

_____ 5. Halley's comet, viewing through a telescope, was quite impressive.
                         A   B   C   D

_____ 6. The state of deep asleep is characterized by rapid eye movement, or REM, sleep.
                      A   B   C   D

_____ 7. Among the disputing sections of the Monteverdi opera are the sinfonia, the
                   A   B   C   D

prologue, and the role of Ottone.

_____ 8. Most probably because of the likable rapport between anchors, the night newscast
              A   B   C

on the local ABC affiliate has recently moved well beyond its competitors in the
                                D

ratings battle.

_____ 9. Signing at the outset of a business deal, a contract offers the participants a certain
           A   B   C

degree of legal protection from costly mistakes.
                                 D

_____ 10. The story presented by Fischer is a headlong tale told so effectively that
                                              A   B

its momentum carries the reader right through the live endnotes.
      C   D

TOEFL REVIEW EXERCISE (Skills 1–51): Choose the letter of the word or group of words that best completes the sentence.

1. During the early nineteenth century, the Spanish missions in Alta, California _____ to be an integral part of the economy and productive capacity of the region.

   (A) proved
   (B) they proved
   (C) they proved it
   (D) proved it

2. Still other hurdles remain before _____ suitable for private cars.

   (A) fuel cells
   (B) become
   (C) fuel cells become
   (D) that fuel cells become

3. The daughters of Joseph LaFlesche were born into the generation of Omaha forced to abandon tribal traditions, _____ on the reservation, and to adapt to the white man's ways.

   (A) they matured
   (B) to mature
   (C) maturing
   (D) to maturity

4. Among the most revealing aspects of mining towns _____ their paucity of public open space.

   (A) was
   (B) were
   (C) it was
   (D) so

Choose the letter of the underlined word or group of words that is not correct.

_____ 5. Factor analysis is used to discover how many abilities are involve in intelligence test
                   A   B   C   D

performance.

_____ 6. One of the early orders of marine mammals, manatees have evolved more than fifty
                    A   B

million years ago from land animals.
    C   D

_____ 7. Dolphins and chimps are like in that they have been shown to have language skills.
                          A B   C   D

_____ 8. In the appendix at the end of the chapter are the instructions to be used for the
                               A   B   C

completion correct of the form.
          D

_____ 9. Used sound that varies not only in time but in space, whales at close range may
          A   B   C

            communicate with sonarlike "pictures."
                      D

_____10. The 1898 Trans-Mississippi International Exposition has the distinction of being the
                                                            A   B

            last major fair which held during the Victorian period.
                              C   D

PROBLEMS WITH ARTICLES

Articles are very difficult to learn because there are many rules, many exceptions, and many special cases. It is possible, however, to learn a few rules that will help you to use articles correctly much of the time.

Nouns in English can be either countable or uncountable. If a noun is countable, it must be either singular or plural. In addition to these general types of nouns, there are two types of articles: definite (specific) and indefinite (general).

ARTICLES	COUNTABLE SINGULAR NOUNS	COUNTABLE PLURAL NOUNS	UNCOUNTABLE NOUNS
INDEFINITE (General)	*a* dollar *an* apple	_____ dollars _____ apples	_____ money _____ juice
DEFINITE (Specific)	*the* dollar *the* apple	*the* dollars *the* apples	*the* money *the* juice

SKILL 52:   USE ARTICLES WITH SINGULAR NOUNS

You can see from the chart that if a noun is either countable plural or uncountable, it is possible to have either the definite article *the* or no article (indefinite). With **all** countable singular nouns, however, you must have an article (unless you have another determiner such as *my* or *each*).

      I have *money.*   (uncountable — no article needed)
      I have *books.*   (countable plural — no article needed)
      I have a *book.*   (countable singular — article needed)

The following chart outlines the key information that you should remember about articles with singular nouns:

ARTICLES WITH SINGULAR NOUNS
A singular noun **must** have an article (*a, an, the*) or some other determiner such as *my* or *each*. (A plural noun or an uncountable noun **may** or **may not** have an article.)

EXERCISE 52: The following sentences contain different types of nouns. Circle only the countable singular nouns. Mark where articles (or determiners) have been omitted. Then indicate if the sentences are correct (C) or incorrect (I).

___I___   1. She is taking ∨(trip) with friends.

___C___   2. In my (yard) there are flowers, trees, and grass.

_____   3. The manager sent memo to his employees.

_____   4. There is car in front of the building.

_____   5. The child and his friends are having milk and cookies.

_____   6. She is studying to be an actress in films.

_____   7. My neighbor was arrested for throwing rocks through windows.

_____   8. We have machinery that prints ten pages each minute.

_____   9. Teacher has many students during a semester.

_____ 10. Can you heat water for tea?

SKILL 53:   DISTINGUISH A AND *AN*

The basic difference between *a* and *an* is that *a* is used in front of consonants and *an* is used in front of vowels (*a, e, i, o, u*):

a book	*an* orange
a man	*an* illness
a page	*an* automobile

In reality, the rule is that *a* is used in front of a word that begins with a consonant *sound* and that *an* is used in front of a word that begins with a vowel *sound*. Pronounce the following examples:

a university	*a* hand	*a* one-way street	*a* euphemism	*a* xerox machine
an unhappy man	*an* hour	*an* omen	*an* event	*an* x-ray machine

These examples show that certain beginning letters can have either a consonant or a vowel sound. A word that begins with *u* can begin with a consonant *y* sound as in *university* or with a vowel sound as in *unhappy.* A word that begins with *h* can begin with a consonant *h* sound as in *hand* or with a vowel sound as in *hour.* A word that begins with *o* can begin with a consonant *w* sound as in *one* or with a vowel sound as in *omen.* A word that begins with *e* can begin with either a consonant *y* sound as in *euphemism* or with a vowel sound as in *event.* A word that begins with *x* can begin with either a consonant *z* sound as in *xerox* or with a vowel sound as in *x-ray.*

The following chart outlines the key information about the use of *a* and *an*:

A AND *AN*	
A	A is used in front of a singular noun with a *consonant* sound.
AN	*An* is used in front of a singular noun with a *vowel* sound.
Be careful of words beginning with letters such as *u, o, e, x,* or *h.* They may begin with either a *vowel* or a *consonant* sound.	

EXERCISE 53: Each of the following sentences contains *a* or *an*. Circle each *a* or *an*. Underline the beginning of the word that directly follows. Pronounce the word. Then indicate if the sentences are correct (C) or incorrect (I).

___I___   1.   The dishwasher quit his job because he was making only four dollars ⓐ <u>h</u>our.

___C___   2.   It was ⓐn <u>u</u>nexpected disappointment to receive ⓐ <u>r</u>ejection letter from the university.

_____   3.   A signature is required wherever you see a X on the form.

_____   4.   He bought a half gallon of milk and a box of a hundred envelopes.

_____   5.   An objection was raised because it was such a unacceptable idea.

_____   6.   There are two trees in the yard, an elm tree and a eucalyptus tree.

_____   7.   The police officer was not wearing an uniform when she arrested the suspect.

_____   8.   If you do not give me a hand, finishing the project on time will be an impossibility.

_____   9.   She was upset when a honest mistake was made.

_____   10.   She opened a account at a local department store during a one-day sale.

SKILL 54:   MAKE ARTICLES AGREE WITH NOUNS

The definite article (*the*) is used for both singular and plural nouns, so agreement is not a problem with the definite article. However, because the use of the indefinite article is different for singular and plural nouns, you must be careful of agreement between the indefinite article and the noun. One very common agreement error is to use the singular indefinite article (*a* or *an*) with a plural noun.

> He saw *a** new *movies*.
> They traveled to *a** nearby *mountains*.
> Do you have *another** *books*?

In these examples, you should not have *a* or *an* because the nouns are plural. The following sentences are possible corrections of the sentences above.

He saw a new movie.	(singular)
He saw new movies.	(plural)
They traveled to a nearby mountain.	(singular)
They traveled to nearby mountains.	(plural)
Do you have another book?	(singular)
Do you have other books?	(plural)

The following chart states the key point for you to remember about the agreement of articles with nouns:

AGREEMENT OF ARTICLES WITH NOUNS
You should never use *a* or *an* with a plural noun.

EXERCISE 54: Each of the following sentences contains *a* or *an*. Circle each *a* or *an*. Draw an arrow to the noun it describes. Then indicate if the sentences are correct (C) or incorrect (I).

    C   1. She went to school in (a) local community.

    I   2. The doctor used (an)other pills.

          3. It is necessary to have a farm or land of your own.

          4. He must contact a members of the club.

          5. You will need a pen or a pencil.

          6. He is responsible for bringing a number of items.

          7. You must write a report on a subjects of your choice.

          8. They crossed through several forests and a stream.

          9. There will be another important lessons tomorrow.

       10. He could not give me a good reasons for what he did.

SKILL 55:   DISTINGUISH SPECIFIC AND GENERAL IDEAS

With countable singular nouns it is possible to use either the definite or the indefinite article, but they have different meanings. The definite article is used to refer to one specific noun.

> Tom will bring *the* book tomorrow.
> (There is one specific book that Tom will bring tomorrow.)
>
> He will arrive on *the* first Tuesday in July.
> (There is only one first Tuesday in July.)
>
> He sailed on *the* Pacific Ocean.
> (There is only one Pacific Ocean.)

The definite article is used when the noun could be one of several different nouns.

> Tom will bring *a* book tomorrow.
> (Tom will bring any one book.)
>
> He will arrive on *a* Tuesday in July.
> (He will arrive on one of four Tuesdays in July.)
>
> He sailed on *an* ocean.
> (He sailed on any one of the world's oceans.)

The following chart outlines the key information that you should understand about specific and general ideas:

SPECIFIC AND GENERAL IDEAS		
ARTICLE	MEANING	USES
A or AN	general idea	Use when there are *many*, and you do not *know* which one it is. Use when there are *many*, and you do not *care* which one it is.
THE	specific idea	Use when it is *the only one*. Use when there are *many*, and you *know* which one it is.

EXERCISE 55: Each of the following sentences contains one or more articles. Circle the articles. Draw arrows to the nouns they describe. Then indicate if the sentences are correct (C) or incorrect (I).

__I__   1. He took (a) trip on (a) Snake River.

__C__   2. I'll meet you at (the) library later.

_____ 3. The ball hit a child on a head.

_____ 4. He had a best grade in the class on the exam.

_____ 5. The people who came here yesterday were here again today.

_____ 6. She was a most beautiful girl in the room.

_____ 7. The trip that I took last year to the Bahamas was the only vacation I had all year.

_____ 8. I need a piece of paper so that I can finish the report that I am working on.

_____ 9. A basketball player threw the ball to a center of the court.

_____ 10. The sixth-grade class went on a field trip to visit a Lincoln Memorial.

EXERCISE (Skills 52–55): Circle the articles in the following sentences. Then indicate if the sentences are correct (C) or incorrect (I).

_____ 1. He took a money from his wallet to pay for sweater.

_____ 2. The notebook that he left had an important assignment in it.

_____ 3. Because of previous disagreements, they are trying to arrive at an understanding.

_____ 4. The appearance of room could be improved by adding a green plants.

_____ 5. The Senate passed law banning smoking in public workplaces.

_____ 6. Each chemistry student should bring laboratory manual to a next class.

_____ 7. She admitted that she made mistake but said that she had made a honest effort.

_____ 8. His absence from the board meeting was a strong indications of his desire to leave the company.

_____ 9. The car needed gas, so the driver stopped at a service station.

_____ 10. Anyone taking group tour to the Hawaiian Islands must pay fee before a first of the month.

TOEFL EXERCISE (Skills 52–55): Choose the letter of the underlined word or group of words that is not correct.

_____ 1. On a trip down to the bottom of the Grand Canyon, the equipment will in all
          A   B   C

probability be carried by a burros.
                D

_____ 2. Ford designed the first large-scale assembly line at plant in
                A   B   C

Highland Park, Michigan.
       D

_____ 3. In the human body, blood flows from a heart through the arteries, and it returns
      A   B   C

through the veins.
      D

_____ 4. The scholarship that Wilson received to study history at Cambridge presented an
        A   B   C   D

unique opportunity.

_____ 5. Observations from Earth indicate that at the solar surface, the outward magnetic
                                 A   B

field is a strongest at the polar regions.
       C   D

_____ 6. A radar images of Venus add details about a planet dominated by
      A   B   C

volcanoes and lava.
      D

_____ 7. In 1863 and 1864, the U.S. Congress passed the National Bank Acts, which set up a
                                  A   B

system of privately owned banks chartered by a federal government.
          C   D

_____ 8. An human ear responds to a wide range of frequencies.
      A   B   C   D

_____ 9. Bacteria that live in soil and water play a vital role in recycling carbon, nitrogen,
                        A   B

sulfur, and another chemical elements used by living things.
          C   D

_____ 10. During the U.S. Civil War, an American balloonist organized a balloon corps in Army.
        A   B   C   D

TOEFL REVIEW EXERCISE (Skills 1–55): Choose the letter of the word or group of words that best completes the sentence.

1. In economics, "diminishing returns" describes _____ resource inputs and production.

   (A) among
   (B) when it is
   (C) among them
   (D) the relationship between

2. When lava reaches the surface, its temperature can be ten times _____ boiling water.

   (A) the temperature
   (B) that of
   (C) it is
   (D) more

3. Rarely _____ remove the entire root of a dandelion because of its length and sturdiness.

   (A) can the casual gardener
   (B) the casual gardener
   (C) the casual gardener will
   (D) does the casual gardener's

Choose the letter of the underlined word or group of words that is not correct.

_____ 4. Operas can be broadly classified as either comedies or they are tragedies.
                        A   B   C   D

_____ 5. Tungsten has the highest melting point of all metals, and for this reason it is often
                      A

use in equipment that must withstand high temperatures.
 B   C   D

_____ 6. Whereas there are forty-three ant species in Great Britain, the same amount of ant
          A   B   C

species can be found in a single tree in Peru.
                          D

_____ 7. People voice theirs opinions first in small groups or among friends and acquaintances.
                     A   B   C   D

_____ 8. Inside the Lincoln Memorial is a large statue of Lincoln make from white marble.
                                       A   B   C   D

_____ 9. Detailed photometric data of the area just north of Triton's equatorial region indicate
                     A   B

the existence of a thin, transparent layers of frost.
                    C   D

_____10. U.S. census figures indicate that people with only an elementary education can earn
                            A   B

just half as much as college graduations.
     C   D

PROBLEMS WITH PREPOSITIONS_____

Prepositions can be used in two ways: in a literal way and in an idiomatic way. In the literal use, the preposition means exactly what you expect.

> The boy ran *up* the hill.
> She went *in* the house.

In the first example, the preposition *up* means that the boy went in the direction *up* rather than *down*. In the second example, the preposition *in* means that she went *into* rather than *out of* the house.

   In the idiomatic use, which is what appears most often on the TOEFL test, the preposition appears in an idiomatic expression; that is, its meaning in this expression has nothing to do with the literal meaning.

> I call *up* my friend.
> He succeeded *in* passing the course.

In the first example, the word *up* has nothing to do with the direction *up*. *To call up someone* means *to telephone* someone. In the second example, the word *in* has nothing to do with the meaning of *into* or *inside*; it is simply idiomatic that the word *in* is used after the verb *succeed*.

   It is impossible to list all potential idiomatic expressions with their prepositions because there are so many expressions that could appear on the TOEFL test. However, in this section you can practice recognizing problems with prepositions in TOEFL-type questions. Then, when you are working in the Written Expression section of the TOEFL test, you should be aware that idiomatic errors with prepositions are common in that section. There are two common types of problems with prepositions that you should expect: (1) incorrect prepositions and (2) omitted prepositions.

SKILL 56:   RECOGNIZE INCORRECT PREPOSITIONS

Sometimes an incorrect preposition is given in a sentence in the Written Expression section of the TOEFL test.

> The game was called *on** because of rain.
> I knew I could count *in** you to do a good job.

The first example should say that the game was *called off* because of rain. The expression *called off* means *canceled,* and that is the meaning that makes sense in this sentence. *To call on someone* is *to visit someone,* and this meaning does not make sense in this example. In the second example, it is not correct in English to *count in someone*. The correct expression is to *count on someone*.

EXERCISE 56: Each of the following sentences contains at least one preposition. Circle the prepositions. Then indicate if the sentences are correct (C) or incorrect (I).

_C_   1. (After) school many students participate (in) sports.

_I_   2. I know I can rely (in) you to be here (on) time.

_____   3. If you need more light to read, turn on the lamp next to you.

_____   4. Parents always try to bring at their children to be thoughtful.

_____   5. I'll have to consult to my attorney before making a decision.

_____   6. Walt has lost his keys, so he must look for them.

_____   7. I just don't approve at your cheating on the exam.

_____   8. Smoking is forbidden, so you should put out your cigarette.

_____   9. Failure to pass the test will result to the loss of your license.

_____   10. It is unlawful for parolees to associate with known felons.

SKILL 57:   RECOGNIZE WHEN PREPOSITIONS HAVE BEEN OMITTED

Sometimes a necessary preposition has been omitted from a sentence in the Written Expression section of the TOEFL test.

> Can you *wait** me after the game?
> I *plan** attending the meeting.

The first example is incorrect because it is necessary to say *wait for me*. The second example is incorrect because it is necessary to say *plan on attending*.

EXERCISE 57: Prepositions have been omitted in some of the following sentences. Mark where prepositions have been omitted. Then indicate if the sentences are correct (C) or incorrect (I).

_I_   1. If you take this job, it will be necessary to deal^V other departments.

_C_   2. Each child took one cookie from the plate.

_____   3. In the discussion, Rob sided the rest.

_____   4. The board turned his suggestion for the project because it was too costly.

_____   5. He can always depend his friends.

_____   6. While Mrs. Sampson went shopping, a baby-sitter looked the children.

_____   7. I know Steve believes what you told him.

_____   8. Children should beware strangers.

_____   9. It was difficult to make a decision about buying a house.

_____   10. Tom blamed his brother the dent in the car.

EXERCISE (Skills 56–57): Circle the prepositions in the following sentences. Mark where they have been omitted. Then indicate if the sentences are correct (C) or incorrect (I).

_____   1. The students must hand in their homework.

_____   2. It will be difficult to forgive you of breaking your promise.

_____   3. Elizabeth excels math and science.

_____   4. She insisted on going to work in spite of her cold.

_____   5. Bob reminds me to his father because he looks just like him.

_____   6. If you are cold, you should put on your sweater.

_____   7. Mr. Sanders is not here now, but he will call you when he returns.

_____   8. I do not want to interfere your plans.

_____   9. Alan waited Marie after school.

_____   10. Bill laughs me whenever he looks me.

TOEFL EXERCISE (Skills 56–57): Choose the letter of the underlined word or group of words that is not correct.

_____ 1. Amelia Earhart, the first woman to fly solo across the Atlantic, disappeared on June
                        A   B   C

1937 while attempting to fly around the world.
                                              D

_____ 2. The occurrence edema indicates the presence of a serious illness.
                        A   B   C   D

_____ 3. Atomic nuclei are believed to be composed by protons and neutrons in equal
                              A   B   C   D

numbers for the lighter elements.

_____ 4. According legend, Betsy Ross designed and sewed the first American flag.
              A   B   C   D

_____ 5. The middle ear is attached for the back of the throat by the Eustachian tube.
                   A   B   C   D

_____ 6. Plants that sprout, grow, bloom, produce seeds, and die within one year are
                                                              A   B   C

classified for annuals.
                   D

_____ 7. A marionette is controlled by means strings connected to wooden bars.
                                    A   B   C   D

_____ 8. In July of 1861, Pat Garrett killed Billy the Kid in a house close Fort Sumner.
              A   B   C   D

_____ 9. Many comfort heating systems using steam as a working fluid operate at the
                                      A   B   C   D

convection principle.

_____ 10. Mars' two small moons are irregularly shaped and covered for craters.
              A   B   C   D

TOEFL REVIEW EXERCISE (1–57): Choose the letter of the word or group of words that best completes the sentence.

1. In any matter, heat tends to flow _____ to the cooler parts.

   (A) hotter parts
   (B) there are hotter parts
   (C) from the hotter parts
   (D) toward the hotter parts

2. Certain authorities claim that the costumes that people wear to parties _____ into their personalities.

   (A) give subtle insights
   (B) they give subtle insights
   (C) which give subtle insights
   (D) subtle insights

3. _____ Army camps near Washington, D.C., in 1861, Julia Ward Howe wrote "The Battle Hymn of the Republic."

   (A) She visited
   (B) After visiting
   (C) When visited
   (D) When was she visiting

Choose the letter of the underlined word or group of words that is not correct.

_____ 4. The body depends in food as its primary source of energy.
                        A   B   C D

_____ 5. Regular programming was interrupted to broadcast a special news bulletins.
                      A   B   C   D

_____ 6. Sulfa drugs had been used to treat bacterial infection until penicillin becomes widely
                                    A   B   C   D

available.

_____ 7. Plans for both the International Monetary Fund or the World Bank were drawn up
              A   B   C   D

at the Bretton Woods Conference.

_____ 8. Seldom Antarctic icebergs will move far enough north to disturb South Pacific
                        A   B   C

shipping lanes.
    D

_____ 9. In 1958, a largest recorded wave, with a height of 500 meters, occurred in Lituya
                A   B   C   D

   Bay, Alaska.

_____ 10. Exercise in swimming pools is particularly helpful because of the buoyant
                                     A   B   C

   effect water.
         D

PROBLEMS WITH USAGE

In English certain groups of words have similar uses, and these words are sometimes confused in the Written Expression section of the TOEFL test. Although various usage problems are possible on the TOEFL test, the following problems are the most common: (1) when to use *make* and *do;* (2) when to use *like, unlike,* and *alike;* and (3) when to use *other, another,* and *others.*

SKILL 58:   DISTINGUISH *MAKE* AND *DO*

Make and *do* can be confused in English because their meanings are so similar. Since the difference between *make* and *do* is tested on the TOEFL test, you should learn to distinguish them.

    Make often has the idea of *creating* or *constructing.* The following expressions show some of the possible uses of *make:*

> She likes to *make* her own clothes.
> Would you like to *make* a cake for dessert?
> If you *make* a mistake, you should correct it.
> He was unable to *make* a response to the threat.

Do often has the idea of *completing* or *performing.* The following expressions show some of the possible uses of *do:*

> This morning she *did* all the dishes.
> The students *are doing* the assignments.
> The janitors *did* the work they were assigned.
> You can *do* your laundry at the laundromat.

These are only some of the uses of *make* and *do.* Many uses of *make* and *do* are idiomatic and therefore difficult to classify.

EXERCISE 58: Each of the following sentences contains *make* or *do.* Circle *make* or *do.* Draw arrows to the nouns that complete the expressions. Then indicate if the sentences are correct (C) or incorrect (I).

__I__   1. The biology student (did) several mistakes in the lab report.

__C__   2. I hope that you will be able to (do) me a favor this afternoon.

_____ 3. 'No matter what job she has, she always makes her best.

_____ 4. The runner did a strong effort to increase her speed in the mile race.

_____ 5. It is comforting to think that your work can make a difference.

_____ 6. His grade was not very good because he had not done his homework.

_____ 7. In this job you will make more money than in your previous job.

_____ 8. He was unable to do dinner because no one had done the lunch dishes.

_____ 9. It is a pleasure to work with someone who always makes the right thing.

_____ 10. If you make a good impression at your job interview, you will get the job.

SKILL 59:   DISTINGUISH *LIKE, ALIKE, UNLIKE,* AND *DISLIKE*

Like, alike, unlike, and *dislike* are easily confused because they look so similar and they have many different uses. There are several structures with *like, alike, unlike,* and *dislike* that you should be familiar with.

The first structures you should already be familiar with are the adjectives *alike* and *like* (see Skill 50). Study the use of *alike* and *like* in the following examples.

> John and Tom are *alike*.
> John and Tom worked in a *like* manner.

In both these examples, *alike* and *like* are adjectives that mean *similar*. In the first example, *alike* is a predicate adjective describing *John* and *Tom*. Because *alike* is a predicate adjective, it can only be used after a linking verb such as *are*. In the second example, *like* is the adjective form that is used immediately before the noun *manner*.

The next structures you should be familiar with are the prepositions *like* and *unlike*, which have opposite meanings. Because they are prepositions, they must be followed by objects.

> John is (*like* Tom).
> John is (*unlike* Tom).

In the first example, the preposition *like* is followed by the object *Tom*. It means that Tom and John are similar. In the second example, the preposition *unlike* is followed by the object *Tom*. It means that Tom and John are not similar.

The prepositions *like* and *unlike* can also be used at the beginning of a sentence.

> (*Like* Tom), John is tall.
> (*Unlike* Tom), John is tall.

In the first example, the preposition *like* is followed by the object *Tom*. It means that Tom is tall. In the second example, the preposition *unlike* is followed by the object *Tom*. It means that Tom is not tall.

The final structures that you should be familiar with are the verbs *like* and *dislike*, which have opposite meanings. Because they are verbs, they are used with subjects.

> John and Tom *like* the course.
> John and Tom *dislike* the course.

In the first example, the verb *like* follows the subject *John and Tom*. It means that both men think that the course is enjoyable. In the second example, the verb *dislike* follows that subject *John and Tom*. It means that both men think that the course is not enjoyable.

The following chart outlines the structures and meanings of sentences with *like, alike, unlike,* and *dislike:*

LIKE, ALIKE, UNLIKE, AND DISLIKE			
	GRAMMAR	MEANING	USE
like *alike*	adjective adjective	similar similar	As an adjective, *like* is used before a noun. As an adjective, *alike* is used after a linking verb.
like *unlike*	preposition preposition	similar different	Both prepositions are followed by objects. They can both be used in many positions, including at the beginning of the sentence.
like *dislike*	verb verb	enjoy not enjoy	Both verbs follow subjects.

EXERCISE 59: Each of the following sentences contains *like, alike, unlike,* or *dislike.* Circle the *like* words. Then indicate if the sentences are correct (C) or incorrect (I).

__I__   1. The two routes you have chosen for the trip are (like.)

__C__   2. The science books this semester are (like) the books used last semester.

_____   3. Alike the restaurant where we usually eat, this new restaurant has early-bird specials.

_____   4. Unlike the traditional red fire engines, the new fire engines are yellow.

_____   5. The two girls disliked the fact that they were wearing alike dresses.

_____   6. The new piece that the pianist is preparing is unlike any she has ever played before.

_____   7. Like the Washington Zoo, the San Diego Zoo has several panda bears.

_____   8. The insurance package offered by that company is exactly alike the package our company offers.

_____   9. Any further work done in a like fashion will be rejected.

_____   10. It is unfortunate that the covers for this year's and last year's albums are so dislike.

Skill 60:   DISTINGUISH *OTHER, ANOTHER,* AND *OTHERS*

Other, another, and *others* are very easy to confuse. To decide how to use each of them correctly, you must consider three things: (1) if it is singular or plural, (2) if it is definite (*the*) or indefinite (*a*), and (3) if it is an adjective (it appears with a noun) or if it is a pronoun (it appears by itself).

	SINGULAR	PLURAL
INDEFINITE	I have *another* book. I have *another.*	I have *other* books. I have *others.*
DEFINITE	I have *the other* book. I have *the other.*	I have *the other* books. I have *the others.*

Notice that you use *another* only to refer to an indefinite, singular idea. *Others* is used only as a plural pronoun (not accompanied by a noun). In all other cases, *other* is correct.

EXERCISE 60: Each of the following sentences contains *other, another,* or *others.* Circle *other, another,* or *others.* Then indicate if the sentences are correct (C) or incorrect (I).

___C___ 1. It is essential to complete the first program before working on the (others.)

___I___ 2. The waitress will bring you (the another) bowl of soup if you want.

_____ 3. You should pack another pair of shoes in case that pair gets soaked.

_____ 4. It is difficult to find others workers who are willing to work such long hours.

_____ 5. Since the lamp you wanted is out of stock, you must choose another.

_____ 6. The other desk clerk must have put that message in your mailbox.

_____ 7. If your identification card is lost or stolen, you cannot get another.

_____ 8. Because they were not pleased with the hotel accommodations last year, they have decided to try a other hotel this year.

_____ 9. As some students moved into the registration area, others took their places in line.

_____ 10. The printer will not function unless it has another cartridges.

EXERCISE (Skills 58–60): Circle the words in the following sentences that are commonly confused on the TOEFL test. Then indicate if the sentences are correct (C) or incorrect (I).

_____ 1. When the car's odometer reached 100,000, she decided that it was time to buy another car.

_____ 2. Every time someone does an error in the program, several extra hours of work are created.

_____ 3. Like the fashions shown in this magazine, the fashions in the other magazine are quite expensive.

_____ 4. Because the main highway is crowded at this hour, the driver should try to find another routes to the stadium.

_____ 5. Although the two signatures are supposed to be exactly the same, they are not at all like.

_____ 6. The decorators did the shopping for the material and made curtains for the windows.

_____ 7. Before the administrator reads the stack of papers on his desk, he should sign the others that are on the file cabinet.

_____ 8. The committee is doing the arrangements for the Saturday evening banquet.

_____ 9. When he made several other big mistakes, he did his apologies to the others in the office.

_____ 10. Perhaps the designer could select others styles if these are inappropriate.

TOEFL EXERCISE (Skills 58–60): Choose the letter of the underlined word or group of words that is not correct.

_____ 1. The buffalo and the bison are like except for the size and shape of the head and
                              A   B   C   D

shoulders.

_____ 2. Other interesting aspect of tachistopic training in recent years has been the
         A   B   C

newfound use by professional teams.
         D

_____ 3. Only about 3 percent of oil wells actually do a profit.
         A   B   C   D

_____ 4. Dislike sumac with red berries, sumac with white berries is poisonous.
         A   B   C   D

_____ 5. Pittsburgh has reduced its smog by requiring more complete oxidation of fuel in
                              A   B

cars, and others cities can do the same thing.
              C   D

_____ 6. Alike all other mammals, dolphins have lungs.
         A   B   C   D

_____ 7. Up to World War II almost all important research in physics had been made in
                            A   B

universities, with only university funds for support.
              C   D

_____ 8. Because the plan that was made yesterday is no longer feasible, the manager had to
                       A   B   C

choose another alternatives.
               D

_____ 9. Particles with unlike charges attract each other, while particles with alike charges
                        A   B   C

repel each other.
         D

_____10. One another surprising method of forest conservation is controlled cutting of trees.
         A   B   C   D

TOEFL REVIEW EXERCISE (Skills 1–60): Choose the letter of the word or group of words that best completes the sentence.

1. Wild Bill Hickok _____ for the Union Army during the Civil War by posing as a Confederate officer.

   (A) spied
   (B) spying
   (C) a spy
   (D) was spied

2. _____ was unusable as farmland and difficult to traverse, the Badlands is an area in South Dakota.

   (A) So named because it
   (B) Because of
   (C) It
   (D) Naming it

Choose the letter of the underlined word or group of words that is not correct.

_____ 3. Titania, photographed by *Voyager 2* in 1986, has significantly fewer craters than
                        A   B   C
another moons of Uranus.
   D

_____ 4. The author Francis Scott Key Fitzgerald is better know as F. Scott Fitzgerald.
              A   B   C D

_____ 5. The result of the failure to plan for the future is that a child from an urban area
                                                              A   B
must be took to the country to see nature.
          C   D

_____ 6. This machine can print on a single pieces of paper, but only if the level is facing the
          A   B   C   D
front of the machine.

_____ 7. The development of permanent teeth, alike that of deciduous teeth, begins before
                                              A   B   C
birth.
   D

_____ 8. A crowd of several hundred fan watched the ceremony from behind a fence.
                     A   B   C   D

_____ 9. Unlike other architects of the early modern movement, Alvar Aalto stressed
          A   B
informality, personal expression, romantic, and regionality in his work.
                                   C   D

_____10. Color blindness may exist at birth or may occur later in life as a result for disease or
          A   B   C   D
injury.

TOEFL POST-TEST

SECTION 2
STRUCTURE AND WRITTEN EXPRESSION
Time—25 minutes
(including the reading of the directions)
Now set your clock for 25 minutes.

This section is designed to measure your ability to recognize language that is appropriate for standard written English. There are two types of questions in this section, with special directions for each type.

Structure

Directions: These questions are incomplete sentences. Beneath each sentence you will see four words or phrases, marked (A), (B), (C), and (D). Choose the **one** word or phrase that best completes the sentence. Then, on your answer sheet, find the number of the question and fill in the space that corresponds to the letter of the answer you have chosen.

Look at the following examples.

Example I   **Sample Answer**

The president _____ the election by a landslide.

(A) won
(B) he won
(C) yesterday
(D) fortunately

The sentence should read, "The president won the election by a landslide." Therefore, you should choose answer (A).

Example II   **Sample Answer**

When _____ the conference?

(A)   the doctor attended
(B)   did the doctor attend
(C)   the doctor will attend
(D)   the doctor's attendance

The sentence should read, "When did the doctor attend the conference?" Therefore, you should choose answer (B).

GO ON TO THE NEXT PAGE →

1. The planet Mercury _____ rotations during every two trips around the Sun.

   (A) three complete
   (B) completes three
   (C) the completion of three
   (D) completing three of the

2. In prehistoric _____ of western Utah was covered by Lake Bonneville.

   (A) times, a large part
   (B) times, there was a large part
   (C) part of the time
   (D) for large parts of time

3. The helicopter is able to hover in _____ powered rotors produce lift even at zero forward speed.

   (A) flight because of the
   (B) flying the
   (C) the flying of the
   (D) flight because the

4. The upper levels of the Sun's atmosphere are of very low _____ heats the gases there to very high temperatures.

   (A) dense and solar
   (B) density, solar activity
   (C) density, but solar activity
   (D) density and activity of the Sun is

5. Lapis lazuli, _____ stone, has been valued for ornamental purposes for more than 6,000 years.

   (A) an opaque deep blue
   (B) is an opaque deep blue
   (C) it is an opaque deep blue
   (D) that is an opaque deep blue

6. Mountaineers _____ climb Mount Everest must make reservations to do so, often up to seven years in advance.

   (A) want to
   (B) they want to
   (C) who want
   (D) wanting to

7. Created by the dissolution of limestone, the underground cave system _____ Mammoth Cave is noted for its stalactites and stalagmites.

   (A) is known as
   (B) it is known to be
   (C) known as
   (D) to be known

8. Most slang terms are simply old words _____ additional new meanings.

   (A) give
   (B) given
   (C) are given
   (D) they are given

9. North Carolina's Outer Banks are a chain of low, narrow islands _____ the mainland from the frequent Atlantic storms in the area.

   (A) they buffer
   (B) that buffer
   (C) to buffer them
   (D) that they buffer

10. It is at the age of approximately eighteen months _____ children begin to make combinations of two or three words.

    (A) when many
    (B) when are many
    (C) when do many
    (D) when have many of the

11. *Story of a Bad Boy*, a semiautobiographical novel by Thomas Bailey Aldrich, ranks high among books _____ have incorporated their boyhood experiences.

    (A) the American authors
    (B) which are American authors
    (C) in which American authors
    (D) are those which American authors

GO ON TO THE NEXT PAGE ➡

12. In the La Brea tar pits of Los Angeles _____ which have been preserved from the Pleistocene period.

    (A) thousands of animals are
    (B) thousands are animals
    (C) the thousands of animals
    (D) are thousands of animals

13. _____ provided a living for nearly 90 percent of the population of the American colonies.

    (A) Farming was what
    (B) What farming
    (C) Farming was
    (D) What was farming

14. Not only _____ more brittle than hard maples, but they are also less able to withstand high winds.

    (A) soft maples are
    (B) are soft maples
    (C) they are soft maples
    (D) soft maples

15. _____ become blocked so that heat and moisture could not escape, death would result.

    (A) Were the skin's pores to
    (B) The pores of the skin were to
    (C) The skin's pores
    (D) If the pores of the skin

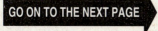
GO ON TO THE NEXT PAGE

Written Expression

Directions: In these questions, each sentence has four underlined words or phrases. The four underlined parts of the sentence are marked (A), (B), (C), and (D). Identify the **one** underlined word or phrase that must be changed in order for the sentence to be correct. Then, on your answer sheet, find the number of the question and fill in the space that corresponds to the letter of the answer you have chosen.

Look at the following examples.

Example I

The four string on a violin are tuned
  A   B   C D
in fifths.

Sample Answer

Ⓐ
●
Ⓒ
Ⓓ

The sentence should read, "The four strings on a violin are tuned in fifths." Therefore, you should choose answer (B).

Example II

The research for the book *Roots* taking
    A   B   C
Alex Haley twelve years.
           D

Sample Answer

Ⓐ
Ⓑ
●
Ⓓ

The sentence should read, "The research for the book *Roots* took Alex Haley twelve years." Therefore, you should choose answer (C).

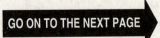

16. The wave <u>lengths</u> of ultraviolet light are <u>short</u> than <u>those</u> of visible light <u>but longer</u>
           A   B   C   D
than those of X-rays.

17. <u>All</u> thoroughbreds are descended <u>from</u> three Arabian <u>stallion</u> imported <u>into</u> England
   A   B   C   D
between 1689 and 1724.

18. By <u>measuring</u> the rate of decay of potassium isotopes in volcanic ash, scientists
      A
can date the layers of volcanic ash and any human <u>remains</u> in <u>they</u>.
   B   C   D

19. <u>Hundreds of</u> partial <u>to complete</u> fossil skeletons of *Triceratops* have been <u>gather</u> in
     A   B   C
North America from <u>rocks</u> of the late Cretaceous period.
                   D

20. By the <u>time</u> of the dinosaurs, turtles <u>have</u> already developed the hard shell
        A   B
<u>into which</u> their heads and legs could be <u>drawn</u>.
   C   D

21. A zoom lens <u>produces</u> an <u>inverted</u> real image, either on the film in a camera <u>and on</u>
 A   B   C   D
the light-sensitive tube of a television camera.

22. The leaves and young twigs of the henna plant are <u>ground</u> into a powder to <u>produce</u> a
                                        A   B
<u>paste</u> that can <u>used</u> as a dye.
 C   D

23. Thirty-one <u>pairs</u> of spinal nerves <u>are</u> <u>present</u> in humans, and each pair <u>have</u> two
         A   B   C   D
roots.

24. William Randolph Hearst <u>built</u> a chain of newspapers <u>that</u> included 25 <u>dailies</u> and 11
                     A   B   C
Sunday editions at <u>their</u> peak in 1937.
             D

25. The electromagnetic <u>spectrum</u> consists <u>in</u> <u>bands</u> of different <u>wavelengths</u>.
                   A   B   C   D

GO ON TO THE NEXT PAGE →

26. Lemon trees are similar in longevity and appear to orange trees but have more upright
                          A   B   C

    growth.
      D

27. Christopher Columbus, alike many other explorers, underestimated the size of the
                              A   B   C

    Earth and overestimated the width of Asia.
                                 D

28. Manganese, found in trace amounts in higher animals, activates a large amount of
                A   B

    the enzymes involved in metabolic processes.
              C   D

29. The remains of *Homo erectus,* an extinct species of early man, was first discovered
                       A   B   C   D

    on the island of Java by Dutch physician Eugene Debois.

30. The Ford Motor Company introduced the moving assembly line in 1914 so that it will
                                    A   B

    be able to meet the huge demand for its Model T.
                            C   D

31. By 1830, approximately 200 steamboats had become operationally on the
     A   B   C   D

    Mississippi River.

32. The huge Meteor Crater was created when a 63,000-ton iron meteorites struck the
         A   B   C   D

    Earth near Winslow, Arizona.

33. Daniel Boone helped to build the Wilderness Road through the Cumberland Gap,
                A   B

    creating a route for settlers heading westerly.
       C   D

34. The Appalachian Mountains extend Georgia and Alabama in the south to Canada in
     A   B   C   D

    the north.

35. Howard Hughes once did more than half a billion dollars in one day in 1966 when he
                 A   B

    received a single bank draft for $546,549,171 for his share of TWA.
             C   D

GO ON TO THE NEXT PAGE →

36. The city of Tampa, Florida, is <u>located</u> on <u>peninsula</u> <u>across</u> Tampa Bay <u>from</u> Saint
    $\quad\quad\quad\quad\quad\quad\quad\quad\quad\quad\quad$ A $\quad\quad$ B $\quad\quad\quad$ C $\quad\quad\quad\quad\quad\quad\quad$ D
    Petersburg.

37. <u>The closer</u> it gets to December 21, the <u>first day</u> of winter, the <u>short</u> the days <u>become</u>.
    $\quad$ A $\quad\quad\quad\quad\quad\quad\quad\quad\quad\quad\quad\quad\quad$ B $\quad\quad\quad\quad\quad\quad$ C $\quad\quad\quad\quad$ D

38. Only about a hundred out of an <u>estimating</u> 3,000 known mineral species
    $\quad\quad\quad\quad\quad\quad\quad\quad\quad\quad\quad\quad\quad$ A
    <u>have been found</u> at least <u>reasonably</u> suitable <u>for</u> use as gems.
    $\quad\quad$ B $\quad\quad\quad\quad\quad\quad\quad$ C $\quad\quad\quad\quad$ D

39. Most of the year San Miguel Island is <u>shrouded</u> in fog, and <u>strong</u> northwest winds
    $\quad\quad\quad\quad\quad\quad\quad\quad\quad\quad\quad\quad\quad\quad\quad$ A $\quad\quad\quad\quad\quad$ B
    <u>batter</u> <u>relentlessly the island</u>.
    $\quad$ C $\quad\quad$ D

40. Women have <u>admitted</u> to the United States Military Academy at West Point <u>since</u>
    $\quad\quad\quad\quad\quad$ A $\quad\quad\quad\quad\quad\quad\quad\quad\quad\quad\quad\quad\quad\quad\quad\quad\quad\quad$ B
    1976, and the <u>first</u> women cadets <u>graduated</u> in 1980.
    $\quad\quad\quad\quad\quad$ C $\quad\quad\quad\quad\quad\quad\quad$ D

**This is the end of Section 2.
If you finish before 25 minutes has ended,
check your work on Section 2 only.**

When you finish the test, you may do the following:
- Turn to the **Diagnostic Chart** on pages 553–555, and circle the numbers of the questions that you missed.
- Turn to **Scoring Information** on pages 549–550, and determine your TOEFL score.
- Turn to the **Progress Chart** on page 559, and add your score to the chart.

SECTION THREE

READING COMPREHENSION

3 △ 3 △ 3 △ 3 △ 3 △ 3 △ 3 △ 3

DIAGNOSTIC PRE-TEST

SECTION 3
READING COMPREHENSION
Time—55 minutes
(including the reading of the directions)
Now set your clock for 55 minutes.

This section is designed to measure your ability to read and understand short passages similar in topic and style to those that students are likely to encounter in North American universities and colleges. This section contains reading passages and questions about the passages.

Directions: In this section you will read several passages. Each one is followed by a number of questions about it. You are to choose the **one** best answer, (A), (B), (C), or (D), to each question. Then, on your answer sheet, find the number of the question and fill in the space that corresponds to the letter of the answer you have chosen.

Answer all questions about the information in a passage on the basis of what is **stated** or **implied** in that passage.

Read the following passage:

> John Quincy Adams, who served as the sixth president of the United States from 1825 to 1829, is today recognized for his masterful statesmanship and diplomacy. He dedicated his life to public service, both in the presidency and in the various other political offices that he *Line* held. Throughout his political career he demonstrated his unswerving belief in freedom of (5) speech, the antislavery cause, and the right of Americans to be free from European and Asian domination.

Example I   **Sample Answer**

To what did John Quincy Adams devote his life?   Ⓐ ● Ⓒ Ⓓ

- (A) Improving his personal life
- (B) Serving the public
- (C) Increasing his fortune
- (D) Working on his private business

According to the passage, John Quincy Adams "dedicated his life to public service." Therefore, you should choose answer (B).

Example II   **Sample Answer**

In line 4, the word "unswerving" is closest in meaning to   Ⓐ Ⓑ ● Ⓓ

- (A) moveable
- (B) insignificant
- (C) unchanging
- (D) diplomatic

The passage states that John Quincy Adams demonstrated his unswerving belief "throughout his career." This implies that the belief did not change. Therefore, you should choose answer (C).

GO ON TO THE NEXT PAGE

TOEFL® test directions and format are reprinted by permission of ETS, the copyright owner. However, all examples and test questions are provided by Pearson Education, Inc.

Questions 1–12

Algae is a primitive form of life, a single-celled or simple multiple-celled organism that is able to conduct the process of photosynthesis. It is generally found in water but can also be found elsewhere, growing on such surfaces as rocks or trees. The various types of algae are classified according to their
Line pigmentation, or coloration.
(5)   Blue-green algae, or *Cyanophyta*, can grow at very high temperatures and under high-intensity light. This is a microscopic type of algae, and some species consist of only one cell. Blue-green algae is the oldest form of life with photosynthetic capabilities, and fossilized remains of this type of algae more than 3.4 billion years old have been found in parts of Africa.

Green algae, or *Chlorophyta*, is generally found in fresh water. It reproduces on the surfaces of
(10) enclosed bodies of water such as ponds or lakes and has the appearance of a fuzzy green coating on the water. In large quantities, this type of algae may reproduce enough to give a green color to an entire lake.

Brown algae, or *Phaeophyta*, grows in shallow, temperate water. This type of algae is the largest in size and is most recognizable as a type of seaweed; kelp is a type of brown algae that has grown to
(15) lengths of up to 200 feet. Its long stalks can be enmeshed on the ocean floor, or it can float freely on the ocean's surface.

Red algae, or *Rhodophyta*, is a small, delicate organism found in the deep waters of the subtropics, where it often grows with coral. This type of algae has an essential role in the formation of coral reefs: it secretes lime from the seawater to foster the formation of limestone deposits.

1. What is the author's main purpose?

   (A) To show what color algae is
   (B) To differentiate the various classifications of algae
   (C) To describe where algae is found
   (D) To clarify the appearance of the different types of algae

2. Which of the following is NOT true about algae?

   (A) All types have only one cell.
   (B) It can be found out of water.
   (C) It can use photosynthesis.
   (D) It is not a relatively new form of life.

3. The word "pigmentation" in line 4 means

   (A) size
   (B) shape
   (C) composition
   (D) color

4. The word "microscopic" in line 6 is closest in meaning to

   (A) mechanical
   (B) tiny
   (C) visual
   (D) bacterial

5. Algae remnants found in Africa are

   (A) still flourishing
   (B) photogenic
   (C) extremely old
   (D) red in color

6. Green algae is generally found

   (A) on the ocean floor
   (B) on top of the water
   (C) throughout ponds and lakes
   (D) surrounding enclosed bodies of water

7. The word "coating" in line 10 could best be replaced by

   (A) clothing
   (B) covering
   (C) warmth
   (D) sweater

8. Brown algae would most likely be found

   (A) on trees
   (B) near green algae
   (C) on rocks
   (D) in the ocean

GO ON TO THE NEXT PAGE

9. According to the passage, red algae is

(A) sturdy
(B) huge
(C) fragile
(D) found in shallow water

10. It can be inferred from the passage that limestone deposits serve as the basis of

(A) coral reefs
(B) red algae
(C) subtropical seawater
(D) secret passages

11. How is the information in the paragraph organized?

(A) Various details supporting a theory are explored.
(B) Various classifications of a specific life form are described.
(C) Various stages of the chronological development of a life form are presented.
(D) Various elements that compose a certain life form are outlined.

12. This passage would most probably be assigned reading in a course on

(A) chemistry
(B) physics
(C) botany
(D) zoology

GO ON TO THE NEXT PAGE

Questions 13–21

Narcolepsy is a disease characterized by malfunctioning sleep mechanics. It can consist of a
sudden and uncontrollable bout of sleep during daylight hours and disturbed sleep during nighttime
hours. It occurs more often in men than in women, and it commonly makes its appearance during
Line adolescence or young adulthood. At least a half million Americans are believed to be affected by
(5) narcolepsy.

Narcolepsy can take a number of forms during daylight hours. One common symptom of the
disease during daytime hours is a sudden attack of REM (rapid-eye movement) sleep during normal
waking hours. This occurs in some people hundreds of times in a single day, while others only have
rare occurrences. During a sleep attack, narcoleptics may experience automatic behavior; even
(10) though asleep, they may continue automatically performing the activity they were involved in prior to
falling asleep. They may, for example, continue walking, or driving, or stirring a pot until the activity
is interrupted by external forces. Others experience cataplexy during daytime hours; cataplexy
involves a sudden loss of muscle tone that may cause the head to droop or the knees to wobble in
minor attacks or a total collapse in more serious attacks. Cataplexy seems to occur most often in
(15) conjunction with intense emotion or excitement.

During sleep hours, narcolepsy can also manifest itself in a variety of ways, During the
transitional phase that precedes the onset of sleep, it is common for hallucinations to occur. These
hallucinations, known as hypnagogic phenomena, consist of realistic perceptions of sights and
sounds during the semi-conscious state between wakefulness and sleep. Narcoleptics may also suffer
(20) from night wakening during sleep, resulting in extremely fragmented and restless sleep. Then, upon
waking, a narcoleptic may experience sleep paralysis, the inability to move, perhaps for several
minutes, immediately after waking.

13. Which of the following would be the most
appropriate title for the passage?

(A) A Good Night's Sleep
(B) A Cure for Narcolepsy
(C) An Unusual Sleep Disturbance
(D) Hallucinations during Sleep

14. The word "malfunctioning" in line 1 is
closest in meaning to

(A) improperly working
(B) regularly waking
(C) incorrectly classifying
(D) harshly interpreting

15. At which of the following ages would a
person be most likely to develop
narcolepsy?

(A) 10
(B) 20
(C) 30
(D) 40

16. Approximately how many narcoleptics are
there in the United States?

(A) Fewer than 500,000
(B) More than 500,000
(C) Fewer than 1,500,000
(D) More than 1,500,000

17. The word "bout" in line 2 is closest in
meaning to

(A) symptom
(B) lack
(C) illness
(D) period

18. Which of the following would be most
likely to occur during daily activities?

(A) Automatic behavior
(B) Hallucinations
(C) Night wakening
(D) Sleep paralysis

GO ON TO THE NEXT PAGE

19. Which of the following involves a complete collapse?

    (A) Automatic behavior
    (B) Cataplexy
    (C) Hallucinations
    (D) REM sleep

20. When would hypnagogic phenomena most likely occur?

    (A) Just after going to bed
    (B) In the middle of the night
    (C) Soon after waking
    (D) After getting up

21. Where in the passage does the author describe what seems to precipitate a sudden loss of muscle tone?

    (A) Lines 12–14
    (B) Lines 14–15
    (C) Lines 16–17
    (D) Lines 20–22

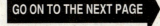
GO ON TO THE NEXT PAGE

Questions 22–30

Whereas literature in the first half of the eighteenth century in America had been largely religious and moral in tone, by the latter half of the century the revolutionary fervor that was coming to life in the colonies began to be reflected in the literature of the time, which in turn served to further
Line influence the population. Although not all writers of this period supported the Revolution, the two
(5) best-known and most influential writers, Ben Franklin and Thomas Paine, were both strongly supportive of that cause.

Ben Franklin first attained popular success through his writings in his brother's newspaper, the *New-England Courant.* In these articles he used a simple style of language and commonsense argumentation to defend the point of view of the farmer and the Leather Apron man. He continued
(10) with the same commonsense practicality and appeal to the common man with his work on *Poor Richard's Almanac* from 1733 until 1758. Firmly established in his popular acceptance by the people, Franklin wrote a variety of extremely effective articles and pamphlets about the colonists' revolutionary cause against England.

Thomas Paine was an Englishman working as a magazine editor in Philadelphia at the time of
(15) the Revolution. His pamphlet *Common Sense*, which appeared in 1776, was a force in encouraging the colonists to declare their independence from England. Then throughout the long and desperate war years he published a series of *Crisis* papers (from 1776 until 1783) to encourage the colonists to continue on with the struggle. The effectiveness of his writing was probably due to his emotional yet oversimplified depiction of the cause of the colonists against England as a classic struggle of good
(20) and evil.

22. The paragraph preceding this passage most likely discusses

    (A) how literature influences the population
    (B) religious and moral literature
    (C) literature supporting the cause of the American Revolution
    (D) what made Thomas Paine's literature successful

23. The word "fervor" in line 2 is closest in meaning to

    (A) war
    (B) anxiety
    (C) spirit
    (D) action

24. The word "time" in line 3 could best be replaced by

    (A) hour
    (B) period
    (C) appointment
    (D) duration

25. It is implied in the passage that

    (A) some writers in the American colonies supported England during the Revolution
    (B) Franklin and Paine were the only writers to influence the Revolution
    (C) because Thomas Paine was an Englishman, he supported England against the colonies
    (D) authors who supported England did not remain in the colonies during the Revolution

26. The pronoun "he" in line 8 refers to

    (A) Thomas Paine
    (B) Ben Franklin
    (C) Ben Franklin's brother
    (D) Poor Richard

27. According to the passage, the tone of *Poor Richard's Almanac* is

    (A) pragmatic
    (B) erudite
    (C) theoretical
    (D) scholarly

GO ON TO THE NEXT PAGE

28. The word "desperate" in line 16 could best be replaced by

    (A) unending
    (B) hopeless
    (C) strategic
    (D) combative

29. Where in the passage does the author describe Thomas Paine's style of writing?

    (A) Lines 4–6
    (B) Lines 8–9
    (C) Lines 14–15
    (D) Lines 18–20

30. The purpose of the passage is to

    (A) discuss American literature in the first half of the eighteenth century
    (B) give biographical data on two American writers
    (C) explain which authors supported the Revolution
    (D) describe the literary influence during revolutionary America

GO ON TO THE NEXT PAGE →

Questions 31–41

Federal Express is a company that specializes in rapid overnight delivery of high-priority packages. The first company of its type, Federal Express was founded by the youthful Fred Smith in 1971, when he was only 28 years old. Smith had actually developed the idea for the rapid delivery
Line service in a term paper for an economics class when he was a student at Yale University. The term
(5) paper reputedly received a less-than-stellar grade because of the infeasibility of the project that Smith had outlined. The model that Smith proposed had never been tried; it was a model that was efficient to operate but at the same time was very difficult to institute.

Smith achieved efficiency in his model by designing a system that was separate from the passenger system and could, therefore, focus on how to deliver packages most efficiently. His strategy
(10) was to own his own planes so that he could create his own schedules and to ship all packages through the hub city of Memphis, a set-up which resembles the spokes on the wheel of a bicycle. With this combination of his own planes and hub set-up, he could get packages anywhere in the United States overnight.

What made Smith's idea difficult to institute was the fact that the entire system had to be
(15) created before the company could begin operations. He needed a fleet of aircraft to collect packages from airports every night and deliver them to Memphis, where they were immediately sorted and flown out to their new destinations; he needed a fleet of trucks to deliver packages to and from the various airports; he needed facilities and trained staff all in place to handle the operation. Smith had a $4 million inheritance from his father, and he managed to raise an additional $91 million dollars
(20) from venture capitalists to get the company operating.

When Federal Express began service in 1973 in 25 cities, the company was not an immediate success, but success did come within a relatively short period of time. The company lost $29 million in the first 26 months of operations. However, the tide was to turn relatively quickly. By late 1976, Federal Express was carrying an average of 19,000 packages per night and had made a profit of $3.6
(25) million.

31. The most appropriate title for this passage is

   (A) The Problems and Frustrations of a Business Student
   (B) The Importance of Business Studies
   (C) The Capitalization of Federal Express
   (D) The Implementation of a Successful Business

32. The word "developed" in line 3 could best be replaced by

   (A) come up with
   (B) come about
   (C) come across
   (D) come into

33. What is stated in the passage about Smith's term paper?

   (A) Smith submitted it through a delivery service.
   (B) It was written by a student of Smith's.
   (C) Its grade was mediocre.
   (D) The professor thought it had great potential.

34. What was a key idea of Smith's?

   (A) That he should focus on passenger service
   (B) That package delivery should be separate from passenger service
   (C) That packages could be delivered on other companies' planes
   (D) That passenger service had to be efficient

GO ON TO THE NEXT PAGE ➤

35. A "hub city" in line 11 is

   (A) a large city with small cities as destinations
   (B) a city that is the final destination for many routes
   (C) a city where many bicycle routes begin
   (D) a centralized city with destinations emanating from it

36. It can be inferred from the passage that Smith selected Memphis as his hub city because it

   (A) was near the middle of the country
   (B) had a large number of passenger aircraft
   (C) already had a large package delivery service
   (D) was a favorite passenger airport

37. The pronoun "they" in line 16 refers to

   (A) aircraft
   (B) packages
   (C) airports
   (D) destinations

38. It is NOT mentioned in the passage that, in order to set up his company, Smith needed

   (A) airplanes
   (B) trucks
   (C) personnel
   (D) faculty

39. How long did it take Federal Express to become profitable?

   (A) Two months
   (B) One year
   (C) Three years
   (D) Six years

40. Which paragraph explains what made Smith's model effective?

   (A) The first paragraph
   (B) The second paragraph
   (C) The third paragraph
   (D) The last paragraph

41. The tone of the passage in describing Smith's accomplishments is

   (A) unflattering
   (B) sincere
   (C) unconvincing
   (D) snobbish

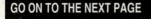
GO ON TO THE NEXT PAGE

Questions 42–50

Perhaps better known than the Cullinan Diamond is the Hope Diamond, a valuable and rare blue gem with a background of more than 300 years as a world traveler. The 112-carat blue stone that later became the Hope Diamond was mined in India sometime before the middle of the seventeenth
Line century and was first known to be owned by Shah Jahan, who built the Taj Mahal in memory of his
(5) beloved wife. From India, the celebrated blue stone has changed hands often, moving from location to location in distant corners of the world.

In the middle of the seventeenth century, a trader from France named Jean Baptiste Tavernier acquired the large blue diamond, which was rumored to have been illegally removed from a temple. Tavernier returned to France with the big blue gem, where the stone was purchased by the Sun King,
(10) Louis XIV. Louis XIV had it cut down from 112 to 67 carats to make its shape symmetrical and to maximize its sparkle. The newly cut diamond, still huge by any standards, was passed down through the royal family of France, until it arrived in the hands of Louis XVI and Marie Antoinette. During the French Revolution, Louis XVI and his wife met their fate on the guillotine in 1793, and the big blue diamond disappeared from public sight.
(15) The diamond somehow managed to get from France to England, where banker Henry Hope purchased it from a gem dealer early in the nineteenth century. The huge blue stone was cut into a 45.5-carat oval, and at this point it took on the name by which it is known today. The diamond stayed in the Hope family for around a century, when deep indebtedness brought on by a serious gambling habit on the part of one of Henry Hope's heirs forced the sale of the diamond.
(20) From England, the Hope Diamond may have made its way into the hands of the Sultan of Turkey; whatever route it took to get there, it eventually went on to the United States when American Evelyn Walsh McLean purchased it in 1911. Mrs. McLean certainly enjoyed showing the diamond off; guests in her home were sometimes astounded to notice the huge stone embellishing the neck of Mrs. McLean's Great Dane as the huge pet trotted around the grounds of her Washington, D.C. home. The
(25) Hope Diamond later became the property of jeweler Harry Winston, who presented the stunning 45.5-carat piece to the Smithsonian in 1958. The Hope Diamond is now taking a well-earned rest following its rigorous travel itinerary and is on display at the Smithsonian Institution in Washington, D.C., where it has been since 1958.

42. The paragraph preceding the passage most likely discussed

    (A) why gems are considered valuable
    (B) how the Hope Diamond was mined
    (C) a diamond other than the Hope Diamond
    (D) methods for mining diamonds

43. The main idea of this passage is that the Hope Diamond

    (A) came from India
    (B) has moved around a lot
    (C) has been cut several times
    (D) now resides in the Smithsonian

44. The pronoun "it" in line 12 refers to

    (A) its shape
    (B) the newly cut diamond
    (C) the royal family
    (D) the French Revolution

45. It can be inferred from the passage that the author is not certain

    (A) who bought the Hope Diamond in England
    (B) who sold the Hope Diamond in England
    (C) how the Hope Diamond went from France to England
    (D) how big the Hope Diamond was in the nineteenth century

GO ON TO THE NEXT PAGE

46. A "dealer" in line 16 is most likely a

   (A) card player
   (B) miner
   (C) cutter
   (D) businessman

47. It can be determined from the passage that Henry Hope most likely had how many carats cut off the Hope Diamond?

   (A) 21.5
   (B) 45.5
   (C) 66.5
   (D) 67

48. According to the passage, Mrs. McLean

   (A) donated the Hope Diamond to the Smithsonian
   (B) let her dog wear the Hope Diamond
   (C) purchased the Hope Diamond from the French
   (D) had the Hope Diamond cut to its present size of 45.5 carats

49. Which country is NOT mentioned in the passage as a place where the Hope Diamond spent some time?

   (A) India
   (B) France
   (C) England
   (D) Denmark

50. Where in the passage does the author describe what happened to the royal French owners of the diamond?

   (A) Lines 7–8
   (B) Lines 10–11
   (C) Lines 12–14
   (D) Lines 15–16

This is the end of the Reading Comprehension Pre-Test.

When you finish the test, you may do the following:

• Turn to the **Diagnostic Chart** on pages 556–558, and circle the numbers of the questions that you missed.

• Turn to **Scoring Information** on pages 549–550, and determine your TOEFL score.

• Turn to the **Progress Chart** on page 559, and add your score to the chart.

READING COMPREHENSION

The third section of the TOEFL test is the Reading Comprehension section. This section consists of fifty questions (some tests may be longer). You have fifty-five minutes to complete the fifty questions in this section.

In this part of the test you will be given reading passages, and you will be asked two types of questions about the reading passages:

1. **Reading Comprehension** questions ask you to answer questions about the information given in the reading passages. There will be a variety of questions about each reading passage, including main idea questions, directly answered detail questions, and implied detail questions.

2. **Vocabulary** questions ask you to identify the meanings of vocabulary words in the reading passages. To answer these questions, you may have to know the meanings of the words. You can also identify the meanings of some of the words by understanding the context surrounding the words, by using structural clues to identify the meanings of the words, or by breaking down the unknown words into known word parts in order to identify them.

GENERAL STRATEGIES

1. **Be familiar with the directions.** The directions on every TOEFL test are the same, so it is not necessary to spend time reading the directions carefully when you take the test. You should be completely familiar with the directions before the day of the test.

2. **Do not spend too much time reading the passages!** You do not have time to read each reading passage in depth, and it is quite possible to answer the questions correctly without first reading the passages in depth. Some students prefer to spend a minute or two on each passage reading for the main idea before starting on the questions. Other students prefer to move directly to the questions without reading the passages first.

3. **Do not worry if a reading passage is on a topic that you are unfamiliar with.** All of the information that you need to answer the questions is included in the passages. You do not need any background knowledge to answer the questions.

4. **Never leave any answers blank on your answer sheet.** Even if you are unsure of the correct response, you should answer each question. There is no penalty for guessing.

— THE READING COMPREHENSION QUESTIONS—

The Reading Comprehension section of the TOEFL test consists of five reading passages, each followed by a number of reading comprehension and vocabulary questions. Topics of the reading passage are varied, but they are often informational subjects that might be studied in an American university: American history, literature, art, architecture, geology, geography, and astronomy, for example.

Time is definitely a factor in the Reading Comprehension section. Many students who take the TOEFL test note that they are unable to finish all the questions in this section. Therefore, you need to make the most efficient use of your time in this section to get the highest score. The following method is the best way of attacking a reading passage to get the most questions correct in a limited amount of time.

STRATEGIES FOR THE READING COMPREHENSION QUESTIONS

1. **Skim the reading passage to determine the main idea and the overall organization of ideas in the passage.** You do not need to understand every detail in each passage to answer the questions correctly. It is therefore a waste of time to read the passage with the intent of understanding every single detail before you try to answer the questions.

2. **Look ahead at the questions to determine what types of questions you must answer.** Each type of question is answered in a different way.

3. **Find the section of the passage that deals with each question.** The question-type tells you exactly where to look in the passage to find correct answers.

   • For *main idea questions,* look at the first line of each paragraph.

   • For *directly* and *indirectly answered detail questions,* choose a key word in the question, and skim for that key word (or a related idea) in order in the passage.

   • For *vocabulary questions,* the question will tell you where the word is located in the passage.

   • For *overall review questions,* the answers are found anywhere in the passage.

4. **Read the part of the passage that contains the answer carefully.** The answer will probably be in the same sentence (or one sentence before or after) the key word or idea.

5. **Choose the best answer to each question from the four answer choices listed in your test book.** You can choose the best answer according to what is given in the appropriate section of the passage, eliminate definitely wrong answers, and mark your best guess on the answer sheet.

The following skills will help you to implement these strategies in the Reading Comprehension section of the TOEFL test.

QUESTIONS ABOUT THE IDEAS OF THE PASSAGE

It is very common for reading passages in the Reading Comprehension section of the TOEFL test to have questions about the overall ideas in the passage. The most common type of question asks about the main idea, topic, title, or subject. Occasionally, there will also be a question about how the information in the passage is organized.

SKILL 1:   ANSWER MAIN IDEA QUESTIONS CORRECTLY

Almost every reading passage on the TOEFL test will have a question about the main idea of a passage. Such a question may be worded in a variety of ways; you may, for example, be asked to identify the *topic, subject, title, primary idea,* or *main idea.* These questions are all really asking what primary point the author is trying to get across in the passage. Since TOEFL passages are generally written in a traditionally organized manner, it is not difficult to find the main idea by studying the topic sentence, which is most probably found at the beginning of a paragraph.

If a passage consists of only one paragraph, you should study the beginning of that paragraph to determine the main idea.

Example I

The passage:

In the philosophy of John Dewey, a sharp distinction is made between "intelligence" and "reasoning." According to Dewey, intelligence is the only absolute way to achieve a balance between
Line realism and idealism, between practicality and wisdom of life.
(5) Intelligence involves "interacting with other things and knowing them," while reasoning is merely the act of an observer, ". . . a mind that beholds or grasps objects outside the world of things. . . ." With reasoning, a level of mental certainty can be achieved, but it is through intelligence that control is taken of events that shape
(10) one's life.

The question:

What is the topic of this passage?

(A)   The intelligence of John Dewey
(B)   Distinctions made by John Dewey
(C)   Dewey's ideas on the ability to reason
(D)   How intelligence differs from reasoning in Dewey's works

---

The first sentence of this passage discusses a distinction between the ideas of "intelligence" and "reasoning" in the philosophy of John Dewey, so this is probably the topic. A quick check of the rest of the sentences in the passage confirms that the topic is in fact the difference between "intelligence" and "reasoning." Now you should check each of the answers to determine which one comes closest to the topic that you have determined. Answer (A) mentions only intelligence, so it is not the topic. Answer (B) mentions distinctions that John Dewey makes, but it does not say specifically what type of distinctions. Answer (C) mentions only reasoning, so answer (C) is incomplete. The best answer is therefore (D); the idea of *how intelligence differs from reasoning* comes from the first sentence of the passage, which mentions *a sharp distinction . . . between "intelligence" and "reasoning."*

If a passage consists of more than one paragraph, you should study the beginning of each paragraph to determine the main idea.

Example II

The passage:

Nitrogen fixation is a process by which nitrogen is continuously fed into biological circulation. In this process, certain algae and bacteria convert nitrogen into ammonia (NH_3). This
Line newly created ammonia is then for the most part absorbed by
(5) plants.

The opposite process of denitrification returns nitrogen to the air. During the process of denitrification, bacteria cause some of the nitrates from the soil to convert into gaseous nitrogen or nitrous oxide (N_2O). In this gaseous form the nitrogen returns to the
(10) atmosphere.

The question:

Which of the following would be the best title for this passage?

(A) The Process of Nitrogen Fixation
(B) Two Nitrogen Processes
(C) The Return of Nitrogen to the Air
(D) The Effect of Nitrogen on Plant Life

In a passage with more than one paragraph, you should be sure to read the first sentence of each paragraph to determine the subject, title, or main idea. In Example II, the first sentence of the first paragraph indicates that the first paragraph is about the process of nitrogen fixation. If you look only at the first paragraph, you might choose the incorrect answer (A), which would be a good title for the first paragraph only. The first sentence of the second paragraph indicates that the process of denitrification is discussed in the second paragraph. Answer (C) is incorrect because *the return of nitrogen to the air* is the process of denitrification, and this is discussed in the second paragraph only. Answer (D) is incorrect because *the effect of nitrogen on plant life* is not discussed in this passage. The best answer to this question is answer (B); the two nitrogen processes are nitrogen fixation, which is discussed in the first paragraph, and denitrification, which is discussed in the second paragraph.

The following chart outlines the key information that you should remember about main idea questions:

MAIN IDEA QUESTIONS	
HOW TO IDENTIFY THE QUESTION	*What is the **topic** of the passage?* *What is the **subject** of the passage?* *What is the **main idea** of the passage?* *What is the author's **main point** in the passage?* *With what is the author **primarily concerned**?* *Which of the following would be the best **title**?*
WHERE TO FIND THE ANSWER	The answer to this type of question can generally be determined by looking at the first sentence of each paragraph.

HOW TO ANSWER THE QUESTION	1. Read the first line of each paragraph.
	2. Look for a common theme or idea in the first lines.
	3. Pass your eyes quickly over the rest of the passage to check that you really have found the topic sentence(s).
	4. Eliminate any definitely wrong answers and choose the best answer from the remaining choices.

TOEFL EXERCISE 1: Study each of the passages and choose the best answers to the questions that follow. In this exercise, each passage is followed by several main idea, topic, or title questions so that the students can practice this type of question. On the TOEFL test, one passage would probably not have two such questions because they are so similar.

PASSAGE ONE (Questions 1–2)

Fort Knox, Kentucky, is the site of a U.S. army post, but it is even more renowned for the Fort Knox Bullion Depository, the massive vault that contains the bulk of the U.S. government's gold deposits. Completed in 1936, the vault is housed in a two-story building constructed of granite, steel, and concrete; the vault itself is made of steel and concrete and has a door that weighs more than twenty tons. Naturally, the most up-to-date security devices available are in place at Fort Knox, and the army post nearby provides further protection.

Line (5)

1. Which of the following best describes the topic of the passage?

    (A) The city of Fort Knox, Kentucky
    (B) The federal gold depository
    (C) The U.S. army post at Fort Knox
    (D) Gold bullion

2. Which of the following would be the best title for this passage?

    (A) The Massive Concrete Vault
    (B) Fort Knox Security
    (C) Where the U.S. Keeps Its Gold
    (D) A Visit to Kentucky

PASSAGE TWO (Questions 3–4)

One identifying characteristic of minerals is their relative hardness, which can be determined by scratching one mineral with another. In this type of test, a harder mineral can scratch a softer one, but a softer mineral is unable to scratch the harder one. The Mohs' hardness scale is used to rank minerals according to hardness. Ten minerals are listed in this scale, ranging from talc with a hardness of 1 to diamond with a hardness of 10. On this scale, quartz (number 7) is harder than feldspar (number 6) and is therefore able to scratch it; however, feldspar is unable to make a mark on quartz.

Line (5)

3. Which of the following best states the subject of this passage?

    (A) The hardness of diamonds
    (B) Identifying minerals by means of a scratch test
    (C) Feldspar on the Mohs' scale
    (D) Recognizing minerals in their natural state

4. The main idea of this passage is that

    (A) the hardness of a mineral can be determined by its ability to make a mark on other minerals
    (B) diamonds, with a hardness of 10 on the Mohs' scale, can scratch all other minerals
    (C) a softer mineral cannot be scratched by a harder mineral
    (D) talc is the first mineral listed on the Mohs' scale

PASSAGE THREE (Questions 5–6)

Hurricanes generally occur in the North Atlantic from May through November, with the peak of the hurricane season in September; only rarely will they occur from December through April in that part of the ocean. The main reason for the occurrence of hurricanes during this period is that the
Line temperature on the water's surface is at its warmest and the humidity of the air is at its highest.
(5)   Of the tropical storms that occur each year in the North Atlantic, only about five, on the average, are powerful enough to be called hurricanes. To be classified as a hurricane, a tropical storm must have winds reaching speeds of at least 117 kilometers per hour, but the winds are often much stronger than that; the winds of intense hurricanes can easily surpass 240 kilometers per hour.

5. The passage mainly discusses

    (A) how many hurricanes occur each year
    (B) the strength of hurricanes
    (C) the weather in the North Atlantic
    (D) hurricanes in one part of the world

6. The best title for this passage would be

    (A) The North Atlantic Ocean
    (B) Storms of the Northern Atlantic
    (C) Hurricanes: The Damage and Destruction
    (D) What Happens from May through November

PASSAGE FOUR (Questions 7–9)

Henry Wadsworth Longfellow (1807–1882) was perhaps the best-known American poet of the nineteenth century. His clear writing style and emphasis on the prevalent values of the period made him popular with the general public if not always with the critics. He was particularly recognized for
Line his longer narrative poems *Evangeline*, *The Song of Hiawatha*, and *The Courtship of Miles Standish*, in
(5) which he told stories from American history in terms of the values of the time.
Evangeline was set during the French and Indian War (1754–1763), when the British forced French settlers from Nova Scotia; two lovers, Gabriel and Evangeline, were separated by the British, and Evangeline devoted her lifetime to the search for Gabriel. With its emphasis on sentimental, undying love, *Evangeline* was immensely popular with the public.
(10)   In *The Song of Hiawatha*, Longfellow depicted the noble life of the American Indian through the story of the brave Hiawatha and his beloved wife Minehaha. The tear-inspiring poem follows Hiawatha through the tragedies and triumphs of life, ending with the death of Minehaha and Hiawatha's departure into the sunset in his canoe.
The Courtship of Miles Standish takes place during the early period of the settlement of New
(15) England, a period which was viewed as a time of honor and romance. In this poem centered around a love triangle, Miles Standish asks his friend John Alden to propose to Priscilla Mullins for him; John Alden ends up marrying Priscilla Mullins himself, and it takes time for his friendship with Miles Standish to recover. As with Longfellow's other narrative poems, the emphasis on high ideals and romance made the poem extremely popular.

7. Which of the following best describes the main idea of the passage?

    (A) American history is often depicted in poetry.
    (B) Longfellow described American history even though people really did not enjoy it.
    (C) The popularity of Longfellow's poems results from his stress on the values of the people.
    (D) Longfellow wrote long narrative poems that were not always popular with the critics.

8. The best title of the passage is

    (A) Longfellow's Popular Appeal
    (B) Historical Narrative Poems
    (C) The Lyric, Dramatic, and Narrative Poems of Longfellow
    (D) Longfellow and the Critics

9. The subject of the fourth paragraph is

    (A) nobility and honor in the poems of Longfellow
    (B) the love triangle involving Miles Standish
    (C) the popular appeal of *The Courtship of Miles Standish*
    (D) the period of the early settlement of New England

Skill 2: RECOGNIZE THE ORGANIZATION OF IDEAS

In the Reading Comprehension section of the TOEFL test, there will sometimes be questions about the organization of ideas in a passage. In this type of question, you will be asked to determine how the ideas in one paragraph (or paragraphs) relate to the ideas in another paragraph (or paragraphs).

Example

The passage:

  If asked who invented the game of baseball, most Americans would probably reply that it was Abner Doubleday. At the beginning of this century, there was some disagreement over how
Line the game of baseball had actually originated, so sporting-goods
(5) manufacturer Spaulding inaugurated a commission to research the question. In 1908 a report was published by the commission in which Abner Doubleday, a U.S. Army officer from Cooperstown, New York, was given credit for the invention of the game. The National Baseball Hall of Fame was established in Cooperstown in
(10) honor of Doubleday.
  Today, most sports historians are in agreement that Doubleday really did not have much to do with the development of baseball. Instead, baseball seems to be a close relation to the English game of rounders and probably has English rather than
(15) American roots.

The question:

The second paragraph

(A) provides examples to support the ideas in the first paragraph
(B) precedes the ideas in the first paragraph
(C) outlines the effect of the idea in the first paragraph
(D) refutes the idea in the first paragraph

To answer this question it is necessary to look at the main ideas of each of the two paragraphs. The main idea of the first paragraph is found in the first sentence of the first paragraph: most people believe that Abner Doubleday invented the game of baseball. The main idea of the second paragraph is found in the first line of the second paragraph: historians generally agree that Doubleday did not invent baseball. The second paragraph therefore *contradicts* or *refutes* the information in the first paragraph. The best answer to this question is answer (D).

The following chart outlines the key information that you should remember about questions on the organization of ideas:

ORGANIZATION OF IDEAS	
HOW TO IDENTIFY THE QUESTION	*How is the information in the passage **organized?*** *How is the information in the second paragraph **related** to the information in the first paragraph?*
WHERE TO FIND THE ANSWER	The answer to this type of question can generally be determined by looking at the first sentence of the appropriate paragraphs.
HOW TO ANSWER THE QUESTION	1. Read the first line of each paragraph. 2. Look for words that show the relationship between the paragraphs. 3. Choose the answer that best expresses the relationship.

TOEFL EXERCISE 2: Study each of the passages and choose the best answers to the questions that follow.

PASSAGE ONE (Questions 1–2)

Conflict within an organization is not always viewed as undesirable. In fact, various managers have widely divergent ideas on the value that conflict can have.

According to the traditional view of conflict, conflict is harmful to an organization. Managers
Line with this traditional view of conflict see it as their role in an organization to rid the organization of
(5) any possible sources of conflict.

The interactionist view of conflict, on the other hand, holds that conflict can serve an important function in an organization by reducing complacency among workers and causing positive changes to occur. Managers who hold an interactionist view of conflict may actually take steps to stimulate conflict within the organization.

1. How is the information in the passage organized?

   (A) The origin of ideas about conflict is presented.
   (B) Contrasting views of conflict are presented.
   (C) Two theorists discuss the strengths and weaknesses of their views on conflict.
   (D) Examples of conflict within organizations are presented.

2. What type of information is included in the third paragraph?

   (A) A comparison of the interactionist and traditional views of conflict
   (B) A discussion of the weaknesses of the interactionist view of conflict
   (C) An outline of the type of manager who prefers the interactionist view of conflict
   (D) A description of one of the opposing views of conflict

PASSAGE TWO (Questions 3–4)

IQ, or Intelligence Quotient, is defined as the ratio of a person's mental age to chronological age, with the ratio multiplied by 100 to remove the decimal. Chronological age is easily determined; mental age is generally measured by some kind of standard test and is not so simple to define.

Line
(5)   In theory, a standardized IQ test is set up to measure an individual's ability to perform intellectual operations such as reasoning and problem solving. These intellectual operations are considered to represent intelligence.

In practice, it has been impossible to arrive consensus as to which types of intellectual operations demonstrate intelligence. Furthermore, has been impossible to devise a test without cultural bias, which is to say that any IQ tests so far produced have been shown to reflect the culture
(10) of the test makers. Test takers from that culture would, nows, score higher on such a test than test takers from a different culture with equal intelligence.

3. What type of information is included in the first paragraph?

   (A) An argument
   (B) A definition
   (C) An opinion
   (D) A theory

4. How does information in the third paragraph from that in the second paragraph?

   (A) It presents a contrasting point of view.
   (B) It follows chronologically from the ideas in the second paragraph.
   (C) It presents real information rather than a premise.
   (D) It presents an example of the ideas in the second paragraph.

PASSAGE THREE (Questions 5–6)

The largest lake in the western United States is the Great Salt Lake, an inland saltwater lake in northwestern Utah, just outside the state capital of Salt Lake City. Rivers and streams feed into the Great Salt Lake, but none drain out of it; this has a major influence on both the salt content and the
Line size of the lake.
(5)   Although the Great Salt Lake is fed by freshwater streams, it is actually saltier than the oceans of the world. The salt comes from the more than two million tons of minerals that flow into the lake each year from the rivers and creeks that feed it. Sodium and chloride—the components of salt— comprise the large majority of the lake's mineral content.

The Great Salt Lake can vary tremendously from its normal size of 1,700 square miles,
(10) depending on long-term weather conditions. During periods of heavy rains, the size of the lake can swell tremendously from the huge amounts of water flowing into the lake from its feeder rivers and streams; in 1980 the lake even reached a size of 2,400 square miles. During periods of dry weather, the size of the lake decreases, sometimes drastically, due to evaporation.

5. How is the information in the passage organized?

   (A) Two unusual characteristics of the Great Salt Lake are discussed.
   (B) Contrasting theories about the Great Salt Lake's salt levels are presented.
   (C) The process by which the Great Salt Lake gets its salt is outlined.
   (D) The reasons for the variations in the Great Salt Lake's size are given.

6. The third paragraph contains information on

   (A) how the size of the lake affects weather conditions
   (B) the effects of contrasting weather conditions on the size of the lake
   (C) the effects of changes in the size of the lake
   (D) the causes of the varied weather conditions in the area of the lake

TOEFL EXERCISE (Skills 1–2):   Study each of the passages and choose the best answers to the questions that follow.

PASSAGE ONE (Questions 1–2)

Common types of calendars can be based on the Sun or on the Moon. The solar calendar is based on the solar year. Since the solar year is 365.2422 days long, solar calendars consist of regular years of 365 days and have an extra day every fourth year, or leap year, to make up for the additional
Line fractional amount. In a solar calendar, the waxing and waning of the moon can take place at various
(5) stages of each month.

The lunar calendar is synchronized to the lunar month rather than the solar year. Since the lunar month is twenty-nine and a half days long, most lunar calendars have alternating months of twenty-nine and thirty days. A twelve-month lunar year thus has 354 days, 11 days shorter than a solar year.

1. What is the main idea of the passage?

   (A) All calendars are the same.
   (B) The solar calendar is based on the Sun.
   (C) Different calendars have dissimilar bases.
   (D) The lunar month is twenty-nine and a half days long.

2. How is the information in the passage organized?

   (A) Characteristics of the solar calendar are outlined.
   (B) Two types of calendars are described.
   (C) The strengths and weakness of the lunar calendar are described.
   (D) The length of each existing calendar is contrasted.

PASSAGE TWO (Questions 3–4)

Vaccines are prepared from harmful viruses or bacteria and administered to patients to provide immunity to specific diseases. The various types of vaccines are classified according to the method by which they are derived.
Line   The most basic class of vaccines actually contains disease-causing microorganisms that have
(5) been killed with a solution containing formaldehyde. In this type of vaccine, the microorganisms are dead and therefore cannot cause disease; however, the antigens found in and on the microorganisms can still stimulate the formation of antibodies. Examples of this type of vaccine are the ones that fight influenza, typhoid fever, and cholera.

A second type of vaccine contains the toxins produced by the microorganisms rather than the
(10) microorganisms themselves. This type of vaccine is prepared when the microorganism itself does little damage but the toxin within the microorganism is extremely harmful. For example, the bacteria that cause diphtheria can thrive in the throat without much harm, but when toxins are released from the bacteria, muscles can become paralyzed and death can ensue.

A final type of vaccine contains living microorganisms that have been rendered harmless. With
(15) this type of vaccine, a large number of antigen molecules are produced and the immunity that results is generally longer lasting than the immunity from other types of vaccines. The Sabin oral antipolio vaccine and the BCG vaccine against tuberculosis are examples of this type of vaccine.

3. Which of the following expresses the main idea of the passage?

   (A) Vaccines provide immunity to specific diseases.
   (B) Vaccines contain disease-causing microorganisms.
   (C) Vaccines are derived in different ways.
   (D) New approaches in administering vaccines are being developed.

4. How many types of vaccines are presented in the passage?

   (A) Two
   (B) Three
   (C) Four
   (D) Five

PASSAGE THREE (Questions 5–7)

A hoax, unlike an honest error, is a deliberately concocted plan to present an untruth as the truth. It can take the form of a fraud, a fake, a swindle, or a forgery, and can be accomplished in almost any field: successful hoaxes have been foisted on the public in fields as varied as politics, religion, science, art, and literature.

Line
(5)

A famous scientific hoax occurred in 1912 when Charles Dawson claimed to have uncovered a human skull and jawbone on the Piltdown Common in southern England. These human remains were said to be more than 500,000 years old and were unlike any other remains from that period; as such they represented an important discovery in the study of human evolution. These remains, popularly known as the Piltdown Man and scientifically named *Eoanthropus dawsoni* after their discoverer,

(10)

confounded scientists for more than forty years. Finally in 1953, a chemical analysis was used to date the bones, and it was found that the bones were modern bones that had been skillfully aged. A further twist to the hoax was that the skull belonged to a human and the jaws to an orangutan.

5. The topic of this passage could best be described as

(A) the Piltdown Man
(B) Charles Dawson's discovery
(C) *Eoanthropus dawsoni*
(D) a definition and an example of a hoax

6. The author's main point is that

(A) various types of hoaxes have been perpetrated
(B) Charles Dawson discovered a human skull and jawbone
(C) Charles Dawson was not an honest man
(D) the human skull and jawbone were extremely old

7. The second paragraph includes

(A) an illustration to support the ideas in the first paragraph
(B) a counterargument to the ideas in the first paragraph
(C) an analogy to the ideas in the first paragraph
(D) a detailed definition of a hoax

DIRECTLY ANSWERED QUESTIONS_____

Many questions in the Reading Comprehension section of the TOEFL test will require answers that are directly stated in the passage. This means that you should be able to find the answer to this type of question without having to draw a conclusion. The common questions of this type are (1) stated detail questions, (2) "unstated" detail questions, and (3) pronoun referent questions.

SKILL 3: ANSWER STATED DETAIL QUESTIONS CORRECTLY

A stated detail question asks about one piece of information in the passage rather than the passage as a whole. The answers to these questions are generally given in order in the passage, and the correct answer is often a restatement of what is given in the passage. This means that the correct answer often expresses the same idea as what is written in the passage, but the words are not exactly the same.

Example

The passage:

Williamsburg is a historic city in Virginia situated on a peninsula between two rivers, the York and the James. It was settled by English colonists in 1633, twenty-six years after the first *Line* permanent English colony in America was settled at Jamestown. In (5) the beginning the colony at Williamsburg was named Middle Plantation because of its location in the middle of the peninsula. The site for Williamsburg had been selected by the colonists because the soil drainage was better there than at the Jamestown location, and there were fewer mosquitoes.

The questions:

1. According to the passage, Williamsburg is located

   (A) on an island
   (B) in the middle of a river
   (C) where the York and the James meet
   (D) on a piece of land with rivers on two sides

2. The passage indicates that Jamestown

   (A) was settled in 1633
   (B) was settled twenty-six years after Williamsburg
   (C) was the first permanent English colony in America
   (D) was originally named Middle Plantation

3. The passage states that the name Middle Plantation

   (A) is a more recent name than Williamsburg
   (B) derived from the location of the colony on the peninsula
   (C) refers to the middle part of England that was home to the colonists
   (D) was given to the new colony because it was located in the middle of several plantations

The answers to the questions are generally found in order in the passage, so you should look for the answer to the first question near the beginning of the passage. Since the first question asks about where *Williamsburg is located,* you should see that the first sentence in the passage answers the question because *situated* means *located.* Answer (A) is an incorrect answer because Williamsburg is not located on an island; the passage states that it is *situated on a peninsula.* Answer (B) is incorrect because Williamsburg is *between two rivers,* not *in the middle of a river.* Answer (C) is incorrect because the passage says nothing about whether or not the two rivers meet at Williamsburg. The best answer to this question is answer (D); *with rivers on two sides* is closest in meaning to *between two rivers.*

The answer to the second question will probably be located in the passage after the answer to the first question. Since the second question is about *Jamestown*, you should skim through the passage to find the part of the passage that discusses this topic. The answer to this question is found in the statement that Williamsburg *was settled by English colonists in 1633, twenty-six years after the first permanent English colony in America was settled at Jamestown.* Answer (A) is incorrect because it was Williamsburg that was settled in 1633. Answer (B) is incorrect because Jamestown was settled *before* rather than *after Williamsburg.* Answer (D) is incorrect because the name *Middle Plantation* referred to Williamsburg. The best answer to this question is answer (C), which is directly stated in the passage about Jamestown.

The answer to the third question will probably be located in the passage after the answer to the second question. Because the third question is about *the name Middle Plantation*, you should skim through the passage to find the part that discusses this topic. The answer to this question is found in the statement *Williamsburg was named Middle Plantation because of its location in the middle of the peninsula.* Answer (B) is correct because it is closest in meaning to this statement. Answer (A) is incorrect because it is false; the area was named Middle Plantation *in the beginning,* and the name Williamsburg is *more recent.* Answer (C) is incorrect because the passage says nothing about naming the area after the colonists' home in England. Answer (D) is incorrect because the passage says nothing about any other plantations in the area of Williamsburg.

The following chart outlines the key information that you should remember about stated detail questions:

STATED DETAIL QUESTIONS	
HOW TO IDENTIFY THE QUESTION	*According* to the passage,... It is **stated** in the passage... The passage **indicates** that... The author **mentions** that... Which of the following is **true**...?
WHERE TO FIND THE ANSWER	The answers to these questions are found in order in the passage.
HOW TO ANSWER THE QUESTION	1. Choose a *key word* in the question. 2. Skim in the appropriate part of the passage for the *key word* or *idea.* 3. Read the sentence that contains the *key word* or *idea* carefully. 4. Look for the answer that restates an idea in the passage. 5. Eliminate the definitely wrong answers and choose the best answer from the remaining choices.

TOEFL EXERCISE 3: Study each of the passages and choose the best answers to the questions that follow.

PASSAGE ONE (Questions 1–3)

Ice ages, those periods when ice covered extensive areas of the Earth, are known to have occurred at least six times. Past ice ages can be recognized from rock strata that show evidence of foreign materials deposited by moving walls of ice or melting glaciers. Ice ages can also be recognized *Line* from land formations that have been produced from moving walls of ice, such as U-shaped valleys, *(5)* sculptured landscapes, and polished rock faces.

1. According to the passage, what happens during an ice age?

   (A) Rock strata are recognized by geologists.
   (B) Evidence of foreign materials is found.
   (C) Ice covers a large portion of the Earth's surface.
   (D) Ice melts six times.

2. The passage covers how many different methods of recognizing past ice ages?

   (A) One
   (B) Two
   (C) Three
   (D) Four

3. According to the passage, what in the rock strata is a clue to geologists of a past ice age?

   (A) Ice
   (B) Melting glaciers
   (C) U-shaped valleys
   (D) Substances from other areas

PASSAGE TWO (Questions 4–6)

The human heart is divided into four chambers, each of which serves its own function in the cycle of pumping blood. The atria are the thin-walled upper chambers that gather blood as it flows from the veins between heartbeats. The ventricles are the thick-walled lower chambers that receive *Line* blood from the atria and push it into the arteries with each contraction of the heart. The left atrium *(5)* and ventricle work separately from those on the right. The role of the chambers on the right side of the heart is to receive oxygen-depleted blood from the body tissues and send it on to the lungs; the chambers on the left side of the heart then receive the oxygen-enriched blood from the lungs and send it back out to the body tissues.

4. The passage indicates that the ventricles

   (A) have relatively thin walls
   (B) send blood to the atria
   (C) are above the atria
   (D) force blood into the arteries

5. According to the passage, when is blood pushed into the arteries from the ventricles?

   (A) As the heart beats
   (B) Between heartbeats
   (C) Before each contraction of the heart
   (D) Before it is received by the atria

6. According to the passage, which part of the heart gets blood from the body tissues and passes it on to the lungs?

   (A) The atria
   (B) The ventricles
   (C) The right atrium and ventricle
   (D) The left atrium and ventricle

PASSAGE THREE (Questions 7–9)

The Golden Age of Railroads refers to the period from the end of the Civil War to the beginning of World War I when railroads flourished and, in fact, maintained a near monopoly in mass transportation in the United States. One of the significant developments during the period was the notable increase in uniformity, particularly through the standardization of track gauge and time.

Line
(5)
At the end of the Civil War, only about half of the nation's railroad track was laid at what is now the standard gauge of 1.4 meters; much of the rest, particularly in the southern states, had a 1.5-meter gauge. During the postwar years, tracks were converted to the 1.4-meter gauge, and by June 1, 1886, the standardization of tracks was completed, resulting in increased efficiency and economy in the rail system.

(10)
A further boon to railroad efficiency was the implementation of standard time in 1883. With the adoption of standard time, four time zones were established across the country, thus simplifying railroad scheduling and improving the efficiency of railroad service.

7. According to the passage, the Golden Age of Railroads

   (A) occurred prior to the Civil War
   (B) was a result of World War I
   (C) was a period when most of U.S. mass transportation was controlled by the railroads
   (D) resulted in a decrease in uniformity of track gauge

8. The passage mentions that which of the following occurred as a result of uniformity of track gauge?

   (A) The Civil War
   (B) Improved economy in the transportation system
   (C) Standardization of time zones
   (D) Railroad schedules

9. The passage indicates that standard time was implemented

   (A) before the Civil War
   (B) on June 1, 1886
   (C) after World War I
   (D) before standardized track gauge was established throughout the United States

Skill 4:   FIND "UNSTATED" DETAILS

You will sometimes be asked in the Reading Comprehension section of the TOEFL test to find an answer that is *not stated* or *not mentioned* or *not true* in the passage. This type of question really means that three of the answers are *stated, mentioned,* or *true* in the passage, while one answer is not. Your actual job is to find the three correct answers and then choose the letter of the one remaining answer.

You should note that there are two kinds of answers to this type of question: (1) there are three true answers and one answer that is not discussed in the passage, or (2) there are three true answers and one that is false according to the passage.

Example

The passage:

In English there are many different kinds of expressions that people use to give a name to anything whose name is unknown or momentarily forgotten. The word *gadget* is one such word. It was
Line   first used by British sailors in the 1850s and probably came from
(5)   the French word *gachette*, which was a small hook. In everyday use, the word has a more general meaning. Other words are also used to give a name to something unnamed or unknown, and these words tend to be somewhat imaginative. Some of the more commonly used expressions are a *what-d'ye-call-it,* a *whatsis,* a *thingamabob,* a
(10)   *thingamajig,* a *doodad,* or a *doohickey.*

The questions:

1.   Which of the following is NOT true about the word "gadget"?

    (A)   It is used to name something when the name is not known.
    (B)   It was used at the beginning of the nineteenth century.
    (C)   It most likely came from a word in the French language.
    (D)   Its first known use was by British sailors.

2.   Which of the following is NOT mentioned in the passage as an expression for something that is not known?

    (A)   A *thingamabob*
    (B)   A *gadget*
    (C)   A *doohickey*
    (D)   A *what-is-it*

The first question asks for the one answer that is *not true,* so three of the answers are true and one answer is *not.* Answer (B) is the one answer that is not true: the word *gadget* was first used in 1850, which is the middle of the nineteenth century, so answer (B) is the best answer. Answer (A) is true according to the second line of the paragraph; answer (C) is true according to the fourth and fifth lines of the paragraph; answer (D) is true according to the fourth line of the paragraph.

The second question asks for the one answer that is *not mentioned,* so three of the answers are listed in the passage and one is not. Since a *thingamabob,* a *gadget,* and a *doohickey* are listed in the passage, answers (A), (B), and (C) are incorrect. However, a *what-is-it* is not listed in the passage, so answer (D) is the best answer to this question.

The following chart outlines the key information that you should remember about "unstated" detail questions:

"UNSTATED" DETAIL QUESTIONS	
HOW TO IDENTIFY THE QUESTION	*Which of the following is **not stated**. . .?* *Which of the following is **not mentioned**. . .?* *Which of the following is **not discussed**. . .?* *All of the following are true **except**. . . .*
WHERE TO FIND THE ANSWER	The answers to these questions are found in order in the passage.
HOW TO ANSWER THE QUESTION	1. Choose *a key word* in the question. 2. Scan in the appropriate place in the passage for the *key word* (or related *idea*). 3. Read the sentence that contains the *key word* or *idea* carefully. 4. Look for answers that are definitely true according to the passage. Eliminate those answers. 5. Choose the answer that is *not true* or *not discussed* in the passage.

TOEFL EXERCISE 4: Study each of the passages and choose the best answers to the questions that follow.

PASSAGE ONE (Questions 1–2)

Blood plasma is a clear, almost colorless liquid. It consists of blood from which the red and white blood cells have been removed. It is often used in transfusions because a patient generally needs the plasma portion of the blood more than the other components.

Line (5) Plasma differs in several important ways from whole blood. First of all, plasma can be mixed for all donors and does not have to be from the right blood group, as whole blood does. In addition, plasma can be dried and stored, while whole blood cannot.

1. All of the following are true about blood plasma EXCEPT

(A) it is a deeply colored liquid
(B) blood cells have been taken out of it
(C) patients are often transfused with it
(D) it is generally more important to the patient than other parts of whole blood

2. Which of the following is NOT stated about whole blood?

(A) It is different from plasma.
(B) It cannot be dried.
(C) It is impossible to keep it in storage for a long time.
(D) It is a clear, colorless liquid.

PASSAGE TWO (Questions 3–4)

    Elizabeth Cochrane Seaman was an American journalist at the turn of the century who wrote for the newspaper *New York World* under the pen name Nellie Bly, a name which was taken from the Stephen Foster song *Nelly Bly*. She achieved fame for her exposés and in particular for the bold and adventuresome way that she obtained her stories.

Line
(5)

    She felt that the best way to get the real story was from the inside rather than as an outside observer who could be treated to a prettified version of reality. On one occasion she pretended to be a thief so that she would get arrested and see for herself how female prisoners were really treated. On another occasion she faked mental illness in order to be admitted to a mental hospital to get the real picture on the treatment of mental patients.

3. Which of the following is NOT true about Nellie Bly?

  (A) Nellie Bly's real name was Elizabeth Cochrane Seaman.
  (B) Nellie Bly was mentally ill.
  (C) The name Nellie Bly came from a song.
  (D) The name Nellie Bly was used on articles that Seaman wrote.

4. Which of the following is NOT mentioned as something that Nellie Bly did to get a good story?

  (A) She acted like a thief.
  (B) She got arrested by the police.
  (C) She pretended to be ill.
  (D) She worked as a doctor in a mental hospital.

PASSAGE THREE (Questions 5–6)

    Dekanawida's role as a supreme lawgiver in the Iroquois tribe has given him the status of demigod within the Indian nation. Born into the Huron tribe, Dekanawida caused great fear in his parents, who tried to drown him in his youth after a prophecy was made indicating that he would bring great sorrow to the Huron nation. Dekanawida was to survive this attempted drowning but later left his parents' home and tribe to live among the Iroquois.

Line
(5)

    One of his achievements with the Iroquois was the institution of a law among the Iroquois that virtually ended blood feuds among the nation's families. Wampum, strings of beads made of polished shells, was a valued commodity in the Iroquois culture; according to policies established by Dekanawida, wampum had to be paid to the family of a murder victim by the family of the killer.

(10)

Since the killer was also put to death, the family of the killer had to pay the victim's family in wampum for two deaths, the death of the murder victim and the death of the killer. These strict policies implemented by Dekanawida helped to establish him as a wise lawgiver and leader of the Iroquois nation.

5. According to the passage, Dekanawida was NOT

  (A) a lawmaker
  (B) a Huron by birth
  (C) a near deity
  (D) drowned when he was young

6. Which of the following is NOT mentioned in the passage about wampum?

  (A) It was used extensively by the Huron.
  (B) It had a high value to the Iroquois.
  (C) It was given to a murder victim's family.
  (D) It was made of polished shells.

SKILL 5:   FIND PRONOUN REFERENTS

In the Reading Comprehension section of the TOEFL test, you will sometimes be asked to determine which noun a pronoun refers to. In this type of question it is important to understand that a noun is generally used first in a passage, and the pronoun that refers to it comes after. Whenever you are asked which noun a pronoun refers to, you should look *before* the pronoun to find the noun.

Example

The passage:

Carnivorous plants, such as the sundew and the Venus flytrap, are generally found in humid areas where there is an inadequate supply of nitrogen in the soil. In order to survive, these
Line   plants have developed mechanisms to trap insects within their
(5)   foliage. They have digestive fluids to obtain the necessary nitrogen from the insects. These plants trap the insects in a variety of ways. The sundew has sticky hairs on its leaves; when an insect lands on these leaves, it gets caught up in the sticky hairs, and the leaf wraps itself around the insect. The leaves of the Venus flytrap function
(10)   more like a trap, snapping suddenly and forcefully shut around an insect.

The questions:

1. The pronoun "they" in line 5 refers to

    (A)   humid areas
    (B)   these plants
    (C)   insects
    (D)   digestive fluids

2. The pronoun "it" in line 8 refers to

    (A)   a variety
    (B)   the sundew
    (C)   an insect
    (D)   the leaf

To answer the first question, you should look before the pronoun *they* for plural nouns that the pronoun could refer to. *Humid areas, insects,* and *these plants* come before the pronoun, so they are possible answers; *digestive fluids* comes after the pronoun, so it is probably not the correct answer. Then you should try the three possible answers in the sentence in place of the pronoun. You should understand from the context that *these plants* have *digestive fluids* to obtain the necessary nitrogen from the insects, so the best answer to this question is answer (B). To answer the second question, you should look before the pronoun *it* for singular nouns that the pronoun could refer to. *A variety, the sundew,* and *an insect* come before the pronoun, so they are possible answers; *the leaf* comes after the pronoun, so it is probably not the correct answer. Next you should try the three possible answers in the sentence in place of the pronoun. *An insect* gets caught up in the sticky hairs, rather than *a variety* or *the sundew,* so the best answer to this question is answer (C).

The following chart outlines the key information that you should remember about pronoun referents:

PRONOUN REFERENTS	
HOW TO IDENTIFY THE QUESTION	*The **pronoun** "..." in line X **refers** to which of the following?*
WHERE TO FIND THE ANSWER	The line where the pronoun is located is generally given in the question. The noun that the pronoun refers to is generally found *before* the pronoun.
HOW TO ANSWER THE QUESTION	1. Find the pronoun in the passage. (The line where the pronoun can be found is generally stated in the question.) 2. Look for nouns that come *before* the pronoun. 3. Read the part of the passage *before* the pronoun carefully. 4. Eliminate any definitely wrong answers and choose the best answer from the remaining choices.

TOEFL EXERCISE 5: Study each of the passages and choose the best answers to the questions that follow.

PASSAGE ONE (Questions 1–2)

The full moon that occurs nearest the equinox of the Sun has become known as the harvest moon. It is a bright moon which allows farmers to work late into the night for several nights; they can work when the moon is at its brightest to bring in the fall harvest. The harvest moon of course occurs at different times of the year in the northern and southern hemispheres. In the northern hemisphere, the harvest moon occurs in September at the time of the autumnal equinox. In the southern hemisphere, the harvest moon occurs in March at the time of the vernal equinox.

Line (5)

1. The pronoun "It" in line 2 refers to

    (A) the equinox
    (B) the Sun
    (C) the harvest moon
    (D) the night

2. The pronoun "they" in line 2 refers to

    (A) farmers
    (B) nights
    (C) times of the year
    (D) northern and southern hemispheres

PASSAGE TWO (Questions 3–4)

Mardi Gras, which means "Fat Tuesday" in French, was introduced to America by French colonists in the early eighteenth century. From that time it has grown in popularity, particularly in New Orleans, and today it is actually a legal holiday in several southern states. The Mardi Gras celebration in New Orleans begins well before the actual Mardi Gras Day. Parades, parties, balls, and numerous festivities take place throughout the week before Mardi Gras Day; tourists from various countries throughout the world flock to New Orleans for the celebration, where they take part in a week of nonstop activities before returning home for some much-needed rest.

Line (5)

3. The pronoun "it" in line 2 refers to

    (A) Mardi Gras
    (B) French
    (C) that time
    (D) New Orleans

4. The pronoun "they" in line 6 refers to

    (A) numerous festivities
    (B) tourists
    (C) various countries
    (D) nonstop activities

PASSAGE THREE (Questions 5–6)

The financial firm Dow Jones and Company computes business statistics every hour on the hour of each of the business days of the year, and these statistics are known as the Dow Jones averages. They are based on a select group of stocks and bonds that are traded on the New York Stock *Line* Exchange. The Dow Jones averages are composed of four different types of averages: the average *(5)* price of the common stock of thirty industrial firms, the average price of the common stock prices of twenty transportation companies, the average price of the common stock prices of fifteen utility companies, and an overall average of all the sixty-five stocks used to compute the first three averages. Probably the average that is the most commonly used is the industrial average; it is often used by an investor interested in checking the state of the stock market before making an investment in an *(10)* industrial stock.

5. The pronoun "They" in line 3 refers to

    (A) the business days
    (B) these statistics
    (C) stocks and bonds
    (D) four different types

6. The pronoun "it" in line 8 refers to

    (A) the industrial average
    (B) an investor
    (C) the state of the stock market
    (D) an investment

TOEFL EXERCISE (Skills 3–5): Study each of the passages and choose the best answers to the questions that follow.

PASSAGE ONE (Questions 1–4)

The United States does not have a national university, but the idea has been around for quite some time. George Washington first recommended the idea to Congress; he even selected an actual site in Washington, D.C., and then left an endowment for the proposed national university in his will. *Line* During the century following the Revolution, the idea of a national university continued to receive the *(5)* support of various U.S. presidents, and philanthropist Andrew Carnegie pursued the cause at the beginning of the present century. Although the original idea has not yet been acted upon, it continues to be proposed in bills before Congress.

1. According to the passage, the national university of the United States

    (A) has been around for a while
    (B) does not exist
    (C) is a very recent idea
    (D) is an idea that developed during the present century

2. The passage indicates that George Washington did NOT do which of the following?

    (A) He suggested the concept for a national university to Congress.
    (B) He chose a location for the national university.
    (C) He left money in his will for a national university.
    (D) He succeeded in establishing a national university.

3. Which of the following is NOT mentioned in the passage about Andrew Carnegie?

    (A) He was interested in doing charity work and good deeds for the public.
    (B) He was a member of Congress.
    (C) He was interested in the idea of a national university.
    (D) He was active in the early twentieth century.

4. The pronoun "it" in line 6 refers to

    (A) the cause
    (B) the beginning of the present century
    (C) the original idea
    (D) Congress

PASSAGE TWO (Questions 5–9)

The La Brea tarpits, located in Hancock Park in the Los Angeles area, have proven to be an extremely fertile source of Ice Age fossils. Apparently, during the period of the Ice Age, the tarpits were covered by shallow pools of water; when animals came there to drink, they got caught in the sticky tar and perished. The tar not only trapped the animals, leading to their death, but also served as a remarkably effective preservant, allowing near-perfect skeletons to remain hidden until the present era.

In 1906, the remains of a huge prehistoric bear discovered in the tarpits alerted archeologists to the potential treasure lying within the tar. Since then thousands and thousands of well-preserved skeletons have been uncovered, including the skeletons of camels, horses, wolves, tigers, sloths, and dinosaurs.

Line
(5)

(10)

5. Which of the following is NOT true about the La Brea tarpits?

   (A) They contain fossils that are quite old.
   (B) They are found in Hancock Park.
   (C) They have existed since the Ice Age.
   (D) They are located under a swimming pool.

6. The pronoun "they" in line 3 refers to

   (A) the La Brea tarpits
   (B) Ice Age fossils
   (C) shallow pools of water
   (D) animals

7. According to the passage, how did the Ice Age animals die?

   (A) The water poisoned them.
   (B) They got stuck in the tar.
   (C) They were attacked by other animals.
   (D) They were killed by hunters.

8. When did archeologists become aware of the possible value of the contents of the tarpits?

   (A) During the Ice Age
   (B) Thousands and thousands of years ago
   (C) Early in the twentieth century
   (D) Within the past decade

9. Which of the following is NOT mentioned as an example of a skeleton found in the tarpits?

   (A) A bear
   (B) A sloth
   (C) A horse
   (D) A snake

PASSAGE THREE (Questions 10–14)

When the president of the United States wants to get away from the hectic pace in Washington, D.C., Camp David is the place to go. Camp David, in a wooded mountain area about 70 miles from Washington, D.C., is the official retreat of the president of the United States. It consists of living space for the president, the first family, and the presidential staff as well as sporting and recreational facilities.

Line
(5)

Camp David was established by President Franklin Delano Roosevelt in 1942. He found the site particularly appealing in that its mountain air provided relief from the summer heat of Washington and its remote location offered a more relaxing environment than could be achieved in the capital city.

When Roosevelt first established the retreat, he called it Shangri-La, which evoked the blissful mountain kingdom in James Hilton's novel *Lost Horizon.* Later, President Dwight David Eisenhower renamed the location Camp David after his grandson David Eisenhower.

(10)

Camp David has been used for a number of significant meetings. In 1943 during World War II, President Roosevelt met there with Great Britain's Prime Minister Winston Churchill. In 1959 at the height of the Cold War, President Eisenhower met there with Soviet Premier Nikita Khrushchev; in 1978 President Jimmy Carter sponsored peace talks between Israel's Prime Minister Menachem Begin and Egypt's President Anwar el-Sadat at the retreat at Camp David.

(15)

10. Which of the following is NOT discussed about Camp David?

    (A) Its location
    (B) Its cost
    (C) Its facilities
    (D) Its uses

11. According to the passage, who founded Camp David?

    (A) George Washington
    (B) The first family
    (C) Franklin Delano Roosevelt
    (D) Dwight David Eisenhower

12. The pronoun "he" in line 10 refers to

    (A) Camp David
    (B) Roosevelt
    (C) James Hilton
    (D) President Dwight David Eisenhower

13. Which of the following is NOT true about President Eisenhower?

    (A) He had a grandson named David.
    (B) He attended a conference with Nikita Khrushchev.
    (C) He named the presidential retreat Shangri-La.
    (D) He visited Camp David.

14. Khrushchev was at Camp David in

    (A) 1942
    (B) 1943
    (C) 1959
    (D) 1978

TOEFL REVIEW EXERCISE (Skills 1–5): Study each of the passages and choose the best answers to the questions that follow.

PASSAGE ONE (Questions 1–4)

    Hay fever is a seasonal allergy to pollens; the term "hay fever," however, is a less than adequate description since an attack of this allergy does not incur fever and since such an attack can be brought on by sources other than hay-producing grasses. Hay fever is generally caused by air-borne pollens, particularly ragweed pollen. The amount of pollen in the air is largely dependent on geographical location, weather, and season. In the eastern section of the United States, for example, there are generally three periods when pollen from various sources can cause intense hay fever suffering: in the springtime months of March and April when pollen from trees is prevalent, in the summer months of June and July when grass pollen fills the air, and at the end of August when ragweed pollen is at its most concentrated levels.

Line (5)

1. Which of the following would be the best title for the passage?

    (A) The Relationship between Season and Allergies
    (B) Misconceptions and Facts about Hay Fever
    (C) Hay Fever in the Eastern United States
    (D) How Ragweed Causes Hay Fever

2. According to the passage, which of the following helps to explain why the term "hay fever" is somewhat of a misnomer?

    (A) A strong fever occurs after an attack.
    (B) The amount of pollen in the air depends on geographical location.
    (C) Hay fever is often caused by ragweed pollen.
    (D) Grass pollen is prevalent in June and July.

3. Which of the following is NOT discussed in the passage as a determining factor of the amount of pollen in the air?

    (A) Place
    (B) Climate
    (C) Time of year
    (D) Altitude

4. Which of the following is NOT true about hay fever in the eastern United States?

    (A) Suffering from hay fever is equally severe year-round.
    (B) Pollen from trees causes hay fever suffering in the spring.
    (C) Grass pollen fills the air earlier in the year than ragweed pollen.
    (D) Ragweed pollen is most prevalent at the end of the summer.

PASSAGE TWO (Questions 5–9)

Line
(5)

(10)

Lincoln's now famous Gettysburg Address was not, on the occasion of its delivery, recognized as the masterpiece that it is today. Lincoln was not even the primary speaker at the ceremonies, held at the height of the Civil War in 1863, to dedicate the battlefield at Gettysburg. The main speaker was orator Edward Everett, whose two-hour speech was followed by Lincoln's shorter remarks. Lincoln began his small portion of the program with the words that today are immediately recognized by most Americans: "Four score and seven years ago our fathers brought forth on this continent a new nation, conceived in liberty and dedicated to the proposition that all men are created equal." At the time of the speech, little notice was given to what Lincoln had said, and Lincoln considered his appearance at the ceremonies rather unsuccessful. After his speech appeared in print, appreciation for his words began to grow, and today it is recognized as one of the all-time greatest speeches.

5. The main idea of this passage is that

(A) the Gettysburg Address has always been regarded as a masterpiece
(B) at the time of its delivery the Gettysburg Address was truly appreciated as a masterpiece
(C) it was not until after 1863 that Lincoln's speech at Gettysburg took its place in history
(D) Lincoln is better recognized today than he was at the time of his presidency

6. Which of the following is true about the ceremonies at Gettysburg during the Civil War?

(A) Lincoln was the main speaker.
(B) Lincoln gave a two-hour speech.
(C) Everett was the closing speaker of the ceremonies.
(D) Everett's speech was longer than Lincoln's.

7. According to the passage, when Lincoln spoke at the Gettysburg ceremonies,

(A) his words were immediately recognized by most Americans
(B) he spoke for only a short period of time
(C) he was enthusiastically cheered
(D) he was extremely proud of his performance

8. When did Lincoln's Gettysburg Address begin to receive public acclaim?

(A) After it had been published
(B) Immediately after the speech
(C) Not until the present day
(D) After Lincoln received growing recognition

9. The pronoun "it" in line 10 refers to which of the following?

(A) His speech
(B) Print
(C) Appreciation
(D) One

PASSAGE THREE (Questions 10–15)

According to the theory of continental drift, the continents are not fixed in position but instead move slowly across the surface of the Earth, constantly changing in position relative to one another. This theory was first proposed in the eighteenth century when mapmakers noticed how closely the
Line continents of the Earth fit together when they were matched up. It was suggested then that the
(5) present-day continents had once been one large continent that had broken up into pieces which drifted apart.

Today the modern theory of plate tectonics has developed from the theory of continental drift. The theory of plate tectonics suggests that the crust of the Earth is divided into six large, and many small, tectonic plates that drift on the lava that composes the inner core of the Earth. These plates
(10) consist of ocean floor and continents that quite probably began breaking up and moving relative to one another more than 200 million years ago.

10. The topic of this passage is

   (A) continental drift
   (B) the theory of plate tectonics
   (C) the development of ideas about the movement of the Earth's surface
   (D) eighteenth-century mapmakers

11. The passage states that the theory of continental drift developed as a result of

   (A) the fixed positions of the continents
   (B) the work of mapmakers
   (C) the rapid movement of continents
   (D) the fit of the Earth's plates

12. The pronoun "they" in line 4 refers to

   (A) mapmakers
   (B) continents
   (C) pieces
   (D) tectonic plates

13. Which of the following is NOT true about the theory of plate tectonics?

   (A) It is not as old as the theory of continental drift.
   (B) It evolved from the theory of continental drift.
   (C) It postulates that the Earth's surface is separated into plates.
   (D) It was proposed by mapmakers.

14. According to the passage, what constitutes a tectonic plate?

   (A) Lava
   (B) Only the continents
   (C) The inner core of the Earth
   (D) The surface of the land and the floor of the oceans

15. Which of the following best describes the organization of the passage?

   (A) Two unrelated theories are presented.
   (B) Two contrasting opinions are stated.
   (C) A theory is followed by an example.
   (D) One hypothesis is developed from another.

PASSAGE FOUR (Questions 16–24)

Charles Lutwidge Dodgson is perhaps not a name that is universally recognized, but Dodgson did achieve enormous success under the pseudonym Lewis Carroll. He created this pseudonym from the Latinization, *Carolus Ludovicus,* of his real given names. It was under the name Lewis Carroll that
Line Dodgson published the children's books *Alice's Adventures in Wonderland* (1865) and its sequel
(5) *Through the Looking Glass* (1872). Though Dodgson achieved this success in children's literature, he was not an author of children's books by training or profession. His education and chosen field of pursuit were far removed from the field of children's literature and were instead focused on theoretical mathematics.

Dodgson graduated with honors from Christ Church, Oxford, in 1854 and then embarked on a
(10) career in the world of academia. He worked as a lecturer in mathematics at Oxford and, later in his career, published a number of theoretical works on mathematics under his own name rather than under the pseudonym that he used for his children's stories. He produced a number of texts for students, such as *A Syllabus of Plane Algebraical Geometry* (1860), *Formulae of Plane Trigonometry* (1861), which was notable for the creativity of the symbols that he used to express trigonometric
(15) functions such as sine and cosine, and *A Guide for the Mathematical Student* (1866). In a number of more esoteric works, he championed the principles of Euclid; in *Euclid and His Modern Rivals* (1879), he presented his ideas on the superiority of Euclid over rival mathematicians in a highly imaginative fashion, by devising a courtroom trial of anti-Euclid mathematicians that he named "Euclid-wreakers" and ultimately finding the defendants guilty as charged. *Curiosa Mathematica* (1888–1893)
(20) made a further defense of Euclid's work, focusing on Euclid's definition of parallel lines. These academic works never had the universal impact of Dodgson's works for children using the name Lewis Carroll, but they demonstrate a solid body of well-regarded academic material.

16. The topic of this passage is

    (A) the works of Lewis Carroll
    (B) Charles Dodgson and Euclid
    (C) the story of *Alice's Adventures in Wonderland*
    (D) Dodgson and Carroll: mathematics and children's stories

17. According to the passage, Dodgson

    (A) did not use his given name on his stories for children
    (B) used the same name on all his published works
    (C) used the name Carroll on his mathematical works
    (D) used a pseudonym for the work about the courtroom trial

18. Which of the following is true, according to the passage?

    (A) "Lewis" is a Latin name.
    (B) "Lutwidge" is part of Dodgson's pseudonym.
    (C) "Carolus" is the Latin version of the name "Charles."
    (D) "Ludovicus" is part of Dodgson's given name.

19. It is NOT stated in the passage that Dodgson

    (A) attended Christ Church, Oxford
    (B) studied children's literature
    (C) was an outstanding student
    (D) was a published author of academic works

20. What is stated in the passage about the work *Formulae of Plane Trigonometry*?

    (A) It portrayed mathematics in a creative way.
    (B) It was written by Euclid.
    (C) It was published in 1860.
    (D) It was one of the texts that Dodgson studied at Oxford.

21. All of the following are stated in the passage about the work *Euclid and His Modern Rivals* EXCEPT that

    (A) it was published in 1879
    (B) it was a highly creative work
    (C) it described an actual trial in which Euclid participated
    (D) it described a trial in which "Euclid-wreakers" were found guilty

22. The passage indicates that which of the following works was about Euclid?

   (A) *A Syllabus of Plane Algebraical Geometry*
   (B) *Formulae of Plane Trigonometry*
   (C) *A Guide for the Mathematical Student*
   (D) *Curiosa Mathematica*

23. The pronoun "they" in line 22 refers to

   (A) parallel lines
   (B) these academic works
   (C) Dodgson's works for children
   (D) children

24. What is stated in the passage about Dodgson's academic works?

   (A) They are all about Euclid.
   (B) They had an impact on his works for children.
   (C) They were published under the name Lewis Carroll.
   (D) They were well received in the academic world.

INDIRECTLY ANSWERED QUESTIONS_____

Some questions in the Reading Comprehension section of the TOEFL test will require answers that are not directly stated in the passage. To answer these questions correctly, you will have to draw conclusions from information that is given in the passage. Two common types of indirectly answered questions are (1) implied detail questions and (2) transition questions.

SKILL 6:   ANSWER IMPLIED DETAIL QUESTIONS CORRECTLY

You will sometimes be asked to answer a question by drawing a conclusion from a specific detail or details in the passage. Questions of this type contain the words *implied, inferred, likely,* or *probably* to let you know that the answer to the question is not directly stated. In this type of question it is important to understand that you do not have to "pull the answer out of thin air." Instead, some information will be given in the passage, and you will draw a conclusion from that information.

Example

The passage:

Line
(5)

(10)

The Hawaiian language is a melodious language in which all words are derived from an alphabet of only twelve letters, the five vowels *a, e, i, o, u* and the seven consonants *h, k, l, m, n, p, w*. Each syllable in the language ends in a vowel, and two consonants never appear together, so vowels have a much higher frequency in the Hawaiian language than they do in English.

This musical-sounding language can be heard regularly by visitors to the islands. Most Hawaiians speak English, but it is quite common to hear English that is liberally spiced with words and expressions from the traditional language of the culture. A visitor may be greeted with the expression *aloha* and may be referred to as a *malihini* because he is a newcomer to the island. This visitor may attend an outside *luau* where everyone eats too much and may be invited afterwards to dance the *hula*.

The questions:

1. Which of the following is probably NOT a Hawaiian word?

    (A) *mahalo*
    (B) *mahimahi*
    (C) *meklea*
    (D) *moana*

2. It is implied that a *luau* is

    (A) a dance
    (B) a feast
    (C) a concert
    (D) a language

To answer the first question, you should refer to the part of the passage where it states that in the Hawaiian language *two consonants never appear together*. From this you can draw the conclusion that answer (C), *meklea*, is probably not a Hawaiian word because the consonants *k* and *l* appear together in this word, so answer (C) is the best answer to this question. To answer the second question, you should refer to the part of the passage where it states that at a luau, *everyone eats too much*. From this you can draw the conclusion that a *luau* is a feast, which is a very large meal. The best answer is therefore answer (B).

The following chart outlines the key information that you should remember about implied detail questions:

IMPLIED DETAIL QUESTIONS	
HOW TO IDENTIFY THE QUESTION	It is **implied** in the passage that . . . It can be **inferred** from the passage that . . . It is most **likely** that . . . What **probably** happened . . . ?
WHERE TO FIND THE ANSWER	The answers to these questions are found in order in the passage.
HOW TO ANSWER THE QUESTION	1. Choose a key word in the question. 2. Scan the passage for the key word (or a related idea). 3. Carefully read the sentence that contains the key word. 4. Look for an answer that *could be* true, according to that sentence.

TOEFL EXERCISE 6: Study each of the passages and choose the best answers to the questions that follow.

PASSAGE ONE (Questions 1–2)

Eskimos need efficient and adequate means to travel across water in that the areas where they live are surrounded by oceans, bays, and inlets and dotted with lakes and seas. Two different types of boats have been developed by the Eskimos, each constructed to meet specific needs.

Line
(5)
The kayak is something like a canoe that has been covered by a deck. A kayak is generally constructed with one opening in the deck for one rider; however, some kayaks are made for two. Because the deck of a kayak is covered over except for the hole (or holes) for its rider (or riders), a kayak can tip over in the water and roll back up without filling with water and sinking. One of the primary uses of the kayak is for hunting.

(10)
The umiak is not closed over, as is the kayak. Instead, it is an open boat that is built to hold ten to twelve passengers. Eskimos have numerous uses for the umiak which reflect the size of the boat; e.g., the umiak is used to haul belongings from campsite to campsite, and it is used for hunting larger animals that are too big to be hunted in a kayak.

1. It is implied in the passage that if a kayak has two holes, then

(A) it accommodates two riders
(B) it is less stable than a kayak with one hole
(C) it is as large as an umiak
(D) it cannot be used on the ocean

2. It can be inferred from the passage that an example of the animal mentioned in lines 11–12 might be

(A) a kangaroo
(B) a snake
(C) a whale
(D) a salmon

PASSAGE TWO (Questions 3–5)

Two types of trees from the same family of trees share honors in certain respects as the most impressive of trees. Both evergreen conifers, the California redwood (*Sequoia sempervirens*) and the giant sequoia (*Sequoiandendron giganteum*) are found growing natively only in the state of California.
Line The California redwood is found along the northern coast of the state, while the giant sequoia is
(5) found inland and at higher elevations, along the western slopes of the Sierra Nevadas.

The California redwood is the tallest living tree and is in fact the tallest living thing on the face of the Earth; the height of the tallest redwood on record is 385 feet (120 meters). Though not quite as tall as the California redwood, with a height of 320 feet (100 meters), the giant sequoia is nonetheless the largest and most massive of living things; giant sequoias have been measured at more than 100
(10) feet (30 meters) around the base, with weights of more than 6,000 tons.

3. It is implied in the passage that

   (A) the leaves of only the California
          redwood turn brown in the autumn
   (B) the leaves of only the giant sequoia
          turn brown in the winter
   (C) the leaves of both types of trees in the
          passage turn brown in the winter
   (D) the leaves of neither type of tree in the
          passage turn brown in the winter

4. It can be inferred from the passage that the
    Sierra Nevadas are

   (A) a type of giant redwood
   (B) a coastal community
   (C) a group of lakes
   (D) a mountain range

5. Which of the following is implied in the
    passage?

   (A) The giant sequoia is taller than the
          California redwood.
   (B) The California redwood is not as big
          around as the giant sequoia.
   (C) The California redwood weighs more
          than the giant sequoia.
   (D) Other living things are larger than the
          giant sequoia.

PASSAGE THREE (Questions 6–8)

Probably the most recognized boardgame around the world is the game of Monopoly. In this game, players vie for wealth by buying, selling, and renting properties; the key to success in the game, in addition to a bit of luck, is for a player to acquire monopolies on clusters of properties in order to force opponents to pay exorbitant rents and fees.

Line
(5)
Although the game is now published in countless languages and versions, with foreign locations and place names appropriate to the target language adorning its board, the beginnings of the game were considerably more humble. The game was invented in 1933 by Charles Darrow, during the height of the Great Depression. Darrow, who lived in Germantown, Pennsylvania, was himself unemployed during those difficult financial times. He set the original game not as might be expected

(10)
in his hometown of Germantown, but in Atlantic City, New Jersey, the site of numerous pre-Depression vacations, where he walked along the Boardwalk and visited at Park Place. Darrow made the first games by hand and sold them locally until Parker Brothers purchased the rights to Monopoly in 1935 and took the first steps toward the mass production of today.

6. The French version of Monopoly might possibly include a piece of property entitled

   (A) Atlantic City, New Jersey
   (B) Germantown, Pennsylvania
   (C) Boardwalk
   (D) the Eiffel Tower

7. It is implied that Darrow selected Atlantic City as the setting for Monopoly because

   (A) it brought back good memories
   (B) his family came from Atlantic City
   (C) the people of Germantown might have been angered if he had used Germantown
   (D) Atlantic City was larger than Germantown

8. Parker Brothers is probably

   (A) a real estate company
   (B) a game manufacturing company
   (C) a group of Charles Darrow's friends
   (D) a toy design company

SKILL 7: ANSWER TRANSITION QUESTIONS CORRECTLY

You will sometimes be asked to determine what probably came before the reading passage (in the *preceding* paragraph) or what probably comes after the reading passage (in the *following* paragraph). Of course, the topic of the *preceding* or *following* paragraph is not directly stated, and you must draw a conclusion to determine what is probably in these paragraphs.

This type of question is a *transition* question. It asks you to demonstrate that you understand that good writing contains *transitions* from one paragraph to the next. A paragraph may start out with the idea of the previous paragraph as a way of linking the ideas in the two paragraphs. A paragraph may also end with an idea that will be further developed in the following paragraph.

Example

The passage:

Another myth of the oceans concerns Davy Jones, who in folklore is the mean-spirited sovereign of the ocean's depths. The name "Jones" is thought by some etymologists to have been derived *Line* from the name "Jonah," the Hebrew prophet who spent three days *(5)* in a whale's belly.

According to tradition, any object that goes overboard and sinks to the bottom of the ocean is said to have gone to Davy Jones's locker, the ocean-sized, mythical receptacle for anything that falls into the water. Needless to say, any sailor on the seas is *(10)* not so eager to take a tour of Davy Jones's locker, although it might be a rather interesting trip considering all the treasures located there.

The questions:

1. The paragraph *preceding* this passage most probably discusses

   (A) the youth of Davy Jones
   (B) Davy Jones's career as a sailor
   (C) a different traditional story from the sea
   (D) preparing to travel on the ocean

2. The topic of the paragraph *following* the passage most likely is

   (A) valuable items located at the bottom of the ocean
   (B) where Davy Jones is found today
   (C) Jonah and the whale
   (D) preventing objects from falling overboard

The first question asks about the topic of the *preceding* paragraph, so you must look at the beginning of the passage and draw a conclusion about what probably came *before*. Since the passage begins with the expression *another myth of the oceans*, you should understand that the new passage is going to present a *second* myth of the oceans and the previous passage probably presented the *first* myth of the oceans. A *myth* is a *traditional story,* so the best answer to this question is answer (C). The second question asks about the topic of the *following* paragraph, so you must look at the end of the passage and draw a conclusion about what probably comes *after.* The passage ends with the mention of *all the treasures located there,* and *there* is in Davy Jones's locker, or at the bottom of the ocean; this is probably going to be the topic of the next paragraph. The best answer to the second question is therefore answer (A).

The following chart outlines the key information that you should remember about transition questions:

TRANSITION QUESTIONS	
HOW TO IDENTIFY THE QUESTION	*The paragraph **preceding** the passage probably . . .* *What is most likely in the paragraph **following** the passage?*
WHERE TO FIND THE ANSWER	The answer can generally be found *in the first line* of the passage for a *preceding* question. The answer can generally be found *in the last line* for a *following* question.

HOW TO ANSWER THE QUESTION	1. Read the *first* line for a *preceding* question.
	2. Read the *last* line for a *following* question.
	3. Draw a conclusion about what comes *before* or *after*.
	4. Choose the answer that is reflected in the *first* or *last* line of the passage.

TOEFL EXERCISE 7: Study each of the passages and choose the best answers to the questions that follow.

PASSAGE ONE (Questions 1–2)

Another program instrumental in the popularization of science was *Cosmos*. This series, broadcast on public television, dealt with topics and issues from varied fields of science. The principal writer and narrator of the program was Carl Sagan, a noted astronomer and Pulitzer Prize-winning author.

1. The paragraph preceding this passage most probably discusses

    (A) a different scientific television series
    (B) Carl Sagan's scientific achievements
    (C) the Pulitzer Prize won by Carl Sagan
    (D) public television

2. The paragraph following this passage most likely contains information on what?

    (A) The popularity of science
    (B) The program *Cosmos*
    (C) The astronomer Carl Sagan
    (D) Topics and issues from various fields of science

PASSAGE TWO (Questions 3–4)

When a strong earthquake occurs on the ocean floor rather than on land, a tremendous force is exerted on the seawater and one or more large, destructive waves called *tsunamis* can be formed. Tsunamis are commonly called tidal waves in the United States, but this is really an inappropriate name in that the cause of the tsunami is an underground earthquake rather than the ocean's tides.

Line (5) Far from land, a tsunami can move through the wide open vastness of the ocean at a speed of 600 miles (900 kilometers) per hour and often can travel tremendous distances without losing height and strength. When a tsunami reaches shallow coastal water, it can reach a height of 100 feet (30 meters) or more and can cause tremendous flooding and damage to coastal areas.

3. The paragraph preceding the passage most probably discusses

    (A) tsunamis in various parts of the world
    (B) the negative effects of tsunamis
    (C) land-based earthquakes
    (D) the effect of tides on tsunamis

4. Which of the following is most likely the topic of the paragraph following the passage?

    (A) The causes of tsunamis
    (B) The destructive effects of tsunamis on the coast
    (C) The differences between tsunamis and tidal waves
    (D) The distances covered by tsunamis

PASSAGE THREE (Questions 5–6)

While draft laws are federal laws, marriage laws are state laws rather than federal; marriage regulations are therefore not uniform throughout the country. The legal marriage age serves as an example of this lack of conformity. In most states, both the man and the woman must be at least eighteen years old to marry without parental consent; however, the states of Nebraska and Wyoming require the couple to be at least nineteen, while the minimum age in Mississippi is twenty-one. If parental permission is given, then a couple can marry at sixteen in some states, and a few states even allow marriage before the age of sixteen, though a judge's permission, in addition to the permission of the parents, is sometimes required in this situation. Some states which allow couples to marry at such a young age are now considering doing away with such early marriages because of the numerous negative effects of these young marriages.

Line (5)

(10)

5. The paragraph preceding the passage most probably discusses

   (A) state marriage laws
   (B) the lack of uniformity in marriage laws
   (C) federal draft laws
   (D) the minimum legal marriage age

6. The topic of the paragraph following the passage is most likely to be

   (A) disadvantages of youthful marriages
   (B) reasons why young people decide to marry
   (C) the age when parental consent for marriage is required
   (D) a discussion of why some states allow marriages before the age of sixteen

TOEFL EXERCISE (Skills 6–7): Study each of the passages and choose the best answers to the questions that follow.

PASSAGE ONE (Questions 1–4)

The most conservative sect of the Mennonite Church is the Old Order Amish, with 33,000 members living mainly today in the states of Pennsylvania, Ohio, and Indiana. Their lifestyle reflects their belief in the doctrines of separation from the world and simplicity of life. The Amish have steadfastly rejected the societal changes that have occurred in the previous three hundred years, preferring instead to remain securely rooted in a seventeenth-century lifestyle. They live on farms without radios, televisions, telephones, electric lights, and cars; they dress in plainly styled and colored old-fashioned clothes; and they farm their lands with horses and tools rather than modern farm equipment. They have a highly communal form of living, with barn raisings and quilting bees as commonplace activities.

Line (5)

1. The paragraph preceding this passage most probably discusses

   (A) other, more liberal sects of Mennonites
   (B) where Mennonites live
   (C) the communal Amish lifestyle
   (D) the most conservative Mennonites

2. Which of the following would probably NOT be found on an Amish farm?

   (A) A hammer
   (B) A cart
   (C) A long dress
   (D) A refrigerator

3. It can be inferred from the passage that a quilting bee

(A) involves a group of people
(B) is necessary when raising bees
(C) always follows a barn raising
(D) provides needed solitude

4. Which of the following is most likely the topic of the paragraph following the passage?

(A) The effects of the communal lifestyle on the Old Order Amish
(B) How the Old Order Amish differ from the Mennonites
(C) The effect of modern technology on the Old Order Amish
(D) The doctrines of the Old Order Amish

PASSAGE TWO (Questions 5–8)

Various other Indian tribes also lived on the Great Plains. The Sioux, a group of seven American Indian tribes, are best known for the fiercely combative posture against encroaching White civilization in the 1800s. Although they are popularly referred to as Sioux, these Indian tribes did not
Line call themselves Sioux; the name was given to them by an enemy tribe. The seven Sioux tribes called
(5) themselves by some variation of the word "Dakota," which means "allies" in their language. Four tribes of the eastern Sioux community living in Minnesota were known by the name Dakota. The Nakota included two tribes that left the eastern woodlands and moved out onto the plains. The Teton Sioux, or Lakota, moved even farther west to the plains of the present-day states of North Dakota, South Dakota, and Wyoming.

5. The paragraph preceding this passage most probably discusses

(A) how the Sioux battled the White man
(B) one of the Plains Indian tribes
(C) where the Sioux lived
(D) American Indian tribes on the East Coast

6. Which of the following represents a likely reaction of the Sioux in the 1800s to the encroaching White civilization?

(A) The Sioux would probably help the Whites to settle in the West.
(B) The Sioux would probably attack the White settlers.
(C) The Sioux would probably invite the Whites to smoke a peace pipe.
(D) The Sioux would probably join together in hunting parties with the White settlers.

7. It is implied in the passage that the seven Sioux tribes called each other by some form of the word "Dakota" because they were

(A) united in a cause
(B) all living in North Dakota
(C) fiercely combative
(D) enemies

8. It can be inferred from the passage that the present-day states of North and South Dakota

(A) are east of Minnesota
(B) are home to the four tribes known by the name Dakota
(C) received their names from the Indian tribes living there
(D) are part of the eastern woodlands

PASSAGE THREE (Questions 9–12)

The extinction of many species of birds has undoubtedly been hastened by modern man; since 1600 it has been estimated that approximately 100 bird species have become extinct over the world. In North America, the first species known to be annihilated was the great auk, a flightless bird that served as an easy source of food and bait for Atlantic fishermen through the beginning of the nineteenth century.

Shortly after the great auk's extinction, two other North American species, the Carolina parakeet and the passenger pigeon, began dwindling noticeably in numbers. The last Carolina parakeet and the last passenger pigeon in captivity both died in September 1914. In addition to these extinct species, several others such as the bald eagle, the peregrine falcon, and the California condor are today recognized as endangered; steps are being taken to prevent their extinction.

9. The number of bird species that have become extinct in the United States since 1600 most probably is

   (A) more than 100
   (B) exactly 100
   (C) less than 100
   (D) exactly three

10. The passage implies that the great auk disappeared

   (A) before 1600
   (B) in the 1600s
   (C) in the 1800s
   (D) in the last fifty years

11. It can be inferred from the passage that the great auk was killed because

   (A) it was eating the fishermen's catch
   (B) fishermen wanted to eat it
   (C) it flew over fishing areas
   (D) it baited fishermen

12. The paragraph following this passage most probably discusses

   (A) what is being done to save endangered birds
   (B) what the bald eagle symbolizes to Americans
   (C) how several bird species became endangered
   (D) other extinct species

TOEFL REVIEW EXERCISE (Skills 1–7): Study each of the passages and choose the best answers to the questions that follow.

PASSAGE ONE (Questions 1–6)

The Mason-Dixon Line is often considered by Americans to be the demarcation between the North and the South. It is in reality the boundary that separates the state of Pennsylvania from Maryland and parts of West Virginia. Prior to the Civil War, this southern boundary of Pennsylvania separated the nonslave states to the north from the slave states to the south.

The Mason-Dixon Line was established well before the Civil War, as a result of a boundary dispute between Pennsylvania and Maryland. Two English astronomers, Charles Mason and Jeremiah Dixon, were called in to survey the area and officially mark the boundary between the two states. The survey was completed in 1767, and the boundary was marked with stones, many of which remain to this day.

1. The best title for this passage would be

   (A) Dividing the North and the South
   (B) The Meaning of the Mason-Dixon Line
   (C) Two English Astronomers
   (D) The History of the Mason-Dixon Line

2. It can be inferred from the passage that before the Civil War

   (A) Pennsylvania was south of the Mason-Dixon Line
   (B) Pennsylvania was a nonslave state
   (C) the states south of the Mason-Dixon Line had the same opinion about slavery as Pennsylvania
   (D) the slave states were not divided from the nonslave states

3. According to the passage, the Mason-Dixon Line was established because of a disagreement

(A) about borders
(B) about slaves
(C) between two astronomers
(D) over surveying techniques

4. The passage states all of the following about Mason and Dixon EXCEPT that

(A) they came from England
(B) they worked as astronomers
(C) they caused the boundary dispute between Pennsylvania and Maryland
(D) they surveyed the area of the boundary between Pennsylvania and Maryland

5. The passage indicates that the Mason-Dixon Line was identified with

(A) pieces of rock
(B) fences
(C) a stone wall
(D) a border crossing

6. The paragraph following the passage most probably discusses

(A) where the Mason-Dixon Line is located
(B) the Mason-Dixon Line today
(C) the effect of the Civil War on slavery
(D) what happened to Charles Mason and Jeremiah Dixon

PASSAGE TWO (Questions 7–12)

Manic depression is another psychiatric illness that mainly affects mood. A patient suffering from this disease will alternate between periods of manic excitement and extreme depression, with or without relatively normal periods in between. The changes in mood suffered by a manic-depressive patient go far beyond the day-to-day mood changes experienced by the general population. In the period of manic excitement, the mood elevation can become so intense that it can result in extended insomnia, extreme irritability, and heightened aggressiveness. In the period of depression, which may last for several weeks or months, a patient experiences feelings of general fatigue, uselessness, and hopelessness and, in serious cases, may contemplate suicide.

Line
(5)

7. The paragraph preceding this passage most probably discusses

(A) when manic depression develops
(B) a different type of mental disease
(C) how moods are determined
(D) how manic depression can result in suicide

8. The topic of this passage is

(A) various psychiatric illnesses
(B) how depression affects the mood
(C) the intense period of manic excitement
(D) the mood changes of manic depression

9. According to the passage, a manic-depressive patient in a manic phase would be feeling

(A) highly emotional
(B) unhappy
(C) listless
(D) relatively normal

10. The passage indicates that most people

(A) never undergo mood changes
(B) experience occasional shifts in mood
(C) switch wildly from highs to lows
(D) become highly depressed

11. The pronoun "it" in line 5 refers to

(A) the general population
(B) the mood elevation
(C) insomnia
(D) heightened aggressiveness

12. The passage implies that

(A) changes from excitement to depression occur frequently and often
(B) only manic-depressive patients experience aggression
(C) the depressive phase of this disease can be more harmful than the manic phase
(D) suicide is inevitable in cases of manic depression

PASSAGE THREE (Questions 13–18)

Line
(5)

(10)

Unlike earlier campaigns, the 1960 presidential campaign featured the politically innovative and highly influential series of televised debates in the contest between the Republicans and the Democrats. Senator John Kennedy established an early lead among the Democratic hopefuls and was nominated on the first ballot at the Los Angeles convention to be the representative of the Democratic party in the presidential elections. Richard Nixon, then serving as vice president of the United States under Eisenhower, received the nomination of the Republican party. Both Nixon and Kennedy campaigned vigorously throughout the country and then took the unprecedented step of appearing in face-to-face debates on television. Political experts contend that the debates were a pivotal force in the elections. In front of a viewership of more than 100 million citizens, Kennedy masterfully overcame Nixon's advantage as the better-known and more experienced candidate and reversed the public perception of him as too inexperienced and immature for the presidency.

13. Which of the following best expresses the main idea of the passage?

   (A) Kennedy defeated Nixon in the 1960 presidential election.
   (B) Television debates were instrumental in the outcome of the 1960 presidential election.
   (C) Television debates have long been a part of campaigning.
   (D) Kennedy was the leading Democratic candidate in the 1960 presidential election.

14. The passage implies that Kennedy

   (A) was a long shot to receive the Democratic presidential nomination
   (B) won the Democratic presidential nomination fairly easily
   (C) was not a front runner in the race for the Democratic presidential nomination
   (D) came from behind to win the Democratic presidential nomination

15. The passage states that the television debates between presidential candidates in 1960

   (A) did not influence the selection of the president
   (B) were the final televised debates
   (C) were fairly usual in the history of presidential campaigns
   (D) were the first presidential campaign debates to be televised

16. Which of the following is NOT mentioned about Richard Nixon?

   (A) He was serving as vice president.
   (B) He was the Republican party's candidate for president.
   (C) He campaigned strongly all over the country.
   (D) He was nominated on the first ballot.

17. The passage states that in the debates with Nixon, Kennedy demonstrated to the American people that he was

   (A) old enough to be president
   (B) more experienced than Nixon
   (C) better known than Nixon
   (D) too inexperienced to serve as president

18. The pronoun "him" in line 11 refers to

   (A) John Kennedy
   (B) Richard Nixon
   (C) Eisenhower
   (D) the better-known and more experienced candidate

PASSAGE FOUR (Questions 19–29)

Line
(5)

(10)

(15)

(20)

Unlike these fish, which are actually extinct, the coelacanth is a type of fish that was believed to be extinct. However, an unexpected twentieth-century rediscovery of living coelacanths has brought about a reassessment of the status of this prehistoric sea creature that was believed to have long since disappeared from the Earth.

From fossil remains of the coelacanth, paleontologists have determined that the coelacanth was in existence around 350 million years ago, during the Paleozoic Era, more than 100 million years before the first dinosaurs arrived on Earth. The most recent fossilized coelacanths date from around 70 million years ago, near the end of the Mesozoic Era and near the end of the age of dinosaurs. Because no fossilized remnants of coelacanths from the last 70 million years have been found, the coelacanth was believed to have died out around the same time as the dinosaurs.

The prehistoric coelacanth studied by paleontologists had distinctive characteristics that differentiated it from other fish. It was named for its hollow spine and was known to have been a powerful carnivore because of its many sharp teeth and a special joint in the skull that allowed the ferocious teeth to move in coordination with the lower jaw. It also had a pair of fins with unusual bony and muscular development that allowed the coelacanth to dart around the ocean floor. These fins also enable the coelacanth to search out prey trying to hide on the ocean bottom.

In 1938, a living specimen of the coelacanth was discovered in the catch of a fishing boat off the coast of South Africa, and since then numerous other examples of the coelacanth have been found in the waters of the Indian Ocean. This modern version of the coelacanth is not exactly the same as its prehistoric cousin. Today's coelacanth is larger than its prehistoric relative, measuring up to six feet in length and weighing up to 150 pounds. However, the modern version of the coelacanth still possesses the characteristic hollow spine and distinctive fins with their unusual bony and muscular structure.

19. The topic of the preceding paragraph is most likely

    (A) various extinct fish
    (B) the discovery of the coelacanth
    (C) a reassessment of the status of a number of kinds of fish
    (D) a particular prehistoric sea creature

20. This passage is about a fish

    (A) that is extinct
    (B) that once was extinct
    (C) that is becoming extinct
    (D) that, surprisingly, is not extinct

21. It can be inferred from the passage that the first dinosaurs most likely appeared on Earth around

    (A) 150 million years ago
    (B) 250 million years ago
    (C) 350 million years ago
    (D) 450 million years ago

22. Coelacanths were believed to have died out after existing for

    (A) 70 million years
    (B) 140 million years
    (C) 280 million years
    (D) 350 million years

23. It can be inferred from the passage that the word *coelacanth* comes from the Greek for

    (A) extinct fish
    (B) hollow spine
    (C) sharp teeth
    (D) bony fingers

24. What is stated in the passage about the prehistoric coelacanth?

    (A) It was a rather feeble fish.
    (B) It lived on plants.
    (C) It had few teeth.
    (D) It moved its teeth in an unusual way.

25. The pronoun "It" in line 14 refers to

    (A) coelacanth
    (B) joint
    (C) coordination
    (D) jaw

26. According to the passage, why are scientists sure that the prehistoric coelacanth was a flesh-eater?

    (A) Because of its hollow spine
    (B) Because of the size of the skull
    (C) Because of the shape and movement of the teeth
    (D) Because of its unusual bony and muscular development

27. How many modern coelacanths have been found?

    (A) Only one
    (B) Only two
    (C) Only a few
    (D) Quite a few

28. What is NOT true about the prehistoric coelacanth, according to the passage?

    (A) It was smaller than the modern coelacanth.
    (B) It measured as much as six feet in length.
    (C) It weighed less than 150 pounds.
    (D) It had a hollow spine and distinctive fins.

29. Which paragraph describes the earlier version of the coelacanth?

    (A) The first paragraph
    (B) The second paragraph
    (C) The third paragraph
    (D) The fourth paragraph

VOCABULARY QUESTIONS

In the Reading Comprehension section of the TOEFL test, there will be a number of vocabulary questions. To answer this type of question, it is of course helpful if you know the meaning of the word that the the TOEFL test is testing. However, it is not always *necessary* for you to know the meaning of the word; often there are skills that you can use to help you find the correct answer to the question: (1) finding definitions from structural clues, (2) determining meanings from word parts, and (3) using context clues to determine meanings.

SKILL 8:   FIND DEFINITIONS FROM STRUCTURAL CLUES

When you are asked to determine the meaning of a word in the Reading Comprehension section of the TOEFL test, it is possible (1) that the passage provides information about the meaning of the word and (2) that there are structural clues to tell you that the definition of a word is included in the passage.

Example

The passage:

One of the leading schools of psychological thought in the twentieth century was <u>behaviorism</u>—the belief that the role of the psychologist is to study behavior, which is observable, rather than
Line conscious or unconscious thought, which is not. Probably the best-
(5) known proponent of behaviorism is B.F. Skinner, who was famous for his research on how rewards and punishments influence behavior. He came to believe that <u>positive reinforcements</u> such as praise, food, or money were more effective in promoting good behavior than <u>negative reinforcement</u>, or punishment.

The questions:

1. In "behaviorism" in line 2, a psychologist is concerned with

    (A) conscious thought patterns
    (B) unconscious thought patterns
    (C) observable actions
    (D) unobservable actions

2. What is "positive reinforcement" in line 7?

    (A) A gift
    (B) A reward
    (C) A bribe
    (D) A penalty

3. What is "negative reinforcement" in line 9?

    (A) A promotion
    (B) A reward
    (C) A surprise
    (D) A punishment

To answer the first question, you should look at the part of the passage following the word *behaviorism*. The dash punctuation (—) indicates that a definition or further information about behaviorism is going to follow. In the information following the dash you should see that the behaviorist is interested in *behavior, which is observable,* so the best answer to this question is answer (C). To answer the second question, you should look at the part of the passage following the expression *positive reinforcements*. The expression *such as* indicates that examples of *positive reinforcement* are going to follow. Your job is to look at the examples of positive reinforcement and draw a conclusion about what positive reinforcement might be. Since *praise, food,* or *money* might be given in return for a job well done, then *positive reinforcement* must be a *reward*. The best answer to this question is therefore answer (B). To answer the third question, you should look at the part of the passage following the expression *negative reinforcement*. The word *or* following *negative reinforcement* tells you that the idea is going to be restated in different words. You can see in the passage that another word for *negative reinforcement* is *punishment,* so answer (D) is the best answer to this question.

The following chart outlines the key information that you should remember about structural clues to help you understand unknown vocabulary words:

STRUCTURAL CLUES	
HOW TO IDENTIFY THE QUESTION	*What is . . . ?* *What is the **meaning** of . . . ?* *What is true about . . . ?*
TYPES OF CLUES	Punctuation: comma, parentheses, dashes Restatement: *or, that is, in other words, i.e.* Examples: *such as, for example, e.g.*
WHERE TO FIND THE ANSWER	Information to help you determine what something means will generally be found after the punctuation clue, the restatement clue, or the example clue.
HOW TO ANSWER THE QUESTION	1. Find the word in the passage. 2. Locate any structural clues. 3. Read the part of the passage after the structural clue *carefully*. 4. Eliminate any definitely wrong answers and choose the best answer from the remaining choices.

TOEFL EXERCISE 8: Study each of the passages and choose the best answers to the questions that follow.

PASSAGE ONE (Questions 1–4)

The teddy bear is a child's toy, a nice, soft stuffed animal suitable for cuddling. It is, however, a toy with an interesting history behind it.

Theodore Roosevelt, or Teddy as he was commonly called, was president of the United States
Line from 1901 to 1909. He was an unusually active man with varied pastimes, one of which was hunting.
(5) One day the president was invited to take part in a bear hunt; and inasmuch as Teddy was president, his hosts wanted to ensure that he caught a bear. A bear was captured, clunked over the head to knock it out, and tied to a tree; however, Teddy, who really wanted to actually hunt, refused to shoot the bear and in fact demanded that the bear be extricated from the ropes; that is, he demanded that the bear be set free.
(10)   The incident attracted a lot of attention among journalists. First a cartoon—drawn by Clifford K. Berryman to make fun of this situation—appeared in the *Washington Post*, and the cartoon was widely distributed and reprinted throughout the country. Then toy manufacturers began producing a toy bear which they called a "teddy bear." The teddy bear became the most widely recognized symbol of Roosevelt's presidency.

1. According to line 1 of the passage, what is a "teddy bear"?

   (A) A ferocious animal
   (B) The president of the United States
   (C) A famous hunter
   (D) A plaything

2. In line 4, "pastimes" could best be replaced by

   (A) things that occurred in the past
   (B) previous jobs
   (C) hunting trips
   (D) leisure activities

3. The word "extricated" in line 8 is closest in meaning to which of the following?

   (A) Released
   (B) Tied up
   (C) Hunted
   (D) Shot

4. In line 10, a "cartoon" could best be described as

   (A) a newspaper
   (B) a type of teddy bear
   (C) a drawing with a message
   (D) a newspaper article

PASSAGE TWO (Questions 5–8)

A supernova occurs when all of the hydrogen in the core of a huge star is transformed to iron and explodes. All stars die after their nuclear fuel has been exhausted. Stars with little mass die gradually, but those with relatively large mass die in a sudden explosion, a supernova. The sudden
Line flash of light can then be followed by several weeks of extremely bright light, perhaps as much light as
(5) twenty million stars.

Supernovae are not very common; they occur about once every hundred years in any galaxy, and in 1987 a supernova that could be seen by the naked eye occurred in the Magellan Cloud, a galaxy close to the Milky Way. Scientists periodically detect supernovae in other galaxies; however, no supernovae have occurred in the Milky Way (the galaxy that includes the Earth) since 1604. One very
(10) impressive supernova occurred in the Milky Way on July 4, 1054. There was a great explosion followed by three months of lighted skies, and historical chronicles of the time were full of accounts and unusual explanations for the misunderstood phenomenon—many people believed that it meant that the world was coming to an end.

5. A "supernova" in line 1 is which of the following?

   (A) The iron component of a star
   (B) The core of a star
   (C) The hydrogen in a star
   (D) The explosion of a star

6. According to the passage, which of the following best describes the "Magellan Cloud" in line 7?

   (A) A galaxy inside the Milky Way
   (B) A cloud composed of hydrogen
   (C) A galaxy near the Earth's galaxy
   (D) A cloud in the sky above the Earth

7. The "Milky Way" in line 9 is

   (A) part of the Earth
   (B) a galaxy close to the Earth
   (C) the galaxy that is home to the Earth
   (D) a creamy-colored cloud in the sky

8. Which of the following is closest in meaning to "phenomenon" in line 12?

   (A) Everyday occurrence
   (B) Misunderstood event
   (C) Common belief
   (D) Unusual occurrence

Skill 9:   DETERMINE MEANINGS FROM WORD PARTS

When you are asked to determine the meaning of a long word that you do not know in the Reading Comprehension section of the TOEFL test, it is sometimes possible to determine the meaning of the word by studying the word parts.

Example

The passage:

>   Ring Lardner himself was born into a wealthy, educated, and cultured family. For the bulk of his career, he worked as a reporter for newspapers in South Bend, Boston, St. Louis, and Chicago.
> *Line* However, it is for his short stories of lower middle-class Americans
> *(5)* that Ring Lardner is perhaps best known. In these stories, Lardner vividly creates the language and the ambiance of this lower class, often using the misspelled words, grammatical errors, and incorrect diction that typified the language of the lower middle class.

The questions:

1.   The word "vividly" in line 6 is closest in meaning to

   (A)   in a cultured way
   (B)   in a correct way
   (C)   in a lifelike way
   (D)   in a brief way

2.   The word "misspelled" in line 7 is closest in meaning to

   (A)   highly improper
   (B)   vulgar
   (C)   incorrectly written
   (D)   slang

3.   The word "diction" in line 8 is closest in meaning to

   (A)   writing
   (B)   sentence structure
   (C)   form
   (D)   speech

In the first question, the word *vividly* contains the word part *viv,* which means *life,* so the best answer is answer (C). In the second question, the word *misspelled* contains the word part *mis,* which means *error* or *incorrect,* so the best answer is answer (C). In the third question, the word *diction* contains the word part *dic,* which means *speak,* so the best answer is answer (D).

The following chart contains a few word parts that you will need to know to complete the exercises in this part of the text. A more complete list of word parts and exercises to practice them can be found in Appendix I at the back of the text.

A SHORT LIST OF WORD PARTS					
PART	MEANING	EXAMPLE	PART	MEANING	EXAMPLE
CONTRA	(against)	contrast	DIC	(say)	dictate
MAL	(bad)	malcontent	DOMIN	(master)	dominant
MIS	(error)	mistake	JUD	(judge)	judgment
SUB	(under)	subway	MOR	(death)	mortal
DEC	(ten)	decade	SPEC	(see)	spectator
MULTI	(many)	multiple	TERR	(earth)	territory
SOL	(one)	solo	VER	(turn)	divert
TRI	(three)	triple	VIV	(live)	revive

TOEFL EXERCISE 9: Study each of the passages and choose the best answers to the questions that follow.

PASSAGE ONE (Questions 1–5)

Juan Rodriguez Cabrillo was a Portuguese-born explorer who is credited with the exploration of the coast of what is today the state of California. Sketchy military records from the period show that early in his career he served with the Spanish army from 1520 to 1524 in Spain's quest for subjugation

Line
(5) of the people in what are today Cuba, Mexico, and Guatemala. Little is known of his activities over the next decades, but apparently he succeeded in rising up through the ranks of the military; in 1541, he was ordered by Antonio de Mendoza, the Spanish ruler of Mexico, to explore the western coast of North America. Cabrillo set out in June of 1542 in command of two ships, the *San Salvador* and the *Victoria*; he reached San Diego Bay on September 28, 1542, and claimed the terrain for Spain. The peninsula where he landed is today named Cabrillo Point in his honor; the area has been established

(10) as a national monument and park, and local residents each year hold a celebration and reenactment of Cabrillo's landing.

From San Diego, Cabrillo continued northward for further exploration of the spectacular California coastline. By November 1542, he had reached as far north as San Francisco Bay, although he missed the entrance of the bay due to a huge storm. Soon after, with the approach of winter, he

(15) veered south and headed back to Mexico. He made it as far south as the Channel Islands off the coast of what is today Santa Barbara. Cabrillo, who died on San Miguel Island in the Channel Islands, never made it back to Mexico.

1. The word "subjugation" in line 3 is closest in meaning to
   (A) religion
   (B) flag
   (C) control
   (D) agreement

2. In line 5, the word "decades" is closest in meaning to
   (A) months
   (B) centuries
   (C) long epoch
   (D) ten-year periods

3. In line 8, the word "terrain" is closest in meaning to
   (A) land
   (B) population
   (C) minerals
   (D) prosperity

4. The word "spectacular" in line 12 is closest in meaning to which of the following?
   (A) Ruggedly handsome
   (B) Visually exciting
   (C) Completely uneven
   (D) Unendingly boring

5. The word "veered" in line 15 is closest in meaning to
   (A) arrived
   (B) ran
   (C) turned
   (D) cooled

PASSAGE TWO (Questions 6–10)

Checks and balances are an important concept in the formation of the U.S. system of government as presented in the Constitution of the United States. Under this conception of government, each branch of government has built-in checks and limitations placed on it by one or
Line more different branches of government in order to ensure that any one branch is not able to usurp
(5) total dominance over the government. Under the Constitution, the United States has a tripartite government, with power divided equally among the branches: the presidency, the legislature, and the judiciary. Each branch is given some authority over the other two branches to balance the power among the three branches. An example of these checks and balances is seen in the steps needed to pass a law. Congress can pass a law with a simple majority, but the president can veto such a law.
(10) Congress can then counteract the veto with a two-thirds majority. However, even if Congress passes a law with a simple majority or overrides a presidential veto, the Supreme Court can still declare the law unconstitutional if it finds that the law is contradictory to the guidelines presented in the Constitution.

6. The expression "dominance over" in line 5 is closest in meaning to

    (A) understanding of
    (B) dispute over
    (C) authority over
    (D) rejection of

7. The word "tripartite" in line 5 suggests that something is

    (A) divided into three
    (B) totally democratic
    (C) powerfully constructed
    (D) evenly matched

8. The "judiciary" in line 7 is

    (A) the electorate
    (B) the authority
    (C) the legal system
    (D) the government

9. The word "counteract" in line 10 is closest in meaning to

    (A) vote for
    (B) debate
    (C) surpass
    (D) work against

10. "Contradictory to" in line 12 is closest in meaning to which of the following expressions?

    (A) In agreement with
    (B) Opposite to
    (C) Supported by
    (D) Similar to

SKILL 10:   USE CONTEXT TO DETERMINE MEANINGS OF DIFFICULT WORDS

On the TOEFL test you will sometimes be asked to determine the meaning of a difficult word, a word that you are not expected to know. In this case, the passage will give you a clear indication of what the word means.

Example

A line in the passage:
. . . The barges headed across the lake . . . .

The question:

A "barge" is probably which of the following?

(A) A train
(B) A plane
(C) A bicycle
(D) A boat

In this type of question, you are not expected to know the meaning of the word *barge*. Instead, you should understand from the context that if the *barge* went across a *lake*, then it is probably a type of boat. Answer (D) is therefore the best answer.

The following chart outlines the key information that you should remember about vocabulary questions containing difficult words:

VOCABULARY QUESTIONS CONTAINING DIFFICULT WORDS	
HOW TO IDENTIFY THE QUESTION	"*What is the* **meaning** *. . . ?*" "*Which of the following is closest in* **meaning** *to . . . ?*" The word is a difficult word, one that you probably do not know.
WHERE TO FIND THE ANSWER	The question usually tells you in which line of the passage the word can be found.
HOW TO ANSWER THE QUESTION	1. Find the word in the passage. 2. Read the sentence that contains the word *carefully*. 3. Look for context clues to help you understand the meaning. 4. Choose the answer that the context indicates.

TOEFL EXERCISE 10: Study each of the passages and choose the best answers to the questions that follow.

PASSAGE ONE (Questions 1–4)

The black widow is the most dangerous spider living in the United States. It is most common in the southern parts of the country, but it can be found throughout the country. The black widow got its name because the female has been known to kill the male after mating and, as a result, becomes a
Line widow.
(5)   The black widow is rather distinctive in appearance; it has a shiny globular body, the size and shape of a pea, and is marked on its underbelly with a red or yellow spot. The female is considerably more ample than the male, roughly four times larger on the average.
    If a human is bitten by a black widow, the spider's poison can cause severe illness and pain. Black widow bites have occasionally resulted in death, but it is certainly not the norm for black
(10) widow bites to be mortal.

1. In line 2, the word "widow" means

    (A) a type of poison
    (B) the dead male spider
    (C) the human victim of the spider
    (D) a female whose mate has died

2. Which of the following is closest in meaning to the word "globular" in line 5?

    (A) Earthen
    (B) Luminescent
    (C) Green in color
    (D) Round

3. The word "ample" in line 7 indicates that the spider is

    (A) feminine
    (B) large in size
    (C) dotted with colors
    (D) normal

4. Which of the following has the same meaning as the word "mortal" in line 10?

    (A) Deadly
    (B) Painful
    (C) Poisonous
    (D) Sickening

PASSAGE TWO (Questions 5–8)

Tornadoes occur throughout the world, but for reasons that scientists are not fully able to discern, the great majority occur in the United States. Approximately 700 tornadoes a year occur within the United States, and this comprises three-quarters of the worldwide total. Most of the U.S.

Line tornadoes take place in the Midwest and in the southern states that border the Gulf of Mexico.

(5)   In general a tornado cuts a path of a few hundred yards and lasts less than an hour; an average tornado might propel itself at a speed of 15 or 20 miles per hour and therefore cover a distance of 20 or so miles. Tornadoes, however, can be much worse than average. The most devastating tornado on record occurred on March 18, 1925, in the states of Missouri, Illinois, and Indiana. The path of this tornado was more than 200 miles long and a mile wide. Traveling at an average speed of 60 miles per

(10) hour, the winds at the center of the storm swirled around at considerably more than 200 miles per hour. A total of 689 people died, and countless more were injured at the hands of this killer storm.

5. The word "discern" in line 2 is closest in meaning to which of the following?

(A) Present
(B) Understand
(C) Cause
(D) Misrepresent

6. The word "propel" in line 6 could best be replaced by

(A) move
(B) develop
(C) destroy
(D) inhibit

7. Which of the following is closest in meaning to the word "devastating" in line 7?

(A) Described
(B) Delicate
(C) Destructive
(D) Determined

8. The word "swirled" in line 10 is closest in meaning to

(A) decreased
(B) rose
(C) settled
(D) circled

Skill 11: USE CONTEXT TO DETERMINE MEANINGS OF SIMPLE WORDS

You will sometimes be asked to determine the meaning of a simple word, a word that you see often in everyday English. In this type of question, you should *not* give the normal, everyday meaning of the word; instead, the TOEFL test wants to know the meaning of the word **in this situation.**

Example

A line from the passage:

. . . He put his answer this way. . . .

The question:

The word "put" is closest in meaning to which of the following?

(A) placed
(B) set
(C) expressed
(D) handed

In this type of question, you should understand that *put* is a normal, everyday word, and you are not being asked to give the regular meaning of a normal, everyday word. Because the primary meaning of *to put* is *to place*, answer (A) is **not** the correct answer. To answer this type of question, you must see which of the answers best fits into the sentence in the passage. You cannot *place an answer* or *set an answer* or *hand an answer*, but you can *express an answer*, so answer (C) is the best answer to this question.

The following chart outlines the key information that you should remember about vocabulary questions containing simple words:

VOCABULARY QUESTIONS CONTAINING SIMPLE WORDS	
HOW TO IDENTIFY THE QUESTION	"What is the **meaning** . . . ?" "Which of the following is closest in **meaning** to . . . ?" The word is a simple word, one that you see often in everyday English.
WHERE TO FIND THE ANSWER	The question usually tells you in which line of the passage the word can be found.
HOW TO ANSWER THE QUESTION	1. Find the word in the passage. 2. Read the sentence that contains the word *carefully*. 3. Look for context clues to help you understand the meaning. 4. Choose the answer that the context indicates.

TOEFL EXERCISE 11: Study each of the passages and choose the best answers to the questions that follow.

PASSAGE ONE (Questions 1–3)

The *piece of eight* was the nickname of the Spanish *peso,* which was the rough equivalent of the American dollar in early America; the peso was accepted coin in much of the Americas, particularly during the period when the stores of Spanish ships were regularly stripped by pirates on
Line the waters off the Americas and "redistributed" throughout coastal towns. The nickname *piece of eight*
(5) derived from the fact that the peso was equal to eight *reals* and therefore had the numeral 8 stamped on it. The piece of eight was sometimes actually cut into pieces, or bits, and one popular size was one-quarter of a piece of eight, or two bits. As a consequence, the U.S. quarter of a dollar is sometimes referred to today as two-bits, particularly in the western part of the country. A visitor to that area, if told "It'll be two-bits," should take it that the price of an item is being given.

1. The word "rough" in line 1 is closest in meaning to

   (A) unsmooth
   (B) mean
   (C) approximate
   (D) heavy

2. "Stores" in line 3 are probably

   (A) departments
   (B) markets
   (C) shops
   (D) supplies

3. The word "take" in line 9 could best be replaced by

   (A) hold
   (B) understand
   (C) possess
   (D) grab

PASSAGE TWO (Questions 4–6)

Although the *Wealth of Nations* by Adam Smith appeared in 1776, it includes many of the ideas that economists still consider the foundation of private enterprise. The ideas put forth by Smith compose the basis of the philosophies of the school of thought called classical economics.

Line
(5)   According to Smith's ideas, free competition and free trade are vital in fostering the growth of an economy. The role of government in the economy is to ensure the ability of companies to compete freely.

Smith, who was himself a Scot, lived during the period of the revolutions in America and in France. During this epoch, the predominant political thought was a strong belief in freedom and independence in government. Smith's economic ideas of free trade and competition are right in line
(10)   with these political ideas.

4. A "school" in line 3 is

   (A) a common belief
   (B) a college
   (C) a university
   (D) an educational institution

5. Which of the following is closest in meaning to the word "free" in line 4?

   (A) Cheap
   (B) No cost
   (C) Uncontrolled
   (D) Democratic

6. The word "line" in line 9 could best be replaced by

   (A) straightness
   (B) directness
   (C) file
   (D) agreement

TOEFL EXERCISE (Skills 8–11): Study each of the passages and choose the best answers to the questions that follow.

PASSAGE ONE (Questions 1–5)

Cardamom is not as widely used as a spice in the United States as it is in other parts of the world. This fruit of the ginger plant provides an oil that basically has been used solely as a stimulant in American and English medicines. Other cultures have recognized the multipurpose benefits of this
Line   aromatic fruit. In Asia it is used to season sauces such as curry; in Middle Eastern countries it is
(5)   steeped to prepare a flavorful golden-colored tea; in parts of Northern Europe it is used as a spice in various types of pastry.

1. The word "solely" in line 2 could best be replaced by

   (A) initially
   (B) only
   (C) reportedly
   (D) healthfully

2. The word "multipurpose" in line 3 is closest in meaning to

   (A) health
   (B) singular
   (C) recognized
   (D) varied

3. Which of the following is closest in meaning to the word "season" in line 4?

   (A) Divide
   (B) Forecast
   (C) Spice
   (D) Put a time limit

4. "Curry" in line 4 is

   (A) the fruit of the ginger plant
   (B) a spicy type of sauce
   (C) a culture in the area of the Middle East
   (D) a type of golden-colored tea

5. The word "steeped" in line 5 is closest in meaning to

   (A) soaked
   (B) dried
   (C) stored
   (D) grown

PASSAGE TWO (Questions 6–13)

The life span of an elephant that dies from natural causes is about sixty-five years. Of course, an elephant can perish from a number of "unnatural causes"; e.g., it can be killed by hunters, most probably for the valuable ivory in its tusks; it can die from diseases that spread throughout an elephant herd; or it can die from drought or from the lack of food that almost certainly accompanies the inadequate supply of water.

Line
(5)

If, however, an elephant survives these disasters, it falls prey to old age in its mid-sixties. Around this age, the cause of death is attributed to the loss of the final set of molars. When this last set of teeth is gone, the elephant dies from malnutrition because it is unable to obtain adequate nourishment. In old age, elephants tend to search out a final home where there is shade for comfort from the sun and soft vegetation for cushioning; the bones of many old elephants have been found in such places.

(10)

6. The word "perish" in line 2 means

   (A) fall ill
   (B) shoot
   (C) die
   (D) get rich

7. The word "unnatural" in line 2 is closest in meaning to

   (A) wild
   (B) violent
   (C) domesticated
   (D) abnormal

8. The word "drought" in line 4 means

   (A) a drowning
   (B) a lack of food
   (C) an inadequate supply of water
   (D) an overabundance of animals

9. Which of the following could be used to replace the word "survives" in line 6?

   (A) Rises to
   (B) Succumbs to
   (C) Denies
   (D) Lives through

10. "Molars" in line 7 are

    (A) germs
    (B) old-age characteristics
    (C) types of food
    (D) teeth

11. In line 8, "malnutrition" is used to describe someone who

    (A) is in good health
    (B) has an illness
    (C) suffers from poor eating
    (D) experiences dental problems

12. The expression "a final home" in line 9 is closest in meaning to

    (A) a place to die
    (B) a comfortable house
    (C) a place for sale
    (D) the only remaining place to live

13. The word "shade" in line 9 is closest in meaning to

    (A) color
    (B) heat
    (C) diminished light
    (D) a front porch

PASSAGE THREE (Questions 14–21)

The American flag is the end product of a long evolution. Each of its component parts has its own history.

Line
(5)
The very first American flag was hoisted in the skies over Boston on January 1, 1776, by the American forces there. This first flag consisted of thirteen red and white stripes representing the number of American colonies. It also included the British Cross of St. George and Cross of St. Andrew. It could be considered rather ironic that these symbols of British rule were included on the American flag in that the American colonists were fighting for independence from the British.

The origin of the stars on the current flag is obscure; that is, the stars could possibly have been taken from the flag of Rhode Island, or they could have been taken from the coat of arms of the
(10)
Washington family. According to legend, this first flag with stars was sewn by Betsy Ross, a Philadelphia seamstress who was famous for her clever needlework. This version of the flag contained thirteen stars and thirteen stripes, one for each of the thirteen colonies battling for independence.

The original idea was to add one star and one stripe for each state that joined the new, young country. However, by 1818, the number of states had grown to twenty, and it did not work well to keep
(15)
adding stripes to the flag. As a result, Congress made the decision to revert to the original thirteen stripes representing the thirteen original colonies and adding a star each time a new state was admitted. This has been the policy ever since.

14. The word "product" in line 1 is closest in meaning to

(A) goods
(B) merchandise
(C) banner
(D) result

15. Something that is "hoisted" (line 3) is

(A) created
(B) found
(C) raised
(D) made

16. The word "ironic" in line 6 could most easily be replaced by

(A) steel-like
(B) normal
(C) unexpected
(D) nationalistic

17. Which of the following is closest in meaning to "obscure" in line 8?

(A) Unclear
(B) Original
(C) Modern
(D) Known

18. In line 11, the word "seamstress" is used to describe someone who

(A) works at home
(B) sews
(C) is a part of high society
(D) practices medicine

19. The word "work" in line 14 could best be replaced by

(A) get a job
(B) function
(C) accomplish
(D) make an effort

20. The word "keep" in line 14 could best be replaced by

(A) continue
(B) maintain
(C) hold
(D) guard

21. The expression "revert to" in line 15 means

(A) return to
(B) add to
(C) rejoice over
(D) forget about

TOEFL REVIEW EXERCISE (Skills 1–11): Study each of the passages and choose the best answers to the questions that follow.

PASSAGE ONE (Questions 1–6)

Bigfoot is a humanlike creature reportedly living in the Pacific Northwest. Bigfoot sightings have been noted most often in the mountainous areas of northern California, Oregon, and Washington in the United States. The creature has also been spotted numerous times in British
Line Columbia in Canada, where it is known as *Sasquatch*.
(5)   The creature described by witnesses is tall by human standards, measuring 7 to 10 feet (2 to 3 meters) in height. It resembles an ape with its thick, powerful, fur-covered arms and short, strong neck; however, its manner of walking erect is more like that of *Homo sapiens*.

Although there have been hundreds of reported sightings of Bigfoot, most experts have not seen enough evidence to be convinced of its existence. The fact that some purported evidence has been
(10) proven fake may have served to discredit other more credible information.

1. Which of the following best states the topic of the passage?

    (A) Differences between Bigfoot and Sasquatch
    (B) A description of Bigfoot
    (C) Where Bigfoot, or Sasquatch, can be found
    (D) The creature Bigfoot and its questionable existence

2. The word "noted" in line 2 is closest in meaning to which of the following?

    (A) Reported
    (B) Written in a letter
    (C) Refuted
    (D) Discussed

3. It is implied in the passage that Bigfoot would probably NOT like to live

    (A) in Oregon
    (B) in the Pacific Northwest
    (C) on coastal plains
    (D) in mountainous areas

4. Which of the following is NOT true about the appearance of Bigfoot?

    (A) Its arms and neck look like those of an ape.
    (B) Its arms are covered with fur.
    (C) It is short-necked.
    (D) It walks like an ape.

5. The expression *Homo sapiens* in line 7 is closest in meaning to

    (A) ape
    (B) creature
    (C) human
    (D) furry animal

6. According to the passage, how do experts feel about the evidence concerning Bigfoot's existence?

    (A) They feel certain as to its existence.
    (B) They are not yet certain.
    (C) They are sure that it does not exist.
    (D) They feel that all the evidence is fake.

PASSAGE TWO (Questions 7–13)

The next hormone is epinephrine, or adrenaline. This hormone is a natural secretion of the adrenal glands in the human body. Its primary function in the human body is to assist the body in coping with sudden surges of stress. When a person unexpectedly finds himself in a stressful situation

Line
(5)   filled with fear or anger, a large amount of epinephrine is released into the blood and the body responds with an increased heartbeat, higher blood pressure, and conversion of glycogen into glucose for energy to enable the body to deal with the stress.

It is possible to extract epinephrine from the adrenal glands of animals or to synthesize it chemically in order to put it to further use. It is used in the treatment of severe asthma, where it relaxes the large muscles of the bronchi, the large air passages leading into the lungs. It is also used in

(10)   cases of severe allergic reaction or cardiac arrest.

7. The paragraph preceding the passage most probably discusses

  (A) further uses of epinephrine
  (B) the treatment of cardiac arrest
  (C) a different hormone
  (D) the secretions of the adrenal glands

8. What is another name for epinephrine?

  (A) Adrenal glands
  (B) Stressful situation
  (C) Bronchi
  (D) Adrenaline

9. Which of the following is NOT mentioned as a result of the release of epinephrine in the blood?

  (A) Severe asthma
  (B) An increase in blood pressure
  (C) Higher heartbeat
  (D) Increased energy

10. It is implied in the passage that increased heartbeat

  (A) harms the body
  (B) causes the release of epinephrine into the body
  (C) is helpful in combating the stressful situation
  (D) is useful in treating asthma

11. The passage indicates that epinephrine is used in the treatment of all of the following EXCEPT

  (A) asthma
  (B) high blood pressure
  (C) serious allergic reactions
  (D) heart problems

12. What are the "bronchi" in line 9?

  (A) A large muscle
  (B) Air passages
  (C) The lungs
  (D) Part of the heart

13. Which of the following best expresses the organization of the information in the passage?

  (A) Epinephrine and adrenaline
  (B) Various effects of epinephrine on the body
  (C) Causes of sudden stress
  (D) Epinephrine's natural functions and further applications

PASSAGE THREE (Questions 14–18)

A massive banking crisis occurred in the United States in 1933. In the two preceding years, a large number of banks had failed, and fear of lost savings had prompted many depositors to remove their funds from banks. Problems became so serious in the state of Michigan that Governor William
Line A. Comstock was forced to declare a moratorium on all banking activities in the state on February 14,
(5) 1933. The panic in Michigan quickly spread to other states, and on March 6, President Franklin D. Roosevelt declared a banking moratorium throughout the United States that left the entire country without banking services.

Congress immediately met in a special session to solve the banking crisis and on March 9 passed the Emergency Banking Act of 1933 to assist financially healthy banks to reopen. By March
(10) 15, banks controlling 90 percent of the country's financial reserves were again open for business.

14. The passage states that all the following occurred prior to 1933 EXCEPT that

(A) many banks went under
(B) many bank patrons were afraid of losing their deposits
(C) a lot of money was withdrawn from accounts
(D) Governor Comstock canceled all banking activities in Michigan

15. The word "moratorium" in line 4 is closest in meaning to which of the following?

(A) Death
(B) Temporary cessation
(C) Murder
(D) Slow decline

16. The passage indicates that the moratorium declared by Roosevelt affected

(A) the banks in Michigan
(B) the banks in most of the United States
(C) only the financially unhealthy banks
(D) all the banks in the United States

17. Which of the following can be inferred from the passage?

(A) Congress did not give any special priority to the banking situation.
(B) The Emergency Banking Act helped all banks to reopen.
(C) Ten percent of the country's money was in financially unhealthy banks.
(D) Ninety percent of the banks reopened by the middle of March.

18. Which of the following best describes the organization of the passage?

(A) A theme followed by an example
(B) A problem and a solution
(C) Opposing viewpoints of an issue
(D) A problem and its causes

PASSAGE FOUR (Questions 19–31)

Benjamin Franklin is famous in the history of the United States because of his many and varied accomplishments later in his life, as a brilliant diplomat, as a scientist, as an inventor, as a philosopher, and as a public official. Early in his life, however, he was headed for a career as a printer.
Line
(5)
He was apprenticed at the age of twelve in a print shop that belonged to his half-brother James. When faced with the unhappy prospect of spending nine years in an intolerable situation, Benjamin devised a way to get out of his contract as an apprentice printer in a rather unusual and creative way.

Benjamin's half-brother James ran a weekly newspaper, the *New-England Courant,* and it was in this paper that young Benjamin worked as an apprentice printer. Unbeknownst to his half-brother James, who owned the paper, a very young Benjamin wrote a series of humorous letters to the paper.
(10)
He did not sign his own name to these letters. Instead, he used the pseudonym Mrs. Silence Dogood. In these letters he mocked the life around Boston. The letters amused the paper's readers, but they did not have the same effect on city officials.

As a result of the letters, city officials forbade James to publish his newspaper. James then decided to continue printing the paper using Benjamin's name rather than his own; in order to do
(15)
this, however, James had to release Benjamin from his contract as an apprentice. After all, a newspaper could not be headed by an apprentice printer. After James had released Benjamin from his apprenticeship, he was to discover that Benjamin had written the letters that had caused so much trouble. He was angry that he had lost the right to publish his paper because of Benjamin. On his part, Benjamin was delighted to have been released from his contract as an apprentice.
(20)
Later in his life, after he had achieved success in so many varied fields of endeavor, Ben Franklin did admit that he had not handled his dissatisfaction with his apprenticeship in the most mature way. However, he still appreciated the creative way that he had dealt with the problem.

19. The main idea of the passage is that Benjamin Franklin

    (A) worked at a newspaper owned by his half-brother James
    (B) was known for his many and varied accomplishments
    (C) was involved in a prank at a New England newspaper
    (D) dealt creatively with a problem early in his amazing career

20. It is NOT mentioned in the passage that Benjamin Franklin was recognized for his achievements in

    (A) diplomacy
    (B) science
    (C) psychology
    (D) public service

21. The expression "headed for" in line 3 could best be replaced by

    (A) moving in the direction of
    (B) serving as a leader of
    (C) at the top of
    (D) climbing up

22. How did young Benjamin feel about the idea of spending time as an apprentice printer?

    (A) He was overjoyed.
    (B) He was discontented.
    (C) He was amused.
    (D) He was satisfied.

23. The expression "unbeknownst to" could best be replaced by which of the following?

    (A) On behalf of
    (B) In regard to
    (C) Without the knowledge of
    (D) Without consideration for

24. It can be determined from the passage that Benjamin and James

    (A) were not related
    (B) had one parent in common
    (C) were distant cousins
    (D) had the same parents

25. The letters that Benjamin wrote

    (A) had a serious tone
    (B) were sent to city officials
    (C) were about life as an inventor
    (D) did not include Benjamin's name

26. The word "mocked" in line 11 is closest in meaning to

   (A) was complimentary
   (B) made fun of
   (C) cried over
   (D) paid attention to

27. The pronoun "they" in line 11 refers to

   (A) citizens
   (B) letters
   (C) readers
   (D) officials

28. It is implied in the passage that, when city officials read the letters, they

   (A) laughed at them
   (B) paid no attention
   (C) got angry
   (D) agreed with the content

29. The word "headed" in line 16 could best be replaced by

   (A) led
   (B) located
   (C) aimed
   (D) mounted

30. What eventually happened as a result of Benjamin's letters?

   (A) Benjamin became an apprentice printer.
   (B) James was given control of the paper.
   (C) James laughed at the joke.
   (D) Benjamin got out of his contract.

31. In which paragraph does the author describe the outcome of Benjamin Franklin's letter-writing campaign?

   (A) The first paragraph
   (B) The second paragraph
   (C) The third paragraph
   (D) The fourth paragraph

OVERALL REVIEW QUESTIONS

Often in the Reading Comprehension section of the TOEFL test the last question (or two) for a particular reading passage is an *overall* question, one that asks about the passage as a whole rather than one small detail. The overall review questions are generally *not* main idea questions; instead they ask about some other aspect of the passage as a whole. The most common types of overall review questions are (1) questions that ask *where* in the passage something is found, (2) questions about the *tone* of the passage, (3) questions about the *author's purpose* in writing the passage, or (4) questions about which *course* the passage might be a part of.

SKILL 12:   DETERMINE WHERE SPECIFIC INFORMATION IS FOUND

Sometimes the final question in a reading passage will ask you to determine where in the passage a piece of information is found. The answer choices will list possible locations for that information. The best way to approach this type of question is to study the question to determine the information that you are looking for and then to go to the lines listed in the answers and skim for that information.

Example

The passage:

Meteor Crater, a great crater approximately 40 miles east of Flagstaff, Arizona, is generally thought by scientists to have formed as a result of the impact of a 60,000-ton meteor about 50,000 years
Line ago. The meteor, made of nickel and iron, disintegrated on impact
(5) and spread half a billion tons of rock over the surface of the land. The massiveness of the meteor can only be imagined from the mammoth size of the crater, which measures a mile in diameter and three miles around the top. The rim of the crater rises more than 150 feet above the plain where the meteor impacted and is
(10) visible for more than ten miles on a clear day.

The questions:

1. Where in the passage does the author discuss the composition of the meteor?

   (A) Lines 1–4
   (B) Lines 4–5
   (C) Lines 6–8
   (D) Lines 8–10

2. Where in the passage does the author mention the distance from which the crater can be seen?

   (A) Lines 1–4
   (B) Lines 4–5
   (C) Lines 6–8
   (D) Lines 9–10

The first question asks you to find information about the *composition* of the crater. You should skim through the lines of the passage listed in the answers to the question looking for the word *composition* or something that means *composition*. In line 4 you should find the expression *made of*, and you should recognize that *composition* is what something is *made of*. The best answer to this question is therefore answer (B). The second question asks you to find information about the *distance from which the crater can be seen*. You should again skim through the lines of the passage listed in the answers to the question looking for the key words or ideas *distance* and *seen*. In lines 9 and 10 you should recognize that *visible* means *seen*, and *ten miles* is a *distance*. The best answer to this question is therefore answer (D).

The following chart outlines the key information that you should remember when you are trying to determine where in the passage something is found:

QUESTIONS ABOUT WHERE IN THE PASSAGE	
HOW TO IDENTIFY THE QUESTION	*Where* in the passage . . . ?
WHERE TO FIND THE ANSWER	The answer can be in any of the lines listed in the answers to the question.
HOW TO ANSWER THE QUESTION	1. Choose a *key word* or *idea* in the question. 2. Skim the lines in the passage that are listed in the answers to the question. You should skim for the *key word* or *idea*. 3. Choose the answer that contains the line numbers of a *restatement* of the question.

TOEFL EXERCISE 12: Study each of the passages and choose the best answers to the questions that follow.

PASSAGE ONE (Questions 1–4)

Beavers generally live in family clusters consisting of six to ten members. One cluster would probably consist of two adults, one male and one female, and four to eight young beavers, or kits. A female beaver gives birth each spring to two to four babies at a time. These baby beavers live with
Line
(5)
their parents until they are two years old. In the springtime of their second year they are forced out of the family group to make room for the new babies. These two-year-old beavers then proceed to start new family clusters of their own.

1. Where in the passage does the author give the name of a baby beaver?

   (A) Line 1
   (B) Line 2
   (C) Line 3
   (D) Lines 4–5

2. Where in the passage does the author mention the time of year when new baby beavers are born?

   (A) Line 1
   (B) Line 2
   (C) Line 3
   (D) Lines 4–5

3. Where in the passage does the author state the age at which beavers must go out on their own?

   (A) Line 1
   (B) Line 2
   (C) Line 3
   (D) Lines 4–5

4. Where in the passage does the author indicate why the young beavers must leave their parents' home?

   (A) Line 1
   (B) Line 2
   (C) Line 3
   (D) Lines 4–5

PASSAGE TWO (Questions 5–7)

Chamber music received its name because it was originally intended to be performed in small rooms in private homes rather than huge concert halls or theaters. Today it has evolved into small ensemble music in which each performer in the ensemble plays an individual part.

Line (5)

The compositions written for this type of performance can easily be classified into three distinct periods, each with its style of music and instrumentation. In the earliest period (1450–1650), the viol and other instrumental families developed considerably, and instrumental music took its first steps toward equal footing with vocal music. In the second period (1650–1750), trio sonatas dominated. These ensemble compositions were often written for two violins and a cello; the harpsichord was also featured in various compositions of this period. In the modern period (after 1750), the preponderance of chamber music was written for the string quartet, an ensemble composed of two violins, a viola, and a cello.

(10)

5. Where in the passage does the author discuss the modern definition of chamber music?

    (A) Lines 2–3
    (B) Lines 4–5
    (C) Lines 8–9
    (D) Lines 9–11

6. Where in the passage does the author discuss the period when ensembles for three instruments predominated?

    (A) Lines 2–3
    (B) Lines 4–5
    (C) Lines 7–9
    (D) Lines 9–11

7. Where in the passage does the author mention music written for four strings?

    (A) Lines 2–3
    (B) Lines 4–5
    (C) Lines 7–9
    (D) Lines 9–11

PASSAGE THREE (Questions 8–10)

It is common practice to coat metals such as iron and steel with a protective layer of zinc or an alloy made from zinc mixed with aluminum, cadmium, or tin in a process known as "galvanization." The purpose of galvanization is to prevent the corrosion of the iron or steel.

Line (5)

The most common method to galvanize metal is the hot-dip galvanizing process. In this process, the iron or steel is dipped into a hot bath of a zinc alloy to form a protective coating approximately .003 inches thick. Another method of galvanizing that is not as common is the process known as electrogalvanizing; in this process the metal is placed in a solution composed of zinc sulphate and water and is then charged electrically. This causes a thin layer of zinc to coat the metal.

(10)

Zinc is effective in galvanizing metals such as iron or steel in that zinc reacts more easily with oxygen than iron does. If iron is unprotected, it reacts with the oxygen in the air to form iron oxide, or rust, which leads to the corrosion of the iron. If, however, the iron is coated with zinc, as it is in the galvanization process, then it is the zinc rather than the iron which interacts with the oxygen to form zinc oxide, and the iron is not subject to corrosion.

8. Where in the passage does the author list the components of a zinc alloy?

(A) Lines 1–2
(B) Lines 4–6
(C) Lines 9–10
(D) Lines 11–13

9. Where in the passage does the author present the less routinely used process of galvanization?

(A) Lines 1–2
(B) Lines 4–6
(C) Lines 6–8
(D) Lines 9–10

10. Where in the passage does the author describe what happens when iron and oxygen interact?

(A) Lines 4–6
(B) Lines 6–8
(C) Lines 10–11
(D) Lines 11–13

Skill 13:   DETERMINE THE TONE, PURPOSE, OR COURSE

Other types of overall review questions occur occasionally in the Reading Comprehension section of the TOEFL test. Possible questions of this type are those that ask about (1) the *tone* of the passage, (2) the *author's purpose* in writing the passage, and (3) the *course* in which the passage might be used.

A question about the *tone* is asking if the author is showing any emotion in his or her writing. The majority of the passages on the TOEFL test are factual passages presented without any emotion; the tone of this type of passage could be simply *informational, explanatory,* or *factual*. Sometimes on the TOEFL test, however, the author shows some emotion, and you must be able to recognize that emotion to answer a question about tone correctly. If the author is being funny, then the tone might be *humorous;* if the author is making fun of something, the tone might be *sarcastic;* if the author feels strongly that something is right or wrong, the tone might be *impassioned*.

A question about *purpose* is asking what the author is trying to do in the passage. You can draw a conclusion about the author's purpose by referring to the main idea and the organization of details in the passage. For example, if the main idea is that George Washington's early life greatly influenced his later career and if the details give a history of his early life, the author's purpose could be *to show how George Washington's early life influenced his later career.* However, the answer to a purpose question is often considerably more general than the main idea. A more general author's purpose for the main idea about George Washington would be *to demonstrate the influence of early experiences on later life* (without any mention of George Washington).

A question about the *course* is asking you to decide which university course might have this passage as assigned reading. You should draw a conclusion about the course by referring to the topic of the passage and the organization of details. For example, if the passage is about George Washington and the details give historical background on his early life, then this would probably be assigned reading in an American history class. However, if the passage is about George Washington and the details show the various influences that he had on the formation of the American government, then the passage might be assigned reading in a government or political science class.

Example

The passage:

Military awards have long been considered symbolic of
royalty, and thus when the United States was a young nation just
finished with revolution and eager to distance itself from anything
Line tasting of monarchy, there was strong sentiment against military
(5)   decoration. For a century, from the end of the Revolutionary War
until the Civil War, the United States awarded no military honors.
The institution of the Medal of Honor in 1861 was a source of great
discussion and concern. From the Civil War until World War I, the
Medal of Honor was the only military award given by the United
(10) States government, and today it is awarded only in the most
extreme cases of heroism. Although the United States is still
somewhat wary of granting military awards, several awards have
been instituted since World War I.

The questions:

1. The *tone* of the passage is

    (A) angered
    (B) humorous
    (C) outraged
    (D) informational

2. The author's *purpose* in this passage is to

    (A) describe the history of military awards from the
         Revolutionary War to the Civil War
    (B) demonstrate an effect of America's attitude toward
         royalty
    (C) give an opinion of military awards
    (D) outline various historical symbols of royalty

3. The passage would probably be assigned reading in a
    course on

    (A) general science
    (B) psychology
    (C) American history
    (D) interior decoration

The first question asks about the *tone* of the passage. To determine the tone of a passage, you should look for any indications of emotion on the part of the author. In this passage, the author uses historical facts to make a point about America's sentiment against military awards; the author does not make any kind of emotional plea. Therefore, the best answer to this question is answer (D). There is nothing in the passage to indicate any anger (A), or humor (B), or outrage (C) on the part of the author.

The second question asks about the author's *purpose* in writing the passage. To answer this question correctly, you should refer to the main idea of this passage as outlined in the first sentence. The main idea is that there has been strong sentiment against military awards in the United States because military awards are symbols of royalty. The author gives historical facts about military awards as details to support the main idea. Since the purpose is determined from the main idea and the overall organization of details, the author's purpose is to describe, explain, or demonstrate that America's sentiment against military awards is because of its negative sentiment against royalty. The best answer to this question is therefore answer (B); you should notice that the correct answer is considerably more general than the main idea: according to answer (B) the purpose is to *demonstrate an effect* (America's dislike of military awards) *of America's attitude toward royalty.*

The third question asks about the *course* in which you might be assigned this reading passage. To draw a conclusion about the course, you should refer to the topic of the passage and the overall organization of details. Since this passage is about American military awards, and the details discuss the history of American military awards from the Revolutionary War until today, the best answer is (C).

The following chart outlines the key information that you should remember about tone, purpose, or course questions:

TONE, PURPOSE, OR COURSE		
HOW TO IDENTIFY THE QUESTION	TONE: PURPOSE: COURSE:	*What is the **tone** of the passage?* *What is the author's **purpose** in this passage?* *In which **course** would this reading be assigned?*
WHERE TO FIND THE ANSWER	TONE: PURPOSE: COURSE:	There will be clues throughout the passage that the author is showing some *emotion* rather than just presenting facts. Draw a conclusion about the *purpose* from the main idea and supporting details. Draw a conclusion about the *course* from the topic of the passage and the supporting details.
HOW TO ANSWER THE QUESTION	TONE: PURPOSE: COURSE:	1. Skim the passage looking for clues that the author is showing some *emotion*. 2. Choose the answer that identifies the emotion. 1. Study the main idea in the topic sentence and the details used to support the main idea. 2. Draw a conclusion about the *purpose*. 1. Study the main idea in the topic sentence and the details used to support the main idea. 2. Draw a conclusion about the *course*.

TOEFL EXERCISE 13: Study each of the passages and choose the best answers to the questions that follow.

PASSAGE ONE (Questions 1–3)

      Truman Capote's *In Cold Blood* (1966) is a well-known example of the "nonfiction novel," a popular type of writing based upon factual events in which the author attempts to describe the underlying forces, thoughts, and emotions that lead to actual events. In Capote's book, the author
Line describes the sadistic murder of a family on a Kansas farm, often showing the point of view of the
(5) killers. To research the book, Capote interviewed the murderers, and he maintains that his book presents a faithful reconstruction of the incident.

1. The purpose of this passage is to

   (A) discuss an example of a particular literary genre
   (B) tell the story of *In Cold Blood*
   (C) explain Truman Capote's reasons for writing *In Cold Blood*
   (D) describe how Truman Capote researched his nonfiction novel

2. Which of the following best describes the tone of the passage?

   (A) Cold
   (B) Sadistic
   (C) Emotional
   (D) Descriptive

3. This passage would probably be assigned reading in which of the following courses?

   (A) Criminal Law
   (B) American History
   (C) Modern American Novels
   (D) Literary Research

PASSAGE TWO (Questions 4–6)

      Up to now, confessions that have been obtained from defendants in a hypnotic state have not been admitted into evidence by courts in the United States. Experts in the field of hypnosis have found that such confessions are not completely reliable. Subjects in a hypnotic state may confess to
Line crimes they did not commit for one of two reasons. Either they fantasize that they committed the
(5) crimes or they believe that others want them to confess.
      A landmark case concerning a confession obtained under hypnosis went all the way to the U.S. Supreme Court. In the case of *Layra* v. *Denno*, a suspect was hypnotized by a psychiatrist for the district attorney; in a posthypnotic state the suspect signed three separate confessions to a murder. The Supreme Court ruled that the confessions were invalid because the confessions had been the only
(10) evidence against him.

4. Which of the following best describes the author's purpose in this passage?

   (A) To explain the details of a specific court case
   (B) To demonstrate why confessions made under hypnosis are not reliable
   (C) To clarify the role of the Supreme Court in invalidating confessions from hypnotized subjects
   (D) To explain the legal status of hypnotically induced confessions

5. The tone of this passage could best be described as

   (A) outraged
   (B) judicial
   (C) hypnotic
   (D) informative

6. This passage would probably be assigned reading in a course on

   (A) American law
   (B) psychiatric healing
   (C) parapsychology
   (D) philosophy

PASSAGE THREE (Questions 7–9)

Line
(5)

(10)

The rate at which the deforestation of the world is proceeding is alarming. In 1950 approximately 25 percent of the Earth's land surface had been covered with forests, and less than twenty-five years later the amount of forest land was reduced to 20 percent. This decrease from 25 percent to 20 percent from 1950 to 1973 represents an astounding 20 million square kilometers of forests. Predictions are that an additional 20 million square kilometers of forest land will be lost by 2020.

The majority of deforestation is occurring in tropical forests in developing countries, fueled by the developing countries' need for increased agricultural land and the desire on the part of developed countries to import wood and wood products. More than 90 percent of the plywood used in the United States, for example, is imported from developing countries with tropical rain forests. By the mid-1980s, solutions to this expanding problem were being sought, in the form of attempts to establish an international regulatory organization to oversee the use of tropical forests.

7. The author's main purpose in this passage is to

(A) cite statistics about an improvement on the Earth's land surface
(B) explain where deforestation is occurring
(C) make the reader aware of a worsening world problem
(D) blame developing countries for deforestation

8. Which of the following best describes the tone of the passage?

(A) Concerned
(B) Disinterested
(C) Placid
(D) Exaggerated

9. This passage would probably be assigned reading in which of the following courses?

(A) Geology
(B) Geography
(C) Geometry
(D) Marine Biology

TOEFL EXERCISE (Skills 12–13): Study each of the passages and choose the best answers to the questions that follow.

PASSAGE ONE (Questions 1–5)

The causes of schizophrenia are not clear, but schizophrenia has long been attributed to faulty parenting. In cases where schizophrenia developed, the parents were often considered responsible and were faulted for having been uncaring, or manipulative, or emotionally abusive. However, recent
Line
(5)
studies are now pointing to heredity and prenatal environmental factors as the chief culprits in this disease.

Recent studies of identical twins have been used to demonstrate that heredity plays a role in the development of schizophrenia. These studies have shown that in cases where one identical twin is afflicted with schizophrenia, the other twin has a 50 percent probability of also suffering from it.

However, heredity is not believed to be the only culprit. Studies of the fingerprints of identical
(10)
twins have lent credence to the theory that prenatal environmental factors are likely contributors to the development of schizophrenia. In studies of pairs of identical twins in which one is afflicted with schizophrenia and one is not, abnormalities were found in the fingerprints of one-third of the twins, always in the afflicted twin. Since fingers develop in the second trimester of pregnancy, the hypothesis has been proposed that the abnormalities in the fingerprints were due to a second-
(15)
trimester trauma that affected only one of the twins and that this same trauma was a factor in the onset of schizophrenia.

1. The author's purpose in this passage is to
   (A) enumerate examples
   (B) cause the development of schizophrenia
   (C) prove that faulty parenting is the main cause of schizophrenia
   (D) refute a common misconception

2. Where in the passage does the author discuss the traditionally held view about the cause of schizophrenia?
   (A) Lines 1–3
   (B) Lines 3–5
   (C) Lines 6–7
   (D) Lines 9–11

3. Where in the passage does the author present the idea that people may inherit the tendency for schizophrenia?
   (A) Lines 2–3
   (B) Lines 6–7
   (C) Lines 11–13
   (D) Lines 13–16

4. Where in the passage does the author give the fraction of twins under study with irregular fingerprints?
   (A) Lines 3–5
   (B) Lines 7–8
   (C) Lines 9–11
   (D) Lines 11–13

5. This passage would probably be assigned reading in which of the following courses?
   (A) Criminology
   (B) Public Administration
   (C) Statistics
   (D) Psychology

PASSAGE TWO (Questions 6–9)

To Americans, the Pony Express was a fixture of the Old West; most Americans are rather surprised to find out that in reality the Pony Express was in existence for only a short period of time, about a year and a half. This forefather of "express" mail service operated between St. Joseph,
Line Missouri, and Sacramento, California, a distance of just under 2,000 miles; letters and small packages
(5) could be delivered in under 10 days instead of the 3 to 4 weeks that it had taken prior to the institution of the Pony Express.

In 1860, St. Joseph was the westernmost terminal of the country's railroad system; mail destined for the West Coast could come to St. Joe by train, but the only way to get it farther west was on horseback. The Pony Express service was established on April 3, 1860, to fill this need: a letter carried
(10) on horseback with only minimal downtime for changes in horses and riders could cover 200 miles in one twenty-four hour period.

The Pony Express system consisted of approximately 80 riders, 400 horses, and 190 stations every 10 to 15 miles along the route. One rider took a mail pouch and carried it for 75 miles, changing his tired horse for a fresh one at every station; he then passed the pouch to another rider. Riders
(15) traveled day and night, and the mail never stopped.

On October 24, 1861, only a year and a half after the start of the Pony Express, the first transcontinental telegraph opened for business, ending the need for the Pony Express. The Pony Express officially closed for business on October 26, 1861; obviously its owners were quick to recognize that the need for their services had just been basically wiped out.

6. In which course would this passage most likely be assigned reading?

(A) Veterinary Medicine
(B) Speech Communication
(C) Audiology
(D) American History

7. Where in the passage does the author mention the amount of time it took to deliver a letter before the Pony Express?

(A) Lines 1–3
(B) Lines 3–6
(C) Lines 9–11
(D) Lines 12–13

8. Where in the passage does the author discuss why the Pony Express was discontinued?

(A) The first paragraph
(B) The second paragraph
(C) The third paragraph
(D) The fourth paragraph

9. What is the author's purpose in writing this passage?

(A) To warn of the dire effects of ending the Pony Express
(B) To describe a little-known reality about a historical subject
(C) To incite readers to action on behalf of the Pony Express
(D) To describe the development of express mail service

PASSAGE THREE (Questions 10–13)

The grand jury is an important part of the American legal system. The grand jury is composed of private citizens who are appointed to serve for a designated period of time. Grand juries, which hold meetings in private, serve one of two functions: charging or investigatory. A grand jury that is serving *Line* a charging function listens to evidence presented by the prosecutor and decides whether or not the *(5)* prosecution has adequate evidence to charge a suspect with a crime; if the grand jury feels that there is adequate evidence, then it issues an indictment, and the suspect must then proceed with a trial. A grand jury that is serving an investigatory function investigates cases of suspected dishonesty, often by public officials.

The primary reason for the existence of the grand jury is that it is supposed to ensure that *(10)* citizens are not subject to unfair prosecution; under the grand jury system, prosectors must first convince an unbiased group of citizens that there is justification for the charges that they want to bring. However, the grand jury system has come under attack from numerous directions. Grand juries are routinely criticized for being too slow and too costly; the grand jury system really means that there are two trials, the grand jury hearing to decide whether or not there should be a trial and then *(15)* the actual trial itself. Another criticism of the grand jury results from the fact that the meetings are held in private; the grand jury is not open to public scrutiny and is therefore not publicly responsible for its actions, and this has cast doubt on some of its findings. A final common criticism of the grand jury is that the evidence it hears is one-sided, from the perspective of the prosecution, so that the grand jury serves as the right arm of the prosecution rather than as a defender of the rights of a *(20)* suspect.

10. In which course might this passage be assigned reading?

   (A) Sociology of Criminal Behavior
   (B) Introduction to Law
   (C) American History
   (D) Research Methodologies

11. Where in the passage does the author mention who serves on a grand jury?

   (A) Lines 1–2
   (B) Lines 6–8
   (C) Lines 9–11
   (D) Lines 15–17

12. Where in the passage does the author discuss the problem associated with holding grand jury meetings in private?

   (A) Lines 3–6
   (B) Lines 6–8
   (C) Lines 12–15
   (D) Lines 15–17

13. How does the author seem to feel about the grand jury system?

   (A) Quite assured as to its usefulness
   (B) Somewhat doubtful about its effectiveness
   (C) Highly supportive of its use
   (D) Extremely negative about all aspects

TOEFL REVIEW EXERCISE (Skills 1–13): Study each of the passages and choose the best answers to the questions that follow.

PASSAGE ONE (Questions 1–6)

Another noteworthy trend in twentieth-century music in the U.S. was the use of folk and popular music as a base for more serious compositions. The motivation for these borrowings from traditional music might be a desire on the part of a composer to return to simpler forms, to enhance patriotic feelings, or to establish an immediate rapport with an audience. For whatever reason, composers such as Charles Ives and Aaron Copland offered compositions featuring novel musical forms flavored with refrains from traditional Americana. Ives employed the whole gamut of patriotic songs, hymns, jazz, and popular songs in his compositions, while Copland drew upon folk music, particularly as sources for the music he wrote for the ballets *Billy the Kid*, *Rodeo*, and *Appalachian Spring*.

Line (5)

1. The paragraph preceding this passage most probably discusses

   (A) nineteenth-century music
   (B) one development in music in the twentieth century
   (C) the works of Aaron Copland
   (D) the history of folk and popular music

2. Which of the following best describes the main idea of the passage?

   (A) Traditional music flavored some American musical compositions in the last century.
   (B) Ives and Copland used folk and popular music in their compositions.
   (C) A variety of explanations exist as to why a composer might use traditional sources of music.
   (D) Traditional music is composed of various types of folk and popular music.

3. It can be inferred from this passage that the author is not sure

   (A) when Ives wrote his compositions
   (B) that Ives and Copland actually borrowed from traditional music
   (C) why certain composers borrowed from folk and popular music
   (D) if Copland really featured new musical forms

4. Which of the following is not listed in the passage as a source for Ives's compositions?

   (A) National music
   (B) Religious music
   (C) Jazz
   (D) American novels

5. Where in the passage does the author list examples of titles of Copland's works?

   (A) Lines 1–2
   (B) Lines 2–4
   (C) Lines 4–6
   (D) Lines 6–9

6. The passage would most probably be assigned reading in which of the following courses?

   (A) American History
   (B) The History of Jazz
   (C) American Music
   (D) Composition

PASSAGE TWO (Questions 7–13)

The rattlesnake has a reputation as a dangerous and deadly snake with a fierce hatred for humanity. Although the rattlesnake is indeed a venomous snake capable of killing a human, its nature has perhaps been somewhat exaggerated in myth and folklore.

Line
(5)
The rattlesnake is not inherently aggressive and generally strikes only when it has been put on the defensive. In its defensive posture the rattlesnake raises the front part of its body off the ground and assumes an S-shaped form in preparation for a lunge forward. At the end of a forward thrust, the rattlesnake pushes its fangs into the victim, thereby injecting its venom.

There are more than 30 species of rattlesnakes, varying in length from 20 inches to 6 feet and also varying in toxicity of venom. In the United States there are only a few deaths annually from
(10)
rattlesnakes, with a mortality rate of less than 2 percent of those attacked.

7. Which of the following would be the best title for this passage?

(A) The Exaggerated Reputation of the Rattlesnake
(B) The Dangerous and Deadly Rattlesnake
(C) The Venomous Killer of Humans
(D) Myth and Folklore about Killers

8. According to the passage, which of the following is true about rattlesnakes?

(A) They are always ready to attack.
(B) They are always dangerous and deadly.
(C) Their fierce nature has been underplayed in myth and folklore.
(D) Their poison can kill people.

9. The word "posture" in line 5 is closest in meaning to which of the following?

(A) Mood
(B) Fight
(C) Position
(D) Strike

10. When a rattlesnake is ready to defend itself, it

(A) lies in an S-shape on the ground
(B) lunges with the back part of its body
(C) is partially off the ground
(D) assumes it is prepared by thrusting its fangs into the ground

11. It can be inferred from the passage that

(A) all rattlesnake bites are fatal
(B) all rattlesnake bites are not equally harmful
(C) the few deaths from rattlesnake bites are from six-foot snakes
(D) deaths from rattlesnake bites have been steadily increasing

12. The word "mortality" in line 10 is closest in meaning to

(A) percentage
(B) illness
(C) death
(D) survival

13. The author's purpose in this passage is to

(A) warn readers about the extreme danger from rattlesnakes
(B) explain a misconception about rattlesnakes
(C) describe a rattlesnake attack
(D) clarify how rattlesnakes kill humans

PASSAGE THREE (Questions 14–21)

For a century before the Erie Canal was built, there was much discussion among the general population of the Northeast as to the need for connecting the waterways of the Great Lakes with the Atlantic Ocean. A project of such monumental proportions was not going to be undertaken and
Line completed without a supreme amount of effort.
(5)   The man who was instrumental in accomplishing the feat that was the Erie Canal was DeWitt Clinton. As early as 1812, he was in the nation's capital petitioning the federal government for financial assistance on the project, emphasizing what a boon to the economy of the country the canal would be; his efforts with the federal government, however, were not successful.

In 1816, Clinton asked the New York State Legislature for the funding for the canal, and this
(10) time he did succeed. A canal commission was instituted, and Clinton himself was made head of it. One year later, Clinton was elected governor of the state, and soon after, construction of the canal was started.

The canal took eight years to complete, and Clinton was on the first barge to travel the length of the canal, the *Seneca Chief*, which departed from Buffalo on October 26, 1825, and arrived in New
(15) York City on November 4. Because of the success of the Erie Canal, numerous other canals were built in other parts of the country.

14. The information in the passage

   (A) gives a cause followed by an effect
   (B) is in chronological order
   (C) lists opposing viewpoints of a problem
   (D) is organized spatially

15. When did Clinton ask the U.S. government for funds for the canal?

   (A) One hundred years before the canal was built
   (B) In 1812
   (C) In 1816
   (D) In 1825

16. The word "boon" in line 7 is closest in meaning to which of the following?

   (A) Detriment
   (B) Disadvantage
   (C) Benefit
   (D) Cost

17. The pronoun "it" in line 10 refers to which of the following?

   (A) The New York State Legislature
   (B) The canal
   (C) The commission
   (D) The state governor

18. In what year did the actual building of the canal get underway?

   (A) In 1812
   (B) In 1816
   (C) In 1817
   (D) In 1825

19. The *Seneca Chief* was

   (A) the name of the canal
   (B) the name of a boat
   (C) Clinton's nickname
   (D) the nickname of Buffalo

20. Where in the passage does the author mention a committee that worked to develop the canal?

   (A) The first paragraph
   (B) The second paragraph
   (C) The third paragraph
   (D) The fourth paragraph

21. The paragraph following the passage most probably discusses

   (A) the century before the building of the Erie Canal
   (B) canals in different U.S. locations
   (C) the effect of the Erie Canal on the Buffalo area
   (D) Clinton's career as governor of New York

PASSAGE FOUR (Questions 22–33)

The Celtic languages are a group of languages of northern Europe that are descendents of the Indo-European family of languages. These languages developed from the language of the Celts, a warlike civilization originating in the eastern part of central Europe, in the northern Alps, and along the Danube during the Bronze Age. The Celts reached the height of their civilization during the Iron Age, the last five centuries B.C., and then fanned out from their original homeland into many parts of continental Europe and across the channel and into the British Isles. Celtic languages were spoken in much of western Europe during Pre-Roman and Roman times. Place names of Celtic origin can be found today all over the British Isles and France, in northern Spain and Italy, and in Switzerland and parts of Germany.

Rather than one language, the Celtic languages consist of two distinct clusters: the Gaelic group and the Brythonic group. These two clusters of languages most likely developed from dialects of the same language, the language of the Celts in their original homeland. These two dialects were most likely mutually intelligible to some degree as late as the fourth century. The Gaelic group of Celtic languages consists of Irish, Scottish, and Manx, the language of the Isle of Man. The Brythonic group of Celtic languages includes Welsh, Cornish, Breton, and Gaulish, the language of Gaul prior to the days of the Roman Empire, with its Latin-speaking population.

Many, though not all, of the Celtic languages are either extinct or are in the process of becoming extinct. Gaulish apparently disappeared around 600 A.D. Cornish and Manx both actually became extinct, the former in the nineteenth century and the latter just a few decades ago, but both are being revived and are now taught in a few schools each. Scottish, Irish, and Breton are all declining in use. There are under a hundred thousand speakers of Scottish Gaelic, mostly on the northern Hebridean Islands; there are more than a hundred thousand speakers of Irish, mainly in the western counties of Ireland; there are about a half million speakers who use Breton on a daily basis. In all these situations, though, the rate of transmission to new generations is low, and this does not bode well for the survival of these languages. Of all the Celtic languages, perhaps only Welsh has a strong hold on the future.

Line (5) and *(10)* and *(15)* and *(20)* and *(25)* mark the line numbers in the left margin.

22. The author's purpose in the passage is to

   (A) describe the past and present of a related set of languages
   (B) list the major characteristics of Celtic languages
   (C) outline the major achievements of the Celts
   (D) explain how languages manage to survive without changing

23. According to the passage, the Celtic languages did NOT

   (A) develop from the Indo-European language family
   (B) originate in the British Isles
   (C) exist before the time of the Roman Empire
   (D) provide any Italian place names

24. The passage states that the Celts were

   (A) peaceful farmers
   (B) unheard of during the Bronze Age
   (C) at their peak during the Iron Age
   (D) at the height of their civilization 1,500 years ago

25. The expression "fanned out" in line 5 could best be replaced by

   (A) spread out
   (B) called off
   (C) got lost
   (D) turned out

26. The Brythonic group of languages does NOT include

   (A) Welsh
   (B) Cornish
   (C) Manx
   (D) Breton

27. It is implied in the passage that Gaulish

   (A) first surfaced after the Roman Empire
   (B) has been revived in the last century
   (C) is declining in use
   (D) was replaced by Latin

28. The main idea of the third paragraph is that

   (A) all Celtic languages are extinct
   (B) a few Celtic languages disappeared
   (C) some Celtic languages are flourishing
   (D) most Celtic languages are either dead or dying

29. It is NOT true according to the passage that both Cornish and Manx

    (A) were once considered extinct
    (B) became extinct in the same century
    (C) are being resuscitated
    (D) may be taught in some academic institutions

30. According to the passage, the percentage of young people learning Scottish, Irish, and Breton is

    (A) nonexistent
    (B) not high
    (C) increasing
    (D) quite robust

31. This passage would most likely be assigned reading in a course on

    (A) archeology
    (B) European literature
    (C) historical linguistics
    (D) Bronze Age civilizations

32. Where in the passage does the author explain when the two clusters of Celtic languages were still understood by members of each group of speakers?

    (A) Lines 2–4
    (B) Lines 6–7
    (C) Lines 10–11
    (D) Lines 12–13

33. The paragraph following the passage most likely discusses

    (A) how Welsh is surviving
    (B) efforts to classify Celtic languages
    (C) languages that preceded Celtic languages in Europe
    (D) the causes of language extinction

TOEFL POST-TEST

SECTION 3
READING COMPREHENSION
Time—55 minutes
(including the reading of the directions)
Now set your clock for 55 minutes.

This section is designed to measure your ability to read and understand short passages similar in topic and style to those that students are likely to encounter in North American universities and colleges. This section contains reading passages and questions about the passages.

Directions: In this section you will read several passages. Each one is followed by a number of questions about it. You are to choose the **one** best answer, (A), (B), (C), or (D), to each question. Then, on your answer sheet, find the number of the question and fill in the space that corresponds to the letter of the answer you have chosen.

Answer all questions about the information in a passage on the basis of what is **stated** or **implied** in that passage.

Read the following passage:

> John Quincy Adams, who served as the sixth president of the United States from 1825 to 1829, is today recognized for his masterful statesmanship and diplomacy. He dedicated his life to public service, both in the presidency and in the various other political offices that he
> *Line* held. Throughout his political career he demonstrated his unswerving belief in freedom of
> (5) speech, the antislavery cause, and the right of Americans to be free from European and Asian domination.

Example I   **Sample Answer**

To what did John Quincy Adams devote his life?   (A) ●
                                                         (C) ○
(A) Improving his personal life   (D) ○
(B) Serving the public
(C) Increasing his fortune
(D) Working on his private business

According to the passage, John Quincy Adams "dedicated his life to public service." Therefore, you should choose answer (B).

Example II   **Sample Answer**

In line 4, the word "unswerving" is closest in meaning to   (A) ○
                                                              (B) ○
(A) moveable   ●
(B) insignificant   (D) ○
(C) unchanging
(D) diplomatic

The passage states that John Quincy Adams demonstrated his unswerving belief "throughout his career." This implies that the belief did not change. Therefore, you should choose answer (C).

GO ON TO THE NEXT PAGE ➡

Questions 1–10

Aspirin's origins go back at least as early as 1758. In that year, Englishman Edward Stone noticed a distinctive bitter flavor in the bark of the willow tree. To Stone, this particular bark seemed to have much in common with "Peruvian Bark," which had been used medicinally since the 1640s to
Line bring down fevers and to treat malaria. Stone decided to test the effectiveness of the willow bark. He
(5) obtained some, pulverized it into tiny pieces, and conducted experiments on its properties. His tests demonstrated that this pulverized willow bark was effective both in reducing high temperatures and in relieving aches and pains. In 1763, Stone presented his findings to the British Royal Society.

Several decades later, further studies on the medicinal value of the willow bark were being conducted by two Italian scientists. These chemists, Brugnatelli and Fontana, determined that the
(10) active chemical that was responsible for the medicinal characteristics in the willow bark was the chemical salicin, which is the active ingredient of today's aspirin.

The name "aspirin" is the trade name of the drug based on the chemical salicin, properly known as acetylsalicylic acid. The trade name "aspirin" was invented for the drug in the 1890s by the Bayer Drug Company in Germany. The first bottles of aspirin actually went on sale to the public just prior to
(15) the turn of the century, in 1899.

1. According to the passage, aspirin originated

   (A) no later than 1758
   (B) sometime after 1758
   (C) definitely sometime in 1758
   (D) no earlier than 1758

2. It can be inferred from the passage that Peruvian Bark

   (A) caused fevers
   (B) was ineffective in treating malaria
   (C) was described to the British Royal Society by Stone
   (D) was in use prior to aspirin

3. The pronoun "it" in line 5 refers to

   (A) malaria
   (B) willow bark
   (C) effectiveness
   (D) the British Royal Society

4. The word "properties" in line 5 could best be replaced by

   (A) ownership
   (B) body
   (C) characteristics
   (D) materials

5. What did the willow bark look like after Stone prepared it for his experiments?

   (A) It was in large chunks.
   (B) It was a thick liquid.
   (C) It was a rough powder.
   (D) It was in strips of bark.

6. The Italian chemists mentioned in the passage most probably conducted their studies on willow bark

   (A) in the 1750s
   (B) in the 1760s
   (C) in the 1770s
   (D) in the 1780s

7. What is true about Brugnatelli and Fontana?

   (A) They were from England.
   (B) They added a chemical to the willow bark.
   (C) They conducted studies on the willow bark.
   (D) They were medical doctors.

8. The expression "prior to" in line 14 could best be replaced by

   (A) at
   (B) before
   (C) during
   (D) after

GO ON TO THE NEXT PAGE →

9. The word "turn" in line 15 could best be replaced by

(A) spin
(B) corner
(C) change
(D) reversal

10. Where in the passage does the author name the scientific compound that makes up aspirin?

(A) Lines 2–4
(B) Line 7
(C) Lines 8–9
(D) Lines 12–13

GO ON TO THE NEXT PAGE

Questions 11–20

Herman Melville, an American author best known today for his novel *Moby Dick*, was actually more popular during his lifetime for some of his other works. He traveled extensively and used the knowledge gained during his travels as the basis for his early novels. In 1837, at the age of eighteen,
Line
(5) Melville signed as a cabin boy on a merchant ship that was to sail from his Massachusetts home to Liverpool, England. His experiences on this trip served as a basis for the novel *Redburn* (1849). In 1841 Melville set out on a whaling ship headed for the South Seas. After jumping ship in Tahiti, he wandered around the islands of Tahiti and Moorea. This South Sea island sojourn was a backdrop to the novel *Omoo* (1847). After three years away from home, Melville joined up with a U.S. naval frigate that was returning to the eastern United States around Cape Horn. The novel *White-Jacket* (1850)
(10) describes this lengthy voyage as a navy seaman.

With the publication of these early adventure novels, Melville developed a strong and loyal following among readers eager for his tales of exotic places and situations. However, in 1851, with the publication of *Moby Dick*, Melville's popularity started to diminish. *Moby Dick*, on one level the saga of the hunt for the great white whale, was also a heavily symbolic allegory of the heroic struggle of
(15) humanity against the universe. The public was not ready for Melville's literary metamorphosis from romantic adventure to philosophical symbolism. It is ironic that the novel that served to diminish Melville's popularity during his lifetime is the one for which he is best known today.

11. The main subject of the passage is

(A) Melville's travels
(B) the popularity of Melville's novels
(C) Melville's personal background
(D) *Moby Dick*

12. According to the passage, Melville's early novels were

(A) published while he was traveling
(B) completely fictional
(C) all about his work on whaling ships
(D) based on his travels

13. In what year did Melville's book about his experiences as a cabin boy appear?

(A) 1837
(B) 1841
(C) 1847
(D) 1849

14. The word "basis" in line 5 is closest in meaning to

(A) foundation
(B) message
(C) bottom
(D) theme

15. The passage implies that Melville stayed in Tahiti because

(A) he had unofficially left his ship
(B) he was on leave while his ship was in port
(C) he had finished his term of duty
(D) he had received permission to take a vacation in Tahiti

16. A "frigate" in line 8 is probably

(A) an office
(B) a ship
(C) a troop
(D) a train

17. How did the publication of *Moby Dick* affect Melville's popularity?

(A) His popularity increased immediately.
(B) It had no effect on his popularity.
(C) It caused his popularity to decrease.
(D) His popularity remained as strong as ever.

GO ON TO THE NEXT PAGE

18. According to the passage, *Moby Dick* is

    (A) a romantic adventure
    (B) a single-faceted work
    (C) a short story about a whale
    (D) symbolic of humanity fighting the environment

19. The word "metamorphosis" in line 15 is closest in meaning to

    (A) circle
    (B) change
    (C) mysticism
    (D) descent

20. The passage would most likely be assigned reading in a course on

    (A) nineteenth-century novels
    (B) American history
    (C) oceanography
    (D) modern American literature

GO ON TO THE NEXT PAGE

Questions 21–31

Although only a small percentage of the electromagnetic radiation that is emitted by the Sun is ultraviolet (UV) radiation, the amount that is emitted would be enough to cause severe damage to most forms of life on Earth were it all to reach the surface of the Earth. Fortunately, all of the Sun's
Line ultraviolet radiation does not reach the Earth because of a layer of oxygen, called the ozone layer,
(5) encircling the Earth in the stratosphere at an altitude of about 15 miles above the Earth. The ozone layer absorbs much of the Sun's ultraviolet radiation and prevents it from reaching the Earth.

Ozone is a form of oxygen in which each molecule consists of three atoms (O_3) instead of the two atoms (O_2) usually found in an oxygen molecule. Ozone forms in the stratosphere in a process that is initiated by ultraviolet radiation from the Sun. UV radiation from the Sun splits oxygen
(10) molecules with two atoms into free oxygen atoms, and each of these unattached oxygen atoms then joins up with an oxygen molecule to form ozone. UV radiation is also capable of splitting up ozone molecules; thus, ozone is constantly forming, splitting, and reforming in the stratosphere. When UV radiation is absorbed during the process of ozone formation and reformation, it is unable to reach Earth and cause damage there.

(15) Recently, however, the ozone layer over parts of the Earth has been diminishing. Chief among the culprits in the case of the disappearing ozone, those that are really responsible, are the chloroflurocarbons (CFCs). CFCs meander up from Earth into the stratosphere, where they break down and release chlorine. The released chlorine reacts with ozone in the stratosphere to form chlorine monoxide (ClO) and oxygen (O_2). The chlorine then becomes free to go through the cycle
(20) over and over again. One chlorine atom can, in fact, destroy hundreds of thousands of ozone molecules in this repetitious cycle, and the effects of this destructive process are now becoming evident.

21. According to the passage, ultraviolet radiation from the Sun

    (A) is causing severe damage to the Earth's ozone layer
    (B) is only a fraction of the Sun's electromagnetic radiation
    (C) creates electromagnetic radiation
    (D) always reaches the Earth

22. The word "encircling" in line 5 is closest in meaning to

    (A) rotating
    (B) attacking
    (C) raising
    (D) surrounding

23. It is stated in the passage that the ozone layer

    (A) enables ultraviolet radiation to reach the Earth
    (B) reflects ultraviolet radiation
    (C) shields the Earth from a lot of ultraviolet radiation
    (D) reaches down to the Earth

24. According to the passage, an ozone molecule

    (A) consists of three oxygen molecules
    (B) contains more oxygen atoms than the usual oxygen molecule does
    (C) consists of two oxygen atoms
    (D) contains the same number of atoms as the usual oxygen molecule

25. The word "free" in line 10 could best be replaced by

    (A) liberal
    (B) gratuitous
    (C) unconnected
    (D) emancipated

26. Ultraviolet radiation causes oxygen molecules to

    (A) rise to the stratosphere
    (B) burn up ozone molecules
    (C) split up and reform as ozone
    (D) reduce the number of chloroflurocarbons

GO ON TO THE NEXT PAGE

27. The pronoun "it" in line 13 refers to

(A) radiation
(B) process
(C) formation
(D) damage

28. The word "culprits" in line 16 is closest in meaning to which of the following?

(A) Guilty parties
(B) Detectives
(C) Group members
(D) Leaders

29. According to the passage, what happens after a chlorine molecule reacts with an ozone molecule?

(A) The ozone breaks down into three oxygen atoms.
(B) Two different molecules are created.
(C) The two molecules combine into one molecule.
(D) Three distinct molecules result.

30. Where in the passage does the author explain how much damage chlorine can do?

(A) Lines 1–3
(B) Lines 12–14
(C) Lines 18–19
(D) Lines 20–22

31. The paragraph following the passage most likely discusses

(A) the negative results of the cycle of ozone destruction
(B) where chloroflurocarbons (CFCs) come from
(C) the causes of the destruction of ozone molecules
(D) how electromagnetic radiation is created

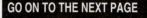
GO ON TO THE NEXT PAGE

Questions 32–40

A number of nonmetric measurements in common use may at first glance seem to lack the logic and clarity of the metric system, with its measurements all neatly based on tens and multiples of tens. However, these nonmetric measurements developed over time from habitual use of commonplace
Line items to make simple measurements. They might not seem like simple measurements today, but such
(5) is their history.

The measurements *foot* and *yard* developed based on average lengths of body parts. As can be inferred from the name, the Romans used the term *foot* to describe the length of a man's foot, from the base of the heel to the tip of the big toe. Though not exactly an accurate measurement, due to the varying lengths of men's feet, a foot was a measurement that was easy to conceptualize and visualize
(10) by most people. The term *yard* was used extensively by the English as the measurement from the tip of a man's nose to the tip of his outstretched thumb. English King Edward I redefined a yard as equivalent to three feet in 1305, and it still has this meaning today.

To describe longer distances, the Romans also invented the use of the term *mile*. The word *mile* comes from the Latin word *mille*, which means *one thousand*. A mile was meant to conform to a
(15) distance of one thousand paces, each pace consisting of two steps or approximately five thousand feet.

On the ocean, speed is measured in knots, with one knot roughly equivalent to one nautical mile per hour. This measurement of speed comes from the days when sailors used a knotted rope to determine their speed while at sea. A rope was knotted at regular intervals and tossed overboard. The rope was let out as sand flowed through an hourglass. When the sand had passed through the hourglass,
(20) the speed of the boat was determined by counting the number of knots that had been let out.

32. The main idea of the passage is that nonmetric measurements

(A) are, in reality, quite illogical
(B) lack the clarity of metric measurements
(C) are actually based on simple concepts
(D) developed from Roman measurements

33. What is stated about the term *foot* as used by the Romans?

(A) It had nothing to do with the body part of the same name.
(B) It was not a standard measurement.
(C) It was equal in length to two footsteps.
(D) It was not very easy for people to understand.

34. The word "visualize" in line 9 is closest in meaning to

(A) picture mentally
(B) describe exactly
(C) sketch roughly
(D) measure precisely

35. It is NOT mentioned in the passage that the term *yard*

(A) was originally used to describe a measurement based on body parts
(B) changed in definition in the 14th century
(C) is now equal to three feet
(D) was in use prior to the term *foot*

36. The word "extensively" in line 10 could best be replaced by

(A) lengthily
(B) precisely
(C) widely
(D) occasionally

37. What is NOT true, according to the passage?

(A) The English word *mile* is derived from a Latin word.
(B) The Latin word *mille* has the same meanings as the English word *mile*.
(C) A distance of a mile is approximately 2,000 steps.
(D) A distance of a mile is roughly equivalent to 5,000 feet.

GO ON TO THE NEXT PAGE

38. What is a "knot" in line 16?

(A) A measure of distance
(B) A measure of force
(C) A measure of time
(D) A measure of speed

39. It is implied in the passage that

(A) a measurement in knots requires information on both distance and time
(B) a knot can be used to make measurements on land
(C) a knotted rope could be used to measure knots without an hourglass
(D) the term *knot* has come to be used only recently

40. Which paragraph discusses examples of measurements based on parts of the body?

(A) The first paragraph
(B) The second paragraph
(C) The third paragraph
(D) The last paragraph

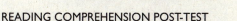
GO ON TO THE NEXT PAGE

Questions 41–50

In the first half of the nineteenth century, the U.S. government decided that it needed to set up a system for protecting its coastline. It then began building a series of forts along the coast of the eastern part of the country to facilitate its defenses.

Line
(5) The largest of these forts was Fort Jefferson, which was begun in 1846. This fort was built on Garden Key, one of a cluster of small coral islands 70 miles west of Key West. At the time of its construction, Fort Jefferson was believed to be of primary strategic importance to the United States because of its location at the entryway to the Gulf of Mexico. Because of its location at the entrance to a great body of water, it became known as the Gibraltar of the Gulf, in reference to the island located at the mouth of the Mediterranean. The fort itself was a massive structure. It was hexagonal in shape,
(10) with 8-foot-thick walls, and was surrounded by a medieval-style moat for added security. Covering most of the Garden Key, it was approximately half a mile in circumference.

In the latter half of the nineteenth century, during the Civil War and its aftermath, the fort was used as a prison rather than a military installation. The most notorious of its prisoners was Dr. Samuel Mudd, a physician who was most probably innocently involved in the assassination of
(15) Abraham Lincoln. The actual assassin, John Wilkes Booth, broke his leg as he lept from the stage of the Ford Theater during the assassination. Dr. Mudd set Booth's broken leg, unaware of Booth's involvement in the assassination. As a result of this action, Dr. Mudd was sentenced to life in prison and remanded to Fort Jefferson. He was pardoned after only four years because of his courageous efforts in combatting an epidemic of yellow fever that ravaged the fort.
(20) Continuous use of Fort Jefferson ended in the 1870s, although the U.S. Navy continued with sporadic use of it into the twentieth century. Today, the massive ruins still remain on the tiny island that stands guard over the entrance to the gulf, undisturbed except for the occasional sightseer who ventures out from the coast to visit.

41. The passage is mainly about
   (A) a series of forts
   (B) a series of events at one fort
   (C) a single event at one fort
   (D) a series of events at several forts

42. All of the following are true about Fort Jefferson EXCEPT that
   (A) it is on an island
   (B) it was built because of its strategic location
   (C) it is in the middle of the Gulf of Mexico
   (D) it has been compared with an island at the opening of the Mediterranean

43. The word "hexagonal" in line 9 is closest in meaning to
   (A) six-sided
   (B) seven-sided
   (C) eight-sided
   (D) irregular in shape

44. The pronoun "it" in line 11 refers to
   (A) fort
   (B) shape
   (C) moat
   (D) circumference

45. All of the following are stated about Dr. Samuel Mudd EXCEPT that
   (A) he was a medical doctor
   (B) he cared for Lincoln's assassin
   (C) he was imprisoned at Fort Jefferson
   (D) he was most likely guilty of Lincoln's assassination

46. How was Fort Jefferson most likely used in 1865?
   (A) As a strategic defensive unit of the U.S. military
   (B) As a penal institution
   (C) As a regularly functioning naval base
   (D) As a destination for tourists

GO ON TO THE NEXT PAGE

47. "Yellow fever" in line 19 is most likely

   (A) an enemy military force
   (B) a prison regimen
   (C) a contagious disease
   (D) a mental illness

48. What is implied about Fort Jefferson today?

   (A) It is a thriving community.
   (B) It is a relatively quiet place.
   (C) It is still in use by the U.S. military.
   (D) It remains in good condition.

49. Where in the passage does the author describe an injury to the man who shot Lincoln?

   (A) Lines 5–7
   (B) Lines 13–15
   (C) Lines 15–16
   (D) Lines 18–19

50. The information in the passage is presented

   (A) in chronological order
   (B) by listing examples of a concept
   (C) in spatial order
   (D) by arguing for a hypothesis

This is the end of Section 3.

When you finish the test, you may do the following:

- Turn to the **Diagnostic Chart** on pages 556–558, and circle the numbers of the questions that you missed.

- Turn to **Scoring Information** on pages 549–550, and determine your TOEFL score.

- Turn to the **Progress Chart** on page 559, and add your score to the chart.

SECTION FOUR

TEST OF
WRITTEN ENGLISH
(TWE)

TEST OF WRITTEN ENGLISH (TWE)

The Test of Written English (TWE) is a writing section that appears on the TOEFL test several times a year. You should check the *Bulletin of Information for TOEFL, TWE, and TSE* for the dates that the TWE will be administered. If you are required to take the TWE, be sure to sign up for the TOEFL test in one of the months in which the TWE is given.

On the TWE you will be given a specific topic and you will be asked to write an essay on that topic in thirty minutes. The TWE will be given at the beginning of the TOEFL test, before the Listening Comprehension, Structure and Written Expression, and Reading Comprehension sections.

Because you must write a complete essay in such a short period of time, it is best for you to aim to write a basic, clear, concise, and well-organized essay. The following strategies should help you to write this type of essay.

STRATEGIES FOR THE TEST OF WRITTEN ENGLISH (TWE)

1. **Read the topic carefully and write about it exactly as it is presented.** Take several minutes at the beginning of the test to be sure that you understand the topic and to outline a response.

2. **Organize your response very clearly.** You should think of having an introduction, body paragraphs that develop the introduction, and a conclusion to end your essay. Use transitions to help the reader understand the organization of ideas.

3. **Whenever you make any general statement, be sure to support that statement.** You can use examples, reasons, facts, or similar details to support any general statement.

4. **Stick to vocabulary and sentence structures that you know.** This is not the time to try out new words or structures.

5. **Finish writing your essay a few minutes early so that you have time to proof what you wrote.** You should spend the last three to five minutes checking your essay for errors.

THE SCORE

The score of the TWE is included on the same form as your regular TOEFL score, but it is not part of your overall TOEFL score. It is a separate score on a scale of 1 to 6, where 1 is the worst score and 6 is the best score. The following table outlines what each of the scores essentially means:

TEST OF WRITTEN ENGLISH (TWE) SCORES
6. The writer has very strong organizational, structural, and grammatical skills.
5. The writer has good organizational, structural, and grammatical skills. However, the essay contains some errors.
4. The writer has adequate organizational, structural, and grammatical skills. The essay contains a number of errors.
3. The writer shows evidence of organizational, structural, and grammatical skills that still need to be improved.
2. The writer shows a minimal ability to convey ideas in written English.
1. The writer is not capable of conveying ideas in written English.

SAMPLE ESSAYS

This section contains six essays, one demonstrating each of the six possible scores. These essays can give you some idea of the type of essay you need to write to achieve a good score. They can also demonstrate some of the major errors you should avoid when you work on the writing section.

The strengths and weaknesses of each essay have been outlined at the end of each. It would be helpful to study each answer in order to understand what is good and what is not so good in each of these essays.

This is the topic that was used:

Sample Essay Topic
Time — 30 minutes

Do you agree or disagree with the following statement?

Some people place a high value on loyalty to the employer. To others, it is perfectly acceptable to change jobs every few years to build a career. Discuss these two positions. Then indicate which position you agree with and why.

Use specific reasons and details to support your answer.

The following essay received a score of 6:

Different cultures place varying values on loyalty to the employer. In some countries, most notably in Asia, there is a high degree of loyalty to one company. However, in most European countries and the United States, loyalty to one's employer is not highly valued; instead it is considered more rationel and reasonable for an employee to change jobs whenever it is waranted to achieve the optimal overall career. Both of these positions have advantages and disadvantages.

In cultures that value loyalty to the employer, a kind of family relationship seems to develop between employer and employee. It is a reciprocal arrangement which the employer is concerned with asisting the employee to develop to his/her full potential and the employee is concerned about optimizing the welfare of the company. The negative aspect to absolute loyalty to one company is that an employee may stay in one job that he/she has outgrow and may miss out on opportunities to develop in new directions. From the employer's point of view, the employee may be burdened with employees whose skills no longer match the needs of the company.

In cultures in which it is quite acceptable to change jobs every few years, employees can build the career they choose for themself. They can stay with one company as long as it is mutually beneficial to company and employee. As long as good relationship exists and the employee's career is advancing at an acceptable pace, the employee can rmain with a company. But at any time the employee is free to move to another company, perhaps to achieve a higher position, to move into a new area, or to find a work situation that is more suitable to his/her personality. The disadvantage of this situation is employees tend to move around a lot.

Although both these systems have advantages and disadvantages, it is much better for employees have the opportunity to move from job to job if it is necessary to have a better career.

THE "6" ESSAY

Strengths of This Essay

1. It discusses all aspects of the topic.

2. It is clearly organized.

3. The ideas are well developed.

4. It has good, correct sentence structure.

5. It has only a few spelling and grammar errors.

Weaknesses of This Essay

1. The concluding paragraph is rather weak.

The following essay received a score of 5:

Some people place high value on loyalty to employer. They believe the company is responsible for the employee's career. The company will make decisions for the employee about his job. The company will decide to raise employee to new position or keep him in the old position. In this way the company will have overall plan for the good of the company and everyone in the company.

Other people believe it is perfectly acceptable to change jobs every few years to build a career. They believe employee is responsible for his own career. The employee will make decisions about his career. Employee will decide when to move to other company. Employee will choose what is good for employee rather than the company.

The best system is one when employer takes responsibility for the careers of employees. Employer should take responsibility. It is his duty. Employee knows that employer is watching out for his career. Then employee will work hard and do good job. He will be loyal to the company. This system works out best for everyone. It is best for both the company and employees.

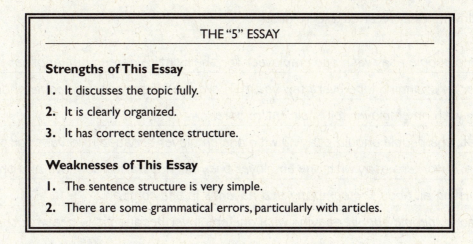

THE "5" ESSAY

Strengths of This Essay

1. It discusses the topic fully.

2. It is clearly organized.

3. It has correct sentence structure.

Weaknesses of This Essay

1. The sentence structure is very simple.

2. There are some grammatical errors, particularly with articles.

The following essay received a score of 4:

Every one is not in agreement about how loyal people should be to their employers. Some people place a high value on loyalty to the employer. These people believe that they should work hard for their employer and so their employer will take care of them. To others it is perfectly acceptable to change jobs every few years to build a career. They believe that having only one employer and one job in a career will not be the best for them.

In my culture people stay with one employer for their whole life. They have a job they will work their hardest at that job because it is the only job they will have. They do not look for another job they already have one because that would be unloyal. This way is better because when you old the company will take care you and your family.

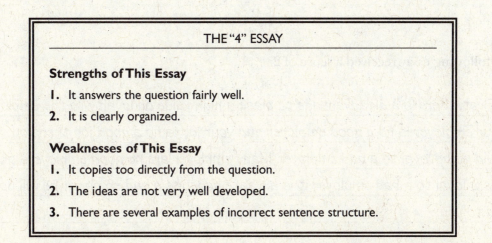

THE "4" ESSAY

Strengths of This Essay

1. It answers the question fairly well.

2. It is clearly organized.

Weaknesses of This Essay

1. It copies too directly from the question.

2. The ideas are not very well developed.

3. There are several examples of incorrect sentence structure.

The following essay received a score of 3:

Some people stay with one employeer for their entire career, but anothers build a career by changing jobs every few years. There are three reasens people should staying with on employer for their entire career.

First, the people should staying with one employer because it is best for the workers. If workers stay with one employer they will not having to move and they can learning all abou the company and advence in the company.

Second, people should staying with one employer because it is best for the compeny. The people will knowing how to do their jobs and they will having a big producton and the compeny will be very success.

Finally, people should staying with one employer because it is best for soceity. If people stay with one compeny then all the compenies will being very success. If all the compenie are very success then soceity will be success.

THE "3" ESSAY

Strengths of This Essay

1. It is clearly organized.
2. It has good, correct sentence structure.

Weaknesses of This Essay

1. It does not discuss the topic completely.
2. There are errors in spelling and grammar.

The following essay received a score of 2:

First, there is a disadvantage to place a high value on loyalty to the employer if your employer is no a good employer and your job is no a good job then you should no be loyal to a bad employer. Many employer are no good employers and if you are loyal to a bad employer it is a waste because a bad employer he will no be good to you.

Next, there is a advantage to change jobs every few years to build a carere if you get boring with your job and you want to move from one job to other so yo can get a better job instead of stay in your old boring job.

Finally, people should decide for themself where they want to work, if they decide one plce when they very young, how can they be sure whe they are older that they will still want to work there?

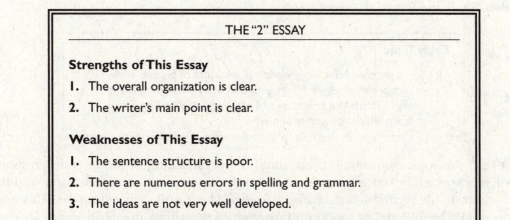

THE "2" ESSAY

Strengths of This Essay

1. The overall organization is clear.

2. The writer's main point is clear.

Weaknesses of This Essay

1. The sentence structure is poor.

2. There are numerous errors in spelling and grammar.

3. The ideas are not very well developed.

The following essay received a score of 1:

I think people should staying only one job for his hole careere. Because it is importent loyal to your jop. If you not loyal. Th company didn't be able has good business. If the employees keep change. New employees alway needs be train, and so on.

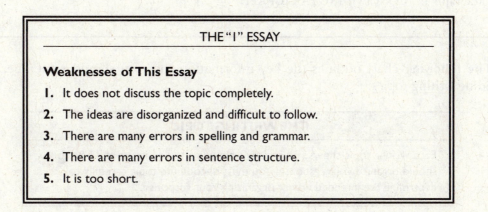

THE "1" ESSAY

Weaknesses of This Essay

1. It does not discuss the topic completely.

2. The ideas are disorganized and difficult to follow.

3. There are many errors in spelling and grammar.

4. There are many errors in sentence structure.

5. It is too short.

BEFORE WRITING

SKILL 1: DECODE THE TOPIC

The first and most important step when writing an essay on the TOEFL test is to decode the topic to determine what the intended outline is. Writing topics generally give very clear clues about how your answer should be constructed. It is important to follow the clear clues that are given in the topic when you are planning your answer. You probably will not be given much credit for a response that does not cover the topic in the way that is intended. Study the following essay topic:

Essay Topic

Some people prefer large weddings with lots of people, while others prefer small weddings with only very close friends and family. Discuss the advantages of each type of wedding. Then indicate which you prefer and why.

As you read this topic, you should think about the organization of the intended response that will be expected by test graders. Your essay should start with an introduction, and that introduction should mention *large weddings, small weddings,* and their *advantages.* This introduction should be followed by supporting paragraphs describing the *advantages of large weddings* and the *advantages of small weddings.* In the final paragraph, you should discuss whether *you prefer large weddings* or *small weddings* and *why.* This final paragraph serves as your conclusion because it brings together the ideas in the previous paragraphs about large and small weddings. The following is an appropriate outline for an essay on the topic above:

Paragraph 1:   INTRODUCTORY PARAGRAPH
(mentioning the advantages of large and small weddings)

Paragraph 2:   FIRST SUPPORTING PARAGRAPH
(listing and discussing the advantages of large weddings)

Paragraph 3:   SECOND SUPPORTING PARAGRAPH
(listing and discussing the advantages of small weddings)

Paragraph 4:   CONCLUDING PARAGRAPH
(whether you prefer large or small weddings and why)

The following chart outlines the key information that you should remember about decoding writing topics:

THE WRITING TOPIC

Each writing topic shows you exactly *what* you should discuss and *how* you should organize your response. You must decode the topic carefully to determine the intended way of organizing your response.

EXERCISE 1: For each of the following writing topics, indicate the type of information that you will include in each paragraph of your response.

> 1. What type of novel do you enjoy reading most? Use reasons and examples to support your response.

INTRODUCTION: *the type of novel I enjoy reading most*
SUPPORTING PARAGRAPH 1:   *the first reason I enjoy this type of novel (with an example)*
SUPPORTING PARAGRAPH 2:   *the second reason I enjoy this type of novel (with an example)*
SUPPORTING PARAGRAPH 3:   *the third reason I enjoy this type of novel (with an example)*
CONCLUSION: *summary of the reasons I enjoy this type of novel*

> 2. Some students prefer to study alone, while other students prefer to study with others. Discuss the advantages of each type of studying. Then indicate which you prefer and why.

> 3. Do you agree or disagree with the following statement?
>   *Patience is the most important characteristic in a boss.*
>   Use specific reasons and examples to support your response.

> 4. Some people work better during the day, while other people work better at night. Which kind of person are you, and why? Use reasons and examples to support your response.

5. Do you agree or disagree with the following statement?

    Time should never be wasted.

    Use specific reasons and examples to support your response.

6. What type of company would you most like to see built in your hometown or city. Give reasons to support your response.

7. Some people live for today, while other people live for the future. Which type of person are you? Use reasons and examples to support your response.

8. Do you agree or disagree with the following statement?

    A knowledge of history is absolutely essential.

    Use specific reasons and examples to support your response.

SKILL 2: DEVELOP SUPPORTING IDEAS

After you have decoded a writing topic to determine the overall organization of your response, you need to plan how to develop your ideas. You need to provide as much support as possible for the ideas in your essay, using reasons and examples and making your answer as personal as possible. To have an effective essay, you need strong support.

Essay Topic

Why is it important to you to learn English? Support your response with reasons and examples.

As you read this topic, you should quickly determine that the overall organization of your response should be an introduction, supporting paragraphs about your reasons for learning English, and a conclusion. You should take a few minutes before you begin writing to develop your ideas.

INTRODUCTION	*my reasons for learning English*
SUPPORTING PARAGRAPH 1	*for educational opportunities*
(examples)	• *going to university abroad, going to graduate school abroad*
(reason)	• *necessary to learn English in order to study abroad*
(personal story)	• *the opportunity that I have to get a graduate degree abroad with a scholarship from my company*
SUPPORTING PARAGRAPH 2	*for professional opportunities*
(examples)	• *getting an entry-level job in a multinational company, advancing to a higher position in the company*
(reason)	• *necessary to learn English in order to succeed in a multinational company*
(personal story)	• *the low, entry-level job in a multinational company that I got after I was interviewed in English*
CONCLUSION	*the educational and professional opportunities that result from learning English*

In this example, there are two main reasons for learning English: *for educational opportunities* and *for professional opportunities*. Each of these ideas is supported by examples, a reason, and personal information.

The following chart outlines the key information that you should remember about the development of supporting ideas.

SUPPORTING IDEAS

Support your essay with *reasons* and *examples*, and *personalize* your essay as much as possible. The more support you have, the stronger your essay will be.

EXERCISE 2: For each of the following topics, develop ideas to support it, using reasons, examples, and personal information.

> 1. What have you done that has most surprised the people around you? Use reasons and examples to support your response.

> 2. Some people like to visit new and different places, while others prefer to remain in places they know. Which type of person are you? Support your response with reasons and examples.

> 3. Do you agree or disagree with the following statement?
>
>   *A teacher should always stick to the subject matter of the course.*
>
>   Use specific reasons and examples to support your response.

> 4. What advice would you give to someone who is just beginning the study of the English language? Give reasons and examples to support your response.

5. Some people prefer to marry when they are young, while others prefer to wait until they are older to marry. Discuss the advantages of each position. Then indicate which you think is better and why.

6. Do you agree or disagree with the following statement?

   It is better to save your money for the future than to enjoy it now.

   Use specific reasons and examples to support your response.

7. At the end of your life, how would you most like to be remembered? Support your response with reasons and examples.

8. Some people dream of reaching unlikely goals, while other people set more reasonable and reachable goals. Which kind of person do you tend to be? Use examples to support your response.

WHILE WRITING

SKILL 3: WRITE THE INTRODUCTORY PARAGRAPH

The purpose of the introduction is first to interest the reader in your topic and then to explain clearly to the reader what you are going to discuss. When finished with your introduction, the reader should be eager to continue on with your essay, and the reader should have an exact idea of your topic and how you are going to organize the discussion of your topic. You do not need to give the outcome of your discussion in the introduction; you can save that for the conclusion.

Essay Topic

Do you agree or disagree with the following statement?

To succeed, you should focus more on cooperation than on competition.

Support your response with specific examples.

The following paragraph shows one possible introduction to an essay on this topic in which the author agrees with the statement.

INTRODUCTION 1

In my work in a marketing company, it is very clear that employees in the company compete with each other in order to be selected to work on the best projects and in order to advance in the company. However, in spite of this intense competition among employees, the most important key to the success of the company, and therefore to the success of the employees working within the company, is for employees to cooperate in order to produce the most effective marketing campaigns. Two examples in which I have taken part, a marketing campaign for an office supply company and a marketing campaign for a dance theater, demonstrate the value of cooperation among employees.

The first part of this introduction gives background information about the writer to interest the reader in the essay. The first two sentences tell the reader that the writer works in a marketing company and recognizes that, while both competition and cooperation exist among the employees of the marketing company, cooperation is the most important. From the last sentence of the introduction, it can be determined that the writer will discuss two examples from the marketing company that demonstrate the value of cooperation.

The next paragraph shows another way that the essay on the above topic could be introduced. In this essay, the author disagrees with the statement.

INTRODUCTION 2

As a student in the university, I find that, while on many occasions it is beneficial to cooperate with other students, it is most important for me always to compete with other students for the top grades in the courses I take. The following two situations from my university studies indicate the importance of competition to a student in my position.

The first part of this introduction informs the reader that the writer is a university student who regularly competes for top grades; it also shows that the writer believes that competition is more important than cooperation. From the last sentence of the introduction, it can be determined that the writer will continue the essay by discussing two situations from the university that demonstrate the importance of competition.

The following chart outlines the key information that you should remember about writing introductory paragraphs.

THE INTRODUCTORY PARAGRAPH
1. Begin the introduction with *background* information about how the topic relates to you in order to get the reader *interested* in your essay.
2. End the introduction with a statement or statements that show the reader how the rest of the essay will be *organized*.

EXERCISE 3: Write introductory paragraphs for essays on the following topics. In each introductory paragraph, circle the *background* information that shows how the topic relates to you. Underline the information that shows how the rest of the essay will be *organized*.

> 1. Do you agree or disagree with the following statement?
>
>   *It is better to stick with what you know than to try out new things.*
>
>   Use specific reasons and examples to support your response.

> 2. What course that you have taken have you enjoyed the most, and why? Use reasons and examples to support your response.

3.   In some courses, there are numerous exams throughout the course, while in other courses there is only one final exam. Discuss the advantages of each type of course. Then indicate which you prefer and why.

4.   Do you agree or disagree with the following statement?

Parents always know what is best for their children.

Use specific reasons and examples to support your response.

5.   What is the strongest advantage that technology can bring us? Support your response with reasons and examples.

6.   Some people are very casual about handling their money, while other people budget their money carefully. Which type of person are you? Support your response with reasons and examples.

7.   Do you agree or disagree with the following statement?

It is the responsibility of government to support the arts.

Use specific reasons and examples to support your response.

8.   What person, other than a family member, has influenced you the most in your life? Support your response with reasons and examples.

SKILL 4: WRITE UNIFIED SUPPORTING PARAGRAPHS

A good way to write a clear and effective supporting paragraph is to begin with a sentence to introduce the main idea of the passage, support the main idea with strong details, and connect the ideas together in a unified paragraph. The following outline shows a paragraph topic and its supporting ideas.

> _to be a good employee, have a good understanding of your job_
> - _understand your responsibilities_
> - _understand the rules you must follow_
> - _understand the decisions you can make_

Various methods can be used to connect ideas together in a unified paragraph: repeating a key word, rephrasing the key word, referring to the key word with a pronoun or possessive, and adding transition expressions or sentences. The paragraph based on the outline above contains examples of each of these methods of unifying the ideas in a paragraph.

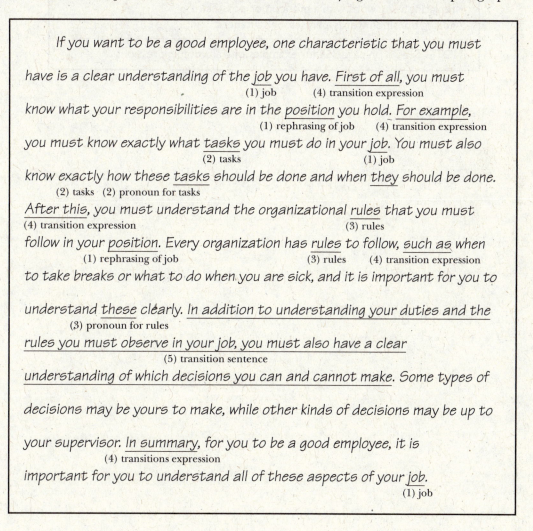

If you want to be a good employee, one characteristic that you must

have is a clear understanding of the job you have. First of all, you must
           (1) job   (4) transition expression

know what your responsibilities are in the position you hold. For example,
          (1) rephrasing of job   (4) transition expression

you must know exactly what tasks you must do in your job. You must also
      (2) tasks   (1) job

know exactly how these tasks should be done and when they should be done.
    (2) tasks (2) pronoun for tasks

After this, you must understand the organizational rules that you must
(4) transition expression   (3) rules

follow in your position. Every organization has rules to follow, such as when
     (1) rephrasing of job   (3) rules   (4) transition expression

to take breaks or what to do when you are sick, and it is important for you to

understand these clearly. In addition to understanding your duties and the
     (3) pronoun for rules

rules you must observe in your job, you must also have a clear
          (5) transition sentence

understanding of which decisions you can and cannot make. Some types of

decisions may be yours to make, while other kinds of decisions may be up to

your supervisor. In summary, for you to be a good employee, it is
     (4) transitions expression

important for you to understand all of these aspects of your job.
              (1) job

This paragraph contains numerous examples of devices that make the paragraph more unified. (1) The key word *job* is repeated numerous times and rephrased as *position*. (2) The key word *tasks* is repeated and is replaced with the pronoun *they*. (3) The key word *rules* is repeated and then is replaced with the pronoun *these*. (4) There are numerous transition expressions: *first of all, for example, after this, such as,* and *in summary.* (5) There is a transition sentence relating the first two supporting ideas about duties and rules to the third supporting idea about decisions.

The following chart outlines the key information that you should remember when you are writing supporting paragraphs.

UNIFIED SUPPORTING PARAGRAPHS

Introduce each supporting paragraph with a *topic sentence* and support that paragraph with lots of *details*. Make sure that the ideas in the paragraph are unified by using a mixture of the following methods:

• repeating a key word
• rephrasing a key word
• replacing a key word with a pronoun or possessive
• adding transition words, phrases, or sentences

NOTE: See 7B on page 364 for examples of transition expressions.

EXERCISE 4: Read the paragraph. Then answer these questions.

1. (A) Find the word *employee* in the passage. How many times does it appear?
    (B) How is the word *employee* restated in the second sentence?

2. (A) Find the word *priorities* in the passage. How many times does it appear?
    (B) Which pronoun refers to the noun *priorities?*

3. (A) Find the word *manner* in the passage. *Manner* is a rephrasing of which word in the previous sentence?
    (B) What pronoun refers to *manner?*

4. (A) Find the transition expression that indicates the first way you must understand your organization.
    (B) Find the transition sentence that relates the first way to the second way you must understand your organization.

5. (A) Find the transition expression that precedes examples of priorities.
    (B) Find the transition expression that precedes examples of manner.
    (C) Find the transition expression that precedes examples of inflexible style.

Another characteristic that you must have if you are going to be a good employee is a clear understanding of your organization. First of all, for you to be a good worker, you must understand where the organization places
Line its priorities. You must, for example, know if the organization most values
(5) product quality, on-time production, customer satisfaction, or cost savings. If you understand the organization's priorities, then you will be able to do your job in accordance with them. However, in addition to understanding an organization's priorities if you want to be a good employee, you must also understand the style for getting work done within
(10) the organization. The manner of getting work done could, for instance, be casual or formal, with perhaps very formal or informal ways of dressing or communicating. It could also be either flexible or inflexible. In a very rigid type of organization, you follow the rules to the letter (i.e., arriving at your desk precisely on time, taking breaks exactly as prescribed, and leaving as the
(15) clock strikes the hour); in a less rigid organization, the rules are not followed so precisely.

Now write a paragraph beginning with *The recent news event that has affected me most*…. Then follow these directions:

1. Circle each key word the first time that it appears in the paragraph. Draw a line from the key word to any repetitions, rephrases, or pronoun references to that key word.
2. Underline any transition phrases once.
3. Underline any transition sentences twice.

SKILL 5: WRITE THE CONCLUDING PARAGRAPH

The purpose of the conclusion is to close your essay by summarizing the main points of your discussion. When finished with your conclusion, the reader should clearly understand your exact ideas on the topic and the reasons you feel the way that you do about the topic.

The ideas in your conclusion should be closely related to the ideas that you began in the introduction. While in the introduction you should indicate what you intend to discuss in the essay, in the conclusion you should indicate the outcome or results of the discussion. Refer to the essay topic and sample introductions in Skill 3 on page 350.

Essay Topic

Do you agree or disagree with the following statement?

To succeed, you should focus more on cooperation than on competition.

Support your response with specific examples.

The following paragraph is a conclusion to the essay that began with INTRODUCTION 1 (in Skill 3) on page 350.

CONCLUSION 1

Even though there is intense competition among employees to advance in the company, the key ingredient for the success of the company is cooperation among employees to complete the company's various projects. The truth of this statement should be clear from the examples of the marketing campaigns for the office supply company and the dance theater, where strong teamwork caused one campaign to succeed and lack of teamwork caused the other campaign to be less successful.

In this conclusion, the writer clearly indicates the belief that cooperation is more important than competition. The writer also refers to the two examples from the essay that support this position.

The next paragraph is a conclusion to the essay that began with INTRODUCTION 2 (in Skill 3) on page 351.

CONCLUSION 2

If I had not competed so strongly in these two situations, my life would be very different from what it is today. I would never have been admitted to the top university in my country, and I would certainly never have earned a scholarship for my studies there. It is because I believe so strongly in competition that I was able to succeed in this way.

In this conclusion, the writer clearly indicates the strong belief that competition is very important. The writer also summarizes the two examples from the essay that support this position.

The following chart outlines the key information that you should remember about writing concluding paragraphs.

THE CONCLUDING PARAGRAPH
1. *Summarize* the key points in your discussion.
2. Be sure that your overall *idea* and the *reasons* for the idea are very clear.

EXERCISE 5: Write concluding paragraphs for the essays that you introduced in Skill 3. In each concluding paragraph, circle your overall idea. Underline the key points of your discussion.

> 1. Do you agree or disagree with the following statement?
>
>   *It is better to stick with what you know than to try out new things.*
>
>   Use specific reasons and examples to support your response.

> 2. What course that you have taken have you enjoyed the most, and why? Use reasons and examples to support your response.

> 3. In some courses, there are numerous exams throughout the course, while in other courses there is only one final exam. Discuss the advantages of each type of course. Then indicate which you prefer and why.

4. Do you agree or disagree with the following statement?

    Parents always know what is best for their children.

    Use specific reasons and examples to support your response.

5. What is the strongest advantage that technology can bring us?
    Support your response with reasons and examples.

6. Some people are very casual about handling their money, while
    other people budget their money carefully. Which type of person
    are you? Support your response with reasons and examples.

7. Do you agree or disagree with the following statement?

    It is the responsibility of government to support the arts.

    Use specific reasons and examples to support your response.

8. What person, other than a family member, has influenced you the
    most in your life? Support your response with reasons and
    examples.

Skill 6: CONNECT THE SUPPORTING PARAGRAPHS IN THE ESSAY

To make your essay as clear as possible, you should show as clearly as you can how the ideas in the supporting paragraphs in your essay are related. This can be accomplished (1) with transition expressions such as *the first, the most important,* or *a final way,* or (2) with transition sentences that include the idea of the previous paragraph and the idea of the current paragraph. It is best to use a combination of these two types of transitions. The following example shows how transitions can be used to show the relationships among the supporting paragraphs in an essay.

ESSAY OUTLINE

(introduction)	*characteristics of a good class*
(supporting paragraph 1)	• *an organized teacher*
(supporting paragraph 2)	• *interesting lectures*
(supporting paragraph 3)	• *clear and reasonable assignments*

TRANSITIONS

(to introduce SP1)	*One important characteristic of a good class is an organized teacher.*
(to introduce SP2)	*In addition to having a teacher who is organized, a good class must also have a teacher who gives interesting lectures.*
(to introduce SP3)	*A final characteristic of a good class is that the assignments are clear and reasonable.*

The first supporting paragraph is introduced with the transition *One important characteristic* to show that this is the first of the characteristics of a good class that you are going to discuss in your essay. The second supporting paragraph is introduced with a transition sentence that shows how this paragraph is related to the previous paragraph; it includes a reference to the first supporting paragraph *a teacher who is organized* and a reference to the second supporting paragraph *a teacher who gives interesting lectures*. The third supporting paragraph is introduced with the transition expression *A final characteristic* to show that this is the last of the three characteristics of a good class.

The following chart outlines the important information to remember about connecting the supporting paragraphs of your essay:

WELL-CONNECTED SUPPORTING PARAGRAPHS

1. The supporting paragraphs of an essay can be connected with *transition expressions* or with *transition sentences*.
2. It is best to use a combination of these two types of transitions.

EXERCISE 6: For each outline of an essay, write sentences to introduce each of the supporting paragraphs. You should use a combination of transition expressions and transitions sentences.

1.   INTRO: *courses I've enjoyed the most*
     SP1:   sociology
     SP2:   philosophy
     SP3:   psychology

     SP1:   *One course I have enjoyed is sociology.* _____

     SP2:   *Even more than sociology, I have really enjoyed philosophy.* _____

     SP3:   *Of all the courses, the one that I have enjoyed the most is psychology.* ____

2.   INTRO: *places in the United States that I would like to see*
     SP1:   • the Grand Canyon
     SP2:   • Niagara Falls
     SP3:   • the Petrified Forest

     SP1:   _____

     SP2:   _____

     SP3:   _____

3.   INTRO: *best type of part-time job while in school*
     SP1:   one that pays a lot
     SP2:   one that is related to my future career
     SP3:   one that has flexible hours

     SP1:   _____

     SP2:   _____

     SP3:   _____

4.   INTRO: *the world's most important priorities*
     SP1:   feeding the hungry
     SP2:   taking care of the environment
     SP3:   finding cures for diseases
     SP4:   ending war and violence

     SP1:   _____

     SP2:   _____

     SP3:   _____

     SP4:   _____

5. INTRO: *assignments I most dislike*
    SP1: writing long research papers
    SP2: working on group assignments
    SP3: giving speeches

    SP1: _____

    SP2: _____

    SP3: _____

6. INTRO: *advantages of learning to cook*
    SP1: saving money
    SP2: preparing exactly what you want
    SP3: being able to cook for family and friends

    SP1: _____

    SP2: _____

    SP3: _____

7. INTRO: *what my parents taught me*
    SP1: to be honest with myself
    SP2: to make the most of what I have
    SP3: to strive for more than I think I can do

    SP1: _____

    SP2: _____

    SP3: _____

8. INTRO: *overused excuses for tardiness*
    SP1: "I overslept."
    SP2: "My alarm clock broke."
    SP3: "My car wouldn't start."
    SP4: "The bus was late."

    SP1: _____

    SP2: _____

    SP3: _____

    SP4: _____

AFTER WRITING _____

SKILL 7: EDIT SENTENCE STRUCTURE

7A. Simple Sentence Structure

A *simple* sentence is a sentence that has only one **clause**.[1] Two types of sentence structure errors are possible in a sentence with only one clause: (1) the clause can be missing a subject or a verb, and (2) the clause can be introduced by a subordinate clause connector.

The first type of incorrect simple sentence is a sentence that is missing a subject or a verb. (Note that an asterisk is used to indicate that the sentence contains an error.)

> Every day it <ins>is</ins> necessary to sign in and sign out.*
>   VERB

> His <u>recommendation</u> about the project.*
>   SUBJECT

The first sentence is incorrect because it has the verb *is* but is missing a subject. The second sentence is incorrect because it has the subject *recommendation* but is missing a verb.

A sentence structure with both a subject and a verb is not always correct. If the one clause in the sentence includes both a subject and a verb but is introduced by a subordinate clause connector, then the sentence is also incomplete.

> When the <u>storm</u> with thunder and lightning <u>will leave</u> the area.*
>   SUBJECT   VERB

> How the <u>driver</u> of the car <u>managed</u> to avoid an accident.*
>   SUBJECT   VERB

The first sentence includes both the subject *storm* and the verb *will leave,* but this sentence is not correct because it is introduced by the subordinate clause connector *When.* The second sentence includes both the subject *driver* and the verb *managed,* but this sentence is not correct because it is introduced by the subordinate clause connector *How.*

The following chart outlines what you should remember about editing simple sentences:

SIMPLE SENTENCES
1. A simple sentence is a sentence with *one clause.*
2. A simple sentence must have both a *subject* and a *verb.*
3. A simple sentence may not be introduced by a *subordinate clause connector.*

---

[1] A **clause** is a group of words that has both a subject and a verb. Simple sentences with only one main clause are covered in great detail in Skills 1–5 of the Structure and Written Expression section on pages 98–107.

EXERCISE 7A: Underline the subjects once and the verbs twice. Put boxes around the subordinate clause connectors. Then indicate if the sentences are correct (C) or incorrect (I).

__I__   1. The vague <u>meaning</u> of the underlined expression.

_____   2. When you finally found out the whole truth.

_____   3. His reaction to the film was priceless.

_____   4. Usually leaves quite early in the morning.

_____   5. An indication to everyone of the importance of the project.

_____   6. Surprisingly, no one has collected the prize.

_____   7. Why the committee met for so long.

_____   8. Absolutely cannot submit the forms today.

_____   9. The refusal of the judge to accept the petition.

_____   10. The idea shocked me.

_____   11. Since each of the participants was fully trained.

_____   12. In a moment of anguish forgot about his promise.

_____   13. A discussion by all interested parties has been scheduled.

_____   14. A situation needing a considerable amount of attention.

_____   15. Only that the books were overdue at the library.

_____   16. The dean finally decided.

_____   17. To put off the announcement for one more day.

_____   18. If the outcome had been better.

_____   19. Actually, the results have not yet been posted.

_____   20. What the other students were able to do.

7B. Compound Sentence Structure

A *compound* sentence is a sentence that has more than one **main clause.**[2] The main clauses in a compound sentence can be connected correctly with either a coordinate conjunction (*and, but, so, or, yet*) and a comma or with a semi-colon (*;*).

> Tom drove too fast. He got a ticket for speeding.
> Tom drove too fast, so he got a ticket for speeding.
> Tom drove too fast; he got a ticket for speeding.

In the first example, the two main clauses *Tom drove too fast* and *He got a ticket for speeding* are not connected into a compound sentence. In the second example, the two main clauses are combined into a compound sentence with the coordinate conjunction *so* and a comma. In the third example, the same two clauses are combined into a compound sentence with a semi-colon.

It is possible to use adverb transitions in compound sentences. It is important to note that adverb transitions are not conjunctions, so either a semi-colon or a coordinate conjunction with a comma is needed.

> Tom drove too fast. As a result, he got a ticket for speeding.
> Tom drove too fast, and he got a ticket for speeding as a result.
> Tom drove too fast; as a result, he got a ticket for speeding.

In the first example, the two main clauses *Tom drove too fast* and *he got a ticket for speeding* are not combined into a compound sentence even though the adverb transition *As a result* is used. In the second example, the two main clauses are combined into a compound sentence with the coordinate conjunction *and* and a comma; the adverb transition *as a result* is included at the end of the compound sentence. In the third example, the same two main clauses are combined into a compound sentence with a semi-colon, and the adverb transition is set off from the second main clause with a comma.

The following chart lists some commonly used adverb transitions:

ADVERB TRANSITIONS			
TIME	CAUSE	CONTRAST	CONDITION
afterwards next then finally	as a result consequently therefore	however in contrast	otherwise

---

[2]A **main clause** is an independent clause that has both a subject and a verb. It is not introduced by a subordinate connector. Compound sentences are covered in Skill 6 of the Structure and Written Expression section on pages 107–108.

EXERCISE 7B: Underline the subjects once and the verbs twice in the main clauses. Put boxes around the punctuation, transitions, and connectors that join the main clauses. Then indicate if the sentences are correct (C) or incorrect (I).

__I__   1. The researcher completed the study, the results were quite surprising.

_____   2. The meeting did not take place today, so it will have to be rescheduled.

_____   3. I expected the exam to be on Tuesday, however it was on Monday instead.

_____   4. The department's sales were very high; as a result, the manager has been given a bonus.

_____   5. We finished the last details and then we submitted the final report.

_____   6. The employees often come late to work, but this does not seem to be a problem.

_____   7. The team won its last three games. Next, it will compete in the championship tournament.

_____   8. The light bulb in the lamp has burned out I need to replace the bulb.

_____   9. The manager is hiring some more employees, then we will not have to work so much.

_____   10. The textbook chapter was quite long, yet I finished it by 10:00.

_____   11. You must turn in the paper by Friday, otherwise your grade will be lowered.

_____   12. The decision has not yet been made. Therefore, we must wait to learn the final outcome.

_____   13. Afterwards construction on the highway was completed, traffic moved more smoothly.

_____   14. This course requires a lot of work; in contrast, the other course required very little.

_____   15. Our flight is scheduled to board soon, we must head over to the gate now.

_____   16. The building has a tower; the tower is on the north side of the building.

_____   17. We have to see the professor now, or we will have to wait until next week.

_____   18. I have worked hard for several months; finally, I will be able to rest.

_____   19. The bookstore is open for another hour we should go there right now.

_____   20. It has been raining steadily for days, consequently, the streets are flooded.

7C. Complex Sentence Structure

A *complex* sentence is a sentence that has at least one main clause and one **subordinate clause**.[3] Noun, adjective, and adverb clauses are all types of subordinate clauses. Each of these sentences is a complex sentence because it contains a subordinate clause:

> They do not understand (what I said).
> NOUN CLAUSE

> The professor (who wrote the book) is giving the lectures.
> ADJECTIVE CLAUSE

> Final grades will be available (after the semester ends).
> ADVERB CLAUSE

The first complex sentence contains the subordinate noun clause *what I said*. The second complex sentence contains the subordinate adjective clause *who wrote the book*. The final complex sentence contains the subordinate adverb clause *after the semester ends*.

A variety of errors with complex sentence structures can occur in student writing, but the following two errors occur with great frequency: (1) repeated subjects after adjective clauses, and (2) repeated subjects after noun clauses as subjects.

> The <u>movie</u> (that we saw last night) <u>it</u>* <u>was</u> really funny.
>   S   ADJECTIVE CLAUSE   S   V

> (<u>What she told me yesterday</u>) <u>it</u>* <u>was</u> quite confusing.
>   NOUN CLAUSE - S   S   V

The first sentence is incorrect because it contains an extra subject. The correct subject *movie* comes before the adjective clause *that we saw last night*, and an extra subject *it* comes after the adjective clause. To correct this sentence, you should omit the extra subject *it*. The second sentence is also incorrect because it contains an extra subject. The noun clause *What she told me yesterday* is a subject, and this noun clause subject is followed by an extra subject *it*. To correct this sentence, you should omit the extra subject *it*.

The following chart outlines what you should remember about editing complex sentences:

+--+
| **COMPLEX SENTENCES** |
+--+
| 1. When a subject comes before an adjective clause, do not |
| add an extra subject after the adjective clause. |
| 2. When a noun clause is used as a subject, do not add an |
| extra subject after the noun clause. |
+--+

---

[3]A **subordinate clause** is a dependent clause. It has both a subject and a verb and is introduced by a subordinate connector. Complex sentences with subordinate noun, adverb, and adjective clauses are covered in great detail in Skills 7–12 of the Structure and Written Expression section on pages 109–121.

EXERCISE 7C: Underline the subjects once and the verbs twice in the main clauses. Put parentheses around the subordinate noun and adjective clauses. Then indicate if the sentences are correct (C) or incorrect (I).

__I__   1.   The tickets (that I ordered) they will be delivered tomorrow.

_____   2.   How I will be able to get all this work done is unclear.

_____   3.   The excuse that you gave me was not very credible.

_____   4.   What the lecturer said it was really quite amusing.

_____   5.   The place where we agreed to meet it was quite secluded.

_____   6.   The person whose friendship I cherish most is a friend from my childhood.

_____   7.   Who is responsible for the accident it is unknown.

_____   8.   That the story is on the front page of the paper it is indisputable.

_____   9.   The contractor who painted the house he did a very careful job.

_____   10.   Why she was the one who got the job is a mystery to me.

_____   11.   What happened just before our arrival it is unknown.

_____   12.   The clothes that we purchased at the sale were quite a good bargain.

_____   13.   The room in which the seminar will be held is rather tiny.

_____   14.   What will happen to her next it is what concerns me the most.

_____   15.   The receptionist who regularly answers the phone is out of the office.

_____   16.   What the manager wrote in the report it was highly complimentary.

_____   17.   The classmate who presented the report he did a great job.

_____   18.   How such a thing could happen is not clear to me.

_____   19.   The situation in which I found myself was one in which all of the facts are not known.

_____   20.   Why he has done what I told him not to do with the money that I gave him it is not

              certain.

EXERCISE 7 (A-C): Find and correct the sentence structure errors in the following essay. (The number in parentheses at the end of each paragraph indicates the number of errors in that paragraph.) The essay discusses the following topic.

> Some people prefer to take vacations in quiet, natural places, while others prefer to spend their vacation time in big cities. Discuss the advantages of each type of vacation. Then indicate which you prefer and why.

1.   *What you need to do before going on a vacation it is to decide where you will go on your vacation. You may decide to go to a quiet place with a quiet and natural setting, instead you may decide to go to a big city with a fast-paced life. Each of these types of vacation something to offer. (3 errors)*

2.   *The reasons that it can be a good idea to go to a quiet and natural location for a vacation they are numerous. First of all, a vacation in a natural setting allowing you to relax and slow down the pace of your life for a while. Instead of hurrying from place to place as you are used to doing. You can spend your time doing nothing more than enjoying the beauty of the location. Then, after are thoroughly relaxed, what you can do it is to take part in outdoor activities such as hiking or swimming. All of this will leave you completely relaxed and free of stress by the end of your vacation. (5 errors)*

3.   *It can be nice to go to a quiet and natural spot for a vacation, however it can also be quite an adventure to go to a big and fast-paced city for a vacation. The main reason that it can be a good idea to take a vacation in a big city it is to take part in so many activities that are unavailable in your hometown. On a big city vacation, numerous cultural events that might not be available in your hometown, such as theatrical performances, concerts, and art and museum exhibits, they are available. On a big city vacation, will also have access to some of the world's finest restaurants and shopping. After your big city vacation has ended. You will have a whole range of new experiences that are not part of your daily life. (5 errors)*

4.   *For me, the type of vacation that I decide to take it depends on my life prior to the vacation. I work as a legal assistant in a law office, this job is often repetitious and dull but is sometimes quite frantic just prior to a major case. After a slow and boring period of work. All I want is to head to a fast-paced vacation in a big city. However, if my job been frantic and busy prior to my vacation, then want to head to a quiet and beautiful place where I can relax. Thus, I enjoy different types of vacations, the type of vacation depends on the pace of my life before the vacation. (6 errors)*

SKILL 8: EDIT WRITTEN EXPRESSION

8A. Inversions and Agreement

Errors in inversions and agreement are covered in the Structure and Written Expression section of this book. You may want to review these skills.

Skills 15–19: Sentences with Inverted Subjects and Verbs
Skills 20–23: Problems with Subject/Verb Agreement

EXERCISE 8A: Find and correct the errors in the following essay. (The number in parentheses at the end of each paragraph indicates the number of errors in that paragraph.) The essay discusses the following topic.

> Some people prefer to work for a company, while others prefer to work for themselves. Discuss the advantages of each position. Then indicate which you prefer and why.

1.   *Something very important for students to decide as they near the end of their studies are whether should they work for another company or go into business for themselves. As a university student, this decision about my future are one that I face soon myself. To me, each of these positions have clear advantages, in particular depending on the stage of your career. (4 errors)*

2.   *There is numerous advantages to working for another company, particularly early in your career. One of the advantages are that working in someone else's company provide a situation with the security of a regular paycheck and less responsibility than you would have you were to be the owner of the company. Also, not until you start your own business you need to come up with the finances to back the company. Thus, all of this indicate that it is better to work for other people early in your career while you are gaining the knowledge and experience you need to start your own company. (6 errors)*

3.   *Then, later in your career, it may be advantageous for you to go into business for yourself. The main reason for going into business for yourself are that in your own company you are able to decide on what direction do you want your company to go. However, only when you have gained enough knowledge and experience are it a good idea to go into business for yourself. This is when will you be ready to deal with the responsibility, pressure, and financial needs of owning a company. (4 errors)*

4.   *Nothing are more important to me than having my own company one day. However, what seems very clear to me now is that beginning my career working in someone else's company are best. In this situation, not only I can work with more security and less pressure, but I can also build up my financial resources and learn from others. Then, I should manage to gain enough experience, knowledge, and confidence and build up my financial resources, I hope eventually to open my own company, where can I determine exactly how would I like the company to operate. (6 errors)*

8B. Parallel, Comparative, and Superlative Structures

Errors in parallel, comparative, and superlative structures are covered in the Structure and Written Expression section of this book. You may want to review these skills.

Skills 24–26: Problems with Parallel Structure
Skills 27–29: Problems with Comparatives and Superlatives

EXERCISE 8B: Find and correct the errors in the following essay. (The number in parentheses at the end of each paragraph indicates the number of errors in that paragraph.) The essay discusses the following topic.

> Do you agree or disagree with the following statement?
>
> *The primary reason to get an education is to succeed financially.*
>
> Support your response with reasons and examples.

1.   I am a university student, and I am studying in the university for a number of reasons. Of course, one of my reasons for going to school, studying hard, and obtain a university degree is to succeed financially; the more money I make, it will be better for me. However, financial success is not my most importantest reason for going to the university. Instead, I am going to the university for a much broad reason than that: I believe that a university education will give me a much rich and better life, not just in a financial way. (5 errors)

2.   One way that a university education makes your life enjoyabler is to give you the opportunity to have a career that you really desire and appreciative. Having a career that you like is much better than a job that just pays the bills. I, for example, am studying to be a marine biologist. I will have the better career for me; I will be rewarded not only in terms of money and also in terms of enjoyment of my career. (5 errors)

3.   Another way that a university education can enrich your life is to provide a broadest knowledge, understand, and appreciation of the world around you than you already have. It provides you with an understanding of both the history of your own culture and to influence history on the present. It also provides you with an understanding of other cultures and shows you that other cultures are neither exactly the same as nor they are completely different from your own culture. Finally, it provides you with an understanding of the universe around you and showing you how the universe functions. (5 errors)

4.   Thus, in getting a university education, I can say that financial success is certainly one goal that I have. However, the goal of financial success is not as important as I have another goal. My primary goal in getting a university education is the goal of achieving a more full life, certainly one with financial security but more importantly one that is rewarding both in terms of professional opportunities or in terms of awareness and understanding of life around me. The closer I get to achieving this goal, I will be happier. (4 errors)

8C. Verbs

Errors in verbs are covered in the Structure and Written Expression section of this book. You may want to review these skills.

> **Skills 30–32: Problems with the Form of the Verb**
> **Skills 33–36: Problems with the Use of the Verb**
> **Skills 37–38: Problems with Passive Verbs**

EXERCISE 8C: Find and correct the errors in the following essay. (The number in parentheses at the end of each paragraph indicates the number of errors in that paragraph.) The essay discusses the following topic.

> When something unexpected happens, how do you react? Use examples to support your response.

1.   When something unexpected happens, different people reacted in a variety of ways. I wish I could reacted calmly to unexpected situations. However, unfortunately, I usually react with panic. The following example shows my usual reaction to situations when I have be completely unprepared for them. (3 errors)

2.   This example of the way that I react to unexpected situations has occurred in history class last week. The professor had told us that we will be covering the material in Chapters 10 through 12 in class on Thursday. By the time I arrived in class, I have read all of the assigned material, and I understood most of what I had study. While I was relax in my chair at the beginning of class, the professor announces that there would be a pop quiz on the material in the assigned chapters. I was preparing on the material because I have studied all of it thoroughly before class. (8 errors)

3.   However, I was face with an unexpected situation, and I do not react well to unexpected situations. Instead of feeling relaxed at the announcement of the unexpected quiz because I was so prepared, I was completely fill with anxiety by the situation. As the professor was write the questions on the board, I become more and more nervous. I was unable to think clearly, and I knew that I would done a bad job on the quiz because this was what always happens to me when I feel panic. As I stared at the questions on the board, I had been unable to think of the correct answers. It was as if I had not prepare at all for class. Then, the professor collected the papers from the class, including my basically blank piece of paper. Just after the papers had been collecting, the answers to all the questions came to me. (9 errors)

4.   You can seen from this example that my usual reaction to something unexpected is to panic. In the future, I hoped that I will learn to react more calmly, but up to now I had not learned to react this way. On the basis of my past behavior, however, it seems that I currently had a stronger tendency to react with panic than with calm. (4 errors)

8D. Nouns and Pronouns

Errors in nouns and pronouns are covered in the Structure and Written Expression section of this book. You may want to review these skills.

> **Skills 39–42: Problems with Nouns**
> **Skills 43–45: Problems with Pronouns**

EXERCISE 8D: Find and correct the errors in the following essay. (The number in parentheses at the end of each paragraph indicates the number of errors in that paragraph.) The essay discusses the following topic.

> What part of your high school experience was the most valuable? Use reasons and examples to support your response.

1.   I was not a very good athleticism in high school, but I wanted with all of mine heart to be on the football team. My desire to be on the team had little to do with athletics and was perhaps not for the best of reasons; the strong stimuli for I to make the team was that team members were well-known in the school and he became very popular. This desire to be on the football team in high school, and the fact that through hard worker I managed to accomplish something that I wanted so much, even if its was something petty, turned out to be the single most valuable experiences of my years in high school. (8 errors)

2.   I had to work very hard to make the football team in high school, and for some time this seemed like an impossible goals. A large amount of students in my school, more than a hundred and fifty of them, spent many of theirs afternoons trying out for a team with less than forty positions. After a lot of hard work on my part, and after I had demonstrated to the coaches that he could count on me to keep going long after everyone was exhausted, I managed to make the team as a secondary play. Even with so many effort, I was never going to be a sports phenomena or even a member of the first team, but I did accomplish my goal of making the team. (8 errors)

3.   The valuable lesson that I learned through this experience was not the joy of competitor or the much benefits of teamwork, several lesson very commonly associated with participation in team sports. Instead, the valuable lesson that I learned was that hard work and determination could be very important in helping I accomplish each goals that I want to reach. Even if others have more talent, I can work harder than it does and still perhaps find successor where them do not. (8 errors)

8E. Adjectives and Adverbs

Errors in adjectives and adverbs are covered in the Structure and Written Expression section of this book. You may want to review these skills.

> **Skills 46–48: Problems with Adjectives and Adverbs**
> **Skills 49–51: More Problems with Adjectives**
> **Skills 52–55: Problems with Articles**

EXERCISE 8E: Find and correct the errors in the following essay. (The number in parentheses at the end of each paragraph indicates the number of errors in that paragraph.) The essay discusses the following topic.

> Some students prepare early, while other students procrastinate. Which type of student are you? Support your response with reasons and examples.

1.   I understand that it seems importantly for a students to prepare early their assignments rather than procrastinate in getting assignments done. However, although I understand this clear, I always seem to wait until the finally minute to get assigning projects done. There are two reasons why I regular procrastinate on my assignments academic in spite of the fact that this is not a best way to get my work done. (9 errors)

2.   One reason that I tend to be a eternal procrastinator is that I work much more efficient under pressure than I do when I am not under pressure. For example, I can accomplish so much more in a two-hour period when I have a definitely deadline in two hours than I can during an alike period without the pressure of a deadline strict. Without a deadline, the two-hour period seems to fly by with minimally accomplishment, but with an rapid approached deadline I seem quite capably of making every minute of the two-hour period count. (10 errors)

3.   Another reason that I tend to procrastinate is that if I start preparing early, it takes generally more of my time. If, for example, I have paper due in six weeks, I can start working on the paper now and work on it on a day basis, and that paper will take up a lot of my time and energy during the followed six weeks. However, if I wait to begin work on the paper until week before it is due, I have to go off some place where I can be lone and spend all of my time and energy that week on the paper, but it will only take one week of my time valuable and not six weeks. (7 errors)

4.   In summary, it seems that I always wait until the last minute to complete an assignments because I am afraid that I will waste too much time by starting early. It would be good idea, however, for me to make a effort to get work done efficient and early so that I do not always have to feel tensely about getting work done at a last minute. (6 errors)

8F. Prepositions and Usage

Errors in prepositions and usage are covered in the Structure and Written Expression section of this book. You may want to review these skills.

> **Skills 56–57: Problems with Prepositions**
> **Skills 58–60: Problems with Usage**

EXERCISE 8F: Find and correct the errors in the following essay. (The number in parentheses at the end of each paragraph indicates the number of errors in that paragraph.) The essay discusses the following topic.

> Some people avoid confrontations at all costs, while other people seem to seek them out. Discuss each type of person. Then indicate which type of person you are and why.

1.   Some people make their best to avoid confrontations, while another people often seem to get involved confrontations. There can be problems with either type of behavior; thus, I always try to be dislike people at either extreme and remain moderate in my approach at confrontation. (5 errors)

2.   To some people, confrontation should be avoided for all costs. These people will make nothing even after something terribly wrong has happened to them. They, for example, stay silent when they are pushed around or when they are blamed something they did not do. Unfortunately, it is quite probable that others will take advantage from people alike this. Thus, people who avoid confrontations will find that they do not get as much out life as they deserve because other always take advantage of them. (7 errors)

3.   Alike people who avoid confrontations, others individuals go to the opposite extreme; they take part for confrontations too easily. When something small happens accidentally, they become enraged and do a big deal of it as if they had been terribly wronged. Perhaps, for example, someone accidentally bumps in them or mistakenly says something offensive; in this type of situation, they create a serious confrontation. While it is true that other people will try hard not to provoke this type of person, it is also true that other will do an effort to avoid spending much time in the company of such a person. Thus, people who get involved in confrontations easily will find it hard to develop close friendships and relationships with anothers. (8 errors)

4.   I try to make the right thing by avoiding either extreme type of behavior. I always try to behave in an alike manner, without overreacting or underreacting. If someone offends me with chance, I try to brush it and keep in going as if nothing had happened me. If someone intentionally succeeds on bothering me, however, I try to react without anger but with a reaction that shows that behavior alike this is unacceptable. In this way, I do not do the mistake of wasting time on unimportant situations, but I prevent others instances of bad behavior toward me for recurring. (11 errors)

PRACTICE TESTS

Essay Topic #1
Time — 30 minutes

Do you agree or disagree with the following statement?

Children should be strongly pushed to achieve their maximum.

Use specific reasons and details to support your answer. Write your answer on a separate sheet of paper.

Essay Topic #2
Time — 30 minutes

People are watching more and more television, and as a result television is having an increasing effect on society. Discuss the beneficial and harmful effects of television on society. Then indicate what you believe the role of television should be and why.

Write your answer on a separate sheet of paper.

Essay Topic #3
Time — 30 minutes

A practical career is not always something that you love to do. Is it better to pursue a practical career or to follow your dreams, even though they may be rather impractical? Discuss each position. Then indicate which you agree with and why.

Write your answer on a separate sheet of paper.

Essay Topic #4
Time — 30 minutes

Do you agree or disagree with the following statement?

It is better to marry for practical reasons than for love.

Use specific reasons and details to support your answer. Write your answer on a separate sheet of paper.

COMPLETE
TESTS

1 □ 1 □ 1 □ 1 □ 1 □ 1 □ 1 □ 1

COMPLETE TEST ONE

SECTION 1
LISTENING COMPREHENSION
Time—approximately 35 minutes
(including the reading of the directions for each part)

In this section of the test, you will have an opportunity to demonstrate your ability to understand conversations and talks in English. There are three parts to this section, with special directions for each part. Answer all the questions on the basis of what is **stated** or **implied** by the speakers you hear. Do **not** take notes or write in your test book at any time. Do **not** turn the pages until you are told to do so.

Part A

Directions: In Part A you will hear short conversations between two people. After each conversation, you will hear a question about the conversation. The conversations and questions will not be repeated. After you hear a question, read the four possible answers in your test book and choose the best answer. Then, on your answer sheet, find the number of the question and fill in the space that corresponds to the letter of the answer you have chosen.

Listen to an example.

Sample Answer

On the recording, you will hear:

(man)   *That exam was just awful.*
(woman)   *Oh, it could have been worse.*
(narrator)   *What does the woman mean?*

In your test book, you will read: (A) The exam was really awful.
(B) It was the worst exam she had ever seen.
(C) It couldn't have been more difficult.
(D) It wasn't that hard.

You learn from the conversation that the man thought the exam was very difficult and that the woman disagreed with the man. The best answer to the question, "What does the woman mean?" is (D), "It wasn't that hard." Therefore, the correct choice is (D).

1. (A) Carla does not live very far away.
   (B) What Carla said was unjust.
   (C) He does not fear what anyone says.
   (D) Carla is fairly rude to others.

2. (A) She thinks it's an improvement.
   (B) The fir trees in it are better.
   (C) It resembles the last one.
   (D) It is the best the man has ever done.

3. (A) He graduated last in his class.
   (B) He is the last person in his family to graduate.
   (C) He doesn't believe he can improve gradually.
   (D) He has finally finished his studies.

4. (A) He thought the dress was so chic.
   (B) He was surprised the dress was not expensive.
   (C) He would like to know what color dress it was.
   (D) The dress was not cheap.

5. (A) Leave the car somewhere else.
   (B) Ignore the parking tickets.
   (C) Add more money to the meter.
   (D) Pay the parking attendant.

6. (A) He does not like to hold too many books at one time.
   (B) There is no bookstore in his neighborhood.
   (C) It's not possible to obtain the book yet.
   (D) He needs to talk to someone at the bookstore.

7. (A) It was incomplete.
   (B) It finished on time.
   (C) It was about honor.
   (D) It was too long.

8. (A) She needs to use the man's notes.
   (B) Yesterday's physics class was quite boring.
   (C) She took some very good notes in physics class.
   (D) She would like to lend the man her notes.

9. (A) It's her birthday today.
   (B) She's looking for a birthday gift.
   (C) She wants to go shopping with her dad.
   (D) She wants a new wallet for herself.

10. (A) He took a quick trip.
    (B) The big boat was towed through the water.
    (C) There was coal in the water.
    (D) He didn't go for a swim.

11. (A) She just left her sister's house.
    (B) Her sister left the sweater behind.
    (C) She believes her sweater was left at her sister's house.
    (D) She doesn't know where her sister lives.

12. (A) She doesn't have time to complete additional reports.
    (B) She cannot finish the reports that she is already working on.
    (C) She is scared of having responsibility for the reports.
    (D) It is not time for the accounting reports to be compiled.

13. (A) He's had enough exercise.
    (B) He's going to give himself a reward for the hard work.
    (C) He's going to stay on for quite some time.
    (D) He would like to give the woman an exercise machine as a gift.

14. (A) He cannot see the huge waves.
    (B) The waves are not coming in.
    (C) He would like the woman to repeat what she said.
    (D) He agrees with the woman.

15. (A) The exam was postponed.
    (B) The man should have studied harder.
    (C) Night is the best time to study for exams.
    (D) She is completely prepared for the exam.

GO ON TO THE NEXT PAGE ➡

16. (A) Students who want to change schedules should form a line.
    (B) It is only possible to make four changes in the schedule.
    (C) It is necessary to submit the form quickly.
    (D) Problems occur when people don't wait their turn.

17. (A) In a mine.
    (B) In a jewelry store.
    (C) In a clothing store.
    (D) In a bank.

18. (A) A visit to the woman's family.
    (B) The telephone bill.
    (C) The cost of a new telephone.
    (D) How far away the woman's family lives.

19. (A) She hasn't met her new boss yet.
    (B) She has a good opinion of her boss.
    (C) Her boss has asked her about her impressions of the company.
    (D) Her boss has been putting a lot of pressure on her.

20. (A) The recital starts in three hours.
    (B) He intends to recite three different poems.
    (C) He received a citation on the third of the month.
    (D) He thinks the performance begins at three.

21. (A) Choose a new dentist.
    (B) Cure the pain himself.
    (C) Make an appointment with his dentist.
    (D) Ask his dentist about the right way to brush.

22. (A) It is almost five o'clock.
    (B) The man doesn't really need the stamps.
    (C) It is a long way to the post office.
    (D) It would be better to go after five o'clock.

23. (A) The article was placed on reserve.
    (B) The woman must ask the professor for a copy.
    (C) The woman should look through a number of journals in the library.
    (D) He has reservations about the information in the article.

24. (A) He needs to take a nap.
    (B) He hopes the woman will help him to calm down.
    (C) The woman just woke him up.
    (D) He is extremely relaxed.

25. (A) She doesn't think the news report is false.
    (B) She has never before reported on the news.
    (C) She never watches the news on television.
    (D) She shares the man's opinion about the report.

26. (A) Management will offer pay raises on Friday.
    (B) The policy has not yet been decided.
    (C) The manager is full of hot air.
    (D) The plane has not yet landed.

27. (A) He doesn't believe that it is really snowing.
    (B) The snow had been predicted.
    (C) The exact amount of snow is unclear.
    (D) He expected the woman to go out in the snow.

28. (A) She's going to take the test over again.
    (B) She thinks she did a good job on the exam.
    (C) She has not yet taken the literature exam.
    (D) She's unhappy with how she did.

29. (A) The door was unlocked.
    (B) It was better to wait outside.
    (C) He could not open the door.
    (D) He needed to take a walk.

30. (A) He nailed the door shut.
    (B) He is heading home.
    (C) He hit himself in the head.
    (D) He is absolutely correct.

GO ON TO THE NEXT PAGE

Part B

Directions: In this part of the test, you will hear longer conversations. After each conversation, you will hear several questions. The conversations and questions will not be repeated.

After you hear a question, read the four possible answers in your test book and choose the best answer. Then, on your answer sheet, find the number of the question and fill in the space that corresponds to the letter of the answer you have chosen.

Remember, you are **not** allowed to take notes or write in your test book.

31. (A) The haircut is unusually short.
    (B) This is Bob's first haircut.
    (C) Bob doesn't know who gave him the haircut.
    (D) After the haircut, Bob's hair still touches the floor.

32. (A) It is just what he wanted.
    (B) He enjoys having the latest style.
    (C) He dislikes it immensely.
    (D) He thinks it will be cool in the summer.

33. (A) A broken mirror.
    (B) The hairstylist.
    (C) The scissors used to cut his hair.
    (D) Piles of his hair.

34. (A) "You should become a hairstylist."
    (B) "Please put it back on."
    (C) "It'll grow back."
    (D) "It won't grow fast enough."

35. (A) Every evening.
    (B) Every week.
    (C) Every Sunday.
    (D) Every month.

36. (A) That she was eighty-five years old.
    (B) That a storm was coming.
    (C) That she was under a great deal of pressure.
    (D) That she wanted to become a weather forecaster.

37. (A) In her bones.
    (B) In her ears.
    (C) In her legs.
    (D) In her head.

38. (A) Call his great-grandmother less often.
    (B) Watch the weather forecasts with his great-grandmother.
    (C) Help his great-grandmother relieve some of her pressures.
    (D) Believe his great-grandmother's predictions about the weather.

GO ON TO THE NEXT PAGE

Part C

Directions: In this part of the test, you will hear several talks. After each talk, you will hear some questions. The talks and questions will not be repeated.

After you hear a question, you will read the four possible answers in your test book and choose the best answer. Then, on your answer sheet, find the number of the question and fill in the space that corresponds to the letter of the answer you have chosen.

Here is an example.

On the recording, you will hear:

(narrator) *Listen to an instructor talk to his class about painting.*
(man) *Artist Grant Wood was a guiding force in the school of painting known as American regionalist, a style reflecting the distinctive characteristics of art from rural areas of the United States. Wood began drawing animals on the family farm at the age of three, and when he was thirty-eight one of his paintings received a remarkable amount of public notice and acclaim. This painting, called "American Gothic," is a starkly simple depiction of a serious couple staring directly out at the viewer.*

Now listen to a sample question.

Sample Answer

(narrator) *What style of painting is known as American regionalist?*

In your test book, you will read: (A) Art from America's inner cities.
(B) Art from the central region of the United States.
(C) Art from various urban areas in the United States.
(D) Art from rural sections of America.

The best answer to the question, "What style of painting is known as American regionalist?" is (D), "Art from rural sections of America." Therefore, the correct choice is (D).

Now listen to another sample question.

Sample Answer

(narrator) *What is the name of Wood's most successful painting?*

In your test book, you will read: (A) "American Regionalist."
(B) "The Family Farm in Iowa."
(C) "American Gothic."
(D) "A Serious Couple."

The best answer to the question, "What is the name of Wood's most successful painting?" is (C), "American Gothic." Therefore, the correct choice is (C).

Remember, you are **not** allowed to take notes or write in your test book.

Wait

39. (A) In a car.
    (B) On a hike.
    (C) On a tram.
    (D) In a lecture hall.

40. (A) It means they have big tears.
    (B) It means they like to swim.
    (C) It means they look like crocodiles.
    (D) It means they are pretending to be sad.

41. (A) They are sad.
    (B) They are warming themselves.
    (C) They are getting rid of salt.
    (D) They regret their actions.

42. (A) Taking photographs.
    (B) Getting closer to the crocodiles.
    (C) Exploring the water's edge.
    (D) Getting off the tram.

43. (A) Water Sports.
    (B) Physics.
    (C) American History.
    (D) Psychology.

44. (A) To cut.
    (B) To move fast.
    (C) To steer a boat.
    (D) To build a ship.

45. (A) To bring tea from China.
    (B) To transport gold to California.
    (C) To trade with the British.
    (D) To sail the American river system.

46. (A) A reading assignment.
    (B) A quiz on Friday.
    (C) A research paper for the end of the semester.
    (D) Some written homework.

47. (A) Writers.
    (B) Actors.
    (C) Athletes.
    (D) Musicians.

48. (A) He or she would see butterflies.
    (B) He or she would break a leg.
    (C) He or she would have shaky knees.
    (D) He or she would stop breathing.

49. (A) By staring at the audience.
    (B) By breathing shallowly.
    (C) By thinking about possible negative outcomes.
    (D) By focusing on what needs to be done.

50. (A) At two o'clock.
    (B) At four o'clock.
    (C) At six o'clock.
    (D) At eight o'clock.

This is the end of Section 1.
Stop work on Section 1.

Turn off the recording.

Read the directions for Section 2 and begin work.
Do NOT read or work on any other section
of the test during the next 25 minutes.

SECTION 2
STRUCTURE AND WRITTEN EXPRESSION
Time—25 minutes
(including the reading of the directions)
Now set your clock for 25 minutes.

This section is designed to measure your ability to recognize language that is appropriate for standard written English. There are two types of questions in this section, with special directions for each type.

Structure

Directions: These questions are incomplete sentences. Beneath each sentence you will see four words or phrases, marked (A), (B), (C), and (D). Choose the **one** word or phrase that best completes the sentence. Then, on your answer sheet, find the number of the question and fill in the space that corresponds to the letter of the answer you have chosen.

Look at the following examples.

Example I   **Sample Answer**

The president _____ the election by a landslide.

  (A) won
  (B) he won
  (C) yesterday
  (D) fortunately

The sentence should read, "The president won the election by a landslide." Therefore, you should choose answer (A).

Example II   **Sample Answer**

When _____ the conference?

  (A) the doctor attended
  (B) did the doctor attend
  (C) the doctor will attend
  (D) the doctor's attendance

The sentence should read, "When did the doctor attend the conference?" Therefore, you should choose answer (B).

GO ON TO THE NEXT PAGE

1. _____ range in color from pale yellow to bright orange.

   (A) Canaries which
   (B) Canaries
   (C) That canaries
   (D) Canaries that are

2. _____ of precious gems is determined by their hardness, color, and brilliance.

   (A) The valuable
   (B) It is the value
   (C) It is valuable
   (D) The value

3. _____ a tornado spins in a counterclockwise direction in the northern hemisphere, it spins in the opposite direction in the southern hemisphere.

   (A) However
   (B) Because of
   (C) Although
   (D) That

4. The Caldecott Medal, _____ for the best children's picture book, is awarded each January.

   (A) a prize
   (B) which prize
   (C) is a prize which
   (D) is a prize

5. The horn of the rhinoceros consists of a cone of tight bundles of keratin _____ from the epidermis.

   (A) grow
   (B) grows
   (C) growing
   (D) they grow

6. Most species of heliotropes are weeds, _____ of them are cultivated.

   (A) some
   (B) but some
   (C) for some species
   (D) some species

7. Thunder occurs as _____ through air, causing the heated air to expand and collide with layers of cooler air.

   (A) an electrical charge
   (B) passes an electrical charge
   (C) the passing of an electrical charge
   (D) an electrical charge passes

8. Researchers have long debated _____ Saturn's moon Titan contains hydrocarbon oceans and lakes.

   (A) over it
   (B) whether it
   (C) whether
   (D) whether over

9. Nimbostratus clouds are thick, dark grey clouds _____ forebode rain.

   (A) what
   (B) which
   (C) what they
   (D) which they

10. _____ in several early civilizations, a cubit was based on the length of the forearm from the tip of the middle finger to the elbow.

    (A) It was used as a measurement
    (B) A measurement was used
    (C) The use of a measurement
    (D) Used as a measurement

GO ON TO THE NEXT PAGE

11. Only when air and water seep through its outer coat _____.

    (A) does a seed germinate
    (B) to the germination of a seed
    (C) a seed germinates
    (D) for a seed to germinate

12. _____ seasonal rainfall, especially in regions near the tropics, is winds that blow in an opposite direction in winter than in summer.

    (A) Causing
    (B) That cause
    (C) To cause
    (D) What causes

13. The extinct Martian volcano Olympus Mons is approximately three times as _____ Mount Everest.

    (A) high
    (B) high as is
    (C) higher than
    (D) the highest of

14. The flight instructor, _____ at the air base, said that orders not to fight had been given.

    (A) when interviewed
    (B) when he interviewed
    (C) when his interview
    (D) when interviewing

15. In the northern and central parts of the state of Idaho _____ and churning rivers.

    (A) majestic mountains are found
    (B) found majestic mountains
    (C) are found majestic mountains
    (D) finding majestic mountains

GO ON TO THE NEXT PAGE

Written Expression

Directions: In these questions, each sentence has four underlined words or phrases. The four underlined parts of the sentence are marked (A), (B), (C), and (D). Identify the **one** underlined word or phrase that must be changed in order for the sentence to be correct. Then, on your answer sheet, find the number of the question and fill in the space that corresponds to the letter of the answer you have chosen.

Look at the following examples.

Example I

The four <u>string</u> on a violin <u>are</u> <u>tuned</u>
  A   B   C   D

in fifths.

Sample Answer

Ⓐ
●
Ⓒ
Ⓓ

The sentence should read, "The four strings on a violin are tuned in fifths." Therefore, you should choose answer (B).

Example II

The <u>research</u> <u>for</u> the book *Roots* <u>taking</u>
    A   B   C

Alex Haley <u>twelve years</u>.
           D

Sample Answer

Ⓐ
Ⓑ
●
Ⓓ

The sentence should read, "The research for the book *Roots* took Alex Haley twelve years." Therefore, you should choose answer (C).

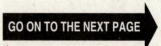

16. Light can travels from the Sun to the Earth in eight minutes and twenty seconds.
       A   B   C   D

17. Every human typically have twenty-three pairs of chromosomes in most cells.
              A   B   C D

18. Most sedimentary rocks start forming when grains of clay, silt, or sandy settle in
     A   B   C

    river valleys or on the bottoms of lakes and oceans.
            D

19. The total thickness of the ventricular walls of the heart are about three times that of
                               A   B C   D

    the atria.

20. The type of jazz known as "swing" was introduced by Duke Ellington when he wrote
                  A   B   C

    and records "It Don't Mean a Thing If It Ain't Got That Swing."
        D

21. The bones of mammals, not alike those of other vertebrates, show a high degree of
                      A   B   C

    differentiation.
     D

22. The neocortex has evolved more recently then other layers of the brain.
     A   B   C D

23. The United States receives a large amount of revenue from taxation of a tobacco
                    A   B   C D

    products.

24. Much fats are composed of one molecule of glycerin combined with three molecules
     A   B

    of fatty acids.
       C   D

25. The capital of the Confederacy was originally in Mobile, but they were moved to
        A   B   C   D

    Richmond.

26. A pearl develops when a tiny grain of sand or stone or some another irritant
               A   B   C

    accidentally enters into the shell of a pearl oyster.
            D

GO ON TO THE NEXT PAGE →

27. The English horn is an alto oboe with a pitch one-fifth lower than the soprano oboe.
              A   B   C   D

28. In the Milky Way galaxy, the most recent observed supernova appeared in 1604.
                              A   B   C   D

29. Never in the history of humanity has there been more people living on this relatively
                           A   B   C   D

    small planet.

30. Because of the mobility of Americans today, it is difficult for they to put down
                   A   B   C

    real roots.
    D

31. For five years after the Civil War, Robert E. Lee served to president of Washington
    A   B

    College, which was later called Washington and Lee.
             C   D

32. The number of wild horses on Assateague is increasing lately, resulting in overgrazed
        A   B   C

    marsh and dune grasses.
                   D

33. Hypnoses was successfully used during World War II to treat battle fatigue.
        A   B   C   D

34. The lobster, like many crustaceans, can cast off a damaging appendage and
                 A   B   C

    regenerate a new appendage to nearly normal size.
                                         D

35. Humans develop normally twenty primary, or deciduous, teeth and thirty-two
               A   B   C

    permanent ones.
    D

36. The curricula of American public schools are set in individual states; they
        A   B

    do not determine by the federal government.
           C   D

37. The fact that the sophisticated technology has become part of revolution in travel
                                              A   B

    delivery systems has not made travel schedules less hectic.
    C   D

GO ON TO THE NEXT PAGE →

38. Balanchine's <u>plotless</u> ballets, <u>such</u> *Jewels* and *The Four Temperaments*, <u>present</u> dance
          A   B   C

  <u>purely</u> as a celebration of the movement of the human body.
  D

39. In a <u>solar battery</u>, a photosensitive <u>semiconducting</u> substance <u>such as</u> silicon crystal
       A   B   C

  is the source of <u>electrician</u>.
                     D

40. In early days, hydrochloric acid was <u>done</u> by <u>heating</u> a mixture of sodium chloride
       A   B   C

  with iron sulfate.
  D

This is the end of Section 2.
If you finish before 25 minutes has ended,
check your work on Section 2 only.

At the end of 25 minutes, go on to Section 3.
Use exactly 55 minutes to work on Section 3.

SECTION 3
READING COMPREHENSION
Time—55 minutes
(including the reading of the directions)
Now set your clock for 55 minutes.

This section is designed to measure your ability to read and understand short passages similar in topic and style to those that students are likely to encounter in North American universities and colleges. This section contains reading passages and questions about the passages.

Directions: In this section you will read several passages. Each one is followed by a number of questions about it. You are to choose the **one** best answer, (A), (B), (C), or (D), to each question. Then, on your answer sheet, find the number of the question and fill in the space that corresponds to the letter of the answer you have chosen.

Answer all questions about the information in a passage on the basis of what is **stated** or **implied** in that passage.

Read the following passage:

> John Quincy Adams, who served as the sixth president of the United States from 1825 to 1829, is today recognized for his masterful statesmanship and diplomacy. He dedicated his life to public service, both in the presidency and in the various other political offices that he
> *Line* held. Throughout his political career he demonstrated his unswerving belief in freedom of
> (5) speech, the antislavery cause, and the right of Americans to be free from European and Asian domination.

Example I   **Sample Answer**

To what did John Quincy Adams devote his life?

(A) Improving his personal life
(B) Serving the public
(C) Increasing his fortune
(D) Working on his private business

According to the passage, John Quincy Adams "dedicated his life to public service." Therefore, you should choose answer (B).

Example II   **Sample Answer**

In line 4, the word "unswerving" is closest in meaning to

(A) moveable
(B) insignificant
(C) unchanging
(D) diplomatic

The passage states that John Quincy Adams demonstrated his unswerving belief "throughout his career." This implies that the belief did not change. Therefore, you should choose answer (C).

TOEFL® test directions and format are reprinted by permission of ETS, the copyright owner. However, all examples and test questions are provided by Pearson Education, Inc.

Questions 1–9

John James Audubon, nineteenth-century artist and naturalist, is known as one of the foremost authorities on North American birds. Born in Les Cayes, Haiti, in 1785, Audubon was raised in France and studied art under French artist Jacques-Louis David. After settling on his father's Pennsylvania estate at the age of eighteen, he first began to study and paint birds.

Line
(5)   In his young adulthood, Audubon undertook numerous enterprises, generally without a tremendous amount of success; at various times during his life he was involved in a mercantile business, a lumber and grist mill, a taxidermy business, and a school. His general mode of operating a business was to leave it either unattended or in the hands of a partner and take off on excursions through the wilds to paint the natural life that he saw. His business career came to an end in 1819
(10)   when he was jailed for debt and forced to file for bankruptcy.

It was at that time that Audubon began to seriously pursue the dream of publishing a collection of his paintings of birds. For the next six years he painted birds in their natural habitats while his wife worked as a teacher to support the family. His *Birds of America*, which included engravings of 435 of his colorful and lifelike watercolors, was published in parts during the period from 1826 to 1838 in
(15)   England. After the success of the English editions, American editions of his work were published in 1839, and his fame and fortune were ensured.

1. This passage is mainly about

   (A) North American birds
   (B) Audubon's route to success as a painter of birds
   (C) the works that Audubon published
   (D) Audubon's preference for travel in natural habitats

2. The word "foremost" in line 1 is closest in meaning to

   (A) prior
   (B) leading
   (C) first
   (D) largest

3. In the second paragraph, the author mainly discusses

   (A) how Audubon developed his painting style
   (B) Audubon's involvement in a mercantile business
   (C) where Audubon went on his excursions
   (D) Audubon's unsuccessful business practices

4. The word "mode" in line 7 could best be replaced by

   (A) method
   (B) vogue
   (C) average
   (D) trend

5. Audubon decided not to continue to pursue business when

   (A) he was injured in an accident at a grist mill
   (B) he decided to study art in France
   (C) he was put in prison because he owed money
   (D) he made enough money from his paintings

6. The word "pursue" in line 11 is closest in meaning to

   (A) imagine
   (B) share
   (C) follow
   (D) deny

GO ON TO THE NEXT PAGE

7. According to the passage, Audubon's paintings

    (A) were realistic portrayals
    (B) used only black, white, and gray
    (C) were done in oils
    (D) depicted birds in cages

8. The word "support" in line 13 could best be replaced by

    (A) tolerate
    (B) provide for
    (C) side with
    (D) fight for

9. It can be inferred from the passage that after 1839 Audubon

    (A) unsuccessfully tried to develop new businesses
    (B) continued to be supported by his wife
    (C) traveled to Europe
    (D) became wealthy

GO ON TO THE NEXT PAGE ➤

Questions 10–19

These stories of killer bees in the news in recent years have attracted a lot of attention as the bees have made their way from South America to North America. Killer bees are reputed to be extremely aggressive in nature, although experts say that their aggression may have been somewhat
Line
(5)   inflated.

The killer bee is a hybrid—or combination—of the very mild European strain of honeybee and the considerably more aggressive African bee, which was created when the African strain was imported into Brazil in 1955. The African bees were brought into Brazil because their aggression was considered an advantage: they were far more productive than their European counterparts in that they spent a higher percentage of their time working and continued working longer in inclement
(10) weather than did the European bees.

These killer bees have been known to attack humans and animals, and some fatalities have occurred. Experts point out, however, that the mixed breed known as the killer bee is actually not at all as aggressive as the pure African bee. They also point out that the attacks have a chemical cause. A killer bee stings only when it has been disturbed; it is not aggressive by nature. However, after a
(15) disturbed bee stings and flies away, it leaves its stinger embedded in the victim. In the vicera attached to the embedded stinger is the chemical isoamyl acetate, which has an odor that attracts other bees. As other bees approach the victim of the original sting, the victim tends to panic, thus disturbing other bees and causing them to sting. The new stings create more of the chemical isoamyl acetate, which attracts more bees and increases the panic level of the victim. Killer bees tend to travel in large
(20) clusters or swarms and thus respond in large numbers to the production of isoamyl acetate.

10. The subject of the preceding paragraph was most likely

(A) ways of producing honey
(B) stories in the media about killer bees
(C) the chemical nature of killer bee attacks
(D) the creation of the killer bee

11. The main idea of this passage is that killer bees

(A) have been in the news a lot recently
(B) have been moving unexpectedly rapidly through the Americas
(C) are not as aggressive as their reputation suggests
(D) are a hybrid rather than a pure breed

12. The word "inflated" in line 4 could best be replaced by

(A) exaggerated
(B) blown
(C) aired
(D) burst

13. It can be inferred from the passage that the killer bee

(A) traveled from Brazil to Africa in 1955
(B) was a predecessor of the African bee
(C) was carried from Africa to Brazil in 1955
(D) did not exist early in the twentieth century

14. Why were African bees considered beneficial?

(A) They produced an unusual type of honey.
(B) They spent their time traveling.
(C) They were very aggressive.
(D) They hid from inclement weather.

15. A "hybrid" in line 5 is

(A) a mixture
(B) a relative
(C) a predecessor
(D) an enemy

GO ON TO THE NEXT PAGE

16. It is stated in the passage that killer bees

    (A) are more deadly than African bees
    (B) are less aggressive than African bees
    (C) never attack animals
    (D) always attack African bees

17. The pronoun "They" in line 13 refers to

    (A) killer bees
    (B) humans and animals
    (C) fatalities
    (D) experts

18. What is NOT mentioned in the passage as a contributing factor in an attack by killer bees?

    (A) Panic by the victim
    (B) An odorous chemical
    (C) Disturbance of the bees
    (D) Inclement weather

19. Where in the passage does the author describe the size of the groups in which killer bees move?

    (A) Lines 2–4
    (B) Lines 5–7
    (C) Lines 11–12
    (D) Lines 19–20

GO ON TO THE NEXT PAGE

Questions 20–28

There is a common expression in the English language referring to a blue moon. When people say that something happens "only once in a blue moon," they mean that it happens only very rarely, once in a great while. This expression has been around for at least a century and a half; there are
Line references to this expression that date from the second half of the nineteenth century.
(5)   The expression "a blue moon" has come to refer to the second full moon occurring in any given calendar month. A second full moon is not called a blue moon because it is particularly blue or is any different in hue from the first full moon of the month. Instead, it is called a blue moon because it is so rare. The moon needs a little more than 29 days to complete the cycle from full moon to full moon. Because every month except February has more than 29 days, every month will have at least one full
(10) moon (except February, which will have a full moon unless there is a full moon at the very end of January and another full moon at the very beginning of March). It is on the occasion when a given calendar month has a second full moon that a blue moon occurs. This does not happen very often, only three or four times in a decade.

The blue moons of today are called blue moons because of their rarity and not because of their
(15) color; however, the expression "blue moon" may have come into existence in reference to unusual circumstances in which the moon actually appeared blue. Certain natural phenomena of gigantic proportions can actually change the appearance of the moon from Earth. The eruption of the Krakatao volcano in 1883 left dust particles in the atmosphere, which clouded the sun and gave the moon a bluish tint. This particular occurrence of the blue moon may have given rise to the expression
(20) that we use today. Another example occurred more than a century later. When Mount Pinatubo erupted in the Philippines in 1991, the moon again took on a blue tint.

20. This passage is about

    (A) an idiomatic expression
    (B) an unusual color
    (C) a month on the calendar
    (D) a phase of the moon

21. How long has the expression "once in a blue moon" been around?

    (A) For around 50 years
    (B) For less than 100 years
    (C) For more than 100 years
    (D) For 200 years

22. A blue moon could best be described as

    (A) a full moon that is not blue in color
    (B) a new moon that is blue in color
    (C) a full moon that is blue in color
    (D) a new moon that is not blue in color

23. The word "hue" in line 7 is closest in meaning to

    (A) shape
    (B) date
    (C) color
    (D) size

24. Which of the following might be the date of a "blue moon"?

    (A) January 1
    (B) February 28
    (C) April 15
    (D) December 31

25. How many blue moons would there most likely be in a century?

    (A) 4
    (B) 35
    (C) 70
    (D) 100

26. According to the passage, the moon actually looked blue

    (A) after large volcanic eruptions
    (B) when it occurred late in the month
    (C) several times a year
    (D) during the month of February

GO ON TO THE NEXT PAGE ➡

27. The expression "given rise to" in line 19 could best be replaced by

(A) created a need for
(B) elevated the level of
(C) spurred the creation of
(D) brightened the color of

28. Where in the passage does the author describe the duration of a lunar cycle?

(A) Lines 1–3
(B) Lines 5–6
(C) Line 8
(D) Lines 12–13

GO ON TO THE NEXT PAGE

Questions 29–40

The organization that today is known as the Bank of America did start out in America, but under quite a different name. Italian American A.P. Giannini established this bank on October 17, 1904, in a renovated saloon in San Francisco's Italian community of North Beach under the name
Line Bank of Italy, with immigrants and first-time bank customers comprising the majority of his first
(5) customers. During its development, Giannini's bank survived major crises in the form of a natural disaster and a major economic upheaval that not all other banks were able to overcome.

One major test for Giannini's bank occurred on April 18, 1906, when a massive earthquake struck San Francisco, followed by a raging fire that destroyed much of the city. Giannini obtained two wagons and teams of horses, filled the wagons with the bank's reserves, mostly in the form of gold,
(10) covered the reserves with crates of oranges, and escaped from the chaos of the city with his clients' funds protected. In the aftermath of the disaster, Giannini's bank was the first to resume operations. Unable to install the bank in a proper office setting, Giannini opened up shop on the Washington Street Wharf on a makeshift desk created from boards and barrels.

In the period following the 1906 fire, the Bank of Italy continued to prosper and expand. By
(15) 1918 there were twenty-four branches of the Bank of Italy, and by 1928 Giannini had acquired numerous other banks, including a Bank of America located in New York City. In 1930 he consolidated all the branches of the Bank of Italy, the Bank of America in New York City, and another Bank of America that he had formed in California into the Bank of America National Trust and Savings Association.

(20) A second major crisis for the bank occurred during the Great Depression of the 1930s. Although Giannini had already retired prior to the darkest days of the Depression, he became incensed when his successor began selling off banks during the bad economic times. Giannini resumed leadership of the bank at the age of sixty-two. Under Giannini's leadership, the bank weathered the storm of the Depression and subsequently moved into a phase of overseas development.

29. According to the passage, Giannini

   (A) opened the Bank of America in 1904
   (B) worked in a bank in Italy
   (C) set up the Bank of America prior to setting up the Bank of Italy
   (D) later changed the name of the Bank of Italy

30. Where did Giannini open his first bank?

   (A) In New York City
   (B) In what used to be a bar
   (C) On Washington Street Wharf
   (D) On a makeshift desk

31. According to the passage, which of the following is NOT true about the San Francisco earthquake?

   (A) It happened in 1906.
   (B) It occurred in the aftermath of a fire.
   (C) It caused problems for Giannini's bank.
   (D) It was a tremendous earthquake.

32. The word "raging" in line 8 could best be replaced by

   (A) angered
   (B) localized
   (C) intense
   (D) feeble

33. It can be inferred from the passage that Giannini used crates of oranges after the earthquake

   (A) to hide the gold
   (B) to fill up the wagons
   (C) to provide nourishment for his customers
   (D) to protect the gold from the fire

34. The word "chaos" in line 10 is closest in meaning to

   (A) legal system
   (B) extreme heat
   (C) overdevelopment
   (D) total confusion

GO ON TO THE NEXT PAGE

35. The word "consolidated" in line 17 is closest in meaning to

(A) hardened
(B) merged
(C) moved
(D) sold

36. The passage states that after his retirement, Giannini

(A) began selling off banks
(B) caused economic misfortune to occur
(C) supported the bank's new management
(D) returned to work

37. The expression "weathered the storm of" in line 23 could best be replaced by

(A) found a cure for
(B) rained on the parade of
(C) survived the ordeal of
(D) blew its stack at

38. Where in the passage does the author describe Giannini's first banking clients?

(A) Lines 2–5
(B) Lines 7–8
(C) Lines 12–13
(D) Lines 14–16

39. How is the information in the passage presented?

(A) In chronological order
(B) In order of importance
(C) A cause followed by an effect
(D) Classifications with examples

40. The paragraph following the passage most likely discusses

(A) bank failures during the Great Depression
(B) a third major crisis of the Bank of America
(C) the international development of the Bank of America
(D) how Giannini spent his retirement

GO ON TO THE NEXT PAGE

Questions 41–50

Thunderstorms, with their jagged bursts of lightning and roaring thunder, are actually one of nature's primary mechanisms for transferring heat from the surface of the earth into the atmosphere. A thunderstorm starts when low-lying pockets of warm air from the surface of the earth begin to rise.

Line
(5)
The pockets of warm air float upward through the air above that is both cooler and heavier. The rising pockets cool as their pressure decreases, and their latent heat is released above the condensation line through the formation of cumulus clouds.

What will happen with these clouds depends on the temperature of the atmosphere. In winter, the air temperature differential between higher and lower altitudes is not extremely great, and the temperature of the rising air mass drops more slowly. During these colder months, the atmosphere,
(10)
therefore, tends to remain rather stable. In summer, however, when there is a high accumulation of heat near the earth's surface, in direct contrast to the considerably colder air higher up, the temperature differential between higher and lower altitudes is much more pronounced. As warm air rises in this type of environment, the temperature drops much more rapidly than it does in winter; when the temperature drops more than four degrees Fahrenheit per thousand feet of altitude,
(15)
cumulus clouds aggregate into a single massive cumulonimbus cloud, or thunderhead.

In isolation, a single thunderstorm is an impressive but fairly benign way for Mother Earth to defuse trapped heat from her surface; thunderstorms, however, can appear in concert, and the resulting show, while extremely impressive, can also prove extraordinarily destructive. When there is a large-scale collision between cold air and warm air masses during the summer months, a squall
(20)
line, or series of thunderheads, may develop. It is common for a squall line to begin when an advancing cold front meets up with and forces itself under a layer of warm and moist air, creating a line of thunderstorms that races forward at speeds of approximately forty miles per hour. A squall line, which can be hundreds of miles long and can contain fifty distinct thunderheads, is a magnificent force of nature with incredible potential for destruction. Within the squall line, often
(25)
near its southern end, can be found supercells, long-lived rotating storms of exceptional strength that serve as the source of tornadoes.

41. The topic of the passage is

   (A) the development of thunderstorms and squall lines
   (B) the devastating effects of tornadoes
   (C) cumulus and cumulonimbus clouds
   (D) the power of tornadoes

42. "Mechanisms" in line 2 are most likely

   (A) machines
   (B) motions
   (C) methods
   (D) materials

43. It can be inferred from the passage that, in summer,

   (A) there is not a great temperature differential between higher and lower altitudes
   (B) the greater temperature differential between higher and lower altitudes makes thunderstorms more likely to occur
   (C) there is not much cold air higher up in the atmosphere
   (D) the temperature of rising air drops more slowly than it does in winter

44. The word "benign" in line 16 is closest in meaning to

   (A) harmless
   (B) beneficial
   (C) ferocious
   (D) spectacular

GO ON TO THE NEXT PAGE ➔

45. The expression "in concert" in line 17 could best be replaced by

    (A) as a chorus
    (B) with other musicians
    (C) as a cluster
    (D) in a performance

46. According to the passage, a "squall line" in line 20 is

    (A) a lengthy cold front
    (B) a serious thunderstorm
    (C) a line of supercells
    (D) a string of thunderheads

47. The pronoun "itself" in line 21 refers to

    (A) a large-scale collision
    (B) a squall line
    (C) an advancing cold front
    (D) a layer of warm and moist air

48. All of the following are mentioned in the passage about supercells EXCEPT that they

    (A) are of short duration
    (B) have circling winds
    (C) have extraordinary power
    (D) can give birth to tornadoes

49. This reading would most probably be assigned in which of the following courses?

    (A) Geology
    (B) Meteorology
    (C) Marine Biology
    (D) Chemistry

50. The paragraph following the passage most likely discusses

    (A) the lightning and thunder associated with thunderstorms
    (B) various types of cloud formations
    (C) the forces that contribute to the formation of squall lines
    (D) the development of tornadoes within supercells

This is the end of Section 3.

**If you finish in less than 55 minutes,
check your work on Section 3 only.
Do NOT read or work on any other section of the test.**

When you finish the test, you may do the following:

- Turn to the **Diagnostic Charts** on pages 551–558, and circle the numbers of the questions that you missed.

- Turn to **Scoring Information** on pages 549–550, and determine your TOEFL score.

- Turn to the **Progress Chart** on page 559, and add your score to the chart.

TEST OF WRITTEN ENGLISH:
TWE ESSAY TOPIC
Time—30 minutes

At what age should parents allow children to begin making their own decisions? Use specific reasons and examples to support your response.

1 □ 1 □ 1 □ 1 □ 1 □ 1 □ 1 □ 1

COMPLETE TEST TWO

SECTION 1
LISTENING COMPREHENSION
Time—approximately 35 minutes
(including the reading of the directions for each part)

In this section of the test, you will have an opportunity to demonstrate your ability to understand conversations and talks in English. There are three parts to this section, with special directions for each part. Answer all the questions on the basis of what is **stated** or **implied** by the speakers you hear. Do **not** take notes or write in your test book at any time. Do **not** turn the pages until you are told to do so.

Part A

Directions: In Part A you will hear short conversations between two people. After each conversation, you will hear a question about the conversation. The conversations and questions will not be repeated. After you hear a question, read the four possible answers in your test book and choose the best answer. Then, on your answer sheet, find the number of the question and fill in the space that corresponds to the letter of the answer you have chosen.

Listen to an example.   **Sample Answer**

On the recording, you will hear:

(man)   *That exam was just awful.*
(woman)   *Oh, it could have been worse.*
(narrator)   *What does the woman mean?*

In your test book, you will read: (A) The exam was really awful.
                                          (B) It was the worst exam she had ever seen.
                                          (C) It couldn't have been more difficult.
                                          (D) It wasn't that hard.

You learn from the conversation that the man thought the exam was very difficult and that the woman disagreed with the man. The best answer to the question, "What does the woman mean?" is (D), "It wasn't that hard." Therefore, the correct choice is (D).

1. (A) They were in the regular room.
    (B) The key was misplaced.
    (C) He's taking a different class.
    (D) He has the key to the classroom.

2. (A) She will lend it to the man.
    (B) She never lent the book to Jim.
    (C) Jim wants to borrow the book.
    (D) Jim has the book.

3. (A) Paying bills.
    (B) Talking to the landlord.
    (C) Turning the lights off.
    (D) Looking for an apartment.

4. (A) She has no time to go to class.
    (B) They are already late for class.
    (C) It's too early to go to class.
    (D) She has to be on time for class.

5. (A) He is resuming his duties one more time.
    (B) He is assuming the class is difficult.
    (C) The class is terrible all the time.
    (D) The class takes a lot of time.

6. (A) She needs a new coat.
    (B) She likes the paint in the dorm rooms.
    (C) She has the same opinion as the man.
    (D) She left her coat in the dorm room.

7. (A) He needs to complete the math assignment first.
    (B) He'll be ready in a couple of hours.
    (C) He is going to history class now.
    (D) He was ready a few minutes ago.

8. (A) She's sorry she moved them.
    (B) She really knows where they are.
    (C) They haven't been moved.
    (D) Someone else moved them.

9. (A) A solution is not apparent.
    (B) The problem can be fixed.
    (C) There is really a pair of problems.
    (D) The problem is difficult to solve.

10. (A) The professor gives quizzes regularly.
    (B) The woman is really quite prepared.
    (C) It is unusual for this professor to give quizzes.
    (D) He doesn't think there's a class today.

11. (A) She could not comprehend the chemistry lecture.
    (B) She has not had time to look at the assignment.
    (C) It was possible for her to complete the problem.
    (D) She could not understand the problem.

12. (A) He doesn't know how far away the exhibit is.
    (B) He's uncertain about the fee.
    (C) The exhibit is not very far away.
    (D) He's sure the exhibit isn't free.

13. (A) Not taking it at all.
    (B) Taking it along with chemistry.
    (C) Taking it later.
    (D) Taking it instead of chemistry.

14. (A) An astronomer.
    (B) A physician.
    (C) A philosopher.
    (D) An engineer.

15. (A) Nothing could surprise her.
    (B) The gift really astonished her.
    (C) She couldn't have gotten more gifts.
    (D) She was expecting the gift.

16. (A) She's wearing a new dress.
    (B) She's ready to study for hours.
    (C) She's exhausted.
    (D) She has studied about the war for hours.

17. (A) He's really tall.
    (B) He's the best.
    (C) He's got a good head on his shoulders.
    (D) He always uses his head.

GO ON TO THE NEXT PAGE

1 □ 1 □ 1 □ 1 □ 1 □ 1 □ 1 □ 1

18. (A) He's already talked to the professor about the assignment.
    (B) There is no assignment for tomorrow.
    (C) He's not sure what the professor will talk about.
    (D) The professor discussed the assignment only briefly.

19. (A) He went to it.
    (B) He knew about it.
    (C) He didn't know about it.
    (D) He gave it.

20. (A) It's hard to lock the room.
    (B) The cloak was delivered on time.
    (C) Someone struck the crockery and broke it.
    (D) It is now midday.

21. (A) That she wouldn't take the trip.
    (B) That she would go to the beach.
    (C) That she really liked the beach.
    (D) That she would take a break from her studies.

22. (A) They were disappointed.
    (B) They didn't get any gifts.
    (C) They were unexcited.
    (D) They were really pleased.

23. (A) She believes she can succeed.
    (B) She's decided to pull out of it.
    (C) She wants to put off the speech for a while.
    (D) She thinks the speech is too long.

24. (A) She'd like to offer the man a scholarship.
    (B) The documents were returned to her with a signature.
    (C) She needs to sign the documents.
    (D) She works in the scholarship office.

25. (A) He doesn't have time to pay the bills.
    (B) The bills weren't paid on time.
    (C) Of course, he paid the bills on time.
    (D) He will pay the bills for the last time.

26. (A) He thinks the lecture was really interesting.
    (B) He's not sure if the ideas are workable.
    (C) He understood nothing about the lecture.
    (D) He's not sure what the woman would like to know.

27. (A) He missed an opportunity.
    (B) He was late for his trip.
    (C) He should take the next boat.
    (D) He should send in his application.

28. (A) He agrees with what she said.
    (B) He thinks she didn't say anything.
    (C) He couldn't hear what she said.
    (D) He did hear what she said.

29. (A) That John would pick them up for the concert.
    (B) That the concert would start earlier.
    (C) That John would not be going to the concert.
    (D) That they would be late to the concert.

30. (A) He enjoyed the trip immensely.
    (B) The boat trip was really rough.
    (C) He couldn't have enjoyed the trip more.
    (D) The water was not very rough.

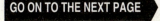

Part B

Directions: In this part of the test, you will hear longer conversations. After each conversation, you will hear several questions. The conversations and questions will not be repeated.

After you hear a question, read the four possible answers in your test book and choose the best answer. Then, on your answer sheet, find the number of the question and fill in the space that corresponds to the letter of the answer you have chosen.

Remember, you are **not** allowed to take notes or write in your test book.

31. (A) Two students.
    (B) Two professors.
    (C) Two sociologists.
    (D) Two lecturers.

32. (A) She wants his opinion of sociologists.
    (B) She wants to hear him lecture.
    (C) She wants to know about a course he took.
    (D) She wants to meet Professor Patterson.

33. (A) A course where the professor lectures.
    (B) A course where the students just listen and take notes.
    (C) A course with Professor Patterson.
    (D) A course where the students take part in discussion.

34. (A) She thinks it'll be boring.
    (B) She doesn't want to take it.
    (C) It sounds good to her.
    (D) She'd prefer a course with more student participation.

35. (A) From a friend.
    (B) From the newspaper.
    (C) From a discussion.
    (D) From the utility company.

36. (A) In a far desert.
    (B) Close by.
    (C) At the utility company's headquarters.
    (D) The man has no idea.

37. (A) It's cheaper in the short run.
    (B) The utility company won't need any extra money.
    (C) The plant's far away.
    (D) It exists in large quantities.

38. (A) She's concerned it'll be too costly.
    (B) She thinks the price is too low.
    (C) She thinks the plant is totally unnecessary.
    (D) She thinks the utility company has a good idea.

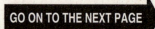
GO ON TO THE NEXT PAGE

Part C

Directions: In this part of the test, you will hear several talks. After each talk, you will hear some questions. The talks and questions will not be repeated.

After you hear a question, you will read the four possible answers in your test book and choose the best answer. Then, on your answer sheet, find the number of the question and fill in the space that corresponds to the letter of the answer you have chosen.

Here is an example.

On the recording, you will hear:

(narrator) *Listen to an instructor talk to his class about painting.*
(man) *Artist Grant Wood was a guiding force in the school of painting known as American regionalist, a style reflecting the distinctive characteristics of art from rural areas of the United States. Wood began drawing animals on the family farm at the age of three, and when he was thirty-eight one of his paintings received a remarkable amount of public notice and acclaim. This painting, called "American Gothic," is a starkly simple depiction of a serious couple staring directly out at the viewer.*

Now listen to a sample question.   **Sample Answer**

(narrator) *What style of painting is known as American regionalist?*

                                                      Ⓐ
     Ⓑ

In your test book, you will read: (A) Art from America's inner cities. Ⓒ
                                   (B) Art from the central region of the ●
                                         United States.
                                   (C) Art from various urban areas in the
                                         United States.
                                   (D) Art from rural sections of America.

The best answer to the question, "What style of painting is known as American regionalist?" is (D), "Art from rural sections of America." Therefore, the correct choice is (D).

Now listen to another sample question.   **Sample Answer**

(narrator) *What is the name of Wood's most successful painting?*

                                                        Ⓐ
     Ⓑ

In your test book, you will read: (A) "American Regionalist." ●
                                     (B) "The Family Farm in Iowa." Ⓓ
                                     (C) "American Gothic."
                                     (D) "A Serious Couple."

The best answer to the question, "What is the name of Wood's most successful painting?" is (C), "American Gothic." Therefore, the correct choice is (C).

Remember, you are **not** allowed to take notes or write in your test book.

39. (A) The Employment Office manager.
    (B) The university registrar.
    (C) The bookstore manager.
    (D) A student working in the bookstore.

40. (A) Prepare a schedule.
    (B) Decide which workers to hire.
    (C) Plan student course schedules.
    (D) Train office workers.

41. (A) What the students' majors are.
    (B) When the students are able to work.
    (C) Why the students want to work.
    (D) In which jobs the students have experience.

42. (A) Cashier.
    (B) Shelf stocker.
    (C) Business office worker.
    (D) Phone operator.

43. (A) Soft, warm clothing.
    (B) Problems in landfills.
    (C) How fleece is obtained.
    (D) Recycling soda bottles.

44. (A) They were left in landfill areas.
    (B) They were reused.
    (C) They were recycled.
    (D) They were refilled.

45. (A) Dye.
    (B) Warm, soft clothing.
    (C) Computer chips.
    (D) Glass bottles.

46. (A) Buying plastic bottles.
    (B) Solving the problems in landfills.
    (C) Buying these recycled products.
    (D) Becoming aware of the environment.

47. (A) The Central Pacific Group.
    (B) The Transcontinental Railroad Company.
    (C) A group from Ogden, Utah.
    (D) Two separate railroad companies.

48. (A) They had to lay tracks across a mountain range.
    (B) They had to cross all of Nebraska.
    (C) They had to work for another railroad company.
    (D) They had to move westward to Sacramento, California.

49. (A) Several days.
    (B) Several weeks.
    (C) Several months.
    (D) Several years.

50. (A) Dynamite was used to blast out access.
    (B) A golden spike was hammered into the last track.
    (C) The workers labored dangerously and exhaustingly.
    (D) The workers traversed the Sierra Nevadas.

This is the end of Section 1.
Stop work on Section 1.

Turn off the recording.

Read the directions for Section 2 and begin work.
Do NOT read or work on any other section
of the test during the next 25 minutes.

SECTION 2
STRUCTURE AND WRITTEN EXPRESSION
Time—25 minutes
(including the reading of the directions)
Now set your clock for 25 minutes.

This section is designed to measure your ability to recognize language that is appropriate for standard written English. There are two types of questions in this section, with special directions for each type.

Structure

Directions: These questions are incomplete sentences. Beneath each sentence you will see four words or phrases, marked (A), (B), (C), and (D). Choose the **one** word or phrase that best completes the sentence. Then, on your answer sheet, find the number of the question and fill in the space that corresponds to the letter of the answer you have chosen.

Look at the following examples.

Example I   **Sample Answer**

    The president _____ the election by a landslide.   ●
                                                     Ⓑ
    (A) won   Ⓒ
    (B) he won   Ⓓ
    (C) yesterday
    (D) fortunately

The sentence should read, "The president won the election by a landslide." Therefore, you should choose answer (A).

Example II   **Sample Answer**

    When _____ the conference?   Ⓐ
                                                    ●
    (A) the doctor attended   Ⓒ
    (B) did the doctor attend   Ⓓ
    (C) the doctor will attend
    (D) the doctor's attendance

The sentence should read, "When did the doctor attend the conference?" Therefore, you should choose answer (B).

GO ON TO THE NEXT PAGE

1. The hard palate _____ between the mouth and nasal passages.

   (A) forming a partition
   (B) a partition forms
   (C) forms a partition
   (D) a form and a partition

2. Sam Spade in *The Maltese Falcon* and Rick Blaine in *Casablanca* _____ of Humphrey Bogart's more famous roles.

   (A) they are two
   (B) two of them are
   (C) two of them
   (D) are two

3. _____, the outermost layer of skin, is about as thick as a sheet of paper over most of the skin.

   (A) It is the epidermis
   (B) The epidermis
   (C) In the epidermis
   (D) The epidermis is

4. During the Precambrian period, the Earth's crust formed, and life _____ in the seas.

   (A) first appeared
   (B) the first to appear
   (C) the first appearance
   (D) appearing first

5. When fluid accumulates against the eardrum, a second more insidious type of _____.

   (A) *otitis media* may develop
   (B) developing *otitis media*
   (C) the development of *otitis media*
   (D) to develop *otitis media*

6. Before the Statue of Liberty arrived in the United States, newspapers invited the public to help determine where _____ placed after its arrival.

   (A) should the statue be
   (B) the statue being
   (C) it should be the statue
   (D) the statue should be

7. A stock _____ at an inflated price is called a watered stock.

   (A) is issued
   (B) issued
   (C) it is issued
   (D) which issued

8. Acidic lava flows readily and tends to cover much larger areas, while basic lava _____.

   (A) viscous
   (B) more viscous
   (C) is more viscous
   (D) it is more viscous

9. Seismic reflection profiling has _____ the ocean floor is underlain by a thin layer of nearly transparent sediments.

   (A) reveal that
   (B) revealed that
   (C) the revelation of
   (D) revealed about

10. _____ and terrifying, coral snakes can grow to 4 feet (1.2 meters) in length.

    (A) They are extremely poisonous
    (B) The poison is extreme
    (C) Extremely poisonous
    (D) An extreme amount of poison

GO ON TO THE NEXT PAGE

11. The leaves of the white mulberry provide food for silkworms, _____ silk fabrics are woven.

(A) whose cocoons
(B) from cocoons
(C) whose cocoons are from
(D) from whose cocoons

12. As _____ in Greek and Roman mythology, harpies were frightful monsters that were half woman and half bird.

(A) described
(B) to describe
(C) description
(D) describing

13. Not only _____ generate energy, but it also produces fuel for other fission reactors.

(A) a nuclear breeder reactor
(B) it is a nuclear breeder reactor
(C) does a nuclear breeder reactor
(D) is a nuclear breeder reactor

14. D.W. Griffith pioneered many of the stylistic features and filmmaking techniques _____ as the Hollywood standard.

(A) that established
(B) that became established
(C) what established
(D) what became established

15. _____ be needed, the water basin would need to be dammed.

(A) Hydroelectric power should
(B) When hydroelectric power
(C) Hydroelectric power
(D) Should hydroelectric power

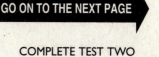
GO ON TO THE NEXT PAGE

Written Expression

Directions: In these questions, each sentence has four underlined words or phrases. The four underlined parts of the sentence are marked (A), (B), (C), and (D). Identify the **one** underlined word or phrase that must be changed in order for the sentence to be correct. Then, on your answer sheet, find the number of the question and fill in the space that corresponds to the letter of the answer you have chosen.

Look at the following examples.

Example I   **Sample Answer**

The four string on a violin are tuned
__A__   __B__   __C__ __D__

in fifths.

The sentence should read, "The four strings on a violin are tuned in fifths." Therefore, you should choose answer (B).

Example II   **Sample Answer**

The research for the book *Roots* taking
____A____   __B__   __C__

Alex Haley twelve years.
                __D__

The sentence should read, "The research for the book *Roots* took Alex Haley twelve years." Therefore, you should choose answer (C).

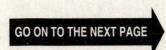

16. Mosquitoes will accepts the malaria parasite at only one stage of the parasite's
A   B   C

complex life cycle.
D

17. The counterpart of a negative electrons is the positive proton.
A   B   C   D

18. Alexander Hamilton's advocacy of a strong national government brought he into
A   B   C

bitter conflict with Thomas Jefferson.
D

19. There are more than eighty-four million specimens in the National Museum of
A   B

Natural History's collection of biological, geological, archeological, and
C

anthropology treasures.
D

20. After George Washington married widow Martha Custis, the couple comes to reside
A   B   C   D

at Mount Vernon.

21. Rubberized asphalt can hardly be classified as cutting edge at this stage in their
A   B   C   D

development.

22. Rhesus monkeys exhibit patterns of shyness similar to that in humans.
A   B   C   D

23. In space, with no gravity for muscles to work against, the body becomes weakly.
A   B   C   D

24. Fort Jefferson, in the Dry Tortugas off the southern tip of Florida, can be reach
A   B   C

only by boat or plane.
D

25. Quarter horses were developed in eighteenth-century Virginia to race on
A   B

courses short of about a quarter of a mile in length.
C   D

26. Supersonic flight is flight that is faster the speed of sound.
A   B   C   D

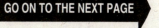
GO ON TO THE NEXT PAGE

27. Since the dawn of agriculture 9,000 years ago, only a few animal species had been
    <u>ago</u> <u>a</u> <u>few</u> <u>had been</u>
         A   B C   D

    domesticated.

28. The Betataken House Ruins at Navajo National Monument is among the largest and
                                                          <u>is</u> <u>largest</u>
                                                           A   B

    most elaborate cliff dwellings in the country.
        <u>elaborate</u>   <u>country</u>
            C   D

29. The island of Kauai has much streams, some of which have worn deep canyons into
                          <u>much</u>   <u>of which</u> <u>worn</u>
                           A   B   C

    the rock.
    <u>rock</u>
     D

30. It is a common observation that liquids will soak through some materials but not
       <u>a common</u>   <u>will soak</u>   <u>but not</u>
        A   B   C

    through other,
    <u>other</u>
     D

31. Surrounded by forested mountain slopes are the town of Telluride, a former
    <u>Surrounded</u>   <u>slopes are</u>   <u>former</u>
     A   B   C

    gold-mining town 7,500 feet above sea level.
                              <u>sea level</u>
                               D

32. The newsreels of Hearst Metronome News, which formed part of every moviegoer's
                                                            <u>every</u>
                                                             A

    experience in the era before television, offer an unique record of the events of the
                          <u>before television</u> <u>an</u>   <u>events</u>
                           B   C   D

    1930s.

33. Probably the best known of all dinosaurs, the *Tyrannosaurus* was larger and last of
    <u>Probably</u> <u>best known</u>   <u>larger</u> <u>last</u>
     A   B   C   D

    the meat-eating carnosaurs.

34. Unlikely gas sport balloons, hot air balloons do not have nets.
    <u>Unlikely</u> <u>sport</u>   <u>have</u> <u>nets</u>
     A   B   C   D

35. Born in Massachusetts in 1852, Albert Farbanks has begun making banjos in Boston
    <u>Born</u>   <u>has begun</u> <u>making</u>
     A   B   C

    in the late 1870s.
    <u>late</u>
     D

36. Methane in wetlands comes from soil bacteria that consumes organic plant matter.
                        <u>comes</u> <u>from</u>   <u>consumes</u>   <u>matter</u>
                         A   B   C   D

GO ON TO THE NEXT PAGE

37. Alois Alzheimer made the first <u>observers</u> of the <u>telltale</u> signs of the disease that today
                                     A   B

    <u>bears</u> <u>his name.</u>
     C   D

38. Edward McDowell <u>remembers</u> as the <u>composer</u> of such <u>perennial</u> <u>favorites</u> as "To a
                          A   B   C   D

    Wild Rose" and "To a Water Lily."

39. Animism is the <u>belief</u> that objects and natural <u>phenomena</u> such as rivers, rocks, and
                     A   B

    wind are <u>live</u> and have <u>feelings.</u>
           C   D

40. Newtonian physics <u>accounts</u> <u>from</u> the <u>observation</u> of the <u>orbits</u> of the planets and
                            A   B   C   D

    moons.

**This is the end of Section 2.
If you finish before 25 minutes has ended,
check your work on Section 2 only.**

**At the end of 25 minutes, go on to Section 3.
Use exactly 55 minutes to work on Section 3.**

SECTION 3
READING COMPREHENSION
Time—55 minutes
(including the reading of the directions)
Now set your clock for 55 minutes.

This section is designed to measure your ability to read and understand short passages similar in topic and style to those that students are likely to encounter in North American universities and colleges. This section contains reading passages and questions about the passages.

Directions: In this section you will read several passages. Each one is followed by a number of questions about it. You are to choose the **one** best answer, (A), (B), (C), or (D), to each question. Then, on your answer sheet, find the number of the question and fill in the space that corresponds to the letter of the answer you have chosen.

Answer all questions about the information in a passage on the basis of what is **stated** or **implied** in that passage.

Read the following passage:

> John Quincy Adams, who served as the sixth president of the United States from 1825 to 1829, is today recognized for his masterful statesmanship and diplomacy. He dedicated his life to public service, both in the presidency and in the various other political offices that he
> *Line* held. Throughout his political career he demonstrated his unswerving belief in freedom of
> (5) speech, the antislavery cause, and the right of Americans to be free from European and Asian domination.

Example I

To what did John Quincy Adams devote his life?

(A) Improving his personal life
(B) Serving the public
(C) Increasing his fortune
(D) Working on his private business

Sample Answer

According to the passage, John Quincy Adams "dedicated his life to public service." Therefore, you should choose answer (B).

Example II

In line 4, the word "unswerving" is closest in meaning to

(A) moveable
(B) insignificant
(C) unchanging
(D) diplomatic

Sample Answer

The passage states that John Quincy Adams demonstrated his unswerving belief "throughout his career." This implies that the belief did not change. Therefore, you should choose answer (C).

GO ON TO THE NEXT PAGE

Questions 1–10

Niagara Falls, one of the most famous North American natural wonders, has long been a popular tourist destination. Tourists today flock to see the two falls that actually constitute Niagara Falls: the 173-foot-high Horseshoe Falls on the Canadian side of the Niagara River in the Canadian

Line province of Ontario and the 182-foot-high American Falls on the U.S. side of the river in the state of
(5) New York. Approximately 85 percent of the water that goes over the falls actually goes over Horseshoe Falls, with the rest going over American Falls.

Most visitors come between April and October, and it is quite a popular activity to take a steamer out onto the river and right up to the base of the falls for a close-up view. It is also possible to get a spectacular view of the falls from the strategic locations along the Niagara River, such as
(10) Prospect Point or Table Rock, or from one of the four observation towers which have heights up to 500 feet.

Tourists have been visiting Niagara Falls in large numbers since the 1800s; annual visitation now averages above 10 million visitors per year. Because of concern that all these tourists would inadvertently destroy the natural beauty of this scenic wonder, the state of New York in 1885 created
(15) Niagara Falls Park in order to protect the land surrounding American Falls. A year later Canada created Queen Victoria Park on the Canadian side of the Niagara, around Horseshoe Falls. With the area surrounding the falls under the jurisdiction of government agencies, appropriate steps could be taken to preserve the pristine beauty of the area.

1. What is the major point that the author is making in this passage?

    (A) Niagara Falls can be viewed from either the American side or the Canadian side.
    (B) A trip to the United States isn't complete without a visit to Niagara Falls.
    (C) Niagara Falls has had an interesting history.
    (D) It has been necessary to protect Niagara Falls from the many tourists who go there.

2. The word "flock" in line 2 could best be replaced by

    (A) come by plane
    (B) come in large numbers
    (C) come out of boredom
    (D) come without knowing what they will see

3. According to the passage, which of the following best describes Niagara Falls?

    (A) Niagara Falls consists of two rivers, one Canadian and the other American.
    (B) American Falls is considerably higher than Horseshoe Falls.
    (C) The Niagara River has two falls, one in Canada and one in the United States.
    (D) Although the Niagara River flows through the United States and Canada, the falls are only in the United States.

4. A "steamer" in line 8 is probably

    (A) a bus
    (B) a boat
    (C) a walkway
    (D) a park

GO ON TO THE NEXT PAGE

5. The expression "right up" in line 8 could best be replaced by

   (A) turn to the right
   (B) follow correct procedures
   (C) travel upstream
   (D) all the way up

6. The passage implies that tourists prefer to

   (A) visit Niagara Falls during warmer weather
   (B) see the falls from a great distance
   (C) take a ride over the falls
   (D) come to Niagara Falls for a winter vacation

7. According to the passage, why was Niagara Park created?

   (A) To encourage tourists to visit Niagara Falls
   (B) To show off the natural beauty of Niagara Falls
   (C) To protect the area around Niagara Falls
   (D) To force Canada to open Queen Victoria Park

8. The word "jurisdiction" in line 17 is closest in meaning to

   (A) view
   (B) assistance
   (C) taxation
   (D) control

9. The word "pristine" in line 18 is closest in meaning to

   (A) pure and natural
   (B) highly developed
   (C) well-regulated
   (D) overused

10. The paragraph following the passage most probably discusses

   (A) additional ways to observe the falls
   (B) steps take by government agencies to protect the falls
   (C) a detailed description of the division of the falls between the United States and Canada
   (D) further problems that are destroying the area around the falls

GO ON TO THE NEXT PAGE

Questions 11–19

What is commonly called pepper in reality comes from two very different families of plants. Black and white pepper both come from the fruit of the *Piper nigrum,* a vine with fruits called peppercorns. The peppercorns turn from green to red as they ripen and finally blacken as they dry
Line
(5) out. The dried-out peppercorns are ground to obtain black pepper. White pepper, which has a more subtle flavor than black pepper, comes from the same peppercorns as black pepper; to obtain white pepper, the outer hull of the peppercorn, the pericarp, is removed before the peppercorn is ground.

Red and green peppers, on the other hand, come from a completely different family from black and white pepper. Red and green peppers are from the genus *Capsicum.* Plants of this type generally have tiny white flowers and fruit which can be any one of a number of colors, shapes, and sizes. These
(10) peppers range in flavor from very mild and sweet to the most incredibly burning taste imaginable. Bell peppers are the most mild, while habaneros are the most burning.

Christopher Columbus is responsible for the present-day confusion over what a pepper is. The *Piper nigrum* variety of pepper was highly valued for centuries, and high demand for pepper by Europeans was a major cause of the fifteenth-century push to locate ocean routes to the spice-
(15) growing regions of Asia. When Columbus arrived in the New World in 1492, he was particularly interested in finding black pepper because of the high price that it would command in Europe. Columbus came across plants from the *Capsicum* family in use among the people of the New World, and he incorrectly identified them as relatives of black pepper. Columbus introduced the spicy *Capsicum* chili peppers to Europeans on his return from the 1492 voyage, and traders later spread
(20) them to Asia and Africa. These *Capsicum* peppers have continued to be called peppers in spite of the fact that they are not related to the black and white pepper of the *Piper nigrum* family.

11. The purpose of this passage is to

    (A) explain why there is confusion today over peppers
    (B) provide the scientific classification of various types of peppers
    (C) demonstrate that it was Columbus who brought peppers to Europe
    (D) classify the variety of sizes, shapes, and colors of peppers

12. The word "turn" in line 3 could best be replaced by

    (A) revert
    (B) exchange
    (C) veer
    (D) change

13. According to the passage, both black and white peppers

    (A) come from different plants
    (B) change colors after they are ground
    (C) are ground from dried out peppercorns
    (D) have the same flavor

14. What part of the *Piper nigrum* is the pericarp?

    (A) The seed inside the fruit
    (B) The outer covering of the fruit
    (C) The pulp inside the vine
    (D) The outer covering of the vine

15. What usually does NOT vary in a *Capsicum* plant?

    (A) The color of the flower
    (B) The size of the fruit
    (C) The shape of the fruit
    (D) The color of the fruit

16. The word "push" in line 14 could best be replaced by

    (A) shove
    (B) strength
    (C) drive
    (D) hit

GO ON TO THE NEXT PAGE

17. The pronoun "them" in line 18 refers to

    (A) plants
    (B) people
    (C) relatives
    (D) Europeans

18. It can be inferred from the passage that chili peppers originally came from

    (A) Europe
    (B) Asia
    (C) America
    (D) Africa

19. Where in the passage does the author explain the mistake that Columbus made?

    (A) Lines 7–8
    (B) Line 12
    (C) Lines 15–16
    (D) Lines 17–18

GO ON TO THE NEXT PAGE →

Questions 20–31

Just two months after the flight of *Apollo 10*, the *Apollo 11* astronauts made their historic landing on the surface of the Moon. This momentous trip for humanity also provided scientists with an abundance of material for study; from rock and soil samples brought back from the Moon, *Line* scientists have been able to determine much about the composition of the Moon as well as to draw (5) inferences about the development of the Moon from its composition.

The Moon soil that came back on *Apollo 11* contains small bits of rock and glass which were probably ground from larger rocks when meteors impacted with the surface of the Moon. The bits of glass are spherical in shape and constitute approximately half of the Moon soil. Scientists found no trace of animal or plant life in this soil.

(10) In addition to the Moon soil, astronauts gathered two basic types of rocks from the surface of the Moon: basalt and breccia. Basalt is a cooled and hardened volcanic lava common to the Earth. Since basalt is formed under extremely high temperatures, the presence of this type of rock is an indication that the temperature of the Moon was once extremely hot. Breccia, the other kind of rock brought back by the astronauts, was formed during the impact of falling objects on the surface of the (15) Moon. This second type of rock consists of small pieces of rock compressed together by the force of impact. Gases such as hydrogen and helium were found in some of the rocks, and scientists believe that these gases were carried to the Moon by the solar wind, the streams of gases that are constantly emitted by the Sun.

20. The paragraph preceding the passage most likely discusses

   (A) astronaut training
   (B) the inception of the *Apollo* space program
   (C) a different space trip
   (D) previous Moon landings

21. What is the subject of this passage?

   (A) The *Apollo* astronauts
   (B) Soil on the Moon
   (C) What the Moon is made of
   (D) Basalt and breccia

22. An "abundance" in line 3 is

   (A) a disorderly pile
   (B) a wealthy bunch
   (C) an insignificant proportion
   (D) a large amount

23. According to the passage, what does Moon soil consist of?

   (A) Hydrogen and helium
   (B) Large chunks of volcanic lava
   (C) Tiny pieces of stones and glass
   (D) Streams of gases

24. The word "spherical" in line 8 is closest in meaning to

   (A) earthen
   (B) circular
   (C) angular
   (D) amorphous

25. Which of the following was NOT brought back to the Earth by the astronauts?

   (A) Basalt
   (B) Soil
   (C) Breccia
   (D) Plant life

26. An "indication" in line 13 is

   (A) an exhibition
   (B) a clue
   (C) a denial
   (D) a dictate

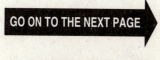

GO ON TO THE NEXT PAGE

27. According to the passage, breccia was formed

    (A) when objects struck the Moon
    (B) from volcanic lava
    (C) when streams of gases hit the surface of the Moon
    (D) from the interaction of helium and hydrogen

28. It is implied in the passage that scientists believe that the gases found in the Moon rocks

    (A) were not originally from the Moon
    (B) were created inside the rocks
    (C) traveled from the Moon to the Sun
    (D) caused the Moon's temperature to rise

29. The word "emitted" in line 18 is closest in meaning to

    (A) set off
    (B) vaporized
    (C) sent out
    (D) separated

30. The author's purpose in this passage is to

    (A) describe some rock and soil samples
    (B) explain some of the things learned from space flights
    (C) propose a new theory about the creation of the Moon
    (D) demonstrate the difference between basalt and breccia

31. It can be inferred from the passage that

    (A) the only items of importance that astronauts brought back from the Moon were rock and soil samples
    (B) scientists learned relatively little from the Moon rock and soil samples
    (C) scientists do not believe that it is necessary to return to the Moon
    (D) rock and soil samples were only some of a myriad of significant items from the Moon

GO ON TO THE NEXT PAGE

Questions 32–40

Today, the most universally known style of trousers for both men and women is jeans; these trousers are worn throughout the world on a variety of occasions and in diverse situations. Also called levis or denims, jeans have an interesting history, one that is intermixed with the derivations of the
Line words *jeans, denims,* and *levis.*
(5)   The word *jeans* is derived from the name of the place where a similar style of pants developed. In the sixteenth century, sailors from Genoa, Italy, wore a rather unique type of cotton trousers. In the French language, the word for the city of Genoa and for the people from that city is Genes; this name became attached to the specific style of pants worn by the sailors from this city and developed into the word *jeans* that today describes the descendents of the Genovese sailors' cotton pants.
(10)   Similar to the word *jeans,* the word *denim* is also derived from a place name. In the seventeenth century, French tailors began making trousers out of a specialized type of cloth that was developed in the city of Nimes, France, and was known as *serge de Nimes.* This name for the cloth underwent some transformations, and it eventually developed into today's *denim,* the material from which jeans are made and an alternate name for these popular pants.
(15)   The word *levis* came from the name of a person rather than a place. In the nineteenth century, immigrant Levi Strauss came to America and tried his hand at selling heavy canvas to miners taking part in the hunt for gold in northern California. Strauss intended for this canvas to be used by miners to make heavy-duty tents. This first endeavor was a failure, but Strauss later found success when he used the heavy canvas to make indestructible pants for the miners. Levi then switched the fabric from
(20)   brown canvas to blue denim, creating a style of pants that long outlived him and today is referred to by his name. A modern-day urban shopper out to buy some levis is searching for a close relative of the product that Strauss had developed years earlier.

32. This passage is developed by

   (A) citing an effect and its causes
   (B) explaining history with three specific cases
   (C) demonstrating the sides of an issue
   (D) developing the biography of a famous person chronologically

33. The word "unique" in line 6 is closest in meaning to

   (A) universal
   (B) solitary
   (C) unusual
   (D) commonplace

34. All of the following are mentioned in the passage about Genoa EXCEPT that it

   (A) was the source of the word *jeans*
   (B) is in Italy
   (C) has a different name in the French language
   (D) is a landlocked city

35. The word "descendents" in line 9 could best be replaced by

   (A) offspring
   (B) bottoms
   (C) antecedents
   (D) derivations

36. The word *denim* was most probably derived from

   (A) two French words
   (B) two Italian words
   (C) one French word and one Italian word
   (D) three French words

37. The pronoun "it" in line 13 refers to

   (A) city
   (B) name
   (C) cloth
   (D) material

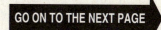
GO ON TO THE NEXT PAGE

38. The word "switched" in line 19 is closest in meaning to

(A) reduced
(B) created
(C) pounded
(D) changed

39. It can be inferred from the passage that, in order to develop the pants for which he became famous, Strauss did which of the following?

(A) He studied tailoring in Nimes.
(B) He used an existing type of material.
(C) He experimented with brown denim.
(D) He tested the pants for destructability.

40. Where in the passage does the author explain how Strauss' first attempt at creating a business with canvas turned out?

(A) Lines 12–14
(B) Lines 15–17
(C) Lines 18–19
(D) Lines 21–22

GO ON TO THE NEXT PAGE

Questions 41–50

During the heyday of the railroads, when America's rail system provided the bulk of the country's passenger and freight transportation, various types of railroad cars were in service to accomplish the varied tasks handled by the railroads. One type of car that was not available for public
Line use prior to the Civil War, however, was a sleeping car; ideas for sleeping cars abounded at the time,
(5) but these ideas were unworkable. It unfortunately took the death of a president to make the sleeping car a viable reality.

Cabinet-maker George M. Pullman had recognized the demand for sleeping cars and had worked on developing experimental models of sleeping cars in the decade leading up to the Civil War. However, in spite of the fact that he had made successful test runs on the Chicago and Alton Railroads
(10) with his models, he was unable to sell his idea because his models were too wide and too high for existing train stations and bridges. In 1863, after spending time working as a storekeeper in a Colorado mining town, he invested his savings of twenty thousand dollars, a huge fortune at that time and all the money that he had in the world, in a luxurious sleeping car that he named the Pioneer. Pullman and friend Ben Field built the Pioneer on the site of the present-day Chicago Union Station.
(15) For two years, however, the Pioneer sat on a railroad siding, useless because it could not fit through train stations and over bridges.

Following President Lincoln's assassination in 1865, the state of Illinois, Lincoln's birthplace, wanted to transport the presidential casket in the finest fashion possible. The Pullman Pioneer was the most elegant car around; in order to make the Pullman part of the presidential funeral train in its
(20) run from Springfield to Chicago, the state cut down station platforms and raised bridges in order to accommodate the luxurious railway car. The Pullman car greatly impressed the funeral party, which included Lincoln's successor as president, General Ulysses S. Grant, and Grant later requested the Pioneer for a trip from Detroit to Chicago. To satisfy Grant's request for the Pioneer, the Michigan Central Railroad made improvements on its line to accommodate the wide car, and soon other
(25) railroads followed. George Pullman founded the Pullman Palace Car Company in partnership with financier Andrew Carnegie and eventually became a millionaire.

41. Which of the following best states the main idea of the passage?

(A) America's railroads used to provide much of the country's transportation.
(B) President Lincoln's assassination in 1865 shocked the nation.
(C) George Pullman was the only one to come up with the idea for a sleeping car.
(D) Pullman's idea for a sleeping car became workable after Lincoln's death.

42. A "heyday" in line 1 is most probably a

(A) time for harvest
(B) a period with low prices
(C) a period of great success
(D) a type of railroad schedule

43. It can be inferred from the passage that before the Civil War, sleeping cars

(A) were used abundantly
(B) were thought to be a good idea
(C) were only used privately
(D) were used by presidents

44. The word "test" in line 9 could best be replaced by which of the following?

(A) Exam
(B) Trial
(C) Inspection
(D) Scientific

45. What was the initial problem that made Pullman's cars unusable?

(A) They were too large.
(B) They were too expensive.
(C) They were too slow.
(D) They were too unusual.

GO ON TO THE NEXT PAGE

46. What is stated in the passage about George Pullman?

    (A) He once had a job in a store.
    (B) He always lived in Chicago.
    (C) He worked in a mine.
    (D) He saved money for his project.

47. The word "site" in line 14 is closest in meaning to which of the following?

    (A) Factory
    (B) View
    (C) Location
    (D) Foundation

48. Why did the state of Illinois want to use the Pullman in Lincoln's funeral train?

    (A) It was superior to other cars.
    (B) It was the only railroad car that could make it from Springfield to Chicago.
    (C) Ulysses S. Grant requested it.
    (D) The Pullman Palace Car Company was a major Illinois business.

49. It can be inferred from the passage that the Michigan Central Railroad

    (A) was owned by George Pullman
    (B) controlled the railroad tracks between Detroit and Chicago
    (C) was the only railroad company to accommodate wide cars
    (D) was the sole manufacturer of the Pioneer

50. This passage would most likely be assigned in which of the following courses?

    (A) Engineering
    (B) Political science
    (C) Finance
    (D) History

This is the end of Section 3.

**If you finish in less than 55 minutes,
check your work on Section 3 only.
Do NOT read or work on any other section of the test.**

When you finish the test, you may do the following:

- Turn to the **Diagnostic Charts** on pages 551–558, and circle the numbers of the questions that you missed.

- Turn to **Scoring Information** on pages 549–550, and determine your TOEFL score.

- Turn to the **Progress Chart** on page 559, and add your score to the chart.

TEST OF WRITTEN ENGLISH:
TWE ESSAY TOPIC
Time—30 minutes

What are the most important characteristics in a teacher? Use specific details and examples to support your opinion.

1 □ 1 □ 1 □ 1 □ 1 □ 1 □ 1 □ 1

COMPLETE TEST THREE

SECTION 1
LISTENING COMPREHENSION
Time—approximately 35 minutes
(including the reading of the directions for each part)

In this section of the test, you will have an opportunity to demonstrate your ability to understand conversations and talks in English. There are three parts to this section, with special directions for each part. Answer all the questions on the basis of what is **stated** or **implied** by the speakers you hear. Do **not** take notes or write in your test book at any time. Do **not** turn the pages until you are told to do so.

Part A

Directions: In Part A you will hear short conversations between two people. After each conversation, you will hear a question about the conversation. The conversations and questions will not be repeated. After you hear a question, read the four possible answers in your test book and choose the best answer. Then, on your answer sheet, find the number of the question and fill in the space that corresponds to the letter of the answer you have chosen.

Listen to an example.   **Sample Answer**

On the recording, you will hear:

(man)   *That exam was just awful.*
(woman)   *Oh, it could have been worse.*
(narrator) *What does the woman mean?*

In your test book, you will read: (A) The exam was really awful.
                                         (B) It was the worst exam she had ever seen.
                                         (C) It couldn't have been more difficult.
                                         (D) It wasn't that hard.

You learn from the conversation that the man thought the exam was very difficult and that the woman disagreed with the man. The best answer to the question, "What does the woman mean?" is (D), "It wasn't that hard." Therefore, the correct choice is (D).

1. (A) He finished the problem at last.
   (B) He hardly worked on the math.
   (C) It was hard for him to assign the math.
   (D) The problem was very difficult.

2. (A) He didn't fail by much.
   (B) He completely failed the exam.
   (C) He had a really high grade.
   (D) His grade was low but passing.

3. (A) The laundry is getting done.
   (B) They are close to the cleaners.
   (C) The woman should close the machine.
   (D) He is watching someone clear the machine.

4. (A) Leaving on Tuesday.
   (B) Cutting their visit short.
   (C) Changing the day of their departure.
   (D) Postponing their visit to a later date.

5. (A) The landlord has raised the rent.
   (B) The landlord has received a letter with some bad news.
   (C) The landlord will not increase the rent.
   (D) The landlord will not rent them an apartment.

6. (A) He is always underappreciated.
   (B) She is thankful for what he did.
   (C) He has made no apparent effort.
   (D) She feels little appreciation for his efforts.

7. (A) Getting dressed.
   (B) Making salad.
   (C) Shopping for groceries.
   (D) Washing clothes.

8. (A) She convinced Jack to go.
   (B) She will not be able to go to the restaurant.
   (C) Jack has convinced her to go to a restaurant.
   (D) Jack is not going.

9. (A) Descend the stairs and go in the second door.
   (B) Step around the building and enter through the first door.
   (C) Go through the first door and go down the steps.
   (D) Go down the hall and enter the doorway.

10. (A) She can see him very clearly.
    (B) He speaks loudly.
    (C) He's very soft-spoken.
    (D) She didn't speak to him.

11. (A) She would like the man to repeat himself.
    (B) The last exam was not very hard.
    (C) She agrees with the man about the exam.
    (D) The man has repeated himself several times.

12. (A) It has probably not been arranged.
    (B) It is ready for the conference.
    (C) It needs a set of chairs.
    (D) It needs to be emptied.

13. (A) She'll be able to stay up until the last moment.
    (B) She's been running for some time.
    (C) She's not sure when the last exam is.
    (D) She's really exhausted.

14. (A) He fascinated the guests.
    (B) The speaker's ideas intrigued him.
    (C) Giving speeches is fascinating.
    (D) He was a guest of the speaker.

15. (A) It is quite humid this week.
    (B) The humidity will last through the week.
    (C) It is drier now.
    (D) It was better just last week.

16. (A) She was extremely understanding.
    (B) She couldn't understand the explanation.
    (C) She did not understand the problem.
    (D) She missed class due to illness.

GO ON TO THE NEXT PAGE ➤

17. (A) She didn't see all of the show.
    (B) The show was unbelievable.
    (C) She doesn't believe that the show really happened.
    (D) The skydivers were pulled off their feet.

18. (A) They were unable to pay the bill.
    (B) The prices were surprisingly low.
    (C) The restaurant was too expensive for them to try.
    (D) They almost didn't have enough to pay for the meal.

19. (A) He has to take microbiology.
    (B) He wishes he could take microbiology this semester.
    (C) He is not enrolling in microbiology this semester.
    (D) He had hoped to take microbiology this semester.

20. (A) That she would take the course.
    (B) That the first lecture would not be tomorrow.
    (C) That he would not be in the course.
    (D) That she would not register.

21. (A) Construction workers.
    (B) Architects.
    (C) Insurance agents.
    (D) Artists.

22. (A) The runner did not fall.
    (B) The team won.
    (C) The loss was the runner's fault.
    (D) The team won't ever win a game.

23. (A) Starting on their exam preparation.
    (B) Leaving for the exam.
    (C) Going home to study.
    (D) Going to her job.

24. (A) She's not a very good manager.
    (B) He'll be able to work reasonably well with her.
    (C) He's unhappy that there is a class project.
    (D) He's happy that she's not part of the group.

25. (A) He was not surprised by the change.
    (B) He didn't expect the change.
    (C) The requirements have not changed.
    (D) He expects to change his major.

26. (A) The bridge is too hard to cross.
    (B) They must pay rent for the bridge.
    (C) They must cross a bridge to get to the house.
    (D) They can decide later.

27. (A) The trip was less than perfect.
    (B) There was nothing at all wrong with the trip.
    (C) There wasn't any way that she could take the trip.
    (D) The trip could have been improved in a number of ways.

28. (A) It received more attention on the exam than it did in the lectures.
    (B) It was a major part of all of the lectures.
    (C) It was not on the exam at all.
    (D) It received more attention in the lectures than it had on the exam.

29. (A) The professor made an early announcement about the exam.
    (B) The professor failed to announce the exam.
    (C) The professor announced the exam too soon.
    (D) The professor did not give enough notice for the exam.

30. (A) That he would remember her birthday.
    (B) That he would bring her a gift.
    (C) That he had forgotten her birthday.
    (D) That he would get her something she didn't like.

GO ON TO THE NEXT PAGE

Part B

Directions: In this part of the test, you will hear longer conversations. After each conversation, you will hear several questions. The conversations and questions will not be repeated.

After you hear a question, read the four possible answers in your test book and choose the best answer. Then, on your answer sheet, find the number of the question and fill in the space that corresponds to the letter of the answer you have chosen.

Remember, you are **not** allowed to take notes or write in your test book.

31. (A) To write his paper.
    (B) To help him decide on a topic.
    (C) To teach him about history.
    (D) To discuss history with him.

32. (A) At the beginning of the semester.
    (B) Before the start of the semester.
    (C) Near the end of the semester.
    (D) One week after the semester is finished.

33. (A) The topic's too general.
    (B) He isn't interested in technology.
    (C) He doesn't have enough time.
    (D) Technology has nothing to do with American history.

34. (A) A month.
    (B) The semester.
    (C) Seven days.
    (D) A day or two.

35. (A) Fire damage to some apartments.
    (B) How to prevent fires.
    (C) An apartment fire and what one can learn from it.
    (D) An early morning news story.

36. (A) One was damaged more severely than the others.
    (B) All the apartments were completely destroyed.
    (C) There was one thousand dollars of damage.
    (D) All twenty apartments suffered some damage.

37. (A) They were killed.
    (B) They were taken to the hospital.
    (C) The damage to the apartments was more serious than the harm to the residents.
    (D) They weren't frightened.

38. (A) Call the fire department.
    (B) Rush to the hospital.
    (C) Listen for a smoke alarm.
    (D) Have an alarm and extinguisher in good condition.

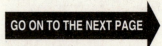

GO ON TO THE NEXT PAGE

1 □ 1 □ 1 □ 1 □ 1 □ 1 □ 1 □ 1

Part C

Directions: In this part of the test, you will hear several talks. After each talk, you will hear some questions. The talks and questions will not be repeated.

After you hear a question, you will read the four possible answers in your test book and choose the best answer. Then, on your answer sheet, find the number of the question and fill in the space that corresponds to the letter of the answer you have chosen.

Here is an example.

On the recording, you will hear:

(narrator) *Listen to an instructor talk to his class about painting.*
(man) *Artist Grant Wood was a guiding force in the school of painting known as American regionalist, a style reflecting the distinctive characteristics of art from rural areas of the United States. Wood began drawing animals on the family farm at the age of three, and when he was thirty-eight one of his paintings received a remarkable amount of public notice and acclaim. This painting, called "American Gothic," is a starkly simple depiction of a serious couple staring directly out at the viewer.*

Now listen to a sample question.

Sample Answer

(narrator) *What style of painting is known as American regionalist?*

In your test book, you will read: (A) Art from America's inner cities.
(B) Art from the central region of the United States.
(C) Art from various urban areas in the United States.
(D) Art from rural sections of America.

The best answer to the question, "What style of painting is known as American regionalist?" is (D), "Art from rural sections of America." Therefore, the correct choice is (D).

Now listen to another sample question.

Sample Answer

Ⓐ
Ⓑ
●
Ⓓ

(narrator) *What is the name of Wood's most successful painting?*

In your test book, you will read: (A) "American Regionalist."
(B) "The Family Farm in Iowa."
(C) "American Gothic."
(D) "A Serious Couple."

The best answer to the question, "What is the name of Wood's most successful painting?" is (C), "American Gothic." Therefore, the correct choice is (C).

Remember, you are **not** allowed to take notes or write in your test book.

39. (A) A professional dancer.
    (B) A student in the dance department.
    (C) The head of the dance department.
    (D) A choreographer.

40. (A) Which dance degree to take.
    (B) Whether or not to major in dance.
    (C) Whether to be a professional dancer
        or choreographer.
    (D) Whether to specialize in dance
        therapy or dance history.

41. (A) Physical therapy.
    (B) Dance history.
    (C) Choreography.
    (D) Dance administration.

42. (A) They are both intended for
        professional dancers.
    (B) They involve mostly the same courses.
    (C) They do not need to be selected until
        later.
    (D) They are both four-year programs.

43. (A) A Cajun.
    (B) A tourist.
    (C) An Acadian.
    (D) A tour guide.

44. (A) They went to Acadia in the eighteenth
        century.
    (B) They came from France in the
        eighteenth century.
    (C) They maintained characteristics of
        their old culture.
    (D) They assimilated completely into the
        new culture.

45. (A) Very spicy.
    (B) Full of sugar.
    (C) Salty.
    (D) Full of tobacco.

46. (A) An Acadian will give a talk.
    (B) The bus ride will continue.
    (C) They will stop in Lafayette.
    (D) They will see the exhibition at
        Acadian Village.

47. (A) The purpose of the FCC.
    (B) The relatively rapid development of
        radio.
    (C) Interference from competing radio
        stations.
    (D) The first U.S. radio station.

48. (A) Introduction to Engineering.
    (B) Popular Radio Programs.
    (C) Ethics in Journalism.
    (D) The History of Communication.

49. (A) The many radio stations were highly
        regulated.
    (B) In 1930 there was only one radio
        station in the United States.
    (C) The existing radio stations were
        totally uncontrolled.
    (D) The FCC was unable to control the
        radio stations.

50. (A) First Communications Committee.
    (B) First Control Committee.
    (C) Federal Control of Communications.
    (D) Federal Communications
        Commission.

**This is the end of Section 1.
Stop work on Section 1.**

Turn off the recording.

**Read the directions for Section 2 and begin work.
Do NOT read or work on any other section
of the test during the next 25 minutes.**

2 • 2 • 2 • 2 • 2 • 2 • 2 • 2

SECTION 2
STRUCTURE AND WRITTEN EXPRESSION
Time—25 minutes
(including the reading of the directions)
Now set your clock for 25 minutes.

This section is designed to measure your ability to recognize language that is appropriate for standard written English. There are two types of questions in this section, with special directions for each type.

Structure

Directions: These questions are incomplete sentences. Beneath each sentence you will see four words or phrases, marked (A), (B), (C), and (D). Choose the **one** word or phrase that best completes the sentence. Then, on your answer sheet, find the number of the question and fill in the space that corresponds to the letter of the answer you have chosen.

Look at the following examples.

Example I   **Sample Answer**

The president _____ the election by a landslide.

(A) won
(B) he won
(C) yesterday
(D) fortunately

The sentence should read, "The president won the election by a landslide." Therefore, you should choose answer (A).

Example II   **Sample Answer**

When _____ the conference?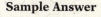

(A) the doctor attended
(B) did the doctor attend
(C) the doctor will attend
(D) the doctor's attendance

The sentence should read, "When did the doctor attend the conference?" Therefore, you should choose answer (B).

GO ON TO THE NEXT PAGE

1. In the late 1880s, Hull House _____ United States' first welfare state.

   (A) to become the
   (B) became the
   (C) becoming one of the
   (D) it became the

2. _____ with the largest alphabet is Cambodian, with 74 letters.

   (A) In the language
   (B) The language is
   (C) The language
   (D) About the language

3. _____ given to the various types of microscopic plants and animals found in water.

   (A) Named plankton
   (B) The name of plankton
   (C) Plankton's name
   (D) Plankton is the name

4. Charles Babbage (1792–1871) drew up the first plans for a programmable digital computer in 1834, but _____ was never completed.

   (A) his invention
   (B) he invented
   (C) to invent him
   (D) for him to invent

5. _____, one of the oldest forms of written communication, was used as early as 3000 B.C.

   (A) Cuneiform writing
   (B) In cuneiform writing
   (C) Cuneiform writing was
   (D) When cuneiform writing

6. As a protection device, an octopus ejects black or purple ink to cloud the water when _____.

   (A) does it escape
   (B) its escape
   (C) it escapes
   (D) escapes it

7. _____ manipulate with their feet as well as with their hands, it is difficult for them to stand upright.

   (A) Apes can, however,
   (B) Apes are able to
   (C) Despite the ability of apes
   (D) Although apes can

8. Approximately 500 varieties of insectivorous plants, which trap animals for their sustenance, _____ in the world.

   (A) and their existence
   (B) exist
   (C) they exist
   (D) that exist

9. Ozone is formed when ultraviolet radiation from the Sun _____ molecules into highly reactive oxygen atoms.

   (A) oxygen breaks up
   (B) oxygen is broken up
   (C) breaks up oxygen
   (D) to break up oxygen

10. The surrealistic movement in art in the 1920s and 1930s placed _____ is pictured in the unconscious and often incorporated dreamlike images.

    (A) to emphasize it
    (B) an emphasis on it
    (C) emphasize what
    (D) an emphasis on what

GO ON TO THE NEXT PAGE

11. Today used to measure the weight of gem-stones or the amount of gold per 24 parts of pure gold, _____ originally the weight of a seed of the carob tree.

    (A) was a carat
    (B) a carat was
    (C) which was a carat
    (D) that a carat was

12. The film *Lawrence of Arabia* is three hours and forty-one minutes long, one minute _____ *Gone with the Wind*.

    (A) in length like
    (B) long is
    (C) is longer than
    (D) longer than is

13. The genus *Equus* became extinct in North America during the glacial period, and it was not reintroduced until _____ by the Spaniards.

    (A) brought there
    (B) was brought there
    (C) bringing it there
    (D) it brought there

14. In _____ several vertically aligned honeycombs with hexagonal wax cells stacked close together.

    (A) a honeybee hive is
    (B) a honeybee hive are
    (C) a honeybee hive of
    (D) a honeybee hive composed of

15. The shapes of snow crystals depend largely _____ temperature and humidity are.

    (A) how high its
    (B) on the height of the
    (C) on how high the
    (D) that the height of the

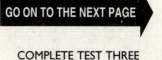
GO ON TO THE NEXT PAGE

Written Expression

Directions: In these questions, each sentence has four underlined words or phrases. The four underlined parts of the sentence are marked (A), (B), (C), and (D). Identify the **one** underlined word or phrase that must be changed in order for the sentence to be correct. Then, on your answer sheet, find the number of the question and fill in the space that corresponds to the letter of the answer you have chosen.

Look at the following examples.

Example I

The four string on a violin are tuned
  A   B   C   D

in fifths.

Sample Answer

Ⓐ
●
Ⓒ
Ⓓ

The sentence should read, "The four strings on a violin are tuned in fifths." Therefore, you should choose answer (B).

Example II

The research for the book *Roots* taking
      A   B   C

Alex Haley twelve years.
            D

Sample Answer

Ⓐ
Ⓑ
●
Ⓓ

The sentence should read, "The research for the book *Roots* took Alex Haley twelve years." Therefore, you should choose answer (C).

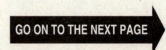

GO ON TO THE NEXT PAGE

16. The price of silver rose to $50.05 per troy ounce in January 1980 and then fell to
    <u>   </u>A   B   <u>   </u>C
    $10.80 two <u>month</u> later.
                   D

17. Most polar seals <u>retreat</u> to open water during the winter, but <u>a few</u> types have <u>learn</u>
                         A   B   C
    to survive on and under the ice all year <u>round</u>.
                                                 D

18. <u>More than</u> half of all stars <u>is</u> in <u>binary</u> or <u>multiple-star</u> systems.
        A   B   C   D

19. The harpsichord is the <u>most complex</u> and <u>most large</u> of all the <u>plucked</u> keyboard
                           A   B   C   D
    instruments.

20. <u>United States</u> <u>forces</u> won the city of Los Angeles in 1847 <u>during</u> the Mexican War and
        A   B   C
    <u>gain</u> all of California in the same year.
     D

21. <u>During</u> fermentation, complex carbohydrates <u>are converted</u> to <u>another</u> chemicals by
      A   B   C
    the action of enzymes <u>produced by</u> molds, yeasts, or bacteria.
                              D

22. The surface of Mars is very <u>complex</u> and <u>consists</u> of a mixture of <u>flat</u> deserts, craters,
                                   A   B   C
    volcanoes, and <u>mountainous</u>.
                        D

23. Hardwood <u>comes from</u> broad-leaved <u>deciduous</u> trees, <u>those that</u> lose <u>theirs</u> leaves in
                 A   B   C   D
    winter.

24. The Washington <u>quarter</u> was <u>first</u> <u>minting</u> by the U.S. government in 1932 on the
                       A   B   C
    200th <u>anniversary</u> of George Washington's birth.
              D

25. W. Somerset Maugham's <u>best-known</u> novel, *Of Human Bondage,* is a <u>partially</u>
                              A   B
    fictionalized account of <u>a</u> unhappy <u>youth</u>.
                              C   D

GO ON TO THE NEXT PAGE ▶

26. The Congressional Medal of Honor, instituted at the <u>height</u> of the Civil War, is today
    $\overset{}{\underset{A}{}}$

    <u>a</u> highest <u>decoration</u> for <u>gallantry</u> in the United States.
    B   C   D

27. High blood pressure <u>results from</u> either an <u>increased</u> output of blood from the heart
                         A   B

    and an increased resistance to its <u>flow</u> through tiny branches of the arteries.
    C   D

28. When the U.S. <u>government's</u> library was <u>burned by</u> the British in 1814, <u>former</u>
                   A   B   C

    President Thomas Jefferson donated 6,487 of <u>their</u> own books to start the present-
                                                D

    day Library of Congress.

29. James A. Garfield <u>has become</u> the <u>twentieth</u> president of the United States in 1881
                       A   B

    and was <u>assassinated</u> <u>later in that</u> year.
            C   D

30. Mambas, <u>poisonous</u> African snakes that <u>come from</u> the same family <u>as</u> cobras,
            A   B   C

    possess an <u>extreme</u> potent venom.
               D

31. Not until <u>the discovery</u> of Pluto's moon Charon <u>was</u> many of the <u>characteristics</u> of
              A   B   C

    the planet Pluto <u>evident</u>.
                     D

32. Scorpions, which are <u>normally</u> <u>lone</u>, have developed a cautious mating ritual
                         A   B

    because they are <u>not immune</u> to <u>their</u> own poison.
                     C   D

33. The diameter of the Sun is <u>more than</u> one hundred <u>times</u> <u>greater</u> than <u>the</u> Earth.
                               A   B   C   D

34. In the <u>mid-18th</u> century, American, Russian, and Canadian hunters <u>on the</u> Pacific
           A   B

    coast of North America <u>annihilated</u> almost the sea otter in order <u>to collect</u> the pelts.
                           C   D

35. Pat Garrett, who <u>shot and killed</u> Billy the Kid on July 14, 1881, <u>later</u> <u>did</u> his living
                     A   B   C

    <u>as</u> a Texas Ranger.
    D

GO ON TO THE NEXT PAGE →

36. Paul Revere was the son of a French <u>immigration</u> named Apollos Rivoire, who <u>later</u>
$\qquad\qquad\qquad\qquad\qquad\qquad$ A $\qquad\qquad\qquad\qquad\qquad\qquad\qquad$ B

began calling <u>himself</u> Revere to make his name <u>easier</u> for Americans to pronounce.
$\qquad\qquad\qquad$ C $\qquad\qquad\qquad\qquad\qquad\qquad$ D

37. <u>Safety glass</u>, a <u>toughened</u> glass sheet, is six <u>times stronger</u> than <u>untreating</u> glass.
$\quad$ A $\qquad\qquad$ B $\qquad\qquad\qquad\qquad\qquad$ C $\qquad\qquad$ D

38. The foxglove is <u>source</u> of the drug digitalis, <u>which</u> is <u>used</u> to treat <u>heart disease</u>.
$\qquad\qquad\qquad$ A $\qquad\qquad\qquad\qquad$ B $\quad$ C $\qquad\qquad$ D

39. Related <u>fungus</u> from a family of yeasts <u>called</u> ascomycetes cause <u>bread</u> to rise, create
$\qquad\qquad$ A $\qquad\qquad\qquad\qquad\qquad$ B $\qquad\qquad\qquad$ C

the veins in blue cheese, and <u>produce</u> penicillin.
$\qquad\qquad\qquad\qquad\qquad\qquad$ D

40. <u>Rival</u> leaders <u>during</u> the American Civil War, Abraham Lincoln and Jefferson Davis
$\quad$ A $\qquad\qquad$ B

<u>both</u> <u>hailed</u> Kentucky.
$\quad$ C $\quad$ D

This is the end of Section 2.
If you finish before 25 minutes has ended,
check your work on Section 2 only.

At the end of 25 minutes, go on to Section 3.
Use exactly 55 minutes to work on Section 3.

SECTION 3
READING COMPREHENSION
Time—55 minutes
(including the reading of the directions)
Now set your clock for 55 minutes.

This section is designed to measure your ability to read and understand short passages similar in topic and style to those that students are likely to encounter in North American universities and colleges. This section contains reading passages and questions about the passages.

Directions: In this section you will read several passages. Each one is followed by a number of questions about it. You are to choose the **one** best answer, (A), (B), (C), or (D), to each question. Then, on your answer sheet, find the number of the question and fill in the space that corresponds to the letter of the answer you have chosen.

Answer all questions about the information in a passage on the basis of what is **stated** or **implied** in that passage.

Read the following passage:

> John Quincy Adams, who served as the sixth president of the United States from 1825 to 1829, is today recognized for his masterful statesmanship and diplomacy. He dedicated his life to public service, both in the presidency and in the various other political offices that he
> *Line* held. Throughout his political career he demonstrated his unswerving belief in freedom of
> (5) speech, the antislavery cause, and the right of Americans to be free from European and Asian domination.

Example I   **Sample Answer**

To what did John Quincy Adams devote his life?   Ⓐ
                                                                  ●
(A) Improving his personal life   Ⓒ
(B) Serving the public   Ⓓ
(C) Increasing his fortune
(D) Working on his private business

According to the passage, John Quincy Adams "dedicated his life to public service." Therefore, you should choose answer (B).

Example II   **Sample Answer**

In line 4, the word "unswerving" is closest in meaning to   Ⓐ
                                                                   Ⓑ
(A) moveable   ●
(B) insignificant   Ⓓ
(C) unchanging
(D) diplomatic

The passage states that John Quincy Adams demonstrated his unswerving belief "throughout his career." This implies that the belief did not change. Therefore, you should choose answer (C).

GO ON TO THE NEXT PAGE

Questions 1–10

The final battle of the War of 1812 was the Battle of New Orleans. This battle gave a clear demonstration of the need for effective communication during wartime; it also showed the disastrous results that can come to pass when communication is inadequate.

Line
(5) The War of 1812 was fought between Great Britain and the very young country of the United States only a relatively few years after the United States had won its independence from Britain. The United States had declared war against Britain in June of 1812, mostly because of interference with U.S. shipping by the British and because of the shanghaiing of U.S. sailors for enforced service on British vessels. The war lasted for a little more than two years, when a peace treaty was signed at Ghent, in Belgium, on the 24th of December, 1814.

(10) Unfortunately, the news that the Treaty of Ghent had been signed and that the war was officially over was not communicated in a timely manner over the wide distance to where the war was being contested. Negotiations for the treaty and the actual signing of the treaty took place in Europe, and news of the treaty had to be carried across the Atlantic to the war front by ship. A totally unnecessary loss of life was incurred as a result of the amount of time that it took to inform the combatants of the
(15) treaty.

Early in January of 1815, some two weeks after the peace treaty had been signed, British troops in the southern part of the United States were unaware that the war had officially ended. Over 5,000 British troops attacked U.S. troops. During the ensuing battle, known as the Battle of New Orleans, the British suffered a huge number of casualties, around 2,000, and the Americans lost 71, all in a
(20) battle fought only because news of the peace treaty that had already been signed in Ghent had not yet reached the battlefield.

1. The main idea of this passage is that

   (A) the War of Independence was unnecessary
   (B) the War of 1812 was unnecessary
   (C) the Treaty of Ghent was unnecessary
   (D) the Battle of New Orleans was unnecessary

2. The pronoun "it" in line 2 refers to

   (A) battle
   (B) demonstration
   (C) communication
   (D) wartime

3. The expression "come to pass" in line 3 could best be replaced by

   (A) happen
   (B) overthrow
   (C) self-destruct
   (D) circumvent

4. According to the passage, when did the United States win its independence from Britain?

   (A) Shortly before the War of 1812
   (B) During the War of 1812
   (C) Just after the War of 1812
   (D) Long after the War of 1812

5. According to the passage, some U.S. sailors were

   (A) taken forcibly to Shanghai
   (B) made to go to Ghent
   (C) forced to work on British ships
   (D) responsible for causing the War of 1812

6. It is NOT stated in the passage that Ghent was

   (A) where negotiations took place
   (B) the site of the final battle
   (C) where the treaty was signed
   (D) far from the battlefield

GO ON TO THE NEXT PAGE

7. The word "contested" in line 12 is closest in meaning to

   (A) played
   (B) fought
   (C) discussed
   (D) examined

8. It can be determined from the passage that, of the following dates, the Battle of New Orleans was most probably fought

   (A) on December 10, 1814
   (B) on December 24, 1814
   (C) on January 1, 1815
   (D) on January 8, 1815

9. Where in the passage does the author indicate when the War of 1812 officially ended?

   (A) Lines 1–3
   (B) Lines 4–5
   (C) Lines 8–9
   (D) Lines 10–12

10. Which paragraph describes the battle that took place after the signing of the treaty?

    (A) The first paragraph
    (B) The second paragraph
    (C) The third paragraph
    (D) The last paragraph

GO ON TO THE NEXT PAGE ➡

Questions 11–21

Mount Rushmore is a well-known monument in the Black Hills of South Dakota that features the countenances of four United States presidents: Washington, Jefferson, Roosevelt, and Lincoln. What is not so well known is that the process of creating this national treasure was not exactly an uneventful one.

Line
(5) Mount Rushmore was the project of the visionary sculptor John Gutzen de la Mothe Borglum, who was born in Idaho but studied sculpture in Paris in his youth and befriended the famous French sculptor Auguste Rodin. In 1927 Borglum was granted a commission by the federal government to create the sculpture on Mount Rushmore. Though he was nearly sixty years old when he started, he was undaunted by the enormity of the project and the obstacles that it engendered. He optimistically
(10) asserted that the project would be completed within five years, not caring to recognize the potential problems that such a massive project would involve, the problems of dealing with financing, with government bureaucracy, and with Mother Nature herself. An example of what Mother Nature had to throw at the project was the fissure—or large crack—that developed in the granite where Jefferson was being carved. Jefferson had to be moved to the other side of Washington, next to Roosevelt
(15) because of the break in the stone. The work that had been started on the first Jefferson had to be dynamited away.

Mount Rushmore was not completed within the five years predicted by Borglum and was in fact not actually completed within Borglum's lifetime, although it was almost finished. Borglum died on March 6, 1941, at the age of seventy-four, after fourteen years of work on the presidents. His son,
(20) Lincoln Borglum, who had worked with his father throughout the project, completed the monument within eight months of his father's death.

11. Which of the following best expresses the main idea of the passage?

    (A) Mount Rushmore was a huge project filled with numerous obstacles.
    (B) Mount Rushmore is a famous American monument.
    (C) Mount Rushmore has sculptures of four United States presidents on it.
    (D) John Gutzen de la Mothe Borglum created Mount Rushmore.

12. Which of the following best describes the relationship between Borglum and Rodin in Borglum's early years?

    (A) Borglum studied about Rodin in Paris.
    (B) Borglum was far more famous than Rodin as a sculptor.
    (C) Borglum and Rodin were born and raised in the same place.
    (D) Borglum and Rodin were friends.

13. The word "nearly" in line 8 could best be replaced by which of the following.

    (A) Over
    (B) Closely
    (C) Almost
    (D) Barely

14. Which of the following is NOT true about Borglum?

    (A) He began Mount Rushmore around the age of sixty.
    (B) He predicted that Mount Rushmore would be finished around 1932.
    (C) Mount Rushmore was finished when Borglum predicted it would be.
    (D) Borglum worked on Mount Rushmore for more than a decade.

GO ON TO THE NEXT PAGE

15. It can be inferred from the passage that Borglum was someone who

    (A) expected the best to happen
    (B) set realistic goals
    (C) never tried anything too challenging
    (D) was always afraid that bad things were going to happen

16. A "fissure" in line 13 is a

    (A) discoloration
    (B) break
    (C) unevenness
    (D) softness

17. Why does the author mention the fact that the carving of Thomas Jefferson was moved?

    (A) It shows what a perfectionist Borglum was.
    (B) It demonstrates Borglum's artistic style.
    (C) It gives insight into Jefferson's character.
    (D) It is an example of a problem caused by nature.

18. The pronoun "it" in line 18 refers to which of the following?

    (A) The first Jefferson
    (B) Mount Rushmore
    (C) Borglum's lifetime
    (D) Fourteen years of work

19. Which of the following is closest in meaning to the expression "within eight months of his father's death" in line 21?

    (A) More than eight months before his father's death
    (B) Less than eight months before his father's death
    (C) Less than eight months after his father's death
    (D) More than eight months after his father's death

20. Where in the passage does the author mention when the Mount Rushmore project got started?

    (A) Lines 1–4
    (B) Lines 7–8
    (C) Lines 9–12
    (D) Lines 17–18

21. This passage would most likely be assigned reading in a course on

    (A) art history
    (B) geography
    (C) management
    (D) government

GO ON TO THE NEXT PAGE

$$3 \triangle 3 \triangle 3 \triangle 3 \triangle 3 \triangle 3 \triangle 3 \triangle 3$$

Questions 22–31

Carbon dating can be used to estimate the age of any organic natural material; it has been used successfully in archeology to determine the age of ancient artifacts or fossils as well as in a variety of other fields. the principle underlying the use of carbon dating is that carbon is a part of all living
Line things on Earth. Since a radioactive substance such as carbon-14 has a known half-life, the amount of
(5) carbon-14 remaining in an object can be used to date that object.

Carbon-14 has a half-life of 5,570 years, which means that after that number of years half of the carbon-14 atoms have decayed into nitrogen-14. It is the ratio of carbon-14 to nitrogen-14 in that substance that indicates the age of the substance. If, for example, in a particular sample the amount of carbon-14 is roughly equivalent to the amount of nitrogen-14, this indicates that around half of the
(10) carbon-14 has decayed into nitrogen-14, and the sample is approximately 5,570 years old.

Carbon dating cannot be used effectively in dating objects that are older than 80,000 years. When objects are that old, much of the carbon-14 has already decayed into nitrogen-14, and the minuscule amount that is left does not provide a reliable measurement of age. In the case of older objects, other age-dating methods are available, methods which use radioactive atoms with longer
(15) half-lives than carbon has.

22. This passage is mainly about

(A) the differences between carbon-14 and nitrogen-14
(B) one method of dating old objects
(C) archeology and the study of ancient artifacts
(D) various uses for carbon

23. The word "estimate" in line 1 is closest in meaning to

(A) understand
(B) hide
(C) rate
(D) approximate

24. The pronoun "it" in line 1 refers to

(A) carbon dating
(B) the age
(C) any organic natural material
(D) archeology

25. Which of the following is NOT true about carbon-14?

(A) It is radioactive.
(B) Its half-life is more than 5,000 years.
(C) It and nitrogen always exist in equal amounts in any substance.
(D) It can decay into nitrogen-14.

26. The word "underlying" in line 3 could best be replaced by

(A) below
(B) requiring
(C) being studied through
(D) serving as a basis for

27. It can be inferred from the passage that if an item contains more carbon-14 than nitrogen-14, then the item is

(A) too old to be age-dated with carbon-14
(B) not as much as 5,570 years old
(C) too radioactive to be used by archeologists
(D) more than 5,570 years old

28. The word "roughly" in line 9 could best be replaced by

(A) harshly
(B) precisely
(C) coarsely
(D) approximately

GO ON TO THE NEXT PAGE

29. The expression "is left" in line 13 could best be replaced by

    (A) remains
    (B) has turned
    (C) changes
    (D) is gone

30. It is implied in the passage that

    (A) carbon dating could not be used on an item containing nitrogen
    (B) fossils cannot be age-dated using carbon-14
    (C) carbon-14 does not have the longest known half-life
    (D) carbon dating has no known uses outside of archeology

31. The paragraph following the passage most probably discusses

    (A) how carbon-14 decays into nitrogen-1
    (B) various other age-dating methods
    (C) why carbon-14 has such a long half-life
    (D) what substances are part of all living things

GO ON TO THE NEXT PAGE

Questions 32–40

Madison Square Garden, a world-famous sporting venue in New York City, has actually been a series of buildings in varied locations rather than a single building in one spot. In 1873, P. T. Barnum built Barnum's Monster Classical and Geological Hippodrome at the corner of Madison Avenue and
Line 26th Street, across from Madison Square Park. Two years later, bandleader Patrick Gilmore bought
(5) the property, added statues and fountains, and renamed it Gilmore's Gardens. When Cornelius Vanderbilt bought the property in 1879, it was renamed Madison Square Garden.

A second very lavish Madison Square Garden was built at the same location in 1890, with a ballroom, a restaurant, a theater, a rooftop garden, and a main arena with seating for 15,000. However, this elaborate Madison Square Garden lasted only until 1924, when it was torn down to
(10) make way for a forty-story skyscraper.

When the second Madison Square Garden had been replaced in its location across from Madison Square Park, boxing promoter Tex Rickard raised six million dollars to build a new Madison Square Garden. This new Madison Square Garden was constructed in a different location, on 8th Avenue and 50th Street and quite some distance from Madison Square Park and Madison Avenue.
(15) Rickard's Madison Square Garden served primarily as an arena for boxing prizefights and circus events until it outgrew its usefulness by the late 1950s.

A new location was found for a fourth Madison Square Garden, atop Pennsylvania Railroad Station, and plans were announced for its construction in 1960. This current edifice, which includes a huge sports arena, a bowling center, a 5,000-seat amphitheater, and a twenty-nine-story office
(20) building, does retain the traditional name Madison Square Garden. However, the name is actually quite a misnomer. The building is not located near Madison Square, nor does it have the flowery gardens that contributed to the original name.

32. The main point of this passage is that Madison Square Garden

   (A) has had a varied history in various locations
   (B) was P. T. Barnum's major accomplishment
   (C) is home to many different sporting events
   (D) was named after an adjacent park

33. Which paragraph discusses the third incarnation of Madison Square Garden?

   (A) The first paragraph
   (B) The second paragraph
   (C) The third paragraph
   (D) The last paragraph

34. What is a "venue" in line 1?

   (A) A place where people come together
   (B) An event in a competition
   (C) An exhibit of various products
   (D) An invitation to a program

35. According to the passage, Patrick Gilmore did all of the following EXCEPT that he

   (A) purchased the property at the corner of Madison Avenue and 26th Street
   (B) made improvements to the property that he bought
   (C) named the property that he bought Madison Square Garden
   (D) sold the property to Cornelius Vanderbilt

36. The word "lavish" in line 7 is closest in meaning to

   (A) simple
   (B) modern
   (C) elaborate
   (D) outlandish

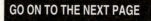
GO ON TO THE NEXT PAGE

37. How long did the second Madison Square Garden last?

    (A) 11 years
    (B) 34 years
    (C) 45 years
    (D) 60 years

38. Which of the following would most likely have taken place at Rickard's Madison Square Garden?

    (A) A ballroom dance
    (B) A theater production
    (C) A basketball game
    (D) A tiger show

39. An "edifice" in line 18 is most likely

    (A) an address
    (B) an association
    (C) a component
    (D) a building

40. What can be inferred about the current Madison Square Garden?

    (A) It is on Madison Avenue.
    (B) It is across from Madison Square Park.
    (C) It has incredible gardens.
    (D) It is above a transportation center.

GO ON TO THE NEXT PAGE

Questions 41–50

It is often the case with folktales that they develop from actual happenings but in their development lose much of their factual base; the story of Pocahontas quite possibly fits into this category of folktale. This princess of the Powhatan tribe was firmly established in the lore of early
Line America and has been made even more famous by the Disney film based on the folktale that arose from
(5) her life. She was a real-life person, but the actual story of her life most probably differed considerably from the folktale and the movie based on the folktale.

Powhatan, the chief of a confederacy of tribes in Virginia, had several daughters, none of whom was actually named Pocahontas. The nickname means "playful one," and several of Powhatan's daughters were called Pocahontas. The daughter of Powhatan who became the subject of the folktale
(10) was named Matoaka. What has been verified about Matoaka, or Pocahontas as she has come to be known, is that she did marry an Englishman and that she did spend time in England before she died there at a young age. In the spring of 1613, a young Pocahontas was captured by the English and taken to Jamestown. There she was treated with courtesy as the daughter of chief Powhatan. While Pocahontas was at Jamestown, English gentleman John Rolfe fell in love with her and asked her to
(15) marry. Both the governor of the Jamestown colony and Pocahontas's father Powhatan approved the marriage as a means of securing peace between Powhatan's tribe and the English at Jamestown. In 1616, Pocahontas accompanied her new husband to England, where she was royally received. Shortly before her planned return to Virginia in 1617, she contracted an illness and died rather suddenly.

A major part of the folktale of Pocahontas that is unverified concerns her love for English
(20) Captain John Smith in the period of time before her capture by the British and her rescue of him from almost certain death. Captain John Smith was indeed at the colony of Jamestown and was acquainted with Powhatan and his daughters; he even described meeting them in a 1612 journal. However, the story of his rescue by the young maiden did not appear in his writings until 1624, well after Pocahontas had aroused widespread interest in England by her marriage to an English
(25) gentleman and her visit to England. It is this discrepancy in dates that has caused some historians to doubt the veracity of the tale. However, other historians do argue quite persuasively that this incident did truly take place.

41. The main idea of the passage is that

    (A) folktales are often not very factual
    (B) Pocahontas did not really exist
    (C) any one of Powhatan's daughters could have been the Pocahontas of legend
    (D) Pocahontas fell in love with John Smith and saved his life

42. The expression "arose from" in line 4 is closest in meaning to

    (A) developed from
    (B) went up with
    (C) was told during
    (D) climbed to

43. What is true about the name Pocahontas, according to the passage?

    (A) It was the real name of a girl named Matoaka.
    (B) It meant that someone was playful.
    (C) Only one girl was known to have used this name.
    (D) Powhatan was one of several people to be given this nickname.

44. How was Pocahontas treated when she was held at Jamestown?

    (A) With respect
    (B) With disdain
    (C) With surprise
    (D) With harshness

GO ON TO THE NEXT PAGE

45. It can be inferred from the passage that Pocahontas

    (A) never intended to return to Virginia
    (B) had a long marriage
    (C) suffered from a long illness
    (D) did not mean to remain in England

46. The word "indeed" in line 21 is closest in meaning to

    (A) therefore
    (B) in fact
    (C) unexpectedly
    (D) in contrast

47. The pronoun "he" in line 22 refers to

    (A) the governor
    (B) Pocahontas
    (C) John Smith
    (D) Powhatan

48. When did John Smith most likely meet Pocahontas?

    (A) In 1612
    (B) In 1613
    (C) In 1616
    (D) In 1624

49. Why are some historians doubtful about the portion of the Pocahontas folktale dealing with John Smith?

    (A) Captain John Smith probably never knew Pocahontas.
    (B) Captain John Smith was never actually in Jamestown.
    (C) His rescue purportedly happened while Pocahontas was in England.
    (D) His account of the rescue did not appear until well after the event supposedly happened.

50. The word "veracity" in line 26 is closest in meaning to

    (A) timing
    (B) location
    (C) understanding
    (D) accuracy

This is the end of Section 3.

**If you finish in less than 55 minutes,
check your work on Section 3 only.
Do NOT read or work on any other section of the test.**

When you finish the test, you may do the following:

- Turn to the **Diagnostic Charts** on pages 551–558, and circle the numbers of the questions that you missed.

- Turn to **Scoring Information** on pages 549–550, and determine your TOEFL score.

- Turn to the **Progress Chart** on page 559, and add your score to the chart.

TEST OF WRITTEN ENGLISH:
TWE ESSAY TOPIC
Time—30 minutes

Do you agree or disagree with the following statement?

You can get a better education from experience than you can in a classroom.

Use specific details and examples to support your opinion.

1 □ 1 □ 1 □ 1 □ 1 □ 1 □ 1 □ 1 □ 1

COMPLETE TEST FOUR

SECTION 1
LISTENING COMPREHENSION
Time—approximately 35 minutes
(including the reading of the directions for each part)

In this section of the test, you will have an opportunity to demonstrate your ability to understand conversations and talks in English. There are three parts to this section, with special directions for each part. Answer all the questions on the basis of what is **stated** or **implied** by the speakers you hear. Do **not** take notes or write in your test book at any time. Do **not** turn the pages until you are told to do so.

Part A

Directions: In Part A you will hear short conversations between two people. After each conversation, you will hear a question about the conversation. The conversations and questions will not be repeated. After you hear a question, read the four possible answers in your test book and choose the best answer. Then, on your answer sheet, find the number of the question and fill in the space that corresponds to the letter of the answer you have chosen.

Listen to an example.   **Sample Answer**

On the recording, you will hear:

(man)	*That exam was just awful.*
(woman)	*Oh, it could have been worse.*
(narrator)	*What does the woman mean?*

In your test book, you will read:
  (A) The exam was really awful.
  (B) It was the worst exam she had ever seen.
  (C) It couldn't have been more difficult.
  (D) It wasn't that hard.

You learn from the conversation that the man thought the exam was very difficult and that the woman disagreed with the man. The best answer to the question, "What does the woman mean?" is (D), "It wasn't that hard." Therefore, the correct choice is (D).

1. (A) Watching a movie.
   (B) Hunting.
   (C) Buying film.
   (D) Taking photos.

2. (A) It's a good idea to be thrifty.
   (B) He's feeling a little dirty.
   (C) He'd like something to drink.
   (D) Stopping for thirty minutes is a good idea.

3. (A) The flight is departing in the near future.
   (B) The plane is taking off early.
   (C) The man needs to make plans soon.
   (D) The plane is taking up space.

4. (A) He has never gone to any games.
   (B) It is rare for the football team to win.
   (C) He doesn't go to games often.
   (D) It is rare for the university team to have a game.

5. (A) They should call out to their neighbors.
   (B) They should visit their neighbors.
   (C) They should phone their neighbors.
   (D) They should look over their neighbors.

6. (A) It is not done yet.
   (B) It was not done carelessly.
   (C) It does not seem to have been done by the accountant.
   (D) It contains a lot of errors.

7. (A) He will be far from the conference tonight.
   (B) He's not quite sure who the speaker will be.
   (C) He knows Dr. Burton well.
   (D) He knows that Dr. Burton will be speaking.

8. (A) Take a short nap.
   (B) Go out now.
   (C) Enjoy the rest of the evening.
   (D) Have a little snack before going out.

9. (A) He's going to say something in the theater.
   (B) What the woman said was magnified out of proportion.
   (C) The size of the theater was magnificent.
   (D) He shares the woman's opinion.

10. (A) They are unconfirmed.
    (B) They are dependent on future research.
    (C) They are most probably correct.
    (D) They are independent of the researchers' ideas.

11. (A) She was less than delighted.
    (B) She was quite pleased.
    (C) She was unable to accept it.
    (D) She wished she could have been more delighted.

12. (A) The lawyer delivered the letter this morning.
    (B) The courier has already made the delivery.
    (C) The letter to the courier has already been received.
    (D) The lawyer's office does not have the letter.

13. (A) The phone is off the hook.
    (B) The man will head the committee.
    (C) The man is no longer responsible.
    (D) The committee meeting has been put off.

14. (A) She must work tonight.
    (B) The shift in her plans is unlucky.
    (C) Her roommate is persuasive.
    (D) Her roommate will work in her place.

15. (A) Put it away.
    (B) Put it off.
    (C) Put it out.
    (D) Put it down.

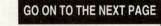
GO ON TO THE NEXT PAGE

16. (A) That the man should not reach out so far.
    (B) That the man can accomplish what he wants.
    (C) That the man will be unable to graduate.
    (D) That the man cannot score a goal.

17. (A) She couldn't afford a new computer.
    (B) The computers were not on sale.
    (C) She was unable to get a new computer.
    (D) She bought a new computer.

18. (A) Visiting a doctor.
    (B) Attending a reception.
    (C) Applying to medical school.
    (D) Interviewing for a job.

19. (A) It met her expectations.
    (B) It was rather mediocre.
    (C) It was what she had hoped to see.
    (D) It was the last performance.

20. (A) Going home on the bus.
    (B) Sleeping on the bus.
    (C) Taking a quick walk.
    (D) Getting some sleep before going home.

21. (A) The course is free.
    (B) The course costs $100 more this semester.
    (C) The course was cheaper last semester.
    (D) She thinks the cost of the course is too low.

22. (A) That he would be at work.
    (B) That he knew a lot about architecture.
    (C) That he did not get the job.
    (D) That he would not be at home.

23. (A) The rider took the road to the hospital.
    (B) An ambulance took the rider to the hospital.
    (C) The ambulance left the hospital with the rider.
    (D) The motorcyclist followed the ambulance to the hospital.

24. (A) He cannot work on the assignment because of a headache.
    (B) He thinks the assignment will take about two hours.
    (C) It would be better to prepare two assignments than one.
    (D) He prefers not to work on it by himself.

25. (A) The project that the woman wants is impossible.
    (B) Two hours is not long enough to complete the project.
    (C) The woman's request can be accomplished.
    (D) The woman should not ask for such a thing.

26. (A) He is not very impressed with it.
    (B) He thinks it is fantastic.
    (C) He does not want more pressure on it.
    (D) It is less impressive than expected.

27. (A) She spent her normal amount of time on it.
    (B) It is rare for her to finish an assignment.
    (C) It is rare for her to put any effort into an assignment.
    (D) She spent more time than usual on it.

28. (A) It was not cold enough.
    (B) The snowball struck him forcefully.
    (C) The snow stayed around too long.
    (D) It was too cold.

29. (A) That she couldn't get into the lab.
    (B) That she wouldn't do the assignment.
    (C) That her lab assignment was already done.
    (D) That she would start working in a couple of hours.

30. (A) She took the stairs out of necessity.
    (B) She didn't want to take the elevator.
    (C) It was only a few flights of stairs.
    (D) She preferred to climb the stairs.

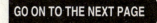
GO ON TO THE NEXT PAGE

Part B

Directions: In this part of the test, you will hear longer conversations. After each conversation, you will hear several questions. The conversations and questions will not be repeated.

After you hear a question, read the four possible answers in your test book and choose the best answer. Then, on your answer sheet, find the number of the question and fill in the space that corresponds to the letter of the answer you have chosen.

Remember, you are **not** allowed to take notes or write in your test book.

31. (A) The price of textbooks.
    (B) History 101.
    (C) The university bookstore.
    (D) Ways to sell used books.

32. (A) He desperately needs the money.
    (B) Reading doesn't interest him.
    (C) He's finished using them.
    (D) He'd rather have cheaper books.

33. (A) The bookstore doesn't want to buy them.
    (B) He wouldn't get enough money.
    (C) He doesn't like the bookstore's advertisements.
    (D) It's too late to sell them to the bookstore.

34. (A) Post some advertisements.
    (B) Take History 101.
    (C) Give the books to the bookstore for nothing.
    (D) Keep the books.

35. (A) That babies sleep thirteen hours a day.
    (B) That the woman was taking a psychology class.
    (C) That more mature people required so much sleep.
    (D) That the need for sleep decreases with age.

36. (A) In psychology class.
    (B) In a discussion with the man.
    (C) From an article that she read.
    (D) From the class textbook.

37. (A) Teens.
    (B) Twenties.
    (C) Thirties.
    (D) Fifties.

38. (A) Thirteen hours.
    (B) Nine hours.
    (C) Eight hours.
    (D) Six hours.

GO ON TO THE NEXT PAGE

1 □ 1 □ 1 □ 1 □ 1 □ 1 □ 1 □ 1

Part C

Directions: In this part of the test, you will hear several talks. After each talk, you will hear some questions. The talks and questions will not be repeated.

After you hear a question, you will read the four possible answers in your test book and choose the best answer. Then, on your answer sheet, find the number of the question and fill in the space that corresponds to the letter of the answer you have chosen.

Here is an example.

On the recording, you will hear:

(narrator) *Listen to an instructor talk to his class about painting.*
(man) *Artist Grant Wood was a guiding force in the school of painting known as American regionalist, a style reflecting the distinctive characteristics of art from rural areas of the United States. Wood began drawing animals on the family farm at the age of three, and when he was thirty-eight one of his paintings received a remarkable amount of public notice and acclaim. This painting, called "American Gothic," is a starkly simple depiction of a serious couple staring directly out at the viewer.*

Now listen to a sample question.   **Sample Answer**

(narrator) *What style of painting is known as American regionalist?*   Ⓐ
                                                                               Ⓑ
In your test book, you will read: (A) Art from America's inner cities.   Ⓒ
                                       (B) Art from the central region of the ●
                                            United States.
                                       (C) Art from various urban areas in the
                                            United States.
                                       (D) Art from rural sections of America.

The best answer to the question, "What style of painting is known as American regionalist?" is (D), "Art from rural sections of America." Therefore, the correct choice is (D).

Now listen to another sample question.   **Sample Answer**

(narrator) *What is the name of Wood's most successful painting?*   Ⓐ
                                                                               Ⓑ
In your test book, you will read: (A) "American Regionalist."   ●
                                       (B) "The Family Farm in Iowa."   Ⓓ
                                       (C) "American Gothic."
                                       (D) "A Serious Couple."

The best answer to the question, "What is the name of Wood's most successful painting?" is (C), "American Gothic." Therefore, the correct choice is (C).

Remember, you are **not** allowed to take notes or write in your test book.

39. (A) How to get a professor's signature.
    (B) The procedure for dropping courses.
    (C) When to come and see the advisor.
    (D) The effect of officially dropping a course.

40. (A) Any time, if the professor is willing to sign.
    (B) Only on the day of the talk.
    (C) During the first three weeks of the semester.
    (D) Up to three weeks before the end of the semester.

41. (A) None.
    (B) One.
    (C) Two.
    (D) Three.

42. (A) The student fails the course.
    (B) The course is removed from the student's schedule.
    (C) The student needs to get the advisor's signature.
    (D) The student receives a warning.

43. (A) A woodcarving business.
    (B) A lumber business.
    (C) A construction business.
    (D) A jewelry business.

44. (A) During the construction of a sawmill.
    (B) After prospectors had arrived.
    (C) Sometime after Sutter's death.
    (D) Before Sutter had the rights to the land.

45. (A) Increased prosperity.
    (B) A large share of gold.
    (C) A healthier lumber business.
    (D) Little or nothing.

46. (A) To show what a terrible life John Sutter had led.
    (B) To show the folly of trying to develop a business.
    (C) To show the effect that the discovery of gold has on individuals.
    (D) To show that the development of the West happened partly by chance.

47. (A) Becoming a university student.
    (B) Managing time.
    (C) Majoring in management.
    (D) Spending a week in a management training program.

48. (A) Relaxation techniques.
    (B) Homework assignments.
    (C) A personal time-management study.
    (D) Keeping an appointment calendar.

49. (A) Ninety-six days.
    (B) Twenty-four days.
    (C) Seven days.
    (D) Fifteen minutes.

50. (A) Make an appointment.
    (B) Begin the time study.
    (C) Write down how they spend their time.
    (D) Attend another seminar.

This is the end of Section 1.
Stop work on Section 1.

Turn off the recording.

Read the directions for Section 2 and begin work.
Do NOT read or work on any other section
of the test during the next 25 minutes.

SECTION 2
STRUCTURE AND WRITTEN EXPRESSION
Time—25 minutes
(including the reading of the directions)
Now set your clock for 25 minutes.

This section is designed to measure your ability to recognize language that is appropriate for standard written English. There are two types of questions in this section, with special directions for each type.

Structure

Directions: These questions are incomplete sentences. Beneath each sentence you will see four words or phrases, marked (A), (B), (C), and (D). Choose the **one** word or phrase that best completes the sentence. Then, on your answer sheet, find the number of the question and fill in the space that corresponds to the letter of the answer you have chosen.

Look at the following examples.

Example I   **Sample Answer**

The president _____ the election by a landslide.   ●
                                                                                                Ⓑ
(A) won   Ⓒ
(B) he won   Ⓓ
(C) yesterday
(D) fortunately

The sentence should read, "The president won the election by a landslide." Therefore, you should choose answer (A).

Example II   **Sample Answer**

When _____ the conference?   Ⓐ
                                                                                                ●
(A) the doctor attended   Ⓒ
(B) did the doctor attend   Ⓓ
(C) the doctor will attend
(D) the doctor's attendance

The sentence should read, "When did the doctor attend the conference?" Therefore, you should choose answer (B).

GO ON TO THE NEXT PAGE

1. Indiana's Lost River _____ underground for a distance of 22 miles.

   (A) travels
   (B) traveling
   (C) to travel
   (D) it travels

2. The 1980 explosion of _____ the first volcanic eruption in the continental United States in over 60 years.

   (A) Mount St. Helens
   (B) was Mount St. Helens
   (C) it was Mount St. Helens
   (D) Mount St. Helens was

3. Static electricity _____ one cloud to another or between clouds and the ground creates lightning.

   (A) flows from
   (B) the flow from
   (C) flowing from
   (D) is flowing from

4. The Model T car, introduced in 1908, _____ $850.

   (A) the price was
   (B) a price of
   (C) to be priced at
   (D) was priced at

5. _____ reacts with a chlorine atom, an electron is transferred from the outer shell of the sodium atom to the outer shell of the chlorine atom.

   (A) A sodium atom
   (B) When a sodium atom
   (C) For a sodium atom
   (D) It is a sodium atom

6. In 1858, the site _____ was to become the city of Denver was settled as a way station for outfitting gold prospectors.

   (A) it
   (B) of it
   (C) what
   (D) of what

7. The light from an electrical lamp includes many different wavelengths, _____ in a laser is concentrated on only one wavelength.

   (A) all the energy
   (B) it is all the energy
   (C) while all the energy
   (D) while all the energy is

8. In the Antarctic Ocean _____ plankton and crustacean forms of life.

   (A) an abundance of
   (B) is an abundance of
   (C) it is abundant
   (D) an abundance is

9. Flintlock muskets _____ sharp bayonets were standard weapons during the American Revolution.

   (A) tip with
   (B) tipped with
   (C) the tips of
   (D) were tipped with

10. Benjamin Franklin believed that the turkey rather than the eagle _____ of the United States.

    (A) should become the symbol
    (B) the symbol becomes
    (C) should symbolize becoming
    (D) becoming the symbol

GO ON TO THE NEXT PAGE ➔

11. _____ to occur in the Earth's crust, push-pull and shake waves would be generated simultaneously.

   (A) Were a break
   (B) If a break
   (C) A break was
   (D) If broken

12. Fossil fuels like coal, oil, and gas produce carbon dioxide when _____.

   (A) are burned
   (B) they burned
   (C) burned
   (D) are they burned

13. Not until Nellie Tayloe Ross was elected governor of Wyoming in 1924 _____ as governor of a U.S. state.

   (A) a woman served
   (B) a woman serving
   (C) to serve a woman
   (D) did a woman serve

14. The temperatures _____ take place vary widely for different materials.

   (A) which melting and freezing
   (B) at which melting and freezing
   (C) which they melt and freeze
   (D) at which they melt and freeze

15. In general, the cells of large animals and plants are only slightly larger than _____ plants and animals.

   (A) smaller
   (B) are smaller
   (C) those smaller
   (D) are those of smaller

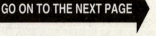
GO ON TO THE NEXT PAGE

Written Expression

Directions: In these questions, each sentence has four underlined words or phrases. The four underlined parts of the sentence are marked (A), (B), (C), and (D). Identify the **one** underlined word or phrase that must be changed in order for the sentence to be correct. Then, on your answer sheet, find the number of the question and fill in the space that corresponds to the letter of the answer you have chosen.

Look at the following examples.

Example I   **Sample Answer**

The four string on a violin are tuned
A   B   C   D

in fifths.

The sentence should read, "The four strings on a violin are tuned in fifths." Therefore, you should choose answer (B).

Example II   **Sample Answer**

The research for the book *Roots* taking
A   B   C

Alex Haley twelve years.
D

The sentence should read, "The research for the book *Roots* took Alex Haley twelve years." Therefore, you should choose answer (C).

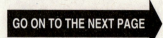
GO ON TO THE NEXT PAGE

2 • 2 • 2 • 2 • 2 • 2 • 2 • 2 • 2

16. The music on a compact disk (CD) is record by lasers.
    A   B   C   D

17. Alaska has more active glaciers as the rest of the inhabited world combined.
                             A   B   C   D

18. Aristotle believed that everything in the universe were composed of four basic
              A   B   C
    elements: earth, water, air, and fire.
                                    D

19. In the cold climate of the far north, mosquito eggs may remains dormant from
    A   B   C   D
    autumn until late June.

20. Passengers have ridden the first Ferris wheel at the Columbian Exposition in
               A   B   C
    Chicago in 1893.
            D

21. One type of Australian frog lays up to 25 eggs at a time and then swallows they for
                                A   B   C
    protection.
    D

22. The Cro-Magnons entered the area that is today Europe and quickly eliminated or
                                     A   B
    absorbed theirs Neanderthal predecessors.
             C   D

23. The Spanish introduced not only horses and also cattle to the North American
                   A   B   C
    continent.
    D

24. The best-known members of the cabbage vegetable group includes head cabbage,
        A   B   C   D
    cauliflower, broccoli, kale, collard, and brussels sprouts.

25. White blood cells are the largest of red blood cells and are more varied in size and in
                    A   B   C   D
    shape.

GO ON TO THE NEXT PAGE

26. An hiccup is a spasmodic contraction of the diaphragm, which leads to a massive
    ‾A‾   ‾‾B‾‾   ‾‾‾C‾‾‾

    intake of air.
    ‾‾D‾‾

27. To make a lithograph, an artist used a flat stone of a kind that will soak up oil and
    ‾‾A‾‾   ‾‾B‾‾   ‾‾C‾‾   ‾‾D‾‾

    water.

28. Alike a bar magnet, the Earth has two magnetic poles.
    ‾‾A‾‾   ‾‾B‾‾   ‾‾C‾‾ ‾‾D‾‾

29. Not until Harvard College was founded in 1636 was there any colleges in America.
        ‾‾A‾‾   ‾‾B‾‾   ‾‾C‾‾   ‾‾D‾‾

30. Antelopes are gregarious animals that travel in herds, ranging in amount from a few
                 ‾‾‾A‾‾‾   ‾‾B‾‾   ‾‾C‾‾

    to several thousand.
       ‾‾D‾‾

31. A supersonic airplane can fly faster than a speed of sound.
      ‾‾‾A‾‾‾   ‾B‾ ‾C‾   ‾D‾

32. In 1821, Emma Willard opened officially the doors of the first school in the United
    ‾A‾   ‾‾‾‾B‾‾‾‾

    States to offer college-level courses for women.
          ‾C‾   ‾D‾

33. The first gummed postage stamps issued in New York City in 1842.
              ‾‾‾A‾‾‾   ‾‾B‾‾ ‾C‾   ‾D‾

34. Typical long bone such as the femur consists of a long shaft with swellings at each
    ‾‾A‾‾   ‾‾B‾‾   ‾‾‾C‾‾‾   ‾‾‾D‾‾‾

    end.

35. The common octopus lives lone in a den just big enough for its body.
                             ‾‾A‾‾   ‾B‾ ‾C‾   ‾D‾

36. The vacuum tube did an important contribution to the early growth of radio and
        ‾‾A‾‾   ‾‾‾B‾‾‾ ‾C‾   ‾‾D‾‾

    television.

37. St. Augustine, Florida, founded in 1565 by Pedro Menendez, was razing 21 years
                           ‾‾A‾‾   ‾B‾   ‾‾C‾‾

    later by Francis Drake.
    ‾D‾

GO ON TO THE NEXT PAGE ➡

38. A bimetallic thermometer relies the different rates of expansion of two types of
       <u>A</u>   <u>B</u>   <u>C</u>

   metal, usually brass and copper.
          <u>D</u>

39. An ice crystal is the nuclei on which a hailstone is built.
         <u>A</u>   <u>B</u>   <u>C</u>   <u>D</u>

40. Tremendous flooding during the summer of 1993 left 8 million acres of nine
              <u>A</u>   <u>B</u>

   midwestern states inundated and proved both expensively and deadly.
                                                <u>C</u>   <u>D</u>

This is the end of Section 2.
If you finish before 25 minutes has ended,
check your work on Section 2 only.

At the end of 25 minutes, go on to Section 3.
Use exactly 55 minutes to work on Section 3.

SECTION 3
READING COMPREHENSION
Time—55 minutes
(including the reading of the directions)
Now set your clock for 55 minutes.

This section is designed to measure your ability to read and understand short passages similar in topic and style to those that students are likely to encounter in North American universities and colleges. This section contains reading passages and questions about the passages.

Directions: In this section you will read several passages. Each one is followed by a number of questions about it. You are to choose the **one** best answer, (A), (B), (C), or (D), to each question. Then, on your answer sheet, find the number of the question and fill in the space that corresponds to the letter of the answer you have chosen.

Answer all questions about the information in a passage on the basis of what is **stated** or **implied** in that passage.

Read the following passage:

John Quincy Adams, who served as the sixth president of the United States from 1825 to 1829, is today recognized for his masterful statesmanship and diplomacy. He dedicated his life to public service, both in the presidency and in the various other political offices that he
Line held. Throughout his political career he demonstrated his unswerving belief in freedom of
(5) speech, the antislavery cause, and the right of Americans to be free from European and Asian domination.

Example I   **Sample Answer**

To what did John Quincy Adams devote his life?

(A) Improving his personal life
(B) Serving the public
(C) Increasing his fortune
(D) Working on his private business

According to the passage, John Quincy Adams "dedicated his life to public service." Therefore, you should choose answer (B).

Example II   **Sample Answer**

In line 4, the word "unswerving" is closest in meaning to

(A) moveable
(B) insignificant
(C) unchanging
(D) diplomatic

The passage states that John Quincy Adams demonstrated his unswerving belief "throughout his career." This implies that the belief did not change. Therefore, you should choose answer (C).

GO ON TO THE NEXT PAGE

Questions 1–10

A rather surprising geographical feature of Antarctica is that a huge freshwater lake, one of the world's largest and deepest, lies hidden there under four kilometers of ice. Now known as Lake Vostok, this huge body of water is located under the ice block that comprises Antarctica. The lake is
Line
(5) able to exist in its unfrozen state beneath this block of ice because its waters are warmed by geothermal heat from the earth's core. The thick glacier above Lake Vostok actually insulates it from the frigid temperatures (the lowest ever recorded on Earth) on the surface.

The lake was first discovered in the 1970s while a research team was conducting an aerial survey of the area. Radio waves from the survey equipment penetrated the ice and revealed a body of water of indeterminate size. It was not until much more recently that data collected by satellite made
(10) scientists aware of the tremendous size of the lake; the satellite-borne radar detected an extremely flat region where the ice remains level because it is floating on the water of the lake.

The discovery of such a huge freshwater lake trapped under Antarctica is of interest to the scientific community because of the potential that the lake contains ancient microbes that have survived for thousands upon thousands of years, unaffected by factors such as nuclear fallout and
(15) elevated ultraviolet light that have affected organisms in more exposed areas. The downside of the discovery, however, lies in the difficulty of conducting research on the lake in such a harsh climate and in the problems associated with obtaining uncontaminated samples from the lake without actually exposing the lake to contamination. Scientists are looking for possible ways to accomplish this.

1. The purpose of the passage is to
   (A) explain how Lake Vostok was discovered
   (B) provide satellite data concerning Antarctica
   (C) discuss future plans for Lake Vostok
   (D) present an unexpected aspect of Antarctica's geography

2. The word "lies" in line 2 could best be replaced by
   (A) sleeps
   (B) sits
   (C) tells falsehoods
   (D) inclines

3. What is true of Lake Vostok?
   (A) It is completely frozen.
   (B) It is not a saltwater lake.
   (C) It is beneath a thick slab of ice.
   (D) It is heated by the sun.

4. Which of the following is closest in meaning to "frigid" in line 6?
   (A) Extremely cold
   (B) Never changing
   (C) Quite harsh
   (D) Rarely recorded

5. All of the following are true about the 1970 survey of Antarctica EXCEPT that it
   (A) was conducted by air
   (B) made use of radio waves
   (C) did not measure the exact size of the lake
   (D) was controlled by a satellite

6. It can be inferred from the passage that the ice would not be flat if
   (A) there were no lake.
   (B) the lake were not so big
   (C) Antarctica were not so cold
   (D) radio waves were not used

GO ON TO THE NEXT PAGE

7. The word "microbes" in line 13 could best be replaced by which of the following?

    (A) Pieces of dust
    (B) Trapped bubbles
    (C) Tiny organisms
    (D) Rays of light

8. The passage mentions which of the following as a reason for the importance of Lake Vostok to scientists?

    (A) It can be studied using radio waves.
    (B) It may contain uncontaminated microbes.
    (C) It may have elevated levels of ultraviolet light.
    (D) It has already been contaminated.

9. The word "downside" in line 15 is closest in meaning to

    (A) bottom level
    (B) negative aspect
    (C) underside
    (D) buried section

10. The paragraph following the passage most probably discusses

    (A) further discoveries on the surface of Antarctica
    (B) problems with satellite-borne radar equipment
    (C) ways to study Lake Vostok without contaminating it
    (D) the harsh climate of Antarctica

GO ON TO THE NEXT PAGE

Questions 11–21

In the American colonies there was little money. England did not supply the colonies with coins and it did not allow the colonies to make their own coins, except for the Massachusetts Bay Colony, which received permission for a short period in 1652 to make several kinds of silver coins. England
Line wanted to keep money out of America as a means of controlling trade: America was forced to trade
(5) only with England if it did not have the money to buy products from other countries. The result during this prerevolutionary period was that the colonists used various goods in place of money: beaver pelts, Indian wampum, and tobacco leaves were all commonly used substitutes for money. The colonists also made use of any foreign coins they could obtain. Dutch, Spanish, French, and English coins were all in use in the American colonies.

(10) During the Revolutionary War, funds were needed to finance the war, so each of the individual states and the Continental Congress issued paper money. So much of this paper money was printed that, by the end of the war, almost no one would accept it. As a result trade in goods and the use of foreign coins still flourished during this period.

By the time the Revolutionary War had been won by the American colonists, the monetary
(15) system was in a state of total disarray. To remedy this situation, the new Constitution of the United States, approved in 1789, allowed Congress to issue money. The individual states could no longer have their own money supply. A few years later, the Coinage Act of 1792 made the dollar the official currency of the United States and put the country on a bimetallic standard. In this bimetallic system, both gold and silver were legal money, and the rate of exchange of silver to gold was fixed by the
(20) government at sixteen to one.

11. The passage mainly discusses

    (A) American money from past to present
    (B) the English monetary policies in colonial America
    (C) the effect of the Revolution on American money
    (D) the American monetary system of the seventeenth and eighteenth centuries

12. The passage indicates that during the colonial period, money was

    (A) supplied by England
    (B) coined by the colonists
    (C) scarce
    (D) used extensively for trade

13. The Massachusetts Bay Colony was allowed to make coins

    (A) continuously from the inception of the colony
    (B) throughout the seventeenth century
    (C) from 1652 until the Revolutionary War
    (D) for a short time during one year

14. The expression "a means of" in line 4 could best be replaced by

    (A) an example of
    (B) a method for
    (C) a result of
    (D) a punishment for

15. Which of the following is NOT mentioned in the passage as a substitute for money during the colonial period?

    (A) Wampum
    (B) Cotton
    (C) Tobacco
    (D) Beaver furs

16. The pronoun "it" in line 12 refers to which of the following?

    (A) The Continental Congress
    (B) Paper money
    (C) The war
    (D) Trade in goods

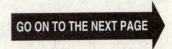
GO ON TO THE NEXT PAGE

17. It is implied in the passage that at the end of the Revolutionary War, a paper dollar was worth

   (A) exactly one dollar
   (B) just under one dollar
   (C) just over one dollar
   (D) almost nothing

18. The word "remedy" in line 15 is closest in meaning to

   (A) resolve
   (B) understand
   (C) renew
   (D) medicate

19. How was the monetary system arranged in the Constitution?

   (A) Only the United States Congress could issue money.
   (B) The United States officially went on a bimetallic monetary system.
   (C) Various state governments, including Massachusetts, could issue money.
   (D) The dollar was made the official currency of the United States.

20. According to the passage, which of the following is NOT true about the bimetallic monetary system?

   (A) Either gold or silver could be used as official money.
   (B) Gold could be exchanged for silver at a rate of sixteen to one.
   (C) The monetary system was based on two metals.
   (D) It was established in 1792.

21. The word "fixed" in line 19 is closest in meaning to

   (A) discovered
   (B) repaired
   (C) valued
   (D) set

GO ON TO THE NEXT PAGE

Questions 22–30

The human brain, with an average weight of 1.4 kilograms, is the control center of the body. It receives information from the senses, processes the information, and rapidly sends out responses; it also stores the information that is the source of human thoughts and feelings. Each of the three main parts of the brain—the cerebrum, the cerebellum, and the brain stem—has its own role in carrying out these functions.

Line
(5)

The cerebrum is by far the largest of the three parts, taking up 85 percent of the brain by weight. The outside layer of the cerebrum, the cerebral cortex, is a grooved and bumpy surface covering the nerve cells beneath. The various sections of the cerebrum are the sensory cortex, which is responsible for receiving and decoding sensory messages from throughout the body; the motor cortex, which sends action instructions to the skeletal muscles; and the association cortex, which receives, monitors, and processes information. It is in the association cortex that the processes that allow humans to think take place.

(10)

The cerebellum, located below the cerebrum in the back part of the skull, is made of masses of bunched up nerve cells. It is the cerebellum that controls human balance, coordination, and posture.

(15)

The brain stem, which connects the cerebrum and the spinal cord, controls various body processes such as breathing and heartbeat. It is the major motor and sensory pathway connecting the body and the cerebrum.

22. What is the author's main purpose?

  (A) To describe the functions of the parts of the brain
  (B) To explain how the brain processes information
  (C) To demonstrate the physical composition of the brain
  (D) To give examples of human body functions

23. The word "stores" in line 3 is closest in meaning to

  (A) shops
  (B) processes
  (C) releases
  (D) stockpiles

24. The passage states that the most massive part of the brain is the

  (A) cerebrum
  (B) cerebellum
  (C) cerebral cortex
  (D) brain stem

25. The "cerebral cortex" in line 7 is

  (A) a layer of the brain beneath the cerebrum
  (B) a layer of nerve cells in the brain
  (C) a part of the brain that makes up 85 percent of the brain
  (D) a ridged layer covering the cerebrum in the brain

26. The sensory cortex

  (A) senses that messages should be sent out to the muscles
  (B) provides a surface covering for nerve cells
  (C) is where the human process of thinking occurs
  (D) receives and processes information from the senses

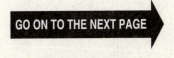

GO ON TO THE NEXT PAGE

27. The word "monitors" in line 11 is closest in meaning to which of the following?

    (A) Keeps track of
    (B) Keeps hold of
    (C) Gets away with
    (D) Gets rid of

28. Which of the following is true about the cerebellum?

    (A) It is located above the cerebrum.
    (B) It controls breathing.
    (C) It is responsible for balance.
    (D) It is the outside layer of the cerebrum.

29. What shape does the brain stem most likely have?

    (A) Small and round
    (B) Long and thin
    (C) Large and formless
    (D) Short and flat

30. Which of the following could best be used in place of "pathway" in line 16.

    (A) Driveway
    (B) Roadway
    (C) Route
    (D) Street

GO ON TO THE NEXT PAGE

Questions 31–41

Though Edmund Halley was most famous because of his achievements as an astronomer, he was a scientist of diverse interests and great skill. In addition to studying the skies, Halley was also deeply interested in exploring the unknown depths of the oceans. One of his lesser-known

Line
(5) accomplishments that was quite remarkable was his design for a diving bell that facilitated exploration of the watery depths.

The diving bell that Halley designed had a major advantage over the diving bells that were in use prior to his. Earlier diving bells could only make use of the air contained within the bell itself, so divers had to surface when the air inside the bell ran low. Halley's bell was an improvement in that its design allowed for an additional supply of fresh air that enabled a crew of divers to remain
(10) underwater for several hours.

The diving contraption that Halley designed was in the shape of a bell that measured three feet across the top and five feet across the bottom and could hold several divers comfortably; it was open at the bottom so that divers could swim in and out at will. The bell was built of wood, which was first heavily tarred to make it water repellent and was then covered with a half-ton sheet of lead to make
(15) the bell heavy enough to sink in water. The bell shape held air inside for the divers to breathe as the bell sank to the bottom.

The air inside the bell was not the only source of air for the divers to breathe, and it was this improvement that made Halley's bell superior to its predecessors. In addition to the air already in the bell, air was also supplied to the divers from a lead barrel that was lowered to the ocean floor close to
(20) the bell itself. Air flowed through a leather pipe from the lead barrel on the ocean floor to the bell. The diver could breath the air from a position inside the bell, or he could move around outside the bell wearing a diving suit that consisted of a lead bell-shaped helmet with a glass viewing window and a leather body suit, with a leather pipe carrying fresh air from the diving bell to the helmet.

31. The subject of the preceding passage was most likely Halley's

   (A) childhood
   (B) work as an astronomer
   (C) many different interests
   (D) invention of the diving bell

32. Which of the following best expresses the subject of this passage?

   (A) Halley's work as an astronomer
   (B) Halley's many different interests
   (C) Halley's invention of a contraption for diving
   (D) Halley's experiences as a diver

33. Halley's bell was better than its predecessors because it

   (A) was bigger
   (B) provided more air
   (C) weighed less
   (D) could rise more quickly

34. The expression "ran low" in line 8 is closest in meaning to

   (A) moved slowly
   (B) had been replenished
   (C) sank to the bottom
   (D) was almost exhausted

35. How long could divers stay underwater in Halley's bell?

   (A) Just a few seconds
   (B) Only a few minutes
   (C) For hours at a time
   (D) For days on end

36. It is NOT stated in the passage that Halley's bell

   (A) was wider at the top than at the bottom
   (B) was made of tarred wood
   (C) was completely enclosed
   (D) could hold more than one diver

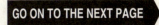
GO ON TO THE NEXT PAGE

37. The expression "at will" in line 13 could best be replaced by

    (A) in the future
    (B) as they wanted
    (C) with great speed
    (D) upside down

38. It can be inferred from the passage that, were Halley's bell not covered with lead, it would

    (A) float
    (B) get wet
    (C) trap the divers
    (D) suffocate the divers

39. Where in the passage does the author indicate how air traveled from the barrel to the bell?

    (A) Lines 8–10
    (B) Lines 11–13
    (C) Lines 17–18
    (D) Line 20

40. In which paragraph does the author describe the diving bells that preceded Halley's?

    (A) In the first paragraph
    (B) In the second paragraph
    (C) In the third paragraph
    (D) In the last paragraph

41. This passage would most likely be assigned reading in a course on

    (A) astronomy
    (B) recreation
    (C) oceanography
    (D) physiology

GO ON TO THE NEXT PAGE

Questions 42–50

Paul Bunyan is perhaps America's best-known folk hero. A fictional logger of incredible strength, he was most likely based on an actual nineteenth-century logger from the northern United States or Canada. As a folk hero, he struck a chord with Americans on some level, perhaps because he *Line* was incredibly strong but also because he was hard-working and capable, ingenious in solving (5) problems, and fun-loving.

Though there is evidence that Paul Bunyan tales were part of oral tradition in the nineteenth century, Paul Bunyan stories did not appear in written form until the early twentieth century. Journalist James McGillivray included descriptions of Bunyan in a series of essays entitled "The Round River Drive," which appeared in a number of Midwestern newspapers between 1906 and 1910. (10) However, it was through an extensive advertising campaign that Paul Bunyan moved solidly into print.

Recognizing the appeal of Paul Bunyan as a figure for his company's advertising, William Laughead, an advertising executive for the Red River Lumber Company, initiated a campaign that consisted of a series of publications featuring Paul Bunyan. For several decades, the company (15) distributed these publications free of charge and made no attempt to obtain a copyright on them. In fact, the company vigorously encouraged other writers to make use of Paul Bunyan because it felt that the use of this character enhanced the name recognition of the Red River Lumber Company inasmuch as the name of the folk hero and the name of the company had become interwoven.

The Bunyan stories published by Red River and further circulated by others were tall tales of (20) gigantic proportions. In these tales, Bunyan is depicted as a man of superhuman proportions, who is strong, hard-working, entrepreneurial, and innovative. In one story, for example, Paul is credited with digging the Great Lakes in order to create a watering hole for his giant ox, Babe. In another of these tales, Paul caused an entire winter of blue snow to fall by swearing a blue streak after he injured himself by smashing his thumb with a large hammer. A third story in the series describes Paul's role (25) in establishing the Mississippi River.

Fascination with Paul Bunyan has continued to grow, and today he is a standard of American folklore. The prevalence of Bunyan as a figure of folklore today is evidenced by references to him in countless stories, cartoons, poems, and songs as well as the numerous community festivals and logging competitions featuring Paul Bunyan that can be found throughout the sections of the country (30) where logging has a strong tradition.

42. The purpose of this passage is to

(A) present the actual feats of a real-life logger
(B) discuss a "larger than life" folk hero
(C) describe logging in North America
(D) provide an overview of American folktales

43. It is NOT stated in the passage that Paul Bunyan is known for his

(A) unusual strength
(B) dedication to work
(C) ingenuity in difficult situations
(D) serious nature

44. The passage states that Paul Bunyan tales first appeared

(A) in oral stories
(B) in a series of essays
(C) in newspapers
(D) in advertising

45. Which of the following CANNOT be inferred about the Red River Lumber Company's advertising campaign featuring Paul Bunyan?

    (A) It endured for quite a time.
    (B) The company did not protect its ownership of the stories.
    (C) The campaign did little to enhance the company's profitability.
    (D) The company wanted the name Paul Bunyan to be known as widely as possible.

46. The pronoun "them" in line 15 refers to

    (A) series
    (B) decades
    (C) publications
    (D) writers

47. The word "interwoven" in line 18 could best be replaced by

    (A) unfashionable
    (B) mixed together
    (C) not compatible
    (D) too separate

48. Where in the passage does the author discuss a weather phenomenon that Paul Bunyan supposedly caused?

    (A) Lines 8–9
    (B) Lines 14–15
    (C) Lines 19–20
    (D) Lines 22–24

49. The word "countless" in line 28 could best be replaced by the expression

    (A) a large number of
    (B) a specified number of
    (C) an insubstantial number of
    (D) an overestimated number of

50. Which paragraph describes the plots of some of the tales of Paul Bunyan?

    (A) The second paragraph
    (B) The third paragraph
    (C) The fourth paragraph
    (D) The fifth paragraph

This is the end of Section 3.

If you finish in less than 55 minutes, check your work on Section 3 only. Do NOT read or work on any other section of the test.

When you finish the test, you may do the following:

- Turn to the **Diagnostic Charts** on pages 551–558, and circle the numbers of the questions that you missed.

- Turn to **Scoring Information** on pages 549–550, and determine your TOEFL score.

- Turn to the **Progress Chart** on page 559, and add your score to the chart.

TEST OF WRITTEN ENGLISH:
TWE ESSAY TOPIC
Time—30 minutes

In difficult situations, some people react calmly, while others react with panic. How do you react in difficult situations? Use specific details and examples to support your answer.

1 □ 1 □ 1 □ 1 □ 1 □ 1 □ 1 □ 1

COMPLETE TEST FIVE

SECTION 1
LISTENING COMPREHENSION
Time—approximately 35 minutes
(including the reading of the directions for each part)

In this section of the test, you will have an opportunity to demonstrate your ability to understand conversations and talks in English. There are three parts to this section, with special directions for each part. Answer all the questions on the basis of what is **stated** or **implied** by the speakers you hear. Do **not** take notes or write in your test book at any time. Do **not** turn the pages until you are told to do so.

Part A

Directions: In Part A you will hear short conversations between two people. After each conversation, you will hear a question about the conversation. The conversations and questions will not be repeated. After you hear a question, read the four possible answers in your test book and choose the best answer. Then, on your answer sheet, find the number of the question and fill in the space that corresponds to the letter of the answer you have chosen.

Listen to an example.   **Sample Answer**

On the recording, you will hear: Ⓐ
                                                                            Ⓑ
                                                                            Ⓒ
                                                                            ●

(man)	*That exam was just awful.*
(woman)	*Oh, it could have been worse.*
(narrator)	*What does the woman mean?*

In your test book, you will read: (A) The exam was really awful.
                                        (B) It was the worst exam she had ever seen.
                                        (C) It couldn't have been more difficult.
                                        (D) It wasn't that hard.

You learn from the conversation that the man thought the exam was very difficult and that the woman disagreed with the man. The best answer to the question, "What does the woman mean?" is (D), "It wasn't that hard." Therefore, the correct choice is (D).

Wait

1. (A) She has rules about how to play.
   (B) Her goal is to pay for school.
   (C) She is praying not to have a low score.
   (D) She'll be acting in a school project.

2. (A) She'd like something to drink.
   (B) She'd like to have thirty.
   (C) She'd like a bite to eat.
   (D) She's a bit thrifty.

3. (A) She's moving in the opposite direction.
   (B) She's wide awake.
   (C) The rest of the people are tired.
   (D) She needs to take a nap.

4. (A) He'll continue to stand in line for texts.
   (B) He has enough to pay for the texts.
   (C) He agrees with the woman about the texts.
   (D) He thinks the woman's in the wrong line to get the texts.

5. (A) He was given the wrong key.
   (B) The key was on top of the clock.
   (C) It was lucky that he got the key.
   (D) The key was at his feet.

6. (A) He went to the conference.
   (B) He saw his friends at the conference.
   (C) He was in his place at the conference.
   (D) He sent a representative.

7. (A) She will see the lawyer tomorrow.
   (B) She needs to phone the lawyer.
   (C) The lawyer will call her tomorrow.
   (D) The lawyer has called off their meeting.

8. (A) There's a lot of difficult homework in it.
   (B) There are not very many exams in it.
   (C) There is little homework.
   (D) There is no homework.

9. (A) Returning to it later.
   (B) Coming back home.
   (C) Finishing the math book.
   (D) Leaving for class.

10. (A) He'll make a charitable contribution.
    (B) He couldn't get into the classroom.
    (C) He didn't have very much to say.
    (D) He was not given the chance to speak.

11. (A) He thought it was extremely fruitful.
    (B) He's happy he didn't attend it.
    (C) A lot of people missed it.
    (D) It was perturbing.

12. (A) He'd like the woman to repeat herself.
    (B) The woman should talk to a physician.
    (C) He shares the woman's position.
    (D) What the woman said was unimportant.

13. (A) To see a dentist.
    (B) To see a cardiologist.
    (C) To see a podiatrist.
    (D) To see an ophthalmologist.

14. (A) She is too scared to try it.
    (B) She would like another opportunity.
    (C) Her time is very scarce.
    (D) She has gone skiing for the last time.

15. (A) He really enjoyed the conference.
    (B) He'll be able to go to the conference.
    (C) He couldn't attend the conference.
    (D) He heard everything at the conference.

16. (A) She doesn't need a jacket for the game.
    (B) She was very uncomfortable last time.
    (C) She will take a jacket with her this time.
    (D) Her jacket does not feel very comfortable.

17. (A) He parked the car to buy the tickets.
    (B) He left the car where he shouldn't have.
    (C) He got a speeding ticket.
    (D) He didn't park the car.

GO ON TO THE NEXT PAGE →

18. (A) She prepared him for what he was going to do.
    (B) She was unprepared for what she had to do.
    (C) She probably didn't spend much time on her presentation.
    (D) She was really ready for her presentation.

19. (A) He has never gone sailing.
    (B) He doesn't like sailing.
    (C) He hasn't had much time for sailing.
    (D) He doesn't have any time to go sailing.

20. (A) That the man had been in class.
    (B) That the man didn't have the notes.
    (C) That she didn't need the notes.
    (D) That the lecture had been canceled.

21. (A) She listened attentively during class.
    (B) She must make the list five pages long.
    (C) She did not attend all of the class.
    (D) She was inattentive during some of the class.

22. (A) He's not quite sure when the projects should be finished.
    (B) He's doing his project for music class now.
    (C) Music class meets for the first time in December.
    (D) He believes the music will be available on December 1.

23. (A) The tuition increase was unexpected.
    (B) She was prepared for the tuition increase.
    (C) She doesn't believe that fees were increased.
    (D) She believes that tuition will not go up.

24. (A) She answered his question a minute ago.
    (B) She just bit her tongue.
    (C) It's hard for her to put the answer into words.
    (D) The tip of her tongue is quite sore.

25. (A) Some of them are lying down.
    (B) Some of them will lose their positions.
    (C) Some of them are choosing part-time jobs.
    (D) Some of them laid down their newspapers.

26. (A) She's unhappy about the score.
    (B) She hasn't seen her score yet.
    (C) She's really pleased with her score.
    (D) She hasn't taken the exam yet.

27. (A) He didn't believe the course was hard.
    (B) He heard that the course was closed.
    (C) It was hard for him to get to the class.
    (D) He registered for the course.

28. (A) He didn't go because he was sleeping.
    (B) He didn't miss the committee meeting.
    (C) He never returned from class.
    (D) He was unable to fall asleep.

29. (A) That he would be working all weekend.
    (B) That no one ever worked on weekends.
    (C) That he would not be in the office this weekend.
    (D) That the office would be open this weekend.

30. (A) They should not let what happened bother them.
    (B) They should keep on trying to talk to Mary.
    (C) They should try to flatter Mary.
    (D) Their project is already as good as it's going to get.

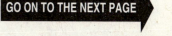

Part B

Directions: In this part of the test, you will hear longer conversations. After each conversation, you will hear several questions. The conversations and questions will not be repeated.

After you hear a question, read the four possible answers in your test book and choose the best answer. Then, on your answer sheet, find the number of the question and fill in the space that corresponds to the letter of the answer you have chosen.

Remember, you are **not** allowed to take notes or write in your test book.

31. (A) To a doctor's appointment.
     (B) To an exercise club.
     (C) To a swimming pool.
     (D) To a school.

32. (A) They're both regular members.
     (B) He likes to go there occasionally.
     (C) She wants him to try it out.
     (D) She hates to exercise alone.

33. (A) A limited number.
     (B) Racquetball courts and a swimming pool.
     (C) Exercise machines, but not classes.
     (D) Just about anything.

34. (A) Visit the club once.
     (B) Take out a membership.
     (C) Try the club unless he hurts himself.
     (D) See if he has time to go.

35. (A) A presentation for political science class.
     (B) How quickly time passes.
     (C) The differences between the various types of courts.
     (D) A schedule for preparing for a political science exam.

36. (A) Three levels of courts.
     (B) Only the municipal courts.
     (C) The state but not the federal courts.
     (D) Only the state and federal courts.

37. (A) On Thursday.
     (B) On Monday.
     (C) In a week.
     (D) Before Monday.

38. (A) Plenty of time.
     (B) Until Monday.
     (C) About one week.
     (D) Until a week from Monday.

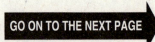

GO ON TO THE NEXT PAGE

Part C

Directions: In this part of the test, you will hear several talks. After each talk, you will hear some questions. The talks and questions will not be repeated.

After you hear a question, you will read the four possible answers in your test book and choose the best answer. Then, on your answer sheet, find the number of the question and fill in the space that corresponds to the letter of the answer you have chosen.

Here is an example.

On the recording, you will hear:

(narrator) *Listen to an instructor talk to his class about painting.*
(man) *Artist Grant Wood was a guiding force in the school of painting known as American regionalist, a style reflecting the distinctive characteristics of art from rural areas of the United States. Wood began drawing animals on the family farm at the age of three, and when he was thirty-eight one of his paintings received a remarkable amount of public notice and acclaim. This painting, called "American Gothic," is a starkly simple depiction of a serious couple staring directly out at the viewer.*

Now listen to a sample question.   **Sample Answer**

(narrator) *What style of painting is known as American regionalist?*   Ⓐ
                                                                              Ⓑ
In your test book, you will read: (A) Art from America's inner cities.   Ⓒ
                                       (B) Art from the central region of the   ●
                                              United States.
                                       (C) Art from various urban areas in the
                                              United States.
                                       (D) Art from rural sections of America.

The best answer to the question, "What style of painting is known as American regionalist?" is (D), "Art from rural sections of America." Therefore, the correct choice is (D).

Now listen to another sample question.   **Sample Answer**

                                                                              Ⓐ
(narrator) *What is the name of Wood's most successful painting?*   Ⓑ
                                                                               ●
In your test book, you will read: (A) "American Regionalist."   Ⓓ
                                       (B) "The Family Farm in Iowa."
                                       (C) "American Gothic."
                                       (D) "A Serious Couple."

The best answer to the question, "What is the name of Wood's most successful painting?" is (C), "American Gothic." Therefore, the correct choice is (C).

Remember, you are **not** allowed to take notes or write in your test book.

1 □ **1** □ **1** □ **1** □ **1** □ **1** □ **1** □ **1**

39. (A) A university administrator.
    (B) A student.
    (C) A librarian.
    (D) A registrar.

40. (A) How to use the library.
    (B) The university registration procedure.
    (C) Services offered by the Student Center.
    (D) Important locations on campus.

41. (A) To provide students with assistance and amusement.
    (B) To assist students in the registration process.
    (C) To allow students to watch movies.
    (D) To provide textbooks for university courses.

42. (A) In administrators' offices.
    (B) In the Student Center.
    (C) In an auditorium.
    (D) In the Student Records Office.

43. (A) Natural soaps.
    (B) Synthetic detergents.
    (C) Biodegradable detergents.
    (D) Phosphates.

44. (A) Synthetic detergents.
    (B) A major cause of water pollution.
    (C) Substances that break down into simpler forms.
    (D) The reason for the foaming water supply.

45. (A) They broke down into simpler forms.
    (B) They caused the water to become foamy.
    (C) They released phosphates into the water.
    (D) They damaged only the underground water supply.

46. (A) Water pollution in the 1950s.
    (B) Nonbiodegradable synthetic detergents.
    (C) The foamy water supply.
    (D) Problems caused by the phosphates.

47. (A) The static atmosphere.
    (B) The cause of changes in the atmosphere.
    (C) The evolution of plant life.
    (D) The process of photosynthesis.

48. (A) Two hundred million years ago.
    (B) Twenty million years ago.
    (C) Two hundred thousand years ago.
    (D) Twenty thousand years ago.

49. (A) The evolution of plants and photosynthesis.
    (B) The variety of gases in the atmosphere.
    (C) The high percentage of nitrogen.
    (D) The ammonia and methane in the original atmosphere.

50. (A) Read about the composition of the atmosphere.
    (B) Study the notes of today's lecture.
    (C) Prepare for a quiz.
    (D) Read the following chapter.

**This is the end of Section 1.
Stop work on Section 1.**

Turn off the recording.

**Read the directions for Section 2 and begin work.
Do NOT read or work on any other section
of the test during the next 25 minutes.**

SECTION 2
STRUCTURE AND WRITTEN EXPRESSION
Time—25 minutes
(including the reading of the directions)
Now set your clock for 25 minutes.

This section is designed to measure your ability to recognize language that is appropriate for standard written English. There are two types of questions in this section, with special directions for each type.

Structure

Directions: These questions are incomplete sentences. Beneath each sentence you will see four words or phrases, marked (A), (B), (C), and (D). Choose the **one** word or phrase that best completes the sentence. Then, on your answer sheet, find the number of the question and fill in the space that corresponds to the letter of the answer you have chosen.

Look at the following examples.

Example I   **Sample Answer**

The president _____ the election by a landslide.

(A) won
(B) he won
(C) yesterday
(D) fortunately

The sentence should read, "The president won the election by a landslide." Therefore, you should choose answer (A).

Example II   **Sample Answer**

When _____ the conference?

(A) the doctor attended
(B) did the doctor attend
(C) the doctor will attend
(D) the doctor's attendance

The sentence should read, "When did the doctor attend the conference?" Therefore, you should choose answer (B).

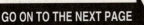
GO ON TO THE NEXT PAGE

1. Different hormones _____ at the same time on a particular target issue.

   (A) usually act
   (B) usually acting
   (C) they usual act
   (D) the usual action

2. The tidal forces on the Earth due to _____ only 0.46 of those due to the Moon.

   (A) the Sun is
   (B) the Sun they are
   (C) the Sun it is
   (D) the Sun are

3. Most radioactive elements occur in igneous and metamorphic _____ fossils occur in sedimentary rocks.

   (A) rocks, nearly all
   (B) rocks, but nearly all
   (C) rocks, nearly all are
   (D) rocks, which nearly all are

4. _____ radioisotope is encountered, the first step in its identification is the determination of its half-life.

   (A) An unknown
   (B) Afterwards, an unknown
   (C) When an unknown
   (D) During an unknown

5. The Missouri _____ longest river in the United States, flows through seven states from its source in Montana to its confluence with the Mississippi.

   (A) River, the
   (B) River is the
   (C) River is one of the
   (D) River, one of the

6. Coral islands such as the Maldives are the tips of reefs built during periods of warm climate, when _____ higher.

   (A) were sea levels
   (B) sea had levels
   (C) having sea levels
   (D) sea levels were

7. Hail forms within large, dense cumulonimbus _____ develop on hot, humid summer days.

   (A) clouds
   (B) clouds that
   (C) clouds that are
   (D) clouds that they

8. Measles is a highly contagious viral disease _____ by a characteristic skin rash.

   (A) accompany
   (B) is accompanied
   (C) accompanied
   (D) it is accompanied

9. Charles Darwin's first scientific book, published in 1842, _____ a since substantiated theory on the origin of coral reefs and atolls.

   (A) to present
   (B) presented
   (C) presenting
   (D) it presents

10. Phytoplanktons thrive where _____ phosphorus into the upper layers of a body of water.

   (A) upwelling currents circulate
   (B) the circulation of upwelling currents
   (C) are upwelling currents
   (D) circulates upwelling currents

GO ON TO THE NEXT PAGE →

11. By the end of 1609, Galileo had a 20-power telescope that enabled him to see _____ planets revolving around Jupiter.

    (A) the call
    (B) he called
    (C) to call him
    (D) what he called

12. On every continent except Antarctica _____ more than 30,000 species of spiders.

    (A) some are
    (B) some of the
    (C) are some of the
    (D) is some

13. Many bugs possess defensive scent glands and emit disagreeable odors when _____.

    (A) disturbed
    (B) are disturbed
    (C) they disturbed
    (D) are they disturbed

14. Hurricanes move with the large-scale wind currents _____ are imbedded.

    (A) that they
    (B) which they
    (C) in that they
    (D) in which they

15. _____ the Earth's ice to melt, the Earth's oceans would rise by about two hundred feet.

    (A) If all
    (B) Were all
    (C) If all were
    (D) All was

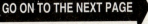

GO ON TO THE NEXT PAGE

Written Expression

Directions: In these questions, each sentence has four underlined words or phrases. The four underlined parts of the sentence are marked (A), (B), (C), and (D). Identify the **one** underlined word or phrase that must be changed in order for the sentence to be correct. Then, on your answer sheet, find the number of the question and fill in the space that corresponds to the letter of the answer you have chosen.

Look at the following examples.

Example I

The four string on a violin are tuned
  A   B   C D

in fifths.

Sample Answer

Ⓐ
●
Ⓒ
Ⓓ

The sentence should read, "The four strings on a violin are tuned in fifths." Therefore, you should choose answer (B).

Example II

The research for the book *Roots* taking
    A   B   C

Alex Haley twelve years.
            D

Sample Answer

Ⓐ
Ⓑ
●
Ⓓ

The sentence should read, "The research for the book *Roots* took Alex Haley twelve years." Therefore, you should choose answer (C).

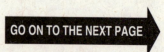

TOEFL® test directions and format are reprinted by permission of ETS, the copyright owner. However, all examples and test questions are provided by Pearson Education, Inc.

2 ● 2 ● 2 ● 2 ● 2 ● 2 ● 2 ● 2

16. The brilliantly colored rhinoceros viper has two or three horns above each nostrils.
    A   B   C   D

17. Most of the outer planets has large swarms of satellites surrounding them.
                A   B   C   D

18. Historical records show that Halley's comet has return about every seventy-six years
                       A   B   C

    for the past 2,000 years.
             D

19. Robert Heinlein was instrumental in popularizing science fiction with a series of
                      A   B   C

    stories that is first published in the *Saturday Evening Post*.
               D

20. Each number on the Richter scale represent a tenfold increase in the amplitude of
         A   B

    waves of ground motion recorded during an earthquake.
                   C   D

21. Lake Tahoe, located on the eastern edge of the Sierra Nevada range, is feed by more
                A   B   C

    than thirty mountain streams.
                          D

22. Established in 1789 and operated by the Jesuits, Georgetown University in
    A

    Washington, D.C. is the older Roman Catholic institution of higher learning in the
                       B   C   D

    United States.

23. The surface of the planet Venus is almost completely hid by the thick clouds that
                                       A   B   C

    shroud it.
    D

24. Present in rocks of all types, hematite is particular abundant in the sedimentary
    A   B   C

    rocks known as red beds.
          D

25. Tropical cyclones, alike extratropical cyclones, which derive much of their energy
                       A   B   C

    from the jet stream, originate far from the polar front.
                                   D

GO ON TO THE NEXT PAGE

COMPLETE TEST FIVE   493

26. Elizabeth Cady Stanton organized the first U.S. women's rights convention in 1848
                                                   A   B

    and was instrumentally in the struggle to win voting and property rights for women.
               C   D

27. Jaguarundis are sleek, long-tailed creatures colored either an uniform reddish brown
                       A   B   C

    or dark grey.
    D

28. It is possible to get a sunburn on a cloudy day because eighty percent of the
                  A   B

    ultraviolet rays from the Sun would penetrate cloud cover.
                           C   D

29. In 1964, GATT established the International Trade Center in order to assist
                                                  A

    developing countries in the promotion of its exports.
      B   C   D

30. Joseph Heller's novel *Catch-22* satirizes both the horrors of war as well as the power
                               A   B   C

    of modern bureaucratic institutions.
               D

31. In *Roots,* Alex Haley uses fictional details to embellish a factual histories of seven
                        A   B   C

    generations of his family.
             D

32. The carbon atoms of the diamond are so strongly bonded that a diamond can only be
          A   B

    scratched with other diamond.
       C   D

33. Viruses are extremely tiny parasites that are able to reproduce only within the cells
      A   B   C

    of theirs hosts.
       D

34. During the last Ice Age, which ended about 10,000 years ago, there was about three
      A   B

    times more ice than is today.
         C   D

GO ON TO THE NEXT PAGE →

35. Melons most probably originated in Persia and were introduced the North American
    $\underline{}$ A $\underline{}$ B $\underline{}$ C

    continent during the sixteenth century.
    $\underline{}$
    D

36. More than 600 million individual bacteria lives on the skin of humans.
     $\underline{}$ $\underline{}$ $\underline{}$ $\underline{}$
     A B C D

37. The more directly overhead the Moon is, the great is the effect that it exhibits on the
     $\underline{}$ $\underline{}$ $\underline{}$ $\underline{}$
     A B C D

    Earth.

38. As the International Dateline at 180 degrees longitude is crossed westerly, it becomes
    $\underline{}$ $\underline{}$
    A B

    necessary to change the date by moving it one day forward.
    $\underline{}$ $\underline{}$
    C D

39. Kilauea's numerous eruptions are generally composed in molten lava, with little
     $\underline{}$ $\underline{}$ $\underline{}$
     A B C

    escaping gas and few explosions.
     $\underline{}$
     D

40. The incubation period of tetanus is usually five to ten days, and the most frequently
     $\underline{}$ $\underline{}$
     A B

    occurred symptom is jaw stiffness.
    $\underline{}$ $\underline{}$
    C D

This is the end of Section 2.
If you finish before 25 minutes has ended,
check your work on Section 2 only.

(STOP) (STOP) (STOP) (STOP) (STOP) (STOP) (STOP)

At the end of 25 minutes, go on to Section 3.
Use exactly 55 minutes to work on Section 3.

SECTION 3
READING COMPREHENSION
Time—55 minutes
(including the reading of the directions)
Now set your clock for 55 minutes.

This section is designed to measure your ability to read and understand short passages similar in topic and style to those that students are likely to encounter in North American universities and colleges. This section contains reading passages and questions about the passages.

Directions: In this section you will read several passages. Each one is followed by a number of questions about it. You are to choose the **one** best answer, (A), (B), (C), or (D), to each question. Then, on your answer sheet, find the number of the question and fill in the space that corresponds to the letter of the answer you have chosen.

Answer all questions about the information in a passage on the basis of what is **stated** or **implied** in that passage.

Read the following passage:

> John Quincy Adams, who served as the sixth president of the United States from 1825 to 1829, is today recognized for his masterful statesmanship and diplomacy. He dedicated his life to public service, both in the presidency and in the various other political offices that he
> *Line* held. Throughout his political career he demonstrated his unswerving belief in freedom of
> (5) speech, the antislavery cause, and the right of Americans to be free from European and Asian domination.

Example I   **Sample Answer**

To what did John Quincy Adams devote his life?   (A)
                                                                                               ●
(A) Improving his personal life   (C)
(B) Serving the public   (D)
(C) Increasing his fortune
(D) Working on his private business

According to the passage, John Quincy Adams "dedicated his life to public service." Therefore, you should choose answer (B).

Example II   **Sample Answer**

In line 4, the word "unswerving" is closest in meaning to   (A)
                                                                                              (B)
(A) moveable   ●
(B) insignificant   (D)
(C) unchanging
(D) diplomatic

The passage states that John Quincy Adams demonstrated his unswerving belief "throughout his career." This implies that the belief did not change. Therefore, you should choose answer (C).

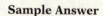

GO ON TO THE NEXT PAGE

TOEFL® test directions and format are reprinted by permission of ETS, the copyright owner. However, all examples and test questions are provided by Pearson Education, Inc.

Questions 1–11

Harvard University, today recognized as part of the top echelon of the world's universities, came from very inauspicious and humble beginnings.

Line
(5)

This oldest of American universities was founded in 1636, just sixteen years after the Pilgrims landed at Plymouth. Included in the Puritan emigrants to the Massachusetts colony during this period were more than 100 graduates of England's prestigious Oxford and Cambridge universities, and these university graduates in the New World were determined that their sons would have the same educational opportunities that they themselves had had. Because of this support in the colony for an institution of higher learning, the General Court of Massachusetts appropriated 400 pounds for a college in October of 1636 and early the following year decided on a parcel of land for the school; this

(10) land was in an area called Newetowne, which was later renamed Cambridge after its English cousin and is the site of the present-day university.

When a young minister named John Harvard, who came from the neighboring town of Charlestowne, died from tuberculosis in 1638, he willed half of his estate of 1,700 pounds to the fledgling college. In spite of the fact that only half of the bequest was actually paid, the General Court

(15) named the college after the minister in appreciation for what he had done. The amount of the bequest may not have been large, particularly by today's standards, but it was more than the General Court had found it necessary to appropriate in order to open the college.

Henry Dunster was appointed the first president of Harvard in 1640, and it should be noted that in addition to serving as president, he was also the entire faculty, with an entering freshman class of

(20) four students. Although the staff did expand somewhat, for the first century of its existence the entire teaching staff consisted of the president and three or four tutors.

1. The main idea of this passage is that

(A) Harvard is one of the world's most prestigious universities
(B) what is today a great university started out small
(C) John Harvard was key to the development of a great university
(D) Harvard University developed under the auspices of the General Court of Massachusetts

2. The passage indicates that Harvard is

(A) one of the oldest universities in the world
(B) the oldest university in the world
(C) one of the oldest universities in America
(D) the oldest university in America

3. It can be inferred from the passage that the Puritans who traveled to the Massachusetts colony were

(A) rather well educated
(B) rather rich
(C) rather supportive of the English government
(D) rather undemocratic

4. The pronoun "they" in line 7 refers to

(A) Oxford and Cambridge universities
(B) university graduates
(C) sons
(D) educational opportunities

5. The "pounds" in line 8 are probably

(A) types of books
(B) college students
(C) units of money
(D) school campuses

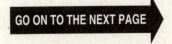
GO ON TO THE NEXT PAGE

6. The "English cousin" in line 10 refers to a

   (A) city
   (B) relative
   (C) person
   (D) court

7. Which of the following is NOT mentioned about John Harvard?

   (A) What he died of
   (B) Where he came from
   (C) Where he was buried
   (D) How much he bequeathed to Harvard

8. The word "fledgling" in line 14 could best be replaced by which of the following?

   (A) Newborn
   (B) Flying
   (C) Winged
   (D) Established

9. The passage implies that

   (A) Henry Dunster was an ineffective president
   (B) someone else really served as president of Harvard before Henry Dunster
   (C) Henry Dunster spent much of his time as president managing the Harvard faculty
   (D) the position of president of Harvard was not merely an administrative position in the early years

10. The word "somewhat" in line 20 could best be replaced by

    (A) back and forth
    (B) to and fro
    (C) side by side
    (D) more or less

11. Where in the passage does it indicate how much money Minister Harvard was really responsible for giving to the university?

    (A) Lines 3–7
    (B) Lines 7–11
    (C) Lines 12–15
    (D) Lines 15–17

GO ON TO THE NEXT PAGE

Questions 12–21

A binary star is actually a pair of stars that are held together by the force of gravity. Although occasionally the individual stars that compose a binary star can be distinguished, they generally appear as one star. The gravitational pull between the individual stars of a binary star causes one to orbit around the other. From the orbital pattern of a binary, the mass of its stars can be determined:
Line
(5) the gravitational pull of a star is in direct proportion to its mass, and the strength of the gravitational force of one star on another determines the orbital pattern of the binary.

Scientists have discovered stars that seem to orbit around an empty space. It has been suggested that such a star and the empty space really composed a binary star. The empty space is known as a "black hole," a star with such strong gravitational force that no light is able to get through. Although
(10) the existence of black holes has not been proven, the theory of their existence has been around for about two centuries, since the French mathematician Pierre Simon de Laplace first proposed the concept at the end of the eighteenth century. Scientific interest in this theory has been intense in the last few decades. However, currently the theory is unproven. Black holes can only be potentially identified based on the interactions of objects around them, as happens when a potential black hole is
(15) part of a binary star; they, of course, cannot be seen because of the inability of any light to escape the star's powerful gravity.

12. A binary star could best be described as

   (A) stars that have been forced apart
   (B) a star with a strong gravitational force
   (C) two stars pulled together by gravity
   (D) a large number of attached stars

13. The word "distinguished" in line 2 is closest in meaning to

   (A) renowned
   (B) tied
   (C) celebrated
   (D) differentiated

14. According to the passage, what happens as a result of the gravitational force between the stars?

   (A) One star circles the other.
   (B) The mass of the binary star increases.
   (C) A black hole is destroyed.
   (D) The gravitational force decreases.

15. The word "proportion" in line 5 is closest in meaning to which of the following?

   (A) Contrast
   (B) Ratio
   (C) Inversion
   (D) Force

16. A "black hole" in line 9 is

   (A) an empty space around which nothing orbits
   (B) a star with close to zero gravity
   (C) a star whose gravitational force blocks the passage of light
   (D) an empty space so far away that no light can reach it

17. Which of the following statements about black holes is NOT supported by the passage?

   (A) A black hole can have a star orbiting around it.
   (B) A binary star can be composed of a black hole and a visible star.
   (C) All empty space contains black holes.
   (D) The gravitational pull of a black hole is strong.

18. The word "get" in line 9 could best be replaced by

   (A) pass
   (B) sink
   (C) jump
   (D) see

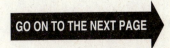

GO ON TO THE NEXT PAGE

19. Which of the following is implied in the passage about the theory of black holes?

    (A) No reputable scientists believe it.
    (B) It has only recently been hypothesized.
    (C) At least some scientists find it credible.
    (D) Scientists are hoping to see a black hole in order to prove the theory.

20. The word "intense" in line 12 is closest in meaning to

    (A) brilliant
    (B) intermittent
    (C) bright
    (D) strong

21. This passage would probably be assigned reading in a course on

    (A) botany
    (B) astrophysics
    (C) geology
    (D) astrology

GO ON TO THE NEXT PAGE

Questions 22–30

Clara Barton is well known for her endeavors as a nurse on the battlefield during the Civil War and for her role in founding the American Red Cross. She is perhaps not as well known, however, for her role in establishing a bureau for tracing missing soldiers following the Civil War.

Line
(5) At the close of the Civil War, the United States did not have in place any agency responsible for accounting for what had happened to the innumerable men who had served in the military during the war, and many families had no idea as to the fate of their loved ones. Families were forced to agonize endlessly over where their loved ones were, what kind of shape they were in, whether or not they would return, and what had happened to them.

Clara Barton developed a system for using print media to publish the names of soldiers known
(10) to have been wounded or killed during various battles of the Civil War. She was prepared to publish names that she herself had gathered on the battlefield as well as information gathered from others. She made numerous unsuccessful attempts to interest various government officials in her plan. However, it was not until Henry Wilson, a senator from the state of Massachusetts, took up her cause and presented her plan to President Lincoln that her plan was implemented.

(15) With Lincoln's assistance, Clara Barton was set up in a small government office with funding for a few clerks and the authority to examine military records. She and her clerks gathered and compiled information from military records and battlefield witnesses and published it in newspapers and magazines. Clara Barton operated this missing persons bureau for four years, from the end of the war in 1865 until 1869. During this period, she and her staff put out more than 100,000 printed lists,
(20) answered more than 60,000 letters, and accounted for more than 20,000 missing soldiers.

22. The purpose of this passage is

    (A) to praise Clara Barton's work as a battlefield nurse
    (B) to outline Clara Barton's role in establishing the American Red Cross
    (C) to malign the role of the U.S. government at the end of the Civil War
    (D) to present one of Clara Barton's lesser-known accomplishments

23. Which of the following is NOT mentioned as one of Clara Barton's accomplishments?

    (A) That she treated wounded Civil War soldiers
    (B) That she was integral to the establishment of the American Red Cross
    (C) That she served as an elected government official
    (D) That she continued to work for the good of soldiers and their families after the Civil War

24. The word "close" in line 4 could best be replaced by

    (A) near
    (B) battle
    (C) end
    (D) shut

25. What is stated in the passage about the issue of missing persons following the Civil War?

    (A) The U.S. government was not officially prepared to deal with the issue.
    (B) President Lincoln did not recognize that there was an issue.
    (C) One U.S. government agency was responsible for the issue.
    (D) U.S. citizens were unaware of the issue.

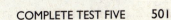
GO ON TO THE NEXT PAGE

26. It can be inferred from the passage that the budget for Barton's missing persons agency was

    (A) quite lavish
    (B) open-ended
    (C) limited in scope
    (D) from private sources

27. The pronoun "it" in line 17 refers to

    (A) funding
    (B) authority
    (C) information
    (D) bureau

28. Which of the following did Clara Barton and her staff accomplish, according to the passage?

    (A) They searched military records.
    (B) They responded to 100,000 letters.
    (C) They printed a list with 100,000 names.
    (D) They talked with 20,000 missing soldiers.

29. Where in the passage does the author indicate the duration of the existence of Clara Barton's missing persons agency?

    (A) Lines 4–6
    (B) Lines 9–10
    (C) Lines 15–16
    (D) Lines 18–19

30. Which paragraph describes Clara Barton's efforts to establish a missing persons bureau?

    (A) The first paragraph
    (B) The second paragraph
    (C) The third paragraph
    (D) The last paragraph

GO ON TO THE NEXT PAGE

Questions 31–40

Mutualism is a type of symbiosis that occurs when two unlike organisms live together in a state that is mutually beneficial. It can exist between two animals, between two plants, or between a plant and an animal. Mutualism is unlike the symbiotic state of commensalism in that commensalism is a
Line one-sided state in which a host gives and a guest takes, while in mutualism both partners live on a
(5) give-and-take basis.

In the African wilds, the zebra and the ostrich enjoy a symbiotic relationship that enhances the ability of each of these large land animals to survive. Both serve as prey for the lion, and neither has the capability alone to withstand an attack from this fierce hunter. However, when the zebra and the ostrich collaborate in their defense by alerting each other to possible danger from an approaching
(10) predator, the lion is rarely able to capture more than the oldest or feeblest of the herd.

The complementary physical strengths and weaknesses of the ostrich and the zebra allow them to work in coordination to avoid succumbing to the lion. The ostrich, the largest flightless bird in the world, possesses great speed and keen eyesight, which enable it to spot large predatory animals long before they are able to position themselves to attack. The zebra, with a running speed equal to that of
(15) the ostrich, has excellent hearing and a good sense of smell but lacks the sharp eyesight of the ostrich. When ostriches and zebras intermix for grazing, each animal benefits from the ability of the other to detect approaching danger. If either animal senses danger, both animals are alerted and take off. With the running speed that both of these animals possess, they are able to outrun any predator except the cheetah.

31. How is the information in the passage organized?

   (A) A concept is explained through an extended example.
   (B) A series of chronological events is presented.
   (C) Two examples are compared and contrasted.
   (D) Two opposing theories are explained.

32. The word "unlike" in line 1 is closest in meaning to

   (A) unfriendly
   (B) dissimilar
   (C) potential
   (D) hated

33. The word "beneficial" in line 2 is closest in meaning to

   (A) distinctive
   (B) meaningful
   (C) helpful
   (D) understood

34. What is "commensalism" in line 3?

   (A) A specific kind of mutualistic relationship
   (B) A relationship that is beneficial to both partners
   (C) A relationship in which both partners are hurt
   (D) A relationship that is beneficial to only one partner

35. What is implied in the passage about the zebra and the ostrich?

   (A) They have a commensalist relationship.
   (B) The lion is prey for both of them.
   (C) They share a mutualistic relationship.
   (D) Their relationship is not symbiotic.

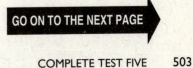

GO ON TO THE NEXT PAGE

36. What is stated in the passage about the lion?

    (A) It is easily able to capture zebras and ostriches.
    (B) It is usually able to catch only weaker zebras and ostriches.
    (C) It never hunts zebras and ostriches.
    (D) It does not hurt old or feeble zebras and ostriches.

37. The word "collaborate" in line 9 is closest in meaning to

    (A) work together
    (B) make observations
    (C) make a stand
    (D) run and hide

38. The pronoun "it" in line 13 refers to

    (A) ostrich
    (B) world
    (C) speed
    (D) eyesight

39. Which of the following is NOT stated in the passage?

    (A) The ostrich is unable to fly.
    (B) The ostrich is able to see better than the zebra.
    (C) The zebra hears and smells well.
    (D) The zebra is able to run faster than the ostrich.

40. Where in the passage does the author mention the one animal that is faster than both the ostrich and the zebra?

    (A) Lines 8–10
    (B) Lines 12–14
    (C) Lines 14–15
    (D) Lines 18–19

GO ON TO THE NEXT PAGE ▶

Questions 41–50

Esperanto is what is called a planned, or artificial, language. It was created more than a century ago by Polish eye doctor Ludwik Lazar Zamenhof. Zamenhof believed that a common language would help to alleviate some of the misunderstandings among cultures.

Line
(5) In Zamenhof's first attempt at a universal language, he tried to create a language that was as uncomplicated as possible. This first language included words such as *ab, ac, ba, eb, be,* and *ce.* This did not result in a workable language in that these monosyllabic words, though short, were not easy to understand or to retain.

Next, Zamenhof tried a different way of constructing a simplified language. He made the words in his language sound like words that people already knew, but he simplified the grammar
(10) tremendously. One example of how he simplified the language can be seen in the suffixes: all nouns in this language end in *o,* as in the noun *amiko,* which means "friend," and all adjectives end in *-a,* as in the adjective *bela,* which means "pretty." Another example of the simplified language can be seen in the prefix *mal-,* which makes a word opposite in meaning; the word *malamiko* therefore means "enemy," and the word *malbela* therefore means "ugly" in Zamenhof's language.

(15) In 1887, Zamenhof wrote a description of this language and published it. He used a pen name, Dr. Esperanto, when signing the book. He selected the name Esperanto because this word means "a person who hopes" in his language. Esperanto clubs began popping up throughout Europe, and by 1905, Esperanto had spread from Europe to America and Asia.

In 1905, the First World Congress of Esperanto took place in France, with approximately 700
(20) attendees from 20 different countries. Congresses were held annually for nine years, and 4,000 attendees were registered for the Tenth World Esperanto Congress scheduled for 1914, when World War I erupted and forced its cancellation.

Esperanto has had its ups and downs in the period since World War I. Today, years after it was introduced, it is estimated that perhaps a quarter of a million people are fluent in it. This may seem
(25) like a large number, but it is really quite small when compared with the billion English speakers and billion Mandarin Chinese speakers in today's world. Current advocates would like to see its use grow considerably and are taking steps to try to make this happen.

41. The topic of this passage is

    (A) a language developed in the last few years
    (B) one man's efforts to create a universal language
    (C) how language can be improved
    (D) using language to communicate internationally

42. According to the passage, Zamenhof wanted to create a universal language

    (A) to resolve cultural differences
    (B) to provide a more complex language
    (C) to build a name for himself
    (D) to create one world culture

43. It can be inferred from the passage that the Esperanto word *malespera* means

    (A) hopelessness
    (B) hope
    (C) hopeless
    (D) hopeful

44. The expression "popping up" in line 17 could best be replaced by

    (A) leaping
    (B) shouting
    (C) hiding
    (D) opening

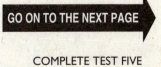
GO ON TO THE NEXT PAGE

45. It can be inferred from the passage that the Third World Congress of Esperanto took place

    (A) in 1905
    (B) in 1907
    (C) in 1909
    (D) in 1913

46. According to the passage, what happened to the Tenth World Esperanto Congress?

    (A) It had 4,000 attendees.
    (B) It was scheduled for 1915.
    (C) It had attendees from 20 countries.
    (D) It never took place.

47. The expression "ups and downs" in line 23 is closest in meaning to

    (A) tops and bottoms
    (B) floors and ceilings
    (C) takeoffs and landings
    (D) highs and lows

48. Which paragraph describes the predecessor to Esperanto?

    (A) The first paragraph
    (B) The second paragraph
    (C) The third paragraph
    (D) The fourth paragraph

49. This passage would most likely be assigned reading in a course on

    (A) European history
    (B) English grammar
    (C) world government
    (D) applied linguistics

50. The paragraph following the passage most likely discusses

    (A) how current supporters of Esperanto are encouraging its growth
    (B) another of Zamenhof's accomplishments
    (C) the disadvantages of using an artificial language
    (D) attempts to reconvene the World Congress of Esperanto in the 1920s

This is the end of Section 3.

**If you finish in less than 55 minutes,
check your work on Section 3 only.
Do NOT read or work on any other section of the test.**

When you finish the test, you may do the following:

- Turn to the **Diagnostic Charts** on pages 551–558, and circle the numbers of the questions that you missed.

- Turn to **Scoring Information** on pages 549–550, and determine your TOEFL score.

- Turn to the **Progress Chart** on page 559, and add your score to the chart.

TEST OF WRITTEN ENGLISH:
TWE ESSAY TOPIC
Time—30 minutes

Some people make decisions quickly. Others arrive at decisions only after long, careful thought. Which type of decision do you most often make? Use specific details and examples to support your answer.

APPENDIXES

APPENDIX A: **Similar Sounds**

DIRECTIONS: In each exercise first read the group of words aloud with the correct pronunciation. Then listen to the statements, each of which contains one of the words. Finally, choose the letter of the word you have heard.

⌒ NOW BEGIN THE RECORDING AT EXERCISE A1.

EXERCISE A1
A. pit	C. pat	E. pout
B. pet	D. put	F. pot

EXERCISE A2
A. heat	C. hut	E. height
B. hit	D. hot	F. hate

EXERCISE A3
A. cat	C. cot	E. kite
B. cut	D. caught	F. coat

EXERCISE A4
A. bill	C. bull	E. bale
B. bell	D. ball	F. bowl

EXERCISE A5
A. cap	C. cup	E. cop
B. cape	D. keep	F. cope

EXERCISE A6
A. bead	C. bed	E. bud
B. bid	D. bad	F. bowed

EXERCISE A7
A. neat	C. net	E. knot
B. night	D. nut	F. note

EXERCISE A8
A. seek	C. sack	E. sock
B. sick	D. soak	F. sake

EXERCISE A9
A. seed	C. sad	E. side
B. said	D. sawed	F. sighed

EXERCISE A10
A. heal	D. hail	G. howl
B. hill	E. hole	H. whole
C. haul	F. hall	I. hull

EXERCISE A11
A. beat	D. bat	G. bait
B. bit	E. but	H. bite
C. bet	F. bought	I. boat

APPENDIX B: **Two- and Three-Part Verbs**

DIRECTIONS: Each of the following sentences contains a two- or three-part verb in italics. Read the sentence and try to understand the italicized expression. Then, find the meaning of the expression in the list that follows the exercise, and write the letter of the answer on the line.

EXERCISE B1

_____ 1. He's been smoking too much. He really needs to *cut down*.

_____ 2. The company had to *cut off* the electricity because the bill was unpaid.

_____ 3. He kept teasing me, so finally I told him to *cut it out*.

_____ 4. He is working hard because he really wants to *get ahead* in his career.

_____ 5. She is such a nice person that she is easily able to *get along* with everyone.

_____ 6. Could you explain a little more clearly? I really don't understand what you are trying to *get at*.

_____ 7. When he stole some money from her, she really wanted to do something to *get back at* him.

_____ 8. We have enough money to *get by* for a few months; we won't have a lot of extras, but we will survive.

_____ 9. She was sick for several weeks, but now she has started to *get over* it.

_____ 10. There are too many clothes in my closet. I need to *get rid of* some of them.

DEFINITIONS—Exercise B1	
A. stop it	**F.** manage
B. get revenge against	**G.** advance
C. recover from	**H.** throw away
D. decrease it	**I.** stop the supply of
E. be friendly	**J.** imply

EXERCISE B2

_____ 1. He read the untrue stories about himself in the newspaper, but he tried not to react. He just tried to *brush it off*.

_____ 2. I haven't played Scrabble in quite some time. I'll have to *brush up on* the rules before we play.

_____ 3. While we were walking in the mountains, we were lucky enough to *come across* a waterfall. It was quite a surprise to find such a beautiful thing.

_____ 4. She is not feeling well; she thinks she is about to *come down with* the flu.

_____ 5. While I'm on my trip, do you think you could *look after* my cats?

_____ 6. The police detective was not sure how the crime was committed. She decided to *look into* it further.

_____   7.   Here is my application. Could you take a few moments to *look it over?*

_____   8.   The brother always used to *pick on* his younger sister. His favorite tricks were to pull her hair, tease her, or scare her.

_____   9.   You have tried on three dresses, but you can't afford all of them. You'll have to *pick out* just one.

_____   10.   Could you *pick* me *up* after school today? I'll wait for you out in front of the school.

DEFINITIONS—Exercise B2	
A. take care of	**F.** bother
B. review; relearn	**G.** not let it have an effect
C. choose	**H.** unexpectedly find
D. get sick with	**I.** come and get
E. look at it briefly	**J.** investigate

EXERCISE B3

_____   1.   We have some new neighbors. I think I'll *call on* them later this afternoon.

_____   2.   The principal had to *call off* the class on Tuesday because the teacher was sick.

_____   3.   The politician should *call for* a decrease in taxes.

_____   4.   Why don't you *call* me *up* about 9:00? I'll be waiting by the phone.

_____   5.   I don't need this bicycle any more. It's not worth too much money, so I think I'll just *give* it *away.*

_____   6.   Here's the book I borrowed from you, and now I think I should *give* it *back.*

_____   7.   I've done all I can. I just can't do anything more. I *give up.*

_____   8.   The teacher has to *put off* the exam until next week because the students are not prepared.

_____   9.   She has to *put on* her coat before she goes out into the cold winter weather.

_____   10.   He's such a mean man that it's difficult to *put up with* him.

DEFINITIONS—Exercise B3	
A. donate	**F.** cancel
B. visit	**G.** delay
C. tolerate	**H.** telephone
D. request; suggest	**I.** dress in
E. return	**J.** surrender

EXERCISE B4

_____ 1. I was scared last night because someone tried to **break into** my house.

_____ 2. He and she have been friends for more than two years, but now they've decided to **break off** their relationship.

_____ 3. I'm really excited to be selected as master of ceremonies. I've never done this before, but I'm really going to try to **carry it off**.

_____ 4. After her husband was killed in an accident, she tried hard to **carry on** with her life.

_____ 5. I'm going to **hold off** taking my vacation. I was scheduled to take my vacation this week, but I'll take it next month instead.

_____ 6. My boss told me that my work had been very good recently and that she wanted me to **keep it up**.

_____ 7. Many of the employees of the company are worried; they've heard a rumor that the company is going to **lay off** a number of employees.

_____ 8. While I was at the market, I was surprised to **run into** a friend I hadn't seen in months.

_____ 9. If I didn't buy milk at the store, we would **run out of** it at breakfast in the morning.

_____ 10. That boy has been playing baseball all day. I know he's going to **wear out** soon.

DEFINITIONS—Exercise B4	
A. postpone	**F.** completely use the supply of
B. succeed	**G.** end
C. fire	**H.** unexpectedly meet
D. tire	**I.** continue
E. unlawfully enter	**J.** continue

EXERCISE B5

_____ 1. The newspapers tend to *play up* sensational stories if they want to improve their circulation.

_____ 2. He knew that it would be difficult to win the tournament, but he worked hard to *pull it off*.

_____ 3. She tends to *show off* a lot. She's very beautiful, and she wants everyone to notice her.

_____ 4. He was supposed to come at 9:00, but he didn't *show up* until 10:00.

_____ 5. Do you know when the wedding will *take place*? I heard that it would be next June.

_____ 6. Neither my roommate nor I like to do the dishes, so we *take turns*.

_____ 7. I don't know how to play golf, but it's a sport that I would like to *take up*.

_____ 8. He applied for the job, but the manager decided to *turn down* his application because he was not really qualified.

_____ 9. The students must *turn in* their papers on Thursday. The teacher has said that the papers can't be even one day late.

_____ 10. Because I swim so many hours every day, I sometimes feel that I'm going to *turn into* a fish.

DEFINITIONS—Exercise B5	
A. try to attract attention	**F.** refuse
B. submit	**G.** succeed
C. happen	**H.** begin (a hobby)
D. increase the significance of	**I.** become
E. arrive	**J.** alternate

APPENDIX C: **Idioms**

DIRECTIONS: Each of the following sentences contains an idiom in italics. Read the sentence and try to understand the idiom. Then find the meaning of the idiom in the list that follows, and write the letter of the answer on the line.

EXERCISE C1

_____ 1. He's holding down two jobs and attending school. He's really *burning the candle at both ends.*

_____ 2. She's buying a lot of new furniture before she even has a job. She's *putting the cart before the horse.*

_____ 3. Every time he opens his mouth, he immediately regrets what he said. He's always *putting his foot in his mouth.*

_____ 4. He's not telling me exactly what happened. He's *beating around the bush.*

_____ 5. She wanted to get that man's phone number, but she wasn't sure of his last name or where he lived. It was like *looking for a needle in a haystack.*

_____ 6. He's always too fast and out of control on his motorcycle. He's *playing with fire.*

_____ 7. She keeps asking if I was the one who was spreading rumors about her, but I wasn't. She's *barking up the wrong tree.*

_____ 8. He took the best portions for himself and didn't leave enough for the others. He's just *looking out for number one.*

_____ 9. She's been working on that assignment for over two months, and I don't think she's ever going to finish it. She's *taking forever and a day.*

_____ 10. She has to go to the bank, and while she's out she'll stop and visit her friend. She's *killing two birds with one stone.*

_____ 11. He was admitted to Harvard, and he would have gone there but he forgot to send in the appropriate form in time. He has really *missed the boat.*

_____ 12. I know that you thought that this part of the program was difficult, but wait until you see the next part. You're *jumping out of the frying pan and into the fire.*

DEFINITIONS—Exercise C1	
A. making a mistake	**G.** missed an opportunity
B. accomplishing two things at once	**H.** saying embarrassing things
C. doing something dangerous	**I.** speaking indirectly
D. doing things in the wrong order	**J.** doing something difficult
E. going from bad to worse	**K.** taking a really long time
F. doing too much	**L.** thinking only about himself

EXERCISE C2

_____ 1. His only two choices are to give up his free time or to pay a lot of money, and he doesn't like either choice. He's **between a rock and a hard place.**

_____ 2. She got 100 percent on the exam and the other students were below 70 percent. She's **head and shoulders above the rest.**

_____ 3. Every day he fixes meals, cleans the apartment, and goes to the market. It's **all in a day's work.**

_____ 4. She's a well-known lawyer, a good skier, a great cook, and a painter. She's a **jack-of-all-trades.**

_____ 5. Every time he puts the toys away, the children just take them out again. Keeping the house clean when the children are there is **like trying to swim upstream.**

_____ 6. Anytime I need help I go to her because I know she'll help me any way she can. She's **one in a million.**

_____ 7. He thought he was going to have to come into the office and work on both Saturday and Sunday, but now he doesn't have to. He's **off the hook.**

_____ 8. She and her classmates all have to read five chapters, write a paper, and prepare for an exam this week. They're **all in the same boat.**

_____ 9. He and his brother have the same hair, the same eyes, the same smile, and the same expressions. They're **like two peas in a pod.**

_____ 10. When I saw him with an older man, I just knew that the man had to be his father. He's **a chip off the old block.**

_____ 11. She's had so much to do to get ready for the trip that she's been running around all day. Now she's **on her last legs.**

_____ 12. I can't think of the answer, but it will come to me in just a minute. It's **on the tip of my tongue.**

DEFINITIONS—Exercise C2

A.	very tired	**G.**	in the same situation
B.	the best	**H.**	nothing out of the ordinary
C.	exactly alike	**I.**	accomplished at many things
D.	really wonderful	**J.**	an idea that is not in words
E.	really difficult or frustrating	**K.**	not responsible any longer
F.	just like his father	**L.**	without any good options

EXERCISE C3

_____ 1. Do you think you could help me out with the math homework? ***Two heads are better than one.***

_____ 2. What was it like when the announcement of the disaster came over the radio? ***You could have heard a pin drop.***

_____ 3. We could either go out to dinner tonight or stay home and cook. ***Six of one, half dozen of the other.***

_____ 4. I know you like the food at this restaurant, but I just don't care for it. ***To each his own.***

_____ 5. I got to the bank just one minute after closing time. ***Just my luck.***

_____ 6. My boss has asked me to respond immediately to this fax. ***No sooner said than done.***

_____ 7. Don't worry about what the boss just said to you. ***His bark is worse than his bite.***

_____ 8. It seems impossible for me to go to graduate school because I just can't afford it. But I'm going to try. ***Where there's a will, there's a way!***

_____ 9. Everything seems to be going the way that it should. ***So far, so good!***

_____ 10. Just think that because you locked your keys in the car, you got to meet that nice, handsome, young locksmith. ***Every cloud has a silver lining!***

_____ 11. I've got to accept the fact that it's going to take more than seven years of school if I want to become a doctor. After all, ***Rome wasn't built in a day.***

_____ 12. She loves my wardrobe, but I wish I had her clothes. ***The grass is always greener on the other side of the fence.***

DEFINITIONS—Exercise C3	
A. It was really quiet.	**G.** Bad things are accompanied by good.
B. It's good to work together.	**H.** You always want what you don't have.
C. It's been going well up to now.	**I.** Everyone has a different opinion.
D. I'm not so fortunate.	**J.** His words are worse than his actions.
E. It doesn't matter.	**K.** If you want something, you can do it.
F. It will be done immediately.	**L.** Everything takes time.

EXERCISE C4

_____ 1. He finally got a job; he couldn't continue to sit around doing nothing. He had to *turn over a new leaf.*

_____ 2. When he told his mother that he didn't need to study for the exam because he knew he would get a good grade, his mother responded, *"Don't count your chickens before they're hatched."*

_____ 3. When I asked my friend to do some of my work for me, she replied that I would have to *stand on my own two feet.*

_____ 4. You've been offered this job, and the offer may not remain on the table for too long, so you'd better take this one while you have the chance. You need to *strike while the iron is hot.*

_____ 5. When you guessed that I would get the promotion, you *hit the nail right on the head.*

_____ 6. Before you accept the position, you should find out everything you can about the company. You should *look before you leap.*

_____ 7. She was appointed to the environmental protection committee, and she's really excited because this is something she's been interested in for some time. This is something she can *sink her teeth into.*

_____ 8. If you want to be the one who gets noticed at work, you need to *dot all the i's and cross all the t's* on every task that you do.

_____ 9. You need to learn to relax. Every time there's a lot of work to do, you just *run around like a chicken with its head cut off.*

_____ 10. I really prepared for that exam. It should *be a piece of cake.*

_____ 11. She thinks she should confess what she did, but no one really seems interested in knowing. Instead, she decides to *let sleeping dogs lie.*

_____ 12. He never has to work for anything because his parents will give him anything he asks for. He seems to *have been born with a silver spoon in his mouth.*

DEFINITIONS—Exercise C4	
A. start over again	**G.** were exactly right
B. be extremely easy	**H.** depend on something you don't have
C. do it myself	**I.** be spoiled
D. pay attention to every detail	**J.** get really involved in
E. think before you act	**K.** take advantage of a good opportunity
F. leave something alone	**L.** act overly nervous and excited

APPENDIX D: **Prepositions**

DIRECTIONS: Study the list of prepositions. Then underline the prepositions in each sentence. Circle the prepositional phrases (prepositions + modifiers + objects). The number in parentheses indicates how many prepositions you should find in each group of sentences.

PREPOSITIONS				
about	behind	except	on	under
above	below	for	onto	underneath
across	beneath	from	outside	unlike
after	beside	in	over	until
against	between	inside	past	up
along	beyond	into	since	upon
among	by	like	through	versus
around	despite	near	throughout	with
as	down	of	to	within
at	during	off	toward	without

EXERCISE D1 (21 prepositions)

1. Advocacy of technology as the panacea for our environmental woes is not without its detractors.

2. State Highway 227 runs east of U.S. Highway 101, from San Luis Obispo in the north to Arroyo Grande in the south.

3. All four components of the Milky Way appear to be embedded in a large, dark corona of invisible material.

4. Over the last three decades, we have seen a consistent worldwide decline in membership of private-sector international trade union federations.

5. There is not complete agreement on the correlation of the various cultures and the glacial sequence, but many think that the Villafranchion, characterized by crudely worked pebble tools, roughly spherical in form, belongs in the early phase of the First Glacial period.

EXERCISE D2 (35 prepositions)

1. A combination of factors appear to have led to the decline of the beetle, all of them directly or indirectly due to human influence but none conclusively proven.

2. At ground level, ozone is produced by a photochemical interaction of the Sun with gases such as nitrogen oxides and unburnt hydrocarbons.

3. The Army of the Potomac under General George Meade and the Army of Northern Virginia under General Robert E. Lee had stumbled upon each other four days earlier at the edge of this little Pennsylvania county seat of 2,400 inhabitants.

4. With this sudden and vast wealth, by the turn of the century, Trinity Church was an ecclesiastical empire with 8,500 communicants and nine chapels scattered around New York City besides the main church itself.

5. Through modern film footage, this video production retraces the route followed by Meriwether Lewis and William Clark during their epochal two-year (1804–1806), eight-thousand-mile round-trip journey by keelboat, on horseback, on foot, and by canoe up the Missouri River, across the Continental Divide, and down the Snake and Columbia Rivers to the Pacific Ocean.

EXERCISE D3 (35 prepositions)

1. During the era from the end of the Civil War to about 1890, there was a land settlement boom within the United States.

2. By coincidence, the Finnish results were released at the same time that an American study confirmed the cancer-fighting potential of a chemical in broccoli known as sulforaphane.

3. At windswept Kitty Hawk, along North Carolina's Outer Banks, the Wright Brothers National Memorial pays tribute to the brothers and their historic first flight on December 17, 1903.

4. A wide central hall, running past the Garden Court, from one end of the building to the other, has four large cases of souvenirs from both palaces, including a program printed for President Warren G. Harding's visit.

5. Like historians raiding an archive of ancient texts, two atmospheric scientists are sifting through old satellite data, looking for a means of extending ozone records back in time in order to prove or disprove a hypothesis; on the basis of ground measurements made in Antarctica since the 1950s, researchers believe that the annual Antarctic ozone hole first appeared in a mild form during the late 1970s and then grew worse in the 1980s.

APPENDIX E: **Word Endings**

Word endings in English often tell you how a word is used grammatically in English; therefore, it is very important for you to recognize some common word endings. If you recognize a word ending on a word that you do not know, you can tell how the word should be used grammatically, even if you do not understand the meaning of the word.

EXERCISE E1: *Noun (Thing) Endings*

The following *noun (thing)* endings are very common in English. It is important for you to study them and become familiar with them.

NOUN (THING) ENDINGS			
-ism	social*ism*	**-ment**	govern*ment*
-nce	excelle*nce*	**-ty**	beau*ty*
-ness	sad*ness*	**-age**	marri*age*
-ion	informat*ion*	**-ship**	friend*ship*

Using one of the endings above, change each of the following words into a *noun (thing)*:

1.	member	_____	9.	alcohol	_____
2.	kind	_____	10.	permanent	_____
3.	real	_____	11.	mile	_____
4.	move	_____	12.	confuse	_____
5.	human	_____	13.	leader	_____
6.	elect	_____	14.	sudden	_____
7.	break	_____	15.	improve	_____
8.	intelligent	_____	16.	equal	_____

EXERCISE E2: *Noun (Person) Endings*

The following *noun (person)* endings are very common in English. It is important for you to study them and become familiar with them.

NOUN (PERSON) ENDINGS			
-er	employer	**-ist**	tourist
-or	actor	**-cian**	musician

Using one of the endings above, change each of the following words into a *noun (person)*:

1.	teach	_____	9.	perfection	_____
2.	type	_____	10.	program	_____
3.	beauty	_____	11.	electricity	_____
4.	ideal	_____	12.	invest	_____
5.	invent	_____	13.	build	_____
6.	clinic	_____	14.	natural	_____
7.	special	_____	15.	advice	_____
8.	ranch	_____	16.	mathematics	_____

EXERCISE E3: *Adjective Endings*

The following *adjective* endings are very common in English. It is important for you to study them and become familiar with them.

ADJECTIVE ENDINGS			
-ent	excellent	**-ive**	expensive
-ant	important	**-ous**	dangerous
-ful	careful	**-al**	natural
-ic	economic	**-able**	capable
-less	careless	**-ible**	possible

Using one of the endings above, change each of the following words into an *adjective:*

1.	heart	_____	9.	courage	_____
2.	nature	_____	10.	use	_____
3.	athlete	_____	11.	enthusiasm	_____
4.	mystery	_____	12.	motion	_____
5.	help	_____	13.	tradition	_____
6.	impress	_____	14.	change	_____
7.	intelligence	_____	15.	permanence	_____
8.	comfort	_____	16.	attract	_____

EXERCISE E4: *Verb Endings*

The following verb endings are very common in English. It is important for you to study them and become familiar with them.

VERB ENDINGS			
-en	soften	**-ize**	memorize
-ate	populate	**-ify**	notify

Using one of the endings above, change each of the following words into a *verb:*

1.	dark	_____	9.	different	_____
2.	final	_____	10.	identity	_____
3.	just	_____	11.	light	_____
4.	separation	_____	12.	glamour	_____
5.	short	_____	13.	person	_____
6.	intense	_____	14.	sweet	_____
7.	investigation	_____	15.	liberal	_____
8.	industrial	_____	16.	demonstration	_____

EXERCISE E5: *Adverb Ending*

The following *adverb* ending is very common in English. It is important for you to become familiar with it.

ADVERB ENDING	
-ly	really

Using the ending above, change each of the following words into an *adverb:*

1.	final	_____	9.	great	_____
2.	careful	_____	10.	complete	_____
3.	obvious	_____	11.	eager	_____
4.	recent	_____	12.	absolute	_____
5.	strong	_____	13.	correct	_____
6.	perfect	_____	14.	sudden	_____
7.	fearful	_____	15.	doubtful	_____
8.	quick	_____	16.	regular	_____

EXERCISE E6: *All Endings Together*

Identify each of the following words as a *noun-thing* (NT), a *noun-person* (NP), an *adjective* (ADJ), an *adverb* (ADV), or a *verb* (V).

_____ 1. heighten
_____ 2. forgetful
_____ 3. imperialism
_____ 4. effusively
_____ 5. cashier
_____ 6. columnist
_____ 7. aggravate
_____ 8. glamorous
_____ 9. vintage
_____ 10. statistician

_____ 11. desertification
_____ 12. submissive
_____ 13. nocturnal
_____ 14. establishment
_____ 15. impertinent
_____ 16. impertinently
_____ 17. togetherness
_____ 18. pharmacist
_____ 19. craftsmanship
_____ 20. manageable

_____ 21. speechless
_____ 22. tremendously
_____ 23. liability
_____ 24. counselor
_____ 25. civic
_____ 26. sensitize
_____ 27. ambiance
_____ 28. justification
_____ 29. interpretive
_____ 30. personify

EXERCISE E7: *All Endings Together*

Circle the letter of the word that correctly completes each sentence.

1. The _____ of the news could not be stressed enough.
   (A) important   (B) importance   (C) importantly

2. The detective _____ that the maid committed the robbery.
   (A) theorized   (B) theoretician   (C) theoretic

3. It is _____ that they live so close to the school.
   (A) convenience   (B) convenient   (C) conveniently

4. The patient responded _____ to the medication.
   (A) weaken   (B) weakness   (C) weakly

5. The psychologist explained his ideas on _____ interaction.
   (A) social   (B) society   (C) socialize

6. Not everyone wants a job as a _____.
   (A) mortal   (B) mortally   (C) mortician

7. You should not _____ the problem.
   (A) minimal   (B) minimize   (C) minimally

8. Because of a traffic _____, he had to appear in court.
   (A) violate   (B) violator   (C) violation

9. The children ran _____ toward the entrance of the park.
   (A) excitedly   (B) excited   (C) excitement

10. The company was unable to _____ enough profit to stay in business.
    (A) generator   (B) generate   (C) generation

11. She picked up a piece of _____ rock.

    (A) volcano   (B) vulcanize   (C) volcanic

12. He responded _____ to the rude question.

    (A) explosively   (B) explosion   (C) explosive

13. Because your medical problem is serious, you need to see a _____.

    (A) specialize   (B) special   (C) specialist

14. The coach was able to _____ the athletes to perform better.

    (A) motivate   (B) motivator   (C) motivation

15. He was not concerned about the _____ of his actions.

    (A) careless   (B) carelessness   (C) carelessly

16. This portion of the report should be completed _____ of the other part.

    (A) independence   (B) independent   (C) independently

17. The view of the mountains was _____.

    (A) magnify   (B) magnificent   (C) magnification

18. It was necessary for the speaker to _____ her message.

    (A) clarify   (B) clarity   (C) clarification

19. The _____ of the village was the soldiers' primary goal.

    (A) liberate   (B) liberation   (C) liberal

20. He gave an _____ incorrect answer to the question.

    (A) obvious   (B) obviously   (C) obviate

EXERCISE E8: *All Endings Together*

The following sentences contain a number of underlined words. Each of the underlined words *may* or *may not* be correct. Circle the underlined words that are incorrect, and make them correct.

1. The police inspect organized an intensively search for the robber.

2. The newspaper reporter did not exact appreciate the negation comments about her article.

3. He became penniless and homeless when a seriousness ill made him unable to work.

4. On the old college campus, the ivy-covered walls of the colonial buildings create an aura of gentility and tradition.

5. Maya Angelou is a poem, composition, and author of two autobiographically works, *I Know Why the Caged Bird Sings* and *My Name*.

6. The process of Americanization encouragement immigrants to assimilation American attitudes, cultural, and citizenship.

7. During the previously war, the national defense establish found itself in greatness need of linguists.

8. The escalate of hostilities between the two nations has proven far more seriousness than analyze had previously expected.

9. Social is becoming increasingly dependence on complex computers for the arrange of its affairs.

10. If someone has an educator in the humanities, he or she is prepared to deal with abstractions or complex and to feel comfortably with subtleties of thought.

11. It is possibly to demonstrate that the mathematical odds for success of the program increase dramatically with the additional of increased financial backing.

12. It would be fatally for the administration to underestimate the determine of the protesters to have the new law overturned.

APPENDIX F: **Irregular Verb Forms**

DIRECTIONS: Fill in the boxes with the correct forms of the verb.

EXERCISE F1

	VERB	PAST	PARTICIPLE		VERB	PAST	PARTICIPLE
1.		beat	beaten	25.		fought	fought
2.	become		become	26.	find		found
3.		began	begun	27.		fit	fit
4.	bet		bet	28.	fly	flew	
5.	bite	bit		29.	forget		forgotten
6.	blow	blew		30.	forgive	forgave	
7.	break		broken	31.		froze	frozen
8.	bring		brought	32.	get		gotten
9.		built	built	33.	give	gave	
10.	buy	bought		34.	go	went	
11.	catch		caught	35.		grew	grown
12.		chose	chosen	36.		had	had
13.	come		come	37.	hear		heard
14.	cost	cost		38.	hide	hid	
15.		cut	cut	39.		hit	hit
16.	dig		dug	40.	hold	held	
17.	do	did		41.	hurt	hurt	
18.	draw	drew		42.	keep		kept
19.		drank	drunk	43.		knew	known
20.	drive	drove		44.		led	led
21.	eat		eaten	45.	leave	left	
22.	fall	fell		46.		lent	lent
23.		fed	fed	47.	let		let
24.	feel	felt		48.		lost	lost

	VERB	PAST	PARTICIPLE		VERB	PAST	PARTICIPLE
49.	make	made		68.		sang	sung
50.		meant	meant	69.	sink		sunk
51.	meet	met		70.	sit	sat	
52.	pay		paid	71.		slept	slept
53.	prove		proven	72.	speak	spoke	
54.		put	put	73.	spend		spent
55.	quit		quit	74.		stood	stood
56.		read	read	75.		stole	stolen
57.	ride	rode		76.	swim	swam	
58.	ring	rang		77.	take		taken
59.		rose	risen	78.	teach	taught	
60.	run	ran		79.	tear		torn
61.	say	said		80.		told	told
62.		saw	seen	81.	think	thought	
63.		sold	sold	82.		threw	thrown
64.	send		sent	83.		understood	understood
65.		shot	shot	84.	wear		worn
66.	show		shown	85.		won	won
67.		shut	shut	86.	write	wrote	

APPENDIX G: **Formation of the Passive**

DIRECTIONS: In the following exercises, sentences are shown in both *active* and *passive*.
Fill in the blanks in the sentences with whatever is needed to complete the sentences.

EXERCISE G1

ACTIVE	PASSIVE
1. He *writes* many letters.	Many letters _____ by him.
2. He *wrote* many letters.	Many letters _____ by him.
3. He *has written* many letters.	Many letters _____ by him.
4. He *had written* many letters.	Many letters _____ by him.
5. He *would write* many letters.	Many letters _____ by him.
6. He *would have written* many letters.	Many letters _____ by him.
7. He *is writing* many letters.	Many letters _____ by him.
8. He *was writing* many letters.	Many letters _____ by him.
9. He *will write* many letters.	Many letters _____ by him.
10. He *will have written* many letters.	Many letters _____ by him.
11. He *is going to write* many letters.	Many letters _____ by him.
12. He *should write* many letters.	Many letters _____ by him.

EXERCISE G2

ACTIVE	PASSIVE
1. Soon the armies _____ the battle.	The battle will be fought by the armies soon.
2. The company is going to buy the equipment.	_____ by the company.
3. Someone _____ in the yard.	A hole was being dug in the yard.
4. The referee had already blown the whistle.	The whistle had _____ by the referee.
5. Parents _____ good values.	Children should be taught good values by parents.
6. She keeps her valuable jewelry in the safe.	_____ in the safe.
7. The enemy's torpedoes _____.	The ship was sunk by the enemy's torpedoes.
8. What you said hurt me.	I _____ hurt by _____.
9. Someone _____ now.	The children are being fed now.
10. You should not have said it so strongly.	_____ so strongly.

EXERCISE G3

ACTIVE	PASSIVE
1. _____ elections _____.	Elections will be held next month by the club.
2. The team won the game in the final seconds.	_____ in the final seconds.
3. Someone is taking photographs of the wedding.	Photographs _____ _____.
4. Someone _____.	The passport had already been stolen.
5. She reads the incoming mail daily.	The incoming mail _____ daily.
6. _____ should not _____ the electricity.	The electricity should not have been shut off.
7. People had bet a lot of money on the game.	A lot _____ on the game.
8. No one _____ in several weeks.	The car has not been driven in several weeks.
9. She would spend many hours on the project.	_____ on the project.
10. They _____ at a large profit.	The house could have been sold at a large profit.

EXERCISE G4

ACTIVE	PASSIVE
1. The guards were bringing the prisoner into court.	The prisoner _____ into court.
2. The agent _____.	The tourists are going to be met by the agent.
3. She _____ several times.	That dress had already been worn several times.
4. Someone tore his clothing during the fight.	_____ during the fight.
5. We are doing everything we can think of.	Everything _____.
6. No one _____.	The money will not ever be found.
7. He would have told me what happened.	I _____ what happened.
8. Someone _____ so much.	The horse should not have been ridden so much.
9 A fisherman caught a shark close to shore.	A shark _____ close to shore.
10. No one _____ really did.	What he really did is not known.

APPENDIX H: **Irregular Plurals**

DIRECTIONS: Study the irregular plurals in the chart in Skill 41 on page 185. Then indicate whether each of the following is correct (C) or incorrect (I).

EXERCISE H1

_____	1. one men		_____	9. several naughty children
_____	2. lots of data		_____	10. an in-depth analyses
_____	3. a surprising hypothesis		_____	11. one hundred alumni
_____	4. one fast-growing fungi		_____	12. lots of bright tooth
_____	5. various criterion		_____	13. various exotic cacti
_____	6. a few mice		_____	14. two required thesis
_____	7. each syllabi for the class		_____	15. the earth's axis
_____	8. a young deer		_____	16. lots of woolly sheep

EXERCISE H2

_____	1. both types of fungus		_____	9. a pair of strong ox
_____	2. a new curricula		_____	10. the X and Y axes
_____	3. two large foot		_____	11. two different theses
_____	4. a new bacteria		_____	12. each beautiful women
_____	5. one terrible crisis		_____	13. a recent alumnus
_____	6. a big, fat salmon		_____	14. two delicious fish
_____	7. many kinds of stimuli		_____	15. the only radius
_____	8. one tiny mouse		_____	16. a scientific syntheses

EXERCISE H3

_____	1. both lengthy syllabus		_____	9. an unexpected diagnoses
_____	2. some strict criteria		_____	10. an aching teeth
_____	3. a fat goose		_____	11. each nuclei of the atom
_____	4. some new hypotheses		_____	12. several fresh trout
_____	5. both young child		_____	13. a thorny cactus
_____	6. a green-colored bacilli		_____	14. each filthy feet
_____	7. many natural phenomenon		_____	15. surrounded by parenthesis
_____	8. each fish in the aquarium		_____	16. some fast-moving deer

APPENDIX I: **Word Parts**

Word parts in English can often give you a clue about the meaning of a word; therefore, it is very important for you to recognize some common word parts. If you recognize one of the word parts in a word that you do not know, you can often get a pretty good idea about the meaning of a word.

EXERCISE I1: *What You Do*

The following word parts describe things you *do*. Study these word parts because they appear in numerous words in English.

WHAT YOU DO					
PART	MEANING	EXAMPLE	PART	MEANING	EXAMPLE
cede/ceed	(go)	pro*ceed*	**rupt**	(break)	e*rupt*
cred	(believe)	*cred*it	**scrib/scrip**	(write)	de*scrib*e
graph	(write)	auto*graph*	**sect**	(cut)	bi*sect*
ject	(throw)	e*ject*	**ven**	(come)	inter*ven*e
mit/miss	(send)	e*mit*	**ver**	(turn)	di*ver*t
mute	(change)	com*mute*	**viv**	(live)	sur*viv*e
port	(carry)	de*port*			

Using the word parts above to help you, match the definitions on the right with the words on the left.

_____	1. *emissary*	A. ideology or *belief*
_____	2. *rupture*	B. cause to *turn*
_____	3. *intersection*	C. the result of a *change*
_____	4. *porter*	D. *write* hastily and messily
_____	5. *permutation*	E. *break* in accustomed friendly relations
_____	6. *convention*	F. study of hand*writing*
_____	7. *vivacious*	G. meeting where many people *come* together
_____	8. *avert*	H. something that is *thrown*
_____	9. *exceed*	I. keenly *alive* and brisk
_____	10. *credo*	J. person who is *sent* to deliver a message
_____	11. *scribble*	K. person who *carries* baggage
_____	12. *graphology*	L. where one road *cuts* through another
_____	13. *projectile*	M. *go* beyond expectations

EXERCISE I2: *Where and When*

The following word parts describe *where* or *when* things happen. Study these word parts because they appear in numerous words in English.

WHERE			WHEN		
PART	MEANING	EXAMPLE	PART	MEANING	EXAMPLE
cir	(around)	circulate	*ante*	(before)	anterior
ex	(out)	exit	*fore*	(before)	foretell
in	(in)	include	*fin*	(end)	finish
re	(back)	return	*pre*	(before)	previous
sub	(under)	subway	*post*	(after)	postpone
tele	(far)	telephone			
trans	(across)	transatlantic			

Using the word parts above to help you, match the definitions on the right with the words on the left.

————	1. *refund*	A. cut *into* something
————	2. *subordinate*	B. occurring *before* the expected time
————	3. *forefather*	C. room that serves as an *entrance* to a larger room
————	4. *transgress*	D. give money *back*
————	5. *postern*	E. apparatus for sending a message over a *distance*
————	6. *incision*	F. *conclusion* of a program
————	7. *premature*	G. *go across* a limit or boundary
————	8. *expel*	H. circular course *around* an area
————	9. *antechamber*	I. occupying a *lower* class, rank, or status
————	10. *telegraph*	J. relative who came *before* you
————	11. *finale*	K. force someone to go *out* of a place
————	12. *circuit*	L. *back* door to a church

EXERCISE I3: *Parts of the Universe and Parts of the Body*

The following word parts describe parts of the *universe* or parts of the *body*. Study these word parts because they appear in numerous words in English.

UNIVERSE			BODY		
PART	MEANING	EXAMPLE	PART	MEANING	EXAMPLE
geo	(earth)	geology	**corp**	(body)	corporation
terr	(earth)	territory	**card**	(heart)	cardiology
hydr	(water)	hydroplane	**derm**	(skin)	dermatologist
aqua	(water)	aquatic	**man**	(hand)	manual
astr	(star)	astronaut	**dent**	(teeth)	dentist
pyr	(fire)	pyrotechnics	**ped/pod**	(feet)	pedestrian
			cap	(head)	captain

Using the word parts above to help you, match the definitions on the right with the words on the left.

_____ 1. *geocentric*

_____ 2. *dentures*

_____ 3. *podiatry*

_____ 4. *capstone*

_____ 5. *dermatitis*

_____ 6. *corpulent*

_____ 7. *aquanaut*

_____ 8. *hydraulic*

_____ 9. *cardiovascular*

_____ 10. *terrace*

_____ 11. *pyrometer*

_____ 12. *manacles*

_____ 13. *asterisk*

A. an under*seas* explorer

B. a series of raised levels of *earth*

C. relating to the *heart* and blood vessels

D. figure of a *star* (*) used as a reference mark

E. having the *earth* as the center

F. *hand*cuffs

G. treatment of *foot* problems

H. having a fleshy *body*

I. *top* or final rock used to complete a structure

J. apparatus for measuring *high temperatures*

K. inflammation of the *skin*

L. operated by *water* under pressure or in motion

M. false *teeth*

EXERCISE I4: *Human States*

The following word parts describe *human states*. Study these word parts because they appear in numerous words in English.

HUMAN STATES					
PART	MEANING	EXAMPLE	PART	MEANING	EXAMPLE
am	(love)	amiable	**path**	(feeling)	sympathy
phil	(love)	Philadelphia	**mania**	(crazy)	maniac
bene	(good)	benefit	**phobia**	(fear)	claustrophobia
eu	(good)	euphemism	**psycho**	(mind)	psychology
mal	(bad)	malcontent	**bio**	(life)	biology
dys	(bad)	dysfunction	**mor**	(death)	mortal

Using the word parts above to help you, match the definitions on the right with the words on the left.

_____ 1. *euphoric*	A.	*fear* of high places
_____ 2. *moribund*	B.	part of the earth's crust where *living* beings exist
_____ 3. *pathetic*	C.	stealing as a result of an *emotional disturbance*
_____ 4. *malign*	D.	any severe form of *mental* disorder
_____ 5. *enamored*	E.	reduced ability or *lack of* ability to read
_____ 6. *acrophobia*	F.	*lover* of books
_____ 7. *benevolent*	G.	in a *dying* state
_____ 8. *biosphere*	H.	speak *negatively* and harmfully about
_____ 9. *kleptomania*	I.	feeling especially *well*
_____ 10. *dyslexia*	J.	evoking pity or *compassion*
_____ 11. *bibliophile*	K.	in *love*
_____ 12. *psychosis*	L.	wanting to do *good* to others

EXERCISE I5: *People and Their Senses*

The following word parts describe *people* or their *senses*. Study these word parts because they appear in numerous words in English.

PEOPLE			SENSES		
PART	MEANING	EXAMPLE	PART	MEANING	EXAMPLE
pater	(father)	*patriarch*	*spec*	(see)	*spectator*
mater	(mother)	*maternity*	*vis/vid*	(see)	*visit/video*
frater	(brother)	*fraternal*	*scope*	(see)	*telescope*
domin	(master)	*domination*	*phon*	(hear)	*telephone*
jud	(judge)	*judgment*	*aud*	(hear)	*audience*
anthro	(people)	*anthropology*	*dic*	(say)	*dictate*
demo	(people)	*democracy*	*loc/loq*	(speak)	*eloquent*

Using the word parts above to help you, match the definitions on the right with the words on the left.

_____	1. *cacophony*		A.	exerting *authority* or influence
_____	2. *judiciary*		B.	*see* in your mind
_____	3. *fraternize*		C.	being ruled or headed by a *woman*
_____	4. *spectacle*		D.	discordant *sound*
_____	5. *audiology*		E.	exceedingly *talkative*
_____	6. *patrimony*		F.	system of *courts* in a country
_____	7. *periscope*		G.	pertaining to a particular *people* or locality
_____	8. *dominant*		H.	instrument to *view* obstructed objects
_____	9. *anthropoid*		I.	farewell *speech* at a graduation ceremony
_____	10. *loquacious*		J.	science of *hearing*
_____	11. *visualize*		K.	estate inherited from a *father* or ancestors
_____	12. *valedictory*		L.	associate in a friendly or *brotherly* way
_____	13. *matriarchal*		M.	impressive *sight* or *view*
_____	14. *endemic*		N.	resembling a *human being*

EXERCISE I6: *Size and Amount*

The following word parts describe *sizes* or *amounts*. Study these word parts because they appear in numerous words in English.

SIZE			AMOUNT		
PART	MEANING	EXAMPLE	PART	MEANING	EXAMPLE
min	(small)	minimum	*ambi*	(both)	ambivalent
micro	(small)	microphone	*multi*	(many)	multiple
macro	(large)	macroeconomics	*poly*	(many)	polygon
mega	(large)	megaphone	*omni*	(all)	omnipotent
magn	(large)	magnify	*auto*	(self)	automatic

Using the word parts above to help you, match the definitions on the right with the words on the left.

_____	1.	*autonomous*	A.	*tiny* plant or animal
_____	2.	*magnum*	B.	*great number* of persons or things
_____	3.	*minuscule*	C.	able to eat *all* types of food
_____	4.	*microorganism*	D.	universe as a *whole*
_____	5.	*polyglot*	E.	*very small*
_____	6.	*ambidextrous*	F.	*self*-governing
_____	7.	*omnivorous*	G.	able to speak or write *many* languages
_____	8.	*macrocosm*	H.	*giant* stone
_____	9.	*multitude*	I.	*large* bottle, for wine or champagne
_____	10.	*megalith*	J.	able to use *both* hands

EXERCISE I7: *Number*

The following word parts describe *numbers*. Study these word parts because they appear in numerous words in English.

NUMBER					
PART	MEANING	EXAMPLE	PART	MEANING	EXAMPLE
sol	(one)	*solo*	*quad*	(four)	*quadruplets*
uni	(one)	*unique*	*oct*	(eight)	*octopus*
mono	(one)	*monologue*	*dec*	(ten)	*decade*
bi	(two)	*bicycle*	*cent*	(hundred)	*century*
du	(two)	*duet*	*mil*	(thousand)	*millimeter*
tri	(three)	*triple*	*semi*	(half)	*semifinal*

Using the word parts above to help you, match the definitions on the right with the words on the left.

_____ 1. *bifocals*

_____ 2. *quadrennial*

_____ 3. *millennium*

_____ 4. *solitaire*

_____ 5. *tripartite*

_____ 6. *duplex*

_____ 7. *decathlon*

_____ 8. *unicorn*

_____ 9. *octogenarian*

_____ 10. *centennial*

_____ 11. *monorail*

_____ 12. *semiprivate*

A. mythical horselike animal with *one* horn

B. card game played by *one* person

C. *eighty*-year-old person

D. *partly* alone and *partly* shared

E. *hundredth* anniversary

F. train on *one* track

G. eyeglass lenses with *two* parts

H. occurring every *four* years

I. athletic contest involving *ten* events

J. period of a *thousand* years

K. building divided into *two* houses

L. divided into *three* sections

EXERCISE I8: *Opposites*

The following word parts describe *opposites*. Study these word parts because they appear in numerous words in English.

OPPOSITES					
PART	MEANING	EXAMPLE	PART	MEANING	EXAMPLE
anti	(against)	antiwar	**im**	(not)	imperfect
contra	(against)	contrast	**il**	(not)	illegal
mis	(error)	misspell	**in**	(not)	incorrect
un	(not)	untrue	**ir**	(not)	irregular
dis	(not)	dislike			

Using the word parts above to help you, match the definitions on the right with the words on the left.

_____	1. *illiterate*		A.	immoral act
_____	2. *inedible*		B.	separate from
_____	3. *contradict*		C.	medicine to counteract the effects of poison
_____	4. *dissociate*		D.	childish
_____	5. *immature*		E.	unable to be cured or solved
_____	6. *misdeed*		F.	unable to read or write
_____	7. *irremediable*		G.	deny or say the opposite
_____	8. *unarmed*		H.	unable to be eaten
_____	9. *antidote*		I.	without weapons

EXERCISE I9: *All Word Parts Together*

Study the word list at the top of each box. Then read each sentence and place the letter of an appropriate word in the sentence. You should use each word one time only, without changing the form.

A.   WHO ARE THESE CHARACTERS?

A. *autobiographer*   E. *introvert*   I. *polygamist*
B. *benefactor*   F. *manicurist*   J. *psychopath*
C. *corpse*   G. *misanthrope*   K. *spectator*
D. *expatriate*   H. *mortician*   L. *triathlete*

1. Someone who lives *outside* of his or her own country is a(n) _____.
2. Someone who works beautifying the *hands* and nails of others is a(n) _____.
3. Someone who *hates other people* is a(n) _____.
4. Someone who works preparing *dead* people for burial is a(n) _____.
5. Someone who is a dead *body* is a(n) _____.
6. Someone who is *writing* the story of his or her *own life* is a(n) _____.
7. Someone who is married to *more than one* person is a(n) _____.
8. Someone who competes in *three* related sports is a(n) _____.
9. Someone who *watches* while others perform is a(n) _____.
10. Someone who does *good* deeds for others is a(n) _____.
11. Someone who, because of *mental illness,* acts without morals is a(n) _____.
12. Someone who *turns* all his or her feelings *inward* is a(n) _____.

B.   WHAT IS IT USED FOR?

A. *aqueduct*   E. *microdot*   I. *terrarium*
B. *hydrant*   F. *missile*   J. *telescope*
C. *kaleidoscope*   G. *monocle*   K. *tripod*
D. *megaphone*   H. *submarine*   L. *unicycle*

1. A(n) _____ is useful when you want to travel *underwater.*
2. A(n) _____ can be used if you want to *see* something from *far* away.
3. A(n) _____ is a little difficult to ride because it has only *one* wheel.
4. A(n) _____ contains *water* that can be used to fight fires.
5. A(n) _____ is used to *send* some explosives to the enemy.
6. A(n) _____ can be used when you want to *grow plants* indoors.
7. A(n) _____ is a *tiny* spot that contains lots of information; spies have been known to use this.
8. A(n) _____ helps you see well out of *one* eye.
9. A(n) _____ is useful if you want to make *a big sound.*
10. A(n) _____ was constructed in older times to *carry water* from place to place.
11. A(n) _____ lets a child look and *see* a variety of shapes and colors.
12. A(n) _____ is a *three-footed* stand that can be used to support a camera.

C.   WHAT ARE THESE THINGS REALLY LIKE?

A.	*antebellum*	E.	*illegible*	I.	*minute*
B.	*audiovisual*	F.	*infinite*	J.	*misfired*
C.	*euphonious*	G.	*invisible*	K.	*portable*
D.	*extraterrestrial*	H.	*irreversible*	L.	*subterranean*

1.   A(n) _____ television is one that can be *carried*.
2.   Ink that is _____ can*not* be *seen* without a special lamp.
3.   A(n) _____ decision is one that can*not* be *changed* back to what it was.
4.   Handwriting that is _____ is *difficult to read*.
5.   A(n) _____ source of water is one that is located *underground*.
6.   A(n) _____ weapon is one that was shot in the *wrong way*.
7.   A(n) _____ house is one that was built *before* the war.
8.   Films or other _____ teaching materials can be both *seen* and *heard*.
9.   Details that are _____ are really, really *small* and *unimportant*.
10. Music that is _____ is really *pleasant sounding*.
11. A(n) _____ supply of money is one that is *never-ending*.
12. A(n) _____ rock is one that came to earth *from outer space*.

D.   WHAT ON EARTH ARE YOU DOING?

A.	*circumvent*	E.	*dissect*	I.	*premeditate*
B.	*decapitate*	F.	*exhale*	J.	*prevent*
C.	*dehydrate*	G.	*interject*	K.	*reverse*
D.	*disinter*	H.	*minimize*	L.	*transmit*

1.   If you _____ something, you take the *water* out of it.
2.   If you _____ something, you *move around* it to avoid it.
3.   If you _____ a murder, you think about it *before* you do it.
4.   If you _____ something, you *turn* it in the *opposite* direction.
5.   If you _____ someone, you cut his or her *head* off.
6.   If you _____ something, you try to make it seem *smaller* and *less important*.
7.   If you _____ when you are smoking, you breathe *out*.
8.   If you _____ a few ideas into a conversation, you *throw* them *in* quickly.
9.   If you _____ a body, you take it *out of the ground*.
10. If you _____ something, you *cut* it in *two*.
11. If you _____ something, you take action *beforehand* to stop it from occurring.
12. If you _____ a message, you *send* it *from one place to another*.

E.   DO YOU KNOW PEOPLE LIKE THIS?

A. *ambivalent*	E. *incredulous*	I. *maternal*
B. *amorous*	F. *indomitable*	J. *omniscient*
C. *antiquated*	G. *introspective*	K. *subtle*
D. *bilingual*	H. *magnanimous*	L. *unselfish*

1. Someone who is _____ has power and control over *everything*.
2. Someone who is _____ can*not believe* what is happening.
3. Someone who is _____ is always *looking inside* for answers.
4. Someone who is _____ acts in a *motherly* fashion.
5. Someone who is _____ is always falling *in love*.
6. Someone who is _____ can*not* be *subjugated*.
7. Someone who is _____ acts in an *under*stated way.
8. Someone who is _____ does what is best *for others*.
9. Someone who is _____ speaks *two* languages.
10. Someone who is _____ comes from an *earlier* time.
11. Someone who is _____ does *not* take *either* side in a discussion.
12. Someone who is _____ would generously give *everything he or she has* to others.

F.   HOW'S YOUR HEALTH?

A. *antibiotic*	E. *epidemic*	I. *revive*
B. *biopsy*	F. *epidermis*	J. *postmortem*
C. *cardiogram*	G. *euthanasia*	K. *psychosomatic*
D. *dentifrice*	H. *malignant*	L. *semiconscious*

1. If you are only *half* awake or aware, you are _____.
2. When *all the people* in an area get a disease, it is a(n) _____.
3. When someone is almost dead and is brought *back* to *life,* the doctor has been able to _____ him or her.
4. A(n) _____ is done when *living* tissue is cut out of a body in order to study it.
5. A(n) _____ tumor is one that is found to be cancerous, or *bad*.
6. You should use a _____ on your *teeth* to keep them healthy.
7. A doctor will use a _____ to test the health of a patient's *heart*.
8. A substance that is used *against* harmful *living* organisms is an _____.
9. A(n) _____ illness occurs when someone *thinks* he or she is sick but really is not.
10. The outer layer of a patient's *skin* is called the _____.
11. If a person is really suffering from an incurable disease, sometimes a loved one might use _____ to put him or her to death for his or her own *good*.
12. *After* someone has *died,* a(n) _____ is conducted.

G.   HOW DO YOU DO THIS?

A. *circumnavigate*	E. *intercede*	I. *reject*
B. *contravene*	F. *postdate*	J. *remit*
C. *inscribe*	G. *preview*	K. *subvert*
D. *inspect*	H. *recede*	L. *transplant*

1. To _____ a book, you *look* at it *ahead of time.*
2. To _____ a tree, you take it out of the ground and *move* it *to another place.*
3. To _____ a machine, you *look into* it very carefully and check for problems.
4. To _____ a check, you write a date that is *after* today's date.
5. To _____ a payment, you *send* it in.
6. To _____ someone, you *undermine* the support that he or she has.
7. To _____ in a problem, you *go* right *into* the middle of it.
8. To _____ a fish that you catch, you *throw* it *back.*
9. To _____ a book, you *write* a message *in* it.
10. To cause something to _____, you make it *go back.*
11. To _____ in a bad situation, you act *against* it or do the *opposite* of what is happening.
12. To _____ an island, you sail all the way *around* it.

H.   WHO NEEDS FRIENDS LIKE THESE?

A. *abrupt*	E. *immutable*	I. *malevolent*
B. *antipathetic*	F. *inaudible*	J. *misinformed*
C. *domineering*	G. *injudicious*	K. *monotonous*
D. *immoral*	H. *judgmental*	L. *morbid*

1. A friend who is _____ wants *bad* things to happen to others.
2. A friend who is _____ always makes *judgments* (often negative) about others.
3. A friend who is _____ always insists on *controlling* every solution.
4. A friend who is _____ can*not* be *heard* when he or she speaks.
5. A friend who is _____ does *not feel* strongly about anything.
6. A friend who is _____ is only concerned with *death.*
7. A friend who is _____ can *never* be persuaded to *change.*
8. A friend who is _____ does *not* make wise or well-thought-out *decisions.*
9. A friend who is _____ does *not* do the *correct* or *right* thing.
10. A friend who is _____ *cuts* off others when they try to speak or act.
11. A friend who is _____ *never has* the *correct* facts.
12. A friend who is _____ always speaks in the *same tone* of voice.

I.   CAN YOU GUESS WHAT IT IS?

A. *antecedent*	E. *controversy*	I. *mutation*
B. *autograph*	F. *foreword*	J. *octave*
C. *benediction*	G. *manuscript*	K. *postscript*
D. *biography*	H. *misnomer*	L. *soliloquy*

1. If you refer to something that came *before,* it is a(n) _____.
2. If you give a *speech* all *by yourself* in a play, it is a(n) _____.
3. Words *written* at the *end* of a letter make up a(n) _____.
4. If you ask a famous person to *write* his name *himself,* you get his _____.
5. At the beginning of the book, *before* the main part of the text, you may find a(n) _____.
6. If you *write* the story of someone's *life,* you write a(n) _____.
7. A musical interval that is *eight* notes apart is a(n) _____.
8. If you *write* something by *hand,* it is a(n) _____.
9. If two people argue *against* each other, they have a(n) _____.
10. If you *say* a few *good* words to close a ceremony, you give a(n) _____.
11. A sudden *change* in the offspring of a plant or animal is a(n) _____.
12. If you call something by an *incorrect name,* it is a(n) _____.

J.   YOU'RE IN BUSINESS?

A. *autocratic*	E. *export*	I. *patron*
B. *bankrupt*	F. *magnate*	J. *semiannual*
C. *bilateral*	G. *monopoly*	K. *subsidiary*
D. *demographics*	H. *multimedia*	L. *visionary*

1. A branch company that comes *under* the control of the parent company is called a(n) _____.
2. When *one* company has control of a particular field of business, it has a(n) _____.
3. A(n) _____ agreement is an equal agreement for *both* sides.
4. Before marketing a product, you must check the _____, the characteristics of the *people* you want to sell to.
5. To send goods *out* of the country is to _____ them.
6. If a company is completely *broke* and has no money or resources left, it is _____.
7. A(n) _____ leader makes all the decisions *alone.*
8. If you have a sale every *six months,* it is a(n) _____ sale.
9. Advertising that is in newspapers, on radio, and on television is _____ advertising.
10. If you believe that "the customer is always right," then you might call a customer a(n) _____.
11. The type of leader who can *see* what is coming in the future and be prepared for it is a(n) _____.
12. A person of *great* influence and importance in a field of business is a(n) _____.

K.   DO YOU SUFFER FROM THIS?

A.	*circumlocution*	E.	*dyspepsia*	I.	*prejudice*
B.	*contradiction*	F.	*egomania*	J.	*pyromania*
C.	*disrespect*	G.	*irrationality*	K.	*solitude*
D.	*duplicity*	H.	*monomania*	L.	*zoophobia*

1. Someone who does *not think* logically suffers from _____.
2. Someone who likes _____ prefers to be *alone.*
3. Someone who is *afraid* of animals suffers from _____.
4. Someone who acts with _____ makes up his or her mind *before* the facts are known.
5. Someone who is able to focus on *only one* thing suffers from _____.
6. Someone who suffers from _____ has a *mental problem* and believes that he or she is the only important person in the world.
7. Someone who has something *wrong* with his or her digestive system suffers from _____.
8. Someone who *speaks indirectly* about something uses _____.
9. Someone who is guilty of *double*-dealing and deception is guilty of _____.
10. Someone who deals with others with _____ does *not* act *politely* with them.
11. Someone who *says* one thing one day and the *opposite* the next day is guilty of a(n) _____.
12. Someone who likes to start *fires* and watch them burn and destroy suffers from _____.

L.   CAN YOU FIGURE THIS OUT?

A.	*amity*	E.	*credibility*	I.	*matricide*
B.	*aquaculture*	F.	*geopolitics*	J.	*paternalism*
C.	*astrology*	G.	*hydrolysis*	K.	*telepathy*
D.	*astrophysics*	H.	*macrobiotics*	L.	*vitality*

1. If you are a good *friend* to people, then you believe in _____.
2. If you divide a compound into other compounds by taking up the elements of *water,* you use _____.
3. If you *kill your mother,* you are guilty of _____.
4. If you grow things in *water,* then you make use of _____.
5. If you lead a business or a country as if you are a *father,* then you believe in _____.
6. If you are *lively* and *active,* then you have _____.
7. If you are interested in the physical properties of the *stars,* then you are interested in _____.
8. If you are *believable,* then you have _____.
9. If you want to *lengthen* your *life* by means of a vegetarian diet, then you believe in _____.
10. If you believe that the *stars* and other heavenly bodies influence your life, you believe in _____.
11. If you use mental _____, you are able to understand what someone is thinking or *feeling* from *far* away.
12. If you are interested in the effect of the layout of the *land* on the power and sovereignty of a country, then you are interested in _____.

SCORES AND CHARTS

SCORING INFORMATION

SCORING YOUR PAPER PRE-TESTS, POST-TESTS, AND COMPLETE TESTS

When your paper TOEFL test is scored, you will receive a score between 20 and 68 in each of the three sections (Listening Comprehension, Structure and Written Expression, and Reading Comprehension). You will also receive an overall score between 217 and 677. You can use the following chart to estimate the scores on your paper Pre-Tests, Post-Tests, and Complete Tests.

NUMBER CORRECT	CONVERTED SCORE SECTION 1	CONVERTED SCORE SECTION 2	CONVERTED SCORE SECTION 3
50	68	–	67
49	67	–	66
48	66	–	65
47	65	–	63
46	63	–	61
45	62	–	60
44	61	–	59
43	60	–	58
42	59	–	57
41	58	–	56
40	57	68	55
39	57	67	54
38	56	65	54
37	55	63	53
36	54	61	52
35	54	60	52
34	53	58	51
33	52	57	50
32	52	56	49
31	51	55	48
30	51	54	48
29	50	53	47
28	49	52	46
27	49	51	46
26	48	50	45
25	48	49	44
24	47	48	43
23	47	47	43
22	46	46	42
21	45	45	41

NUMBER CORRECT	CONVERTED SCORE SECTION 1	CONVERTED SCORE SECTION 2	CONVERTED SCORE SECTION 3
20	45	44	40
19	44	43	39
18	43	42	38
17	42	41	37
16	41	40	36
15	41	40	35
14	37	38	34
13	38	37	32
12	37	36	31
11	35	35	30
10	33	33	29
9	32	31	28
8	32	29	28
7	31	27	27
6	30	26	26
5	29	25	25
4	28	23	24
3	27	22	23
2	26	21	23
1	25	20	22
0	24	20	21

You should first use the chart to determine your converted score for each section. Suppose that you got 30 correct in the first section, 28 correct in the second section, and 43 correct in the third section. The 30 correct in the first section means a converted score of 51. The 28 correct in the second section means a converted score of 52. The 43 correct in the third section means a converted score of 58. (See the chart below.)

	SECTION 1	SECTION 2	SECTION 3
NUMBER CORRECT	30	28	43
CONVERTED SCORE	51	52	58

Next, you should determine your overall score in the following way:

1. <u>Add the three converted scores together.</u> $51 + 52 + 58 = 161$

2. <u>Divide the sum by 3.</u> $161/3 = 53.7$

3. <u>Then multiply by 10.</u> $53.7 \times 10 = 537$

The overall TOEFL score in this example is 537.

DIAGNOSTIC CHARTS

LISTENING COMPREHENSION _____

DIRECTIONS: After you take each Listening Comprehension test, circle the number of each of the questions that you answered incorrectly. In this way, you can keep track of which language skills need more attention.

		PRE-TEST	POST-TEST	COMPLETE TEST 1	COMPLETE TEST 2	COMPLETE TEST 3	COMPLETE TEST 4	COMPLETE TEST 5
Strategies								
	SKILL 1		5		26	17	10	11
	SKILL 2	2 3 8	4 7 19	3 22	2 7 20	1 9	3 19	1 7 14
	SKILL 3	1 22	3 8	1 10	5	3	2	2
Who, What, Where								
	SKILL 4	5	9 13	17 18 21	3 14	7 21	1 18	4 13
	SKILL 5	6 10 13	2 16	11 23	1 8	5 14	12 23	5 17
	SKILL 6	9 14	10 20 27	6 8 9	24	8	14	6

	PRE-TEST	POST-TEST	COMPLETE TEST 1	COMPLETE TEST 2	COMPLETE TEST 3	COMPLETE TEST 4	COMPLETE TEST 5
Negatives							
SKILL 7	4 15 18	1 6 14	4 7	4 11	2 10 15	6 21	3 21
SKILL 8	7 24	15 25	27	9 28	6 25	16 25	16 23
SKILL 9	12 28	23	12	10 18	18 28	4 27	8 19
SKILL 10	27	17 28	19	15 22	16 27	11 26	18 26
Functions							
SKILL 11	11	12	14 25	6	11	9	12
SKILL 12	17 19	21 24	2 5 20	12 13	4 23	7 20	9 22
SKILL 13	30	29	29	21 29	20 30	22 29	20 29
Contrary Meanings							
SKILL 14	16 25	11 26	28	25	19 29	28	15 27
SKILL 15	29	30	24	19 30	22	17 30	28
Idiomatic Language							
SKILL 16	21 26	18 22	13 15 16	16 23	12 24	5 15	25 30
SKILL 17	20 23		26 30	17 27	13 26	13 24	10 24

STRUCTURE AND WRITTEN EXPRESSION _____

DIRECTIONS: After you take each Structure and Written Expression test, circle the number of each of the questions that you answered incorrectly. In this way, you can keep track of which language skills need more attention.

	PRE-TEST	POST-TEST	COMPLETE TEST 1	COMPLETE TEST 2	COMPLETE TEST 3	COMPLETE TEST 4	COMPLETE TEST 5
Sentences with One Clause							
SKILL 1	1	1	1	1	1	1	1
SKILL 2		2	2	2	2	2	2
SKILL 3	2	5	4	3	5		5
SKILL 4	6	6	5			3	
SKILL 5	10	8		7	3	9	8
Sentences with Multiple Clauses							
SKILL 6	3	4	6	4	4		3
SKILL 7		3	7	5	9	5	4
SKILL 8	7		3	8	7	7	10
More Sentences with Multiple Clauses							
SKILL 9	14		8	9	15	10	11
SKILL 10	12	13	12		10	6	
SKILL 11	13	11		11		14	14
SKILL 12	5	9	9	14	8		7
Sentences with Reduced Clauses							
SKILL 13	11	7	10	10	11	4	9
SKILL 14	8		14	12	13	12	13
Sentences with Inverted Subjects and Verbs							
SKILL 15	4	10		6	6		6
SKILL 16	9	12	15		14	8	12
SKILL 17		14	11	13		13	
SKILL 18	15	15		15		11	15
SKILL 19			13		12	15	
Problems with Subject/Verb Agreement							
SKILL 20		29	19	28		24	
SKILL 21	19				18		17
SKILL 22	32		29	31	31	29	
SKILL 23		23	17			18	20

	PRE-TEST	POST-TEST	COMPLETE TEST 1	COMPLETE TEST 2	COMPLETE TEST 3	COMPLETE TEST 4	COMPLETE TEST 5
Problems with Parallel Structure							
SKILL 24	18	26	18	19	22		
SKILL 25	29	21			27	23	30
SKILL 26			27	22	33		34
Problems with Comparatives and Superlatives							
SKILL 27	17	16	22	26	19	17	
SKILL 28				33		25	22
SKILL 29		37					37
Problems with the Form of the Verb							
SKILL 30	23				17		18
SKILL 31	16	19		24		16	21
SKILL 32		22	16	16		19	
Problems with the Use of the Verb							
SKILL 33	31		20	20	20		19
SKILL 34	29			27			
SKILL 35	27	20	32	35	29	20	
SKILL 36		30				27	28
Problems with Passive Verbs							
SKILL 37	30				24	37	23
SKILL 38	38	40	36	38		33	
Problems with Nouns							
SKILL 39		17			16		16
SKILL 40	25	28	24	29		30	
SKILL 41			33	36	39		36
SKILL 42	33		39	37	36	39	
Problems with Pronouns							
SKILL 43		18	30	18		21	
SKILL 44	24				23	22	33
SKILL 45	21	24	25	21	28		29
Problems with Adjectives and Adverbs							
SKILL 46	20		28		30		24
SKILL 47	37	31		23		40	26
SKILL 48		39	35	25	34	32	

	PRE-TEST	POST-TEST	COMPLETE TEST 1	COMPLETE TEST 2	COMPLETE TEST 3	COMPLETE TEST 4	COMPLETE TEST 5
More Problems with Adjectives							
SKILL 49		33					38
SKILL 50	34			39	32	35	
SKILL 51	22	38	34		37		40
Problems with Articles							
SKILL 52	36	36	37		38	34	
SKILL 53				32	25	26	27
SKILL 54		32	23	17			31
SKILL 55	28				26	31	
Problems with Prepositions							
SKILL 56		25	31	40			39
SKILL 57	30	34	38		40	38	35
Problems with Usage							
SKILL 58	40	35	40		35	36	
SKILL 59		27	21	34		28	25
SKILL 60	39		26	30	21		32

READING COMPREHENSION

DIRECTIONS: After you take each Reading Comprehension test, circle the number of each of the questions that you answered incorrectly. In this way, you can keep track of which language skills need more attention.

	PRE-TEST	POST-TEST	COMPLETE TEST 1	COMPLETE TEST 2	COMPLETE TEST 3	COMPLETE TEST 4	COMPLETE TEST 5
Questions about the Ideas of the Passage							
SKILL 1	13 31 43	11 32 41	1 3 20 41	1 21 41	1 11 22 32 41	32	1 41
SKILL 2	11 40	40 50	39	32	10 33	11 40 50	30 31 48
Directly Answered Questions							
SKILL 3	5 6 9 16 19 27 33 34 39 48	1 5 7 12 13 17 18 21 23 24 26 29 33	5 7 14 16 21 22 26 29 30 36 46	3 7 13 14 23 27 45 46 48	4 5 12 43 44 49	3 8 12 13 19 24 26 28 33 35	2 8 12 14 25 28 36 42 46
SKILL 4	2 38 49	35 37 42 45	18 31 48	15 25 34	6 14 25 35	5 15 20 36 43 44	7 17 23 39
SKILL 5	26 37 44	3 27 44	17 47	17 37	2 18 24 47	16 46	4 27 38

	PRE-TEST	POST-TEST	COMPLETE TEST 1	COMPLETE TEST 2	COMPLETE TEST 3	COMPLETE TEST 4	COMPLETE TEST 5
Indirectly Answered Questions							
SKILL 6	8	2	9	6	8	6	3
	10	6	13	18	15	17	9
	15	15	24	28	17	29	19
	18	39	25	31	27	45	26
	20	46	33	36	30		35
	25	48	43	39	37		43
	36			43	38		45
	45			49	40		
	47				45		
					48		
SKILL 7	22	31	10	10	31	10	50
	42		40	20		31	
			50			38	
Vocabulary Questions							
SKILL 8	3	38	15		16	4	16
	35	47				25	34
SKILL 9	4	8	2	8	26	7	32
	14	19	35	24	28	9	33
		22	44	29	34	47	37
		34		38	46	49	
		36			50		
		43					
SKILL 10	17	4	6	2	3	14	5
	23	14	12	4	7	18	6
	28	16	23	9	19	27	10
	32	28	27	22	23	34	13
	46		32	26	36		15
			34	33	39		20
			37	35	42		
			42	42			
				47			
SKILL 11	7	9	4	5	13	2	18
	24	25	8	12	29	21	24
			45	16		23	44
				44		30	47
						37	

	PRE-TEST	POST-TEST	COMPLETE TEST 1	COMPLETE TEST 2	COMPLETE TEST 3	COMPLETE TEST 4	COMPLETE TEST 5
Overall Review Questions							
SKILL 12	21	10	19	19	9	39	11
	29	30	28	40	20	48	29
	50	49	38				40
SKILL 13	1	20	11	11	21	1	21
	12		49	30		22	22
	30			50		41	49
	41					42	

PROGRESS CHART

Each time that you take a Pre-Test, a Post-Test, or a Complete Test, you should record the results in the chart that follows. In this way, you will be able to keep track of the progress that you are making.

DIRECTIONS: Fill in your score on each test section as you take it. Then, after you have taken all three sections of a particular test, compute your overall score and add it to the chart.

	LISTENING COMPREHENSION	STRUCTURE AND WRITTEN EXPRESSION	READING COMPREHENSION	OVERALL SCORE
Pre-Test				
Post-Test				
Complete Test 1				
Complete Test 2				
Complete Test 3				
Complete Test 4				
Complete Test 5				

ANSWER SHEETS

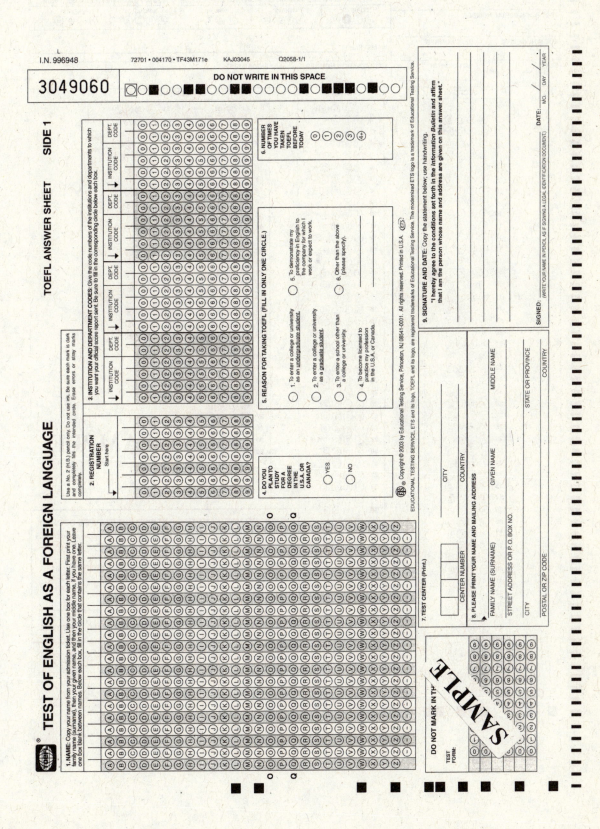

SIDE 2

TEST FORM

Choose only one answer for each question. Carefully and completely fill in the circle corresponding to the answer you choose so that the letter inside the circle cannot be seen. Completely erase any other marks you may have made.

TEST BOOK SERIAL NUMBER

CORRECT	WRONG	WRONG	WRONG	WRONG
Ⓐ Ⓑ ● Ⓓ	Ⓐ Ⓑ ⊘ Ⓓ	Ⓐ Ⓑ ⊗ Ⓓ	Ⓐ Ⓑ ◓ Ⓓ	Ⓐ Ⓑ ◉ Ⓓ

ROOM NUMBER	SEAT NUMBER

NAME (Print)

FAMILY NAME (SURNAME)   GIVEN NAME   MIDDLE NAME

SEX ◯ Male ◯ Female

DATE OF BIRTH
MO.   DAY   YEAR

REGISTRATION NUMBER

SIGNATURE

SECTION 1

1 Ⓐ Ⓑ Ⓒ Ⓓ
2 Ⓐ Ⓑ Ⓒ Ⓓ
3 Ⓐ Ⓑ Ⓒ Ⓓ
4 Ⓐ Ⓑ Ⓒ Ⓓ
5 Ⓐ Ⓑ Ⓒ Ⓓ
6 Ⓐ Ⓑ Ⓒ Ⓓ
7 Ⓐ Ⓑ Ⓒ Ⓓ
8 Ⓐ Ⓑ Ⓒ Ⓓ
9 Ⓐ Ⓑ Ⓒ Ⓓ
10 Ⓐ Ⓑ Ⓒ Ⓓ
11 Ⓐ Ⓑ Ⓒ Ⓓ
12 Ⓐ Ⓑ Ⓒ Ⓓ
13 Ⓐ Ⓑ Ⓒ Ⓓ
14 Ⓐ Ⓑ Ⓒ Ⓓ
15 Ⓐ Ⓑ Ⓒ Ⓓ
16 Ⓐ Ⓑ Ⓒ Ⓓ
17 Ⓐ Ⓑ Ⓒ Ⓓ
18 Ⓐ Ⓑ Ⓒ Ⓓ
19 Ⓐ Ⓑ Ⓒ Ⓓ
20 Ⓐ Ⓑ Ⓒ Ⓓ
21 Ⓐ Ⓑ Ⓒ Ⓓ
22 Ⓐ Ⓑ Ⓒ Ⓓ
23 Ⓐ Ⓑ Ⓒ Ⓓ
24 Ⓐ Ⓑ Ⓒ Ⓓ
25 Ⓐ Ⓑ Ⓒ Ⓓ
26 Ⓐ Ⓑ Ⓒ Ⓓ
27 Ⓐ Ⓑ Ⓒ Ⓓ
28 Ⓐ Ⓑ Ⓒ Ⓓ
29 Ⓐ Ⓑ Ⓒ Ⓓ
30 Ⓐ Ⓑ Ⓒ Ⓓ
31 Ⓐ Ⓑ Ⓒ Ⓓ
32 Ⓐ Ⓑ Ⓒ Ⓓ
33 Ⓐ Ⓑ Ⓒ Ⓓ
34 Ⓐ Ⓑ Ⓒ Ⓓ
35 Ⓐ Ⓑ Ⓒ Ⓓ
36 Ⓐ Ⓑ Ⓒ Ⓓ
37 Ⓐ Ⓑ Ⓒ Ⓓ
38 Ⓐ Ⓑ Ⓒ Ⓓ
39 Ⓐ Ⓑ Ⓒ Ⓓ
40 Ⓐ Ⓑ Ⓒ Ⓓ
41 Ⓐ Ⓑ Ⓒ Ⓓ
42 Ⓐ Ⓑ Ⓒ Ⓓ
43 Ⓐ Ⓑ Ⓒ Ⓓ
44 Ⓐ Ⓑ Ⓒ Ⓓ
45 Ⓐ Ⓑ Ⓒ Ⓓ
46 Ⓐ Ⓑ Ⓒ Ⓓ
47 Ⓐ Ⓑ Ⓒ Ⓓ
48 Ⓐ Ⓑ Ⓒ Ⓓ
49 Ⓐ Ⓑ Ⓒ Ⓓ
50 Ⓐ Ⓑ Ⓒ Ⓓ

SECTION 2

1 Ⓐ Ⓑ Ⓒ Ⓓ
2 Ⓐ Ⓑ Ⓒ Ⓓ
3 Ⓐ Ⓑ Ⓒ Ⓓ
4 Ⓐ Ⓑ Ⓒ Ⓓ
5 Ⓐ Ⓑ Ⓒ Ⓓ
6 Ⓐ Ⓑ Ⓒ Ⓓ
7 Ⓐ Ⓑ Ⓒ Ⓓ
8 Ⓐ Ⓑ Ⓒ Ⓓ
9 Ⓐ Ⓑ Ⓒ Ⓓ
10 Ⓐ Ⓑ Ⓒ Ⓓ
11 Ⓐ Ⓑ Ⓒ Ⓓ
12 Ⓐ Ⓑ Ⓒ Ⓓ
13 Ⓐ Ⓑ Ⓒ Ⓓ
14 Ⓐ Ⓑ Ⓒ Ⓓ
15 Ⓐ Ⓑ Ⓒ Ⓓ
16 Ⓐ Ⓑ Ⓒ Ⓓ
17 Ⓐ Ⓑ Ⓒ Ⓓ
18 Ⓐ Ⓑ Ⓒ Ⓓ
19 Ⓐ Ⓑ Ⓒ Ⓓ
20 Ⓐ Ⓑ Ⓒ Ⓓ
21 Ⓐ Ⓑ Ⓒ Ⓓ
22 Ⓐ Ⓑ Ⓒ Ⓓ
23 Ⓐ Ⓑ Ⓒ Ⓓ
24 Ⓐ Ⓑ Ⓒ Ⓓ
25 Ⓐ Ⓑ Ⓒ Ⓓ
26 Ⓐ Ⓑ Ⓒ Ⓓ
27 Ⓐ Ⓑ Ⓒ Ⓓ
28 Ⓐ Ⓑ Ⓒ Ⓓ
29 Ⓐ Ⓑ Ⓒ Ⓓ
30 Ⓐ Ⓑ Ⓒ Ⓓ
31 Ⓐ Ⓑ Ⓒ Ⓓ
32 Ⓐ Ⓑ Ⓒ Ⓓ
33 Ⓐ Ⓑ Ⓒ Ⓓ
34 Ⓐ Ⓑ Ⓒ Ⓓ
35 Ⓐ Ⓑ Ⓒ Ⓓ
36 Ⓐ Ⓑ Ⓒ Ⓓ
37 Ⓐ Ⓑ Ⓒ Ⓓ
38 Ⓐ Ⓑ Ⓒ Ⓓ
39 Ⓐ Ⓑ Ⓒ Ⓓ
40 Ⓐ Ⓑ Ⓒ Ⓓ

SECTION 3

1 Ⓐ Ⓑ Ⓒ Ⓓ   31 Ⓐ Ⓑ Ⓒ Ⓓ
2 Ⓐ Ⓑ Ⓒ Ⓓ   32 Ⓐ Ⓑ Ⓒ Ⓓ
3 Ⓐ Ⓑ Ⓒ Ⓓ   33 Ⓐ Ⓑ Ⓒ Ⓓ
4 Ⓐ Ⓑ Ⓒ Ⓓ   34 Ⓐ Ⓑ Ⓒ Ⓓ
5 Ⓐ Ⓑ Ⓒ Ⓓ   35 Ⓐ Ⓑ Ⓒ Ⓓ
6 Ⓐ Ⓑ Ⓒ Ⓓ   36 Ⓐ Ⓑ Ⓒ Ⓓ
7 Ⓐ Ⓑ Ⓒ Ⓓ   37 Ⓐ Ⓑ Ⓒ Ⓓ
8 Ⓐ Ⓑ Ⓒ Ⓓ   38 Ⓐ Ⓑ Ⓒ Ⓓ
9 Ⓐ Ⓑ Ⓒ Ⓓ   39 Ⓐ Ⓑ Ⓒ Ⓓ
10 Ⓐ Ⓑ Ⓒ Ⓓ   40 Ⓐ Ⓑ Ⓒ Ⓓ
11 Ⓐ Ⓑ Ⓒ Ⓓ   41 Ⓐ Ⓑ Ⓒ Ⓓ
12 Ⓐ Ⓑ Ⓒ Ⓓ   42 Ⓐ Ⓑ Ⓒ Ⓓ
13 Ⓐ Ⓑ Ⓒ Ⓓ   43 Ⓐ Ⓑ Ⓒ Ⓓ
14 Ⓐ Ⓑ Ⓒ Ⓓ   44 Ⓐ Ⓑ Ⓒ Ⓓ
15 Ⓐ Ⓑ Ⓒ Ⓓ   45 Ⓐ Ⓑ Ⓒ Ⓓ
16 Ⓐ Ⓑ Ⓒ Ⓓ   46 Ⓐ Ⓑ Ⓒ Ⓓ
17 Ⓐ Ⓑ Ⓒ Ⓓ   47 Ⓐ Ⓑ Ⓒ Ⓓ
18 Ⓐ Ⓑ Ⓒ Ⓓ   48 Ⓐ Ⓑ Ⓒ Ⓓ
19 Ⓐ Ⓑ Ⓒ Ⓓ   49 Ⓐ Ⓑ Ⓒ Ⓓ
20 Ⓐ Ⓑ Ⓒ Ⓓ   50 Ⓐ Ⓑ Ⓒ Ⓓ
21 Ⓐ Ⓑ Ⓒ Ⓓ
22 Ⓐ Ⓑ Ⓒ Ⓓ
23 Ⓐ Ⓑ Ⓒ Ⓓ
24 Ⓐ Ⓑ Ⓒ Ⓓ
25 Ⓐ Ⓑ Ⓒ Ⓓ
26 Ⓐ Ⓑ Ⓒ Ⓓ
27 Ⓐ Ⓑ Ⓒ Ⓓ
28 Ⓐ Ⓑ Ⓒ Ⓓ
29 Ⓐ Ⓑ Ⓒ Ⓓ
30 Ⓐ Ⓑ Ⓒ Ⓓ

SAMPLE

IF YOU DO NOT WANT THIS ANSWER SHEET TO BE SCORED

If you want to cancel your scores from this administration, complete A and B below. The scores will not be sent to you or your designated recipients, and they will be removed from your permanent record.

To cancel your scores from this test administration, you must:

A. fill in both circles here   and   B. sign your name below

◯—◯ _____

ONCE A SCORE IS CANCELED, IT CANNOT BE REPORTED AT ANY TIME.

1R	2R	3R	TCS
1CS	2CS	3CS	
		FOR ETS USE ONLY	M

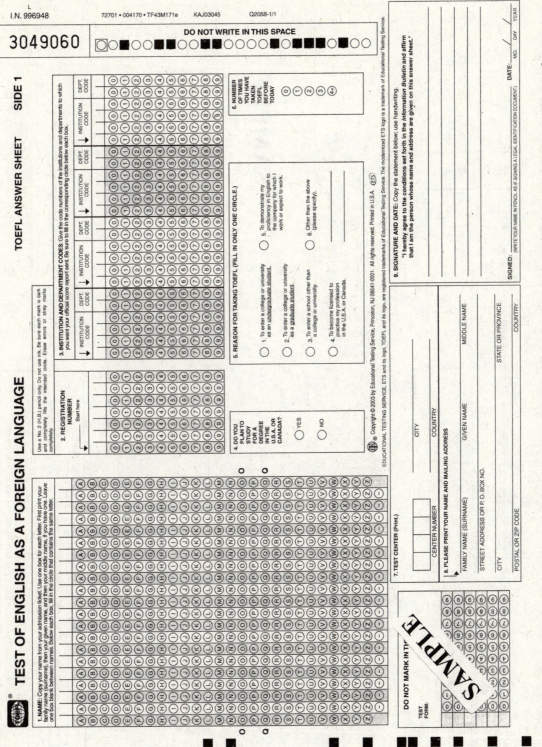
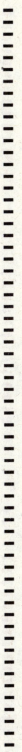

SIDE 2

TEST FORM

TEST BOOK SERIAL NUMBER

ROOM NUMBER   SEAT NUMBER

SEX
○ Male
○ Female

DATE OF BIRTH
___/___
MO. DAY YEAR

Choose only one answer for each question. Carefully and completely fill in the circle corresponding to the answer you choose so that the letter inside the circle cannot be seen. Completely erase any other marks you may have made.

CORRECT	WRONG	WRONG	WRONG	WRONG
Ⓐ	Ⓐ	Ⓐ	Ⓐ	Ⓐ
Ⓑ	Ⓑ	Ⓑ	Ⓑ	Ⓑ
●	Ⓒ⊘	⊗	Ⓒ	●
Ⓓ	Ⓓ	Ⓓ	Ⓓ	Ⓓ

NAME (Print) _____
FAMILY NAME (SURNAME)   GIVEN NAME   MIDDLE NAME

REGISTRATION NUMBER

SIGNATURE _____

SAMPLE

SECTION 1

SECTION 2

SECTION 3

IF YOU DO NOT WANT THIS ANSWER SHEET TO BE SCORED

If you want to cancel your scores from this administration, complete A and B below. The scores will not be sent to you or your designated recipients, and they will be removed from your permanent record.

To cancel your scores from this test administration, you must:

A. fill in both circles here   and   B. sign your name below

○—○
○

ONCE A SCORE IS CANCELED, IT CANNOT BE REPORTED AT ANY TIME.

FOR ETS USE ONLY

1R	2R	3R	TCS
1CS	2CS	3CS	

L

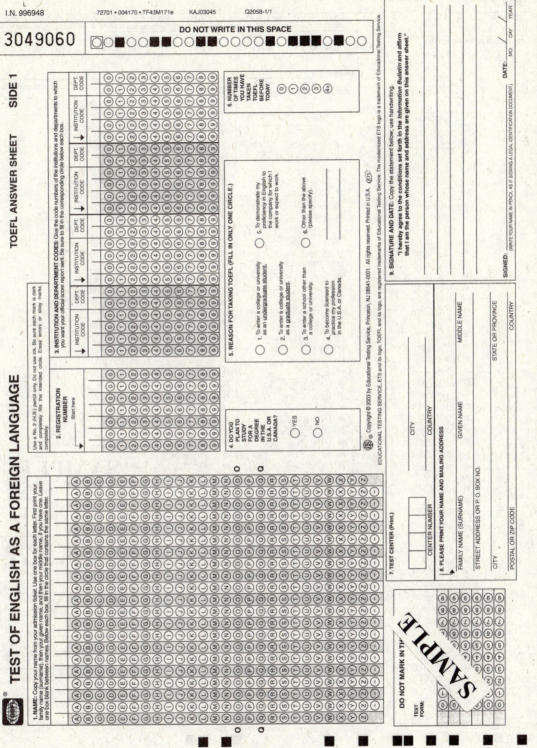

SIDE 2

| TEST FORM | | CORRECT | WRONG | WRONG | WRONG | WRONG |

Choose only one answer for each question. Carefully and completely fill in the circle corresponding to the answer you choose so that the letter inside the circle cannot be seen. Completely erase any other marks you may have made.

CORRECT (A)(B)●(D)   WRONG (A)(B)(Ø)(D)   WRONG (A)(B)(X)(D)   WRONG (A)(B)(C)(D)   WRONG (A)(B)(C)(D)

TEST BOOK SERIAL NUMBER

ROOM NUMBER   **SEAT NUMBER**

NAME (Print)

FAMILY NAME (SURNAME)   GIVEN NAME   MIDDLE NAME

SEX ○ Male ○ Female   **DATE OF BIRTH**   MO.   DAY   YEAR

REGISTRATION NUMBER   **SIGNATURE**

SECTION 1

1 (A)(B)(C)(D)
2 (A)(B)(C)(D)
3 (A)(B)(C)(D)
4 (A)(B)(C)(D)
5 (A)(B)(C)(D)
6 (A)(B)(C)(D)
7 (A)(B)(C)(D)
8 (A)(B)(C)(D)
9 (A)(B)(C)(D)
10 (A)(B)(C)(D)
11 (A)(B)(C)(D)
12 (A)(B)(C)(D)
13 (A)(B)(C)(D)
14 (A)(B)(C)(D)
15 (A)(B)(C)(D)
16 (A)(B)(C)(D)
17 (A)(B)(C)(D)
18 (A)(B)(C)(D)
19 (A)(B)(C)(D)
20 (A)(B)(C)(D)
21 (A)(B)(C)(D)
22 (A)(B)(C)(D)
23 (A)(B)(C)(D)
24 (A)(B)(C)(D)
25 (A)(B)(C)(D)
26 (A)(B)(C)(D)
27 (A)(B)(C)(D)
28 (A)(B)(C)(D)
29 (A)(B)(C)(D)
30 (A)(B)(C)(D)
31 (A)(B)(C)(D)
32 (A)(B)(C)(D)
33 (A)(B)(C)(D)
34 (A)(B)(C)(D)
35 (A)(B)(C)(D)
36 (A)(B)(C)(D)
37 (A)(B)(C)(D)
38 (A)(B)(C)(D)
39 (A)(B)(C)(D)
40 (A)(B)(C)(D)
41 (A)(B)(C)(D)
42 (A)(B)(C)(D)
43 (A)(B)(C)(D)
44 (A)(B)(C)(D)
45 (A)(B)(C)(D)
46 (A)(B)(C)(D)
47 (A)(B)(C)(D)
48 (A)(B)(C)(D)
49 (A)(B)(C)(D)
50 (A)(B)(C)(D)

SECTION 2

1 (A)(B)(C)(D)
2 (A)(B)(C)(D)
3 (A)(B)(C)(D)
4 (A)(B)(C)(D)
5 (A)(B)(C)(D)
6 (A)(B)(C)(D)
7 (A)(B)(C)(D)
8 (A)(B)(C)(D)
9 (A)(B)(C)(D)
10 (A)(B)(C)(D)
11 (A)(B)(C)(D)
12 (A)(B)(C)(D)
13 (A)(B)(C)(D)
14 (A)(B)(C)(D)
15 (A)(B)(C)(D)
16 (A)(B)(C)(D)
17 (A)(B)(C)(D)
18 (A)(B)(C)(D)
19 (A)(B)(C)(D)
20 (A)(B)(C)(D)
21 (A)(B)(C)(D)
22 (A)(B)(C)(D)
23 (A)(B)(C)(D)
24 (A)(B)(C)(D)
25 (A)(B)(C)(D)
26 (A)(B)(C)(D)
27 (A)(B)(C)(D)
28 (A)(B)(C)(D)
29 (A)(B)(C)(D)
30 (A)(B)(C)(D)
31 (A)(B)(C)(D)
32 (A)(B)(C)(D)
33 (A)(B)(C)(D)
34 (A)(B)(C)(D)
35 (A)(B)(C)(D)
36 (A)(B)(C)(D)
37 (A)(B)(C)(D)
38 (A)(B)(C)(D)
39 (A)(B)(C)(D)
40 (A)(B)(C)(D)

SECTION 3

1 (A)(B)(C)(D)   31 (A)(B)(C)(D)
2 (A)(B)(C)(D)   32 (A)(B)(C)(D)
3 (A)(B)(C)(D)   33 (A)(B)(C)(D)
4 (A)(B)(C)(D)   34 (A)(B)(C)(D)
5 (A)(B)(C)(D)   35 (A)(B)(C)(D)
6 (A)(B)(C)(D)   36 (A)(B)(C)(D)
7 (A)(B)(C)(D)   37 (A)(B)(C)(D)
8 (A)(B)(C)(D)   38 (A)(B)(C)(D)
9 (A)(B)(C)(D)   39 (A)(B)(C)(D)
10 (A)(B)(C)(D)   40 (A)(B)(C)(D)
11 (A)(B)(C)(D)   41 (A)(B)(C)(D)
12 (A)(B)(C)(D)   42 (A)(B)(C)(D)
13 (A)(B)(C)(D)   43 (A)(B)(C)(D)
14 (A)(B)(C)(D)   44 (A)(B)(C)(D)
15 (A)(B)(C)(D)   45 (A)(B)(C)(D)
16 (A)(B)(C)(D)   46 (A)(B)(C)(D)
17 (A)(B)(C)(D)   47 (A)(B)(C)(D)
18 (A)(B)(C)(D)   48 (A)(B)(C)(D)
19 (A)(B)(C)(D)   49 (A)(B)(C)(D)
20 (A)(B)(C)(D)   50 (A)(B)(C)(D)
21 (A)(B)(C)(D)
22 (A)(B)(C)(D)
23 (A)(B)(C)(D)
24 (A)(B)(C)(D)
25 (A)(B)(C)(D)
26 (A)(B)(C)(D)
27 (A)(B)(C)(D)
28 (A)(B)(C)(D)
29 (A)(B)(C)(D)
30 (A)(B)(C)(D)

SAMPLE

IF YOU DO <u>NOT</u> WANT THIS ANSWER SHEET TO BE SCORED

If you want to cancel your scores from this administration, complete A and B below. The scores will not be sent to you or your designated recipients, and they will be removed from your permanent record.

To cancel your scores from this test administration, you must:

A. fill in both circles here   and   B. sign your name below

○—○ _____

ONCE A SCORE IS CANCELED, IT CANNOT BE REPORTED AT ANY TIME.

1R	2R	3R	TCS
1CS	2CS	3CS	
		FOR ETS USE ONLY	M

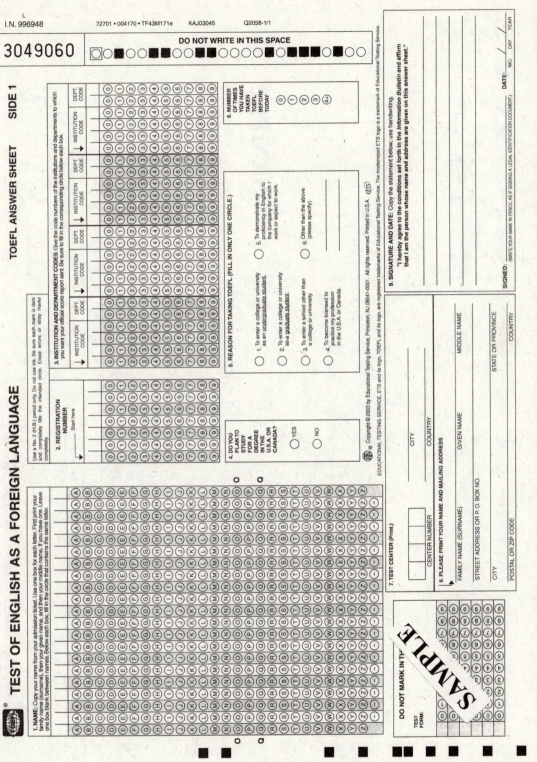
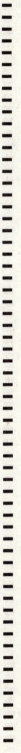

SIDE 2

TEST FORM

TEST BOOK SERIAL NUMBER

ROOM NUMBER   SEAT NUMBER

SEX
○ Male
○ Female

DATE OF BIRTH
MO. DAY YEAR

Choose only one answer for each question. Carefully and completely fill in the circle corresponding to the answer you choose so that the letter inside the circle cannot be seen. Completely erase any other marks you may have made.

NAME (Print)
FAMILY NAME (SURNAME)   GIVEN NAME   MIDDLE NAME

REGISTRATION NUMBER

SIGNATURE

CORRECT	WRONG	WRONG	WRONG	WRONG

SAMPLE

SECTION 1

SECTION 2

SECTION 3

IF YOU DO NOT WANT THIS ANSWER SHEET TO BE SCORED

If you want to cancel your scores from this administration, complete A and B below. The scores will not be sent to you or your designated recipients, and they will be removed from your permanent record.

To cancel your scores from this test administration, you must:

A. fill in both circles here   and   B. sign your name below

ONCE A SCORE IS CANCELED, IT CANNOT BE REPORTED AT ANY TIME.

FOR ETS USE ONLY

1R	2R	3R	TCS
1CS	2CS	3CS	

L

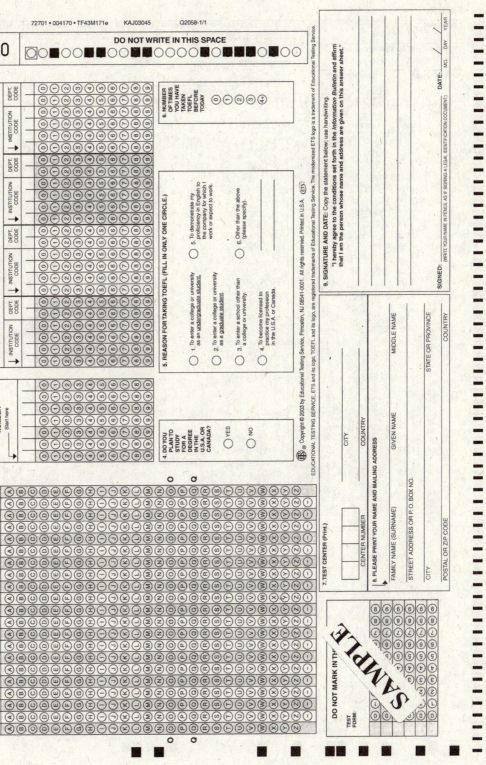

SIDE 2

TEST FORM		Choose only one answer for each question. Carefully and completely fill in the circle corresponding to the answer you choose so that the letter inside the circle cannot be seen. Completely erase any other marks you may have made.

	CORRECT	WRONG	WRONG	WRONG	WRONG
TEST BOOK SERIAL NUMBER	(A)(B)●(D)	(A)(B)(∅)(D)	(A)(⊗)(C)(D)	(A)(B)(⊙)(D)	(A)(B)(●)(D)

ROOM NUMBER   **SEAT NUMBER**

NAME (Print) _____

FAMILY NAME (SURNAME)   GIVEN NAME   MIDDLE NAME

SEX ○ Male ○ Female   **DATE OF BIRTH** MO. / DAY / YEAR

REGISTRATION NUMBER   **SIGNATURE**

SECTION 1

1 (A)(B)(C)(D)
2 (A)(B)(C)(D)
3 (A)(B)(C)(D)
4 (A)(B)(C)(D)
5 (A)(B)(C)(D)
6 (A)(B)(C)(D)
7 (A)(B)(C)(D)
8 (A)(B)(C)(D)
9 (A)(B)(C)(D)
10 (A)(B)(C)(D)
11 (A)(B)(C)(D)
12 (A)(B)(C)(D)
13 (A)(B)(C)(D)
14 (A)(B)(C)(D)
15 (A)(B)(C)(D)
16 (A)(B)(C)(D)
17 (A)(B)(C)(D)
18 (A)(B)(C)(D)
19 (A)(B)(C)(D)
20 (A)(B)(C)(D)
21 (A)(B)(C)(D)
22 (A)(B)(C)(D)
23 (A)(B)(C)(D)
24 (A)(B)(C)(D)
25 (A)(B)(C)(D)
26 (A)(B)(C)(D)
27 (A)(B)(C)(D)
28 (A)(B)(C)(D)
29 (A)(B)(C)(D)
30 (A)(B)(C)(D)
31 (A)(B)(C)(D)
32 (A)(B)(C)(D)
33 (A)(B)(C)(D)
34 (A)(B)(C)(D)
35 (A)(B)(C)(D)
36 (A)(B)(C)(D)
37 (A)(B)(C)(D)
38 (A)(B)(C)(D)
39 (A)(B)(C)(D)
40 (A)(B)(C)(D)
41 (A)(B)(C)(D)
42 (A)(B)(C)(D)
43 (A)(B)(C)(D)
44 (A)(B)(C)(D)
45 (A)(B)(C)(D)
46 (A)(B)(C)(D)
47 (A)(B)(C)(D)
48 (A)(B)(C)(D)
49 (A)(B)(C)(D)
50 (A)(B)(C)(D)

SECTION 2

1 (A)(B)(C)(D)
2 (A)(B)(C)(D)
3 (A)(B)(C)(D)
4 (A)(B)(C)(D)
5 (A)(B)(C)(D)
6 (A)(B)(C)(D)
7 (A)(B)(C)(D)
8 (A)(B)(C)(D)
9 (A)(B)(C)(D)
10 (A)(B)(C)(D)
11 (A)(B)(C)(D)
12 (A)(B)(C)(D)
13 (A)(B)(C)(D)
14 (A)(B)(C)(D)
15 (A)(B)(C)(D)
16 (A)(B)(C)(D)
17 (A)(B)(C)(D)
18 (A)(B)(C)(D)
19 (A)(B)(C)(D)
20 (A)(B)(C)(D)
21 (A)(B)(C)(D)
22 (A)(B)(C)(D)
23 (A)(B)(C)(D)
24 (A)(B)(C)(D)
25 (A)(B)(C)(D)
26 (A)(B)(C)(D)
27 (A)(B)(C)(D)
28 (A)(B)(C)(D)
29 (A)(B)(C)(D)
30 (A)(B)(C)(D)
31 (A)(B)(C)(D)
32 (A)(B)(C)(D)
33 (A)(B)(C)(D)
34 (A)(B)(C)(D)
35 (A)(B)(C)(D)
36 (A)(B)(C)(D)
37 (A)(B)(C)(D)
38 (A)(B)(C)(D)
39 (A)(B)(C)(D)
40 (A)(B)(C)(D)

SECTION 3

1 (A)(B)(C)(D)   31 (A)(B)(C)(D)
2 (A)(B)(C)(D)   32 (A)(B)(C)(D)
3 (A)(B)(C)(D)   33 (A)(B)(C)(D)
4 (A)(B)(C)(D)   34 (A)(B)(C)(D)
5 (A)(B)(C)(D)   35 (A)(B)(C)(D)
6 (A)(B)(C)(D)   36 (A)(B)(C)(D)
7 (A)(B)(C)(D)   37 (A)(B)(C)(D)
8 (A)(B)(C)(D)   38 (A)(B)(C)(D)
9 (A)(B)(C)(D)   39 (A)(B)(C)(D)
10 (A)(B)(C)(D)   40 (A)(B)(C)(D)
11 (A)(B)(C)(D)   41 (A)(B)(C)(D)
12 (A)(B)(C)(D)   42 (A)(B)(C)(D)
13 (A)(B)(C)(D)   43 (A)(B)(C)(D)
14 (A)(B)(C)(D)   44 (A)(B)(C)(D)
15 (A)(B)(C)(D)   45 (A)(B)(C)(D)
16 (A)(B)(C)(D)   46 (A)(B)(C)(D)
17 (A)(B)(C)(D)   47 (A)(B)(C)(D)
18 (A)(B)(C)(D)   48 (A)(B)(C)(D)
19 (A)(B)(C)(D)   49 (A)(B)(C)(D)
20 (A)(B)(C)(D)   50 (A)(B)(C)(D)
21 (A)(B)(C)(D)
22 (A)(B)(C)(D)
23 (A)(B)(C)(D)
24 (A)(B)(C)(D)
25 (A)(B)(C)(D)
26 (A)(B)(C)(D)
27 (A)(B)(C)(D)
28 (A)(B)(C)(D)
29 (A)(B)(C)(D)
30 (A)(B)(C)(D)

SAMPLE

IF YOU DO NOT WANT THIS ANSWER SHEET TO BE SCORED

If you want to cancel your scores from this administration, complete A and B below. The scores will not be sent to you or your designated recipients, and they will be removed from your permanent record.

To cancel your scores from this test administration, you must:

A. fill in both circles here   and   B. sign your name below

○—○ _____

ONCE A SCORE IS CANCELED, IT CANNOT BE REPORTED AT ANY TIME.

1R	2R	3R	TCS
1CS	2CS	3CS	
		FOR ETS USE ONLY	M

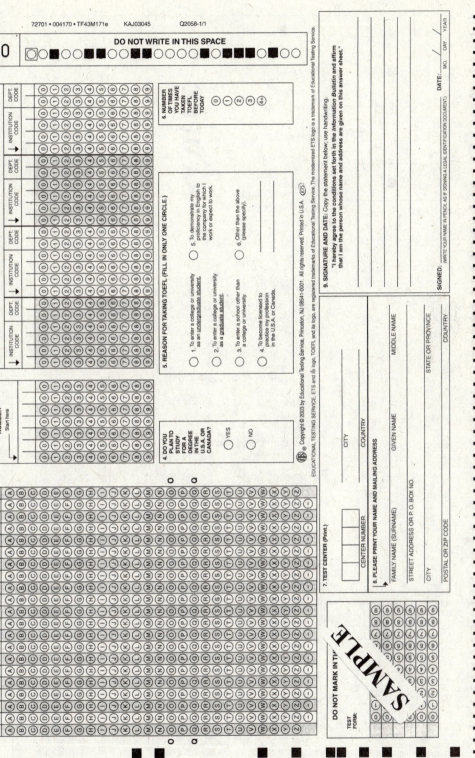

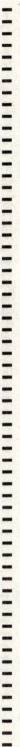

SIDE 2

TEST FORM

TEST BOOK SERIAL NUMBER

ROOM NUMBER   SEAT NUMBER

SEX
○ Male
○ Female

DATE OF BIRTH
MO. DAY YEAR

Choose only one answer for each question. Carefully and completely fill in the circle corresponding to the answer you choose so that the letter inside the circle cannot be seen. Completely erase any other marks you may have made.

NAME (Print)
FAMILY NAME (SURNAME)   GIVEN NAME   MIDDLE NAME

REGISTRATION NUMBER

SIGNATURE

CORRECT	WRONG	WRONG	WRONG	WRONG
Ⓐ	Ⓐ	Ⓐ	Ⓐ	Ⓐ
Ⓑ	Ⓑ	Ⓑ	Ⓑ	Ⓑ
●	Ⓒ	Ⓧ	Ⓒ	●
Ⓓ	Ⓓ	Ⓓ	Ⓓ	Ⓓ

SECTION 1

SECTION 2

SECTION 3

SAMPLE

IF YOU DO NOT WANT THIS ANSWER SHEET TO BE SCORED

If you want to cancel your scores from this administration, complete A and B below. The scores will not be sent to you or your designated recipients, and they will be removed from your permanent record.

To cancel your scores from this test administration, you must:

A. fill in both circles here   and   B. sign your name below

○ — ○

ONCE A SCORE IS CANCELED, IT CANNOT BE REPORTED AT ANY TIME.

FOR ETS USE ONLY

1R	2R	3R	TCS
1CS	2CS	3CS	

L

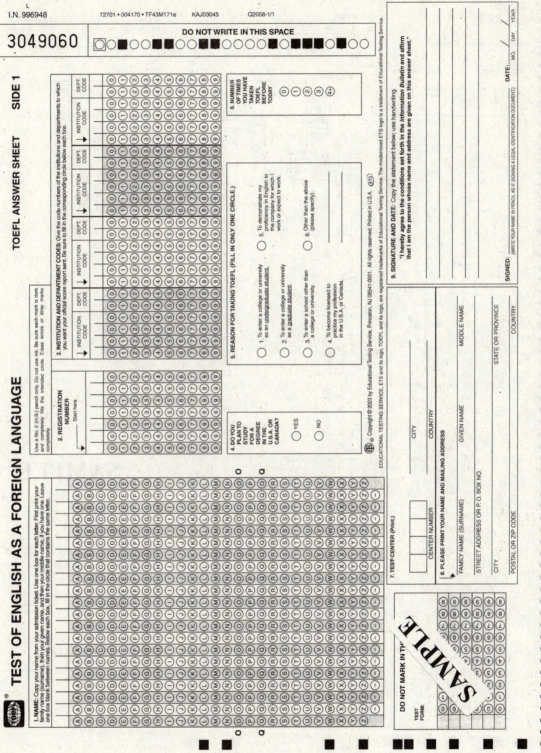

TEST OF ENGLISH AS A FOREIGN LANGUAGE

TOEFL ANSWER SHEET   SIDE 1

I.N. 996948   72701 • 004170 • TF43M171e   KAJ03045   Q2058-1/1

3049060   DO NOT WRITE IN THIS SPACE

SAMPLE

SIDE 2

TEST FORM

TEST BOOK SERIAL NUMBER

ROOM NUMBER   SEAT NUMBER

SEX   ○ Male   ○ Female

DATE OF BIRTH
MO.   DAY   YEAR

Choose only one answer for each question. Carefully and completely fill in the circle corresponding to the answer you choose so that the letter inside the circle cannot be seen. Completely erase any other marks you may have made.

CORRECT	WRONG	WRONG	WRONG	WRONG
Ⓐ Ⓑ ● Ⓓ	Ⓐ Ⓑ ⊘ Ⓓ	Ⓐ Ⓑ ⊗ Ⓓ	Ⓐ Ⓑ ⊙ Ⓓ	Ⓐ Ⓑ ◉ Ⓓ

NAME (Print) _____
FAMILY NAME (SURNAME)   GIVEN NAME   MIDDLE NAME

REGISTRATION NUMBER   SIGNATURE

SECTION 1

1 Ⓐ Ⓑ Ⓒ Ⓓ
2 Ⓐ Ⓑ Ⓒ Ⓓ
3 Ⓐ Ⓑ Ⓒ Ⓓ
4 Ⓐ Ⓑ Ⓒ Ⓓ
5 Ⓐ Ⓑ Ⓒ Ⓓ
6 Ⓐ Ⓑ Ⓒ Ⓓ
7 Ⓐ Ⓑ Ⓒ Ⓓ
8 Ⓐ Ⓑ Ⓒ Ⓓ
9 Ⓐ Ⓑ Ⓒ Ⓓ
10 Ⓐ Ⓑ Ⓒ Ⓓ
11 Ⓐ Ⓑ Ⓒ Ⓓ
12 Ⓐ Ⓑ Ⓒ Ⓓ
13 Ⓐ Ⓑ Ⓒ Ⓓ
14 Ⓐ Ⓑ Ⓒ Ⓓ
15 Ⓐ Ⓑ Ⓒ Ⓓ
16 Ⓐ Ⓑ Ⓒ Ⓓ
17 Ⓐ Ⓑ Ⓒ Ⓓ
18 Ⓐ Ⓑ Ⓒ Ⓓ
19 Ⓐ Ⓑ Ⓒ Ⓓ
20 Ⓐ Ⓑ Ⓒ Ⓓ
21 Ⓐ Ⓑ Ⓒ Ⓓ
22 Ⓐ Ⓑ Ⓒ Ⓓ
23 Ⓐ Ⓑ Ⓒ Ⓓ
24 Ⓐ Ⓑ Ⓒ Ⓓ
25 Ⓐ Ⓑ Ⓒ Ⓓ
26 Ⓐ Ⓑ Ⓒ Ⓓ
27 Ⓐ Ⓑ Ⓒ Ⓓ
28 Ⓐ Ⓑ Ⓒ Ⓓ
29 Ⓐ Ⓑ Ⓒ Ⓓ
30 Ⓐ Ⓑ Ⓒ Ⓓ
31 Ⓐ Ⓑ Ⓒ Ⓓ
32 Ⓐ Ⓑ Ⓒ Ⓓ
33 Ⓐ Ⓑ Ⓒ Ⓓ
34 Ⓐ Ⓑ Ⓒ Ⓓ
35 Ⓐ Ⓑ Ⓒ Ⓓ
36 Ⓐ Ⓑ Ⓒ Ⓓ
37 Ⓐ Ⓑ Ⓒ Ⓓ
38 Ⓐ Ⓑ Ⓒ Ⓓ
39 Ⓐ Ⓑ Ⓒ Ⓓ
40 Ⓐ Ⓑ Ⓒ Ⓓ
41 Ⓐ Ⓑ Ⓒ Ⓓ
42 Ⓐ Ⓑ Ⓒ Ⓓ
43 Ⓐ Ⓑ Ⓒ Ⓓ
44 Ⓐ Ⓑ Ⓒ Ⓓ
45 Ⓐ Ⓑ Ⓒ Ⓓ
46 Ⓐ Ⓑ Ⓒ Ⓓ
47 Ⓐ Ⓑ Ⓒ Ⓓ
48 Ⓐ Ⓑ Ⓒ Ⓓ
49 Ⓐ Ⓑ Ⓒ Ⓓ
50 Ⓐ Ⓑ Ⓒ Ⓓ

SECTION 2

1 Ⓐ Ⓑ Ⓒ Ⓓ
2 Ⓐ Ⓑ Ⓒ Ⓓ
3 Ⓐ Ⓑ Ⓒ Ⓓ
4 Ⓐ Ⓑ Ⓒ Ⓓ
5 Ⓐ Ⓑ Ⓒ Ⓓ
6 Ⓐ Ⓑ Ⓒ Ⓓ
7 Ⓐ Ⓑ Ⓒ Ⓓ
8 Ⓐ Ⓑ Ⓒ Ⓓ
9 Ⓐ Ⓑ Ⓒ Ⓓ
10 Ⓐ Ⓑ Ⓒ Ⓓ
11 Ⓐ Ⓑ Ⓒ Ⓓ
12 Ⓐ Ⓑ Ⓒ Ⓓ
13 Ⓐ Ⓑ Ⓒ Ⓓ
14 Ⓐ Ⓑ Ⓒ Ⓓ
15 Ⓐ Ⓑ Ⓒ Ⓓ
16 Ⓐ Ⓑ Ⓒ Ⓓ
17 Ⓐ Ⓑ Ⓒ Ⓓ
18 Ⓐ Ⓑ Ⓒ Ⓓ
19 Ⓐ Ⓑ Ⓒ Ⓓ
20 Ⓐ Ⓑ Ⓒ Ⓓ
21 Ⓐ Ⓑ Ⓒ Ⓓ
22 Ⓐ Ⓑ Ⓒ Ⓓ
23 Ⓐ Ⓑ Ⓒ Ⓓ
24 Ⓐ Ⓑ Ⓒ Ⓓ
25 Ⓐ Ⓑ Ⓒ Ⓓ
26 Ⓐ Ⓑ Ⓒ Ⓓ
27 Ⓐ Ⓑ Ⓒ Ⓓ
28 Ⓐ Ⓑ Ⓒ Ⓓ
29 Ⓐ Ⓑ Ⓒ Ⓓ
30 Ⓐ Ⓑ Ⓒ Ⓓ
31 Ⓐ Ⓑ Ⓒ Ⓓ
32 Ⓐ Ⓑ Ⓒ Ⓓ
33 Ⓐ Ⓑ Ⓒ Ⓓ
34 Ⓐ Ⓑ Ⓒ Ⓓ
35 Ⓐ Ⓑ Ⓒ Ⓓ
36 Ⓐ Ⓑ Ⓒ Ⓓ
37 Ⓐ Ⓑ Ⓒ Ⓓ
38 Ⓐ Ⓑ Ⓒ Ⓓ
39 Ⓐ Ⓑ Ⓒ Ⓓ
40 Ⓐ Ⓑ Ⓒ Ⓓ

SECTION 3

1 Ⓐ Ⓑ Ⓒ Ⓓ   31 Ⓐ Ⓑ Ⓒ Ⓓ
2 Ⓐ Ⓑ Ⓒ Ⓓ   32 Ⓐ Ⓑ Ⓒ Ⓓ
3 Ⓐ Ⓑ Ⓒ Ⓓ   33 Ⓐ Ⓑ Ⓒ Ⓓ
4 Ⓐ Ⓑ Ⓒ Ⓓ   34 Ⓐ Ⓑ Ⓒ Ⓓ
5 Ⓐ Ⓑ Ⓒ Ⓓ   35 Ⓐ Ⓑ Ⓒ Ⓓ
6 Ⓐ Ⓑ Ⓒ Ⓓ   36 Ⓐ Ⓑ Ⓒ Ⓓ
7 Ⓐ Ⓑ Ⓒ Ⓓ   37 Ⓐ Ⓑ Ⓒ Ⓓ
8 Ⓐ Ⓑ Ⓒ Ⓓ   38 Ⓐ Ⓑ Ⓒ Ⓓ
9 Ⓐ Ⓑ Ⓒ Ⓓ   39 Ⓐ Ⓑ Ⓒ Ⓓ
10 Ⓐ Ⓑ Ⓒ Ⓓ   40 Ⓐ Ⓑ Ⓒ Ⓓ
11 Ⓐ Ⓑ Ⓒ Ⓓ   41 Ⓐ Ⓑ Ⓒ Ⓓ
12 Ⓐ Ⓑ Ⓒ Ⓓ   42 Ⓐ Ⓑ Ⓒ Ⓓ
13 Ⓐ Ⓑ Ⓒ Ⓓ   43 Ⓐ Ⓑ Ⓒ Ⓓ
14 Ⓐ Ⓑ Ⓒ Ⓓ   44 Ⓐ Ⓑ Ⓒ Ⓓ
15 Ⓐ Ⓑ Ⓒ Ⓓ   45 Ⓐ Ⓑ Ⓒ Ⓓ
16 Ⓐ Ⓑ Ⓒ Ⓓ   46 Ⓐ Ⓑ Ⓒ Ⓓ
17 Ⓐ Ⓑ Ⓒ Ⓓ   47 Ⓐ Ⓑ Ⓒ Ⓓ
18 Ⓐ Ⓑ Ⓒ Ⓓ   48 Ⓐ Ⓑ Ⓒ Ⓓ
19 Ⓐ Ⓑ Ⓒ Ⓓ   49 Ⓐ Ⓑ Ⓒ Ⓓ
20 Ⓐ Ⓑ Ⓒ Ⓓ   50 Ⓐ Ⓑ Ⓒ Ⓓ
21 Ⓐ Ⓑ Ⓒ Ⓓ
22 Ⓐ Ⓑ Ⓒ Ⓓ
23 Ⓐ Ⓑ Ⓒ Ⓓ
24 Ⓐ Ⓑ Ⓒ Ⓓ
25 Ⓐ Ⓑ Ⓒ Ⓓ
26 Ⓐ Ⓑ Ⓒ Ⓓ
27 Ⓐ Ⓑ Ⓒ Ⓓ
28 Ⓐ Ⓑ Ⓒ Ⓓ
29 Ⓐ Ⓑ Ⓒ Ⓓ
30 Ⓐ Ⓑ Ⓒ Ⓓ

SAMPLE

IF YOU DO NOT WANT THIS ANSWER SHEET TO BE SCORED

If you want to cancel your scores from this administration, complete A and B below. The scores will not be sent to you or your designated recipients, and they will be removed from your permanent record.

To cancel your scores from this test administration, you must:

A. fill in both circles here   and   B. sign your name below

○—○ _____

ONCE A SCORE IS CANCELED, IT CANNOT BE REPORTED AT ANY TIME.

1R	2R	3R	TCS
1CS	2CS	3CS	
		FOR ETS USE ONLY	M

REGISTRATION NUMBER

Start here

TEST CENTER NUMBER

TOPIC

Ⓐ

Ⓑ

Ⓒ

Test of Written English (TWE)

Answer Sheet

SIDE 3

TEST DATE

Begin your essay here. If you need more space, use the other side.

SAMPLE

ADDITIONAL SPACE IS AVAILABLE ON THE REVERSE SIDE.

CHW02010   Q2035-3

3049060

SIDE 4

Continuation of essay

SAMPLE

THE AREA BELOW IS FOR ETS USE ONLY. DO NOT MARK.

	READER NO.						
1		⓪①②③④⑤⑥⑦⑧⑨ ⓪①②③④⑤⑥⑦⑧⑨ ⓪①②③④⑤⑥⑦⑧⑨	1		Ⓐ Ⓑ Ⓒ Ⓓ Ⓔ Ⓕ Ⓖ Ⓗ Ⓘ Ⓙ Ⓚ Ⓛ Ⓜ Ⓝ Ⓞ Ⓟ Ⓠ Ⓡ Ⓢ Ⓣ Ⓤ Ⓥ Ⓦ Ⓧ Ⓨ Ⓩ	
2		⓪①②③④⑤⑥⑦⑧⑨ ⓪①②③④⑤⑥⑦⑧⑨ ⓪①②③④⑤⑥⑦⑧⑨	2		Ⓐ Ⓑ Ⓒ Ⓓ Ⓔ Ⓕ Ⓖ Ⓗ Ⓘ Ⓙ Ⓚ Ⓛ Ⓜ Ⓝ Ⓞ Ⓟ Ⓠ Ⓡ Ⓢ Ⓣ Ⓤ Ⓥ Ⓦ Ⓧ Ⓨ Ⓩ	
3		⓪①②③④⑤⑥⑦⑧⑨ ⓪①②③④⑤⑥⑦⑧⑨ ⓪①②③④⑤⑥⑦⑧⑨	3		Ⓐ Ⓑ Ⓒ Ⓓ Ⓔ Ⓕ Ⓖ Ⓗ Ⓘ Ⓙ Ⓚ Ⓛ Ⓜ Ⓝ Ⓞ Ⓟ Ⓠ Ⓡ Ⓢ Ⓣ Ⓤ Ⓥ Ⓦ Ⓧ Ⓨ Ⓩ	

ETS